D0450051

REGION AND REGIONALISM
IN THE UNITED STATES

GARLAND REFERENCE LIBRARY
OF SOCIAL SCIENCE
(VOL. 204)

REGION AND REGIONALISM IN THE UNITED STATES

A Source Book
for the
Humanities and Social Sciences

Michael Steiner
Clarence Mondale

GARLAND PUBLISHING, INC. • NEW YORK & LONDON
1988

Library of Congress Cataloging-in-Publication Data

Steiner, Michael
    Region and regionalism in the United States : a source book for
the humanities and social sciences / Michael Steiner, Clarence Mondale.
      p. cm. — (Garland reference library of social science : vol.
204)
    Includes index.
    ISBN 0–8240–9048–9 (alk. paper)
    1. Regionalism—United States—Bibliography. 2. United States—
Historical geography—Bibliography. 3. Anthropo-geography—United
States—Bibliography. I. Mondale, Clarence. II. Title.
III. Series: Garland reference library of social science ; v. 204.
Z1247.M66   1988
[E179.5]
016.973—dc19   88-22793
                                                                            CIP

Printed on acid-free, 250-year-life paper
Manufactured in the United States of America

To
Lucy and Virginia

ACKNOWLEDGMENTS

M.S. expresses his thanks to John Fraser Hart, Yi-Fu-Tuan, and Mary C. Turpie. C.M. expresses his to Carl Abbott, Howard Gillette, James O. Horton, and John Vlach, for reviewing portions of the manuscript. For that and for tutoring in geography and in the excitement of the cultural landscape, he expresses his special thanks to Peirce Lewis and Joseph Wood.

The manuscript would never have found its way to print without meticulous editing by Peggy Ann Brown and the careful work done on short notice by Sally Weber, Alex Mondale, and Nan Ernst.

Contents

Introduction

The divisions of America—North, South, East, West—have long been blurred. We have moved too much, inter-married with too many other split levels, cars and freezers to leave behind anything more than pockets of the past.[1]

Lillian Hellman

All events and experiences are local, somewhere. And all human enhancements of events and experiences ... are regional in the sense that they derive from immediate relation to felt life.[2]

William Stafford

Region and regionalism in the United States is an immense topic. We have attempted to make a vast body of knowledge accessible to a wide scholarly audience in the humanities and social sciences. This introduction explains why we think such a project worthwhile; how we have defined our terms; and how the text itself is organized.

General Significance

Lillian Hellman and William Stafford touch upon a paradox that has gripped American culture from the beginning and that informs much of this book. Americans seem the least likely of regionalists, yet region has always played a central role in their lives. They have always been on the move, breaking the bonds of place and tradition, leveling the landscape, and erasing differences among people. Yet the rootless, homogenizing nature of American experience engenders a counter-desire for stability and more intimate places of identity. The ideals of mobility and the melting pot are counterbalanced by the need for a sense of place and a pluralism rooted in region and in "the immediate relation to felt life."

We continue to be devoted to particular patches of American soil at the same time that we are pulled away from them. Regions and questions of regionalism are intimately tied to our personal and cultural identities. The sheer immensity of the United States seems to require a search for subnational places of belonging. It may be that the larger and more expansive a nation, the more urgent is the need of its citizens for distinctive regional identities. A continental nation, bristling with physical and cultural variety, America may be said to loom too large to understand and embrace as whole.

Nathaniel Hawthorne may have echoed the feelings of many Americans when he lamented that, "We have so much country that we have no country at all," and concluded that, "New England is quite as large a lump of this earth as my heart can really take in." John Dewey carried these sentiments into the twentieth century by noting the local and regional realities beneath the veneer of mass culture and by arguing that "the country is a spread of localities, while the nation is something that exists in Washington and other seats of government.... The wider the formal, the legal entity, the more intense becomes the local life."[3] As this book amply demonstrates, region and regionalism remain pressing concerns despite, perhaps even *because of*, American expansiveness, mobility, and mass culture.

There are historical rhythms in regional self-consciousness. During our formative period, Hector St. John de Crevecoeur could delight in our spatial variety; George Washington found it necessary to warn against sectional frictions. The antebellum period witnessed an American (generally a New England) literary renaissance and sectional divisions that led to the Civil War. The late nineteenth century became a time of regional achievements in architecture, literature and conservation, as well as the era of Populist provincialism. The 1920–40 period abounded with regional concerns of every kind: Southern Agrarians, midwestern regionalist painters, New Deal regional planners, and the government-sponsored rediscovery by writers, artists, and musicians of American "native grounds."

In the two decades following World War II, regional concerns were given short shrift as intellectuals and the general public fixed upon visions of American consensus. However, any notion of America as a seamless whole was shattered in the 1960s. The civil rights and anti-war protests, urban riots and environmental disasters, and the coming-to-consciousness of women and minority groups of all kinds have forced upon all of us a sense of the essential segmentation and pluralism of American culture.

A revived popular interest in region, as the spatial dimension of cultural pluralism, is part of this development. The general culture has become familiar with discussions of Sunbelt and Rustbelt; shown a remarkable interest in cultural "roots" and preservation; and, more insistently with time, pressed for a new understanding of the environmental consequences of a commitment to unbridled economic growth. As the pages of this book make clear, there has been a revival of interest in region in every relevant academic discipline. A number of regional study centers have emerged since the mid-1970s, including the Center for Great Plains Study at the University of Nebraska, the Appalachian Center at the University of Kentucky, the Center for the Study of Southern Culture at the University of Mississippi, the Center for New England Culture at the University of Massachusetts, the Mountain West Center for Regional Studies at Utah State University, and the Program for Regional Studies at Baylor University. The commencement of the publication of the *Dictionary of American Regional English* in 1985 is a further example of the continuing appeal of things regional.

We have assembled this book as a discipline-by-discipline guide to the recent groundswell of scholarly interest in region and regionalism. We emphasize the "new regionalism"[4] of the last two decades, but with attention to what new ideas, discipline by discipline, owe to past scholarship. Grounded in the American Studies training of the authors, this book surveys the meaning of region and regionalism in some sixteen disciplines and fields in the humanities and social sciences. We trust that the historical depth and disciplinary breadth of the book will provide a useful overview of a vast and vital subject.

Definitions and Distinctions

"Region" and "regionalism" are words with many popular meanings and connotations. Critics as varied as Benjamin Botkin, Eudora Welty, and Wendell Berry have rightly complained about indiscriminate, catch-all usage of the words.[5] It is instructive to be aware of this welter of popular meanings. In this book, however, we are concerned with those key terms as they are used within the academy. Introductions to each of the chapters and subchapters of the book review their meanings, by discipline and subdiscipline. Our own usage of the key terms, in the introductions and the annotations, is, we think, consistent, but it requires explanation.

The most general meaning of "region" is coextensive with the discipline of geography. A geographer places events within some "regional" scheme as a means of understanding spatial interconnections and variations in land and life. Treated in this general way, region simply means area.

Our interest is in a subtype of region, the cultural region. Often, students of cultural regions have in mind a "traditional" region or area. The ideal form of such a region involves a perfect coincidence between culture and topography, between "blood" and "land." It is often supposed that that ideal form is most nearly approached in primitive and prehistorical cultures in which the dependence of man on land is most complete. Cultural persistence and areal distribution are the phenomena to be described. A "historical-geographical" approach to cultural traditions maps patterns of "diffusion" from particular "cultural hearths," e.g., a particular folk tale is traced as to origins and later geographical distribution. Diffusion of traditional traits is represented as following the pattern made by the waves when a stone is thrown in water, a rippling out from the cultural hearth to occupy successive contiguous areas. The image is only approximate, of course, in that such diffusion is channeled in relation to actual or perceived physical or cultural conditions.

This bibliographical guide has to do with cultural regions in the United States. American culture has always been relatively mobile and so any perfect coincidence between blood and land has always been out of the question. Scholars speak, however, of American "culture areas," understood to be a looser form of the traditional region, behaving in a generally similar way.[6] American culture areas are said to have formed as traits brought from England were transplanted to New England, the Middle Colonies and the Southern Tidewater areas, and then carried west from each of these hearth areas to successive contiguous areas. Thus, particular traditional house forms in Michigan are similar to house forms in New England, and forms in Tennessee similar to those in Virginia. Boundaries can be drawn on the basis of such patterns of diffusion.

If the idea of culture area is much more flexible and indefinite than that of the traditional region, it still depends upon the same general approach: a study of the historical-geographical diffusion of traditional traits. And it still looks for homogeneity in human-land relationships—if of a less stringent sort. For example, we speak of a Mormon culture area in spite of the many diversities within it, because, we say, it is more Mormon than areas outside its boundaries.

Another limited but still very general concept of region, with very different concerns and implications for cultural geography, is that of the "nodal" region. This, again, is an ideal type. It is most perfectly realized in a modern urban-industrial economy, like that in the United States today. Over time, the argument goes, the nation divides up into urban nodes and their hinterlands. The size of the hinterland is largely decided by economic or demographic measures, as disclosed, for example, in patterns of financial transactions or migration flow. Mapping such patterns yields a complex of nodal regions and a hierarchial ordering of urban centers, with Fargo subordinate to Minneapolis, for example, and Minneapolis subordinate to Chicago. A yet further abstraction of such patterns is said to yield an historical "core" region (roughly the New York-Chicago axis) and a "periphery" (the rest of the country). Changes since World War II have, of course, altered that historical pattern. The Sunbelt—the South and the Pacific West—is now sometimes represented as an "emergent" core area.

These two ideal types of region, traditional and nodal, may be represented as polar extremes within which to locate a currently relevant concept of cultural region. Surely in modern times and in the United States, movement in and out of any given area—not to mention the influence of mass communications—radically modifies any notion of historical-geographical homogeneity among cultures and subcultures. The idea of a culture area may be relatively flexible, compared to that of a traditional region, but it still has limited application in the American case. It works better for the years before 1850 than since, and better for east of the Mississippi than west. The idea of nodal region is, likewise, an ideal type with limited application to an understanding of American cultural regions. It works better when applied to Los Angeles than it does when applied to Natchez, and is more relevant to middle class migration patterns than to those of the lower class. The emphasis by students of traditional regions and culture areas on relatively unchanging (even relict) cultural patterns seems to argue, in a country and over a period of great change, that nothing happens for the first time. The emphasis by students of nodal regions upon economic change and innovation and upon the present moment suggests that nothing happens twice.

The recent revival of interest in cultural region coincides with a new interest in how tradition and change interact. To illustrate the general principle: Relocation from New England to upper New York state, before the coming of the Erie Canal, approximates traditional patterns of diffusion. A movement into eastern New York came out of western Massachusetts and Connecticut, with pioneer migrants shuttling back and forth between the frontier settlement and their homes in western New England. The New England culture area could be represented as expanding into successive contiguous areas of its neighboring states.

Once the canal came, movement was much more varied in pattern and cultural uniformities much more scattershot. People moving from Massachusetts into New York might stop in Rochester, but, also, they might go on to Michigan or Illinois. One could say that with the post-canal era patterns of movement approximate the "nodal" pattern, dependent upon the development of a hierarchical network of urban centers. But, just as clearly, any such pattern was attended by a geographical clustering of cultural groups, even if in a scattershot pattern. Thus Massachusetts people moving to Illinois tended to search out (often moved with) their own kind.

Movement to Los Angeles is recent and would seem to carry nodal patterns to their extreme. Yet cultural clustering also characterizes this very mobile population, even as the clusters themselves become more scattershot. Migrants to Pasadena come from a particular, if good-sized, section of Iowa; for many years, Chicago was known to be the prime market for tourists to Southern California. In thinking of cultural region today one must think of the two ideal types of region (traditional, nodal) in combination.

In assembling this bibliography we have tried to be sensitive to contemporary scholarship that describes the geographical interplay between change and tradition. The instances just cited come from migration studies of a particular kind which focus upon such interplay. Present-day studies of the "vernacular" landscape are just as interested in the built environment of the commercial strip as they are in the building traditions of Appalachia. Current environmental research design incorporates a new concern for the inner geography of "home" and "perception," both important to what we have just described as cultural clustering. Revived interest in folk studies turns on a new sensitivity to how folk culture is "carried" by popular culture emanating from the cities, e.g., the way the record industry catered to and affected black folk music; and how, under modern conditions, an individual belongs simultaneously to several folk groups.

Emphasis upon place is attended by emphasis upon perception and the "perspective of experience."[7] It is now common to speak of "vernacular" or "popular" regions as a means of describing how individuals and the populace generally perceive territorial distinctions. An ascendant phenomenological approach to regional studies embeds perception in the taken-for-granted geographical dimensions of human experience.

In popular usage, a region is often thought to be of a certain scale, smaller than the nation and larger than the locality. Geographers argue that a region can be nearly any size. The recent revival of cultural geography has emphasized the very small scale ("place") as its fundamental unit of meaning and has thereby blurred conventional understanding of what size an area must be to be called a region. The recent revival of "community" history also emphasizes the small scale in attempting to understand regional culture. Our discussion of region, reflecting that shift and blurring of meaning, incorporates recent relevant study of place and community. In popular usage, a region is thought to be relatively homogeneous, combining a cluster of culture-traits. Geographers have always insisted that a region can be defined by a single trait. They would say, for example, that the area within which a plurality of people listen to broadcasts about a particular baseball team constitutes a (single-factor) region.

The interconnections between geography and history are central to this book. Whereas the geographer asks *where*, the historian asks *when*. An historian speaks chronologically (of periods or epochs) in much the same way a geographer speaks chronologically (of regions). In recent years, there has been a renewed interest in history among geographers, and a new level of interest in geography among historians, and overlaps between the disciplines are becoming unusually rich and varied. We therefore devote considerable space to an inventory of work in those two disciplines.

In this volume, we distinguish between "regionalism" (region as concept) and "region" (region as object of study). This distinction is particularly evident in subchapters under History and Geography, but it also informs our selections under other headings.

Region as concept varies from discipline to discipline, within any given discipline, and from time to time. Regionalism in American art in the 1930s was tied to a range of regional ideas in the work of such artists as Thomas Hart Benton and Grant Wood. Frederick Jackson Turner made a kind of regionalism (and sectionalism) basic to his ordering of American history. Region in university urban and regional planning departments has a different vocabulary and object than the regionalisms of the 1930s artists or the Turner school of historians. Regionalism, as the term is used here, has to do with such shifting and varied *concepts* of region.

Region as object of study has to do, rather, with (1) studies of region not centered upon conceptual questions; and, (2) within each academic discipline, strands of geographically oriented inquiry that underlay concepts of region and make the study of region important to the discipline. To illustrate the logic of the second category: one strand of geographical thought emphasizes perception of place and region; another, areal differentiation and cultural landscape; still another, statistical distributional patterns in relation to selected social and cultural categories. Such subdisciplinary strands of thought supply the logic for the subchapters under Geography and History. Chapters without subdivisions are understood to incorporate such subdisciplinary concerns under a single heading.

Structure and Organization

Because this is a guide to scholarship, and scholarship is organized according to discipline, our general practice is to group entries according to academic discipline. Generally, if the author of a given entry received a Ph.D. in psychology, the entry appears under Psychology. By the same logic, if a geographer writes about economics, the entry is placed under Geography; if an economist writes about geography, that entry is placed under Economics. There are exceptions. When an individual shifts or divides academic allegiances, we may place a given author or entry under a disciplinary heading other than that in which he/she received a doctorate. On occasion an individual in one discipline writes "in" another. The same principle applies in deciding the placement of entries among subdisciplines, in the subsections of Geography and History. In some cases, where an entry is important to more than one topic, we place the entry under more than one heading or subheading. Those "duplicate" entries are given separate numbers, and the fact of duplication is noted in the index.

Furthermore, it is not always clear what constitutes a discipline. Folk Studies is developing a significant corpus of work following certain scholarly traditions, and so is treated as a discipline, as is the study of Language. American Studies is by its very nature interdisciplinary, so special considerations had to apply there (although we generally looked for a doctorate in that interdisciplinary field). The grouping under Philosophy and Religion is yet more diffuse in focus. On occasion, we know our practice to be arbitrary but unavoidable given the general scheme, as when we place J.B. Jackson "under" Geography, or Lewis Mumford "under" Architecture and Planning and "under" American Studies. Journalists such as Carey McWilliams, Wilbur J. Cash, and Joel Garreau had to be included. They are placed "under" particular disciplines according to our best judgment (e.g., Cash under History: Perception Studies). We hope that our indexing and cross-referencing will help readers thread their way through such ambiguities.

We have assessed the current status of region and regionalism within each of the disciplines in brief introductions to chapters and subchapters as well as in our annotations to particular entries. In those introductions and annotations we have also attempted to supply the user of this guide with some sense of the history of regional concerns within the particular disciplines. Thus we have included work of historical as well as current relevance under each heading. The introductions, entries and annotations have been jointly reviewed, but each chapter or subchapter is the particular responsibility of one or the other of the editors, as indicated by initials at the conclusion of each introduction.

Entries have been selected because of their relevance to the study of cultural regions throughout the United States. We make no attempt to survey work on particular regions. When a study of a particular region is included, it is there because we think it important to regional studies generally. On occasion we include "secondarily relevant" work. For example, Clifford Geertz in *The Interpretation of Cultures* (item 91, under Anthropology) does not have much to say about regions per se, but his comments on the connections between primordial loyalties and modernization are important to our general concerns. The recent surge of interest in region-related topics in history and geography called for sustained attention to secondarily relevant work in those two disciplines. On occasion we include popularizations and textbooks when they seem to us to contribute to an understanding of the scholarship being reviewed. And on occasion we include model studies, not because they are unique or representative but because we think them unusually good.

The length of this guide goes beyond our plans or intentions. It represents years of work. For all that, it is not comprehensive. We could well have included lists of bibliographies, teaching aids, and journals, had time and space permitted. Because of our training, we tend to emphasize cultural history and a qualitative approach, although we have tried to stay alert to relevant quantitative work. Within such constraints, we have attempted to provide a review of all important work on our general topic in the humanities and the social sciences.

Michael Steiner
Department of American Studies
California State University,
Fullerton

Clarence Mondale
Program in American Civilization
George Washington University

[1]Lillian Hellman, review of *The Provincials* by Eli N. Evans in *The New York Review of Books* (November 11, 1973): 5.

[2]William Stafford, "Regionalism, Localism and Art," *South Dakota Review* 13 (August 1975): 47.

[3]Nathaniel Hawthorne to Henry Wadsworth Longfellow, 29 October 1854, cited in Merle Curti, *The Roots of American Loyalty* (New York: Columbia University Press, 1946), 32, and Hawthorne to Horatio Bridge, 15 January 1857, cited in Randall Stewart, *Regionalism and Beyond: The Essays of Randall Stewart*, ed. George Core (Nashville: Vanderbilt University Press, 1973, 157. John Dewey, "Americanism and Localism," *Dial* 68 (1920): 685–86.

[4]Important analyses of the "new regionalism" include Richard Maxwell Brown, "The New Regionalism in America, 1970–1981," in *Regionalism in the Pacific Northwest*, ed. William G. Robbins et al. (Corvallis: Oregon State Univ. Press, 1983), 37–96; David R. Goldfield, "The New Regionalism," *Journal of Urban History* 10 (February 1984): 171–86; and Jim Wayne Miller, "Anytime the Ground is Uneven: The Outlook for Regional Studies and What to Look Out For," in *Geography and Literature: A Meeting of Disciplines*, ed. William E. Mallory and Paul Simpson Housley (Syracuse: Syracuse Univ. Press, 1987), 1–20.

[5]Benjamin Botkin, "Regionalism: Cult or Culture?" *English Journal* 25 (March 1936): 181–85; Eudora Welty, "Place in Fiction," in *The Eye of the Story: Selected Essays and Reviews* (New York: Random House, 1978), 116–33; Wendell Berry, "The Regional Motive," in *A Continuous Harmony: Essays Cultural and Agricultural* (New York: Harcourt, Brace, Jovanovich, 1970), 63–70.

[6]An influential statement as to distinctions between a traditional region and a culture area can be found in Wilbur Zelinsky, *The Cultural Geography of the United States* (Englewood Cliffs, N.J.: Prentice-Hall, 1973), 110–13. In some ways more interesting is Zelinsky's later and briefer statement in "General Cultural and Popular Regions," in *This Remarkable Continent: An Atlas of the United States and Canadian Society and Culture*, ed. John F. Rooney et al. (College Station: Texas A&M Press, 1982), 3. There he describes as "the holiest of professional grails" the "division of the entire world into a set of strictly defined *total* geographic regions, that is tracts of territory that are congruent in terms of everything—physical features as well as social, economic, political, and other human traits." For Zelinsky, the idea of culture area is a necessary but impoverished approximation of that ideal.

[7]The phrase comes from Yi-Fu Tuan. See his *Space and Place: The Perspective of Experience* (Minneapolis: Univ. of Minnesota Press, 1977).

REGION AND REGIONALISM
IN THE UNITED STATES

American Studies

Region and regionalism have been central themes in American Studies scholarship from the 1920s until the present. The American Studies movement emerged in the early 1920s as a cross-disciplinary effort to breach formal boundaries of intellectual inquiry in order to understand American culture as a whole. As part of the revolt against formalism and the search for a usable past that concerned so many intellectuals after the First World War, American Studies scholars helped initiate a Whitmanesque rediscovery of the profusion of American life.[1] As if fulfilling Whitman's call to "study out the land" and appreciate the indigenous, many of the founders of the American Studies movement, including Vernon Louis Parrington, Lewis Mumford, Van Wyck Brooks, Constance Rourke, Bernard DeVoto, and Howard Mumford Jones, pushed beyond a simple celebration of cultural nationalism to a deeper understanding of America's regional diversity.

A regional orientation continued as American Studies gained institutional recognition in the 1930s, 40s, and 50s. Beginning at Yale in 1933, American Studies programs were launched across the country. By 1947 more than sixty colleges and universities had undergraduate programs while fifteen had graduate programs in American Studies, and regionalism became an important part of American Studies curriculum and scholarship.[2] The graduate programs at Harvard (1936) and Minnesota (1945) became particularly important centers of regional scholarship. At Harvard, Perry Miller, F.O. Matthiessen, Kenneth Murdock, Bernard DeVoto, and Howard Mumford Jones fostered New England and regional studies in general. Three of the first graduates of the Harvard program and earliest recipients of Ph.D.s in American Studies—Henry Nash Smith (1940), Edmund Morgan (1942), and Richard Dorson (1944)—wrote dissertations on images of the American West, the seventeenth century New England family, and New England folklore, respectively, and each scholar proceeded to make important contributions to American regional studies. At Minnesota, Tremaine McDowell, Theodore Blegen, Robert Penn Warren, and Henry Nash

3

Smith pursued a variety of regional scholarship that was carried on by their students Leo Marx, Scott Donaldson, Peter Schmitt, Alan Trachtenberg, and others.

If one theme united this second generation of regional American Studies, it was a focus upon the symbolic or psychological significance of the region or the land within the national experience. Paralleling Wilbur J. Cash's profound analysis of regional consciousness in *The Mind of the South* (1941), Americanists such as Henry Nash Smith, Leo Marx, William R. Taylor, Scott Donaldson, Edward G. White, and William H. Goetzmann examined regional images, myths, and personality types and their relationship to the national character.

A third generation of regional American Studies seems to have emerged since the late 1960s when at least two historical crises reoriented and revitalized regional thought. First, the environmental crisis brought much of the regional symbol-myth-image analysis down to earth, and Americanists such as Donald Worster, Kai Erikson, and William Cronon have focused upon specific examples of environmental abuse and have used ecological principles to enhance our understanding of the significance of place and region. Second, the general cultural turmoil of the late sixties—the civil rights and anti-war protests, the assassinations and urban riots, the insistent demands of young people, women, blacks, Hispanics, Native Americans, and others—shattered the comfortable myth of America as a monolithic, homogeneous culture and compelled American Studies scholars to perceive regionalism as an essential component of America's abiding pluralism. David Whisnant, Robin Winks, Michael Steiner, Werner Sollers, and Jay Mechling are some of the Americanists who have recently explored the relationship between cultural pluralism and regionalism, between place and identity.

Rediscovery of regionalism as the spatial dimension of pluralism and renewed appreciation of place inform this important revival of regional American Studies. At the same time that a sophisticated symbol-myth-image analysis of landscape and region continues in the work of Alan Trachtenberg, Richard Slotkin, Sacvan Bercovitch, and Myra Jehlen, other Americanists are looking beneath regional images and myths for the more immediate reality and experienced texture of regional life through the interpretation of material culture, cultural landscapes, and everyday life. The materials by Michael Barton, Thomas Schlereth, and Robert Sklar reflect this grounded, contextual approach to regional studies.

The interdisciplinary nature of American Studies makes it extremely difficult to draw precise boundaries between it and other academic fields. As already mentioned, the American Studies movement grew out of the revolt against traditional disciplinary constraints, and

Parrington, Mumford, Brooks, and Rourke drew freely from literature, history, art history, sociology, geography, and other fields to comprehend American culture as a whole. This holistic impulse has characterized American Studies scholarship even after it emerged as an academic discipline by the late 1930s.

As with the other disciplinary divisions in our book, we have weighed at least three criteria for placing a piece of scholarship in this area: (1) the author's academic training, (2) his or her departmental or professional affiliation, and (3) the method and subject-matter of the work being considered. Our task would be relatively simple if these variables coincided for every entry; unfortunately, a scholar can be trained in one area, teach in another, and write about a third. Such academic hybridization is especially common in American Studies where some scholars, such as Edmund Morgan or Richard Dorson, have moved on to cultural history and folk studies after being trained in American Studies, while others, such as Sacvan Bercovitch or David Whisnant, are active in American Studies after being trained in literature. With these and other problems in mind, we have carefully applied the above criteria to each piece of scholarship; in cases where more than one disciplinary category offered itself, we have chosen the discipline to which the work in question makes the greatest contribution.

Mindful of the inevitable flaws in boundary making—the difficulties inherent in the *regionalization* of knowledge, ironically enough!—we have tried to indicate, both in the headnotes and in specific entries where disciplinary territories overlap, where related sources can be found within other categories. There are many connections between regional scholarship in American Studies and regional studies in art, folk studies, history, and literature. The symbol-myth approach, pioneered in American Studies, has been especially useful for historians and literary scholars. Paralleling work in American Studies, historians such as Ray Billington, Frank Kramer, Roderick Nash, and Henry Shapiro, and literary scholars such as Annette Kolodny, Lewis Simpson, Cecelia Tichi, and David Wyatt have examined the symbols, myths, and images associated with American landscapes and regions. See History: Perception Studies (items 858, 871, 874, 881) and Literature (items 1232–1233, 1278–1279, 1305, 1325).

M.S.

[1]See, for example, Gene Wise, "Paradigm Dramas in American Studies: A Cultural and Institutional History of the Movement," *American Quarterly* 31 (Bibliography Issue 1979), 293–337 and Robert Sklar, "American Studies and the Realities of America," *American Quarterly* 22 (Summer 1970), 597–605.

[2]Tremaine McDowell's *American Studies* (Minneapolis: Univ.of Minnesota Press, 1948) is an important account of the regional dimension of the discipline in its formative years. Articles by Lawrence Veysey, Marshall Fishwick, Jay Mechling, and Robin Winks, annotated in this chapter, trace the significance of regionalism in American Studies from the 1940s to the 1980s.

*   *   *

1. Ahlstrom, Sidney. "On the Purpose and Significance of Regional Study With Special Reference to New England." In *Reports and Speeches of the Seventh* Yale Conference on the Teaching of the Social Sciences, 47–50. New Haven: Master of Arts in Teaching Program, 1962.

A vigorous appeal for grounded regional scholarship to balance sweeping and often superficial national perspectives. "Regional study," Ahlstrom argues, "allows one to move from the thin, over-generalized falsifications of any broad survey to a confrontation of concrete historical relationships on a smaller scale. . . . we need smaller units of study if we are to grapple with the historical process itself."

2. Barton, Michael, ed. "The Study of American Everyday." *American Quarterly* 34 (Bibliography Issue 1982).

Essays providing useful advice for studying the immediate experience of regional life include John L. Caughey, "The Ethnography of Everyday Life: Theories and Methods for American Culture Studies," pp. 222–43; Jack Larkin, "The View from New England: Notes on Everyday Life in Rural America to 1850," pp. 244–61; Peter O. Muller, "Everyday Life in Suburbia," pp. 262–77; and Charles Camp, "Foodways and Everyday Life," pp. 278–89.

3. Bercovitch, Sacvan. *The Puritan Origins of the American Self.* New Haven: Yale Univ. Press, 1975.

Bercovitch argues that a vision of the New World landscape as a source of redemption lies at the heart of the seventeenth-century New England imagination and that this image of a "new man in a paradisiacal world" continues to influence national identity. "The Myth of America," pp. 136–86, contains a perceptive comparison between southern, Latin American, and New England interpretations or "hermeneutics" of landscape and describes how the prevailing American vision emerged from such New England spokesmen as Cotton Mather, Jonathan Edwards, and Ralph Waldo Emerson.

4. Brooks, Van Wyck. "Regionalism and Nationalism." In *The Opinions of Oliver Allston*, 256–72. New York: E.P. Dutton. 1941.

In this perceptive analysis of the relationship between regionalism, nationalism, and internationalism, Brooks contrasts the immediacy of local experience and expression to rootless cosmopolitanism and argues that regional diversity is the key to a healthy nationalism and a harmonious world order. This is Brooks' most explicit discussion of the connection between two central themes in his work: the cultural nationalism of *America's Coming of Age* (1915) and *Letters and Leadership* (1918) and the regional focus of *The Flowering of New England* (1936) and *New England: Indian Summer* (1940).

5. Cronon, William. *Changes in the Land: Indians, Colonists, and the Ecology of New England.* New York: Hill & Wang, 1983.

A masterful study of the complex interplay between nature and culture in New England during the seventeenth and eighteenth centuries. From an impressive theoretical foundation in plant ecology, historical anthropology, and cultural geography, Cronon carefully compares Native American and European responses to the New England environment. In many ways a model of regional portraiture and analysis, this book is part of a continuing tradition of ecologically oriented cultural history that includes the work of George Perkins Marsh, Fernand Braudel, Jacquetta Hawkes, Carl Sauer, Walter Prescott Webb, James C. Malin, and Donald Worster.

6. ————. "Revisiting the Vanishing Frontier: The Legacy of Frederick Jackson Turner." *Western Historical Quarterly* 28 (April 1987): 157–76.

After reviewing the barrage of criticism leveled at Turner's frontier thesis, Cronon explores reasons for the persistence of this much-maligned theory and suggests that other elements of Turner's thought could lend new unity to the writing of western history. Although Turner's own efforts to write regional history lacked a sense of dynamic narrative and unity, his vision of the interaction between nature and humanity and his "emphasis on the importance of regional

environments to our understanding the course of American history"
make him "one of the pathfinders whose well-blazed trail we continue
to follow."

7. Donaldson, Scott. *The Suburban Myth.* New York: Columbia Univ.
Press, 1969.

A vivid, interdisciplinary study of the meaning of suburbs in
American culture from the late nineteenth to the mid-twentieth century.
Donaldson argues, in part, that the Jeffersonian yeoman myth lies
behind the general disillusionment found in literature about suburbia
written after 1945. Critical of the supposed conformity of suburban life,
that literature dwells upon unrepresentative cases studies. "City and
Country: Marriage Proposals," pp. 23–44, is a valuable analysis of the
cultural forces fueling twentieth century English and American urban
and regional planning.

8. Fishwick, Marshall. "What Ever Happened to Regionalism?"
Southern Humanities Review 2 (Summer 1968): 393–401.

After comparing the surge in regional interest during the 1930s
with the relative dearth of regional concerns in the 1960s, Fishwick
surveys more than one hundred scholars and writers concerning this
apparent decline. Insightful comments by John Kouwenhoven, Oscar
Handlin, Norman Holmes Pearson, Robert Spiller, C. Vann Woodward,
and others are analyzed.

9. Fryer, Judith. "Women and Space: The Flowering of Desire." In
Prospects: An Annual of American Culture Studies. vol. 9, edited by
Jack Salzman, 187–230. New York: Cambridge Univ. Press, 1984.

This essay examines the culturally ascribed meanings of space,
especially built environments, for women and men in the late
nineteenth century. Fryer draws upon the writings of Edith Wharton,
Willa Cather, Charlotte Perkins Gilman, Kate Chopin, Henry James,
and Henry Adams; the architecture of Louis Sullivan, Frank Lloyd
Wright, and Daniel Burnham; and the spatial theories of Yi-Fu Tuan,
Edward Hall, Shirley Ardener, and Virginia Woolf to analyze
significance of public and private realms, movement, and sense of place
for men and for women in American Victorian culture. This argument
has been expanded in Fryer's *Felicitous Space: The Imaginative
Structures of Edith Wharton and Willa Cather* (Chapel Hill: Univ. of
North Carolina Press, 1986).

10. Goetzmann, William H. *Exploration and Empire: Explorer and Scientist in the Winning of the West.* New York: Vintage Books, 1966.

This prize-winning history represents exploration as a more or less systematic process with its objectives defined by the home society sponsoring its activity. Reminiscent of Slotkin, Smith, and White (items 43–44, 45–48, 62), Goetzmann depicts how explorers—from mountain men to members of the U.S. Geological Survey—perceive new environments in terms of their cultural backgrounds and how their discoveries both mirror and transform the home culture. The general topic is the trans-Mississippi West, and Goetzmann draws upon a stunning array of sources (travel charts, scientific reports, lithographs and photographs, specimen collections, contemporary geographies, etc.). Goetzmann describes three historical phases: the Lewis and Clark period (to 1845), the period of settlement and investment (1845–60), and the period of the great surveys (1860–90).

11. ———. *New Lands, New Men: America and the Second Great Age of Discovery.* New York: Viking Press, 1987.

In *Exploration and Empire* (1966), Goetzmann examined the charting of new land within the American West; in this detailed, lavishly illustrated book, he analyzes American exploration within a global context. American explorers are seen as part of a larger "transnational culture of science" that surveyed every corner of America and the far reaches of the world in the eighteenth and nineteenth centuries. Goetzmann's analysis of the perception and meaning of various portions of the new world landscape to the international scientific community during these years is discussed in his opening section, "The Book of the Continent," pp. 19–193.

12. Goetzmann, William H. and William N. Goetzmann. *The West of the Imagination.* New York: W.W. Norton, 1986.

This book, companion to a TV series, is aimed at a popular audience and attempts to connect the development of myths about the West to its visual representations. What is involved, the authors argue, is often good art as well as a message with mythic import. The book is interestingly varied in presentation, moving from painters such as Peale and then Catlin, to Currier and Ives, to popular culture and then to the movies. The midwestern regionalists like Benton and the southwestern artists like Georgia O'Keefe are represented. See W.H. Goetzmann and Becky Duval Reese, *Texas Images and Visions* (Austin: Univ. of Texas Press, 1983) for a similar treatment of one state.

13. Jehlen, Myra. *American Incarnation: The Individual, The Nation and the Continent*. Cambridge: Harvard Univ. Press, 1986.

Paralleling Sacvan Berkovitch, Jehlen argues that the uniqueness of American culture, especially its foundation in liberal individualism, is rooted in perceptions of the New World landscape as an open field for individual achievement. The open land allowed the realization or "incarnation" of liberal individualism; Jehlen traces expressions of this theme in Crevecoeur, Franklin, Emerson, Hawthorne, Melville, and other eighteenth and nineteenth century American writers.

14. Jones, Howard Mumford. *O Strange New World. American Formative Years*. New York: Viking Press, 1964.

"The Image of the New World," pp. 1–34, and "the Anti-Image," pp. 35–70, are masterful analyses of the myriad of myths and images Europeans have used to understand newly discovered American landscapes. Jones's final chapter, "The American Landscape," pp. 351–89, carries the theme of initial discovery into various regions across the continent and discusses the impact of such variegated yet open space upon the national character.

15. Lamar, Howard R. "The Concept of Regionalism in the Teaching of the History of the American West." In *Reports and Speeches of the Seventh Yale Conference on the Teaching of the Social Sciences*, 55–62. New Haven: Master of Arts in Teaching Program, 1962.

After tracing the history of the regional concept in teaching and research, from John Wesley Powell and Frederick Jackson Turner to Howard Odum and Theodore Blegen, Lamar suggests that states may be more significant than regions as cultural containers. "Settlers and their cultural heritage operating within state boundaries," he writes," offer a deeper explanation to the student than do physiographic regions or even artificial regionalism."

16. Lerner, Max. "Regions: The Fusion of People and Place." In *America as a Civilization*, 182–306. New York: Simon & Schuster, 1957.

This useful survey of regional cultures contains a perceptive discussion of the fluctuating interplay between the forces of mobility and attachment to place in American life.

17. McDowell, Tremaine. "Region, Nation, World." In *American Studies*, 82–96. Minneapolis: Univ. of Minnesota Press, 1948.

Drawing from Josiah Royce, John Dewey, and Walt Whitman, McDowell eloquently argues that regionalism as opposed to sectionalism is an outward looking, integrative force and that American Studies scholarship and teaching ought to encourage an ever-expanding consciousness of region, nation, and world.

18. Marcell, David W. "Regions and Regionalism." In *American Studies: A Guide to Information Sources*, 143–147. Detroit: Gale Research Co., 1982.

This is a useful, although unannotated, bibliography.

19. Marx, Leo. "American Institutions and the Ecological Ideal." In *Arts of the Environment* (item 276), 78–97.

After placing the environmental crisis of the late 1960s within a larger cultural-historical context, Marx argues that classic American writers such as Cooper, Emerson, Thoreau, Melville, Whitman, and Twain have lamented the environmental destructiveness of their culture and provided visions of a countervailing ecological ideal. This literary-ecological vision should allow us to consider the "deep-seated, institutional causes of our distress," confront the destructive power of our society, and realize that "To arrest the deterioration of the environment it will be necessary to control many of the same forces that have prevented us from ending the war in Indochina or giving justice to black Americans."

20. ———. *The Machine in the Garden: Technology and the Pastoral Idea in America*. New York: Oxford Univ. Press, 1964.

This influential study of the symbols and myths associated with the American landscape focuses upon the meanings of wilderness, garden, and city and examines the persistent lure of the pastoral ideal—the urge to withdraw to a rural-agrarian refuge away from the demands of the city and the uncertainties of the wilderness. Marx traces the profound impact of this rural myth upon American culture from the seventeenth to the twentieth century, especially as it has been challenged by the equally alluring force of industrial technology.

21. ———. "Pastoral Ideals and City Troubles." *Journal of General Education* 20 (1968–69): 251–71. Reprinted in *Western Man and Environmental Ethics*, edited by Ian G. Barbour, 93–115. Menlo Park, Calif.: Addison-Wesley, 1973.

After describing a pervasive pastoral pattern in American culture—a symbolic journey between urban, rural, and wild landscapes—Marx suggests how an understanding of these symbolic landscapes can be applied to urban and regional planning. For a related essay, see his "The Pastoral and Its Guises," *Sewanee Review* 82 (Spring 1974), pp. 351–62.

22. Matthiessen, F.O. *American Renaissance: Art and Expression in the Age of Emerson and Whitman.* New York: Oxford Univ. Press, 1941.

Consciously building upon the earlier work of Lewis Mumford and Van Wyck Brooks and using the vehicles of literary criticism and intellectual history, Matthiessen's monumental portrait of the New England mind parallels Wilbur Cash's *Mind of the South* published in the same year. Matthiessen's brilliant discussions of "New England Landscapes," pp. 157–65; and "The Problem of the Artist as New Englander," pp. 192–241, as well as asides on the genre paintings of William Sidney Mount and the organic principles of sculptor Horatio Greenough and clipper ship builder Donald McKay, contribute to a profound portrait of the regional dimensions of cultural expression.

23. Mechling, Jay. "If They Can Build a Square Tomato: Notes Toward a Holistic Approach to Regional Studies." In *Prospects: An Annual of American Culture Studies.* vol. 3, edited by Jack Salzman, 59–77. New York: Burt Franklin, 1978.

A perceptive argument for reviving and expanding the study of region and place within American Studies. Beyond effectively connecting regional studies to larger issues of cultural pluralism and modernization, Mechling discusses how regional courses can make vital contributions to American Studies curricula.

24. ———. "Minds, Messages, and Madness: Gregory Bateson Makes a Paradigm for American Culture Studies." In *Prospects: An Annual of American Culture Studies.* vol. 8, edited by Jack Salzman, 11–30. New York: Burt Franklin, 1983.

A central portion of this essay describes how Bateson's concepts of "mind" and "ecology" can enhance regional studies. To conceive of the "region as a mind" possessing "the mental qualities that we associate with all cybernetic systems" encourages students and teachers alike to appreciate the diversity of ideas and cultures that constitute every regional household.

25. Minshull, Roger. "The Function of Geography in American Studies." *Journal of American Studies* 7 (December 1973): 267–78.

After describing the problems commonly encountered in connecting geography and American Studies, this British geographer suggests how four major themes—regional variations, landscape development, manland relationships, and spatial relationships—might be fruitfully studied by both disciplines. All of these themes, furthermore, converge in "the study of the geography of the American city"—a concern that should be central to American Studies.

26. Mumford, Lewis. *The Brown Decades: A Study of the Arts in America, 1865-1895*. New York: Harcourt, Brace, 1931.

Beneath the aggressive expansionism and sooty industrialization of the Gilded Age, Mumford locates hints of environmental consciousness and sources for the much-needed regional renewal of America in the work of John Burroughs, George Perkins Marsh, Frederick Law Olmsted, John Muir, Nathaniel Southgate Shaler, Winslow Homer, Albert Pinkham Ryder, Henry Hobson Richardson, Louis Sullivan, and others. "The Renewal of the Landscape," pp. 59–106, is crucial for understanding an important source of American regional thought and practice. Mumford's contributions to regional thought are indispensable and ubiquitous: his most important and accessible studies in the cultural history of American regionalism are listed here (items 27–28); his seminal work in regional planning is located under Architecture and Regional Planning (items 196–201). See Elmer S. Newman, *Lewis Mumford: A Bibliography, 1914–1970* (New York: Harcourt, Brace, Jovanovich, 1971) for a complete listing of Mumford's voluminous work until 1970.

27. ———. *The Golden Day: A Study of American Experience and Culture*. New York: Boni and Liveright, 1926.

In this neglected regional masterpiece, Mumford condemns the churning, rootless frontier and exalts the sense of place and creativity found in New England during the 1830s, 1840s, and 1850s. This "Golden Day" of creative stability is offered as a model for the regional renewal of American life in the twentieth century.

28. ———. "Roots in the Region." In *Faith For Living*, 259–79. New York: Harcourt, Brace, 1940.

This vividly written survey of the strengths and weaknesses of American regionalism contains a passionate argument that regionalism, rightly practiced, is the ultimate source of national purpose in the fight against fascism.

29. Mussell, Kay, ed. *American Studies/Regional Studies: A Report.*
Washington, D.C.: American University, 1980.

A summary of the work of the NEH-sponsored Regional American
Studies Information Clearinghouse from 1978 until 1980, this report is
useful for constructing regional courses from an American Studies
perspective. It contains information concerning domestic student
exchange programs and regional studies centers; lists of regionally-
related summer programs and workshops; a nationwide sampling of
sixteen course outlines on regional theory, regions, and cities; brief
descriptions of regional course offerings and activities at some 123
colleges and universities; and an extensive bibliography on American
regionalism by Michael Steiner.

30. Noble, David W. "American Studies and the Burden of Frederick
Jackson Turner: The Case of Henry Nash Smith and Richard
Hofstadter." *Journal of American Culture* 4 (Winter 1981): 34–45.

An intricate discussion of the strengths and weaknesses of the
symbol-myth strain in American Studies with oblique reference to the
regional orientation of much of that scholarship. Noble argues that an
implicit acceptance of Turner's dichotomy between a mythic nineteenth
century agrarian America and a utilitarian twentieth century industrial
America has made it difficult for scholars such as Smith and Hofstadter
to perceive symbols and myths as operative in contemporary American
society. Cultural anthropology, he concludes, may provide a path for
"symbol-myth humanists" to bring "a sense of cultural wholeness into
the twentieth century."

31. Parrington, Vernon Lewis. *Main Currents in American Thought.* 3
vols. New York: Harcourt, Brace, 1927.

This massive landmark in American Studies scholarship balances
national and regional visions of American culture. Considerations of
regionalism dominate Volume Two, *The Romantic Revolution in
America,* which is divided into three "books": "The Mind of the South,"
"The Mind of the Middle East," and "The Mind of New England."
Volume Three, *The Beginnings of Critical Realism in America,*
contains valuable discussions on the intellectual climates of the
Midwest, the South, and the urban-industrial scene in late nineteenth
and early twentieth centuries. Parrington's discussions of the
intellectual-psychological dimensions of regional identity have deeply
influenced American regional studies.

32. Rock, Virginia J. "They Took Their Stand: The Emergence of the Southern Agrarians." In *Prospects: An Annual of American Culture Studies*. vol. 1, edited by Jack Salzman, 205–95. New York: Burt Franklin, 1975.

In this thorough analysis of the most visible and vocal group of regionalists during the 1920s and 1930s, Rock discusses the background to the Agrarian protest as well as the contemporary relevance of their thought. See Rock's "Agrarianism: Agrarian Themes in Southern Writing," *Mississippi Quarterly* 21 (Spring 1968), pp. 145–50 for a highly perceptive bibliographical narrative.

33. Rourke, Constance. *American Humor: A Study of the National Character*. New York: Harcourt, Brace & Co., 1931.

In this brilliant inventory of America's "usable past," Rourke uncovers a rich accumulation of largely comic folklore that has sustained American art forms and American culture in general. The first three chapters, pp. 3–104, introduce an enduring trio of regional comic figures who emerged during the early national period: the Yankee pedlar, the backwoodsman or "gamecock of the wilderness," and the Negro minstrel or "long-tail'd blue." "Facing West From California's Shores," pp. 204–34, analyzes the rise of distinct cultural forms in the West and the creative tension between regionalism and nationalism in the late nineteenth century. The final chapter, "Roundup," pp. 266–302, traces the relationship between folk culture and regionalism and nationalism into the early twentieth century literature.

34. ———. *The Roots of American Culture and Other Essays*. Edited by Van Wyck Brooks. New York: Harcourt, Brace & World, 1942.

The majority of the eight essays collected here shed light upon the folk-regional roots of American expressive forms. "The Roots of American Culture," pp. 3–59, cogently modifies John Fiske's influential "transit of culture" thesis by pointing out the vitality of indigenous American folk forms and their diffusion from "many radial centers along the Atlantic seaboard and even inland." "The Rise of Theatricals," pp. 60–160, and "Early American Music," 161–94, trace, in part, regional patterns in these early expressive forms. "A Note on Folklore," pp. 238–50, promotes the teaching of folk studies, especially on a regional basis, and "American Art: A Possible Future," pp. 275–96, examines the relationship between nationalism and regionalism in the arts into the 1930s. Other sources by Rourke are listed under Art (items 301–302).

35. ———. "The Significance of Sections." *New Republic* 76 (September 20, 1933): 147–51.

In this insightful review of Frederick Jackson Turner's book on sectionalism, Rourke argues in the same vein as B.A. Botkin and Meridel LeSueur that regionalism can sustain progressive, even "proletarian," causes.

36. Salzman, Jack, ed. "Regionalism and Ethnicity in American Literature." *Prospects: An Annual of American Culture Studies*, 433–77. vol. 9. New York: Cambridge University Press, 1984.

This symposium of papers selected from a 1981 American Studies Association convention devoted to "Regionalism in American Culture" contains four useful essays. Jules Chametsky's "Styron's *Sophie's Choice*, Jews and Other Marginals and the Mainstream," pp. 433–40, uses Victor Turner's concepts of "liminality," "marginality," and "communitas" to understand the process by which regional writers like Styron and Twain have moved from the edges to the center of the literary establishment and cultural mainstream. Werner Soller's "Region, Ethnic Group, and American Writers . . . ," pp. 441–62, traces the impact of Josiah Royce's notion of "wholesome provincialism" upon theories of regionalism and cultural pluralism propounded by Horace Kallen, Randolph Bourne, Howard Odum, David Potter, and Ludwig Lewisohn. Virginia Yans-McLaughlin and David Balwin offer highly perceptive comments upon Chametsky's and Sollers's arguments, pp. 463–69 and 471–77, respectively.

37. Schlereth, Thomas J. "Regional Studies in America: The Chicago Model." *American Studies: An International Newsletter* 13 (Autumn 1974): 20–34. Updated in *Sources for American Studies*, edited by Jefferson B. Kellogg and Robert H. Walker, 518–32. Westport, Conn.: Greenwood Press, 1983.

Although largely a bibliographic survey of materials related to Chicago, this essay effectively argues that a course structured around "the cultural history of Chicago from the 1870s to the 1920s provides a striking microcosm of the political, economic, literary, and artistic developments in the nation at large."

38. ———, ed. "American Studies and Students of American Things." *American Quarterly*, 35 (Bibliography Issue, 1983).

Important essays stressing the use of landscape and material culture studies in American studies include: Peirce Lewis, "Learning From Looking: Geographic and Other Writing About the American Cultural

Landscape," pp. 242–61; Dell Upton, "The Power of Things: Recent Studies in American Vernacular Architecture," pp. 262–79; Kenneth L. Ames, "American decorative Arts/Household Furnishings," pp. 280–303; Carroll W. Pursell, "The History of Technology and the Study of Material Culture," pp. 304–15; and Simon Bronner, "'Visible Proofs': Material Culture Studies in American Folkloristics," pp. 316–38. For an expanded version of this issue with extensive bibliographical essays by Schlereth, see Thomas J. Schlereth, ed., *Material Culture: A Research Guide* (Lawrence: Univ. Press of Kansas, 1985).

39. ———, ed. *Material Culture Studies in America*. Nashville: American Association for State and Local History, 1982.

This richly detailed anthology contains twenty-five essays, ranging from general theoretical statements, such as John L. Kouwenhoven's "American Studies: Words or Things?," pp. 79–92, to studies of specific artifacts such as gravestones, Coca-Cola bottles, and service stations.

40. Schmitt, Peter J. *Back to Nature: The Arcadian Myth in Urban America*. New York: Oxford Univ. Press, 1969.

A brisk, insightful analysis of the pervasive desire to bring "nature" to urban America from 1880 until 1920. This "arcadian" impulse gripped intellectuals as varied as John Burroughs, Liberty Hyde Bailey, and G. Stanley Hall, influenced the growth of suburbs, inspired the Country Life Movement, playground movement, Boy Scouts, and bird watchers. Most significantly for the students of American regionalism, Schmitt examines the arcadian roots of the regional planning movement in chapter 17, "The New Frontier," pp. 177–89.

41. Shapiro, Edward S.. "Southern Agrarians and the TVA." *American Quarterly*, 22 (Winter 1970): 791–806.

Shapiro points out that, with the exception of Donald Davidson, the Vanderbilt Agrarians had relatively favorable reactions to the Tenneseee Valley Authority.

42. Sklar, Robert. "American Studies and the Realities of America." *American Quarterly* 22 (Summer 1970): 597–605.

Sklar urges American Studies scholars to adopt a pluralistic vision of culture rather than the monolithic perspective perpetuated by most national character and symbol-myth-image studies. His call for "a recognition that a variety of cultures exist in America, each one creating its separate institutions and forms, its alternative vision of reality," is conducive to regional American Studies scholarship since the 1960s. See Sklar's "Cultural History and American Studies: Past, Present, and Future," *American Studies: An International Newsletter* 11 (Autumn 1971), pp. 3–9, for a closely related argument.

43. Slotkin, Richard. *The Fatal Environment: The Myth of the Frontier in the Age of Industrialization, 1800–1890*. New York: Atheneum, 1985.

In this sweeping symbol-myth analysis of the meanings of the ever retreating frontier in the nineteenth century America, Custer's Last Stand is carefully examined as the central fable of a revised Frontier Myth used to explain the contradictions inherent in the industrial conquest of the wilderness. "It is this industrial and imperial version of the Frontier Myth," Slotkin argues, "whose categories still inform our political rhetoric of pioneering progress, world mission, and eternal strife with the forces of darkness and barbarism. It is this myth whose fictive fatalities lurk in the cultural environment we inhabit, whose significance can still be seen behind the silhouettes of skyscrapers, casinos, pipelines, gantries, and freeways." Slotkin's analysis of the "landscape of myth" and its environmental and political consequences, his narration of the morality play between the forces of the Wilderness and the Metropolis in American culture, and his discussion of southern and eastern uses of the Western frontier are valuable contributions to American regional thought.

44. ———. *Regeneration Through Violence: The Mythology of the American Frontier, 1600–1860*. Middletown, Conn.: Wesleyan Univ. Press, 1973.

In this influential study of the violent undertones of the myth of the frontier, Slotkin describes how Europeans gained fresh identity in America through aggressive conquest—violent, transforming acts against the wilderness and its dark inhabitants—and how such behavior is embedded in our national character. A detailed analysis of captivity and hunter narratives lies at the heart of Slotkin's argument, and chapter twelve, "The Fragmented Image: The Boone Myth and Sectional Cultures, 1820–1850," describes regional permutations of frontier mythology.

45. Smith, Henry Nash. "The Dilemma of Agrarianism." *Southwest Review* 14 (April 1934): 215–21.

Stressing that industrialization is an inseparable part of Southern society, Smith underscores the quixotic quality of Agrarian hopes.

"When the Agrarians," he writes, "talk about agriculture as a way of life able to foster the spiritual values destroyed by industrialism, they must be thinking of something besides the kind of farming which is now usual in the South: an ideal, not an actual, Agrarianism." This and the following articles reflect Smith's thorough backgound in regional theory.

46. ———. "The Feel of the Purposeful Earth: Mary Austin's Prophecy." *New Mexico Quarterly* 1 (February 1931): 17–33.

Smith praises Austin's efforts to find the essential rhythms of a regional landscape in its aboriginal myths and folklore, and he argues that this is part of the necessary task of building a truly indigenous American civilization.

47. ———. "Localism in Literature." *Folk-Say: A Regional Miscellany* 2 (1930): 298–310.

This is a generally positive appraisal of the aesthetic and economic implications of the "new regionalism" of the late 1920s.

48. ———. *Virgin Land: The American West as Symbol and Myth.* Cambridge, Mass.: Harvard Univ. Press, 1950.

A masterful study of the symbols and myths surrounding the trans-Mississippi West from the Lewis and Clark expedition (1803–5) to Turner's frontier elegy (1893). Smith's vivid analysis of environmental imagery found in explorers' accounts, dime novels, popular orations, and creative literature; his discussion of changing perceptions of the West, from forbidding desert to beckoning garden; his description of northern and southern versions of the myths of the garden and the yeoman farmer; his efforts to connect regional symbols and myths to physical and social realities—all are vital models for regional American Studies.

49. Sollers, Werner. "The Ethics of Wholesome Provincialism." In *Beyond Ethnicity: Consent and Descent in American Culture, 174–207.* New York: Oxford Univ. Press, 1986.

In this expanded version of an earlier article (Salzman, item 36), Sollers criticizes a tendency among American intellectuals to simplify the "messy" reality of multiple and overlapping regional and ethnic loyalties. As exemplified by Josiah Royce's vision of "wholesome provincialism," a long line of so called "cultural pluralists" have betrayed their hidden desires for comfortable consensus by yearning for cultural homogeneity within uniform regional and ethnic provinces.

50. ———. "A Critique of Pure Pluralism." In *Reconstructing American Literary History*. Edited by Sacvan Bercovitch, 250–79. Cambridge: Harvard Univ. Press, 1986.

Sollers urges students of American culture and literature to adopt a more critical understanding of the sources and implications of cultural pluralism. By closely analyzing Horace Kallen's background and intent in developing the concept of cultural pluralism, Sollers reveals the static, compartmentalized, and potentially racist implications of this theory. "Pluralism," he writes, "is not a redemptively transcendent category that removes its advocates from prejudice. . . . In the current cultural debates pluralism often implies purism" that can build barriers between ethnic groups.

51. Steiner, Michael C. "Regionalism in the Great Depression." *Geographical Review* 73 (October 1983): 430–46.

This article examines the function of regionalism both as a self-conscious ideology among a variety of intellectuals and as a less reflective, though equally compelling, sensibility among ordinary Americans during the 1930s. In addition to beginning a much needed social or vernacular history of American regionalism, Steiner also explores the relationship between regionalism and the need for a sense of place amid the disorder and stress of the Great Depression.

52. ———. "The Significance of Turner's Sectional Thesis." *Western Historical Quarterly* 10 (October 1979): 437–66.

This article draws attention to a surprisingly neglected yet major portion of Turner's work: his growing conviction from 1893 until his death in 1932 that sectionalism was the natural sequel to the dying frontier and that the growth of sectional or regional identity would "offer a counterforce to many of the destructive cultural traits engendered by the frontier and an antidote to the homelessness of mass society." Stressing the contrast between the frontier and sectional theses, Steiner concludes that the latter has more relevance for the present, that "Our heightened awareness in recent years of dwindling global resources and the inefficiency of large-scale organization and massive centralization should open our eyes to the value of Turner's sectional concept."

53. Stott, William. *Documentary Expression and Thirties America*. New York: Oxford Univ. Press, 1973.

Using James Agee and Walker Evans's *Let Us Now Praise Famous Men* (1941) as the apotheosis of the documentary imagination, Stott explains the popularity of documentary films and reportage, of regional guides and photo-text books during the 1930s as a reflection of the search for something stable and certain beneath the social and economic turmoil of the times. This incisive analysis provides a vital glimpse of the social history of American regionalism.

54. Taylor, William R. *Cavalier and Yankee: The Old South and the American National Character.* New York: George Brazillier, 1961.

This important symbol and myth analysis of American regional character types focuses upon the meaning of two regional stereotypes in the first half of the nineteenth century: the gracious Southern planter and the grasping utilitarian Yankee. Analyzing an impressive variety of ante-bellum literature, Taylor effectively explores the social problems and tensions in the North and South that engendered "this legendary past and this fictive sociology."

55. ———. "'The Disappearing South': Progress or Tragedy?" In *Reports and Speeches of the Seventh Yale Conference on the Teaching of the Social Sciences*, 63–70. New Haven: Master of Arts in Teaching Program, 1962.

Taylor argues that in order to fully grasp the significance of regional cultures, scholars and teachers must, like anthropologist Oscar Lewis, engage in close-range fieldwork "in which the texture of human lives and human relationships is revealed and in which there is the historical depth of the rooted traditions which still form part of contemporary life."

56. Trachtenberg, Alan. *The Incorporation of America: Culture and Society in the Gilded Age.* New York: Hill and Wang, 1982.

In this important symbol and myth analysis of the "incorporation" of America into a more tightly-knit, centralized society during the final decades of the nineteenth century, Trachtenberg describes, in part, how regional myths of the South and especially of the West served to unify the nation. "The Westward Route," pp. 11–37, while predictably stressing the national rather than the sectional dimension of Turner's thought, perceptively describes the West as palimpsest for the spread of Eastern capitalism and a symbolic safety valve for industrial discontent. Though the book concludes with the image of monolithic nationalism and hegemony symbolically triumphant in the Great White City at the Chicago World's Fair (1893), it also offers glimpses of a decentralized "alternative America" in the Populist and labor movements and in the ideas of Henry George, Eugene Debs, and Clarence Darrow.

57. Veysey, Lawrence. "Myth and Reality in Approaching American Regionalism." *American Quarterly* 12 (Spring 1960): 31–43.

Vesey begins by urging students of American culture to question the image of America as a "seamless" whole by examining regional diversity. He then argues that to grasp the "reality" of American regionalism, one must search for "deeper," less ethereal sources than those usually used in symbol and myth studies. This essay contains a stimulating discussion of two regional masterpieces: Henry Nash Smith's *Virgin Land* (1950) and Carey McWilliams's *Southern California* (1946).

58. ———. "The Autonomy of American History Reconsidered." *American Quarterly* 31 (Fall 1979): 455–77.

Veysey challenges the long standing assumption that the nation-state is the most significant container for historical inquiry and urges historians to shift their attention both outward to perceive global patterns between nations and inward to grasp the immediate pluralistic reality of American life. This "new awareness that we are but one fractional (and internally fractionated) unit in a polyglot world" suggests that global and regional perspectives might replace the nation-state as the historian's primary focus.

59. Whisnant, David E. *All That Is Native and Fine: The Politics and Culture of an American Region.* Chapel Hill: Univ. of North Carolina Press, 1983.

This perceptive critique of "cultural intervention" explains how outsiders have perceived and manipulated Appalachian culture since the late nineteenth century. Focusing upon three examples—the Hindman Settlement School, the work of Olive Dame Campbell, and the White Top Folk Festival of the 1930s—Whisnant describes not only how well-intentioned intervenors usually misperceived and warped the very culture they hoped to revive, but also how these "cultural" efforts often directed attention away from the serious structural realities of colonial subjugation and resource exploitation. Whisnant's book abounds with further examples of the often exploitative relationships between dominant cultures and regional-ethnic enclaves.

60. ———. "Ethnicity and the Recovery of Regional Identity in Appalachia." In *The Rediscovery of Ethnicity*, edited by Sallie TeSelle, 124–138. New York: Harper and Row, 1973.

Whisnant describes the surge of regional identity in Appalachia as part of a rising sense of indignation and struggle against a dominant culture that subverts their way of life and plunders their land. This essay contains a sensitive discussion of the relationships between ethnicity, regionalism, and cultural pluralism; it also imaginatively compares Frantz Fanon's analysis of colonization to regional exploitation in America.

61. ———. *Modernizing the Mountaineer: People, Power, and Planning in Appalachia.* Boone, North Carolina: Appalachian Consortium Press, 1980.

A sharp-edged study of how Appalachia has served as a mecca for outside reformers and do-gooders from missionaries and local colorists in the late nineteenth century to folk school advocates and TVA planners in the 1920s and 30s to the poverty warriors of the 1960s. Whisnant's final chapter, "Cultural Values and Regional Development," raises vital questions about the uses and and abuses of regional planning.

62. White, Edward G. *The Eastern Establishment and the Western Experience: The West of Frederick Remington, Theodore Roosevelt, and Owen Wister.* New Haven: Yale Univ. Press, 1968.

In analyzing how the West served the imaginative and emotional needs of three representative Easterners from 1870 until 1910, White depicts the West as a blank tablet for Eastern wish fulfillment. Examining the imaginative significance of the East, South, and West during these years, White argues that of the three "the West has had the most dramatic impact upon the American imagination."

63. Winks, Robin W. "Regionalism in Comparative Perspective." In *Regionalism and the Pacific Northwest,* edited by William G. Robbins, Robert J. Frank, and Richard E. Ross, 13–36. Corvallis: Oregon State Univ. Press, 1983.

In this wide-ranging, insightful discussion of the continued vitality of American regionalism, Winks suggests that American regions can best be studied in a comparative perspective. By first comparing two or more regions within the United States and then moving to a global scale by comparing "regions of recent settlement" in the United States, Australia, Canada, or Argentina, regional scholars could forge an important intellectual frontier.

64. Worster, Donald. *Dust Bowl: The Southern Plains in the 1930s.* New York: Oxford Univ. Press, 1979.

A brilliant analysis of the often perilous relationship between nature and culture on the Southern Plains culminating in the 1930s Dust Bowl disaster. Worster's work exemplifies recent regional American Studies scholarship that delves beneath abstract symbols and myths to the lived experiences of place and region. Worster's deeply informed portrait of the Plains ecosystem; his detailed descriptions of how a variety of Native American cultures, capitalistic wheat growers, ranchers and subsistence farmers responded to this delicate ecology; and vivid use of local and oral history are vital models for regional studies. "A Sense of Place," pp. 164–80, contains a valuable discussion of the tension between the security of place and the exhilaration of mobility in our culture; "Epilogue: On a Thin Edge," pp. 231–43, places the American Dust Bowl experience within the global context of recent worldwide water and food shortages.

65. ———. *Nature's Economy: The Roots of Ecology.* Garden City, New York: Anchor Books, 1979.

An invaluable account of the growth of the idea of ecology in Europe and America from the work of Gilbert White, Carl Linnaeus, and Alexander von Humboldt in the eighteenth century to the contrasting visions of Thoreau, Haeckel, and Darwin in the mid-nineteenth century to the concepts of Frederick Clements, Alfred North Whitehead, Aldo Leopold, and others in the early twentieth century. Worster's discussion of the connections between American theories of plant ecology and cultural regionalism in Part Four, "O Pioneers: Ecology on the Frontier," pp. 190–253, is an important contribution to the history of regional theory.

66. ———. "New West, True West: Interpreting the Region's History." *Western Historical Quarterly* 28 (April 1987): 141–56.

In this lucid discussion of the pleasures and perils of regional history, Worster suggests several guidelines and principles that might encourage scholars "to push ahead toward a deeper, fuller, and more intellectually complex regionalism." Among others things, he urges regionalists to avoid Turner's slippery notion of region as process in favor of Webb's geographically grounded conception; to stress regional uniqueness and diversity; to carefully distinguish between ethnic and regional influences; to be aware of the interaction between region, nation, and world; and to be sensitive to the environmental-economic basis of regional culture.

67. ———. *Rivers of Empire: Water, Aridity, and the Growth of the American West.* New York: Pantheon Books, 1985.

Worster continues the work begun in *Dust Bowl* by tracing the ever-expanding impact of irrigation culture upon the arid West, particularly upon the Central and Imperial Valleys of California. In the tradition of George Perkins Marsh, John Wesley Powell, and Walter Prescott Webb, Worster has written a passionate, often polemical, account of the tragic collision between a stubbornly manipulative, profit-oriented culture and a fragile, harshly beautiful landscape. Worster's grim vision of a region encased in a "hydraulic trap" of grandiose engineering projects is countered with a glimpse of a profoundly regional alternative: a utopian vision of a "decentralized, localized, non-hydraulic West," a landscape redesigned "as a network of more or less discrete, self-contained watershed settlements."

Anthropology

American anthropologists have been keenly interested in how groups of people arrange themselves in space, and theories of regionalism, initially in the form of the culture area concept, have been central to their discipline since the late nineteenth century. Partially influenced by Adolph Bastian's theory of "geographical provinces" and Friedrich Ratzel's encyclopedic studies of the spatial patterns of cultural diffusion, early American anthropologists such as John Wesley Powell, Otis T. Mason, and Franz Boas were interested in mapping and explaining the territorial distribution of Native American cultures. They were intrigued by the apparent clustering of similar cultures in regional archipelagoes or "culture areas" across the continent, and their work bore fruit in important ethnological monographs and museum exhibits.

These early ethnological efforts to locate groups of American Indian cultures through the geographical distribution of languages and artifacts quickly flowered into full-fledged theories and debates concerning the nature of culture areas. Beginning with Clark Wissler's formulation of the culture area concept in 1917 and culminating with Alfred Kroeber's magisterial refinement of this concept in 1939, the interwar decades marked a peak of anthroplogical interest in regionalism. Alexander Goldenweiser's environmental theories, Melville Herskovitz's studies of the diffusion of African cultures, and Robert Redfield's early analysis of peasant societies and the "folk-urban continuum" also emerged from this period of intense interest in the spatial dynamics and configurations of preindustrial cultures.

The culture area paradigm has faded in significance since World War II, although some anthropologists, including Harold Driver and his associates at Indiana University, have continued to apply it to Native American groups with increasingly complex models of cultural element distribution. Since the 1940s most regionally oriented anthropologists have either greatly modified or moved beyond the Wissler-Kroeber concept of culture area. They seem to have followed at least four often overlapping paths. First, a number of anthropologists, including Conrad Arensberg, John Bennett, John Gillin, Walter Goldschmidt, and

Evon Vogt and her colleagues, have drawn complex regional portraits of contemporary America. Such large-scale, multi-community regional studies of contemporary society—so frequently pursued in other social sciences—have yet to gain a strong following in anthropology where the general focus remains upon individual small-scale communities whether preindustrial or urban.

Anthropology's primary contribution to regional studies is in the realm of theory, and this characterizes a second group, including Shirley Ardener, Robert Ardrey, Frederik Barth, Mary Douglas, Edward Hall, Joseph Jorgensen, Rik Pinxten, and others who help clarify the spatial dimensions of cultural pluralism and the nature of boundary maintenance between groups. Related to this proxemics and boundary maintenance approach is a third anthropological perspective, that of cultural ecologists Julian Steward, Clifford Geertz, John Bennett, Roy Rappaport, Andrew Vayda, and others who use selected biological principles to visualize human beings as integral parts of complex ecosystems. A fourth and final path, the "regional systems" approach of Robert Redfield, Joseph Casagrande, Elmer Miller, Stephen Olsen, Carol Smith, and others, uses the insights of cultural ecology and systems theory, geography and regional science, to understand how regional constellations of communities function as "intermediate societies" within national societies.

Anthropology has, then, contributed at least five important perspectives to our understanding of region and regionalism. For all of its weaknesses, the culture area concept and its many permutations continue to spark valuable regional speculation. As noted, many anthropologists have transcended their discipline's traditional focus upon individual preindustrial communities in uniform culture regions to portray the interaction of more complex communities within more complex regional settings. Others have enhanced our understanding of the dynamics of regionalism through studies of proxemics and boundary maintenance, cultural ecology, and regional systems.

This chapter provides a more detailed picture of how these and other anthropological perspectives provide an invaluable cultural dimension to the ongoing study of regionalism. Because of space limitations, small-scale community studies have been largely excluded from our list unless they stand as models for more recent conceptions of region or are explicitly connected to larger regional systems.[1] Once again, there is considerable overlap between regional scholarship in this chapter and regional studies in economics, folk studies, geography, and sociology.

M.S.

[1]For a recent survey of the hundreds of anthropological studies of American comunities (and of national character) see George F. Spindler and Louise Spindler, "Anthropologists View American Culture," *Annual Review of Anthropology* 12 (1983), pp. 49–78.

*   *   *

68. Ardener, Shirley, ed. *Women and Space: Ground Rules and Social Maps.* New York: St. Martin's Press, 1981.

This collection of essays by British anthropologists examines questions concerning women and the social and symbolic uses of space in a variety of settings. Essays consider concepts of time and space among the Quechua Indians of Peru, the role of women in the British House of Commons, the relationships of urban Greek women to their environment, the concept of privacy in anthropology, sexual prohibitions and uses of space in Iran, sexual divisions of domestic space among two Soviet minorities, racial divisions and physical arrangements of space in urban South Africa, and how actresses provide public performances of idealized sexuality.

69. Ardrey, Robert. *The Territorial Imperative: A Personal Introduction to the Animal Origins of Property and Nations.* New York: Atheneum, 1966.

An important although hyperbolic discussion of the powerful affinities between people and place—the ever-widening topophilic ties to personal property, locality, region, and nation—that help explain regionalism. "It may come to us as the strangest of thoughts," Ardrey argues, "that the bond between a man and the soil he walks on should be more powerful than his bond with the woman he sleeps with.... we may test the supposition with a single question: How many men have you known of, in your lifetime, who have died for their country? How many for a woman?" Two other highly popular anthropological-ethnological studies of human territoriality and aggressiveness were published within a year of Ardrey's book: Konrad Lorenz's *On Aggression* (New York: Harcourt, Brace, and World, 1966) and Desmond Morris's *The Naked Ape* (New York: McGraw-Hill, 1967).

70. Arensberg, Conrad. "American Communities." *American Anthropologist* 57 (1955): 1143–60.

Drawing upon Lewis Mumford's portraits of cities as ideal types in *The Culture of Cities* (1938), Arensberg portrays four American regional community types: the New England town, the southern county, the crossroads hamlet, and the main street town. This entire issue is devoted to the anthropological study of American culture.

71. Arensberg, Conrad and Solon T. Kimball. *Culture and Community.* New York: Harcourt, Brace, Jovanovich, 1965.

In Part Two, "American Communities and Their Variations," pp. 95–210, the authors compare Arensberg's four regional community types to field studies of specific places: a rural village and a suburban "fringe" community in the Midwest, a southern town, and an eastern metropolitan community.

72. Barclay, Harold B. "On Culture Areas and Regions in Anthropology." In *Perspectives on Regions and Regionalism.* Edited by B.Y. Card, 3–9. Edmonton, Alberta: Western Association of Sociology and Anthropology, 1969.

A thorough and perceptive evaluation of the culture area concept from its earliest use by Otis Mason in 1895 to the sophisticated formulations of Julian Steward in 1955. Barclay concludes that although the traditional culture area approach has "minimal theoretical significance" in the present, regionalization remains a crucial tool because "every anthropologist finds it necessary to chop the world into manageable areas for research and pedagogical purposes."

73. Barth, Fredrik, ed. *Ethnic Groups and Boundaries.* Boston: Little, Brown and Co., 1969.

An influential collection of essays by Scandinavian anthropologists interested in the nature of boundaries between ethnic groups. Barth's "Introduction," pp. 9–38, is a succinct summary of his influential belief in the overriding significance of social and spatial boundaries as sources of group identity. To understand the dynamics of cultural diversity, Barth argues that the critical focus of investigation "becomes the ethnic boundary that defines the group, not the cultural stuff that it encloses."

74. Bateson, Gregory. *Steps to an Ecology of the Mind.* New York: Ballantine Books, 1972.

Bateson's often abstruse discussions of systems theory and cybernetics and his notion of individual minds and cultures as ecosystems that flourish under conditions of flexibility and diversity can be applied to a larger understanding of regionalism. Particularly useful chapters include "Conscious Purpose Versus Nature," pp. 426–39; "The Roots of Ecological Crisis," pp.488–93; and "Ecology and Flexibility in Urban Civilization," pp. 494–505. Some of these ideas are further developed in Bateson's *Mind and Nature: A Necessary Unity* (New York: Bantam Books, 1979). Lawrence B. Slobodkin's "Mind, Bind, and Ecology: A Review of Gregory Bateson's Collected Essays," *Human Ecology* 2 (1974), pp. 67–74, is a useful interpretation. See Mechling under American Studies (item 24) and Berman under Philosophy and Religion (item 1329) for discussions of Bateson's contributions to regional studies.

75. Bennett John W. *The Ecological Transition: Cultural Anthropology and Human Adaptation.* New York: Pergamon Press, 1976.

A richly documented survey of how natural and social sciences can be used by anthropologists to enhance their understanding of the relationship between nature and culture. Along with an almost encyclopedic grasp of anthropological, ecological, geographical, and cybernetic approaches to the culture/environment relationship, Bennett discusses the importance of a regional perspective in human ecology in the final chapter, "Ecology, Culture, and Anthropology," pp. 306–11.

76. ———. *Northern Plainsmen: Adaptive Strategy and Agrarian Life.* Chicago: Aldine Publishing Co., 1969.

In this outstanding regional analysis, in many ways an update of Walter Prescott Webb's *The Great Plains* (1931), Bennett carefully examines the environmental adaptations and interactions of four cultures in a portion of Saskatchewan. Bennett's sensitive portraits of Indian tribal culture, cattle ranchers, wheat farmers, and Hutterites and their varied responses to the same regional environment are coupled with a valuable discussion of anthropological environmental theories.

77. Boas, Franz. "The Principles of Ethnological Classification." In *The Shaping of American Anthropology, 1883–1911: A Franz Boas Reader,* edited by George W. Stocking, 61–67. New York: Basic Books, 1974.

Written in 1887, Boas's argument that museum artifacts should be arranged according to their place of origin rather than with similar artifacts from other places helped encourage several generations of anthropologists to think in terms of "culture areas."

78. Brues, Alice. "Regional Differences in the Physical Characteristics of an American Population." *American Journal of Physical Anthropology* 4 (New Series: December 1946): 463–81.

Differences in the physical traits of regional groups are explained in terms of the spatial diffusion of ethnic groups. Brues's study of the spatial distribution of physiological features serves as a useful balance to the much more common examination of regional artifacts, values systems, or personality types.

79. Casagrande, Joseph B. "Some Observations on the Study of Intermediate Societies." In *Intermediate Societies, Social Mobility, and Communication,* edited by Verne F. Ray, 1–10. Seattle: American Ethnological Society, 1959.

An important discussion of an emerging anthropological interest in studying social groups that stand between small local communities and national mass societies, this essay also contains a useful analysis of the relationship between subculture, folk culture, and region. Building upon Robert Redfield's suggestions in 1955, Casagrande and others in this volume prefigure the more intricate "regional systems" approach advocated by Carol Smith and others in 1976.

80. Chaney, Richard Paul. "On the Concepts of 'Culture Area' and 'Languange Culture'." In *Comparative Studies by Harold E. Driver and Essays in His Honor,* edited by Joseph E. Jorgenson, 237–45. New Haven: HRAF Press, 1974.

This perceptive analysis of Harold Driver's contributions to regional culture studies contains a thorough and useful bibliography.

81. Despres, Leo A. "Anthropological Theory, Cultural Pluralism, and the Study of Complex Societies." *Current Anthropology* 9 (February 1968): 3–26.

Despres places regionalism within a wider context by tracing how anthropologists have dealt with the issue of unity and diversity in complex societies. His model for distinguishing local subcultural traits and activities from culture-wide traits and activities is useful for regional studies. Insightful responses by John Bennet, Marvin Harris, Julian Steward, and others are included.

82. Devereux, George. *Reality and Dream: Psychotherapy of a Plains Indian.* New York: International Universities Press, 1951.

Based upon intensive psychotherapy provided an American Indian at a veterans' hospital in Kansas, ethnopsychologist Devereux attempts to reconstruct the subjective and emotional contours of Plains Indian culture. At the heart of the analysis is Devereux's belief that the patient's personality and neurosis are more deeply molded by Plains culture and ethos than by his specific tribe. The section, "Areal Culture Pattern and Areal Basic Personality," pp. 25–49, weaves together various theories of culture area, culture pattern, and culture and personality to discuss the notion of "areal ethos" and to argue that cultural regions deeply influence basic personality formation.

83. Douglas, Mary, ed. *Rules and Meanings: The Anthropology of Everyday Life*. New York: Penguin Books, 1973.

Building upon the phenomenological insights of Wittgenstein, Schutz, and Husserl, Douglas analyzes the cultural constructions of reality in everyday life. This collection of essays shows, among other things, how cultures structure domestic space, classify animals, and mirror in play the values insisted upon in everyday life.

84. Douglas, Mary and Aaron Wildavsky. *Risk and Culture: An Essay on the Selection of Technical and Environmental Dangers*. Berkeley: Univ. of California Press, 1982.

An important part of this analysis of the cultural meaning of risk examines how the perception of environmental threat often evokes sense of place and regional consciousness. Douglas and Wildavsky's distinctions between the general complacency of the cultural center and the sensitivity of the border is useful for regional studies. "The Border Fears for Nature," pp. 126–51, and "America is Border Country," pp. 152–73, contain perceptive discussions of the grass roots, decentralized, sectarian nature of the American environmental movement and American protest groups in general. Douglas has continued this work in *Risk Acceptability According to the Social Sciences* (New York: Russell Sage Foundation, 1985).

85. Driver, Harold E. "The Contribution of A.L. Kroeber to Culture Area Theory and Practice." *Indiana University Publications in Anthropology and Linguistics Memoir* 18 (1962): 1–28.

A detailed, thoroughly documented account of the evolution of Kroeber's concept of culture area and age area from 1904 until 1960. Driver discusses the similarities and differences between Kroeber's, Wissler's, and Steward's regional theories; examines various critiques of the culture area concept by Boas, Lowie, Woods, and others; and suggests that despite such criticisms the concept remains relevant, especially when reinforced by quantitative methods.

86.———. *Indians of North America*. 2d ed., rev. Chicago: Univ. of Chicago Press, 1967.

"Culture Areas," pp. 17–28, contains a clear, non-technical discussion of the meaning of culture areas and brief descriptions of thirteen such areas in North America. Also useful is an appended series of maps depicting the pre-Columbian distribution of vegetation, subsistence methods, housing, language, population density, and other variables. Readers interested in Driver's technical and statistical refinements of culture area theory should consult Joseph G. Joregensen, ed., *Comparative Studies by Harold E. Driver and Essays in His Honor* (New Haven, Conn.: HRAF Press, 1974). This volume also contains a complete bibliography of Driver's work.

87. Ehrich, Paul W. and Gerald M. Henderson. "Culture Area." In *International Encyclopedia of the Social Sciences.* vol, 3. Edited by David L. Sills, 563–68. New York: Macmillan, 1968.

A wide-ranging, well-documented survey that locates fresh relevance for the culture area concept, especially in light of the persistence of the same generalized geographical boundaries for different groups of cultures over time. The "close correspondence between the regionalization of contemporary Anglo-American civilization in the United States and the culture areas of the North American Indians" is offered as a striking example of this thesis.

88. Ellen, Roy. *Environment, Subsistence and System: The Ecology of Small-Scale Social Formations.* New York: Cambridge Univ. Press, 1982.

This detailed survey of contemporary research in cultural ecology contains extensive discussions of the culture area concept and environmental theories. It also includes detailed analyses of the work of American cultural ecologists Julian Steward, John Bennett, Clifford Geertz, Andrew Vayda, and Roy Rappaport.

89. Geertz, Clifford. "Comments." In *Rural Politics and Social Change in the Middle East*, edited by Richard Antoun and Iliya Harik, 460–67. Bloomington: Indiana Univ. Press, 1972.

In a manner reminiscent of Robert Redfield and later regional systems theorists Joseph Casagrande and Carol Smith, Geertz urges anthropologists to lift their focus from hyperintensive studies of separate communities to a larger vision of regional networks of communities within the national whole. Anthropologists interested in complex societies, he argues, should "discard the the community study genre, for both town and village, in favor of a regional focus that can include both rural and urban systems in a common framework, a larger system."

90. ———. "The Ecological Approach in Anthropology." In *Agricultural Involution: The Process of Ecological Change in Indonesia*, 1–11. Berkeley: Univ. of California Press, 1963.

After describing the limitations of environmental determinism and possibilism, Geertz succinctly explains the advantages of cultural ecology as an anthropological model. By urging anthropologists to delineate "an ecosystem within which certain selected cultural, biological, and physical variables are determinately inter-related," Geertz makes a valuable contribution to regional analysis.

91. ———. *The Interpretation of Cultures*. New York: Basic Books, 1973.

Geertz's influential advocacy of the importance of interpreting immediate, ordinary events and behaviors as cultural texts in "Thick Description: Toward an Interpretive Theory of Culture," pp. 3–30, and "Deep Play: Notes on a Balinese Cockfight," pp. 412–53, has encouraged an ethnographic, text-oriented approach in a number of social sciences and humanities that is also conducive to regional studies. Other essays examine the relationship between primordial loyalties, regionalism, nationalism, and modernization. In "After the Revolution: The Fate of Nationalism in the New States", pp. 234–54, and "The Integrative Revolution: Primordial Sentiments and Civil Politics in the New States," pp. 255–310, Geertz analyzes the tension between local attachments—regional, ethnic, religious—and national identity in Indonesia, Malaya, India, Lebanon, Morocco, and Nigeria.

92. ———. *Local Knowledge: Further Essays in Interpretive Anthropology*. New York: Basic Books, 1983.

Building upon the *The Interpretation of Culture*, this collection of occasional pieces argues that anthropology is moving away from notions of a unified science toward a pluralistic orientation emphasizing how people use particular or "local" terms and frameworks to lead their lives. Drawing upon the ideas of Heidegger, Wittgenstein, Gadamer, Ricoeur, Burke, Foucault, Habermas, Barthes, Kuhn, and others, Geertz stresses the inadequacy of grand theories and the ineluctably local nature of understanding and experience. The title essay examines law as a cultural construct, comparing western, Islamic, and Malayo-Indonesian legal systems. Other essays address questions of art, common sense, and ethnography of high culture.

93. Gillin, John P. "More Complex Cultures for Anthropologists." *American Anthropologist* 69 (1969): 301–5.

In this appeal for more concerted anthropological study of "modern systems," Gillin offers shrewd advice concerning the nature of cultural pluralism and the need to examine regional subcultures in complex societies.

94. ———. "National and Regional Culture Values in the United States." *Social Forces* 34 (December 1955): 107–13. Reprinted in John P. Gillin. *Human Ways: Selected Essays in Anthropology*, 268–80. Pittsburgh: Univ. of Pittsburgh Press, 1969.

Following Odum and Moore's regional division of the nation into the Northeast, Southeast, Middle States, Southwest, Northwest, and Far West, Gillin draws from a wealth of community studies to draw sweeping value and personality profiles for each region.

95. Gillin, John P. and and Emmett J. Murphy. "Notes on Southern Culture Patterns." *Social Forces* 29 (May 1951): 422–32. Reprinted in Gillin's *Human Ways: Selected Essays in Anthropology*, 254–67. Pittsburgh: Univ. of Pittsburgh Press, 1969.

Through detailed field studies, Gillin and Murphy describe the value orientations of five southern subregions: the Alabama Black Belt, South Carolina Piedmont, Alabama Pinebelt, North Carolina Mountains, and North Carolina Coast.

96. Goldenweiser, Arnold. *History, Psychology, and Culture*. New York: Knopf, 1933.

Goldenweiser's discussion of "Cultural Anthropology," pp. 121–76, contains a detailed and perceptive analysis of concepts of diffusion and culture area developed by German theorists Bastain, Ratzel, and Graebner and American anthropologists Boas, Wissler, Kroeber, and others. Goldenweiser's own influential "law of limited possibilities" is outlined on pp. 35–55. See Goldenweiser's *Anthropology: An Introduction to Primitive Cultures* (New York: F.S. Crofts and Co., 1937), especially "The Spread of Culture," pp. 475–95, for another effective overview of culture area theory.

97. Goldschmidt, Walter. *As You Sow: Three Studies in the Social Consequences of Agribusiness*. Glencoe, Ill.: Free Press, 1947.

This detailed participant observation of three agricultural communities in California's Central Valley continues a tradition of politically engaged social science found in Paul Taylor and Dorothea Lange's *American Exodus* (1939) and Carey McWilliams's *Factories in the Fields* (1939). Goldschmidt's analysis of three American farming traditions, northern small landholding pattern, southern plantation system, and southwestern industrial farming—as well as his vivid portrait of the debilitating impact of agribusiness upon Central Valley culture, make this a valuable regional study.

98. Gorer, Geoffrey. "Cultural Community and Cultural Diversity in the North Atlantic Nations." In *The Danger of Equality and Other Essays*, 48–62. New York: Weybright and Talley, 1966.

Gorer describes the "resistence, vitality, and persistence of local cultures" in Northern Europe and North America and argues that such seeds might develop into "autonomous regional societies" constituting the "units that would determine the shape and actions of the North Atlantic community."

99. Hall, Edward T. *The Hidden Dimension*. Garden City, N.Y.: Doubleday, 1966.

Of Hall's several influential books, this pioneering study of "proxemics"—a branch of anthropology he defines as "the interrelated observations and theories of man's use of space as a specialized elaboration of culture"—is most essential for the study of regionalism. By drawing attention to the largely unconscious although ubiquitous spatial dimension of culture, Hall enhances our understanding of how groups of people shape nature and arrange themselves in space. Personal space and territoriality can be perceived as microcosms and building blocks of regionalism. Hall's masterful analysis of the meanings of personal space and territoriality in American, German, French, English, Japanese, and Arab cultures; discussion of the subcultural diversity of spatial needs within American culture, and plea for the uses of proxemics in urban and regional planning are all valuable contributions to regional studies.

100. ———. *The Silent Language*. Garden City, N.Y.: Doubleday, 1959.

"Space Speaks," pp. 162–85, is a succinct preview of Hall's later work in proxemics and a valuable discussion of the quiet pervasiveness of space and place in human affairs. "Man has developed his territoriality to an almost unbelievable extent," Hall argues. "Yet we treat space somewhat as we treat sex. It is there but we don't talk about it."

101. Hallowell, A. Irving. "Cultural Factors in Spatial Organization." In *Culture and Behavior*, Philadelphia: Univ. of Pennsylvania Press, 1955.

Hallowell speculates about the cultural dimensions of spatial orientation by contrasting the spatial framework of the Saulteaux Indians to that of modern western Europeans, emphasizing the fact that all humans develop a map of their world that organizes the relationship between the near-at-hand and the distant, and that all people provide for cosmic as well as pragmatic dimensions.

102. Hardesty, Donald L. *Ecological Anthropology*. New York: John Wiley and Sons, 1977.

A highly perceptive, clearly written survey of environmentally oriented anthropology. Hardesty's introduction, pp. 1–18, succinctly summarizes models of the man/environment relationship from environmental determinism to possibilism to the ecological perspectives of Julian Steward, Clifford Geertz, and others. Various theories of culture area and diffusion, cultural adaptation and the human ecological niche are analyzed, and an extensive bibliography is included. "Ethnoecology" by Catherine S. Fowler, pp. 215–43, is a valuable introduction to a more subjective branch of cultural ecology that studies the environment from the participant or native's point of view.

103. Harris, Marvin. *America Now: The Anthropology of a Changing Culture*. New York: Simon and Schuster, 1981.

In "Why America Changed," pp. 166–83, Harris promotes the growth of a new regionalism: an "egalitarian, decentralized" society that will "slowly tip the balance against the thralldom of hyper-industrialization."

104. Herskovitz, Melville J. *Cultural Anthropology*. New York: Knopf, 1958.

Pages 396–410 contain an intelligent appraisal of the culture area concept and its relevance to understanding complex societies. Herskovitz stresses problems implicit in the core/margin distinction and urges anthropologists to use the culture area simply as a useful organizing device realizing that "the area, as such, exists in the mind of the student and has little meaning to those who inhabit it."

105. Howard, James H. "The Culture-Area Concept: Does It Diffract Anthropological Light?" *Indian Historian* 8 (Spring 1975): 22–26.

After tracing the evolution of the culture area concept, Howard stresses several basic flaws in this theory, namely that such regionalization has tended to elevate those cultures at the "core" and denigrate those at the margins and that the culture area concept lacks historical depth.

106. Jorgensen, Joseph G. "Land Is Cultural, So Is Commodity: The Locus of Differences Among Indians, Cowboys, Sodbusters, and Environmentalists." *Journal of Ethnic Studies* 12 (Fall 1984): 1–21.

Paralleling the pioneering work of Evon Vogt and others in *The People of Rimrock* (item 138), Jorgensen traces varying definitions and perceptions of the land that have been held by western American Indians, farmers, ranchers, environmentalists, and entrepreneurs.

107. Keesing, Felix M. "Culture in Space." In *Cultural Anthropology: The Science of Custom*, 107–37. New York: Rinehart and Co., 1958.

This thoughtful summary of environmental thought in anthropology from Ratzel to Kroeber contains a clear evaluation of the culture area concept.

108. Kroeber, Alfred. *Cultural and Natural Areas of North America.* Berkeley: Univ. of California Publications in Archeology and Ethnology, 1939.

This study is a magnificent refinement and reformulation of the culture area concept. It is primarily concerned with the regional distribution of aboriginal American cultures, yet its speculation about the relationships between the environmental and the cultural has universal meaning. See his "History of Concepts," pp. 3–7, "Relations of Environmental and Cultural Factors," pp. 205–17, and the series of maps depicting the correspondence between the plant, climate, physiographic, and indigenous culture areas of the continent.

109. ⸺. "The Culture Area and Age Area Concepts of Clark Wissler." In *Methods in Social Sciences*, edited by Stuart Rice, 248–65. Chicago: Univ. of Chicago Press, 1931.

In this essay, Kroeber stresses the need for historical depth in culture area studies: the need to see that the spatial configurations of culture shift over time. Wissler's age area theory—the notion that the wider a cultural trait is distributed the older it must be—was carefully developed in Kroeber's own work.

110. ———. "Culture Element Distributions: Area and Climax." *University of California Publications in Archeology and Ethnology*. vol. 37, 101–15. Berkeley: Univ. of California Press, 1939.

Building upon Wissler's notion of a cultural core and using concepts from plant ecology, Kroeber explains how an area's cultural traits intensify at certain points in space as well as during certain periods of history.

111. Kuper, Hilda. "Tha Language of Sites in the Politics of Space." *American Anthropologist* 74 (June 1974): 411–25.

After reviewing anthropological theories of the significance of space in the structuring of human societies, Kuper demonstrates, through field work in Southeast Africa, how particular sites that are invested with sacred and political symbolism can be manipulated for the purpose of social control.

112. Mason, Otis T. "Influences of Environment Upon Human Industries or Arts." In *Annual Report of the Smithsonian Institution for 1895*, 639–65. Washington, D.C.: U.S. Government Printing Office, 1896.

In this early formulation of the culture area concept, Mason argues that culture is largely shaped by physical environment, and maps twelve "ethnic" culture areas in pre-Columbian North America that reflect this relationship.

113. Maxwell, Robert J. *Contexts of Behavior: Anthropological Dimensions*. Chicago: Nelson-Hall, 1983.

In this effective review of social scientific literature regarding the relationship between culture and nature, Maxwell posits three types of ecosystems: natural, interpersonal, and built. He also discusses the general significance and function of clothes, food, disasters, and constructed environments (social and built).

114. Miller, Elmer S. "Regional Systems." In *Introduction to Cultural Anthropology*, 343–62. Englewood Cliffs, N.J.: Prentice-Hall, 1979.

A perceptive, wide-ranging discussion of the need for a regional perspective in contemporary anthropology. Miller carefully uses

Redfield's, Geertz's, Barth's, and Smith's studies of networks of communities as models for a "regional systems" approach to replace the narrower local community paradigm that he believes is inadequate for understanding complex societies.

115. Newman, James L. "The Culture Area Concept in Anthropology." *Journal of Geography* 70 (January 1971): 8–15.

Written from a geographical perspective, this is a useful discussion of the rise and fall of the culture area concept from Franz Boas to Julian Steward.

116. O'Brien, Michael J., ed. *Grassland, Forest and Historical Settlement: An Analysis of Dynamics in Northeast Missouri.* Lincoln: Univ. of Nebraska Press, 1984.

This series of essays, most of them by O'Brien as author or co-author, examines on a small scale the interaction between social relationships, built environments, and frontier householding in one corner of the Midwest. After tracing the migration from Kentucky to Missouri, the essays depict the evolution of a cultural landscape from the discovery of an economic niche by frontiersmen to the development of roads and towns to the investment by Easterners in prairie land, ahead of settlers, and a shift toward larger, commercially viable farms.

117. Peet, Richard. "The Destruction of Regional Cultures." *A World in Crisis: Geographical Perspectives.* (item 474), 150–72.

Written from a geographical perspective, this essay effectively uses a world-systems, center-periphery model developed by anthropologist Eric Wolf and sociologist Immanuel Wallerstein to analyze the destructive impact of European-American capitalism upon Third World regional cultures.

118. Perin, Constance. *Everything in its Place: Social Order and Land Use in America.* Princeton: Princeton Univ. Press, 1977.

Based upon extensive interviews with suburban and urban homeowners, bankers, real estate agents, and people involved in zoning and planning policies, anthropologist Perin analyzes the cultural, social, and economic factors behind the pervasive American preference for the single family detached dwelling. Perin's discussion of the changing meanings of housing and home during various stages of the life cycle is especially insightful. Perin applies anthropological insights to questions of urban planning and design in *With Man in Mind: An*

Interdisciplinary Prospectus for Environmental Design (Cambridge, MIT Press, 1970).

119. Pinxten, Rik, Ingrid van Dooren, and Frank Harvey. *Anthropology of Space: Explorations into the Natural Philosophy and Semantics of the Navajo.* Philadelphia: Univ. of Pennsylvania Press, 1983.

Focusing upon Navajo perceptions of space, this book employs a general method for measuring spatial perceptions that has general application to regional studies. See in particular Pinxten's Appendix B, "'The Device': A Synoptic and Revised Edition of the Universal Frame of Reference for Spatial Analysis," pp. 183–225.

120. Rapoport, Amos. *House Form and Culture.* Englewood Cliffs, N.J.: Prentice-Hall, 1969.

This brief, immensely suggestive book draws useful distinctions between folk, popular, and elite forms of architecture and then centers upon preindustrial housing patterns. The house is analyzed as a cultural product reflecting how people see themselves in relationship to the environment. Housing reflects the human need for security, visual and social complexity, and communication. Rapoport concludes, in part, that preindustrial and traditional housing is in many respects superior to contemporary popular housing.

121. ———. *The Meaning of the Built Environment: A Nonverbal Communications Approach.* Beverly Hills, Calif.: Sage Publications, 1982.

Drawing from a wide variety of sources, Rapoport argues for user-oriented as opposed to expert-devised planning of the built environment. Using Edward Hall's distinction between fixed, semi-fixed, and non-fixed structures, Rapoport argues that semifixed stuctures—e.g., ornaments, add-ons—are central sources of associational meaning, and he finds this sort of analysis more valuable than semiotic attention to the "syntax" of built form.

122. Redfield, Robert. "Civilizations as Societal Structures? The Development of Community Studies." In *Human Nature and the Study of Society: The Papers of Robert Redfield.* vol. 1, edited by Margaret Park Redfield, 375–91. Chicago: Univ. of Chicago Press, 1962.

After arguing that traditional participant observation studies of isolated primitive cultures should be widened or replaced by field studies of complex communities embedded within larger regions, nations, and civilizations, Redfield offers four anthropological models for studying such complex systems. Redfield's belief that local communities can only be understood within the context of larger regional or national communities—a foreshadowing of the recent "regional systems" approach—is also developed in "Societies and Cultures as Natural Systems" (item 124) and in "A Community Within Communities" in *The Little Community: Viewpoints for the Study of the Human Whole* (Chicago: Univ. of Chicago Press, 1955) pp. 113–31.

123. ———. "The Regional Aspect of Culture." *Publications of the American Sociological Society* 34 (May 1930): 34–41. Reprinted in *Human Nature and the Study of Society: The Papers of Robert Redfield.* vol 1, edited by Margaret Park Redfield, 145–51. Chicago: Univ. of Chicago Press, 1962.

After offering a succinct summary of the culture area paradigm, Redfield gives qualified support to regional analysis of culture. Using examples from his study of the Mexican village of Tepoztalan, Redfield shrewdly suggests that "the cultural process is rather a matter of communication than of geography" and that "the homogeneity of culture within a definable range" may be dwindling in complex, industrial societies where a diversity of cultural messages are communicated from vast distances. For a closely related argument, see Robert Redfield, "Folk and Regional Conflict as a Field of Sociological Study," *Publications of the American Sociological Society* 35 (May 1931), pp. 1–17.

124. ———. "Societies and Cultures as Natural Systems." In *Human Nature and the Study of Society: The Papers of Robert Redfield.* vol. 1, edited by Margaret Park Redfield, 121–41. Chicago: Univ. of Chicago Press, 1962.

Redfield gently urges anthropologists to perceive local cultures as parts of ever-widening "compound systems." In words that have greatly influenced recent regional systems theory, Redfield predicted "an increasing interest in those social systems which connect people scattered over a wide area and living in many different local communities. . . . I think we shall study regional systems. We shall study such systems not, as we now tend to, from the viewpoint of some one small local community looking outward, but from the viewpoint of an observer who looks down upon the whole larger regional system."

125. Sahlins, Marshall. "Culture and Environment: The Study of Cultural Ecology." In *Horizons of Anthropology*. 2d ed., edited by Sol Tax and Leslie G. Freeman, 215–31. Chicago: Aldine Publishing Co., 1977.

A perceptive, clearly written survey of increasingly subtle anthropological models of the culture/nature relationship, from environmental determinism to possibilism to reciprocity between cultures and their environments. Sahlins stresses the seeming paradox that environmentally aggressive cultures often dominate nature and other cultures at their own risk, for specialization and extension of power render them less adaptable and more vulnerable to environmental change. "The more adapted a culture," he writes, "the less . . . it is adaptable."

126. Smith, Carol A. "Analyzing Regional Social Systems." In *Regional Analysis*. vol. 2, 3–20. (item 128), vol. 2, 3–20.

In this effective introduction to the field of regional systems analysis, Smith urges anthropologists to adopt a bird's-eye rather than a worm's-eye view of social systems through the geographer's concept of region as well as the insights of regional science, cultural ecology, and systems theory. A succinct sense of the contributions from each of these areas is offered. Stressing the need to understand social and cultural systems between the community and national levels, Smith asserts that "the standard anthropological monograph on a small community suffers theoretical limitations because of its narrow parochialism, and that studies of large-scale, national systems do little to illuminate the lives of people who live in small rural communities—the majority of mankind."

127. ———. "Regional Economic Systems: Geographical Models and Socioeconomic Problems." In *Regional Analysis*. (item 128), vol 1, 2–62.

A thorough survey of how economic geography, especially the central place and location theories of Thunen, Christaller, Losch, G. William Skinner, Brian Berry, Immanuel Wallerstein and others, can contribute to the anthropological understanding of regional societies.

128. Smith, Carol A. *Regional Analysis*. 2 vols. New York: Academic Press, 1976.

This important collection of essays by anthropologists and sociologists is divided into two parts: Volume one explores the regional analysis of economic systems and Volume two covers the regional analysis of social systems. Responding to the calls of Geertz, Redfield, G. William Skinner, and others to examine networks of communities that constitute "intermediate societies," the majority of the essays in both volumes regard the regional understanding of rural, Third World societies. Several of the general theoretical essays—especially those by Olsen, Smith, and Verdery (items 126–127, 137) and by Olsen under Sociology (item 1613)—contribute directly to the regional analysis of complex, industrial societies.

129. Smith, Russell Gordon. "The Concept of Culture Area." *Social Forces* 7 (March 1929): 421–32.

In this positive appraisal of the culture area concept as a distinct and unifying theory of American anthropology, Smith argues that Boas, Wissler, Goldenweiser, Herskovitz, and Kroeber have sharpened the vague ruminations of German anthropologists into a precise scientific tool for the study of simple and complex societies.

130. Spindler, George D. and Louise Spindler. "Anthropologists View American Culture." *Annual Review of Anthropology* 12 (1983): 49–78.

This detailed survey reveals the range and depth of anthropological analyses of American culture, from single community to national character studies.

131. Spoehr, Alexander. "The Part and the Whole: Reflections on the Study of the Region." *American Anthropologist* 68 (June 1966): 629–40.

With the study of Oceania as an example, Spoehr urges anthropologists to use their investigations of particular communities to understand larger cultural wholes. Echoing Redfield, Spoehr argues that "our first step is to attain greater proficiency in analyzing and comparing a variety of present-day regional sociocultural systems. Contemporary work on peasant and intermediate societies points in this direction. Yet I think it is even more important to determine the place of such societies in specific regional systems and to compare these systems than to concentrate undue attention on the typologies of peasant societies as such."

132. Steward, Julian H. *Area Research: Theory and Practice.* New York: Social Science Research Council, 1950.

A central statement of the area studies movement that flowered during and immediately after World War II and a brilliant, interdisciplinary overview of regional theory and practice. Steward argues, in part, that area researchers and regionalists need to balance their penchant for compiling facts with greater theoretical rigor. As a step in this direction he carefully relates concepts of culture and society to the notion of culture area and speculates that in complex societies many "vertical" local and regional loyalties are being replaced by "horizontal" interests groups transcending ties of place. Especially insightful are "Some Practices of Area Research," pp. 20–94, which discusses the relationships between community, regional, and national studies, and "Some Concepts and Methods of Area Research," pp. 95–125, which contains a penetrating summary of regional theory and practice in the natural and social sciences.

133. ———. *Theory of Culture Change: The Methodology of Multilinear Evolution.* Urbana: Univ. of Illinois Press, 1955.

At least four chapters of this important anthropological text offer essential discussions of post World War II developments in regional theory. Steward coined the phrase "cultural ecology" in 1937, and in "The Concept and Method of Cultural Ecology," pp. 30–42, outlines how biological principles can be applied to portions of human activities and describes how a particular environment or region influences various cultures in various ways according to the levels of technology they bring to bear upon it. "Levels of Sociocultural Integration," pp. 43–63, develops a scheme for analyzing cultural systems from local to regional to national levels, while "National Sociocultural Systems," pp. 64–77, carefully examines the interaction between national and subcultural identities. "Culture Area and Cultural Type in Aboriginal America," pp. 78–97, is a sophisticated reformulation of the culture area concept.

134. _____ "'Region'—An Heuristic Concept." *Rural Sociology* 20 (September-December 1955): 297–98.

Faced with an extreme variability of meaning and the fact that the region "cannot represent any inherent features of objective reality that may be defined in absolute and universal terms," Steward argues that the region exists primarily as a useful device for describing and explaining localized subcultures in both premodern and modern societies.

135. Turner, Victor. "The Center Out There: Pilgrim's Goal." *History of Religions* 12 (February 1973): 191–230. Expanded and republished as "Pilgrimages as Social Processes." In *Dramas, Fields, and Metaphors: Symbolic Action in Human Society*, 166–230. Ithaca: Cornell Univ. Press, 1974.

Part of this stimulating analysis of pilgrimage underscores how ritualized movement from a localized home base to a universalized sacred center encourages wider sense of place at regional and transnational levels—a spatial sensibility that has little to do with the political state. This theme is further developed in Victor and Edith Turner's *Image and Pilgrimage in Christian Culture: Anthropological Perspectives* (New York: Columbia Univ. Press, 1978).

136. Vallee, Frank G. "Regionalism and Ethnicity: The French Canadian Case." In *Perspectives on Regions and Regionalism*, edited by B.Y. Card, 19–26. Edmonton, Alberta: Western Association of Sociology and Anthropology, 1969.

A useful discussion of how territorial and ethnic identity can reinforce each other. See Barth and Verdery in this chapter (items 73, 138), Sollers under American Studies (items 49–50), and Greeley (item 1567) and Reed (items 1617–1621) under Sociology for closely related sources.

137. Vayda, Andrew A. and Roy A. Rappaport. "Ecology, Cultural and Noncultural." In *Introduction to Cultural Anthropology*, edited by James A. Clifton, 477–96. Boston: Houghton-Mifflin, 1968.

This insightful survey of anthropological environmental theory focuses upon the rise and fall of the culture area concept from the 1890s to the 1940s and then examines the strengths and weaknesses of the cultural ecology paradigm that emerged in the 1950s.

138. Verdery, Katherine. "Ethnicity and Local Systems: The Religious Organization of Welshness." In *Regional Analysis*. vol. 2, 191–227 (item 128).

Verdery's use of Barth's theories of boundary maintenance and Hechter's concepts of "internal colonialism" and "peripheral sectionalism" to help explain spatial variations in the intensity of Welsh enthnicity can enhance our understanding of other ethnic-regional groups.

139. Vogt, Evon Z. and Ethel M. Albert, eds. *People of Rimrock: A Study of Values in Five Cultures*. Cambridge: Harvard Univ. Press, 1966.

This vivid collection of essays and photographs is a product of the intensive cultural study of the Four Corners region of the Southwest led by Clyde Kluckhohn and other Harvard anthropologists from 1949 until 1955. Five distinct cultures—Zuni, Navaho, Hispanic, Mormon, and

Texan—inhabit Rimrock, and their varied perception of and responses to the region are carefully examined. Chapters that are especially useful for understanding the dynamics of regionalism include "Ecology and Economy," by Evon Vogt, pp. 160–90, and "Expressive Values," by Clyde Kluckhohn with an introduction by Ethel M. Albert, pp. 265–298.

140. Werbner, R. P., ed. *Regional Cults.* New York: Academic Press, 1977.

This collection of essays devoted to understanding the dynamics of African and Near Eastern religious cults that are "more far-reaching than any parochial cult of the little community, yet less inclusive in belief and membership than a world religion" contains useful elaborations of Turner's theories of pilgrimage and Smith's call for regional systems analysis.

141. Wissler, Clark. *The American Indian: An Introduction to the Anthropology of the New World.* New York: McMurtrie and Co., 1917.

Wissler's landmark formulation of the culture area concept, this book provided a method for identifying areas of similar cultures—a method based upon tracing the distribution and clustering of central cultural traits. Ten North American culture areas are identified. Later in *Man and Culture* (New York: Thomas Y. Crowell, 1923), Wissler developed the notion of a cultural center from which trait complexes spread—a concept later elaborated by anthropologists Kroeber and Steward and geographer Donald Meinig.

142. ———. "The Culture-Area Concept as Research Lead." *American Journal of Sociology* 33 (May 1928): 894–900.

In this essay Wissler urges social scientists to begin to apply the culture area concept to complex, contemporary societies. He suggests that regional patterns may be uncovered by examining the spatial distribution of folk architecture, household arts, crops, and field patterns.

143. ———. "The Culture-Area Concept in Social Anthropology." *American Journal of Sociology* 32 (May 1927): 881–91.

In addition to describing the evolution of a regional perspective in the study of aboriginal America, Wissler encourages social anthropologists to explore three areas: the fundamental relationships between culture and the physical environment, the spatial distribution of nonmaterial aspects of culture, and the significance of regions within complex, industrial nations.

144. ———. *The Relation of Nature to Man in Aboriginal America.* New York: Oxford Univ. Press, 1926.

The most germane portion of this book in terms of its contributions to regional theory is Wissler's effort to explain the relationship between vegetation, climate, and culture areas—an analysis that anticipates Kroeber's, Steward's, and Driver's more sophisticated discussions. See "The Ecological Basis," pp. 211–22.

145. Wolf, Eric R. *Europe and the People Without History.* Berkeley: Univ. of California Press, 1982.

Influenced by Immanuel Wallerstein's and Fernand Braudel's models of a capitalist world-system with a dominant European core subjugating an underdeveloped periphery, Wolf describes in encyclopedic detail the global impact of the expansion of European mercantilism and capitalism from the fifteenth century to the present. Wolf's sweeping portrait of global cultural patterns and core-periphery relationships, his grasp of cultural ecology, and analyses of the impact of European expansion upon indigenous cultures in the Americas, Africa, and Asia provide a useful vision of transnational and transcultural regional processes and interactions. For a focused study of human ecology, see John W. Cole and Eric R. Wolf, *The Hidden Frontier: Ecology and Ethnicity in an Alpine Village* (New York: Academic Press, 1974).

146. Wood, W. Raymond and Margot Liberty, eds. *Anthropology of the Great Plains.* Lincoln: Univ. of Nebraska Press, 1980.

The essays in this collection attempt to sum up much of what is known about Great Plains Indian culture by discussing the plains setting, the uses of the culture area concept, plains linguistics and ethnohistory, and Indian ethnography.

Architecture and Planning

This chapter surveys regionalism in two closely related disciplines: architecture and planning. Both disciplines have deep ties with each other and with regionalism. Israeli architect and planner, Artur Glikson, has described the "logical sequence" in which "architects have proceeded from the design of individual houses for the family or the small community to planning the environment of these basic cells: street, square, park, neighborhood, the town as a whole. From here a further step has led to the problems of whole regions."[1]

It is with this logical and natural sequence in mind that architecture and planning have been integrated here. Architecture, planning, and region are naturally merged in the thought and work of Frederick Law Olmsted, Frank Lloyd Wright, Lewis Mumford, Benton MacKaye, Clarence Stein, Albert Mayer, Richard Neutra, Constantinos Doxiadis, Paolo Soleri, Chistopher Alexander, and many others aware of the ever-widening framework of built environments. As with Philosophy and Religion (Chapter eleven), so many important sources and central figures are involved in both architecture and planning that it is difficult to treat them separately. In joining such vast areas, we have had to be unusually selective, and the following paragraphs briefly discuss the general regional orientation and specific themes pursued within each discipline.

Architecture

Regionalism is an inevitable concern for architects. Architecture and region, built and natural environments, are inextricably linked. Even the seemingly placeless products of the International Style are influenced by their natural and cultural surroundings. The sheer wealth of material related to architecture and regionalism underscores the essential nature of the subject. A vast amount of scholarship is devoted to the architecture

of particular places in the United States. Scores of books and articles
have been written about the architecture of every region, state, and
major city of the United States. Wayne Andrews alone has written
separate books about the architecture of New England, the South,
Michigan, New York, and Chicago and Mid-America; Chicago
architecture alone has been analyzed by such distinguished scholars as
Montgomery Schuyler, Lewis Mumford, Sigfried Giedion, Carl Condit,
H. Allen Brooks, William Jordy, and Gwendolyn Wright.

Regional schools and styles of architecture—including Shingle
styles in New England; Prairie styles in the Midwest; Craftsmen,
Spanish Revival, and Case Study styles in Southern California, Bay
Region styles; and many other regional forms, both self-conscious and
vernacular—have been extensively analyzed. And many American
architects, from Andrew Jackson Downing and Frederick Law Olmsted
to Frank Lloyd Wright and Richard Neutra, have written eloquently
about regional influences in their work.

Regionalism in architecture is an immense topic, and rather than
attempt to catalogue every architectural study of regional and place
related issues, only the most relevant sources from three important areas
of scholarship have been selected for this chapter. The first area is
concerned with general theoretical discussions and overviews of
regionalism in architecture. Single region studies have been included
when they contain explicit discussions of regionalism in general.
Among the scholars included in this group, Lewis Mumford, Sibyl
Moholy-Nagy, Rexford Newcomb, Wayne Andrews, and William
Curtis contribute vital theoretical analyses of the relationship between
built environments and regions; Hugh Morrison, Alan Gowans, Jim
Kemp, Lester Walker, David De Long, and others provide surveys and
special exhibits of the evolution of various regional architectures within
a national framework.

A second group analyzes the relationship between architecture,
sense of place, and regionalism. Christian Norberg-Schulz, Wolf Von
Eckert, Ian Nairn, Vincent Scully, Barrie Greenbie, Dolores Hayden,
Phoebe Cutler, Robert Riley, and other architectural critics add to our
theoretical understanding of the links between built and natural
environments, between manmade structures and regional landscapes.

A third group of architects and scholars is actively involved in an
extensive contemporary revival of regional architecture. Growing
dissatisfaction with the cold universalism of much of modern
architecture, especially with the ahistorical and placeless pretensions of
the Bauhaus and the International Style, has inspired an important
counter movement toward self-conscious regionalism and historicism.
Since the 1960s, a growing number of architects and critics, including

Charles Moore, Vincent Scully, Michael Graves, John Morris Dixon, William Curtis, Kenneth Frampton, Peter Buchanan, Chris Abel, Suzanne Stephens, Colin St. John Wilson, and others, have vigorously promoted a pluralistic architecture responsive to local historical, cultural, and environmental conditions. Revival of vernacular architecture is a central element of the new regionalism of the past two decades, and there has been extensive discussion of the meaning of the term "vernacular," its various folk, industrial, and consumerist forms, and their relationship to "neo-vernacular" architecture. John Kouwenhoven, Sibyl Moholy-Nagy, J.B. Jackson, Robert Venturi, Denise Scott Brown, John Chase, Margaret King, Suzanne Stephens, Jim Kemp, Richard Guy Wilson, and others contribute to our understanding of vernacular and regional architecture. The regional-vernacular revival is especially potent among Third World architects eager to throw off the architectural imperialism of the International Style, and vital discussions of this and related topics are found in evocative special issues of *Progressive Architecture, Architectural Review,* and *Mimar: Architecture in Development.*

Planning

Planning, particularly regional planning, constitutes a second major focus of this chapter. As we have already seen, the concerns of architects and planners are often inseparable, and many important figures—including Frank Lloyd Wright, Lewis Mumford, Clarence Stein, Sibyl Moholy-Nagy, Barrie Greenbie, and Christopher Alexander—contribute to both fields. There is a vast literature devoted to regional planning, and a catalogue of all the relevant sources could easily fill an entire book.[2] From this immense literature, only those books and articles that concentrate upon the physical or built environment and enhance our general understanding of regionalism have been chosen. Studies of the political and administrative aspects of regional planning have been omitted along with highly technical analyses. Of the many studies of the Tennessee Valley Authority, for example, only the most general and environmentally-oriented sources have been included; the large literature on regional science is omitted here and discussed briefly under Economics.

The planning sources chosen include classic contributions to regional theory by Ebenezer Howard, Frank Lloyd Wright, Lewis Mumford, and Benton MacKaye and only slightly lesser masterpieces by David Lilienthal, Clarence Stein, Albert Mayer, Artur Glikson, Christopher Tunnard and Henry Hope Reed, John Friedmann and Clyde

Weaver, Ian McHarg, Kevin Lynch, and Christopher Alexander. All of
the sources in this chapter—the general surveys of regional architecture,
the studies of sense of place, the new regionalism, and regional
planning—amplify our understanding of the relationship between built
environments and regionalism. All contribute to our general
understanding of American regionalism.

As always, readers should be aware of a large number of related
sources in other chapters. American planning has had a complex
history, including such disparate sources as William Penn's gridiron
plan of Philadelphia (1682), Pierre Charles L'Enfant's plan of
Washington (1791), John Wesley Powell's plan for the arid regions of
the United States (1878), Daniel Burnham's plan for Chicago (1909),
the Garden and Greenbelt Cities of the 1920s and 1930s, and the New
Towns of 1960s and 1970s. Useful histories of regional planning by
Joseph Arnold, Roy Lubove, John Reps, MelSoctt, and others are
included under History: Other (items 1035, 1071, 1076–1077, 1082).

Questions of regional planning are often brilliantly discussed by
utopian thinkers such as Ralph Borsodi, Paul and Percival Goodman,
E.F. Schumacher, and others listed under Economics (items 321, 339–
340, 381–382), and Murry Bookchin, Karl Hess, Kirkpatrick Sale, and
others listed under Political Science (items 1410–1411, 1431–1432,
1460–1462). The discussion of neo-vernacular and regional architecture
in this chapter is enhanced by references to folk and vernacular buildings
listed under Folk Studies and Geography: Landscape and Settlement.
Analyses of sense of place in architecture here can be linked to similar
discussions under Geography: Region as Concept, Geography:
Landscape and Settlement, Philosophy and Religion, and Psychology.

M.S.

---

[1]Artur Glikson, "Toward Regional Landscape Design," in *The Ecological
Basis of Planning*, ed. by Lewis Mumford (The Hague: Martinus-Nijhoff,
1971), 79.

[2]A glimpse at the extensive literature of regional planning can be found in
two valuable books: John Friedmann and Clyde Weaver's *Territory and
Function: The Evolution of Regional Planning* (Berkeley: University of
California Press, 1979), with extensive bibliographies after each chapter,
and Clyde Weaver's *Regional Development and the Local Community:
Planning, Politics, and the Social Context* (New York: John Wiley and
Sons, 1984), bibliography, 164–88.

*   *   *

147. Abel, Chris. "Regional Transformations." In Special Issue. "Anatomy of Regionalism." *Architectural Review* (item 214), 36–43.

In this favorable survey of the international resurgence of regional architecture, Abel offers perceptive advice to an emerging generation of regionalists, particularly Third World architects challenging the hegemony of western modernism. Regional architects, he argues, should be wary of the romantic assumption that all anonymous architecture is purely indigenous and admirable and all colonial architecture completely foreign and worthless as regional models. "In these confusing times of the global village," he writes, "the true grist of regional architecture often lies in the cross-fertilization and localization of imported models, rather than in the purified identities associated with the usual references."

148. Alexander, Christopher. *The Timeless Way of Building*. New York: Oxford Univ. Press, 1979.

In this companion volume to *A Pattern Language* (item 149), Alexander provides a theoretical foundation for understanding basic patterns of events and space that sustain all "timeless," inherently satisfying built environments. See Alexander's *Notes on the Synthesis of Form* (Cambridge: MIT Press, 1964) for an earlier discussion of this theory. A bibliography of Alexander's writings is contained in Stephen Grabow, *Christopher Alexander: The Search for a New Paradigm in Architecture* (Boston: Oriel Press, 1983), pp. 229–37.

149. Alexander, Christopher, Sara Ishikawa, and Murray Silverstein. *A Pattern Language: Towns, Building, Construction*. New York: Oxford Univ. Press, 1977.

An encyclopedic yet elegantly structured and lyrically written guide to the construction of life-enhancing environments, from large-scale regions to personal spaces. The 253 "patterns" or general principles of construction constitute a language that can be used by planners, architects, and laymen to create a multitude of built environments. "Independent Regions" constitute the largest such environment, and the first third of the book, pp. 3–457, outlines the patterns that constitute such balanced regions, including the distribution of towns, city country fingers, agricultural valleys, mosaic of subcultures, web of shopping, activity nodes, industrial ribbon, holy ground, and common land. Alexander and his associates visualize global regionalization in which independent region "can become the modern polis—the new commune—that human entity which provides the sphere of culture, languages, laws, services, economic exchange, variety, which the old walled city of the polis provided for its members."

150. Alonso, William. "Aspects of Regional Planning Theory in the United States." In *Regional Policy: Readings in Theory and Application* (item 167), 3–17.

In reviewing recent trends in American regional planning, Alonso criticizes the "nostalgic vision of small-town America" which has colored much planning theory at the same time that he implicitly praises public resistance to rigid master schemes and preference for incremental, open-ended plans. Another source by Alonso is listed under Economics (item 314).

151. Andrews, Wayne. *Architecture, Ambition, and Americans: A Social History of American Architecture*. Rev. ed. New York: Free Press, 1978.

Regionalism is an important dimension of Andrew's survey of American architectural taste. "The Southern Triumph: Architecture in the Southern Colonies," pp. 1–31, and "The Northern Struggle: Architecture in the Northern Colonies," pp. 32–54, discuss the evolution of regional mentalities and corresponding architectural tastes. "The Chicago Story," pp. 198–244, emphasizes the regionally-rooted work of Frank Lloyd Wright and the Prairie School. "Modern Times," pp. 246–88, focuses upon the contrast between the destructive regional indifference of Walter Gropius, Ludwig Mies van der Rohe, and other Bauhaus exiles in the East and Midwest and the triumphant regional sensitivity of Bernard Maybeck, the Greene brothers, William Wilson Wurster, Harwell H. Harris, Charles W. Moore, and other architects in California.

152. Banham, Reyner. *Los Angeles: the Architecture of Four Ecologies*. Baltimore: Penguin Books, 1972.

Banham's imaginative, somewhat quirky, analysis stands above most studies of regional architecture because of its vivid sense of how particular buildings and environments are connected to a larger regional context. Banham anatomizes Southern California into four "ecologies"—the coastline, the freeways, the flatlands, and the hillsides—and examines the deliberately regional architecture of the Greene brothers, Irving Gill, Frank Lloyd Wright, Rudolph Schindler, Richard Neutra, Charles and Rae Eames, and others. An equally perceptive guide to the peculiarities of the region's architecture is Charles W. Moore, Peter Becker, and Regula Campbell's *The City*

Observed: Los Angeles (New York: Random House, 1984). A rousing critique of Banham's book which also contains a vivid sense of the regional built environment is Peter Plagen's "Los Angeles: The Ecology of Evil," *Artforum* 11 (December 1972): 67–76.

153. Brown, Denise Scott. "Invention and Tradition in the Making of American Place." In *American Architecture: Innovation and Tradition* (item 162), 158–70.

Brown describes the persistence of colonial cultural landscapes in America and their subtle adaptation to American conditions over time. Her study with Robert Venturi of "the everyday American environment" of Las Vegas and Levittown revealed the dialectic between tradition and innovation in the ongoing creation of American places. "American architects," she concludes, "are cultural immigrants who must face the American hinterland yet make our roads return to Rome."

154. Buchanan, Peter. "Only Connect." In Special Issue. "Regional Identity." In *Architectural Review* (item 213), 23–25.

Like a latter day Lewis Mumford, Buchanan promotes regionalism as the salvation of modern architecture and a key to global survival. After describing the "tragically ruinous impact" of much of modern architecture, Buchanan outlines a strategy for global regional renewal that avoids the pitfalls of nostalgia, kitsch, and provincialism—a renewal that connects the best of the universal with the best of the local.

155. ———. "With Due Respect: Regionalism." In Special Issue. "Regionalism." In *Architectural Review* (item 212), 15–16.

Buchanan vigorously champions "healthy Regionalism" as a necessary response to the crass commercialism and crushing uniformity fostered by the International Style. "Once the whole wide range of the world's cultures is treated with respect and humility," he writes, "and every spot on earth is treasured for more than its commercial value then the dangers of global destruction ... will be averted. Any Regionalism informed by this sense of love, and with a determination to do the best for local culture and global civilization is a powerful step in the right direction."

156. Chase, John. "Unvernacular Vernacular: Contemporary American Consumerist Architecture." *Design Quarterly* 131 (1986): 5–32.

Unlike many advocates of neo-vernacular regional architecture, Chase praises the mass produced "consumerist vernacular" of fast food restaurants, discount stores, shopping malls, and commercial strips. Such "unvernacular vernacular" environments are devoid of folk regional references except when they can be used to attract consumers.

157. Curtis, William J.R. *Modern Architecture Since 1900.* Englewood Cliffs, N.J.: Prentice-Hall, 1982.

"The Problem of Regional Identity," pp. 331–42, examines the rise of interest in "the indigenous, the variable, and the regional" in architecture throughout the world since the 1940s. Examples of "modern regional" architecture in Latin America, the West Coast of the United States, Australia, and Japan are analyzed in detail.

158. ———. "Towards an Authentic Regionalism." In Special Issue. "Regionalism and Architectural Identity." *Mimar: Architecture in Development* (item 215), 24–31.

After cataloging many of the possible shortcomings of the worldwide resurgence of regional architecture, Curtis provides guidelines for the growth of an "authentic" or "modern regionalism" in which "Rigorous modernity and rigorous understanding of the vernacular can be powerful allies in the search for a non-arbitrary architecture." Selected works by Frank Lloyd Wright, Alvar Aalto, Corbusier, Louis Kahn, Luis Barragan, Hassan Fathy, and others are used to illustrate the possibility of "authentic regionalism" throughout the world. This is a highly perceptive, wide-ranging essay.

159. Cutler, Phoebe. *The Public Landscape of the New Deal.* New Haven: Yale Univ. Press, 1985.

Cutler describes "the pervasive and often powerful ways the Depression inscribed itself upon the landscape" through extensive government sponsored projects in landscape architecture. Franklin Roosevelt's agrarian efforts in the Hudson Valley and the Appalachian hills of Georgia were microcosms of eventual New Deal efforts to shape and conserve local and regional landscapes. Cutler's analysis of the enduring signature of these projects—from urban rose gardens and playgrounds to national parks and recreation areas to shelter belts and kudzu plantings—is an important contribution to the history of landscape architecture and regionalism.

160. Dahir, James. *Region Building: Community Development Lessons from the Tennessee Valley*. New York: Harper and Brothers, 1955.

This book contains an insightful discussion of the strengths and weaknesses of sectionalism and metropolitan regionalism with the notion of a third force—"the natural region as a development unit"—as a basic building block for the nation. While lacking some of the critical perspective found in Jane Jacob's discussion of the TVA in *Cities and the Wealth of Nations* (item 356). Dahir is deeply sensitive to the intellectual traditions that contributed to the TVA.

161. Darling, F. Fraser and John P. Milton, eds. *Future Environments of North America*. Garden City, N.Y.: The Natural History Press, 1966.

In many ways a companion volume to William Thomas's *Man's Role in Changing the Face of the Earth* (1955), this extensive anthology contains important essays on natural regions of North America and the human impact upon these habitats. Especially important for regional planning are "Social and Cultural Purposes" and "Regional Planning and Development," pp. 315–612, with essays by Raymond Dasmann, Clarence Glackens, William Vogt, Pierre Dansereau, Ian McHarg, and Christopher Tunnard. Lewis Mumford's "Closing Statement," pp. 718–29, is an eloquent summation of his planning philosophy.

162. De Long, David G., Helen Searing, and Robert A.M. Stern, eds. *American Architecture: Innovation and Tradition*. New York: Rizzoli, 1986.

This important anthology contains the proceedings of a 1982 Columbia University symposium and exhibition that featured the resurgence of regional and vernacular architecture in the United States. Valuable discussions of regional issues in architecture include Vincent Scully's "American Architecture: The Real and the Ideal" (item 207); a section devoted to "The Building: Vernacular and Monumental," pp. 83–140, with perceptive essays on the architecture of Boston, Chicago, and Los Angeles by James O'Gorman, Donald Hoffmann, and Thomas Hines and comments by William Jordy, Rosemary Bletter, and Kenneth Frampton; J.B. Jackson's "Vernacular" (item 176); Denise Scott Brown's "Innovation and Tradition in the Making of American Place" (item 153); Dolores Hayden's "The American Sense of Place and the Politics of Space" (item 173); and the summary of the symposium's exhibition which features the distinctive architecture of six American regions (item 165).

163. Dixon, John Morris et al. "Regionalism Lives." *Progressive Architecture* 55 (March 1974): 59–77.

In his succinct introduction to the the first of a series of special sections devoted to regionalism, Dixon argues that a new regional architecture is emerging in reaction to the rigid universalism of modern architecture and in response to environmental imperatives. "There has always been a dialogue in architecture," he writes, "between the universal and the particular, the ideal and the pragmatic, between academic models and popular sources.... Right now, the preponderance of force seems to be opposing the universal."

164. Doxiadis, Contantinos A. *Ekistiks: An Introduction to the Science of Human Settlement.* New York: Oxford Univ. Press, 1968.

This is a massive, visionary guidebook to the building of neighborhoods, cities, and regions within a global framework. Doxiadis further develops his vision of global regionalization in *Ecumenopolis: the Inevitable City of the Future* (New York: W.W. Norton, 1974).

165. "Exhibition." In *American Architecture: Innovation and Tradition* (item 162), 231–75.

This detailed synopsis of a 1982 exhibition devoted to sense of place and region in American architecture contains an insightful introduction by Suzanne Stephens and separate essays on the distinctive architecture of "The East" by Deborah Nevins, pp. 234–40; "The South" by Gerald Allen, pp. 241–45; "The Midwest" by John Zukowsky, pp. 246–52; "The Plains and Rockies" by Richard Longstreth, pp. 253–59; "the Southwest" by Lawrence Speck, pp. 260–64; and "The West Coast" by Sally Woodbridge. Ann Kaufman's analysis of national traits, "America as a Region," pp. 271–75, ends the section.

166. Frampton, Kenneth. "Prospects for a Critical Regionalism." *Perspecta: The Yale Architectural Journal* 20 (1983): 147–61.

After carefully distinguishing between "critical regionalism and the simplistic evocation of a sentimental or ironic vernacular" and between locally responsive architecture that challenges mass culture and consumerist populism, Frampton describes examples of such radical regionalism in Europe, Japan, North America and Latin America. "The universal Megalopolis," he concludes, "is patently antipathetic to a dense differentiation of culture. It intends, in fact, the reduction of the environment to nothing but commodity.... Critical Regionalism would seem to offer the sole possibility of resisting the rapacity of this tendency." For a closely related argument, see Frampton's "Towards a Critical Regionalism: Six Points for an Architecture of Resistance," in *The Anti-Aesthetic: Essays on Postmodern Culture* (Port Townsend, Washington: Bay Press, 1983), edited by Hal Forster.

167. Friedmann, John and William Alonso, eds. *Regional Development and Planning: A Reader.* Cambridge: MIT Press, 1964.

This anthology, along with Friedmann and Alonso's more recent, *Regional Policy: Readings in Theory and Application* (Cambridge: MIT Press, 1975), contains essential background sources for the multivarious field of regional planning.

168. Friedmann. John and Clyde Weaver. *Territory and Function: The Evolution of Regional Planning.* Berkeley: Univ. of California Press, 1979.

This important book contains a comprehensive survey of American regional planning theory from the 1920s and 1930s to the 1970s. In a series of concise, thoroughly documented chapters, the authors weigh the merits and flaws of the Regional Planning Association of America (1923–1933), the southern regionalists at the University of North Carolina and Vanderbilt, the New Deal Planners, the Chicago human ecologists, and the Regional Science movement. The final chapters bravely propose a new paradigm for regional studies: "the recovery of territorial life" through "agropolitan" planning. While such planning— which involves the development of local self-sufficiency, the uses of small-scale technology, and the communalization of productive wealth—seems most appropriate for densely populated, agrarian societies, it is suggested that post-industrial societies may also be moving toward such regional "recovery."

169. Glikson, Artur. *The Ecological Basis of Planning: Collected Essays.* Edited by Lewis Mumford. The Hague: Martinus-Nijhoff, 1971.

In these posthumous essays, Israeli architect and planner Glikson masterfully discusses the connections between architecture, planning, and regionalism. In such essays as "Man's Relationship to His Environment," pp. 1–16, "The Planner Geddes," pp. 45–51, "Social Trends in Planning," pp. 52–66, "The Relationship Between Landscape

Planning and Regional Planning, pp. 67–78, and "Toward Regional Landscape Design," pp. 78–86, Glikson develops a profound theoretical framework for regional planning that continues many of the ideas developed by Lewis Mumford, Benton MacKaye, Clarence Stein, and other members of the Regional Planning Association of America.

170. Gowans, Alan. *Images of American Living: Four Centuries of Architecture and Furniture as Cultural Expression.* Philadelphia: Lippincott, 1964.

In Part One, "Medieval America: The Seventeenth Century," pp. 3–114, Gowans devotes separate chapters to the regionally distinctive building and furniture styles of New Spain, New Netherlands, New England, Pennsylvania, and the South. "Diversity Within Unity: The Classical Mind as Regional and Class Expression," pp. 173–223, examines stylistic diversity in the eighteenth century by carefully comparing the material culture of three regional social groups: southern plantation society, upper class Philadelphia, and the mercantile society of New York, Newport, and Boston.

171. Greenbie, Barrie B. *Design for Diversity: Planning for Natural Man in the Neo-technic Environment: An Ethological Approach.* Amsterdam: Elsevier Scientific Publishing, 1976.

This is an ingenious effort to apply the studies of territoriality, crowding, and aggression by an ethologist and anthropologists Konrad Lorenz, John Calhoun, Robert Ardry, Edward Hall and others to architecture and regional planning. Greenbie's wide-ranging discussion of regional planning in "A New Look at New Towns," pp. 155–80, is especially insightful.

172. ———. *Spaces: Dimensions of the Human Landscape.* New Haven: Yale Univ. Press, 1981.

Like Christopher Alexander and Christian Norberg-Schulz, Greenbie analyzes the elements of satisfying environments, from intimate to increasingly large scale public domains. The text is gracefully written, well-documented, and amply illustrated with photographs of everyday human habitations in the United States and Europe, ranging from private dwellings to public places to regional landscapes.

173. Hayden, Dolores. "The American Sense of Place and the Politics of Space." In *American Architecture: Innovation and Tradition* (item 162), 184–97.

In this important, highly perceptive essay, Hayden contrasts the sense of place evoked by preindustrial vernacular architecture with the sense of placelessness and control exerted by commercial vernacular architecture. She urges greater awareness of the "politics of space"—the hegemonic, exploitative power of the commercial landscapes as stressed by Henri Lefebvre, Edward Soja and others—and that scholars should encourage the growth of a more pluralistic, locally-defined, sense of place and community based in part on resilient folk, regional, ethnic, and feminist expressions. "The American spatial tradition established by Ford, Levitt, Moses, and Disney," she concludes, "is reshaping parts of the rest of the world, but it is not too late for the United States to import some well-reasoned social concern as well."

174. Howard, Ebenezer. *Garden Cities of Tomorrow*. Edited by F.J. Osborn. Cambridge: MIT Press, 1965.

Originally published in 1898, Howard's sweeping vision of urban decentralization through the careful development of a constellation of garden cities within permanent green belts has had a profound impact upon twentieth century regional thought and practice. For an alternative, somewhat less influentially regional scheme, see Frank Lloyd Wright's Broadacre City proposal (item 230).

175. Jackson, J.B. "Urban Circumstances." *Design Quarterly* 128 (1985): 5–32.

After uncovering the root meaning of the word "vernacular," Jackson analyzes three important American vernacular environments. Southern slave quarters, northern working class dwellings, and mobile homes are discussed as folk variations of larger, more powerful spatial orders, namely the plantation, the factory, and the freeway.

176. ———. "Vernacular." In *American Architecture: Innovation and Tradition* (item 162), 143–51.

Jackson carefully analyzes various meanings of the word "vernacular" and stresses that since its earliest manifestations in the eleventh century, vernacular architecture has been characterized by extraordinary flexibility and adaptability rather than "timeless" traditionalism as argued by many scholars. The general qualities of American domestic vernacular architecture and its many regional permutations are discussed. Other important sources by Jackson are listed under Geography: Landscape and Settlement (items 641–643). Closely related sources in this chapter include Brown, Chase, Kemp,

Kouwenhoven, Stephens, Venturi, and Wilson (items 153, 156, 177, 180, 218, 221, 227).

177. Kemp, Jim. *American Vernacular: Regional Influences in Architecture and Interior Design.* New York: Viking, 1987.

This attractively illustrated guide abounds with useful information regarding the evolution of American regional and vernacular domestic styles with emphasis upon the surge of self-conscious regional architecture in the 1970s and 1980s. Part Two, "A Portfolio of Regional Styles," pp. 29–157, examines a wide variety of historical and contemporary regional house forms with separate chapters devoted to New England, the Mid-Atlantic, South, Southwest, Midwest, West, and National Styles. Part Three, "Furnishings and Objects," pp. 158–205, discusses regional furniture and artifacts from the Northeast, South, Southwest, Midwest, and West. Part Four, "Details and Flourishes," pp. 206–39, illustrates exterior and interior housing details from each of these regions.

178. King, Margaret J. "McDonald's and the New American Landscape." *USA Today* 108 (January 1980): 46–48.

The replacement of uniform golden arches by local and regional architectural motifs in MacDonald's restaurants is analyzed as an example of the commercialization of regionalism in the late 1970s. For closely related sources, see Chase and Stephens (items 156, 218).

179. Kirker, Harold. *California's Architectural Frontier: Style and Tradition in the Nineteenth Century.* Santa Barbara: Peregrine-Smith, 1973.

At the heart of this influential study of architectural colonialism is Kirker's vivid analysis of how two European building traditions— Mediterranean masonry and northern European wood construction—were slowly influenced by regional conditions. This theme is followed into the twentieth century by many scholars, most successfully in Esther Coy's *Five California Architects* (New York: Reinhold Books, 1968); Thomas Hines's "Los Angeles Architecture: The Issue of Tradition in a Twentieth Century City," in David De Long et al., eds. *American Architecture: Innovation and Tradition* (item 162), 112–29; and Reyner Banham's *Los Angeles: The Architecture of Four Ecologies* (item 152).

180. Kouwenhoven, John A. *Made in America: The Arts in Modern American Civilization.* New York: Doubleday 1948.

Kouwenhoven's discussion of the vernacular tradition in American architecture, painting, music, language and industrial design has had a pervasive influence upon American architectural theory and shed light upon the relationship between vernacular, folk, and regional forms. Expanding upon Sigfried Giedion's admiration of American vernacular architecture in *Space, Time and Architecture* (1941), Kouwenhoven praises a pragmatic, functional, and non-elitist approach to art and architecture—a "democratic technological vernacular"—that enabled Americans "to create patterns of clean, organic, and indigenous beauty out of the crude materials of the technological environment."

181. Lilienthal, David E. *TVA: Democracy on the March.* New York: Pocket Books, 1944.

This classic piece of advocacy sums up the New Deal vision of regional planning and, along with MacKaye and Mumford's work, stands as a starting point for considerations of comprehensive regional planning today. Echoing Roosevelt, Norris, and Arthur Morgan, Lilienthal describes the TVA as an effort to appreciate a region as a "seamless web" of land, water, and people: "to envision in its entirety the potentialities of the whole river system, for navigation, for power, for flood control, and for recreation." The eventually tragic shortcomings of this brave effort—its support of strip mining and environmentally disruptive "conservation" projects—have been amply demonstrated by many writers, including Authur E. Morgan in *The Making of the TVA* (Buffalo, N.Y.: Prometheus Books, 1974); Harry Caudill in *My Land Is Dying* (New York: E.P. Dutton, 1971); Wendell Berry in "Mayhem in Industrial Paradise," in *A Continuous Harmony* (New York: Harcourt, Brace, Jovanovich, 1970); and essays by Wilmon H. Droze and Craufurd D. Goodwin in *TVA: Fifty Years of Grass-Roots Bureaucracy* (Urbana: Univ. of Illinois Press, 1983), edited by Erin C. Hargrove and Paul K. Conkin.

182. Longstreth, Richard. *On the Edge of the World: Four Architects in San Francisco at the Turn of the Century.* Cambridge: MIT Press, 1983.

Longstreth's wide-ranging study of the architecture of Ernest Coxhead, Willis Polk, A.C. Schweinfurth, and Bernard Maybeck makes an important contribution to our understanding of American regional architecture. "Academic Eclecticism: The Question of Style," pp. 9–39, effectively analyzes regionalism's central role in late nineteenth century academic architecture, focusing upon examples of academic regionalism in New Mexico, Florida, Philadelphia, Boston, and

Northern California. "Schweinfurth: The Cause of Regional Expression," pp. 258–95, carefully examines the self-conscious use of Hispanic motifs in California regional architecture. A longer, more technical version of "Academic Eclecticism" appeared as "Academic Eclecticism in American Architecture," *Winterthur Portfolio* 17 (Spring 1982), pp. 55–82.

183. Lynch, Kevin. *Good City Form.* Cambridge: MIT Press, 1984.

This masterful summation of Lynch's widespread work in physical planning theory abounds with important regional insights. "Between Heaven and Hell," pp. 51–72, is a valuable study of utopian and dystopian environmental imagery and design from William Morris to Ebenezer Howard to Paolo Soleri. Separate chapters carefully analyze such physical components of "good city form" as vitality, sense of place, fit, access, and control. "A Place Utopia," pp. 293–317, carries forward the vision of a regionalized society started by Paul and Percival Goodman's *Communitas* (1947). Extensive appendices and bibliographies on urban design and regional planning are included.

184. ———. *The Image of the City.* Cambridge: MIT Press, 1960.

Lynch's pioneering and immensely influential "image" study develops a method and terminology for describing how people perceive the city in terms of boundaries, paths, and central landmarks. Boston, Jersey City, and Los Angeles are emphasized. Especially useful are "The City Image and Its Elements" and Appendix B, "The Use of the Method."

185. ———. *Managing the Sense of a Region.* Cambridge: MIT Press, 1976.

Using the chaotic development of San Diego's Mission Valley as a starting point, Lynch argues that planners must be sensitive to how a new environment "affects the everyday lives of the people who use it, that is, how it affects them in an immediate sense, through their eyes, ears, nose, and skin." He also argues that such experimental planning must occur at a regional scale, "since Mission Valleys occur for regional reasons, and people now live their lives at that scale." Lynch's wide-ranging, well documented discussion of how to grasp and maintain "The Sensory Quality of Regions" is a valuable contribution to regional theory and practice. Other useful books by Lynch include *The Image of the City* (Cambridge: MIT Press, 1960), with its influential excursion into mental mapping, and *What Time Is This Place?*

(Cambridge: MIT Press, 1976), which examines the impact of geographical mobility upon sense of place.

186. MacKaye, Benton. "An Appalachian Trail: A Project in Regional Planning." *Journal of the American Institute of Architects* 9 (October 1921): 325–30.

In addition to inspiring the construction of the Appalachian Trail, this important essay contains a vision of the regional reordering of society based upon awareness of the indigenous, primeval basis of society.

187. ———. *Expedition Nine: Return to a Region.* Washington, D.C.: National Geographic Society, 1969.

Based upon eighty years of living in and exploring the land around Shirley Center, Massachusetts, this intimate account of the natural and social ecology of a small corner of New England is the fullest demonstration of MacKaye's regional vision and philosophy.

188. ———. *The New Exploration: A Philosophy of Regional Planning.* Urbana: Univ. of Illinois Press, 1962.

Originally published in 1928 and prefiguring later concerns of bioregionalism, this important book urges Americans to plan within the "indigenous" framework of the continent: to develop an understanding of the primal harmony and balance of each region and to build within that framework so as to elicit the full promise of the land. Many of MacKaye's less accessible essays are collected by Paul T. Bryant in *From Geography to Geotechnics* (Urbana: Univ. of Illinois Press, 1968). A full bibliography of MacKaye's published work is contained in a special "Tribute to Benton MacKaye," *Living Wilderness* 39 (January/March 1976), pp. 33–34.

189. McHarg, Ian. *Design With Nature.* Garden City, N.Y.: Doubleday, 1966.

This is a sweeping guide to community and regional planning full of philosophical, ethical, and ecological speculation echoing George Perkins Marsh, Patrick Geddes, Carl Sauer, and Benton MacKaye. Using the Potomac River Basin as an example, McHarg urges "a simple sequential examination" from the ground up, using insights from geology, botany, biology, and other disciplines to perceive how people might "fit" most harmoniously within the regional system.

190. Mayer, Albert. *The Urgent Future: People, Housing, City, Region.* New York: McGraw-Hill, 1967.

Mayer, a veteran of the regional planning efforts of the 1930s, envisions the growth of New Towns, both within cities and within larger decentralized regional frameworks, as solutions to urban problems in the 1960s. Echoing Clarence Stein and Artur Glikson's work, this book works from the ground up, masterfully connecting the concerns of architecture with regional planning. Insightful chapters include: "New Towns and Fresh In-City Communities," pp. 76–93; "Twentieth Century Pioneering: Restructuring Regions and New Regions," pp. 130–48; and "Synthesis and Sublimation: Organic Architecture," pp. 149–66.

191. Moholy-Nagy, Sibyl. *Matrix of Man: An Illustrated History of the Urban Environment.* New York: Praeger, 1968.

Like economist Jane Jacobs, architectural historian Sibyl Moholy-Nagy is deeply critical of scientific, often ahistorical, approaches to urban and regional planning. In tracing the development of such fundamental settlement forms as primeval geomorphic and concentric environments, the Roman gridiron, the linear merchant city, and modern cluster developments, she pays homage to historical precedent. "Clusters and the End of Origins," pp. 241–82, contains a particularly forceful, if somewhat misdirected, critique of the Patrick Geddes-Ebenezer Howard-Lewis Mumford vision of regional planning.

192. ———. *Native Genius in Anonymous Architecture.* New York: Horizon Press, 1957.

This classic study protests the cold sterility and crushing uniformity of much of the modern built environment and praises the human warmth, variability, and sense of place often found in anonymous or folk architecture. Moholy-Nagy's text is vividly illustrated with a wide variety of American folk dwellings, and her discussion of the need for a sense of "at-homeness on this factory-strewn earth" has influenced the rise of neo-vernacular and regional architecture since the 1970s.

193. Moore, Charles W. and Gerald Allen. *Dimensions: Space, Shape and Scale in Architecture.* New York: Architectural Books, 1976.

Two essays by Moore, offered as regional "walking tours," examine distinctive qualities of architecture in California and the South. "You Have to Pay for the Public Life," pp. 105–30, playfully examines how monuments and public buildings create sense of place in the Bay

Area, Southern California, and small towns in between. Disneyland, freeways, movie palaces, and roadside statuary are respectfully analyzed. "Southerness: A Regional Dimension," pp. 143–56, discusses the architectural design and ambience of Charleston, New Orleans, Williamsburg, Charlottesville, and other southern places, praising their small-scale urban and urbane vivacity.

194. Moore, Charles W., Kathryn Smith, and Peter Becker. *Home Sweet Home: American Domestic Vernacular Architecture*. New York: Rizzoli for the Los Angeles Craft and Folk Art Museum, 1983.

This is a useful source regarding the resurgence of interest in regional and vernacular domestic architecture in the 1970s and 1980s.

195. Morrison, Hugh. *Early American Architecture: From the First Colonial Settlement to the National Period*. New York: Oxford Univ. Press, 1952.

This classic study contains highly perceptive discussions of the regional variations of early American architecture. The first half of the book carefully analyzes seventeenth century regional colonial styles in New England, New York, the South, the Spanish Southwest and California and the French settlements in the Mississippi Valley. The second half of the book examines regional permutations of eighteenth century Georgian architecture from New England to South Carolina.

196. Mumford, Lewis. *The Culture of Cities*. New York: Harcourt, Brace & Co., 1938.

This is Mumford's regional masterpiece and an indispensable contribution to American regional theory. All of this vividly illustrated, powerfully argued book contributes to our understanding of the connections between architecture, city form, and regionalism, but "The Regional Framework of Civilization," pp. 300–47, and "The Politics of Regional Development," pp. 348–401, are especially valuable. Here Mumford provides a sweeping history of regional movements in the western world and argues that civilization can only flourish by decentralizing the metropolis and planning cities within regional frameworks. Beyond replacing the overweening metropolis, this "regional renewal of life" will serve as an antidote to the imperialistic belligerence and environmental insensitivity of the nation-state. *Technics and Civilization* (New York: Harcourt, Brace & World, 1934), articulates Mumford's related vision of the regional decentralization of industrial technology.

197. ———. *Roots of Contemporary American Architecture.* New York: Grove Press, 1959.

Regionalism is a central feature of this important collection of essays on American architecture from the 1850s to the 1950s. Mumford's opening essay, "A Backward Glance," pp. 1–30, provides a sweeping vision of the evolution of American culture and architecture from colonial dependency and environmental defiance toward appreciation of the indigenous, natural, and regional realities of the land. Section Two, "Roots in the Region," pp. 83–149, documents the theme of regional renewal with excerpts from Thoreau's *Walden* (1854) and Downing's *Landscape Architecture* (1844); Mumford's "Frederick Law Olmsted's Contributions," pp. 101–106, and "The Regionalism of Richardson," pp. 117–131; Frank Lloyd Wright's "Nature as Architect," pp. 132–40; and Benton MacKaye's "Environment as a Natural Resource," pp. 141–49. Further relevant essays by Horatio Greenough, Louis Sullivan, Clarence Stein, Catherine Bauer, Wright, and Mumford are included.

198. ———. *The South in Architecture.* New York: Da Capo Press, 1967.

Originally published in 1941, this book discusses the nature of regional architecture and culture with an emphasis upon the work of Thomas Jefferson and Henry Hobson Richardson. Mumford contrasts universal and regional architectural impulses and stresses that both are essential to a lively culture. Regional forms "are those which most closely meet the actual conditions of life and which most fully succeed in making a people feel at home in their environment," and the regional impulse involves a continuous coming to terms with the present rather than nostalgia for the past. The final chapter examines Frank Lloyd Wright as the most accomplished American regional architect.

199. ———. "Status Quo." *New Yorker* 23 (October 11, 1948): 104–110.

In this prescient critique of the mechanical sterility that often passes for modern architecture, Mumford promotes the more humane and regionally responsive work of California Bay Region architects Bernard Maybeck and William Wurster as a path of the future. Their work, he argues, is "a product of the meeting of Oriental and Occidental architectural traditions, and is far more truly a universal style than the so-called international style of the 1930s, since it permits regional adaptations and modifications." Mumford's article sparked a formal symposium devoted to the question "What is Happening to Modern

Architecture?" in February 1948 at the Museum of Modern Art (item 216).

200. ———. *Sticks and Stones: A Study of American Architecture and Civilization.* New York: Boni and Liveright, 1924.

Mumford's book is a masterful reading of built environments—from the New England village to the southern country manor to the Chicago skyscraper—as mirrors of American regional cultures. "The Age of the Machine," pp. 71–89, and "Architecture and Civilization," pp. 91–112, explain the need for regional planning in an urban-industrial society, and Mumford locates the sources of that regional vision in the examples of the seventeenth century New England village and the social theories of Frederick Le Play, Peter Kropotkin, Patrick Geddes, and Ebenezer Howard.

201. ———. *The Urban Prospect.* New York: Harcourt, Brace & World, 1968.

This collection of essays abounds with practical advice and theoretical perspectives for urban and regional planning. Important practical discussions include "Planning for the Phases of Life," pp. 24–43; "Quarters for an Aging Population," pp. 44–55; "Neighborhood and Neighborhood Unit," pp. 56–78; and "The Highway and the City," pp. 92–107. Theoretical essays include highly perceptive analyses of the regional planning visions of Le Corbusier, Frank Lloyd Wright, and Ebenezer Howard, respectively in "Yesterday's City of Tomorrow," pp. 116–27, "Megalopolis as Anti-City," pp. 128–41; and "Beginnings of Urban Integration," pp. 142–52. "Metropolitan Dissolution vs. Regional Integration," pp. 167–81, is an effective summary of Mumford's regional planning philosophy, and "Home Remedies for Urban Cancer," pp. 182–207, documents his debate with Jane Jacobs regarding the relative merits of wholesale and piecemeal urban and regional planning. Other sources by Mumford are listed under American Studies (items 26–28).

202. Nairn, Ian. *The American Landscape: A Critical View.* New York: Random House, 1965.

This architectural-environmental jeremiad by a visiting Englishman condemns the American cultural landscape as the "most characterless and least differentiated mess that man has ever made for himself," and urges Americans to live up to the promise of their land by achieving greater spatial coherence and appreciation of place. "The whole of America, from Pacific to Atlantic," Nairn believes, "could be built up

organically and sensitively.... America is a great big heap of artifacts—
the most varied and exciting heap that the world has ever seen, dumped
down in the most monotonous and dreary way that the world has ever
seen. If they could be given pattern, the result would be the most
varied, exciting and unregimented set of places that the world has ever
seen."

203. Newcomb, Rexford. "Regionalism in American Architecture." In
Regionalism in America, edited by Merrill Jensen, 273–95. Madison:
Univ. of Wisconsin Press, 1951.

In a somewhat piecemeal fashion, Newcomb describes the
evolution of building styles and techniques in New England, the Middle
Atlantic States, the South, the Mississippi Valley, and the Southwest.

204. Norberg-Schulz, Christian. *Existence, Space, and Architecture.*
New York: Praeger, 1971.

This important book effectively analyzes the primal human need
for sense of place, the hazards of rootless mobility, and how built
environments can enhance our sense of place, self, and community.
"The Concept of Space," pp. 9–16, explores the basic "spatiality of
human life" through the phenomenology of Martin Heidegger, Maurice
Merleau-Ponty, Gaston Bachelard, Otto Bollnow, and others.
"Existential Space," pp. 17–36, uses the insights of theologian Mircea
Eliade, psychologists Jean Piaget and Kurt Lewin, and architectural
theorists Sigfried Giedion, Christopher Alexander, and Kevin Lynch to
develop concepts of "center," "path," "area," and "domain" as well as a
hierarchical model of experienced environments for understanding
human uses of space. "Architectural Space," pp. 37–114, surveys the
basic components of humane, environmentally sensitive architecture.
Two other important and related studies by Norberg-Schulz are *Genius
Loci: Towards a Phenomenology of Architecture* (New York: Rizzoli,
1980) and *The Concept of Dwelling: On the Way to a Figurative
Architecture* (New York: Rizzoli, 1985).

205. Perloff, Harvey S. *The Art of Planning: Selected Essays of
Harvey S. Perloff.* Edited by Leland S. Burns and John Friedmann.
New York: Plenum Press, 1985.

Although Perloff's contributions to planning have been primarily
in the area of regional economics, this volume contains some important
work in physical and environmental planning as well. Such essays as
"New Towns Intown" (1966), pp. 5–12; "The Central City in the Post
Industrial Age" (1978), pp. 29–46; "Using the Arts to Improve Life in

the City" (1979), pp. 47–62; and "Key Features of Regional Planning" (1968), pp. 205–19, are useful discussions of the relationship between built environments and regional planning. Other sources by Perloff are listed under Economics (items 374–375).

206. Riley, Robert B. "Speculations on the New American Landscapes." *Landscape* 24 (1980): 1–9.

Riley sensitively describes the gradual dissolution of traditional regional landscapes and the rise of a welter of "pluralistic," often "packaged," landscapes designed to appeal to a myriad of consumer-oriented groups. The role of nostalgia and subcultural identity in the design of shopping malls, strips, and recreation areas is effectively analyzed.

207. Scully, Vincent. "American Architecture: The Real and the Ideal." In *American Architecture: Innovation and Tradition* (item 162), 3–23. New York: Rizzoli, 1986.

In this keynote address, Scully traces four traditions in American architecture: Native American (epitomized by the Southwest pueblo); European colonial architecture; the more organic "realist" tradition of Downing, Richardson, and Wright; and the formal, monumental classicism of Jefferson and L'Enfant. The environmentally responsive forms of the Native American and realist traditions are effectively contrasted to the ever-dominant colonial and classical forms which turn away from nature.

208. ———. *Pueblo: Mountain, Village, Dance.* New York: Viking, 1975.

At the conclusion of this powerful study of the relationship between nature, architecture, and ritual among contemporary Pueblo Indians of New Mexico and Arizona, Scully suggests that such indigenous forms might serve as models for the growth of a more regionally-responsive Euro-American architecture. Scully's *American Architecture and Urbanism* (New York: Praeger, 1969) portrays the expansive urge to dominate and transform nature that has characterized much of Euro-American architecture; his *The Shingle Style: Architectural Theory and Design from Richardson to the Origins of Wright* (New Haven: Yale Univ. Press, 1955) and *The Shingle Style Today, Or, The Historians Revenge* (New York: George Braziller, 1974) trace the development of an important form of regional domestic architecture in the late nineteenth century and its revival in the late twentieth.

209. Sharky, Bruce G. "Strong Attitudes on Regionalism.... But No Consensus." *Landscape Architecture* 75 (March/April 1985): 78–81.

After summarizing recent literature promoting regionalism "as a theoretical and educational focus" in landscape architecture, Sharky analyzes the mixed results of a nationwide survey designed to measure the actual significance of regionalism among practicing landscape architects.

210. Special Issues. "Regionalism: The Southwest." *Progressive Architecture* 55 (March 1974): 60–77.

Progressive Architecture started a series of special sections devoted to American regional architecture in 1974. This first special issue is prefaced by John Morris Dixon's manifesto, "Regionalism Lives" (item 163) and contains photographic essays on the regionally responsive work of Antoine Predock in New Mexico and Bennie M. Gonzales in Arizona. Subsequent regional issues and articles in *Progressive Architecture* include "The Great Northwest Revival," 55 (August 1974), pp. 46–63; "Chicago Architecture," 61 (June 1980), pp. 71–98; "Regionalism and the Vernacular Tradition," 62 (June 1981), pp. 75–114 (item 211); "California Homes," 64 (March 1983), pp. 105–17; and "Radical Regionalism," on the Bay Area, 68 (May 1987), pp. 29, 32.

211. Special Issue. "Regionalism and the Vernacular Tradition." *Progressive Architecture* 62 (June 1981): 75–114.

Suzanne Stephen's important lead essay (item 218) provides a perceptive overview. Sally Woodbridge's "Against Nature," pp. 78–85, analyzes the neo-primative domestic architecture of Andrew Baley and Mark Mack in California's Napa Valley. David Morton discusses neo-vernacular-regional architecture in Tampa, Florida in "'Dog Trot' House," pp. 86–89; Arizona in "Desert Forms," pp. 90–97; the Seattle area in "Timber and Glass," pp. 98–101, and near Miami in "Institutional Redefined," pp. 102–05. Richard Bush examines New Mexican architecture in "Hacienda con Vistas," pp. 106–09, and Peter C. Papademetriou discusses New Orleans forms in "Simmering Mix," pp. 110–14.

212. Special Issue. "Regionalism." *Architectural Review* 173 (May 1983): 14–61.

Peter Buchanan's powerful lead essay, "With Due Respect: Regionalism" (item 155), vigorously promotes regional renewal in architecture. The remaining regionally-specific essays in this seven-article anthology include a discussion of contemporary regional architecture in Sri Lanka in "Bawa's Parliament" , pp. 17–23, and "Hotel Ahungalla, Sri Lanka," pp. 24–29; Denys Lasdun's analysis of Israeli regionalism in "Nurva Synagogue," pp. 30–33; Reyner Banham's examination of "Santa Cruz Shingle Style," pp. 34–38; and discussions of twentieth century Italian regionalisms in "Milano Novecente," pp. 39–45, and "Botta in the City," pp. 46–51.

213. Special Issue. "Regional Identity." *Architectural Review* 176 (October 1984): 23–71.

Peter Buchanan's "Only Connect" (item 154) expands his earlier appeal for regionalism. Other regionally focused essays in this ten-article anthology include Rory Spence's "Three Australian Homes," pp. 26–33; Jonathan Glanery's analysis of Imre Makovecz's Hungarian regionalism in "Makovecz Embrace," pp. 34–40; Bodil Kjaer's study of American architect Martin Price in "How Nature Forms," pp. 42–44; Peter Davey's "Arctic Response," pp. 46–51; John Pastier's study of Michael Graves' response to Southern California in "Missionary Graves," pp. 52–57; Robert Harbison's "With Pevsner in England," pp. 58–61; Aldo van Eyck's discussion of Surinam/Dutch architecture in "Tropical Lafour," pp. 62–67; and Colin St. John Wilson's penetrating essay, "The Historical Sense" (item 226).

214. Special Issue. "Anatomy of Regionalism." *Architectural Review* 180 (November 1986): 36–84.

Chris Abel's "Regional Transformations" (item 154) discusses the relationship between regional, vernacular, and colonial architecture. Other regional cases studies in this six-article anthology include Michael Brawne's discussion of Geoffrey Bawa's Sri Lanka regionalism in "Bawa at Ruhunu," pp. 38–51, Chris Abel's examination of neo-Muslim architecture in "Work of El-Wakil," pp. 52–60; Winfried Nerdinger's study of turn of the century German regionalist, Theodore Fischer, pp. 61–64; Rory Spence on the northern Australian work of Rex Addison, pp. 66–76; and Richard Guy Wilson's highly perceptive "Learning from the American Vernacular" (item 227).

215. Special Issue. "Regionalism and Architectural Identity." *Mimar: Architecture in Development* 19 (January-March 1986): 18–71.

In his succinct lead essay, "Perspectives and Limits on Regionalism and Architectural Identity," pp. 18–21, Brian Bruce Taylor observes that most architects are either intensely local or international rather than regional in their sense of building style, and he urges greater precision in the use of such vague terms as "regionalism" and "identity." The other essays in this eight-article anthology are largely devoted to the emergence of Third World regionalism and include Sumet Jumsai's "The West Pacific Region versus Punk Architecture," pp. 22–23, which urges Southeast Asian regional architects to resist western oriented Post-Modern and Punk styles; William J.R. Curtis's brilliant analysis, "Toward an Authentic Regionalism" (item 158); Yuswadi Saliya's "Notes on Architectural Identity in the Cultural Context," pp. 32–33; Balikrishna Doshi's discussion of contemporary Indian regionalism in "Bohra Houses of Gujarat," pp. 34–40; Kamil Khan Mumtaz's "The Islamic Debate: Architecture in Pakistan," pp. 41–44; and discussion of contemporary regional architecture in Sri Lanka and Malaysia, pp. 45–67 and 68–71.

216. Special Issue. "What is Happening to Modern Architecture?" *The Museum of Modern Art Bulletin* 15 (January 1948): 1–21.

On February 11, 1948, twenty architects and architectural critics gathered at the Museum of Modern Art to debate Lewis Mumford's criticisms of the mechanistic rigor of the International Style and his call for a more regionally responsive architecture (item 199). The published comments of Alfred H. Barr, Henry Russell-Hitchcock, Walter Gropius, Christopher Tunnard, Marcel Breuer, Peter Blake, Talbot Hamlin, Lewis Mumford, and others provide valuable insights to the relationship between architectural regionalism and internationalism. Some proponents of the International Style, including Gropius and Breuer, argued that modernism rightly practiced is compatible with regionalism; Mumford asserted, in part, that "Any local effort, if worth anything, is worth reproducing elsewhere; and any universal formula that is worth anything must always be susceptible of being brought back home—otherwise it lacks true universality."

217. Stein, Clarence S. *Toward New Towns for America*. Cambridge: MIT Press, 1966.

This valuable book documents many of the practical achievements of the Regional Planning Association of America, with chapters devoted to such successful regional communities as Sunnyside Gardens in New York City (1924), Radburn, New Jersey (1928–33), Greenbelt, Maryland (1935–37); and Baldwin Hills Village in Los Angeles (1941). Detailed plans for each project are included. Stein's theoretical discussions in the opening and closing chapters, as well as Lewis

Mumford's introduction, stress the relevance of Ebenezer Howard's Garden City concept and the continued need for regional planning.

218. Stephens, Suzanne. "Regionalism and the Vernacular Tradition." In *Progressive Architecture* (item 211), 75–77.

Stephens quickly traces the dialectic between universal and particular, international and regional approaches in American architecture since 1900. The relationship between the current cult of nostalgia and regional flourishes on domestic, commercial, and even franchise architecture is perceptively analyzed.

219. Sussman, Carl, ed. *Planning the Fourth Migration: The Neglected Vision of the Regional Planning Association of America.* Cambridge: MIT Press, 1976.

Sussman's anthology is the best single documentary source regarding the increasingly influential thought and work of the Regional Planning Association of America (1923–33). In addition to Sussman's detailed introduction, the book contains most of the 1925 regional planning issue of *Survey Graphic*, with important essays by Lewis Mumford, Clarence Stein, Stuart Chase, Benton MacKaye, and others; excerpts from Henry Wright's 1926 report on regional planning for the state of New York; statements by Mumford and Chase from the 1931 Virginia Round Table on Regionalism; and excerpts from the 1932 regional planning debate between Mumford and Thomas Adams.

220. Tunnard, Christopher and Henry Hope Reed. *American Skyline: The Growth and Form of Our Cities and Towns.* New York: New American Library, 1956.

This standard history of American urban patterns and plans ends with an appeal for the planned growth of regional cities to replace urban sprawls. "Just as Royce thought the province could save the individual in the early 1900s," the authors argue, "so today the Regional City can encourage individual development and social cooperation—if it is once recognized as the new unit of social and national life."

221. Venturi, Robert, Denise Scott Brown, and Stephen Izenour. *Learning from Las Vegas: The Forgotten Symbolism of Architectural Form.* rev. ed. Cambridge: MIT Press, 1977.

This important book challenged many of the tenets of modern architecture and encouraged the use of a variety of neo-vernacular architectural forms. The authors find the sources of much needed populist idiom in the commercial vernacular architectural forms of Las

Vegas and Levittown. "To find our symbolism," they write, "we must go to the suburban edges of the existing city that are symbolically rather than formalistically attractive and represent the aspirations of almost all Americans.... Then the archetypal Los Angeles will be our Rome and Las Vegas our Florence, and, like the archetypal grain elevator some generations ago, the Flamingo sign will be the model to shock our sensibilities towards a new architecture."

222. Von Eckert, Wolf. *A Place to Live: The Crisis of the Cities.* New York: Delacorte Press, 1967.

In this prescient critique, Von Eckert argues that modern architecture "has failed to respond to the needs of our time or the varied requirements of its surroundings. It is shouting in isolation. Lacking a sense of time and space, it fails to give our environment a sense of place." Part One, "A Sense of Place," pp. 3–62, documents how architects, often proponents of the International Style, destroy rather than create a sense of place. Part Six, "The New Community," pp. 347–87, describes how a sense of time, place, and community might be restored through flexible regional planning, urban restoration, and community development.

223. Walker, Lester. *American Shelter: An Illustrated Encyclopedia of the American Home.* Woodstock, N.Y.: Overlook Press, 1981.

This engagingly illustrated and effectively organized book is a valuable resource for understanding the wide spectrum of regional domestic architecture in the United States. Walker's brief introduction describes the geographical distribution of Native American housing styles as well as the diffusion of European housing types from various coastal regional hearths. The text contains hundreds of crisp, detailed drawings and careful descriptions of ninety-eight American housing styles, ranging from the southwestern pueblo to the Delaware Valley log cabin, from the New England farmhouse to the midwestern prairie house, from the California ranch house to nationwide Post Modern dwellings. The distribution of each housing style in time and space is carefully delineated.

224. Weimer, David R., ed. *City and Country in America.* New York: Appleton-Century-Crofts, 1962.

This anthology contains a spectrum of important regional statements by American architects and planners from Andrew Jackson Downing to Victor Gruen. Significant regional documents include excerpts from L'Enfant's plan for Washington (1791) and Burnham's and Bennett's *Plan of Chicago* (1909), as well as glimpses of the utopian regional visions of Ebenezer Howard, Peter Kropotkin, Patrick Geddes, Paul and Percival Goodman, Camillo Sitte, Le Corbusier, Ralph Borsodi, Frank Lloyd Wright, and Baker Brownell. Much emphasis is given to the Regional Planning Association of America and the regional perspectives of the work of Benton MacKaye, Clarence Perry, Clarence Stein, and Lewis Mumford.

225. Whyte, William H. *The Last Landscape.* Garden City, N.Y.: Doubleday, 1968.

This wide-ranging book abounds with perceptive advice for regional planning and landscape design. Separate chapters are devoted to the strengths and weaknesses of greenbelts, various forms of cluster developments, and new towns. In "The Design of Nature," pp. 182–95, Whyte echoes MacKaye and McHarg by arguing that "Instead of laying down an arbitrary design for a region," designers ought to "find the plan that nature has already laid down." In the final section, "Design and Density," pp. 331–54, Whyte argues that carefully planned higher density cluster settlements are needed to maintain the regional landscape. For related sources, see Whyte's classic suburban study, *The Organization Man* (New York: Simon and Schuster, 1965) as well as his *The Social Life of Small Urban Spaces* (Washington, D.C.: The Conservation Foundation, 1980).

226. Wilson, Colin St. John. "The Historical Sense: T.S. Eliot's Concept of Tradition and its Relevance to Architecture." In Special Issue. "Regional Identity." *Architectural Review* (item 213), 68–70.

Wilson stresses the need for historical and regional continuity in architecture at the same time recognizing the many misuses of historicism by citing Herbert Read's comment that "In the back of every Dictator there is a bloody Doric Column." Wilson suggests that Eliot's "paradoxical interpretation of tradition as the springboard for innovation" might point toward a constructive, life-affirming use of history in architecture that fuses the old and the new in order to face the future.

227. Wilson, Richard Guy. "Learning from the American Vernacular." In *Architectural Review* (item 214), 77–84.

Wilson carefully traces the earliest uses of the term "vernacular" among American architects to the 1870s when it implied a rejection of academic styles and return to indigenous folk sources. He then describes how vernacular forms were utilized between 1870 and 1930 in the wooden domestic architecture of George Woodward, Henry Hudson Holly, H.H. Richardson, Charles McKim, Frank Lloyd Wright, Walter Burley Griffin, William Gray Purcell, George Grant Elmslie, and John Lloyd Wright. The relationship between this self-conscious use of the "vernacular" and a larger "regionalist response" is discussed.

228. Wright, Frank Lloyd. *An American Architecture: Frank Lloyd Wright*. Edited by Edgar Kaufmann. New York: Horizon Press, 1955.

Frank Lloyd Wright's many published works abound with appeals for greater sense of place and regionalism in architecture, and this lavishly illustrated anthology includes vivid samples of Wright's regional work and writing. The section, "Out of the Ground and Into the Light," pp. 186–202, is especially valuable, containing photographs and Wright's insightful discussions of "Earth," "Wisconsin," "Prairie," "Desert," and "Site."

229. ————. *Frank Lloyd Wright: Selected Writings and Buildings*. Edited by Edgar Kaufmann and Ben Raeburn. Cleveland, Ohio: World Publishing, 1960.

This useful anthology and handbook contains several of Wright's most important regional statements including a discussion of "Prairie Architecture" (1931), pp. 38–55; "The Art and Craft of the Machine" (1901), pp. 55–73; and "The Sovereignty of the Individual" (1910), pp. 84–106. In these essays, Wright discusses the regional roots of his work and the positive influences of the arts and crafts movement and of indigenous folk forms upon architecture.

230. ————. *The Living City*. New York: New American Library, 1958.

This book along with *When Democracy Builds*, rev. ed. (Chicago: Univ. of Chicago Press, 1945), contains Wright's most thorough discussion of the need for decentralization and regional planning through the construction of Broadacre Cities. Wright's original utopian proposal is found in "Broadacre City: A New Community Plan, *Architectural Record* 77 (April 1935), pp. 243–54, and Robert Twombly's "Undoing the City: Frank Lloyd Wright's Planned Communities," *American Quarterly* 24 (October 1972), pp. 538–49, is an insightful analysis of Wright's community and regional planning.

Art

Regionalism has been an important force in American creative expression. Many of our greatest achievements in architecture, literature, and painting have been imbued with a sense of place and region. Chapters four and eleven document this theme in architecture and literature; this chapter underscores the power of regionalism in American painting.

A large number of American painters have been deeply influenced by a regional sense of place. A sense of New England lies at the heart of the work of Winslow Homer, Marsden Hartley, John Marin, and many others. The Midwest imbues the paintings of Charles Burchfield or Ivan Albright just as the Southwest is inseparable from the work of Georgia O'Keefe or Peter Hurd. The works of Morris Graves and Mark Tobey would lose much of their meaning apart from the Northwest as would the paintings of Richard Diebenkorn, Edward Ruscha, and David Hockney apart from Southern California. The list could continue indefinitely, but the point is clear: an immediate, often unconscious, sense of place often informs the greatest art, and the vast space and sprawling diversity of the American scene strongly encourage regional rather than national creative focus.

From the Hudson River School to the present, regionalism has been a persistent force in American painting, but discussions of regional aesthetics reached a peak during the 1920s and 1930s—an unparalleled era of self-conscious Regionalist art. The debate over the strengths and weaknesses of Regionalist art—especially the work of Thomas Hart Benton, Grant Wood, and John Steuart Curry—has generated a large body of literature, much of it relevant for contemporary regional studies. With this in mind, the following list contains at least four groups of sources that are important to understanding regionalism in American painting.

As in the chapter on Architecture and Planning, a fairly small group of art critics and historians—including Matthew Baigel, Peyton Boswell, Alexander Eliot, Alan Gussow, Nancy Heller and Julia Williams, Oliver Larkin, and E.P. Richardson—provide general surveys of regionalism in American art. A second group of scholars—including Martin Heidegger, Arnold Hauser, Gyorgy Kepes, Paul Shepard, Barbara Novak, Harold Rosenberg, Alan Gussow, and Ronald Rees—develop general theories of the relationship between art and nature, between sense of place, region, and artistic expression.

A third group of sources has been selected from the vast literature devoted to the Regionalist and American Scene art of the 1920s and 1930s. (The immensity of this area is underscored by the fact that an entire book by Mary Guedon is devoted to listing the scholarship surrounding the regionalist work of Thomas Hart Benton, Grant Wood, and John Steuart Curry.) The vigorous regional manifestoes of Benton, Wood, Thomas Craven, and Holger Cahill are included in this chapter along with related materials on the American Scene and cultural nationalism by Constance Rourke, Waldo Frank, and others. Benton's running controversies with Alfred Stieglitz, Stuart Davis, and W.H. Janson are documented, as is part of the extensive secondary literature on the Regionalist and American Scene movements. A number of contemporary scholars—including Charles Alexander, Matthew Baigel, Wanda Corn, John Denis, Karal Ann Marling, M. Sue Kendall, Joseph Czestochowski, Hilton Kramer, and William Jordy—have reevaluated these earlier regional enthusiasms, and their valuable work is included in this chapter.

A final group of sources reflects a recent revival of self-conscious regionalism among artists and critics. The regional revival in painting parallels a regional renewal in architecture documented in chapter four. Just as dissatisfaction with the placeless universalism of the International Style has sparked interest in regional and vernacular architectural forms, so discontent with the free floating cosmopolitanism of abstract expressionism and the domination of New York has encouraged the rise of a more pluralistic, representational, and place-specific art in the hinterlands. This contemporary movement, including a related movement of environmental or "earth" art, is analyzed by Bill Berkson, Dan Cameron, Charlotte Moser, Lee Fleming, Donald Kupsit, Peter Plagens, Robert Smithson, and others.

In addition to these four general areas of interest, this chapter also includes biographies of Benton, Wood, Curry, Charles Burchfield, Edward Hopper, Charles Sheeler, Andrew Wyeth, Peter Hurd, and Georgia O'Keefe—all of which analyze questions of regionalism in art. Decorative arts and furnishings are touched upon by Charles Montgomery and Constance Rourke, and the vast field of regionalism in photography and music is discussed by Charles Alexander and William Jordy.

M.S.

231. Abrahams, Edward. "Alfred Stieglitz and/or Thomas Hart Benton." *Arts Magazine* 55 (June 1981): 108–13.

Abrahams analyzes Benton's 1935 essay, "America and/or Alfred Stieglitz," as symbolizing a final parting of ways between two approaches to American cultural nationalism. Both men saw themselves as apostles of "an authentically American art, created by Americans for Americans," but Stieglitz's relatively abstract and rarefied aesthetics were ultimately at odds with Benton's straightforward populist regionalism.

232. Alexander, Charles C. *Here the Country Lies: Nationalism and the Arts in the Twentieth Century.* Bloomington: Indiana Univ. Press, 1980.

This is a wide-ranging, insightful survey of the rise and decline of "genuinely native, nationally representative" art in the United States between 1900 and 1950. Cultural nationalism motivated a wide variety of painters, photographers, architects, novelists, poets, playwrights, dancers, composers, directors, and intellectuals during these years, and Alexander skillfully relates this impulse to the regional concerns of the period. "This Hot Chaos of America," pp. 109–51, contains an especially insightful discussion of the regional thrust of American Scene painters Burchfield, Hopper, Benton, Curry, and Wood, architects Frank Lloyd Wright and Louis Sullivan, and composers Aaron Copeland, Roy Harris, Virgil Thomson, and others. Alexander's earlier study, *Nationalism in American Thought, 1930–45* (Chicago: Rand-McNally, 1969), gives greater attention to the relationship between regional and national ideologies during the Depression Era, and his discussion of "Toward a National Culture: Visual Arts and Music," pp. 60–84, is perceptive.

233. Alloway, Lawrence. "The Recovery of Regionalism: John Steuart Curry." In Special Issue. "Art Across America." *Art in America* (item 305), 70–73.

Alloway argues that in order to reach a deeper understanding of the regionalist paintings of the 1920s and 1930s, critics must be aware of how leading regionalists such as Curry and Wood used European conventions to enhance their seemingly homespun art.

234. Baigel, Matthew. "American Art and National Identity: The 1920s." *Arts Magazine* 61 (February 1987): 48–55.

Baigel carefully describes how the American Scene and Regionalist painting emerged in the wake of World War I and dominated American art until the emergence of Abstract Expressionism after World War II. The relationship between cultural nationalism and regionalism is analyzed as well as the attitudes of Sheeler, Burchfield, Demuth, Hopper, and others toward these aesthetic currents.

235. ———— *The American Scene: American Painting of the 1930s.* New York: Praeger, 1974.

Baigel's discussion of 1930s regionalism, pp. 43–45 and 55–61, places the aesthetic concerns of Benton, Curry, Wood, Hopper, Burchfield, and others into a larger cultural and historical context. Baigell's lavishly illustrated, book-length studies of Benton and Burchfield are also valuable sources. See his *Thomas Hart Benton* (New York: Harry N. Abrams, 1974), especially pp. 83–165, and *Charles Burchfield* (New York: Watson-Guptill, 1976), especially pp. 122–35.

236. ————. "The Beginnings of 'The American Wave' and the Depression." *Art Journal* 27 (1968)A: 387–96, 398.

This is an insightful account of how the "American Wave" or "American Scene" movement gathered force during the 1920s, partially influenced by reactionary nativism and the promotional efforts of Thomas Craven, partially inspired by more progressive concerns. Baigel then demonstrates that by the mid-1930s, this movement split into two, often antagonistic schools: regionalism and social realism.

237. ————. *A Concise History of American Painting and Sculpture.* New York: Harper and Row, 1984.

"Between the World Wars," pp. 242–96, contains a richly detailed survey of the many varieties of social realist, American Scene, and regionalist art of the 1920s and 1930s and stands as an effective summation of Baigell's scholarship in this area since the 1960s.

238. ———— "Grant Wood Revisited." *Art Journal* 26 (Winter 1966–1967): 116–22.

This useful essay emphasizes the sardonic, satirical dimension of Wood's art and its relationship to the often harsh midwestern literary realism of Hamlin Garland, Herbert Quick, Ruth Suckow, and Sherwood Anderson.

239. Barker, Virgil. "Americanism in Painting." *Yale Review* 25 (1936): 778–93.

Barker examines the relationship between colonialism, nationalism, and regionalism in American painting from the eighteenth to the twentieth century. The rediscovery of the American scene in the regionalist works of Curry, Wood, O'Keefe, Marin, Hopper, Burchfield, Sheeler, and others is depicted as "the heart of a new realism by which America can be saved in painting as in its other activities; wherever it stirs, there is in process the creation of a spiritually durable country."

240. Benton, Thomas Hart. *A Thomas Hart Benton Miscellany: Selections From His Published Opinions, 1916-1960.* Edited by Matthew Baigel. Lawrence: Univ. Press of Kansas, 1971.

Benton was the most vocal and colorful of the American regionalist painters, and this highly useful anthology contains some of his most striking regional utterances from the 1920s until the 1960s. His essays, "My American Epic in Paint" (1928), pp. 16–21; "Art and Nationalism" (1934) (item 244); "America and/or Alfred Stieglitz" (1935) (item 241); "Benton Protests" (1943), pp. 84–86; "Art vs. The Mellon Gallery" (1941), pp. 172–73; and a series of flamboyant interviews, pp. 58–65 and 74–79, underscore the sources and controversial nature of his regionalist aesthetic.

241. ———. "America and/or Alfred Stieglitz." *Common Sense* 4 (January 1935): 22–25. Reprinted in *A Thomas Hart Benton Miscellany* (item 240), 66–74.

In this scathing review of *America and Alfred Stieglitz* (1934), Benton describes Stieglitz and his circle of "blind devotees," including Waldo Frank and Lewis Mumford, as recondite mystics out of touch with the realities of American life. Stieglitz's strain of art, Benton argues, is dead, and now "the flow of American art has run toward a socially and environmentally conditioned expression."

242. ———. "American Regionalism: A Personal History of the Movement." *University of Kansas City Review* 13 (1951): 41–75. Reprinted in *An American in Art: A Professional and Technical Autobiography*, 147–92. Lawrence: Univ. Press of Kansas, 1969.

Written in Benton's sturdy, outspoken, vernacular manner, this backward glance at the regional enthusiasms of the 1920s and 1930s is a crucial historical document and central aesthetic statement comparable in significance to Wood's "Revolt Against the City" (1935).

243. ———. *An Artist in America.* 4th rev. ed. Columbia: Univ. of Missouri Press, 1983.

First published in 1937 and updated several times during Benton's long and productive career, this vivid autobiography narrates the more personal, intimate side of his life, while the companion volume, *An American in Art* (1969), traces the more technical aspects of his artistic development. From Benton's powerful account of growing up in southwest Missouri in the 1890s to his dynamic descriptions of the land and folk of the Southern Mountains, the Mississippi and Missouri Rivers, the South, and the West, *An Artist in America* is an invaluable panorama of America's folk-regional cultures in the twentieth century. The final three chapters, "Back to Missouri," pp. 247–76; "After," pp. 277–324; and "And Still After," pp. 325–69, provide vital insights to the regionalist controversies of the 1930s and 1940s, including Benton's bitter disillusionment with the New York art establishment and with urbanism in general, criticisms of abstract expressionism, thoughts about the fate and resiliency of regionalist art, and comments regarding his student, Jackson Pollack, who, had he remained a regionalist, "would have injected a more mystic strain into the generally prosaic characteristics of regionalism." Matthew Baigel's "Foreword" and "Afterword" to this edition contain useful comments on Benton's regionalist art. A thorough bibliography of writing by and about Benton is included, pp. 390–95.

244. ———. "Art and Nationalism." *The Modern Monthly* 8 (May 1934): 232–36. Reprinted in *A Thomas Hart Benton Miscellany* (item 240), 49–58.

Originally a lecture that raised a furor of protest when given to the New York section of the John Reed Club, this article urges radical artists to set aside abstract doctrines and submit their work to the realities of local experience. Warning against abstract, often bellicose, forms of nationalism based upon "fictions of the national will," Benton promotes a form of nationalism that slowly develops out of the immediate experience of regional folk culture.

245. Berkson, Bill. "Reports from Seattle." Parts 1 ("Seattle Sites"), 2 ("In the Studios"). *Art in America* 74 (July, September 1986): 68–82, 133–35; 28–45.

This two-part series carefully analyzes the regional art of the Seattle area from the "Pacific Northwest School" of Mark Tobey, Morris Graves, Kenneth Callahan, and Guy Anderson with its roots in the 1930s to the less explicitly regional work of Galen Hansen, Norie Sato, Jeffrey Bishop, and others in the 1980s. The first article focuses upon the plethora of regionally flavored public arts programs and earthworks in the Seattle area; the second article concentrates upon regional painting, sculpture, and photography. Berkson concludes in part that "What Tom Robbins called in 1968 'a curious spectrum of provincialism and hip' has been transmuted to ... 'regional pluralism'—i.e., the same plethora of styles as elsewhere but with markedly regional twists and limitations."

246. Bonesteel, Michael. "The 39th Corcoran Biennial: The Death Knell of Regionalism?" *Art in America* 73 (October 1985): 31–37.

Reviewing the Corcoran Gallery's exhibit of contemporary painters from the Midwest, Bonesteel disagrees with other critics who see "nothing specifically Midwestern" in their art and who argue that "regionalism is no longer a significant factor" in today's art world. Highly critical of this "bandwagon cosmopolitan view"—this "postmodern continuation of modernism's old antiregionalist position" that art is the same everywhere—Bonesteel argues that subtle regional influences are inevitable in all art. Specifically, he locates distinctive traits of contemporary midwestern art—its debts to central European expressionism and concern with narration and subjective imagery—and describes how these and other midwestern overtones appear in the paintings of Ivan Albright, Roger Brown, Jim Nutt, Ed Paschke, Nicholas Africano, Hollis Sigler, and others.

247. Boswell, Peyton, Jr. *Modern American Painting.* New York: Dodd and Mead, 1940.

"The American Scene," pp. 58–62, heralds the rise of art "based solidly on nationalism and its subdivision, regionalism" as "the most healthy development in the entire three hundred years of American art history." Major and lesser known regionalist painters analyzed in this lavishly illustrated book include Ogden Pleissner, Joe Jones, Millard Sheets, Phil Dyke, and Peter Hurd.

248. Cahill, Holger. *New Horizons in American Art.* New York: Museum of Modern Art, 1936.

In this catalog of work produced during the first year of the Federal Artists' Project, Cahill praises the regional content and style encouraged by the Project and argues that it will change the direction of American art in general.

249. Cameron, Dan. "Springtime on the Fringe." *Art Magazine* 60 (September 1985): 64–67.

In this review of contemporary regional art from the South and microscopic "neighborhood art" from New York's Lower East Side, Cameron raises important questions concerning the relationship between art and the physical environment. Recognizing that geography has an indelible yet elusive impact upon all art, Cameron argues that it is "counter-productive to act as if the qualities which typify a regional response to contemporary issues are somehow too oblique or too mercurial to deserve scrutiny" and urges more thoughtful critical consideration of this issue.

250. Corn, Wanda M. *The Art of Andrew Wyeth*. Boston: New York Graphic Society, 1973.

Corn's essay, "The Art of Andrew Wyeth," pp. 92–165, perceptively analyzes Wyeth's ties to regionalism, both as an art form and as an ideological perspective. Describing regionalism's Whitmanesque "preoccupation with the ordinary and commonplace in quest of wider truths," Corn describes how "Burchfield, Hopper, and later, Wyeth, took the ordinary houses of rural America as seriously as Henry Adams had taken Chartres Cathedral, creating haunting and poignant symbols of man's loneliness."

251. ———. *Grant Wood: the Regionalist Vision*. New Haven: Yale University Press, 1983.

This book accompanied the important Grant Wood retrospective of 1983, and Corn's narrative examines the midwestern and European roots of Wood's art as well as the final meaning of his "regionalist vision." "Hometown Artist, 1901–1930," pp. 5–33, contains a vivid portrait of Wood's regional background: his life in Cedar Rapids and brief stint in Europe, the influence of the Arts and Crafts Movement, and the impact of Iowa writers such as Ruth Suckow, Jay Sigmund, and Frank Luther Mott upon his painting. "The Regionalist, 1930–42," pp. 35–62, depicts the culmination of Wood's art, his relationship with Benton and Curry, his work at the Stone City art colony and the University of Iowa. Underscoring the tension between nostalgia and satire in Wood's art, Corn argues that he was "the *compleat* regionalist, the one who defined and promoted the movement in every aspect of his life."

252. Craven, Thomas. *Modern Art: The Men, the Movements, and the Meaning*. New York: Simon and Schuster, 1940.

This book represents the peak of Craven's tireless, often strident, advocacy of American Scene and Regionalist art during the 1920s and 1930s. "The New Gospel," "Preaching America," and "Benton," pp.

311–59, contain his most sweeping endorsement of the "American spirit" of nationalism and regionalism in painting.

253. Czestochowski, Joseph S., ed. *John Steuart Curry and Grant Wood: A Portrait of Rural America*. Columbia: University of Missouri Press, 1981.

This richly illustrated anthology contains a number of central regionalist manifestos from the 1930s as well as several retrospective studies of the movement. Curry's "What Should the American Artist Paint?" (1935), Wood's "Revolt Against the City" (1935), and Benton's "Afterword: On Regionalism" (1951) are reprinted. Czestochowski's "Introduction," pp. 9–15, evaluates the social and cultural function of rural regional art during the 1930s. Also includes M. Sue Kendall's "Curry's Kansas Pastoral: the Modern American Family on the Middle Border" (item 276).

254. Davis, Stuart. "The New York American Scene in Art." *Art Front* 1 (February 1935): 6. Reprinted in *Stuart Davis*, edited by Diane Kelder, 151–54. New York: Praeger, 1971.

In this particularly vitriolic criticism of regionalist art, Davis accuses Benton and others of producing a "third rate vaudeville cliche with the humor omitted," and of painting "gross caricatures of Negroes" and farmers. "The slight burp which this school of the U.S. scene in art has made," Davis concludes, "may not indicate the stomach ulcer of Fascism. I am not a political doctor, but I have heard the burp and as a fellow artist I would advise those concerned to submit themselves to a qualified diagnostician ...." Benton responded to these charges in the next issue of *Art Front* 1 (April 1935), p. 2, and Davis continued his critique in "Davis's Rejoinder," *Art Digest* 9 (April 1, 1935), pp. 12–12, 26–27.

255. Denis, James M. *Grant Wood: A Study in American Art and Culture*. New York: Viking Press, 1975.

This outstanding, in-depth study of Wood's art and life contains detailed analyses of paintings that have become regional icons in such sections as "*American Gothic* and the Late Gothic," pp. 67–86, and "*Stone City* and the Fantasy Farmscape," pp. 87–105. Perceptive discussions of the relationship between regionalist art and American regionalism in general are found in "The Regionalist Revolt Against the City" and "The Painters and the Agrarian Myth," pp. 141–228. Wood's manifesto, "The Revolt Against the City" (1935), is reprinted, pp. 229–35.

256. Doss, Erika L. "Borrowing Regionalism: Advertising's Use of American Art in the 1930s and 40s." *Journal of American Culture* 5 (Winter 1982): 10–19.

Doss describes how such powerful culture brokers as the Time-Life Corporation, Walt Disney Studios, and Twentieth Century Fox utilized the mass appeal of regionalist motifs. By the late 1930s, it was clear that "profits were to be made by showing the safe, homebound dreamland of the Regionalists." Benton's role, both as advocate and critic of such commercialization, is discussed.

257. Eliot, Alexander. "From the Heartland." In *Three Hundred Years of American Painting*, 212–19. New York: Time, Inc., 1957.

This chapter is a succinct introduction to Benton, Curry, and Wood, the most self-conscious of American regionalists. Eliot's discussions in other chapters of artists' environments—of O'Keefe's New Mexico, Hartley's and Marin's Maine, Marsh's New York City, Burchfield's Ohio—provide further regional insights.

258. Fleming, Lee V. "Art." *American Quarterly* 35 (Spring/ Summer 1983): 130–40.

An important feature of Fleming's argument is that in the 1980s "Land has regained its role as a source of inspiration, with the earthworks and earth-tied art of Robert Smithson, Walter DeMaria, Robert Morris, Dennis Openheim, and others." "The artist hero of the fifties," he writes, "was divorced from this vision of the land.... Now, it seems that separate experiments in the 'true' territory of an artist conjoin as he finds himself restored to, and restoring, the abandoned landscape."

259. Frank, Waldo et al. *America and Alfred Stieglitz: A Collective Portrait*. New York: Literary Guild, 1934.

A tribute to Stieglitz's lifelong efforts to promote and create art "in American terms and on American soil," this book stands as a classic expression of cultural nationalism. It also documents the regional orientation that often accompanied the search for a truly American art. Of the twenty-three contributors—including William Carlos Williams, Lewis Mumford, Paul Rosenfield, Dorothy Newman, Waldo Frank, John Marin, Marsden Hartley, Charles Demuth, Gertrude Stein, Jean Toomer, and Sherwood Anderson—Williams, Mumford, and Anderson discuss most clearly the indigenous, local-regional roots of cultural nationalism. See Williams's, "The American Background," pp. 9–32,

Mumford's "The Metropolitan Milieu," pp. 33–58, and Anderson's "City Plowman," pp. 303–8.

260. Gabrielson, Walter. "Why Suck the Mainstream If You Don't Live in New York?" *Art in America* 62 (January-February 1974): 37–38.

In the spirit of Benton and Wood, this is a vigorous appeal for a more pluralistic and decentralized art in America. "In this land of immense beauty and diversity," Garbrielson asks, "why should art have all the excitement of coal production figures in *Pravda* or the art page of the good, grey New York *Times?*" Important signs of regional artistic vitality, he argues, are emerging in Los Angeles, Chicago, Texas, and the Southwest.

261. Gibson, Arrell Morgan. *The Sante Fe and Taos Colonies: Age of the Muses, 1900–1942.* Norman: Univ. of Oklahoma Press, 1983.

Between 1900 and 1942, northern New Mexico flourished as a vital center of American art, and Gibson documents the historical, geographical, and cultural factors behind this regional aesthetic renaissance. Painters John Sloan, Robert Henri, Marden Hartely, Andrew Dasburg, Frank Applegate, and Ernest Blumenschien, and writers Mary Austin, Mabel Dodge Luhan, D.H. Lawrence, Oliver LaFarge, Lynn Riggs, and Willa Cather are some of the Sante Fe and Taos artists Gibson discusses. His analysis of the creative impact of the landscape and of Spanish and Native American cultures is especially useful.

262. Goodman, Calvin J. "A Return to Regional Art: 'Acres of Diamonds' Revisited." *American Artist* 46 (June 1982): 68–71.

Using Thomas Hart Benton, Georgia O'Keefe, and Harry Jackson as models, Goodman urges aspiring artists to consider the land around them as a starting point and worthy subject matter of their work.

263. ———. "In Defense of Grant Wood and American Regionalism." *American Artist* 48 (May 1984): 72–75, 106–7.

Goodman analyzes the mixed reactions of art critics to the 1983 Grant Wood retrospective. Focusing upon Hilton Kramer's particularly vitriolic review (item 280), Goodman refutes most of his objections and suggests that "Kramer and his city friends" are blinded by provincial elitism and "ideological narrowness."

264. Goodrich, Lloyd. "What Is American in American Art?" In *What Is American in American Art?*, edited by Jean Lipman, 8–27. New York: McGraw-Hill, 1963.

Goodrich traces indigenous themes from colonial portraiture to abstract expressionism and argues that the American Scene and social realist paintings of the interwar decades "achieved the most far-reaching visual exploration and evaluation of our civilization to date, and made an enormous contribution to our national self-knowledge." Goodrich sees the continuation of regionalist themes in Ben Shahn, Philip Evergood, and Jack Levine, and he foresees a revival of regional art. Goodrich has also written full-length studies of regionally-oriented artists, including, with Doris Bry, *Georgia O'Keefe* (New York: Praeger, 1970) and *Edward Hopper* (New York: Abrams, 1971).

265. Guedon, Mary Scholz. *Regionalist Art: Thomas Hart Benton, John Steuart Curry, and Grant Wood: A Guide to the Literature.* Metuchen, N.J.: Scarecrow Press, 1982.

An essential resource for students of American regional art, this carefully constructed guide contains a perceptive foreword by Karal Ann Marling, useful introductory essays by Guedon, and 556 meticulously annotated entries. The opening chapter on "Regionalism," pp. 3–36, is an effective general introduction to regionalism in the arts; the subsequent chapters, devoted to each of the three artists, are thorough.

266. Gussow, Alan. *A Sense of Place: The Artist and the American Land.* San Francisco: Friends of the Earth, 1971.

Gussow's book contains a vivid collection of American landscape paintings and artistic commentary, ranging from John White in Virginia in 1585 to Richard Diebenkorn in California in the 1970s. Representative paintings and words of sixty landscape artists are included, and the large format color plates and skillfully edited, often eloquent, commentary underscores the pervasive significance of sense of place and regionalism in American art. In addition to White and Diebenkorn, the artists include Thomas Cole, Asher B. Durand, John James Audubon, George Catlin, Albert Bierstadt, Alfred Jacob Miller, George Inness, and others in the nineteenth century; and Thomas Hart Benton, Charles Burchfield, Edward Hopper, Charles Sheeler, Marsden Hartley, John Marin, Georgia O'Keefe, Sidney Goodman, Reuben Tam, and others in the twentieth century. Also useful are Richard Wilbur's "Introduction" (item 1320) and Gussow's "Sense of Place," pp. 27–33, which surveys the American landscape tradition and discusses its present significance as "acts of salvage in a desperate time."

267. Hauser, Arnold. *The Sociology of Art.* Translated by Kenneth J. Northcott. Chicago: Univ. of Chicago Press, 1982.

This influential study analyzes regionalism in art from several perspectives. First, Hauser's discussion of "Natural Factors," pp. 97–118, explores the relationship between cultural expression and the natural environment. His insightful analysis of the influence of particular geographical circumstances—e.g., isolation from or proximity to other areas, the presence of oceans, mountains, rivers, and open land, the impact of various climates—upon creative expression, and his discussion of "a firm map of culture areas and their spheres of influence" are important contributions to the study of regionalism and art. Second, Hauser's analysis of "Folk-Art," pp. 562–79, explores the relationship between folk-regional, provincial, urban, and national art forms. For further analysis of folk art, provincial art, and regionalism, see Hauser's "Folk Art and Popular Art," in *The Philosophy of Art History* (New York: Knopf, 1958), pp. 279–365.

268. Heidegger, Martin. "Art and Space." Translated by Charles H. Seibert. *Man and World* 6 (1969): 3–8.

Beginning with a discussion of the interplay between art and space in sculpture, Heidegger compares the shaping of space in art with the creation of "regions"—with the "settling" of and "dwelling" in places in everyday life. In cryptic, evocative language, Heidegger stresses that in its largest sense, "Sculpture would be the embodiment of places. Places, in preserving and opening a region, hold something free gathered around them which grants the tarrying of things under consideration and a dwelling for man in the midst of things." Other sources by Heidegger are listed under Philosophy and Religion (items 1358–1359).

269. Heller, Nancy and Julia Williams. "Portrait of America: The American Land and its People as Celebrated by Eight American Painters." *American Artist* 40 (January 1976): 34–81, 107.

In this special issue, Heller and Williams discuss the regional visions of eight major artists. Their essays include "Winslow Homer: The Great American Coast," pp. 34–39; "John Sloan: Life in the American City," pp. 40–45; John Steuart Curry: The American Farmlands," pp. 46–51; Albert Bierstadt: The American Wilderness," pp. 52–57; "Charles Sheeler: American Industry as Landscape," pp. 58–63; "Eastman Johnson: A Nostalgic View of the Old South," pp. 64–69; "Edward Hopper: Alone in America," pp. 70–75; and "Georgia O'Keefe: The American Southwest," pp. 76–81 and 107.

270. ———. *The Regionalists.* New York: Watson-Guptil, 1976.

This book is a thoughtful, well-illustrated introduction to the panorama of regional painting in the 1920s and 1930s. In addition to discussing the Benton-Curry-Wood triumvirate, Heller and Williams also consider regional dimensions in the work of Charles Burchfield, Aaron Bohrod, Edward Hopper, Reginald Marsh, Peter Hurd, Georgia O'Keefe, and others. The chapters concerning "Concept of Regionalism," pp. 13–33, and "Myth, History, and Social Commentary," pp. 135–73, provide a glimpse of the relationships between aesthetic regionalism and the wider regional impulse of the interwar decades.

271. Horgan, Paul. *Peter Hurd: A Portrait Sketch From Life.* Austin: Univ. of Texas Press for the Amon Carter Museum of Western Art, 1965.

This brief biography of an eminent southwestern painter by an equally eminent southwestern writer touches upon important issues in regional aesthetics. Hurd's cross-regional experiences—his childhood in New Mexico, his years at Chadds Ford studying under N.C. Wyeth, his marriage to Henrietta Wyeth in 1929, and their move back to New Mexico in the late 1930s—says much about conditions for the growth of lasting regional expression. Horgan's discussion of Hurd's "humble love of the land and his lifelong worship of the light upon it" and of the artist's ability to "enter with all his power into the localisms of the Southwest, and to enfold these within the world he paints" contributes to our understanding of regional art. Other sources by Horgan are listed under Literature (items 1219–1220).

272. Huth, Hans. *Nature and the American.* Berkeley: Univ. of California Press, 1957.

Huth's wide-ranging, handsomely illustrated art-historical approach to the subject discusses city parks, vacationers' retreats, botanical gardens, camping, reports from the West, and conservation.

273. Janson, H.W. "Benton and Wood, Champions of Regionalism." *Magazine of Art* 39 (May 1946): 184–86, 198.

This is a penetrating critique of the anti-urban, anti-intellectual, narrowly chauvinistic elements of Benton's and Wood's art. In Janson's opinion, their regional work has ominous similarities to the aesthetics championed by European fascism.

274. ———. "The International Aspects of Regionalism." *College Art Journal* 2 (May 1943): 110–14.

In this succinct summary of the debate regarding the merits of regionalist art, Janson suggests that much of that art is less indigenous than its practitioners would have people believe. The American regionalists, he argues, are deeply indebted to German neo-objectivism of the 1920s, and Grant Wood's work, in particular, has been heavily influenced by reactionary artistic developments "accompanying the rise of nationalism in Europe since the 1920s."

275. Jordy, William H. "Four Approaches to Regionalism in the Visual Arts of the 1930s." In *The Study of American Culture: Contemporary Conflicts*, edited by Luther S. Luedtke, 19–61. DeLand, Fla.: Everett/Edwards, 1977.

In this outstanding essay, Jordy surveys a wide variety of regional expressions in American painting, photography, architecture, and public planning during the 1930s and locates four general regional approaches that attracted artists and intellectuals throughout the decade. First, planners and social theorists including David Lilienthal, Lewis Mumford, and Benton MacKaye used regionalism as a technological tool for reform; second, emigre architects like Walter Gropius and Marcel Breuer used regionalism to adapt or acclimatize their work to the American scene; third, conservative Southern Agrarians used regionalism as an alternative to nationalism and a means of rejecting the dominant culture; and a final group of artists, including Benton, Wood, Curry, Frank Lloyd Wright, Walker Evans, and Dorothea Lange used regionalism to deepen their sense of American nationalism.

276. Kendall, M. Sue. "Curry's Kansas Pastoral: the Modern American Family on the Middle Border," in *John Steuart Curry and Grant Wood: A Portrait of Rural America* (item 253), 34–41.

Kendall analyzes a portion of Curry's murals for the Kansas State Capitol, focusing upon rural family life and its relationship to regionalism.

277. ———. *Rethinking Regionalism: John Steuart Curry and the Kansas Mural Controversy.* Washington, D.C.: Smithsonian Institution Press, 1985.

Looking closely at the controversy surrounding Curry's murals for the Kansas Statehouse between 1937 and 1942, Kendall offers a fresh interpretation of Curry's regionalist aesthetic. Curry's finest regional work, Kendall stresses, was done during a twenty year absence from

Kansas and the Midwest, and his much-heralded return to the Midwest in the late 1930s brought to the surface a deep-seated ambivalence toward his native region—an ambivalence that greatly enhanced his work.

278. Kepes, Gyorgy, ed. *Arts of the Environment.* New York: George Braziller, 1972.

The issues introduced in Kepes's 1956 anthology are brought to an even higher pitch in light of the environmental crisis in this volume. Important essays discussing the relationship between art and nature include Kepes's "Art and Ecological Consciousness," pp. 1–12; Rene Dubos's "The Perils of Adaptation," pp. 32–39; Edward T. Hall's "Art, Space, and Human Experience," pp. 52–59; Erik Erikson's "Environment and Virtues," pp. 60–77; Leo Marx's "American Institutions and Ecological Ideals" (item 19); Kevin Lynch's "The Openness of Open Space," pp. 108–24; and Robert Smithson's "The Spiral Jetty," pp. 222–39.

279. ———, ed. *The New Landscape in Art and Science.* Chicago: Paul Theobald and Co., 1956.

Like John Ruskin and William Morris a century earlier, Kepes and his contributors argue that "The technical landscape must be brought into harmony with the rhythms of the seasons, the breadth of the sky, the resources of the land" and describe how artists, architects, and designers can encourage such environmental renewal. Section Three, "The Industrial Landscape," makes a particularly effective appeal for environmentally sensitive art and architecture through photographic essays and perceptive articles on "Inner and Outer landscape" by Richard Neutra, pp. 83–85; "Poetry and the Landscape" by Richard Wilbur (item 1321); and shorter comments by Fernand Leger, Jean Helion, and Sigfried Giedion.

280. Kramer, Hilton. "The Return of the Nativist." *The New Criterion* 2 (October 1983): 58–63.

Reviving earlier criticisms by Stuart Davis, W.H. Janson, and others, Kramer blasts Grant Wood's art in particular and regionalist art in general. Condemning the contemporary revival of regionalism as a dangerous "revenge of the philistines" and depicting regional art as inherently xenophobic, rancorously anti-cosmopolitan, and "parochial and insipid" when compared with the accomplishments of the New York School, Kramer saves his sharpest barbs for Grant Wood. Wood's life and art, he argues, were "abysmally phoney," constituting "a calculated lie from start to finish." Particularly troubling are Wood's "immaculate marzipan landscapes in which no farmer could ever soil his hands and where the only disaster likely to occur is a stomach ache from too many sweets."

281. Kupsit, Donald B. "Regionalism Reconsidered." In Special Issue. "Art Across America." *Art in America* (item 305), 64–67.

This stimulating essay locates a persistent "provincial spirit" in American art that has roots in the overtly regional work of the 1920s and 1930s and is now flourishing in American expressionism, both abstract and representational. At the heart of this important essay is Kupsit's claim that "Abstract expressionism, not American Scene art, made the crucial transition from a regionalism of physical locale to one of psychic and spiritual locale." Kupsit's sense of the deep-seated tension between the forces of pluralism and cosmopolitanism in our culture and regionalism's role in that dialectic is especially insightful, and he analyzes regional artists such as Mark Tobey, Morris Graves, Jim Nutt, William Wiley, Edward Kienholz, and Bruce Comer to illustrate his argument.

282. Larkin, Oliver W. *Art and Life in America.* rev. and enl. New York: Holt, Rinehart and Winston, 1960.

Larkin's text traces vernacular influences throughout the history of American art. "American Self-Portrait," pp. 412–29, focuses upon the American Scene and regionalist art of the 1930s and echoes Alfred Kazin's equally evocative analysis of cultural nationalism in *On Native Grounds* (1943) (item 1228). Larkin discusses the impact of the Federal Art Project, the rise of regional painting in New England, the Midwest, the Southwest, and the South (analyzing a host of lesser known regionalists along the way), the work of urban regionalists such as Ernest Fiene, Reginald Marsh, and Edward Hopper, and the photography of Paul Strand, Ansel Adams, Bernice Abbott, and Walker Evans.

283. Levin, Gail. *Edward Hopper: The Art and the Artist.* New York: W.W. Norton, 1980.

Levin's carefully researched introduction, "The Identity of the Artist," pp. 5–64, skillfully links Hopper to the American Scene and Regionalist movements of the interwar decades. The extensive illustrations, footnotes, and bibliography are useful. For a parallel biography with less reference to regionalism, see Lloyd Goodrich's *Edward Hopper* (New York: Abrams, 1971).

284. Marling, Karal Ann. "A Note on New Deal Iconography: Futurology and the Historical Myth." *Prospects: An Annual of American Culture Studies.* vol. 4, edited by Jack Salzman, 421–40. New York: Burt Franklin, 1979.

This thoughtful analysis of the sense of time conveyed by New Deal Post Office murals is expanded in *Wall-to-Wall America* (item 288). Marling argues that during the Depression large numbers of Americans yearned for a secure past of happiness and plenty as well as a blissful future of contentment and prosperity. Sordid present day realities were largely omitted from the murals and dismissed from the minds of many.

285. ———. "Don't Knock Wood." *Artnews* 82 (September 1983): 94–99.

Through careful analysis of such paintings as *The Midnight Ride of Paul Revere, Parson Weem's Fable, American Gothic,* and *Daughters of Revolution,* Marling argues that a subtle sense of humor and American history, conveyed in a desire to debunk pretentious images of the past, lies at the heart of Wood's art.

286. ———. "Thomas Hart Benton's *Boomtown*: Regionalism Redefined." *Prospects: An Annual of American Culture Studies.* vol. 6, edited by Jack Salzman, 73–137. New York: Burt Franklin, 1981.

This wide-ranging article focuses upon the late 1920s when Benton's discovery of Turner's frontier thesis and a sketching trip through the Ozarks, Texas, and the Southwest inspired his first full-fledged regional painting. Benton's vivid impressions of Bolger, Texas in 1927, the composition of *Boomtown* in 1928, and the tension between frontier expansiveness and regional rootedness in Benton's subsequent work, and his efforts to popularize his regional vision are carefully discussed.

287. ———. *Tom Benton and His Drawings: A Biographical Essay and a Collection of his Sketches, Studies, and Mural Cartoons.* Columbia: University of Missouri Press, 1985.

Marling's carefully researched account of Benton's colorful career and personal life abounds with fresh information regarding regionalist art. In many ways a tribute to Benton's indomitable spirit, Marling's text documents, among other things, the urban-industrial elements of Benton's regional art, his folk-populist ideology, and his struggles both with New York "assthetes" and midwestern philistines. Hundreds of

Benton's drawings and mural sketches done from the early 1920s until his death in 1975 are analyzed in great detail.

288. ———. *Wall-to-Wall America: A Cultural History of Post Office Murals in the Great Depression*. Minneapolis: Univ. of Minnesota Press, 1982.

Between 1934 and 1943, the Treasury Section of the Fine Arts sponsored a multitude of post office murals depicting local history and events, and Marling analyzes the resulting continental panorama of American life as an index to American culture during the Great Depression. Regionalism, both as an art form and as a social impulse, was a central force behind the murals, and Marling's perceptive case studies of the relationship between visiting artists' regional visions and the desires of local townspeople provide an invaluable grass roots perspective to regionalism. Equally insightful are Marling's discussions of the regional stereotypes borrowed from mass media in the murals and their vision of local history with a stable folk past, a beckoning prosperous future, and a missing present.

289. Mathews, Jane DeHart. "Grant Wood's Vision of the American Scene." *Reviews in American History* 4 (December 1976): 588–93.

This extensive review of James Denis's biography of Grant Wood effectively connects regional aesthetics to other currents of cultural nationalism during the interwar decades. Wood's art, Mathews argues, epitomized "and even helped shape some of the most significant cultural goals of the era."

290. Montgomery, Charles F. "Regional Preferences and Characteristics in American Decorative Arts: 1750–1800." In *American Art: 1750–1800. Toward Independence*, edited by Charles F. Montgomery and Patricia E. Kane, 50–65. Boston: New York Graphic Society, 1976.

After mentioning John Kirk's notion of distinct "furniture regions" corresponding to American dialect regions, Montgomery carefully describes furniture, pewter, and silverware design in five colonial and early national regions. The increasing deviation from English patterns, especially during the Federalist period, documents the growth of cultural independence and regional diversity.

291. Moser, Charlotte. "Regional Revisions: Houston and Chicago." *Art in America* 73 (July 1985): 90–99.

Moser analyzes the strengths and weaknesses of the self- conscious regional art that has emerged in Chicago and Houston since the 1970s.

The desire for artistic pluralism and decentralization, the impact of folk and ethnic art, the movement from abstraction to imagistic painting, and the possible perils of narrow provincialism are insightfully analyzed.

292. Nash, Anedith. "Death on the Ridge Road: Grant Wood and Modernization in the Midwest." *Prospects: An Annual of American Culture Studies.* vol. 8, edited by Jack Salzman, 281–301. New York: Burt Franklin, 1983.

Nash's detailed examination of one painting reveals Wood's complex and ambivalent attitude toward modernization in his native region.

293. Novak, Barbara. *Nature and Culture: American Landscape and Painting, 1825–1875.* New York: Oxford Univ. Press, 1980.

Novak analyzes the philosophical, spiritual, and scientific dimensions of the great epoch of American landscape painting between 1825 and 1875 in this important interdisciplinary study. Although there is little explicit discussion of the regional influences—Novak stresses that Cole, Durand, Church, Cropsey, Kennsett, and others found an "iconography of nationalism" in the natural landscape—her insightful analysis of the tension between wilderness and civilization in American painting contributes to our understanding of the relationship between sense of place and aesthetics. Especially useful in this regard is "Man's Traces: Axe, Train, Figure," pp. 157–200.

294. Park, Marlene and Gerald E. Markovitz. *Democratic Vistas: Post Offices and Public Art in the New Deal.* Philadelphia: Temple Univ. Press, 1984.

Although without the penetrating cultural analysis of Marling's *Wall-to-Wall America* (item 288), this book does contain detailed descriptions of the regional motifs in WPA post office murals throughout the nation. Especially helpful are "regionalism," pp. 68–103, and an extensive appendix listing murals, state-by-state.

295. Plagens, Peter. *Sunshine Muse: Contemporary Art on the West Coast.* New York: Praeger, 1974.

This is a useful study of the historical and social forces that have influenced regionally-flavored art in California, Oregon, and Washington in the 1960s and early 1970s. Plagens has also written several powerfully evocative analyses of contemporary Los Angeles art, architecture, and culture, particularly, "Los Angeles: The Ecology of

Evil," *Artforum* 11 (December 1972), pp. 67–76 and "Bee-Bob Da Reebok in L.A.," *Art in America* 73 (April 1985), pp. 138–49.

296. Rees, Ronald. "Landscape in Art." In *Dimensions of Human Geography: Essays on Some Familiar and Neglected Themes*, edited by Karl W. Butzer, 48–68. Chicago: Univ. of Chicago, Department of Geography, Research Paper 186, 1978.

Analyzing the relationship between painting and place, Rees briefly traces the rise of landscape painting in northern Europe in the sixteenth century and the emergence of self-conscious regionalist art in Great Britain, Canada, and the United States in the nineteenth and twentieth centuries. The significance of naivete and nostalgia in regional art is effectively discussed

297. Richardson, E.P. *Painting in America*. New York: Thomas Y. Crowell, 1956.

"The Twentieth Century: The Second Generation," pp. 382–407, perceptively analyzes a spectrum of American Scene and regionalist art during the 1920s and 1930s, from the urbane regionalism of Stieglitz and his circle to the bombastic efforts of Craven, Benton, and Wood, and from the introspective regionalism of Hopper, Burchfield, Albright, and Tobey to the public murals of the Federal Art Project. Describing a ubiquitous regional impulse in the arts transcending coterie manifestos, Richardson writes, "Regionalism was a word of power.... the mood of rediscovery of America was something wider, deeper, more pervasive and intangible in the whole country than this one shrill chauvinistic outcry."

298. ———. "Regionalism in Painting." In *Regionalism in America*, edited by Merrill Jensen, 261–72. Madison: Univ. of Wisconsin Press, 1951.

After pointing out the difficulties of discerning regional patterns in the fine arts—stressing that "there is no automatic connection between the rivers, mountains, or plains of man's habitat and the imaginative life of man's mind"—Richardson shrewdly observes that painting is particularly aloof from natural influences and "needs no adaptation to a Wisconsin winter or a Texas summer, as does the form of a house." He then briefly sketches the often subtle regional flavor of early painting in New England, the Hudson Valley, Pennsylvania, and the South. After mentioning the self-conscious regional efforts of the 1930s, Richardson concludes that although regionalism remains weak in terms of formal theory and deeply rooted schools, there are healthy signs of decentralization and diversity in American art.

299. Rosenberg, Harold. *Discovering the Present: Three Decades in Art, Culture, and Politics.* Chicago: Univ. of Chicago Press, 1973.

Part Two, "The Geography of Art," contains two essays particularly relevant to understanding the relationship between art and region. "On Space" (1949), pp. 71–73, stresses the special meaning of space in abstract expressionism—an art form in which "there is no use looking for silos or madonnas. They have all melted into the void. But, as I said, the void itself, you have that, just as surely as your grandfather had a sun-speckled lawn." "Tenth Street: A Geography of Modern Art" (1954), pp. 100–09, vividly describes the significance of a place upon the seemingly "placeless" art of abstract expressionism.

300. ———. "Parable of American Painting." In *The Tradition of the New*, 13–22. New York: Horizon Press, 1959.

Like Kouwenhoven, Rourke, and others, Rosenberg depicts the history of American art as the struggle between cultivated and vernacular traditions. In the ongoing battle between "redcoats" and "coonskins," between imitators of European styles and indigenous free spirits, Rosenberg argues that the fresh, anti-formal coonskins, responding to the raw realities of the American landscape rather than the dream world of an imported style, have been the major shapers of American art. "Coonskin doggedness" characterizes the work of Audubon, Eakins, Ryder, Homer, Marin, Stuart Davis, and De Kooning, and by implication informs the best of regional art.

301. Rourke, Constance. "American Art: A Possible Future." *American Magazine of Art*, 28 (1935): 390–405. Reprinted in *The Roots of American Culture and Other Essays*, 275–96. New York: Harcourt, Brace, & World, 1942.

Focusing upon painting, folk art, architecture, and the practical arts, Rourke describes the ongoing tension between indigenous and cultivated traditions in American culture from the seventeenth century to the present. While warning against the excesses of a "militant regionalism," Rourke finds promise of a truly American art—both in subject matter and in style—in the work of Burchfield, Marin, Hopper, Benton, and Wood.

302. ———. *Charles Sheeler: Artist in the American Tradition.* New York: Harcourt, Brace, & World, 1938.

Sheeler's relationship with the American Scene and Regionalist movements of the interwar decades is carefully described in chapter three, pp. 59–88. A sense of the artist's attachment to and inspiration drawn from southeastern Pennsylvania informs much of Rourke's narrative. Sheeler's eclectic enthusiasm for things American—ranging from Shaker architecture to the River Rouge auto plant—and his ability to depict native materials in an indigenous style could stand as a model of cultural nationalism and regionalism in the arts. "The fact that he had chosen an American subject," Rourke argues, "was not in itself significant, for the subject alone is never a solution for the artist.... The determinant is form." Other sources by Rourke are listed under American Studies (items 33–35).

303. Shepard, Paul. "Place in American Culture." *North American Review* 262 (Fall 1977): 22–32.

This wide-ranging, provocative essay masterfully analyzes the regional roots of the Hudson River School and also explores the larger significance of sense of place—especially sense of wilderness—for the healthy development of individuals and entire societies. Portions of Shepard's *Man in the Landscape* (New York: Knopf, 1967), particularly "The Virgin Dream," use American landscape painting as an index to psychological and social development.

304. Smithson, Robert. *The Writings of Robert Smithson: Essays With Illustrations.* Edited by Nancy Holt. New York: NYU Press, 1979.

Smithson, best known for his massive earth work, *Spiral Jetty* (1970), was perhaps the most articulate of a group of earth artists that includes Dennis Openheim, Robert Morris, and James Terrell. This anthology contains a number of highly imaginative, regionally and environmentally oriented essays including "A Tour of the Monuments of Passaic, New Jersey" (1967), pp. 52–57; "A Sedimentation of the Mind: Earth Projects" (1968), pp. 82–91; "The Spiral Jetty" (1972), pp. 109–16; and especially "Frederick Law Olmsted and the Dialectical Landscape" (1973), pp. 117–28.

305. Special Issue. "Art Across America." *Art in America* 64 (July-August 1976).

In addition to the important reconsiderations of regionalism by Alloway and Kupsit (items 233, 281), this issue contains articles analyzing the renaissance of regional art in the South, the Northwest, New Mexico, Texas, California, Chicago, and Philadelphia. Interviews with six regional artists—Robert Gordy, Ellen Lanyon, Roland Ginzel, Craig Kauffman, Dick Wray, and Phil Reneria—are included.

306. Special Issue. "American Landscape." *Art in America* 64 (January-February 1976).

Insightful regionally-related articles include Barbara Novak's "The Double-Edged Axe," pp. 44–50, which examines the tension between devotion to nature and to progress in Hudson River School paintings; Donald Kupsit's "Nineteenth Century Landscape: Poetry and Property," pp. 64–71; Sanford Schwartz's "A Northern Seascape," pp. 72–76, concerning Marsden Hartley's evolving sense of place; and Amy Goldin's "Abstract Expressionism: No Man's Land," pp. 77–79. Other essays regarding images of redwoods, Route 66, and earthworks are pertinent.

307. Special Issue. "Midwest Art: A Special Report." *Art in America* 67 (July-August 1977).

Four articles describe the reemergence of regional art in the Midwest: Carrie Rickey analyzes painting and sculpture in Chicago; Sarah McFadden describes art in Detroit, Minneapolis, Kansas City, and St. Louis; Donald Kupsit treats Columbus; and Holliday T. Day examines Indianapolis, Cincinnati, and Dayton.

308. Wientraub, Linda, ed. *Thomas Hart Benton: Chronicler of America's Folk Heritage*. Annandale-on-Hudson, N.Y.: Edith C. Blum Art Institute, 1984.

This anthology contains three regionally-related essays: Matthew Baigel's "Recovering America for American Art: Benton in the Early Twenties," pp. 12–31; Archie Green's "Tom Benton's Folk Depictions," pp. 32–67: and Alan C. Buechner's "Thomas Hart Benton and American Folk Music," pp. 68–77. Green's essay is particularly insightful because it counters those who criticize Benton as a false regionalist content to depict mainstream America. "Melting pot images of 'gathered multitudes'," Green concludes, "did not shore his populism, nor did he impose a mainstream vision on those caught in backwaters."

309. Wood, Grant. "A Definition of Regionalism." *Books at Iowa* 3 (November 1965): 3–4.

In this brief essay, written at the request of his colleague Norman Foerster in 1937, Wood reiterates Foerster's statement that regionalism is rooted in the "belief that writers who draw their materials from their own experience and the life they know best are more likely to attain universal values than those who do not." He also stresses regionalism is not the same as cultural nationalism and that it "is not ... a revolt against industrial civilization (in the William Morris sense), though it has re-emphasized the fact that America is agrarian as well as industrial."

310. ———. *Revolt Against the City*. Whirling Wind Series, no. 1. Iowa City: Clio Press, 1935. Reprinted in *Grant Wood: A Study in American Art and Culture*, edited by James M. Denis, 229–35. New York: Viking Press, 1975.

In this pamphlet, a central regionalist document, Wood forcefully outlines his aesthetic credo, compares his work to parallel efforts in drama, literature, and social criticism, and effectively places the regional movement of the 1930s within a larger historical context. Strident anti-urban sentiments are balanced by a critical affection for his native region. "I believe in the Middle West in spite of abundant knowledge of its faults," he writes. "Your true regionalist is not a mere eulogist; he may even be a severe critic."

311. Young, Mahonri Sharp. "Other Regionalisms in American Painting." *Apollo* 120 (November 1984): 327–34.

Young points out that regionalism has always been a vigorous force in American painting that has extended far beyond the self-conscious regionalism of Benton, Wood, and Curry. Boston, Philadelphia, New Orleans, the Hudson Valley, New Mexico, San Francisco, Carmel, Los Angeles, the Northwest, Maine, Cape Cod, even Brown County, Indiana, have all supported regional schools of art and underscore the persistence of local accents in American painting.

Economics

Regionalism has always been an important although often implicit theme of American economic thought. Of the three traditional factors of economic production—land, labor, and capital—land and labor change dramatically in essence from one place to another. The geographical distribution of wealth and the spatial variability of national and global economies are crucial economic concerns, and full-fledged theories of economic regionalism have been developed with ever-widening interest since the 1920s.

Economic regionalism has been studied from at least four points of view from the 1920s to the 1980s. In the early 1920s, Norman S.B. Gras initiated the economic analysis of regionalism with his theoretical model of the "metropolitan community" in which a large urban center dominates a far-flung rural hinterland. Gras's vision of metropolitan regionalism rapidly spread beyond economics to influence an emerging generation of regional planners and urban sociologists. By the late 1920s, another influential regional perspective was developed by agricultural economists. Whereas the metropolitan economists perceived regions in terms of commodity flows between rural peripheries and urban cores, agricultural economists such as Oliver Baker, R.L. Mangus, Paul S. Taylor, and others visualized homogeneous agricultural regions dominated by particular crop and farming systems.

After World War II, interest in the economic dynamics of metropolitan and agricultural regions was supplemented by a third paradigm: a "regional analysis" perspective that grew out of the abstract models of economic space found in location theory and regional science. Within this tradition of regional analysis, August Losch, Francois Perroux, Walter Isard, Douglass North, and others have developed abstract models of the effects of space on economic growth. Regions are perceived as networks of "nodes" and "linkages," and various methods— including input-output and comparative cost analysis—are used to eventually plan economic development of particular regions and places. The work of this diverse regional analysis paradigm culminated in the publication of four important books in 1960: *Economic Areas of the United States* by Donald Bogue and Calvin Beale, *Metropolis and Region* by Otis Dudley Duncan and associates, *Methods of Regional Analysis* by Walter Isard, and *Regions, Resources, and Economic Growth* by Harvey Perloff and associates. By the 1960s regional economics had become an established academic field with separate textbooks and courses.

A fourth and equally vital regional perspective has flourished since the 1960s. Stimulated by the rediscovery of regional poverty in the early 1960s and the apparent south and westward shift of America's economic base by the early 1970s, many economists have examined the phenomenon of uneven regional development. This perspective has spawned an abundance of speculation regarding the power shift from frostbelt to sunbelt and such issues as of reindustrialization, deindustrialization, and regional economic disparity and has drawn the attention of economists as varied as Gunnar Myrdal, Walt Rostow, Jane Jacobs, and Ann Markusen. (Items by Bluestone and Bennett, Fallows, Hall, Hall and Markusen, Rifkin and Barbour, Sawers and Tabb, Weinstein and Firestine also analyze this theme.)

All four academic approaches are generally concerned with objectively explaining the way things are; a fifth and final perspective offers more utopian visions of the way the economy ought to be. A long line of "utopian" economic theorists have advocated regional solutions to economic problems: Troy Jesse Cauley, Ralph Borsodi, Herbert Agar, Paul and Percival Goodman, Robert Goodman, Hazel Henderson, E.F. Schumacher, Gar Alperovitz and Jeff Faux, and many others have promoted a spectrum of such regional ideologies as agrarianism, distributism, decentralism, regional socialism, and bioregionalism. (A closely related group of normative regional theorists, including Murray Bookchin, Kirkpatrick Sale, Karl Hess, and others, is represented in Political Science.)

Economists have deepened our general understanding of regionalism by examining the spatial distribution of material wealth. More specifically, they have developed theories of metropolitan and agricultural regions, created a science of regional analysis, explored the dynamics of uneven regional development, and advocated regional solutions to economic problems. There is an overwhelming amount of material related to these issues, and the following list is highly selective. For this reason, only the most representative sources have been selected, and single region studies, textbooks, and highly technical analyses have largely been excluded.[1] Finally, there is an immense amount of overlap between regional scholarship in this chapter and regional scholarship listed under Architecture and Planning, Geography:

Distributional Studies, Political Science, and Sociology. The work of economic geographers Brian Berry, Michael Conzen, David Harvey, Allan Pred, and others listed under Geography: Distributional Studies as well as the scholarship of William Alonso, John Friedmann, Harvey Perloff, and others listed under Architecture and Planning should be read in conjunction with this chapter.

M.S.

---

[1]Readers interested in references to more focused and technical studies of economic regionalism should consult Brian J.L. Berry and Thomas D. Hankin, *A Bibliographic Guide to the Economic Regions of the United States* (Chicago: Univ. of Chicago Press, 1963) and Jean A. Shackelford, *Urban and Regional Economics: A Guide to Information Sources* (Detroit: Gale Research Co., 1980).

*   *   *

312. Advisory Commission on Intergovernmental Relations. *Regional Growth: Historic Perspective.* Washington, D.C.: U.S. Government Printing Office, 1980.

In this clearly written summation of historical trends in economic regionalism a large body of statistics and relevant economic theories are presented in a highly useful, lucid form. Two general patterns emerge over the past century: an overall reduction in regional economic disparities and the pervasive geographical dispersion of economic activities. An extensive bibliography is included.

313. Agar, Herbert and Allen Tate, eds. *Who Owns America? A New Declaration of Independence.* Boston: Houghton-Mifflin, 1936.

The sequel to *I'll Take My Stand* (1930), this manifesto is the most accessible discussion of the Southern Agrarian's adaptation of distributist economic theory. Essays relevant to economic regionalism include David Cushman Doyle's opening discussion of the need for small scale decentralized industry in "The Fallacy of Mass Production," pp. 3–17; Agar's discussion of the Swedish economy as a model for American reform in "'But Can It Be Done?,'" pp. 94–109; and Andrew Lytle's paean to the family farm in "The Small Farm Secures the State," pp. 237–50. Other important essays include Donald Davidson on political regionalism, Robert Penn Warren on literary regionalism, and Hilaire Belloc's critique of large-scale industrial capitalism.

314. Alonso, William. "Urban and Regional Imbalances in Economic Development." *Economic Development and Cultural Change* 17 (1968): 1–14.

Alonso carefully challenges two assumptions of regional economic and planning theory: that the rapid growth of central cities threatens national economic growth, and that governments should intervene to restore income differences between booming urban centers and lagging rural regions. Polarization, regional inequality, and the "primacy" of metropolitan centers, Alonso suggests, "are normal aspects of the early stages of development, corrected by natural processes.... Primacy, overurbanization, and giantism are not diseases but growing pains." Another item by Alonso is listed under Architecture and Planning (item 150).

315. Alperovitz, Gar and Jeff Faux. *Rebuilding America*. New York: Pantheon Books, 1984.

This important book argues that the "beggar-thy-neighbor individualism" of neoconservative economics that has dominated American society since the 1970s must be replaced by a "community-sustaining economics." At the heart of this vision of a more cooperative, decentralized economic system is the need for localized planning and grass roots economic democracy. Sections that are especially relevant to economic regionalism include "A Community-Sustaining Economics," pp. 71–86, which examines the local community as the foundation of economic and political democracy; "Toward Democratic Planning," pp. 257–70, which describes how to encourage dynamic, participatory local community planning as the foundation for a national vision; and "Rebuilding America," pp. 271–81, which reiterates that a sense of local community and commitment is the cornerstone of long-term economic stability and that such communal commitment can only thrive within a regional context that mediates between the local community and the nation.

316. Baker, Oliver E. "Agricultural Regions of North America." Parts 1–12. *Economic Geography* (October 1926–October 1932): 2: 459–93; 3: 50–86; 3:309–39; 3: 447–65; 4: 44–73; 4: 399–433; 5: 36–67; 6: 166–90; 6: 278–308; 7: 109–54; 7: 325–64; 8: 325–77; 9: 167–97.

In this series of twelve articles published over six years, Baker describes nine primary agriculture regions. The lead article, "The Basis for Classification," vol. 2 (October 1926) pp. 460–93, remains a useful introduction to the concept of the agricultural region. For related sources on agricultural regions see Haystead and Fite, Lange and Taylor, and Mangus in this chapter (items 348, 359, 365) and Carl Taylor under Sociology (item 1634).

317. Baker, Oliver E., Ralph Borsodi, and M.L. Wilson. *Agriculture and Modern Life*. New York: Harper and Brothers, 1939.

This collection of essays, many of them concerned with economics and agricultural regions, underscores the pervasiveness of decentralist thought and the back-to-the-land impulse during the 1930s.

318. Berry, Brian J.L. and Thomas D. Hankins, eds. *A Bibliographic Guide to the Economic Regions of the United States*. Chicago: Univ. of Chicago Press, 1963.

This impressive reference book covers much more than economic regionalism. It contains an impressive introduction to regional theory and nearly four hundred carefully annotated entries in such categories as single region economic studies and the development of the regional concept in geography, economics, regional science, and planning. It is a vital source for both economics and geography.

319. Bluestone, Barry and Bennett Harrison. *The Deindustrialization of America: Plant Closings, Community Abandonment, and the Dismantling of Basic Industries*. New York: Basic Books, 1982.

This passionate analysis of the wrenching economic consequences of frostbelt-sunbelt shift advocates public policy promoting the reindustrialization of the declining Northeast. "Boomtown and Busttown: How the Market Produces Reindustrialization," pp. 82–107, contains a vivid portrait of the economic forces fueling Houston, the quintessential boomtown, and draining Youngstown, the epitome of regional decline. For closely related sources in this chapter, see Fallows, Hall and Markusen, Rifkin and Barbour, Sawers and Tabb, and Weinstein and Firestine (items 335, 346, 378, 380, 386).

320. Bogue, Donald J. and Calvin L. Beale. *Economic Areas of the United States*. Glencoe, Ill.: Free Press, 1960.

In this important example of regional analysis, Bogue and Beale divide the United States into five basic economic provinces and thirteen economic regions defined as "clusters of land that are... homogeneous in their general livelihood and socio-economic characteristics." The economic patterns of each area are described in detail.

321. Borsodi, Ralph. *This Ugly Civilization*. New York: Simon and Schuster, 1929.

In this vigorous and influential critique of the massive congestion, inefficiency, and servility imposed by urban-industrial society, Borsodi advocates economic decentralization based upon small-scale domestic production. Related books by Borsodi include *The Distribution Age*, (New York: D. Appleton and Co., 1927) and *Flight From the City*, (Suffern, N.Y.: School of Living, 1947).

322. Brocard, Lucian. "Regional Economy and Economic Regionalism." *The Annals of the American Academy of Political and Social Sciences* 163 (June 1932): 81–92.

Regional and local economies are vital, Brocard argues, for at these levels people have an immediate sense of how to make the wisest, most balanced use of available resources. As social organization expands geographically and becomes more complex, economic decentralization will become increasingly necessary.

323. Broude, Henry W. "The Significance of Regional Studies for the Elaboration of National Economic History." *Journal of Economic History* 20 (1960): 588–96.

Broude argues that the national economy can only be understood in terms of its regional parts and that the mathematical models and empirical measures developed by Isard and others in regional science can be applied to this inductive process.

324. Browett, John. "On the Necessity and Inevitability of Uneven Spatial Development Under Capitalism." *International Journal of Urban and Regional Research* 8 (1984): 155–76.

Browett argues that uneven economic development is not a necessary condition of capitalist accumulation and that regionalism is a largely useless category for economic analysis. Browett's argument is vigorously refuted by Neil Smith, "On the Necessity of Uneven Development," *International Journal of Urban and Regional Research* 10 (March 1986), pp. 87–104. Smith asserts that regionalism is an essential economic issue and that uneven spatial development has intensified in recent years.

325. Buck, Trevor W. "Regional Class Differences: An International Study of Capitalism." *International Journal of Urban and Regional Research* 3 (December 1979): 516–26.

Beginning with the thesis that regional grievances "may owe their existence to class conflict rather than to economic disparities," Buck demonstrates that nations like Australia and West Germany with even distribution of occupations have fewer regional tensions than nations like France and Great Britain with marked contrasts in regional work forces.

326. Castells, Manuel. *The Urban Question: A Marxist Approach.* Translated by Alan Sheridan. Cambridge: MIT Press, 1977.

A central portion of this influential book analyzes the dynamics of large-scale metropolitan regions and the networks of small-scale subcultural neighborhoods within capitalist metropolises. See for, example, "The Formation of Metropolitan Regions in Capitalist Societies," pp. 20–38; "The Urban Sub-Cultures," pp. 96–112; and "The Debate on the Theory of Space," pp. 115–28.

327. Cauley, Troy Jesse. *Agrarianism: A Program for Farmers* Chapel Hill: Univ. of North Carolina Press, 1935.

Although Cauley, an economics professor at the Georgia School of Technology, admits that his book is written "in the nature of an exhortation," it stands as the most competent discussion of Southern Agrarian economics.

328. Chase, Stuart. *Rich Land, Poor Land: A Study of Waste in the Natural Resources of America.* New York: Whittlesey House, 1936.

At the heart of this powerful region-by-region account of environmental despoliation is Chase's advocacy of regional economic planning. See "Planning With Nature" and "Tennessee Valley," pp. 243–61 and 262–87, respectively, for a vision paralleling the theories of Lewis Mumford and Benton MacKaye, Chase's colleagues in the Regional Planning Association of America.

329. Clark, Gordon L. "Capitalism and Regional Inequality." *Annals of the American Association of Geographers* 70 (June 1980): 226–37.

In this detailed overview of the extensive uneven regional development debate, Clark modifies the usual Marxist position that geographical economic disparity is an inevitable consequence of capitalism. Although regional disparity is not a necessary requirement of capitalism, "pockets of high unemployment and economic distress are likely features of the capitalist spatial system."

330. Crichton, Kyle, John Gould Fletcher, Dudley Wynn, and T.M. Pearce. "Economic Aspects of Southwestern Regionalism." *New Mexico Quarterly* 5 (May 1935): 71–87.

This symposium is the most explicit statement describing the economic principles of a New Mexico centered regional movement that is often overshadowed by the Southern Agrarians.

331. Duncan, Otis Dudley et al. *Metropolis and Region.* Baltimore: Johns Hopkins Univ. Press, 1960.

Building upon the insights of economic historian Norman Gras and the work of human ecologists Robert Park and R.D. McKenzie, Duncan and his associates analyze the economic structure and function of metropolitan communities and their relationships to surrounding regions as well as the nation. Perloff's *Regions, Resources, and Economic Growth* (item 375) is a closely related study.

332. Edel, Candace Kim. "Uneven Regional Development: An Introduction to the Issue." *Review of Radical Political Economics* 10 (Fall 1978): 1–12.

In this, the lead essay of a valuable symposium on uneven regional development, Edel urges radical economists to develop a firmer spatial sensibility. Edel assesses Marx's impact upon regional thought, discusses the concept of internal colonialism, and analyzes the complex relationship between class and regional consciousness. See Fox, Goldsmith, and Markusen (items 336, 338, 366) for other essays in this special issue.

333. Editorial Research Reports. *American Regionalism: Our Economic, Cultural, and Political Makeup.* Washington, D.C.: Congressional Quarterly, Inc., 1980.

This somewhat simplistic economic and social profile of each major region distinguished by the Census Bureau contains fairly useful bibliographies focused upon the sunbelt/frostbelt debate.

334. Estall, Robert. "The Changing Balance of the Northern and Southern Regions of the United States. *Journal of American Studies* 14 (December 1980): 365–86.

This effective summary of the sunbelt/frostbelt debate concludes with the possibility that "By the middle of the next century... the old Southern periphery will have become the new national heartland, the old core a new 'Northern periphery'—albeit well-developed and affluent."

335. Fallows, James. "The Changing Economic Landscape." *Atlantic* 255 (March 1985): 47–68.

In this highly effective analysis of the recent regional dislocations in the American economy, Fallows compares various scenarios of reindustrialization and deindustrialization, interviews unemployed steel workers in the Midwest and prospering high tech entrepreneurs in Texas, and discusses the incessant tension between attachment to place and migration in American culture.

336. Fox, Kenneth. "Uneven Regional Development in the U.S." *Review of Radical Political Economics* 10 (Fall 1978): 68–86.

Contrary to the image projected by the popular press, Fox argues that regional economic disparities have decreased in the United States after reaching a peak in the late nineteenth century. The shift from competitive to monopoly capitalism at the turn of the century helped transfer uneven spatial development from the regional level within the United States to an international level through the exploitation of Third World nations.

337. Friedmann, John and William Alonso, eds. *Regional Planning and Development: A Reader*. Cambridge: MIT Press, 1964.

This anthology is an invaluable collection of readings in regional economics and regional planning. In addition to essential essays in regional economics by Losch, North, Perloff and Wingo (items 363, 373, 374) this reader also contains such useful essays as William Alonso's "Location Theory," pp. 78–106; Brian Berry's "Cities as Systems Within Systems of Cities," pp. 116–137; and William Nicholls's "Southern Tradition and Regional Economic Progress," pp. 462–73. Other sources by Friedmann and Alonso are listed under Architecture and Planning (items 150, 167, 168).

338. Goldsmith, William W. "Marxism and Regional Policy: An Introduction." *Review of Radical Political Economics* 10 (Fall 1978): 13–17. Reprinted with some changes as "Marxism and Regional Policy: An Introduction." In *Urban and Regional Planning in an Age of Austerity*, edited by Pierre Clavel, et al., 22–52. New York: Pergamon Press, 1980.

Goldsmith vigorously argues that it is in the very nature of capitalism that regional problems arise—that regional differences within capitalistic nations are accentuated through the exploitation of raw materials and labor.

339. Goodman, Paul and Percival Goodman. *Communitas: Means of Livelihood and Ways of Life*. New York: Random House, 1960.

Originally published in 1947, this book contains a vital critique of twentieth century economic and planning theory as well as a utopian vision of a decentralized and regionally reconstructed American economy. This lively, often humorous yet earnest, manifesto contains a rich synthesis of more than a century of anarchist-decentralist thought and is an indispensable source for regional economics, regional planning, architecture, and bioregionalism.

340. Goodman, Percival. *The Double E*. New York: Anchor Press, 1977.

In what is essentially a revision of *Communitas* in light of the related concepts of economy and ecology, Percival Goodman believes that regionalism is increasingly needed in a crowded world of limited resources. "The Double E," pp. 110–79, contains a vivid discussion of community, urban, and regional planning theory.

341. Goodman, Robert. *The Last Entrepreneurs: America's Regional Wars for Jobs and Dollars*. New York: Simon & Schuster, 1979.

At the heart of this vigorous critique of laissez-faire capitalism is Goodman's alternative vision of the growth of a grass roots "regional socialism." "Regional Socialism: An American Alternative," pp. 171–205, is a vital, maverick contribution to regional economic theory paralleling William Appleman Williams's vision of regional socialism in American history.

342. Gras, Norman S.B. *An Introduction to Economic History*. New York: Harper and Brothers, 1922.

"Metropolitan Economy, Chiefly in England" and "Metropolitan Economy, Chiefly in America," pp. 181–280 and 281–340, respectively, contain Gras's landmark analysis of the rise of metropolitan regions in the western world from the early modern era to the twentieth century.

343. ———. "Regionalism and Nationalism." *Foreign Affairs* 7 (April 1929): 454–67.

Gras traces the historical relationship between region and nation and argues that the hopes that the rise of metropolitan regionalism in the twentieth century "will help form a social point of view which is broader, more rational and economic, and more progressive than the national point of view." In contrast to many later critics of uneven regional development, Gras asserts that "Just as socialism came in to correct the class emphasis, so regionalism will have to rise ... to offset the tendency to favor one region and neglect another."

344. ——. "The Rise of the Metropolitan Community." In *The Urban Community*, edited by Ernest W. Burgess, 183–91. Chicago: Univ. of Chicago Press, 1926.

After succinctly describing the economic dynamics and global dominance of metropolitan regions, Gras suggests an economic and political structure to suit this reality: an international order that is a mosaic of metropolitan regions rather than an archaic patchwork of provinces and nation-states.

345. Hall, Peter. "Keys to Regional Growth." *Society* 19 (July/ August 1982): 183–91.

In clear, lively prose, Hall applies theories of economic cycles and technological innovation developed by Nicolai Kondratief and Joseph Schumpeter to the current regional relocation of the American economy. "New waves of innovation," Hall writes, "are likely to come in just those places that are already buoyant as a result of the last industrial revolution—the one that began in the 1930s. They are highly unlikely to come to America's depressed areas: the Frostbelt cities that were the outcome of earlier waves of industrialization."

346. Hall, Peter and Ann Markusen, eds. *Silicon Landscapes*. Boston: Allen and Unwin, 1985.

This important collection of essays evaluates the significance of a central belief in the burgeoning field of regional economics: the "new economic Holy Grail, industrial renaissance through high technology job creation." The essays focus upon the short- and long-term consequences of high tech industry in the Silicon Valley near San Jose, California and in the M 4 Corridor west of London. Especially useful essays include Peter Hall's "The Geography of the Fifth Kondratieff," pp. 1–19, and Hall and Markusen's "High Technology and Regional-Urban Policy," pp. 144–51. The important question of whether high technology can be successfully transplanted in older industrial cities and regions is carefully examined.

347. Hansen, Niles M. *Rural Poverty and the Urban Crisis: A Strategy for Regional Development*. Bloomington: Indiana Univ. Press, 1970.

In this important book, Hansen applies the tools of economic analysis to the problems of rural regional poverty that Michael Harrington, Robert Coles, and others brought to national attention in the 1960s. In addition to examining the causes of poverty in the South, Appalachia, and the Southwest, Hansen also investigates northern urban ghettos and the economic conditions of Native Americans and Mexican Americans. A somewhat more technical refinement of this book is found in Hansen's *Location Preferences, Migration, and Regional Growth: A Study of the South and Southwestern United States* (New York: Praeger Publishers, 1973).

348. Haystead, Ladd and Gilbert C. Fite. *The Agricultural Regions of the United States.* Norman: Univ. of Oklahoma Press, 1955.

This standard text contains vivid portraits of the history, culture, and economics of eleven agricultural regions. For related sources see Baker, Lange and Taylor, and Mangus in this chapter (items 316, 359, 365) and Carl Taylor under Sociology (item 1634).

349. Henderson, Hazel. "Thinking Locally, Acting Globally: Ethics for the Dawning Solar Age." In *The Politics of the Solar Age: Alternatives to Economics*, 355–405. Garden City, N.Y.: Doubleday, 1981.

In many ways a popularization of the decentralist-anarchist thought of Ralph Borsodi, Paul and Percival Goodman, E.F. Schumacher, and other economists, this essay surveys the worldwide resurgence of decentrist-regional movements and predicts the eventual "denouement of the nation-state as a viable unit of governance; becoming too big for the problems of its own local populations and at the same time too small for the big problems of global relations and ecosystems."

350. Hoepfner, Theodore C. "Economics of Agrarianism." *Mississippi Quarterly* 13 (Spring 1960): 61–68.

Looking back at the arguments of people like Herbert Agar, Allen Tate, and Troy Jesse Cauley, this essay is a useful introduction to the economic principles of the Southern Agrarian and distributist protest.

351. Holland, Stuart. *The Regional Problem.* New York: St. Martin's Press, 1976.

This lucidly-written overview of current regional economic theory focuses upon the European and American debate concerning uneven regional development. Useful discussions include "Politics, Economics and Regions," pp. 1–20, an insightful survey of regional economics from the 1940s to the 1970s; "Capitalism and Regional Imbalance," pp. 21–42; and "Federalism and the Regional Problem," pp. 96–120, which examines American regional growth.

352. Isard, Walter. *Location and Space Economy.* Cambridge: MIT Press, 1956.

This text, written by one of the founders of the regional science movement, is a highly abstract effort to "improve the spatial and regional framework of the social sciences, particularly economics, through the development of a more general theory of location and space economy." The first two chapters, pp. 1–54, are a useful introduction to the construction of regional models and general theories of economic location. Isard's initial book-length exploration of regional science has been followed by two increasingly technical works: *Methods of Regional Analysis* (Cambridge: MIT Press, 1960) and *General Theory: Social, Political, Economic, and Regional,* (Cambridge: MIT Press, 1969).

353. ———. "Regional Science, the Concept of Region and Regional Structure." *Papers and Proceedings of the Regional Science Association* 2 (1956): 13–26.

In this fairly accessible introduction to a fresh discipline, Isard describes how the regional concept is modified by the practice of regional science. Rather than working with a standard set of regions, the regional scientist confronts a fresh configuration for each problem considered. As regional science is refined, however, a "true" set of regions will emerge.

354. Jackson, Gregory et al. *Regional Diversity: Growth in the United States, 1960–1990.* Boston: Auburn House, 1981.

This fairly detailed analysis of regional economic and demographic patterns since 1960 concludes that the dramatic regional divergence of the 1970s will persist in the 1980s with the South and West continuing to outgrow the North. Several important subtrends are detected within the general pattern of divergence: New England and the West North Central regions will grow faster than the rest of the North, and the Pacific and South Atlantic regions will lag behind the rest of the West and South. The book also contains insightful discussions of the revival of nonmetropolitan growth, the changing racial and ethnic mix of central cities, and other issues.

355. Jackson, Gregory and George S. Masnick. "Take Another Look at Regional U.S. Growth." *Harvard Business Review* 61 (March–April 1983): 76–87.

An effective condensation of the findings of *Regional Diversity,* this article addresses the possibility of economic-political conflicts between regions. "So long as the nation grows," they argue, "regional differences imply unequal shares of new activity. As total growth slows, however, one section gains only when another loses—a much more sensitive situation politically."

356. Jacobs, Jane. *Cities and the Wealth of Nations: Principles of Economic Life.* New York: Random House, 1984.

In this major contribution to regional economic theory, Jacobs argues that cities and their regions rather than nations are the "basic salient entities of economic life," and she urges economists to realize that "most nations are composed of collections or grab bags of very different economies, rich regions and poor ones within the same nation." Much of the book is devoted to analyzing regional economic models throughout the world including prosperous import-replacing city regions, "supply regions" exporting natural resources, regions that workers abandon, "clearance regions" dominated by agribusiness, "transplant regions" attracting outside technologies, and "artificial city regions" like the TVA that are planned from the outside. Jacobs's biting critique of political and economic nationalism and her praise of small-scale regional economics have profound implications for regional theory.

357. ———. *The Death and Life of Great American Cities.* New York: Random House, 1961.

At the heart of this influential vision of the centrality of cities in civilization is Jacobs's biting critique of American urban redevelopment and regional planning as dangerous exercises in anti-urban wholesale social engineering. See Chase in this chapter (item 328) and MacKaye, Mumford, Stein, and Sussman under Architecture and Planning for perceptive counter arguments (items 186–188, 196–201, 217, 219).

358. ———. *The Question of Separatism: Quebec and the Struggle Over Sovereignty.* New York: Random House, 1980.

Jacobs uses the issue of separatism in Canada to examine the economic impact of separatism elsewhere—particularly the secession of Norway from Sweden—and concludes that division into smaller units often enhances economic wealth and vitality. Especially useful chapters, in many ways echoing Schumacher's small-is-beautiful message, include "National Size and Economic Development," pp. 52–64, and "Paradoxes of Size," pp. 65–77.

359. Lange, Dorothea and Paul Schuster Taylor. *An American Exodus: A Study of Human Erosion.* New York: Reynal and Hitchcock, 1939; rev. ed., New Haven: Yale Univ. Press, 1969.

Comparable to Agee and Evans's *Let Us Now Praise Famous Men* (1941), Lange and Taylor's masterful documentary study contains vivid, region-by-region portraits of economic dislocation during the Great Depression. Lange's classic photographs of farm folk and migrants, Taylor's incisive economic analysis, and the first person testimony of the people themselves combine to make this an invaluable regional study. For directly related sources see Hansen (item 347), Steiner and Stott under American Studies (items 51, 53), and Goldschmidt under Anthropology (item 97).

360. Lessinger, Jack. *Regions of Opportunity: A Bold New Strategy for Real Estate Development.* New York: Times Books, 1986.

Written for a mass audience, Lessinger's book uses theories of uneven regional economic growth as guidelines for real estate investment. Lessinger places the spatial dimensions of the American economy in a wide historical context, describing the fluctuating lure of "regions of opportunity" and the repulsion of "regions of obsolescence" from the 1730s to the 1980s. "Predicting Regions of Opportunity," pp. 51–77, analyzes the regional dimensions of four overlapping economic paradigms: the economies of the "Mercantile Aristocrat" (1735–1846), the "Bantam Capitalist" (1789–1900), the corporate "Colossus" (1846–1958), and the suburban consumer culture (1900–present). "Predicting Penturbia—the Fifth Region of Opportunity," pp. 78–94, argues that the next important region of economic growth will occur in the "penturbs"—small cities and towns beyond the normal commuting range of major metropolitan centers and populated with "caring conservers" critical of suburban mass-consumption.

361. Loomis, Mildred J. *Alternative Americas.* New York: Universe Books, 1982.

Heavily influenced by Ralph Borsodi, this collection of twenty-four concise essays stands as a guidebook to American decentralist thought. Loomis's chapters focus upon such subjects as the problems of American centralization, the significance of the Green Revolution, the Rodale movement, subsistence homestead and cooperative experiments throughout the world, and the influence of Borsodi, Henry George, Arthur E. Morgan, Peter van Dresser, and others upon decentralist economics.

362. Losch, August. *The Economics of Location.* Translated by W.H. Waglom. New Haven: Yale Univ. Press, 1954.

This highly technical analysis of location theory contains a detailed examination of "Economic Regions," pp. 101–220. The most useful portion of this analysis for the non-expert is where Losch sets his abstract models aside and discusses "Economic Regions in Reality," pp. 215–20. Economics, he writes, is simply one of many intertwining spatial variables that create the "bewildering individuality of various places and events in space." "The economic sphere is simply added to the many other spheres of life that overlap, neither dominating nor merely tolerated."

363. ———. "The Nature of Economic Regions." *Southern Economic Journal* 5 (July 1938): 71–78. Reprinted in *Regional Development and Planning: A Reader* (item 337), 107–115.

In this influential study, Losch develops an abstract hexagonal model of the "independent" or "ideal" economic region free of geographical and political variables; he then compares this ideal type to the more complex reality of economic groupings subject to a myriad of non-economic forces.

364. Mandel, Ernest. "Capitalism and Regional Disparities." *South-West Economy and Society* 1 (1976): 41–47.

Mandel argues that regional disparities are inevitable within capitalist economies because such systems encourage the exploitation of cheap labor reserves in underdeveloped regions. The "construction of socialism" requires the end of such inequities and enhances the lives of people in all regions.

365. Mangus, R.L. *Rural Regions of the United States.* Washington, D.C.: Works Progress Administration, 1940.

Economic regionalism from an agrarian perspective, this is a carefully worked division of the United States into thirty-two "rural culture" regions. For related sources see Baker, Haystead and Fite, Lange and Taylor (items 316, 317, 348, 359) and Carl Taylor under Sociology (item 1634).

366. Markusen, Ann R. "Class, Rent and Sectional Conflict: Uneven Development in Western U.S. Boomtowns." *Review of Radical Political Economics* 10 (Fall 1978): 119–29.

Using the economics of western boomtowns in the 1970s as an example, Markusen argues that uneven regional development divides workers across regions and frustrates efforts toward nationwide solidarity and equality.

367. ———. *Profit Cycles, Oligopoly and Regional Development.* Cambridge: MIT Press, 1985.

Pointing out that the prolonged economic slump of heartland industrial regions in advanced capitalist nations over the past fifteen years contradicts standard theories of regional growth, Markusen develops an alternative explanation for this profound economic dislocation. Several important conclusions stand out from her detailed surveys of American regions and their industries: that "dramatic long-run regional change is a normal part of capitalist developmental dynamics"; that oligopoly or the predominance of one or two basic industries in a region is particularly harmful to regional development because it fosters overspecialization at the same time that it crowds out a variety of indigenous industries; and that "new mechanisms for industrial planning" must be developed to counter regional obsolescence and community dislocation that result from "capitalist expansion with its preoccupation with innovation and profitability." A symposium devoted to this important book is contained in *Urban Geography* 8 (March-April 1987), pp. 161–91 with review essays by Robert W. Lake, Gordon L. Clark, John Rees, Rodney A. Erickson, Edward W. Soja, and à response by Markusen.

368. ———. "Regionalism and the Capitalist State: The Case of the United States." *Kapitalistate* 7 (Winter 1979): 39–62. Revised and reprinted in *Urban and Regional Planning in an Age of Austerity,*edited by Pierre Clavel et al., 31–52. New York: Pergamon Press, 1980.

In this perceptive article, Markusen offers a concise summary of Marxist theory of uneven development and its distinction between temporal, sectoral, and spatial inequalities; she reviews the regional concept and its application to the American experience; and she perceptively evaluates the cultural and economic significance of the "new regionalism" of the 1970s. Although there are possible progressive elements in the American regionalism—especially as a model for a decentralized and locally controlled economy—the "new regionalism" functions largely on a cultural level as a nostalgic substitute for working class identity, as "a powerful device for bailing out capitalism yet one more time."

369. ————. *Regions: The Economics and Politics of Territory.* Totowa, N.J.: Rowman and Littlefield, 1987.

This important book presents the political counterpart to the economic analysis developed in *Profit Cycles, Oligopoly, and Regional Development.* Markusen's masterful study of the "construction" and significance of American regions and regionalism is designed to "offer both scholars and regional protagonists some methods of attack which are interdisciplinary, historically minded, and empirically weighed, and which facilitate an evaluation of the human potential of regionalism." Valuable chapters discuss such subjects as "Ten Theses" concerning the making of American regionalism; the economic, political, and cultural foundations of American regions; the history of American regional cultures, movements, and ideas from colonial times to the 1980s; the significance of regionalism as a contemporary socio-political force. A highly perceptive appendix surveys basic approaches to the subject, and a thorough bibliography is included.

370. Massey, Doreen. "Regionalism: Some Current Issues." *Capital and Class* 6 (1978): 106–125.

This detailed survey of radical regional social theory effectively links Marxist theories of uneven development to sociological models of core-periphery and internal colonization in order to understand the significance of ethnic separatist movements.

371. Meyer, John R. "Regional Economics: A Survey." *American Economic Review* 53 (March 1963): 19–54.

In this detailed survey of the rise of a regional economics from the 1940s to the 1960s, Meyer explains the relationship between regional economics and regional science, discusses the public policy applications of these new fields, and evaluates the use of location theory, multiplier theory, input-output analysis, and mathematical programming.

372. Myrdal, Gunnar. *Rich Lands and Poor: The Road to World Prosperity.* New York: Harper and Brothers, 1957.

Published in England in the same year as *Economic Theory and Underdeveloped Regions*, this important book examines regional disparity from two interrelated perspectives: regional economic inequality *within* nations and global inequality *between* nations. "The Drift toward Regional Economic Inequalities in a Country," pp. 23–38, lucidly illustrates how within a free market system disadvantaged areas are preyed upon by more prosperous areas in a cumulative fashion creating expanding negative "backwash effects" in poor regions and positive "spread effects" in rich ones. Such ever-expanding, parasitical imbalance is unhealthy, and, in "The Role of the State," pp. 39–49, Myrdal advocates national planning of a "created harmony" to counteract these forces. "International Inequalities," pp. 50–66, expands the analysis to the level of global economic disparities, pointing out, in part, that regional equalities are even greater in poorer portions of the world than in richer ones.

373. North, Douglass C. "Location Theory and Regional Economic Growth," *Journal of Political Economy* 63 (June 1955): 243–58. Reprinted in *Regional Development and Planning: A Reader* (item 337), 240–55.

After demonstrating that standard theories of regional economic growth have little relevance for American regional development, North proposes a more empirical and historically grounded model for American economists. In addition to delineating economic regions in terms of unifying export bases, North argues that such regions generally pass through five stages of growth, from basic subsistence to a "mature regional economy exporting capital, skills, and specialized services to less-well-developed regions." For a significant debate regarding North's definition of regions in terms of export bases, see Charles M. Tiebout's "Exports and Regional Economic Growth," North's reply, and Tiebout's rejoinder in *Journal of Political Economy* 64 (April 1956). This is also reprinted in Friedmann and Alonso (item 337), pp. 256–65.

374. Perloff, Harvey S. and Lowdon Wingo, Jr. "Natural Resources Endowment and Regional Economic Growth." In *The Art of Planning: Selected Essays of Harvey S. Perloff*, edited by Leland S. Burns and John Friedmann, 166–85. New York: Plenum Press, 1983.

Building upon some of the findings of *Regions, Resources, and Economic Growth* (1960), Perloff and Wingo provide a historical sketch of American regional economic growth, describing a persistent and dynamic relationship between the industrial heartland in the Middle Atlantic-Great Lakes Corridor and the resource-dominant regional hinterlands in the South and West. The analysis of the heartland-hinterland relationship as well as the discussion of how hinterland regions gain greater economic self-sufficiency are valuable contributions to regional economics. Another source by Perloff is listed under Architecture and Planning (item 205).

375. Perloff, Harvey S. et al. *Regions, Resources, and Economic Growth*. Baltimore: Johns Hopkins Univ. Press, 1960.

In this important companion volume to Duncan's study, Perloff and his associates examine the significance of the larger multi-state economic region. Especially useful are the early chapters, pp. 3–62, dealing with the history of regional economic growth and outlining theories—especially the heartland-hinterland concept—to explain this process. See Harvey S. Perloff with Vera W. Dodds, *How a Region Grows: Area Development in the United States Economy* (New York: Committee for Economic Development, 1963) for a condensed, more accessible version of the earlier study.

376. Perroux, Francois. "Economic Space: Theory and Applications." *Quarterly Journal of Economics* 64 (February 1950): 89–104.

This influential critique of the traditional perspective of the nation-state as the essential container of economic activities proposes a more rational, global vision of economic space that might help "resolve *the* problem of our time, that is to say, *transcending the nation and the national economy.*"

377. Perry, David C. and Alfred J. Watkins, eds. *The Rise of the Sunbelt Cities*. Beverly Hills, Calif.: Sage Publications, 1978.

Perceptive essays in this collection include Watkins and Perry's "Regional Change and the Impact of Uneven Urban Development," pp. 19–54; Walt W. Rostow's "Regional Change in the Fifth Kondratieff Upswing" (item 379); and Murray Bookchin's "Toward a Vision of the Urban Future," pp. 259–76.

378. Rifkin, Jeremy and Randy Barbour. *The North Will Rise Again: Pensions, Politics, and Power in the 1980s*. Boston: Beacon Press, 1979.

After chronicling the decline of organized labor as economic power that has shifted south and westward, the authors outline a plan for the revitalization labor and realignment of the economy by placing pension funds under the control of workers. "For union workers facing unemployment lines and for Graybelt states facing severe economic hardships," they write, "the question is whether they will continue to allow their own capital to be used against them or whether they will assert direct control over these funds in order to save their jobs and their communities."

379. Rostow, Walt W. "Regional Change in the Fifth Kondratieff Upswing." In *The Rise of the Sunbelt Cities* (item 377), 83–103.

Based partially upon Kondratieff's belief that capitalist economies pass through fifty- to sixty-year cycles triggered by technological innovations, Rostow's essay is full of pithy observations concerning uneven regional development within both a global and an American context. Rostow traces the roots of the frostbelt to sunbelt powershift to the decentralization of war industries in the 1940s and outlines suggestions for the economic revival of the North.

380. Sawers, Larry and William K. Tabb, eds. *Sunbelt/Snowbelt: Urban Development and Regional Restructuring.* New York: Oxford Univ. Press, 1984.

Most of the contributors to this anthology advocate vigorous public policy and grass roots planning to counter the regional disparities so often generated by the drive for private profit. Perceptive overview essays include David Wilmoth's "Regional Economic Policy and the New Corporatism," pp. 235–58; Goetz Wolf's "Reindustrialization: A Debate Among Capitalists," pp. 259–68; and William K. Tabb's "Economic Democracy and Regional Restructuring: An International Perspective," pp. 403–16. There are also useful discussions of economic development in New England, Houston, the Silicon Valley, Detroit, and England.

381. Schumacher, E.F. *Small is Beautiful: Economics as if People Mattered.* New York: Harper and Row, 1973.

In this influential book, which abounds with decentralist-regional implications, the author declares that "A most important problem in the second half of the twentieth century is the geographical distribution of the population, the question of 'regionalism.' But regionalism, not in the sense of combining states into free-trade systems, but in the opposite sense of developing all the regions within each country." See especially "A Question of Size," pp. 63–75.

382. Schumacher, E.F. with Peter Gillingham. *Good Work.* New York: Harper and Row, 1979.

"Toward a Human-Scale Technology," pp. 23–65, outlines Schumacher's utopian proposal for small-scale, decentralized regional economies.

383. Shackelford, Jean A. *Urban and Regional Economics: A Guide to Information Sources.* Detroit: Gale Research Co., 1980.

Part Two, "Regional Economics," pp. 101–53, is an extensive compilation of scholarship in the areas of regional policy and planning, location theory, and regional models and techniques.

384. Weinstein, Bernard L. and John Rees. "Reaganomics, Reindustrialization, and Regionalism." *Society* 19 (July/August 1982): 33–38.

A succinct analysis of the regional implications of such key elements of Reaganomics as deregulation, supply-side economics, and the New Federalism. Deregulation of energy prices and decentralization of social programs under the New Federalism are likely to increase regional tensions, and supply-side economics is "principally a reiteration of the reindustrialization theme sounded in the last year of the Carter administration." With such policies in place "regional tensions will remain high during the balance of the 1980s" despite the decline of the sun belt-frost belt conflict of the 1970s.

385. ———. "Sunbelt/Frostbelt Confrontation?" *Society* 17 (May/June 1980): 17–21.

After providing a brief summary of regional economic and demographic patterns between 1950 and 1980, the authors foresee a possible "resurgence of sectionalism" based upon conflict over energy resources.

386. Weinstein, Bernard L. and Robert E. Firestine. *Regional Growth and Decline in the United States: The Rise of the Sunbelt and the Decline of the Northeast.* New York: Praeger, 1978.

The most useful portion of this heavily statistical overview of economic and demographic shifts since the 1940s, is "Regional Economic Change in the United States: A Historic and Theoretical Perspective," pp. 44–67, which briefly compares regional development theories of Schumpeter, Myrdal, North, Rostow, and others.

Folk Studies

Folklore has been used as a term for the study of the traditions of oral expressive life. Folklife, emphasizing the study of material culture, is a recent American import, but it has taken on great momentum of its own in the work of such individuals as Fred Kniffen, Don Yoder and Henry Glassie. An older style of folklore/folklife study emphasized cultural survivals in backward areas. Not surprisingly, such an approach went along with the notion of a traditional culture area (see Introduction). The emphasis recently is less upon the "folk" than upon the group, and more upon how folklife functions ("performs") than upon traditional texts and objects in isolation. An older habit of flatly opposing folk to popular culture is being replaced by an interest in how traditional and popular aspects of our culture interrelate. Discussion of "vernacular" housing and "ordinary" landscape are likely to derive from and overlap with subjects that formerly had been subsumed under folk studies. The study of region has shifted accordingly. Region is perceived relatively, in relation to other group loyalties and activities (e.g., under certain circumstances an individual identifies with regional values; under others with, say, occupational values). New and old, folk studies is centrally concerned with cultural persistence and coherence (with "traditionalizing," to use Dell Hymes's word).

The selections below are intended to illustrate the evolution in the last half century, from studies more or less literary in focus (e.g., Walter Blair's book); to the proto-discipline given shape, largely, as relates to American topics, by Richard Dorson; to the more recent developments just described. The selection of entries also illustrates how the discipline remains interdisciplinary: historians (like Joyner), geographers (like Kniffen), and anthropologists (like Rapoport) all make their continuing contributions. Crossovers between language study and folk study are common, and, in matters of theory, more important now than in the past. The selections are also intended to illustrate the current range of subject-matter studied, from barns, to legends, to foodways, to music.

C.M.

387. Abrahams, Roger D. *Deep Down in the Jungle: Negro Narrative from the Streets of Philadelphia.* 2d ed. Chicago: Aldine Publishing Co., 1970.

Originally published in 1963, study of a Philadelphia neighborhood ("Camingerly") as stage for toasts, jokes, verbal contests, and heroes among young black males. The preface to the new edition discusses the many changes since 1963. The emphasis is on performance in an urban setting.

388. ———. "Moving in America." In *Prospects: An Annual of American Culture Studies.* vol. 2, edited by Jack Salzman, 63–82. New York: Burt Franklin, 1977.

Discussion of how values of home, family and place become transvalued by "vanners," retirees on the road devoted to consuming and to camaraderie with their own kind. They emphasize equality and open membership but reject wandering youngsters because they have not "earned" their leisure.

389. Bauman, Richard and Roger D. Abrahams. "American Folklore and American Studies." *American Quarterly* 28 (Bibliography Issue 1976): 360–77.

Argues that there has been a pastoral bias in folklore studies. Folkloristics must be made to suit urban conditions, which can be achieved if focus is on communication and performance. A bibliographical review and essay.

390. Blair, Walter. *Native American Humor (1800–1900).* New York: American Book Co., 1937.

Subject handled historically, with a literary focus. Regional types of humor (Down East, Old Southwest) mature, finding culmination in the artistry of a Mark Twain. The book includes representative selections and a bibliography.

391. Boatright, Mody. *Folk Laughter on the American Frontier.* New York: Collier, 1961.

In the tradition of Walter Blair. The book describes kinds of frontier humor: the boast, Davy Crockett, ridicule of greenhorns, the tall tale, the stump speech, humor in relation to lawyers and ministers, and reckless coinage of words.

392. Botkin, Benjamin A. "The Folk and the Individual: Their Creative Reciprocity." *The English Journal* 27 (February 1938): 121–35.

Botkin wrote scores of essays on regional topics in the 1930s, depicting the common folk as a primal source of creative expression for the individual artist. See Bruce Jackson, ed., *Folklore & Society: Essays in Honor of Benjamin A. Botkin* (Hatboro, Penn.: Folklore Associates, 1966), for bibliography. In the 1940s Botkin published a series of book-length "treasuries" of regional lore, editing books on New England, the South, the West, the Mississippi River and New York City, as well as slave lore and lore about the Civil War.

393. Bronner, Simon J. *Chair Carvers: Old Men Crafting Meaning.* Lexington, Ky.: Univ. Press of Kentucky, 1985.

Studies chair carvers in Southern Indiana, focusing upon how their craft grows out of their life-histories, as well as upon the development of technique, and how the crafting of chairs thereby becomes the crafting of cultural meaning.

394. Brown, Linda Keller and Kay Mussell, eds. *Ethnic and Regional Foodways in the United States: The Performance of Group Identities.* Knoxville: Univ. of Tennessee Press, 1984.

Collection of essays has to do with use of foodways in relation to group (ethnic and regional) identity. Individuals voluntarily subscribe to patterns·of behavior that identify them as members of a group. Foodways is a powerful "marker" in group self-definition. They also serve "rhetorically," in communication with outsiders.

395. Clark, Thomas D. *The Rampaging Frontier: Manners and Humors of Pioneer Days in the South and the Middle West.* Westport, Conn.: Greenwood, 1975.

Originally published in 1964, concentrates on the eastern frontier, up to about 1830. The book draws upon foreign observers, newspapers, and diaries. It discusses humor in relation to hunting, city slickers, travel, outlaws, class differences, and romance.

396. Cochrane, Timothy. "The Concept of Ecotypes in American Folklore." *Journal of Folklore Research* 24 (January-April 1987): 33–55.

Historical review of the concept of ecotypes, from the originator, Carl Wilhelm von Sydow, in 1948, to initial hostility on the part of historical-geographical folklore scholars, to varied use since, by

Dorson, Abrahams and Dundes. Cochrane sees the idea as useful to issues of regional folklore study, and explores how issues of relation between habit and habitat and of diachronic study need further development.

397. ————. "Place, People and Folklore: An Isle Royale Case Study." *Western Folklore* 46 (January 1987): 1–20.

Analyzes narratives of individuals familiar with the fishing culture that developed on Isle Royale, borrowing terminology from humanistic geographers Tuan and Relph. People most attached to the island were least articulate; those used to talking to outsiders were more articulate but less attached. Isle Royale fishing was in process of closing down, so narratives had a special flavor.

398. Dewhurst, C. Kurt and Marsha MacDowell. "Region and Locality." In *American Folk Art: A Guide to Sources*, edited by Simon J. Bronner, 117–38. New York: Garland Press, 1984.

A bibliography emphasizing folk art in more than one medium or genre, in relation to political-geographical and cultural-geographical patterns, including an extended introduction to the subject.

399. Dorson, Richard Mercer. *Bloodstoppers and Bearwalkers: Folk Traditions of the Upper Peninsula*. Cambridge: Harvard Univ. Press, 1952.

A study of the Upper Peninsula in Michigan, an area combining vigorous folklife (frontier, ethnic, occupational) with marginal economic status.

400. ————. *Buying the Wind: Regional Folklore in the United States*. Chicago: Univ. of Chicago Press, 1964.

Amplifies upon Dorson, *American Folklore* (Chicago: Univ. of Chicago Press), chapter 3. The book presents texts derived from oral presentation, from Maine Down Easters, Pennsylvania Dutch, Southern Mountains, Louisiana Cajuns, Illinois Egyptians, Southwest Mexicans, and Utah Mormons.

401. ————. *Folklore and the Historian*. Chicago: Univ. of Chicago Press, 1971.

Collection of Dorson essays, over many years, on connection between folklore and the study of history (oral as against written evidence, research opportunities in folklore, nationalism and folklore, "fakelore," local history, and folklore).

402. ———. *Land of the Millrats*. Cambridge: Harvard Univ. Press, 1981.

Dorson's attempt to describe urban folklore, centering on the Calumet region of Indiana. The book contains chapters on region and lore relating to steelworkers, ethnicity, blacks, and crime. Dorson states interest in landscape and cognitive maps.

403. ———, ed. *Handbook of American Folklore*. Bloomington: Indiana Univ. Press, 1983.

See especially Jan Harold Brunvand, "Regional Folk Speech and Sayings," pp. 201–7; Edward D. Ives, "The Study of Regional Songs and Ballads," pp. 208–15; and William E. Lightfoot, "Regional Folkloristics," pp. 183–93.

404. Evans, E. Estyn. "The Cultural Geographer and Folklife." In *Folklore and Folklife: An Introduction*, edited by Richard M. Dorson, 517–32. Chicago: Univ. of Chicago Press, 1972.

A brief, pithy, gracious statement by an influential European geographer. Evans talks of both Europe and the U.S. cultural geography, he says, studies *genre de vie*. It and folklore share an interest in the detailed study of small areas, e.g., patterns of settlement, patterns of vernacular housing.

404A. Ferris, William R. *Blues from the Delta: An Illustrated Documentary on the Music and Musicians of the Missisippi Delta*. Garden City, N.Y.: Anchor Books, 1979.

Study of Mississippi Delta region as origin of a black musical tradition. The book emphasizes circumstances of performance: social settings, cultural context (in relation to religion, for example), the influence of the record industry, and the relation between generations in terms of music.

405. ———. *Local Color: A Sense of Place in Folk Art*. New York: McGraw-Hill, 1982.

A study of Mississippi folk arts (cane-making, quilting, painting, basket-making, etc.), arguing that black and white artists share a sense of history and place, and that understanding the lives of folk artists is crucial to understanding their art.

406. Glassie, Henry. "Eighteenth-Century Cultural Process in Delaware Valley Folk Housing." *Winterthur Portfolio* 7 (1972): 29–54.

A model study of a region in terms of its vernacular housing. Glassie argues that traditional forms persisted in the Delaware Valley, although disguised. Georgian exteriors (full, two-thirds, one-third) covered Germanic interiors and I-house adaptations of hall-and-parlor houses. The interiors were traditional, the facades "fashionable."

407. ———. *Folk Housing in Middle Virginia: A Structural Study of Historical Artifacts.* Knoxville: Univ. of Tennessee Press, 1975.

A rigorous analysis of the "deep structure" of house forms in up-country Virginia. The structuralist analysis becomes the means for describing a transformation in house form and culture in a given region, as traditional gives way to modern values.

408. ———. "Meaningful Things and Appropriate Myths: The Artifact's Place in American Studies." In *Prospects: An Annual of American Culture Studies.* vol. 3, edited by Jack Salzman, 1–49. New York: Burt Franklin, 1977.

A spirited "Emersonian" plea for seeing history and culture as matters of collective personalities, means people have worked out collectively to give meaning to life. A proper approach is ethnographical; a proper emphasis is upon central myths; a proper subject is vernacular culture and landscape. Person, context and action (informed by a basic drive for freedom) are central to the kind of ethnography Glassie advocates. The theory is worked out in detail in *Passing the Time* (item 409).

409. ———. *Passing the Time in Ballymenone: Culture and History of an Ulster Community.* Philadelphia: Univ. of Pennsylvania Press, 1982.

This model study of a four square mile area in Northern Ireland combines an analysis of folk history and song with an analysis of farm tools, building styles, domestic furnishings, and cooking. Glassie relates the analysis to the Catholic-Protestant struggle and to modernization of the surrounding culture.

410. ———. *Pattern in the Material Folk Culture of the Eastern United States.* Philadelphia: Univ. of Pennsylvania Press, 1968.

Describes regions in terms of material folk culture, emphasizing formal rather than merely functional analysis. This influential book examines house types, outbuildings (especially barns), tools, musical instruments, decoys, etc., mapping distributional patterns. On that basis, it traces diffusion of folk-culture regions from east coast hearths.

411. ——— et al., eds. *Folk Songs and Their Makers.* Bowling Green: Bowling Green Popular Press, 1971.

Three essays on three singers, emphasizing connections between folk and popular sources for repertoire and performance.

412. Green, Archie. *Only a Miner: Studies in Recorded Coal-Mining Songs.* Urbana: Univ. of Illinois Press, 1972.

Discusses miner songs in eastern Kentucky and their relation to the record industry and the larger culture. Green uses "poplore" as a term to describe popular culture picked up by traditional performers. Folklore occurs when any two people share folk forms.

413. ———. "Regionalism Is a Forever Agenda." *The Appalachian Journal* 9 (1982): 172–80.

Final comments in volume devoted to status of Appalachian studies. Green is impressed by the intellectual sophistication of contributors to the book. He sees a need for regionalists to take political stand for appropriate technology, survival, a land ethic, community identity, industrial democracy, diffused power, and participatory government. The study of region should relate to that political agenda.

414. Hufford, Mary. *One Space, Many Places: Folklife and Land Use in New Jersey's Pinelands National Reserve.* Washington, D.C.: American Folklife Center, Library of Congress, 1986.

A sophisticated argument for the importance of folklife studies in regional cultural conservation. The book details how the Pinelands region is understood, named, and used by people native to the area, and how the insider knowledge and practice of old-timers is important to a continuing sense of connectedness with the past and with the region. Good bibliography and good illustrations.

415. Hymes, Dell. "Folklore's Nature and the Sun's Myth." *Journal of American Folklore* 88 (1975): 345–69.

Generally argues the usefulness of linguistic theory for folkloristics. In the process Hymes recommends analysis of "traditionalizing" as a process, to discover the means by which traditions are invented. By studying tradition, we universalize human experience, enter into the life of the traditors, and better understand the consequences of tradition. We should study performance, situation, and creativity.

416. Jones, Michael Owen. "Another America: Toward a Behavioral History Based on Folkloristics." *Western Folklore* 41 (1982): 43–51.

Part of special section on "Historical Methodology in Folkloristics," a critique of Dorson. Dorson studied folklore thematically. Microcosmic study reveals another America than that revealed through themes. There is a new attention to storytelling, dance events, personal experience narratives, networks, etc., that emphasizes that the more specific and localized the study, the greater the subtleties of behavior observed.

417. ———. *The Handmade Object and Its Maker.* Berkeley: Univ. of California Press, 1965.

Study of one chairmaker in Eastern Kentucky, mostly. Jones tries to fully understand how and why particular kinds of chairs are made. The actor, not just the object, and the action, are the focus.

418. Jones, Suzi. "Regionalization: A Rhetorical Strategy." *Journal of the Folklore Institute* 13 (November 1976): 105–20.

Uses concepts from cultural geographers Yi-Fu Tuan and Philip Wagner. Jones urges folklorists to observe how people imbue folklore with meaning from their regional environments, to look for "signs of the local environment in folklore, that is, the regionalization of lore." A critique of Dorson, to which Dorson replies, in "Editor's Comment," *ibid*, pp. 219–20.

419. Jordan, Terry G. *German Seed on Texas Soil: Immigrant Farmers in Nineteenth-Century Texas.* Austin: Univ. of Texas Press, 1966.

Study by a geographer tracing the replication in certain areas of Texas of settlement patterns from western Germany. Jordan studies the size of farms, crops, kinds of productivity, and frequency of ownership. Humid East Texas yields different patterns than the dry West. He theorizes that German practices were abandoned in the first days of settlement, as the price of survival, but that they came back into use once settlement was secure.

420. ———. *Texas Log Buildings: A Folk Architecture.* Austin: Univ. of Texas Press, 1978.

A geographical study of log folk architecture in Texas, tracing subtypes in relation to geographical distribution. Jordan makes out lower southern, upper southern, German, and Anglo-western regions, based upon detailed analysis of notching, the construction of various features (e.g., fireplaces), and outbuildings.

421. Joyner, Charles. *Down by the Riverside: A South Carolina Slave Community.* Urbana: Illinois Univ. Press, 1984.

A study of slave life in All Saints Parish in South Carolina, combining the techniques of the "new" social historian with those of the folklorist. Joyner tries to reconstruct the texture of slave life, including its range of emotions. He examines the process of cultural change over time as the blacks become a single community by a process of creolization. Joyner is trained in history as well as folklore.

422. Kniffen, Fred. "Folk Housing: Key to Diffusion." *Annals of the Association of American Geographers* 55 (December 1965): 549–57.

Argues that folk housing is crucial to the mapping of settlement geography. Folk housing adheres to type and is abundant. Kniffen's subject is the initial occupance in wooded areas up to 1850. He maps paths of diffusion from the east on p. 560. The I-house with an adapted barn occupies a huge area. New England tended to follow popular fashion, except for barns.

423. Lomax, Alan. *Folk Song Style and Culture.* Washington D.C.: American Association for the Advancement of Science, 1968.

An attempt to establish a new science of cantometrics. Lomax analyzes cultures throughout the world by means of study of films and recordings, thus tracing patterns of performance, themes, texts, and movements, then plots out cantometric regions. Specific traits in performance are seen as communications about specific traits of the societies.

424. ———. *The Folk Songs of North America, in the English Language.* New York: Doubleday, 1975.

Originally published in 1960, an encyclopedic collection of collections, many from earlier Lomax books. It is organized regionally, containing 617 songs.

425. Lomax, Alan and Sidney Robertson Colwell, eds. *American Folk Songs and Folk Lore: A Regional Bibliography.* New York: Hinds, Hayden and Eldredge, 1942.

In addition to listing sources of information about at least ten folk regions ranging from New England to the Appalachians and Ozarks to the Spanish Southwest, this pamphlet also contains bibliographies of general folksong collections and folklore scholarship.

426. Marshall, Howard Wight. *American Folk Architecture: A Selected Bibliography*. Washington, D.C.: American Folklife Center, Library of Congress, 1981.

A wide-ranging listing of sources on its subject, with a useful general introduction, organized under five headings: theory and general works, antecedents of American building, regional works, museums and historic preservation, and field documentation.

427. ———. *Folk Architecture in Little Dixie: A Regional Culture in Missouri*. Columbia: Univ. of Missouri Press, 1981.

Studies an eight-county area southwest of Hannibal, which combines midwest with southern building types (houses and barns). Migrants to the area come from Virginia, North Carolina and Kentucky. The final chapter on "Architecture and Sense of Place," pp. 105–115, summarizes what region means ("insider" notions, vague in boundaries, are quietly persistent). Good bibliography.

428. Marshall, Howard Wight and John Michael Vlach. "Toward a Folklife Approach to American Dialects." *American Speech* 48 (1973): 163–91.

Argues that folklife and dialect study reinforce one another. The emphasis is upon Indiana, but the essay involves discussion as to how historical movements, dialect, and folklife interrelate (e.g., how a middle southern corridor of dialect conforms to a route followed by hog drivers to the deep South).

429. Montell, William Lloyd. *Don't Go Up Kettle Creek: Verbal Legacy of the Upper Cumberland*. Knoxville: Univ. of Tennessee Press, 1983.

An interweaving of "traditional" and "personal" oral narratives about the past of a distinct cultural region.

430. ———. *The Saga of Coe Ridge*. Knoxville: Univ. of Tennessee Press, 1970.

History of a rural and isolated black community as determined by its oral traditions. Montell argues that because it was isolated, the oral tradition of the community had special force. He attempts to determine which traditions are most useful in determining the likely course of history (viz., those evidencing widespread agreement among variant social groups).

431. Nicolaisen, W.F.H. "Variant, Dialect and Region." *New York Folklore* 6 (Winter 1980): 137–49.

Argues for use of linguistic terms in folkloristics, with "register" (use in certain situations) and "isogloss" (boundaries of usage patterns) examples in point. "Dialect" applies to material culture as well as to language.

432. ———. "Folklore and Geography: Toward an Atlas of American Folk Culture." *New York Folklore Quarterly* 29 (March 1973): 3–20.

An appeal to folklorists to trace systematically the spatial distribution of traditional lore and material culture in order to map various folk regions. See also "The Folk and the Region," *New York Folklore* 2 (Winter 1976), pp. 143–49, which introduces folklorists to Odum and Moore's definition of region as well as to the distinction between formal and functional regions.

433. Rapoport, Amos. *House Form and Culture*. Englewood Cliffs, N.J.: Prentice-Hall, 1969.

An influential work by an anthropologist and planner, analyzing the home as a cultural product, focusing upon preindustrial housing. Home bespeaks the human need for security, visual and social complexity, and communication. In Latin cultures, settlement is primary, housing secondary; in our culture, housing is primary, settlement secondary.

434. Stoeltje, Beverly J. "A Helpmate for Man Indeed: The Image of the Frontier Woman." In *Women and Folklore*, edited by Claire R. Farrer, Austin: Univ. of Texas Press, 1975.

In the folklore of the West, types of women are paired off against types of men: the refined lady with the cowboy, helpmate with the settler, and bad woman with bad man. Stories and songs are used as evidence.

435. Swaim, Doug, ed. *Carolina Dwelling: Towards Preservation of Place*. [Raleigh]: North Carolina State Univ.: Student Publication, 1978.

Model survey of North Carolina from east to west, with attention to house types, tobacco barns, churches, siting of farms, and unusual building complexes.

436. Titon, Jeff. *Early Downhome Blues: A Musical and Cultural Analysis.* Champaign: Univ. of Illinois Press, 1977.

Down-home music was sung by males to neighbors (as against vaudeville blues, usually sung by women to commercial audiences). The music comes from the Mississippi Delta. Chapters deal with sense of place, singers, songs, the race record industry, and musicology.

437. Toelken, Barre. "Northwest Regional Folklore." In *Northwest Perspectives: Essays on the Culture of the Pacific Northwest,* edited by Ewin R. Bingham and Glen A. Love, 21–42. Seattle: Univ. of Washington Press, 1979.

Regional folklore emerges when people share regionally specific cultural postulates: it is dynamic and changing, generally conservative. Regional is one kind of folklore, occupation another, etc. The focus is on the Pacific Northwest.

438. Upton, Dell. "The Power of Things: Recent Studies in American Vernacular Culture." *American Quarterly* 35 (1983): 262–79.

The best recent bibliographical review of the literature on vernacular architecture and landscape.

439. Upton, Dell and John Michael Vlach, eds. *Common Places: Readings in American Vernacular Architecture.* Athens: Univ. of Georgia Press, 1985.

A superb anthology of classic essays representing many disciplines but sharing a common focus. See especially "Introduction," pp. xiii-xxiv, where the editors argue for a definition of vernacular architecture and landscape studies that takes off from language studies (a subtype of house can be seen as a "dialectal" form of that house).

440. Vlach, John Michael. *Afro-American Tradition in the Decorative Arts.* Cleveland: Cleveland Museum of Art, 1978.

An examination of the interplay between African and American tradition as represented in the crafts: baskets, quilts, ironwork, houses, and boats. The book is richly illustrated.

441. ———. *Charleston Blacksmith: The Work of Philip Simmons.* Athens: Univ. of Georgia Press, 1981.

Combines field notes and interviews with close analysis of Simmons's work, interrelating Afro-American decorative arts traditions and the Charleston milieu. The idea is to integrate the craft, the craftsman, and the product. A portfolio of Simmons's work is included.

442. Yoder, Don, ed. *American Folklife.* Austin: Univ. of Texas Press, 1976.

Folklife denotes artifacts as against the emphasis in folklore upon the spoken word. Yoder's lead article, pp. 3–18, calls folklife "regional ethnography." The need in that kind of study is to accumulate "micro-regional-ethnological studies" amassing detail. Such an examination must have a historical dimension, in the tradition of American Studies. The article ends with a good bibliography. The book includes essays on boats, coil basketry, tollgates, and New Year customs.

443. ———. "Historical Sources for American Traditional Cookery." *Pennsylvania Folklore* 22 (1971): 16–29.

Examines Pennsylvania German cookery in relation to the experience of migration, acculturation to the dominant culture, a general dietary profile, the effect of the temperance crusade, and the interchange between Pennsylvania Germans and Philadelphia. Yoder discusses more generally the problems of cookery research and the values and problems of historical research of the subject, and proposes a model for a regional archive of traditional cookery.

Geography

Geographers have contributed more to regional studies than any other scholars, for understanding the natural and cultural variations of the earth's surface lies at the heart of their discipline. All fields of knowledge, as we have seen, are affected by the spatial variations of experience and are involved with the basic fact that land and life differ from place to place. The explicit study of spatial variation, however, is geography's primary responsibility and its very reason for being.

The regional essence of the discipline has been underscored by many, including Carl Sauer who defined geography as "the study of the areal or habitat differentiation of the earth" and Richard Hartshorne who perceived it as the "description and interpretation of the variable character of the earth's surface."[1] Others have been even more forthcoming, declaring, for example, that "the regional concept constitutes the core of geography" or that "geography is the art of recognizing and describing the personality of regions."[2] After asserting that the "study of areas" is geography's central responsibility and justification for existence, John Fraser Hart has argued that "Regional geography, the skillful description of areas and places, is the highest form of the geographer's art."[3]

All students of regionalism are indebted, in one way or another, to geographical scholarship, for it contains both the foundation and the cutting edge of regional inquiry. American geographers, immersed in a continent-sized nation bristling with physical and cultural diversities, have devoted much energy to defining regions and explaining the many spatial configurations of their culture. From Jedidiah Morse's tripartite division of the United States into northern, middle, and southern regions in the late eighteenth century to intricate schemes of interlocking hierarchies of nodal regions in the late twentieth century, American geographers have searched for spatial order. A complete list of their efforts would easily fill several large volumes. Because of this almost unmanageable wealth of material, the following bibliography is highly selective and is divided into four categories.

The first category concentrates on *region as concept* and includes basic geographical sources that define regions and regionalism, examine theories and methods of regionalization, and discuss the causes and significance of regionalism in American culture. Moving beyond regionalism as a general conceptual issue, the other categories examine *region as an object of study* and focus upon specific ways of analyzing areal differentiation: through the study of regional perception in terms of mental or cognitive maps, through the study of landscape and settlement, and through the distribution of social variables.

M.S

---

[1]Carl O. Sauer, "The Morphology of Landscape" (1925), ed. John Leighly in *Land and Life: A Selection from the Writings of Carl Ortwin Sauer* (Berkeley: Univ. of California Press, 1863), 316; Richard Hartshorne, *Perspective on the Nature of Geography* (Chicago: Rand McNally, 1959), 21.

[2]Preston James, "Toward a Further Understanding of the Regional Concept," *Annals of the Association of American Geographers* 42 (September 1952): 195; E.W. Gilbert, "Geography and Regionalism," ed. Griffith Taylor, *Geography in the Twentieth Century* (New York: Philosophical Library, 1951), p. 346. See Neven Fenneman, "The Circumference of Geography," *Annals of the Association of American Geographers* 9 (March 1919): 3–11, for an even earlier discussion of "regional geography as the core of the science."

[3]John Fraser Hart, "The Highest Form of the Geographer's Art," *Annals of the Association of American Geographers* 72 (March 1982): 1 and "Introduction," ed. John Fraser Hart in *Regions of the United States* (New York: Harper and Row, 1972), n. p.

Geography: Region as Concept

A firm theoretical foundation and sharp conceptual vision are essential to understanding a subject as pervasive and amorphous as regionalism. More than any other field, geography provides the conceptual orientation and starting point necessary for regional studies. More than other scholars, theoretically inclined geographers provide an understanding of the fundamental impulse behind all regional inquiry.

Curious about the rich variability of land and life—by the fact that every place on earth is distinct, its physical, organic, and cultural features woven in a matchless pattern—students of regionalism are immediately challenged by theoretical questions concerning spatial diversity. The bewildering profusion of people and place evokes a desire for order and a search for explanatory patterns and configurations in the landscape. Order is achieved by segmenting space into regions: by mentally drawing boundaries around portions of the earth's surface that seem to stand apart from other areas. Regions, as many geographers have pointed out, are ultimately *mental* constructs satisfying a human rage for order. Commenting on our "exceptional fondness for cutting up space,"Yi-Fu Tuan has observed that "Boundaries satisfy because they contain. In the attempt to discern pattern, people feel uncomfortable with things that have fuzzy edges."[1]

This process of segmentation or regionalization is an essential yet endlessly intricate human activity, for countless types and sizes of regions can be created according to countless characteristics. Although one may begin by perceiving regions as the most significant spatial-cultural divisions of modern nations, further thought reveals a more complex and ambiguous picture. We have already seen, for example, how academic disciplines partition space in a variety of ways according to a variety of subjects: how anthropologists create culture areas, economists map the distribution of material wealth, folklorists describe spatial patterns of oral expression, and so on. All people, furthermore, divide the world into innumerable compartments: into private, public, and sacred realms; into personal property, neighborhoods, communities, and states; into places for work, consumption, worship, and play. Geographers, whose explicit subject matter is regionalism or the phenomenon of areal differentiation, provide a larger understanding of this human impulse and a theoretical overview of the regional perspectives of particular disciplines.

In addition to imparting a wider understanding of regionalism as a general concept and impulse, the sources in this section also accomplish three specific tasks. First, a large number of entries are concerned with problems of *definition*: with defining region and regionalism in general, with outlining schemes of regionalization, and with explaining particular regional types—including natural, cultural, formal, functional, vernacular, voluntary, and world culture regions. (An increasingly important type of region—the symbolic or perceptual region—is treated separately in the next section.)

A second, highly selective, group of sources in this section explores possible *causes* of regionalism. To explain the fact of regional variations in culture, one is forced to examine the relationship between land and life, between physical environment and culture. In addition to understanding basic theories of the culture/nature relationship such as environmental determinism, possibilism, and probabilism, one must also consider more subjective causes of regionalism, particularly the affective bonds between people and place—what might be called sense of place or topophilia—as well the human propensity for segmenting space. References to George Perkins Marsh, Ellen Churchill Semple, Paul Vidal de la Blache, Carl Sauer, Robert Platt, and others trace the historical development of regional-environmental theory. References in this and other sections to Pierce Lewis, Yi-Fu Tuan, Edward Relph, Thomas Saarinen, David Lowenthal, Anne Buttimer, David Seamon, and others explore the more subjective sources of regionalism.

A final group of materials explores the general *significance* of regionalism in geography in particular and in American culture in general. For much of this century, the region has sparked intense, often polemical, debate in which it has been exalted as the pinnacle of geographical scholarship and also scorned as childish doodling. Regional champions and detractors from both sides of the Atlantic are included in this list, and their continuing debate has generated a profound intellectual legacy for all students of regionalism. In the work of Nevin Fenneman, Harlan Barrows, Carl Sauer, Richard Hartshorne, Walter Kollmorgen, Edward Ackerman, Fred Schaefer, Derwent Whittlesey, E.W. Gilbert, George Kimble, Preston James, and others, one can outline the rise and decline of regional geography between the 1920s and the 1950s. The work of Philip Wagner, D.W. Meinig, R.J.

Johnston, Derek Gergory, Leonard Guelke, Yi-Fu Tuan, John Fraser Hart, Wilbur Zelinsky, and others indicates renewed interest in and refinement of regional concepts since the 1960s. A smaller group of geographers—including J. Trenton Kostbade, W.R. Mead, J.H. Paterson, S.W. Woolridge, Bob J. Walter, and Frank E. Bernard—contribute spirited defenses of the teaching of regional geography.

M.S.

---

[1] Yi-Fu Tuan, "Continuity and Discontinuity," *Geographical Review* 74 (July 1984): 248.

*   *   *

444. Ackerman, Edward A. "Regional Research—Emerging Concepts and Techniques in the Field of Geography." *Economic Geography* 29 (July 1953): 189–97.

After asserting that geographers "reach their highest good in the contribution they make to a final understanding of regions—regions as part of man's life and activity on earth,"Ackerman advocates more systematic regional analysis through several concepts and methods. Geographers must use historical understanding of the evolution of a region to help plan future regional growth. They must also develop more precise models of regional hierarchies, develop quantitative techniques, focus upon key features or topical specialties within regions rather than attempt to complete regional description, explore the significance of nodal regions, and make cross-regional comparisons.

445. Barrows, Harlan. "Geography as Human Ecology." *Annals of the Association of American Geographers* 13 (March 1923): 1–14.

Barrows argues that the distinctive domain of geography is human ecology or the study of the "mutual relations between man and his natural environment." Geography's primary concern is the cultural rather than the natural landscape, and regional cultural geography ought to be the "culminating branch of the science." Building upon Neven Fenneman's assertion that "the center of geography is the study of areas,"Barrows advances the idea that "the center of geography is the study of human ecology in specific areas."

446. Berry, Brian J.L. "Approaches to Regional Analysis: A Synthesis." *Annals of the Association of American Geographers* 54

(March 1964): 2–11. Reprinted in Berry, Brian J.L. and Duane F. Marble, eds. *Spatial Analysis: A Reader in Statistical Geography*, 24–34. Englewood Cliffs, N.J.: Prentice-Hall, 1968.

Berry outlines a possible creative partnership between traditional regional geography and regional science by developing a three-dimensional matrix considering place, characteristics, and time. Describing the possible rapport between regional and systematic or topical concerns, he argues that "neither a topical specialty nor a study of a particular region can be sufficient unto itself. More profound understanding of spatial associations can only come from comparative systematics cutting across several topical fields, from an understanding of local variables, and from an appreciation of the development of patterns through time." See Berry's "Cities as Systems Within Systems of Cities,"*Regional Science Association Papers* 13 (1964) pp. 147–63, for a related argument.

447. Birkenhauer, Josef. "Notes Toward a Transformed Regional Geography: A West German View."*Geography* 71 (April 1986): 131–35.

In this incisive survey of crucial flaws of regional geography as practiced in England, France, and Germany, Birkenhauer argues that "the notion of 'region' . . . is nothing but a cognitive concept used by the human mind to cut a defined track through a vast potential of variables. As a concept of the mind, 'region' can never be applied to the totality of an area." In place of the impossible goal of comprehensive regions, he calls for a fresh notion of "territorial geography"with a system of six "regional types"encompassing vital human uses of the earth.

448. Dickinson, Robert E. *City and Region: A Geographical Approach.* London: Routledge and Kegan Paul, 1964.

In this detailed discussion of the changing relationship between regions, cities, and metropolitan areas in Western Europe and the United States, Dickinson synthesizes an impressive range of geographical and planning theory.

449. ———. *Regional Concept: The Anglo-American Leaders.* London: Routledge and Kegan Paul, 1976.

Dickinson pieces together the history of various strains of regional thought in England and America from the 1880s until the 1960s through the biographies of more than fifty regional theorists including Patrick Geddes, Halford Mackinder, Andrew Herbertson, William Morris

Davis, Ellen Churchill Semple, Isaiah Bowman, Carl Sauer, John Leighly, John K. Wright, Robert Platt, Preston James, and others.

450. ————. *Regional Ecology: The Study of Man's Environment.* New York: John Wiley and Sons, 1970.

A wide-ranging, interdisciplinary outline of the history, theory, and practice of regionalism, this book is particularly useful as an introduction to the immense breadth of regional thinking. Especially useful are "Regional Units and Regional Systems,"pp. 41–63, with its succinct discussion of the regional concept; "Regionalization of Social Processes,"pp. 77–89; and "The Regional Concept in Education,"pp. 167–186.

451. Dunbar, Gary S. "Geographical Personality." In *Geoscience and Man.* vol. 5, edited by H.J. Walker and W.G. Haag, 25–33. Baton Rouge: School of Geoscience, Louisiana State Univ., 1974.

A perceptive survey of the rise and decline of theories of "regional personality"from Michelet and Vidal in the nineteenth century to H.J. Fleure, Cyril Fox, Estyn Evans, E.W. Gilbert, Carl Sauer, Jean Gottmann, and other geographers into the late twentieth century. For closely related sources see Finch, Gilbert, Hall, and Hartshorne in this section (items 455, 457, 458, 463, 466–467) and Campbell, Rubenstein and others under Psychology (items 1489, 1523).

452. English, Paul Ward and Robert C. Mayfield. "The Region." In *Man, Space, and Environment: Concepts in Contemporary Human Geography,* 425–28. New York: Oxford Univ. Press, 1972.

This effective overview of the long-standing debate among geographers concerning the existence and nature of regions wisely concludes that the "region is a spatial definition by the mind, not an objective reality."

453. Entrikin, J. Nicholas. "Philosophical Issues in the Scientific Study of Regions."In *Geography and the Urban Environment.* vol. 4, edited by D.T. Herbert and R.J. Johnston, 1–27. Chichester: John Wiley, 1981.

After carefully examining the positivist critique of regional geography that was mounted during the 1950s and 1960s, Entrikin describes how the tone of geographical debate shifted by the 1970s to an anti-positivist position encouraging once again the study of "historically specific regions." This essay contains detailed analyses of the philosophical orientations of regional geographers Hartshorne, Gregory, and Guelke and their critics Schaefer and Harvey. Other sources by Entrikin are listed under Philosophy and Religion (items 1352–1353).

454. Fenneman, Nevin M. "The Circumference of Geography." *Annals of the Association of American Geographers* 9 (March 1919): 3–11.

Fenneman argues that regional geography is the "core"of geography and that the discipline ought to open out from that center to other academic fields. After arguing that "Without regional geography there is no reason why geography should be treated as a separate discipline,"Fenneman sketches the creative relationship between geography thus defined and other natural and social sciences.

455. Finch, Vernon. "Written Structures for Presenting the Geography of Regions." *Annals of the Association of American Geographers* 24 (June 1934): 113–20.

A prime example of the belief in the existence of all-purpose "organic"regions that motivated many American geographers during the interwar decades, this essay proposes an ingenious classification system of four regional types ranged in a continuum from regions dominated by nature to regions dominated by culture. Finch argues that "a geographic region, or even an arbitrarily chosen portion of the earth's surface, may be thought of as having some of the qualities of a human being. It is a thing ... with physical and cultural elements so interwoven as to give individualism to the organism." See Dunbar, Gilbert, Hall, Hartshorne, and Vidal in this section for closely related discussions of organic regions and regional personality (items 451, 457–458, 463, 466–467, 523).

456. Fisher, C.A. "Whither Regional Geography?" *Geography* 55 (1970): 373–89.

Fisher reviews the sources of twentieth century regional geography in the works of Ratzel, Vidal, and Herbertson and urges geographers to utilize this ever vital body of scholarship.

457. Gilbert, E.W. "Geography and Regionalism." In *Geography in the Twentieth Century*. 3d ed., edited by Griffith Taylor, 345–71. New York: Philosophical Library, 1957.

After succinctly tracing the meanings of "region"and "regionalism,"Gilbert vigorously argues that "It is through the region that new life has been given to the dead bones of geography"and that "geography is the art of recognizing and describing the personalities of regions." Fairly thorough discussions of the significance of political and cultural regionalism in France, Germany, Spain and Portugal, Great Britain, and the United States are included.

458. ———. "The Idea of the Region." *Geography* 45 (1960): 157–75.

In this effective response to Kimble's critique of the regional concept, Gilbert vividly traces the history of regionalism and its relationship to nationalism and suggests, in part, that regional geographers might learn more from regional novelists who evoke "a living picture of the unity of place and people"than they might learn from regional scientists. For closely related arguments in this chapter, see Hart, James, Kimble, Leighly, Paterson, and Spate (items 465, 469–472, 479, 484, 496, 513).

459. Gregory, Derek. *Ideology, Science and Human Geography*. New York: St. Martin's Press, 1978.

After underscoring many of the weaknesses of the positivist-systematic paradigm in geography, Gregory urges geographers to consider the reflexive, phenomenological aspects of human interaction with space and the regional structures within which this takes place. Geographers, he argues, "need to know more about the constitution of *regional* social formations, of *regional* articulations and *regional* transformations,"and doing so they reaffirm "geography's long-standing commitment to places and the people that live in them or to the regional structures which persist in contemporary economies."

460. Grigg, David. "The Logic of Regional Systems." *Annals of the Association of American Geographers* 55 (September 1965): 373–89. Reprinted in *Man, Space, and Environment*, edited by Paul Ward English and Robert C. Mayfield, 450–81. New York: Oxford Univ. Press, 1972.

After describing the need for a universal system of regional classification and division, Griggs carefully uses ten principles of classification derived from the work of logicians and taxonomists to construct a consistent system of regionalization. See Philbrick in this chapter for a closely related argument (item 498).

461. ——. "Regions, Models and Classes." In *Models in Geography*, edited by Richard J. Chorley and Peter Haggett, 462–509. London: Methuen and Co., 1967.

In addition to elaborating generic principles of regionalization applicable to all disciplines concerned with areal differentiation, this essay contains a detailed history of the regional concept among French, English, Russian, and American social scientists from the early nineteenth to the mid-twentieth century. An extensive bibliography is included.

462. Guelke, Leonard. "Regional Geography." *Professional Geographer* 29 (February 1977): 1–7.

After discussing the fate of the regional concept from Hartshorne's seminal work in the 1930s and 1940s to the rise of systematic geography in the 1950s and 1960s, Guelke suggests, among other things, that closer attention to the historical dimension in geography might reinvigorate the regional concept.

463. Hall, Robert B. "The Geographical Region: A Resumé." In Special Issue. "A Conference on Regions." *Annals of the Association of American Geographers* (item 514), 122–30.

In addition to being an extremely insightful survey of the growth of the regional concept in American geography, Hall's essay underscores the belief that regions exist as distinct entities—as organisms with individual characteristics and personalities. For closely related arguments, see Dunbar, Finch, Gilbert, Hartshorne, and Vidal in this chapter (items 451, 455, 457–458, 466–467, 523).

464. Hare, F. Kenneth. "Man's World and Geographers: A Secular Sermon." In *Geographic Humanism, Analysis, and Social Action: Proceedings of a Symposia Celebrating a Half Century of Geography at Michigan*. Michigan Geographical Publication no. 17. Edited by Donald R. Deskins et al., 259–73. Ann Arbor: Univ. of Michigan, Department of Geography, 1977.

This academic jeremiad urges geographers to move beyond "inward-looking navel-gazing"and become more engaged in environmental issues and politics. More specifically, Hare advocates a return to the basic study of the interaction between culture and nature, a deeper understanding of biological-ecological theory, a cultivation of regional understanding, and greater involvement in environmental and regional politics. "Another perspective that we have almost lost, because we listened to methodological exorcists,"Hare warns, "is that of regional synthesis. In politics and environmental management it is very much alive. Trying to demonstrate that regions are some kind of organic reality almost emasculated the (geographical) profession. Realizing that regional perspectives are necessary in politics is to get one's manhood back."

465. Hart, John Fraser. "The Highest Form of the Geographer's Art." *Annals of the Association of American Geographers* 72 (March 1982): 1–29.

In this seminal and wide-ranging essay, Hart champions regional description and analysis as the paragon of geographical scholarship. In the process of describing the region and regional concept as unifying themes for the discipline of geography, he examines many other vital issues, including the relationship between systematic and regional concerns; the tension between quantification and art in geography; the need for fieldwork in regional geography that encompasses a sense of the past and sensitivity to the values of non-academic, "ordinary"people; and the need to visualize the city as a regional subject. Concerning the vexing question of regional definition, Hart argues that "Regions are subjective artistic devices, and they must be shaped to fit the hand of the individual user. There can be no standard definition of a region, and there can be no universal rules for recognizing, delimiting, and describing regions."See Gilbert, Hare, Johnston, Leighly, Paterson, and Spate for directly related sources (items 457–458, 464, 475–477, 484, 496, 513).

466. Hartshorne, Richard. *The Nature of Geography: A Critical Survey of Current Thought in Light of the Past*. Lancaster, Penn.: Association of American Geographers, 1949. Originally published in *Annals of the Association of American Geographers* 29 (1939): 173–658.

This densely researched, brilliantly argued monograph remains an indispensable resource for any serious student of regionalism. This book contains the most thorough account available of the development of regional thought among French, English, American, and especially German geographers; it also offers continually perceptive advice regarding the elusive nature of the region. Valuable portions include "The Nature of Geography According to Its Historical Development,"pp. 35–101, which outlines the history of the regional concept; "The Justification for the Historical Concept of Geography as a Chorographic Science,"pp. 130–48, which asserts the primacy of regional analysis in geography; "'Landschaft' and 'Landscape',"pp. 149–74, which clarifies semantic difficulties surrounding these words; and, especially, "The Concept of the Region as a Concrete Unit Object,"pp. 250–84 and "Methods of Organizing the World Into Regions,"pp. 285–365, in which Hartshorne vigorously argues that the earth is not a mosaic of distinct organic regions, and that geographers "divide the world arbitrarily into areal parts"as a device for understanding, not as a map of reality.

467. ———— . *Perspective on the Nature of Geography*. Chicago: Rand McNally, 1959.

Two chapters are particularly relevant to regional theory: "What Is Meant by Geography as the Study of Areal Differentiation?"pp. 12–21 and "Is Geography Divided Between 'Systematic' and 'Regional' Geography?"pp. 108–45. In the latter, Hartshorne carefully outlines a productive working relationship between perspectives that often seem at odds; he also connects more recent research in regional hierachies, formal and functional regions, to his earlier view of the function of regional geography.

468. Herbertson, A.J. "The Major Natural Regions: An Essay in Systematic Geography." *Geographical Journal* 25 (March 1905): 300–12.

An early and influential effort to perceive the earth's surface as a mosaic of natural regions rather than nations. Herbertson's ambitious definition of the natural region as "the complex of land, water, air, plant, animal, and man, regarded in their special relationship as together constituting a definite characteristic portion of the Earth's surface"represents a strain of regional theory. For closely related discussions of "natural regions,"see Powell, Roxby, and Unstead in this chapter (items 502, 504, 522).

469. James, Preston E. "The Concept of Occupied Space." In *All Possible Worlds: A History of Geographical Ideas*, 457–82. New York: Odyssey Press, 1972.

This impressive survey of the regional concept in the twentieth century, focuses upon problems with the "mosaic of spaces"approach and refinements brought by post World War II criticisms. James's book also contains a valuable bibliography.

470. ———— . "The World and Its Regions."Part III in *On Geography: Selected Writings of Preston E. James*, edited by D.W. Meinig, 280–319. Syracuse: Syracuse Univ. Press, 1971.

This collection of James's essays regarding world culture regions demonstrates the increasing complexity of the regional concept from the 1930s to the 1960s. An especially imaginative framework of global regionalization is outlined in "World Culture Regions and Revolutionary Change"(1964), pp. 314–19, and further theoretical discussion of this scheme is found in P.E. James and T.J. Wilbanks, "World Culture Regions and Patterns of Change,"*Proceedings of the Association of American Geographers* 2 (1970), pp. 77–81.

471. ———— . "The Region as a Concept." *Geographical Review* 52 (January 1962): 127–29.

James's appreciative review of Gilbert's "The Idea of the Region"(1960) ends with a plea for reconciliation between "geography conceived as a science and geography conceived as an art"despite the fact that "the great majority of those who have mastered the mathematical methods cannot use the English language effectively, and most of those who have some facility with language are left speechless in the presence of multiple regressions."

472. ————. "Toward a Further Understanding of the Regional Concept." *Annals of the Association of American Geographers* 42 (September 1952): 195–222. Reprinted in *On Geography: Selected Writings of Preston E. James*, edited by D.W. Meinig, 78–116. Syracuse: Syracuse Univ. Press, 1971.

After asserting that "The regional concept constitutes the core of geography,"James carefully describes the ever increasing sophistication of regional theory during the first half of the twentieth century. The region will remain the "common denominator"of geography if it is perceived as a mental construct rather than an objective reality and if regional geographers push beyond simple description to the more complex task of explaining underlying processes—a task which may require a certain amount of topical specialization.

473. Joerg, W.L.G. "The Geography of North America: A History of its Regional Exposition." *Geographical Review* 26 (October 1936): 640–63.

After stressing that the "real mainsprings"of regional theory and method are rooted in European geography—especially in the work of Vidal, Ratzel, and their followers in France and Germany—Joerg discusses the applications of these ideas to the North American continent. The concept of geographical personality is discussed and a detailed bibliography is included.

474. ———— . "The Subdivision of North America Into Natural Regions: A Preliminary Inquiry." *Annals of the Association of American Geographers* 4 (1914): 55–83.

Joerg describes the surge of interest in delimiting North American "natural regions" that began in the 1880s and prefigured interest in "cultural regions"that would develop after World War I. Scores of regional divisions are analyzed—including those of John Wesley Powell, Mark Jefferson, and William Morris Davis. A useful bibliography and a series of maps are included.

475. Johnston, R.J. and P.J. Taylor, eds. *A World in Crisis? Geographical Perspectives.* New York: Basil Blackwell, 1986.

Many of the essays in this useful anthology apply Immanual Wallerstein's influential world-systems model to regional theory in geography. Essays directly relevant to regional theory within a global framework include Richard Peet's "The Destruction of Regional Cultures"(item 117); Colin H. Wilson's "The Question of National Congruence,"pp. 196–230, which analyzes the tension between state nationalism and ethnic regionalism throughout the world; and Peter J. Taylor's "The World-Systems Project,"pp. 269–88, which carefully discusses the geographical implications of Wallerstein's theory. Extensive bibliographies are included. For closely related sources, see Peet and Wolf under Anthropology (items 117, 145), Braudel under History: Region as Concept (item 798), and Hechter and Wallerstein under Sociology (items 1575–1576, 1642–1643).

476. Johnston, R.J. *Geography and Geographers: Anglo-American Human Geography Since 1945.* 2d ed. London: Edward Arnold, 1983.

This text, especially "Foundations,"pp. 37–49, and "The Growth of Systematic Studies and the Adoption of 'Scientific Method,'"50–93, contains an unusually thorough and perceptive account of the fate of regionalism in English and American geography in the 1940s, 1950s, 1960s, and 1970s. An extensive bibliography is included.

477. ———— . "To the Ends of the Earth." *The Future of Geography*, 326–38. New York: Methuen, 1985.

In this strongly worded essay, Johnston condemns the universalizing reductionism of systematic or positivist geography and champions a fresh commitment to the study of regional diversity throughout the world—an orientation that will foster multicultural sensitivity and appreciation of "the richness of the world's mosaic." Arguing that "without re-engagement with the complexity and variety of the world, geographers will contribute to the ultimate demise of the world,"Johnston promotes instead "a discipline which recognizes and emphasizes the variety of human responses to environment, space, place, and different people and which presents the world as a complex mosaic of different places, not as a series of examples of some general models of behavior."

478. Juillard, Etienne. "The Region: An Essay of Definition." In *Man, Space, and Environment*, edited by Paul Ward English and Robert C. Mayfield, 429–41. New York: Oxford Univ. Press, 1972.

Reflecting French geographical tradition and experience, Juillard develops a definition of region based upon a functional organization of urban cores and peripheral networks. Observing that in common usage "the region is a territorial subdivision ... placed after the state in the hierarchy,"Juillard defines the region as a subnational entity "endowed with a certain self-sufficiency ... in the sense that most of the functions and services of primary importance are represented there in such a way that the region is capable of satisfying most of the needs of its inhabitants."

479. Kimble, George H.T. "The Inadequacy of the Regional Concept." *In London Essays in Geography*, edited by Lawrence Dudley Stamp and Sidney William Woolridge, 151–74. London: Longmans, Green and Co., 1951.

While vigorously attacking the regional concept on a number of fronts—that regionalism is largely an eighteenth century concept applicable only to "fossil"medieval communities and that "Man's 'region' is now the world,"that the earth's surface is too complex to be divided into a simple matrix of regions, that complete description or understanding of any portion of the earth is impossible, and that regional geographers are often mere doodlers "trying to put boundaries that do not exist around areas that do not matter"—Kimble admits that regional study can have substantial merit as a personal work of art whose value lies "in the realm of illumination and suggestion rather than definitive analysis and synthesis." See Kollmorgen and Wrigley for closely related criticisms (items 481, 530).

480. Kohn, C.F. "Regions and Regionalizing." *Journal of Geography* 69 (1970): 134–40.

A straightforward discussion of three basic regional models—the formal or uniform region, the functional or nodal region, and the worldwide functional region—with suggestions for teaching these concepts more effectively.

481. Kollmorgen, Walter M. "Crucial Deficiencies of Regionalism." *American Economic Review* 35 (May 1945): 377–89.

In this scathing indictment that transcends issues of geographical theory, Kollmorgen depicts regionalism as an inherently reactionary, irrational, and divisive impulse. More specifically, he portrays regionalism as a dangerous social and political force that nurtures selfish sectionalism and narrow tribalism and undermines the hope for global unity through science and technology.

482. Kostbade, J. Trenton. "The Regional Concept and Geographic Education." *Journal of Geography* 67 (January 1968): 6–12.

After describing the inevitability of regional classification in geography and outlining central regional concepts, Kostbade urges greater attention to conceptual issues in teaching and better balance between often slighted theoretical tools and factual content.

483. Larkin, Robert P. and Gary L. Peters. "Region."In *Dictionary of Concepts in Human Geography*, 199–205. Westport, Conn.: Greenwood, 1983.

A succinct and thoughtful introduction to the regional concept comparable to classic introductory treatments by Hedwig Hintze in political science and Rupert Vance in sociology. Similarly insightful introductions to "Region"and "Regional Geography"are found in R.J. Johnston, ed., *Dictionary of Human Geography*. New York: Free Press, 1981, pp. 284–85 and 286–88.

484. Leighly, John. "Some Comments on Contemporary Geographic Method." *Annals of the Association of American Geographers* 27 (September 1937): 125–41.

A biting and prescient critique of efforts to launch a "science of regions"with an all-purpose anatomy of the earth's surface, this essay suggests that "Literary art, not systematic description, is the proper medium for regional analysis." Human regional systems are so complex that "there may be today regional sciences of parts of Antarctica . . . but little or none of Ohio." Leighly concludes that "A vision of the whole surface of the earth plastered with topographic descriptions—like the luggage of a round-the-world tourist with hotel stickers—is one that must terrify even the most tolerant reader of regional descriptive literature."

485. Lewis, Pierce. "Defining a Sense of Place." *The Southern Quarterly* 17 (Spring-Summer 1979): 24–46.

Using the South as his primary case study, Lewis brilliantly discusses the significance of sense of place in American culture and the relationship between this sensibility and regionalism. The strengths and weakness of sense of place, the ever-present tension between place and mobility in our culture, and the resurgence of interest in preservation are some of the issues analyzed. Other sources by Lewis are listed under Geography: Landscape and Settlement (items 658–663).

486. McDonald, James R. *A Geography of Regions*. Dubuque, Iowa: William C. Brown, 1972.

An extremely useful book-length introduction to the history of regional thought as well as a guided tour through the maze of contemporary theory, McDonald's book can be read as an American companion piece to Minshull's English text.

487. ———. "The Region: Its Conception, Design, and Limitations." *Annals of the Association of American Geographers* 65 (September 1966): 516–28.

Moving from the region defined by single factors toward a consideration of the "total"region, in which all factors are considered, this essay demonstrates the utter complexity and virtual impossibility of grasping a region in its entirety. Yet McDonald praises the quest for regional definition despite all odds, arguing that "geographers seek regions as alpinists seek unconquered peaks: 'because they are there;' . . . and as the region has represented a challenge to each generation of geographers it may, in a sense, be said to be part of the soul of geography: forever sought, forever undefined."

488. Marsh, George Perkins. *Man and Nature*. Edited by David Lowenthal. Cambridge: Harvard Univ. Press, 1965.

Originally published in 1864, Marsh's encyclopedic analysis of environmental change promoted a novel idea for the time: the notion that human beings were largely free to mold the earth and that much of the earth, for better or for worse, was a manmade product. See Marsh's introduction, pp. 7–52, for a sweeping portrait of man as the dominant, often destructive, force in changing the physical world. For a mid-twentieth century homage to and elaboration of Marsh's vision, see *Man's Role in Changing the Face of the Earth* (Chicago: Univ. of Chicago Press, 1956), edited by William L. Thomas. For related discussions of regionalism in terms of the culture/nature relationship see sources by Platt, Sauer, Semple, and Vidal in this section (items 499–501, 506–508, 512, 523).

489. Mead, W.R. "Geography and Area Studies."In *Trends in Geography*, edited by Ronald U. Cooke and James H. Johnson, 247–52. New York: Pergamon Press, 1969.

A spirited defense of regional course work as the heart of geographic education. Noting that regional study provides a much needed opportunity for synthesis, Mead encourages teachers to use creative literature, autobiography, and introspective exercises to allow students "to put into words the strength of their feeling for a particular place and the reasons for this."

490. ———. "Regional Geography."In *Geography Yesterday and Tomorrow*, edited by E.H Brown, 292–302. New York: Oxford Univ. Press, 1980.

A lively discussion of the relevance of regional description and analysis in contemporary society. Mead argues that the persistence of personal feelings for place——the desire for regional identity and consciousness——underscores the need for geographers to evoke a "splendour of earth"that is rarely found in the abstract equations of systematic geography.

491. Meinig, D.W. "Environmental Appreciation: Localities as a Humane Art." *Western Humanities Review* 25 (Winter 1971): 1–11.

As a response to the environmental crisis, Meinig urges the humanistic development of environmental appreciation and regional consciousness in university curricula. In addition to providing "training in how to look at an area, how to open the eyes and become keenly sensible of one's environment,"such education will also help us "discover that we are less of a standardized people than we had thought, that underneath our national veneer there is an array of sub-societies whose tell-tale marks are revealed in the nuances of daily life ... " Meinig has developed several of these ideas in "The Beholding Eye: Ten Versions of the Same Scene,"*The Interpretation of Ordinary Landscapes* (New York: Oxford Univ. Press 1979), edited by D.W. Meinig, pp. 33–48 and "Geography as Art,"*Transactions, Institute of British Geographers* New Series, 8 (1983), pp. 314–28.

492. ———. "The Mormon Culture Region: Strategies and Patterns in the Geography of the American West, 1847–1964." *Annals of the Association of American Geographers* 56 (September 1966): 191–220.

Meinig's anatomy of the Mormon culture region into three parts—a core, domain, and sphere—has deeply influenced recent perceptions of the structure and function of American regions. Another influential essay by Meinig concerned with the definition of the regional concept is "American Wests: Preface to a Geographical Interpretation,"*Annals of the Association of American Geographers,* 62 (1972), pp. 159–184. Other sources by Meinig are listed under Geography: Perception Studies and Geography: Landscape and Settlement (items 576–577, 670–673).

493. Minshull, Roger. *Regional Geography: Theory and Practice.* Chicago: Aldine Publishing, 1967.

Like McDonald's book, this is an effective, clearly written introduction to the intricacies of European and American regional theory. Especially useful discussions include "Regions As Real Objects,"pp. 26–37; "Formal and Functional Regions,"pp. 38–45; "Regionalism,"pp. 60–67; "Alternatives to an Inadequate Concept,"pp. 85–105, which responds to Kimble's influential critique; and "The Compage,"pp. 120–45, which elaborates Whittlesey's regional concept.

494. Morgan, F.W. "Three Aspects of Regional Consciousness." *Sociological Review* 31 (January 1939): 68–88.

In this highly perceptive survey of the rise of regional awareness in the western world since the 1890s, Morgan interprets manifestations of "regional consciousness"in politics, literature, and geographical technique as parts of a larger reaction against the centralized State and a yearning for a lost sense of community.

495. Parsons, James J. "Geography as Exploration and Discovery." *Annals of the Association of American Geographers* 67 (March 1977): 1–16.

Parsons describes his lifelong interest in a region in Colombia to illustrate his sense of what regional study is and how it proceeds. Man-land relationships are fundamental to regional geography. "The geography that has most appealed to me,"he writes, "has been a kind of historically based 'landscape appreciation,' and I confess a certain uneasiness with the current compulsion for precision of analysis, the often sterile straining for statistical content and significance."

496. Paterson, J.H. "Writing Regional Geography: Problems and Progress in the Anglo-American Realm." In *Progress in Geography.* vol. 6, 3–26. New York: St. Martin's Press, 1975.

Paterson's insightful, often witty, account of the strengths and weaknesses of regional geography since the 1940s contains a vigorous plea for the revitalization of "regional studies which are less bound by old formulae; less obliged to tell all about the region; more experimental and, in the proper sense of the word, more imaginative than in the past.... " By practicing their art in this manner regionalists will retain their special place in the discipline and avoid being perceived as "the last of the handloom weavers."

497. Pfeifer, Gottfried. *Regional Geography in the United States Since the War: A Review of Trends in Theory and Method.* Translated by John Leighly. New York: American Geographical Society, 1938.

Just as American geographer Richard Hartshorne was largely inspired by reading German regional theory during the 1930s, German geographer Gottfried Pfeifer pays critical tribute to American regional theory of the same era. His thirty-seven-page monograph is a remarkably thorough survey of the regional enthusiasms of the 1920s and 1930s found in the work of Harlan Barrows, Carl Sauer, Robert Hall, Derwent Whittlesey, Preston James, Fred Kniffen, and others.

498. Philbrick, Allen K. "Principles of Areal Functional Organization in Regional Human Geography." *Economic Geography* 33 (October 1957): 299–336.

Based upon empirical field studies under Robert Platt, Philbrick develops a general scheme of regional organization based upon a "nested hierarchy"of ever-larger units of occupance. These units of occupance build outward from "first order centers"of individual establishments— e.g., farms, stores, dwellings—to "seventh order centers"of major cities dominating world regions.

499. Platt, Robert S. "A Review of Regional Geography." *Annals of the Association of American Geographers* 47 (June 1957): 187–90.

An important, ever-relevant, essay describing the state of regional theory since the post World War II rise of systematic studies. Platt succinctly describes the perceived differences between systematic and regional efforts: "systematic geography deals with *something* about *every* part of the world, and regional geography deals with *everything* about *some* part of the world."He explains the limitations inherent in each of these goals and advocates a synthesis resulting in a "selective systematic regional geography, increasingly concerned with dynamic processes of human occupation in their spatial relations."

500. ———— . "Environmentalism Versus Geography." *American Journal of Sociology* 53 (March 1948): 251–58.

This classic essay brilliantly summarizes possible causes of regionalism. After calling for the "extermination"of environmental determinism as an explanation for the spatial variation of culture, Platt suggests that what people do with their lives in various environments is largely shaped by their cultural background. As Vidal and other possibilists have argued, the physical resources of a region set certain limits on people's freedom of choice; Platt pushes this reasoning further to argue that cultural programming limits choices even further. See Erhard Rostlund's "Twentieth Century Magic,"*Readings in Cultural Geography* (Chicago: Univ. of Chicago Press, 1962), edited by Philip L. Wagner and Marvin W. Mikesell, pp. 48–53, for an even wider-ranging, more iconoclastic attack on environmental determinism, and G.R. Lewthwaite's "Environmentalism and Determinism: A Search for Clarification,"*Annals of the Association of American Geographers* 56 (March 1966) for a useful overview. For other classic discussions of environmental-regional theory in this section see Marsh, Sauer, Semple, and Vidal (items 488, 506–508, 512, 523).

501. ———— . "Field Approach to Regions." In Special Issue. "A Conference on Regions." *Annals of the Association of American Geographers* (item 514), 153–74.

With meticulous detail Platt describes his recent traverse and field study of Canadian regions between Hudson's Bay and Lake Ontario; in the process, he defends an experiential, on-site, inductive approach to regional analysis that has deeply influenced American geographers since the early 1920s. "Sooner or later,"he argues, "geographers need to go to the field just as the general practitioner in medicine needs to go to his patient." A fuller outline of this approach is contained in Platt's *Field Study in American Geography*. Research Paper no. 61. (Chicago: Univ. of Chicago, Department of Geography, 1959.)

502. Powell, John Wesley. "Physiographic Regions of the United States." In *The Physiography of the United States*, 66–106. Chicago: National Geographic Society, 1886.

This influential division of the United States into sixteen physiographic regions derived from major slopes and river basins reflects late nineteenth century interest in locating "natural"regions underlying the artificial framework of nations. For closely related discussions in this section, see Herbertson and Roxby (items 468, 504).

503. Robinson, G.W.S. "The Geographical Region: Form and Function." *Scottish Geographical Magazine* 69 (September 1953): 49–58.

Robinson reviews mid-century concepts of formal and functional regions and compares these models with earlier regional theories developed by Herbertson, Unstead, and others.

504. Roxby, P.M. "The Theory of Natural Regions." *Geography* 13 (1925–1926): 376–83.

Building upon Herbertson's work, Roxby asserts his faith in the primacy "natural"rather than political regions in human life.

505. Sack, Robert David. "Chorology and Spatial Analysis." *Annals of the Association of American Geographers* 64 (September 1974): 439–52.

After carefully analyzing the Hartshorne-Schaefer dispute, Sack concludes that the contrast between the chorological or regional and spatial or systematic schools of geography has been exaggerated. He argues that these seemingly disparate perspectives can be brought together in a working continuum in which spatial analysis is used to explain situations where general laws can be reached and regional study is used to understand that which is unique and irreducible to general hypotheses.

506. Salter, Christopher. "The Organization of Space."In *The Cultural Landscape*, 143–47. Belmont, Calif.: Duxbury Press, 1971.

Salter compares the ways geographers and historians are compelled to invent convenient "containers"for time and space. Succinctly echoing Hartshorne, Salter writes, "The region for the geographer is as the period is to the historian; both disciplines realize that borders are difficult to define, but in the broad sense, the representative containers of space and time yield more efficient scholarship and teaching." Other sources by Salter are listed under Literature (items 1275–1276).

507. Sauer, Carl Ortwin. "The Education of a Geographer." *Annals of the Association of American Geographers* 46 (1956): 287–299. Reprinted in *Land and Life: A Selection from the Writings of CarlOrtwin Sauer*, edited by John Leighly, 389–404. Berkeley: Univ. of California Press, 1969.

Drawing upon his personal predilections and academic background, Sauer suggests general guidelines for geographical training that refine the scope of regional analysis in the discipline. He argues that "It is neither necessary nor desirable that we consider the totality of region as the common basis of geographic study." While warning against excessive interest in regional classification and encouraging greater attention to topical rather than regional concerns, Sauer concludes that "Really good regional geography is finely representational art, and creative art is not circumscribed by pattern or method."

508. ———. "Foreword to Historical Geography." *Annals of the Association of American Geographers* 31 (1941): 1–24. Reprinted in *Land and Life: A Selection from the Writings of Carl Ortwin Sauer*, edited by John Leighly, 351–79. Berkeley: Univ. of California Press, 1969.

In the process of urging cultural geographers to develop greater historical sensitivity, expand their understanding of physical geography, and forge stronger links with their "sister discipline"of anthropology, Sauer re-emphasizes the centrality of regionalism in cultural geography. Stressing the relevance of the culture area concept and alluding to his cross-disciplinary work with anthropologist Alfred Kroeber, Sauer argues that "The whole task of human geography is nothing less than the comparative study of localized cultures"and that the time-depth study of culture areas is the heart of historical geography.

509. ———. "The Morphology of Landscape."*University of California Publications in Geography* 2 (1925): 19–54. Reprinted *Land and Life: A Selection from the Writings of Carl Ortwin Sauer*, edited by John Leighly, 315–50. Berkeley: Univ. of California Press, 1969.

Sauer's definition of geography as "the study of areas"or science of "areal differentiation"and his analysis of the interaction of natural and culture factors within regional settings have helped inspire generations of American regional geographers. This classic monograph asserts the importance of cultural features in geographical scholarship, links the concepts of cultural landscape and region, sets out a method of regional analysis, and vividly explains the combination of forces that shape cultural landscapes or regions. "The cultural landscape,"he writes, "is fashioned from the natural landscape by a culture group. Culture is the agent, the natural area is the medium, the cultural landscape the result."

510. Scargill, D.I. "Space, Place and Region: Towards a Transformed Regional Geography." *Geography* 70 (April 1985): 138–41.

Describing the "positivist paradigm" emphasizing spatial models and their manipulation that has dominated geography since the 1960s, Scargill seeks to "restore balance"to geography by giving attention to the themes of "place"and "region." In terms of "place,"he advocates further study and teaching of mental mapping and perception. Regarding "region,"he advocates a fresh perspective in which "The region must *not* be seen as some artificial compartment imposed on the earth's surface by tidy-minded geographers, but as a set of active agents, conditioning the impact of the social, economic and political processes that are at work in the world." Effective teaching of regions involves the use of mental maps and awareness of the extreme variability of regional boundaries and hierarchies.

511. Schaefer, Fred K. "Exceptionalism in Geography." *Annals of the Association of American Geographers* 53 (September 1953): 226–49.

In this influential critique of Hartshorne's *The Nature of Geography* (1939), Schaefer essentially urges geographers to shift attention from the more subjective and descriptive orientation of regional analysis to the more objective and scientific efforts of systematic study. He argues that Hartshorne's affirmation of regional or chorological analysis as the core of geography and notion that every region is unique or exceptional reduce geography to a "naive science"incapable of formulating general laws.

512. Semple, Ellen Churchill. *Influences of Geographic Environment.* New York: Russell and Russell, 1968.

Originally published in 1911, Semple's book presents a straightforward vision of environmental determinism that is the antithesis of Marsh's explanation of the variable character of the face of the earth. See Marsh, Platt, Sauer, and Vidal in this section for related sources (items 488, 499–501, 506–508, 523).

513. Spate, O.H.K. "'Region' as a Work of Art."In *Let Me Enjoy: Essays Partly Geographical.* London: Methuen and Co., 1966.

Although geographers should not pretend that the earth's surface is a neat mosaic of "comprehensive"regions, they should continue to develop the art of regional description. Concerning the search for regions as objective realities, Spate asserts that "The geographer's region, unless more narrowly defined by an adjective ('climatic region,' 'market region,' and so on) is really an approximation for the sake of working convenience ... from a strictly objective point of view, there may be nothing in the actual phenomena which is a true referent for any given fully comprehensive region; but if such regions do not exist, we have to invent them to manage our data. They are in fact isolates for study." For related sources see Gilbert, Hart, Leighly, and Paterson in this section (items 457–458, 465, 484, 496).

514. Special Issue. "A Conference on Regions." *Annals of the Association of American Geographers* 25 (September 1935).

This collection of important papers marks a high point of interest in regional geography often marked by a determined search for "organic"regions invested with distinct personalities. Perceptive essays include Robert B. Hall, "The Geographic Region: A Resume"(item 463); George T. Renner, "A Statistical Approach to Regions,"pp. 137–52; and Robert S. Platt, "A Field Approach to Regions"(item 501). Perceptive criticisms by W.L.G. Joerg, Derwent Whittlesey, Richard Hartshorne, Richard E. Dodge, and others are included.

515. Steel, R.W. "Regional Geography in Practice." *Geography* 67 (January 1982): 2–8.

Steel essentially argues that the best regional geography is both descriptive and analytical: that it is anchored to specific facts as well as well as directed toward solving general problems.

516. Symanski, Richard and James L. Newman. "Formal, Functional, and Nodal Regions: Three Fallacies." *Professional Geographer* 25 (November 1973): 350–52.

A crisp exposition of three fallacies common among geographers: the belief that functional and nodal regions are equivalent; the notion that formal regions are always static and functional ones dynamic; and the sense that nodal regions are necessarily "superior"to formal ones.

517. Tuan, Yi-Fu. "Continuity and Discontinuity." *Geographical Review* 74 (July 1984): 245–56.

As in all of his work, Tuan vividly analyzes a vital human trait: in this case, the tendency "to see and organize reality into polarized categories of the continuous and discontinuous, the linked and the discrete." The persistent partitioning of space into discrete regions is an expression of this impulse, an urge that "is developed into a fine art by geographers who show an exceptional fondness for cutting up space. Once they recognize differences within space, they will accent them by drawing boundaries around them to create what they call formal regions. . . . Sometimes the partitioning serves an obviously useful purpose. . . . Often it has no practical value and satisfies an intellectual desire for order." Tuan masterfully explores related themes, although without an explicit regional focus, in *Segmented Worlds and Self: Group Life and Individual Consciousness* under Geography: Perception Studies (item 599).

518. ———— . "Place: An Experiential Perspective." *Geographical Review* 65 (1975): 151–65.

Perhaps Tuan's most focused analysis of region and regionalism, this lucid essay locates regional consciousness within a spectrum of spatial experience ranging outward from places within the home to one's home, city, neighborhood and region, and nation-state. Because the region, unlike more intimate places, is too large to be known directly by most of its inhabitants, it exists primarily as a "construct of thought"sustained "by symbolic means." In a footnote, Tuan wryly observes that "Geographers have constructed many regions, although relatively few are recognized by the people who live in them as distinctive spatial units." The general theme of this essay is expanded in Tuan's *Space and Place: the Perspective of Experience* (item 600, under Geography: Perception Studies), in "Intimate Experiences of Place,"pp. 136–48, and "Attachment to Homeland,"pp. 49–60.

519. ———— . *Topophilia: A Study of Environmental Perception, Attitudes, and Values.* Englewood Cliffs, N.J.: Prentice-Hall, 1974.

Tuan's wide-ranging analysis of humanity's love of place helps explain the subjective, psychological dimensions of regionalism: the emotional need for a sense of place which is often in regional identity. Particularly useful is "Topophilia and Environment,"pp. 92–112, in which Tuan compares the nature of human affections for home regions, nations, empires, and the whole earth. Tuan's *Landscapes of Fear* (New York: Pantheon, 1979), provides a vivid counterpoint to *Topophilia*. Tuan's "Rootedness versus Sense of Place,"*Landscape* 24 (1980), pp. 3–8, develops a useful distinction between unreflective immersion in place (rootedness) and conscious yearning for place (sense of place). Further references to Tuan are Geography: Perception Studies (items 596–601), Literature (item 1308) and Philosophy and Religion (items 1392–1394).

520. Turnock, D. "The Region in Modern Geography." *Geography* 52 (1967): 374–83.

After reviewing theories of environmentalism and regionalism in Germany, France, and England from the mid-nineteenth to the mid-twentieth century, Turnock concludes that regional study can throw light upon modern conditions and can enhance the "locational approach"found in the fields of spatial organization and regional science.

521. Ullman, Edward L. "Human Geography and Area Research." *Annals of the Association of American Geographers* 43 (1953): 54–66.

Ullman emphasizes the relevance of geographic concepts, especially regional ones, to work in the interdisciplinary field of area studies. He wisely stresses the extreme variability of regionalization—that "the purpose of the study controls the type of regions to be set up"—and that many regions "exist around each person and each place."

522. Unstead, J.F. "A System of Regional Geography." *Geography* 18 (1933): 175–87.

522. Unstead, J.F. "A System of Regional Geography." *Geography* 18 (1933): 175–87.

In contrast to Herbertson's global framework of "major natural regions,"Unstead proposes that regional geographers turn their attention to the close description of intimate, small-scale human regions and then construct larger regional configurations from these primal units. In "Classification of Regions of the World,"*Geography* 22 (1937), pp. 253, Unstead and his colleagues extend this inductive approach.

523. Vidal de la Blache, Paul. *Tableau de la Geographie de la France.* Vol. 1 of *Histoire de France* by Ernest Lavisse et al. Paris: Librarie Hachette et cie, 1903.

The early pages of this book contain Vidal's classic formulation of the possibilist explanation of regional variation: that people are free to function and make choices within the possibilities and limits offered by each region or "pays."It also voices Vidal's belief in and ability to portray the distinct personality or "genre de vie"of each region. Also see Vidal's "Les conditions geographique des faits sociaux,"*Annales de geographie* 11 (1902): pp. 13–23. The possibilist tradition is further articulated by Vidal's colleagues and students, including Jean Brunhes in *Human Geography* (London: Harrap, 1910) and Lucien Febvre in *A Geographic Introduction to History* (New York: Knopf, 1925).

524. Wagner, Philip L. "Cultural Landscapes and Regions: Aspects of Communication." In *Man, Space, and Environment,* edited by Paul Ward English and Robert C. Mayfield, 55–68. New York: Oxford Univ. Press, 1972. Reprinted in *Geoscience and Man.* vol. 5, edited by H.J.

Walker and W.G. Haag, 133–42. Baton Rouge: School of Geoscience, Louisiana State Univ., 1974.

Wagner wisely asserts that "The cultural divisions of the world . . . have evolved through communication of ideas—from father to son; among neighbors; through emigrants and traders; by way of pictures, songs, and books." Every region, furthermore, becomes a subtle map of a people's attitudes, values, and beliefs—an artifact or assemblage of expressive landscape features embodying a group's notion of the "good life." Cultural geographers can fully understand this process and interpret "the morality of the landscape"through a firm grounding in culture and communication theory.

525. ———— . "The Themes of Cultural Geography Rethought." *Yearbook, Association of Pacific Coast Geographers* 37 (1975): 7–14.

Essentially an update of the definitions of cultural geography and culture area offered in the introduction to Wagner and Mikesell's *Readings in Cultural Geography* (1962), this essay stresses that most concepts of culture area and region are relevant only to rustic, pre-industrial communities. In order to fit the regional concept into the reality of modern society, cultural geographers must account for how people are "bound together by their manifold communication systems"and must deal with the geography of "institutional subcultures."

526. Walter, Bob J. and Frank E. Bernard. "A Thematic Approach to Regional Geography." *Journal of Geography* 72 (November 1973): 14–28.

The authors outline a regional course that counters many of the criticisms leveled at the regional approach. By focusing upon a number of "process-related themes"within particular places, regional courses can evoke general as well as specific knowledge.

527. ———— . "Ash Pile or Rising Phoenix? A Review of the Status of Regional Geography." *Journal of Geography* 77 (September/October 1978): 192–97.

After reviewing the deficiencies of regional research and teaching, the authors argue that regional concerns are increasingly vital. The emerging importance of area studies in the Third World, the persisting concern for environmental problems, and the need for a "real world testing ground for theoretical systematic geography"all indicate the continuing importance of regional geography.

528. Whittlesey, Derwent. "The Regional Concept and the Regional Method." In *American Geography: Inventory and Prospect*, edited by Preston E. James and Clarence F. Jones, 19–68. Syracuse: Syracuse Univ. Press, 1954.

The summation of five years of information gathering by a special committee on regional geography, Whittlesey's essay remains one of the most comprehensive summations of regional theory in print. After reviewing the history of regional speculation in geography and other disciplines, Whittlesey proposes a definition of the region stressing its heuristic function rather than its objective existence. The region is "a device for selecting and studying areal groupings of the complex phenomena found on the earth. Any segment of the earth's surface is a region if it is homogeneous in terms of such an areal grouping. . . . So defined a region is not an object . . . It is an intellectual concept, an entity for the purposes of thought. . . ." Particular types of regions— including single factor, multiple factor, uniform, and nodal regions—are described, and the concept of the "compage"is introduced to describe a composite region which is "something less than spatial totality; but it does include all of the features of the physical, biotic, and societal environments that are functionally associated with man's occupance of the earth."

529. Woolridge, S.W. "Reflection on Regional Geography in Teaching and Research." In *The Geographer as Scientist: Essays on the Scope and Nature of Geography*, 51–65. New York: Thomas Nelson and Sons, 1956.

In this ringing defense of regional geography as the "central objective"and keystone of the discipline, Woolridge traces the longstanding tension between systematic and regional fields and praises the interdisciplinary breadth necessary for regional synthesis at the same time that he advises regionalists to "abandon pseudo-organic analogies." The basic goal of regional geography, he argues, "is to gather up the disparate strands of the systematic studies, the geographical aspects of other disciplines, into a coherent and focused unity, to see nature, physique and personality as closely related and inter-dependent elements in specific regions."

530. Wrigley, E.A. "Changes in the Philosophy of Geography." In *Frontiers in Geographical Teaching*. 2d ed., edited by R.J. Chorley and Peter Haggett, 3–20. London: Methuen, 1970.

This essay places regional geography within an historical context, arguing that regional studies peaked in the early twentieth century works of Vidal de la Blache and that such evocations of the personality of place do not apply to complex, industrial society. Like Kimble, Kollmorgen, and others, Wrigley argues that "All variants of the 'regional' view of geography are at their best when dealing with areas of rural, local economies. All are ill at ease when dealing with areas thoroughly caught up in the Industrial Revolution."

531. Zelinsky, Wilbur. *The Cultural Geography of the United States.* Englewood Cliffs, N.J.: Prentice-Hall, 1973.

Although it shows the strain of covering such an immense topic in 140 pages, this is an important book and recommended starting point for students of American regions and regionalism. Early chapters masterfully summarize the historical geography of the nation, elements of the national character, and the environmental and social forces that have forged American culture. "Structure,"pp. 109–40, makes an important contribution to regional theory by perceptively evaluating a wide-range of regional research, by classifying various types of American regions into a "multi-tiered, nested hierarchy of culture areas,"beginning with five major regions—New England, the Midland, the South, the Middle West, and the the West—and by developing a fresh concept concerning the emergence of the "voluntary region"in the United States.

532. ———— . "General Cultural and Popular Regions." In *In This Remarkable Continent: An Atlas of the United States and Canadian Societies and Cultures,* edited by John F. Rooney, Wilbur Zelinsky, and Dean R. Louder, 3–24. College Station: Texas A&M Press, 1983.

A lively and insightful introduction to the state of thought about American regions and regionalism in the early 1980s. Zelinsky describes the general purpose of regional classification and delineates three highly useful regional types: the general cultural region, the voluntary region, and the popular or vernacular region. A series of maps illustrates his argument and prepares the reader for subsequent chapters.

533. ———— . "Personality and Self Discovery: The Future Social Geography of the United States." In *Human Geography in a Shrinking World,* edited by Ronald Abler et al., 108–21.

North Scituate, Mass.: Duxbury Press, 1975, 108–21. An evocative discussion of the emergence of "voluntary regions"in late twentieth century American society. Zelinsky's descriptions of military subregions, education subregions, and a panoply of "pleasuring places"based upon retirement, recreation, and lifestyle clustering is extremely insightful. Zelinsky's "Selfward Bound? Personal Preference Patterns and the Changing Map of American Society,"*Economic Geography* 50 (April 1974), pp. 145–79, is an earlier, more thorough discussion of the emergence of "voluntary regions."Other references to Zelinsky are listed in the next three sections as well as under Philosophy and Religion (items 605, 717–719, 1401).

Geography: Perception Studies

Over the past two decades, there has been a remarkable growth of interest among geographers in place as perceived. One can make out, in the entries in this subcategory, two main currents of thought. One concentrates upon images of place and region as cultural phenomena, almost for their own sake. Here we would include those in the tradition of John K. Wright, who sketch the historical career of ideas about place and region (and, especially in the work of Lowenthal, about time); the concern about vernacular regions (regions as popularly perceived), in the manner of Zelinsky (item 605) and many others named below; and the interest in symbolic and generic landscapes, as found in Meinig (item 576) and Hart (item 557). The other main current of interest is in images or perceptions as embedded in experience, as represented in the expanding literature of "humanistic" geographers such as Tuan and Buttimer. For such thinkers, "place" is basic, "region" an abstraction or extrapolation therefrom. Related to both currents of thought is a concern as to how perceptions should be taken into account in architectural and urban design and in planning (as in Relph and Saarinen).

Here and in subsequent subsections under geography, there is an emphasis upon "secondarily relevant" entries, including reviews of literature useful to an understanding of the entries under the subheading and works concerned with developing the theoretical bases for strands of thought there represented.

See also History: Perception Studies, American Studies, Literature, Philosophy and Religion, and Architecture and Planning for closely related entries.

C.M.

534. Aiken, Charles S. "Faulkner's Yoknapatawpha County: A Place in the American South." *Geographical Review* 69 (1979): 331–48.

Examines Faulkner's fictional Yoknapatawpha County in relation to actual conditions in his part of Mississippi at the time he wrote. Clearly the fictional creation was not meant to be the South in microcosm but a description of a particular place in the South. A nice combination of literary appreciation and geographical know-how.

535. Allen, John L. *Passage Through the Garden: Lewis and Clark and the Image of the American Northwest.* Urbana: Univ. of Illinois Press, 1975.

Inspired by Bowden and Wright. Allen examines the literature available to Lewis and Clark about the area they were to explore, and how the resulting image entered into the conduct and results of their explorations. Their report gave the Northwest form and structure. See also Allen, "Lands of Myth, Waters of Wonder: The Place of the Imagination in the History of Geographical Exploration," in *Geographies of the Mind* (New York: Oxford Univ. Press, 1976), edited by David Lowenthal and Martyn J. Bowden, pp. 41–61, which describes the interplay between imagined and real geographies among the first European explorers of Africa and the New World.

536. Appleton, Jay. *The Experience of Landscape.* London: John Wiley and Sons, 1975.

Argues that landscape beauty derives from a primitive need to be sheltered and to observe without being observed. No doubt the need is derived from its usefulness to human survival in the prehistoric past. On the basis of that theory, Appleton reviews theories about beauty and patterns in painting and literature, as well as in the real world.

537. Blouet, Brian W. and Merlin P. Lawson. *Images of the Plains: The Role of Human Nature in Settlement.* Lincoln: Univ. of Nebraska Press, 1975.

Essays emphasizing the role of perception in relation to the Great Plains, most based upon a careful study of the topography. They draw upon diaries, government reports, promotional material, and reports from scientific expeditions. Headings include exploratory images, early resource evaluation, government appraisal of the frontier, early ideas about climate, images of desert and garden, and adaptations to reality. Includes item 538.

538. Bowden, Martyn J. "Desert Wheat Belt, Desert Corn Belt: Environmental Cognition and Behavior of Settlers on the Plains Margin." In *Images of the Plains* (item 537), 189–201.

Studies one county at the margin between wheat and corn belts. Bowden contrasts the eastern view of the desert with the lack of the desert idea on the part of people who had actually been there (e.g., appraisers of land). Real estate boomers of the 1870s and after publicize the idea of subduing the desert and so make the desert idea common currency.

539. ————. "The Great American Desert and the American Frontier, 1800–1882: Popular Images of the Plains and Phases of the Westward Movement." In *Anonymous Americans*, edited by Tamara Hareven, 48–79. Englewood Cliffs, N.J.: Prentice-Hall, 1971.

Survey of nineteenth-century textbooks, newspaper accounts, journals, and diaries. The idea of the great desert reigns in eastern textbooks but not in diaries or journals and is no longer found in textbooks after 1870. See also Bowden, "The Great American Desert in the American Mind, 1890–1972: The Historiography of a Geographical Notion," *Geographies of the Mind* (item 574), pp. 119–47, which surveys historians of the "desert" (many in the Turner tradition).

540. Brown, Ralph H. *Mirror for Americans: Likeness of the Eastern Seaboard, 1810.* New York: American Geographical Society, 1943.

Concerned about how geography was conceived and perceived by people of past times. Brown here created a fictional character who takes a tour along the seaboard in 1810, writing in the language and with the understanding of the time. In *Historical Geography of the United States* (New York: Harcourt Brace Jovanovich, 1948), Brown relies heavily on changes in how people describe their landscapes in surveying his subject.

541. Burton, Ian and R.W. Kates. "The Perception of Natural Hazards in Resource Management." *Natural Resources Journal* 3 (1964): 412–41.

This somewhat specialized study of how natural hazards are perceived involves implications as to how people and cultures order and value the space around them. It argues that there is no perception at all unless a hazard affects central uses and recurs with some frequency. Resource users and scientists have very different perceptions. "Compensations" involved: people deny the existence of the hazard or the likelihood of its recurring; or they ascribe patterns to its recurrence, or put their trust in God. The work of Burton and Kates is summed up in *The Environment as Hazard* (New York: Oxford Univ. Press, 1978).

542. Buttimer, Anne. "Grasping the Dynamism of Lifeworld." *Annals of the Association of American Geographers* 66 (1976): 277–92.

Dense and lucid argument for a phenomenological approach to geography, one that grounds the discipline in the experience and perceptions of the individual, by one of its foremost exponents. Buttimer develops the concepts of life-world, social space, and time-space rhythms as bases for dialogue with more traditional approaches. Literature cited is wide in range and precise in aptness. See also "Social Space in Interdisciplinary Perspective," *Geographical Review* 59 (1969), pp. 417–426.

543. Buttimer, Anne and David Seamon, eds. *The Human Experience of Space and Place*. New York: St. Martin's Press, 1980.

A collection of essays in the phenomenological mode, most of which had been published before. See especially Buttimer, "Home, Reach, and the Sense of Place," pp. 166–87, which describes her own conversion from an "outside" to an "inside" perspective for planners and geographers.

544. Carr, Stephen and Dal Schissler. "The City as a Trip: Perceptual Selection and Memory in the View from the Road." *Environment and Behavior* 1 (1969): 7–35.

Interesting as a sample of work among individuals interested in how the fact that urbanites see much of the world from inside a car, thus powerfully affecting how that world is experienced. This study assumes with Bruner (item 1488) that perceptual expectations prepare people for a trip. What then stands out for the driver is what varies from those expectations, after allowing for the ordinary distractions of driving (curves, intersections, etc.)

545. Cosgrove, Dennis. "Place, Landscape and the Dialectics of Cultural Geography." *The Canadian Geographer* 22 (1978): 66–72.

A critique of recent geographical thought, arguing that the positivist emphasis has run its course in the thought of David Harvey (item 757), and phenomenological thought, while valuable, does not take into account the dialectic between idea and world and between idea and social group. Cosgrove proposes the incorporation of phenomenological contributions within the larger compass of a Marxist approach. The argument is buttressed by a wide-ranging review of the literature.

546. ———. "Prospect, Perspective and the Evolution of the Landscape Idea." *Transactions of the Institute of British Geographers* 10 (1985): 45–62.

Dense article surveying connections among the development of perspective in the Renaissance with the growth of cities, the mapping of territories, landscape painting, and maps themselves, as part of a more general argument for more attention to visual evidence.

547. Craik, Kenneth H. and Ervin H. Zube, eds. *Perceiving Environmental Quality.* New York: Plenum Press, 1976.

Report on research and attending workshop debating perceived environmental quality indices (PEQIs) and their use, e.g., as basis for regional delimitation. Sections are devoted to scene and recreation environments, residential and institutional environments, and air, water and sonic environments. The articles combine geographical and psychological perspectives.

548. Downs, Roger M. and David Stea. *Maps in Minds: Reflections on Cognitive Mapping.* New York: Harper and Row, 1977.

A general introduction to cognitive mapping and its uses, discussing the nature of sense of place, the psychological genesis of maps, how mental mapping is done and the function of mapping in everyday life (what might be called "behavioral regions"). Downs is a geographer, Stea a planner. See also Downs and Stea, *Image and Environment: Cognitive Mapping and Spatial Behavior* (Chicago: Aldine Publishing Co., 1973).

549. Duncan, James S. "The Social Construction of Unreality: An Interactionist Approach to the Tourist's Cognition of Environment." In *Humanistic Geography: Prospects and Problems,* edited by David Ley and Marwyn S. Samuels, 269–82. Chicago: Maaroufa Press, 1978.

One introduction to the general topic of tourist regions. Duncan argues that the tourist is always a stranger to the local scene, and that therefore tourism becomes a way of celebrating inauthenticity. The essay involves a review of relevant literature.

550. Francaviglia, Richard V. "Main Street U.S.A.: The Creation of a Popular Image." *Landscape* 21 (Spring 1977): 18–22.

An exercise in the evolution of a generic region (main street) into a symbolic landscape. The article compares the main street of Disneyland with the Missouri town in which Walt Disney grew up. The

Disneyland version is entirely upbeat. It has no cemeteries, jails, or taverns. It is built to five-eighths size, which artfully enhances the nostalgia experience by the visitors. The street is framed by squares at each end and is designed for pedestrians. The Disney version is in many ways similar to that of a modern shopping mall.

551. Glacken, Clarence. *Traces on the Rhodian Shore.* Berkeley: Univ. of California Press, 1967.

This monumental history of geographical ideas describes the evolution of western thought about design in nature, man in relation to nature, and man as shaper of nature, from classical times down to the eighteenth century. The Hellenistic period (200–300 A.D.) was especially influential. Christianity made nature a creation. From medieval times on, man comes to see nature as more and more under his control. The journey of Captain Cook made necessary a radical recasting of the traditional "world." See also Glacken, "Changing Ideas of the Habitable World," in *Man's Role in Changing the Face of the Earth* (item 700), pp. 70–92.

552. Good, James K. "The Vernacular Regions of Arkansas." *Journal of Geography* 80 (September/October 1981): 179–85.

Results from questionnaire taken by college students about the relation of their own locales to intrastate and interstate regional names. Student ability to respond seemed to depend upon at least one year's residence in the state. Areal identities were confused, with large areas having no regional names. Good recommends the administering of such questionnaires as a useful student exercise.

553. Goodey, Brian and John R. Gold. "Behavioral and Perceptual Geography: From Retrospect to Prospect." *Progress in Human Geography* 9 (December 1985): 585–95.

Argues that geographers have not contributed much to planning and policy, and that current interest in environmental perception is sluggish, with courses on the subject drawing upon old material. See also Gold and Goodey, "Behavioral and Perceptual Geography," *Progress in Human Geography* 7 (1983), pp. 578–86.

554. Gould, Peter and Rodney White. *Mental Maps.* Middlesex, England: Penguin Books, 1974.

See especially the first chapter, "The Image of Places," and chapters four and five on regional images and ignorance among Americans. The book also discusses England and Sweden. It reviews methods for constructing mental maps, subjects amenable to mapping (preference, ignorance), methodology and practical applications. See also Gould, "On Mental Maps," *Man, Space and Environment* (New York: Oxford Univ. Press, 1972), edited by P. W. English and R. C. Mayfield, pp. 260–292, a 1966 paper representing mental maps as a new field of study.

555. Graber, Linda. *Wilderness as Sacred Space.* Washington D.C.: Association of American Geographers Monograph Series, no. 8, 1976.

An analysis of the wilderness ethic: strains of thought and their sources and justifications of wilderness users (practical, custodial, aesthetic, secular). Graber argues that the ethic is finally based upon a religious impulse.

556. Hale, Ruth F. "Vernacular Regions of America." *Journal of Cultural Geography* 5 (Fall/Winter 1984): 131–40.

A study of "vernacular local regions," smaller than states yet larger than counties, based upon a questionnaire sent newspaper editors, county agents, and postmasters throughout the United States, asking them to name the local area in which they lived. The results are mapped and tabulated.

557. Hart, John Fraser. "The Bypass Strip as Symbolic Landscape," *Geographical Review* 72 (1982): 218–23.

An addendum to Meinig's article on symbolic landscapes (item 577) arguing that the strip (and shopping center) constitutes a fourth principal symbolic type of landscape and as a generic region, not differing significantly from place to place. Nostalgia for "community" leads intellectuals to ignore the commercial strip, but it is very popular, to the point of displacing many downtown areas.

558. Hart, Roger. *Children's Experience of Place.* New York: Irvington Publishers, 1979.

A phenomenological study of the real-life behavior of children (up to sixth grade), combining ethnography with some experimental techniques, discussing place-knowledge, place-use, and patterns of space-activity. The locale being studied is a rapidly urbanizing New England town. See also entries under Psychology, on similar topics.

559. Hugill, Peter J. "English Landscape Tastes in the United States." *Geographical Review* 76 (October 1986): 408–23.

A sophisticated historical sketch of how English landscape tastes have fared in the U.S., popularly and in the arts. Hugill argues that the colonial and early national periods were not much influenced by English tastes, but that a re-Anglicization occurred in the late nineteenth century among the well-to-do, in reaction to the ugliness of cities, and because of the effects of steamship travel and the popular press. Hugill makes continuous and interesting reference to Cazenovia, New York, in making his argument.

560. Jackson, Richard H. and Roger Henrio. "Perception of Sacred Space." *Journal of Cultural Geography* 3 (1983): 94–107.

Discusses Mormon perception of sacred space, on the basis of results from a questionnaire. The authors make out distinctions among places as mystico-religious, homeland and locus of historical events. The Utah temple is ranked as high as the heavenly home. Places important to family history rate below the mystico-religious places. Distinct pattern of distance decay: all else equal, places are sacred and near to home, both.

561. Jakle, John A. *Images of the Ohio Valley: A Historical Geography of Travel, 1740–1860.* New York: Oxford Univ. Press, 1977.

An account of how early travelers to the Ohio Valley region described what they saw, so far as possible in their own words. Jakle describes reactions to travel itself, nature, Indians, military life, pastoral and rural landscape, and the urban landscape of Cincinnati. Modes of travel change and make for changes in travel routes and in the travel experience itself. See also Jakle, *The American Small Town: Twentieth Century Place Images* (Hamden, Conn.: Archon Books, 1982), which, on the basis of photographs and fictional accounts, constructs the typology of the small town as a symbolic landscape.

562. ———. *The Tourist: Travel in Twentieth-Century North America.* Lincoln: Univ. of Nebraska Press, 1985.

An analysis of the "roots of modern tourism," emphasizing the 1920–30 period and the advent of touring by automobile. Jakle draws upon accounts by the tourists themselves. He is interested in the tourist role, in the self-conscious effort to explore the landscape, and in the development of touristic landscapes as pleasure travel became widespread.

563. Johnson, Hildegard Binder and Gerald R. Pitzl. "Viewing and Perceiving the Rural Scene: Visualization in Human Geography." *Progress in Human Geography* 5 (1981): 211–33.

Review of literature on (especially rural) landscape: how it relates to countryside, how it is described, how it is seen, relation to aesthetics, pictorialization, assessment and evaluation, use of maps, and airviews, with bibliography.

564. Jordan, Terry G. "Perceptual Regions in Texas." *Geographical Review* 68 (1978): 293–307.

Studies perceptual regions in Texas on basis of questionnaires given to four thousand college students. Finds "sunbelt" an urban term, and "Bible Belt" restricted to north Texas and to Anglo-Saxons. Promotional terms ("Golden Triangle") are progressively displacing topographical terms ("Piney Woods").

565. Kollmorgen, Walter M. "The Woodman's Assault on the Domain of the Cattlemen." *Annals of the Association of American Geographers* 59 (1969): 215–39.

The story of how west-bound farmers had no knowledge of range economy and kept hoping for rain, experimenting with irrigation and dry-farming, and establishing inappropriate laws for land alienation. The range idea, coming from Spanish-American culture, came in through the back door and exactly suited western grasslands. Out of differing notions came long-standing confusions.

566. Lammé, Ary J. and Raymond K. Oldakowski. "Vernacular Areas in Florida." *Southeastern Geographer* 22 (1982): 100–09.

Results of questionnaire given to attendees at a Florida folklife festival. The authors finds "sunbelt" an urban term, "bible belt" a rural term, and "deep South" as a term restricted to the northern part of the state. Popular regions are mostly ahistorical ("Space Coast," "Surf Coast," etc.), which may have to do with recency of the settlement of the area.

567. Leighly, John. "John Muir's Image of the West." *Annals of the Association of American Geographers* 48 (1948): 309–18.

An appreciation of Muir as scientist and observer of the Sierra Nevada country, placing the man in his historical and scientific context. Leighly contrasts Muir, as one who combined the literary and personal with the scientific, to the severely unimaginative "Baconian" scientist.

He quotes liberally from Muir, arguing that he has left behind some marvelous descriptions of natural phenomena.

568. Lewis, G. Malcolm. "Regional Ideas and Reality in the Cis-Rocky Mountain West." *Institute of British Geographers, Transactions and Papers*, no. 38 (1966): 135–50.

Argues that much has been written about region as concept, but not much about the evolution of ideas about particular regions. Lewis surveys the successive and overlapping versions of the area to the east of the Rockies. He finds that regional descriptions vary according to the interest and attitude of the describer but often oversimplify and hang on to outworn notions in characterizing their subject matter.

569. Ley, David. "Social Geography and the Taken-for-granted World." *Transactions of the Institute of British Geographers*, NS2 (1977): 498–512.

A review of the history of theory about social geography, arguing that it needs to transcend the false distinction between subjective and objective by turning to phenomenological thought in the tradition of Husserl, Schutz, Merleau-Ponty, and Max Weber. Ley then reviews the concepts of lifeworld and the taken-for-granted world, as basic concepts in a phenomenological approach to social geography.

570. Lowenthal, David. "The American Scene." *Geographical Review* 58 (1968): 61–88.

Asserts that landscape is formed by landscape taste, and then turns to literature and art to describe that taste, for large size, wildness, formlessness and extremes, as well as a preference for present over past. See also Lowenthal and H.C. Price, "English Landscape Tastes," *Geographical Review* 55 (1965), pp. 186–222, applying the same approach to English subjects.

571. ———. "The American Way of History." *Columbia University Forum* 9 (1966): 27–32.

Argues that Americans disconnect their past from their present in ways peculiar to themselves. They set historical artifacts aside, clean them up, museumize them, and turn them into forms of entertainment, in these various ways artificially creating an imaginary past.

572. ———. "Geography, Experience and Imagination: Toward a Geographic Epistemology." *Annals of the Association of American Geographers* 51 (1961): 241–60.

A lucid and learned review of literature from a very wide range of sources as a means of arguing a set of postulates about perception (personal, public) of topography as shaped by cultural, personal, and historical circumstances. The shape of the body and an egocentric orientation filter sensations. Emotions color thoughts. See also Lowenthal, ed., *Environmental Perception and Behavior* (Chicago: Department of Geography, Univ. of Chicago, Research Paper no. 109, 1967).

573. ———. *The Past is a Foreign Country*. Cambridge, England: Cambridge Univ. Press, 1985.

This wide-ranging study surveys a vast literature having to do with the past (especially the American and English past) as a cultural-historical creation, related to certain psychological needs. Lowenthal discusses the need to repossess the past, the means of knowing the past (memory, history and artifacts), and the ways in which we change and alter our collective and individual pasts. For an early version of this argument, see Lowenthal, "Past Time, Present Place: Landscape and Memory," *Geographical Review* 65 (1975), pp. 1–36. See also Lowenthal, "The Bicentennial Landscape: A Mirror Held Up to the Past," *Geographical Review* 67 (1977), pp. 253–67, on slogans, reenactments and historic preservation incident to the Bicentennial.

574. Lowenthal, David and Martyn J. Bowden, eds. *Geographies of the Mind: Essays in Historical Geosophy in Honor of John Kirtland Wright*. New York: Oxford Univ. Press, 1976.

Geosophy is a mental map, especially of unknown terrain. This Festschrift for John K. Wright addresses a fascinating array of topics: Tuan on "geopiety," Lowenthal on the place of past, Bowden on the Great American Desert (item 539), and Zelinsky on cemetery names, as well as an excellent article on the geography of American utopias.

575. McManis, Douglas R. *The Initial Evaluation and Utilization of the Illinois Prairies, 1815–1840*. Chicago: Univ. of Chicago Press, 1964.

Tests the theory about prairie avoidance by looking at early accounts of the Illinois prairie and checking them against patterns of settlement and use. McManis says the early evaluation was not particularly negative, and that inaccessibility rather than avoidance stalled settlement. Southerners were less given to prairie than Yankees, he says.

576. Meinig, Donald W. "Environmental Appreciation: Localities as a Humane Art." *Western Humanities Review* 25 (1971): 1–11.

Urges humanistic development of environmental appreciation and regional consciousness in the university curriculum as the means of impressing students with the fact that we are far less a standardized people than the media would have us believe.

577. ———. "Symbolic Landscapes." In *The Interpretation of Ordinary Landscapes: Geographical Essays*, edited by Donald W. Meinig, 164–92. New York: Oxford Univ. Press, 1979.

Suggests that there have been three major symbolic landscapes in American cultural history: the New England town, the midwestern main street, and the Southern California suburb. See also Hart (item 557).

578. Merrens, H. R. "The Physical Environment of Early America: Images and Image Makers in Colonial South Carolina," *Geographical Review* 59 (1969): 530–556.

Describes early accounts of South Carolina as a contribution to the description of the evolution of regional description and geographical thought. Divides those accounts into types: promotional tracts, travelers' accounts, settlers' accounts, and descriptions by individuals interested in natural history. Each type is valuable in certain ways, and they all contributed to geographical understanding.

579. Moore, Gary T. and Reginald G. Golledge, eds. *Environmental Knowing: Theories, Research and Methods*. Stroudsburg, Penn.: Dowden, Hutchinson and Ross, 1976.

An encyclopedic collection of articles having to do with environmental cognition. For annotation see item 1518 under Psychology.

580. Pocock, Douglas C.D. "City of the Mind: A Review of Mental Maps of Urban Areas." *Scottish Geographical Magazine* 88 (1972): 115–24.

Lucid summary of meanings and principles of mental maps in the tradition of Kevin Lynch, as applied to Dundee, Scotland. Evaluates patterns of distortion, dependence on mode of travel, and gender differences in relation to how space is perceived.

581. ———, ed. *Humanistic Geography and Literature: Essays on the Experience of Place*. London: Croom Helm, 1981.

Essays by geographers who see literary evidence as an important neglected source for description of place and region in humanistic geography. Pocock argues in his introduction that literature is valuable to geographers because it is both holistic and universal.

582. Pocock, Douglas C.D. and Ray Hudson. *Images of the Urban Environment.* New York: Columbia Univ. Press, 1978.

A brisk survey of the subject, reviewing literature on images and mental maps as related to the urban environment, describing means of analysis and measurement in relation to such maps, and concluding with a discussion of the implications for policy and planning of particular environmental images.

583. Porteous, J. Douglas. "Home: The Territorial Core." *Geographical Magazine* 66 (1976): 383–90.

Argues that home supplies the point of orientation to the larger world and that it is finally a psychological place, providing identity, security, and stimulation and behavioral and regional focus.

584. Prince, Hugh C. "Three Realms of Historical Geography: Real, Imagined and Abstract Worlds of the Past." *Process in Geography* 3 (1971): 4–86.

An exhaustive review of historical geography, European and American, distinguishing among attempts to reconstruct the past world (e.g., Brown, item 540) or describe patterns of change (e.g., in relation to frontier); the imagining of past worlds; and the geography of statistics and models. The article is especially good on worlds of perception.

585. Raitz, Karl and Richard Ulack. "Cognitive Maps of Appalachia." *Geographical Review* 71 (1981): 201–13.

Based upon a questionnaire administered to 2,397 students. Regional boundaries are distorted toward where one lives (e.g., toward New York for New Yorkers). There is a vague fit in student maps between physiographical region and concept (general Northeast-Southwest orientation). See also Raitz and Ulach, "Appalachian Vernacular Regions," *Journal of Cultural Geography* 2 (Fall/Winter 1981), pp. 106–109.

586. Relph, E.C. *Place and Placelessness.* London: Pion Limited, 1976.

Phenomenological in approach. Relph develops a series of polar contrasts to describe the world as experienced by the individual: authentic/inauthentic; inside/outside; intersubjective/sacred. He says "placelessness" is a chronic modern condition making for a chaotically confused habitat. He hopes to inspire a new kind of urban planning attuned to the the lifeworld of its inhabitants.

587. Richardson, Miles, ed. *Place: Experience and Symbol.* Baton Rouge: Dept. of Geography and Anthropology, Louisiana State Univ., 1984.

A collection of papers from a 1982 conference at LSU by geographers friendly to the phenomenological perspective, including essays by Tuan, Buttimer, and Seamon.

588. Robinson, Brian S. "Some Fragmented Forms of Space." *Annals of the Association of American Geographers* 67 (1977): 549–563.

Argues that disorder and chaos, chance and indeterminacy, are characteristic of the modern sense of space. Robinson discusses the work of Ann Douglas, Mircea Eliade, and Kevin Lynch.

589. Rowles, Graham D. *Prisoners of Space? Exploring the Geographic Experience of Older People.* Boulder, Colo.: Westview Press, 1978.

A detailed examination of the lifeworlds of five elderly people in a rundown urban neighborhood. Rowles's approach is oral-historical, concentrating on what is said by his subjects about sense of place, rootedness, memory, boundaries, etc. This study is often cited. See also Rowles, "Geographical Dimensions of Social Support in Rural Appalachia," in *Aging and Milieu* (New York: Academic Press, 1983), edited by Rowles and Russel J. Ohta, pp. 112–30.

590. Rubin, Barbara. "Aesthetic Ideology and Urban Design." *Annals of the Association of American Geographers* 69 (September 1979): 339–61.

Describes the historical connection between money and power on the one hand, and one kind of symbolic landscape, on the other. An argument that "old" money, identified with preindustrial values,and corporate money, with a distaste for the pettiness of small business, have helped dictate popular taste. At the Chicago Columbian Exposition of 1893, the white city was designed in a precommercial way and was given the place of honor; on the same grounds, the unplanned Little Cairo, which had to turn a profit, was organized as a commercial strip. At the present day, corporate advertisement attempts to identify big business with "refined" taste.

591. Saarinen, Thomas F. *Environmental Planning: Perception and Behavior*. Boston: Houghton-Mifflin, 1976.

Meant as an introduction to the subject. Discussion moves from room and architecture (emphasizing psychology): to small town and neighborhood (emphasizing sociology): to city, region, nation, and world. Perception is related to ecology, design, and communications.

592. ———, et al., eds. *Environmental Perception and Behavior: An Inventory and Prospect*. Chicago: Univ. of Chicago, Dept. of Geography, Research Paper no. 109, 1984.

A general assessment of the field in North America and Europe: microscale and urban environments (children's environment, hazards, sense of place, historic preservation) and wider philosophical issues (with essays by Seamon, Buttimer, and others). See also Saarinen and James L. Sell, "Environmental Perception," *Progress in Human Geography* 4 (1980), pp. 525–48, which includes fourteen pages of bibliography.

593. Seamon, David and R. Mugerauer, eds. *Dwelling, Place and Environment*. The Hague: Martinus-Nijhoff, 1985.

A collection of essays derived from papers before the Society for Phenomenology and the Human Sciences. Contributors come from a variety of disciplines, and, among geographers, include Relph, Buttimer and Seamon. Architects, planners, and psychologists are included. The introduction pays special tribute to Heidegger.

594. ———. *A Geography of the Lifeworld: Movement, Rest and Encounter*. New York: St. Martin's Press, 1979.

Tries to develop a phenomenological scheme for the world as experienced by the individual. Much is made of the taken-for-granted world (and of Merleau-Ponty). Seamon works out language to describe states of attention or inattention, and degrees of involvement in the social environment.

595. Shortridge, James R. "The Vernacular Middlewest." *Annals of the Association of American Geographers* 75 (March 1985): 48–57.

Survey of college students over a wide area, asking them to map the Middlewest and list its qualities. Maps vary greatly: people in the

Old Northwest call themselves Midwesterners. People outside the area identify the Midwest with the Nebraska-Kansas area and with rural and small-town values. See also Shortridge, "The Emergence of 'Middle West' as an American Regional Label," *Annals of the Association of American Geographers* 74 (1984), pp. 209–20.

596. Tuan, Yi-Fu. "Geography, Phenomenology and the Study of Human Nature." *The Canadian Geographer* 15 (1971): 181–92.

Important as an early manifesto for a "new" geography on the part of an individual later to become a leading figure among the phenomenologists. So far as a quest for scientific status trivializes behavior, Tuan says, it becomes "scientism." Geography should be dedicated to enlarging the concept of man, and is not finally an earth science.

597. ———. "Images and Mental Maps." *Annals of the Association of American Geographers* 65 (1975): 205–13.

An attempt to clarify language about the two terms. We navigate space without maps, like other animals, so we should not overemphasize the mental dimension of spatial understandi..g. A mental map is a special construct, to aid as a help in finding our way, remembering, etc. An image is a likeness called to mind in the absence of the object. Current usage is sometimes imprecise and confusing.

598. ———. "Literature, Experience, and Environmental Knowing." In *Environmental Knowing: Theories, Research and Methods* (item 1518), 260–72. Stroudsburg, Penn.: Dowden, Hutchinson & Ross, 1976.

Implicitly a comment upon excessive emphasis on merely cognitive knowledge, as in science. Experience, Tuan says, is the sum of the means we have to know reality, and includes feeling, perception, and cognition. Literature embodies experience, and addresses the basic polarities of life (male/female, heaven/earth, life/death). It articulates experience in all its complexity, making us see things anew. The writer is thus a representative man.

599. ———. *Segmented Worlds and Self.* Minneapolis: Univ. of Minnesota Press, 1982.

Argues that modern history is characterized by an increasing segmentation of self and world, climaxing, in the nineteenth century, in separation of one social class from another, work from leisure, downtown from suburbs, and room from room. Synthetic versions of home, neighborhood and community (the bungalow, the suburban complex, and the shopping mall) attempt to reintegrate modern life.

600. ———. *Space and Place: The Perspective of Experience.* Minneapolis: Univ. of Minnesota Press, 1977.

A reworking of the materials in *Topophilia* (item 601). The approach is more systematic than in the earlier book, emphasizing the perspective of experience as the organizing principle. Discussion progresses from the spatial experience of the child to that of the adult, and from the experience of the individual to perceptions of the world.

601. ———. *Topophilia: A Study of Perception, Attitudes and Values.* Englewood Cliffs, N.J.: Prentice-Hall, 1974.

The first book-length statement by the foremost of the "humanistic" geographers. Tuan reviews an amazingly diverse literature to arrive at generalizations about the connections between locale and cosmos, individual and world. He is especially good on how the various senses convey particular aspects of experience (touch as immediate, e.g., and sight as more distant). For discussion of threatening environments see Tuan, *Landscapes of Fear* (New York: Pantheon, 1979).

602. Watson, J. Wreford and Timothy O'Riordan, eds. *The American Environment: Perceptions and Policies.* London: John Wiley and Sons, 1976.

Watson argues that images of progress, the frontier, middle landscape and a democratic people are central to American history. See especially Watson on "Image Regions," pp. 15–28; "The Image of Nature in America," pp. 63–75; and "The City and the American Way of Life," pp. 79–92. Contributors to the collection come from England as well as the United States. See also Watson, "Image Geography: The Myth of America in the American Scene," *The Advancement of Science* 27 (1970–71), pp. 71–79, which describes characteristic "traits" of the American landscape. Watson is clearly in debt to Wright and Lowenthal.

603. Wright, John K. *Human Nature in Geography: Fourteen Papers, 1925–1945.* Edited by David Lowenthal. Cambridge, Mass.: Harvard Univ. Press, 1966.

A collection of essays by a geographer who long ago insisted that ideas and their history were important to geography. They include an essay on terrae incognitae, pp. 68–88; polar seas, pp. 89–118;

measuring and counting in early American geography, especially by Jefferson and Morse, pp. 205–249; and pieties related to natural wonders. What Wright called "geosophy" anticipated present-day work by Tuan and Lowenthal.

604. Zdorkowski, R. Todd and George O. Carney. "This Land is My Land: Oklahoma's Changing Vernacular Regions." *Journal of Cultural Geography* 5 (1985): 97–106.

Results of a questionnaire sent to county historical societies, yielding dominant, secondary and remembered (past) terms for vernacular areas. Many respondents (48%) used terms coined by the state tourist agency.

605. Zelinsky, Wilbur. "North America's Vernacular Regions." *Annals of the Association of American Geographers* 70 (1980): 1–16.

Surveys telephone books to determine how frequently regional terms are used as names by businesses in different parts of the country. On the basis of that evidence, the author maps out vernacular regions of the United States (North, South, Dixie, etc.), as well as areas that seem to have weak regional identity (e.g., northern Ohio)

Geography: Landscape and Settlement

Entries under this subheading have in common a focus upon areal differentiation. They depend upon field-study of landscape and settlement and/or upon documents that reveal actual use and settlement patterns, as against, say, statistical analysis of distributional patterns. They tend to emphasize man-land relationships, and to be sensitive to considerations of terrain and climate. The size of the area is almost a matter of indifference, as are rural-urban distinctions (although there is a tradition of preferring rural subjects). Ordinarily, students of landscape are also sensitive to historical patterns as they affect morphology or structure. (On "perceptual" landscapes, see the previous subsection.)

The emphasis on landscape goes back to Vidal (item 706) and is continued in the work of Sauer and his students. During the post-World War II period an emphasis upon numbers and scientific method among geographers nearly displaced the tradition of landscape study, although it persisted even during those lean years, and has reasserted itself in the last decade or so, under the leadership of Pierce Lewis and Wilbur Zelinsky. Along with a resurgence of landscape study has come a resurgence of historical geography, as is reflected in the anthologies compiled by Ward and by Mitchell and Groves.

This subheading seemed to be the right place for related concerns: general approaches to geography from a regional perspective; treatments of land survey and alienation; and debates about the nature and prospects for historical geography. Also included are basic atlases and bibliographies important to the study of landscape and region.

The rebirth of interest in historical geography is reinforced by the ascendancy of a localized kind of history (see especially History: Frontier and Landscape). Interest in landscape shades off into interest in vernacular architecture and ordinary landscape (see Folk Studies): and in fact the geographer Kniffen was one of the founding fathers of that kind of vernacular study.

C.M.

606. Baerwald, Thomas. "The Emergence of a New 'Downtown.'" *Geographical Review* 68 (1978): 308–18, 378.

Studies the landscape of a new regional type, the suburban freeway corridor strip. The subject is an area in Minneapolis over the 1953–76 period. It has its own pattern: building was for the first time and for altogether mixed uses, with a gradual succession from residential to high-value industrial-commercial use, but with bargain stores filling in left-over land.

607. Bjorklund, Elaine M. "Ideology and Culture Exemplified in Southwestern Michigan." *Annals of the American Association of Geographers* 54 (1964): 227–41.

A study in region-building. Bjorklund describes the continuing landscape effects of colonization by strict Calvinist Dutch Reformed immigrants in Michigan. The immigrants bought up two tiers of townships in the 1840s and have kept control of the land since. They adapted to American conditions in selected ways, dropping the old-world language and building in the American way, but developing a distinct segregation of commercial from other activities, making the church central to settlement patterns.

608. Blouet, Brian and Frederick C. Luebke, eds. *The Great Plains: Environment and Culture.* Lincoln: Univ. of Nebraska Press, 1979.

Twelve essays presented at a Cultural Heritage of the Plains Symposium in 1977. In the introduction, Luebke contrasts culturalists (Webb, Malin and, Kraenzel) to environmentalists (Pomeroy, Berkhofer, and Mather). He recommends Meinig's study of Texas as an example of how one need not adopt one approach to the neglect of the other.

609. Borchert, John R. *America's Northern Heartland: An Economic and Historical Geography of the Upper Midwest.* Minneapolis: Univ. of Minnesota Press, 1987.

A general survey of an American region, with excellent maps, photographs, and bibliography. The region is described period by period over the course of its history. The concern is with general patterns rather than with close description of particular cases, with the overall focus upon the development of a central place network and attendant transportation. Regional topography, settlement history, urban development and demography are the principal themes.

610. Bowman, Isaiah. "Our Expanding and Contracting Desert." *Geographical Review* 25 (1935): 43–61.

This study of climate over time emphasizes the indeterminacy of regional boundaries. It compares and contrasts cycles of rainfall, availability of glaciers, and evidence of sun-spot cycles, and on that basis develops a map of zones in the American West according to their place on a continuum between dry and humid conditions.

611. Brigham, Albert Perry. *Geographic Influences in American History.* Port Washington N.Y.: Kennikatt Press, 1970.

Originally published in 1903. A pioneer attempt to bring geography to bear upon history. Brigham surveys the social and economic effects of topography, rainfall, soil types, etc., going east to west by region. He argues that the reasons for sectional distinctions lack their old authority.

612. Brodsly, David. *L.A. Freeway: An Appreciative Essay.* Berkeley: Univ. of California Press, 1981.

A lively description of what might be called a freeway region. Brodsly traces the continuity from footpaths to railroads to electric railroads to early highways to freeways. He shows how freeways link big business to recreation and to industrial districts. The freeways, he argues, bespeak commitment to individual freedom, liberation from place, and the democracy of mobility.

613. Broek, Jan O.M. *The Santa Clara Valley, California: A Study in Landscape Changes.* Utrecht: Oosthoek, 1932.

Often cited. Broek describes valley landscape at four different time periods, as historical cross-sections (primitive, Spanish-Mexican, early American, present). Description of period landscapes are followed by discussion of socioeconomic determinants of change from one period to the next.

614. Bryan, Patrick Walter. *Man's Adaptation of Nature: Studies of the Cultural Landscape.* New York: Henry Holt & Co., 1933.

The first half of the book develops terminology and methodology for the study of cultural landscapes and regions; the second examines various kinds of American landscapes (e.g., the corn belt, the effects of the railroad, the urban environment). The study is an early effort at interdisciplinary human geography.

615. Clark, Andrew H. *Three Centuries and an Island: An Historical Geography of Settlement and Agriculture in Prince Edward Island, Canada.* Toronto: Univ. of Toronto Press, 1959.

A model work by a great historical geographer. Clark makes an exhaustive study of land, cultural background, and agricultural practices over three centuries. The island is almost uniform in its physical qualities, so differences in agricultural practice are a function of which group (English, Scotch, "Americans," etc.) is involved. See also Clark, *Acadia: The Geography of Early Nova Scotia to 1760* (Madison: Univ. of Wisconsin Press, 1968), a similarly detailed study of French settlement in Nova Scotia.

616. Conzen, M.R.G. *The Urban Landscape: Historical Development and Management.* Edited by J.W.R. Whitehead. London: Academic Press, 1981.

Conzen was trained in Germany and has spent his professional life in England. His best-known book is *Alnwick, Northumberland: A Study in Town Plan Analysis.* Whitehead describes his "morphogenetic" approach to urban landscape in the preface to this collection of essays.

617. Conzen, Michael, ed. "Fashioning the American Landscape." *The Geographical Magazine* 52 (1979–1980).

A good collection of essays on the general subject. Topics include topography, Indian landscape, Spanish borderland, New France, English colonies, southern plantations, woodland clearings, utopias, industrial landscapes, cowboy landscapes, central business districts, and gentrified landscapes.

618. Darby, H.C. "The Changing English Landscape." *Geographical Journal* 117 (1951): 377–98.

A model synoptic study of English landscape and regional changes since the coming of the Saxons, describing deforestation, draining of marshes, tillage and enclosure, country gardens, growth of watering places, migration to cities and growth of manufactures. Attendant maps and illustrations are very helpful. Beresford and Hoskins cited (q.v., under History: Frontier and Landscape, items 894, 914).

619. ———, ed. *A New Historical Geography of England.* Cambridge, England: Cambridge Univ. Press, 1973.

Essays reconstructing the English cultural landscape at six different moments in English history (1086, 1334, 1600, 1800, 1850, 1900), along with essays describing changes in the intervening periods. See also Darby, *Domesday England* (London: Cambridge Univ. Press, 1977): for a summary of information gleaned from the survey of England done in the eleventh century.

620. Dodge, Stanley D. "Bureau and the Princeton Community." *Annals of the American Association of Geographers* 22 (1932): 159–210.

A thorough regional study of a rural area surrounding Princeton, Illinois. Careful study of geography and of the impress of woods, prairies and streams, as well as seasonal variations, becomes the basis for discussion of roads, patterns of travel on those roads, homes, layout of towns, and the impact of the railroad on settlement patterns.

621. Dunbar, G.S. "Illustrations of the American Earth: A Bibliographical Essay on the Cultural Geography of the United States." In *American Studies: Topics and Sources*, edited by Robert H. Walker, 50–58. Westport, Conn.: Greenwood, 1971.

A general bibliography, in debt to Zelinsky. See also its follow-up, Christopher Salter, "Recent Views of the American Landscape," in *Sources for American Studies* (Westport, Conn.: Greenwood, 1983), edited by Jefferson B. Kellogg and Robert H. Walker, pp. 418–23

622. Duncan, James S. "Landscape Taste as a Symbol of Group Identity: A Westchester County Village." *Geographical Review* 63 (July 1973): 344–55.

This study of the landscape of a suburban community within commuting distances of New York City detects three landscape types related to three different social networks: one imitating England landscape taste, removed from public view; a second in an ostentatiously colonial revival style, exposed to the road; and a third and town landscape created by Italian tradesmen with no social pretensions.

623. Evans, Emyr Estyn. *Personality of Ireland: Habitat, Heritage and History*. Cambridge: Cambridge Univ. Press, 1973.

Evans, one of the great cultural geographers of our time, here reviews his life's work on Ireland. He places himself in the tradition of Vidal, Sauer, and Fleure. See also Evans, "The Ecology of Peasant Life in Western Europe," *Man's Role in Changing the Face of the Earth* (item 699), pp. 217–39.

624. ———. "The Cultural Geographer and Folklife Research." In *Folklore and Folklife, an Introduction*, edited by Richard M. Dorson, 517–32. Chicago: Univ. of Chicago Press, 1972.

Annotated under Folk Studies (item 404).

625. Francaviglia, Richard V. *The Mormon Landscape: Existence, Creation and Perception of a Unique Image in the American West*. New York: AMS Press, 1978.

Describes how the Mormons created a particular landscape, with its own architecture, street plan, and logic of community. An analysis of art and literature is included.

626. Gaustad, Edwin Scott. *Historical Atlas of Religion in America*. rev. ed. New York: Harper and Row, 1976.

Originally published in 1962. The standard work of its kind, covering the United States only. Gaustad maps out distributional patterns of major denominations over time. The revised edition substitutes county distribution patterns for earlier maps on a state-by-state basis. It includes large fold-out maps of distribution of denominational "families" and of church members as a percentage of total population.

627. Gibson, James R., ed. *European Settlement and Development in North America: Essays on Geographical Change in Honour and Memory of Andrew Hill Clark*. Toronto: Univ. of Toronto Press, 1978.

First-rate essays on a wide range of subjects in historical geography: the extension of France into rural Canada, Russia in the New World, the formation of culture regions (item 677): antebellum rice culture, Hudson Bay Company in the eighteenth century, territory and identity (item 669), the Victorian city in England and the U.S., and weakness of community in early Pennsylvania.

628. Gottman, Jean. "Why the Skyscraper." *Geographical Review* 56 (1966): 190–212.

An elegant appreciation of a kind of structure that has become the focal point for many nodal regions. The skyscraper attended the development of a commercial life that had become newly intricate; it provided an appropriate and efficient way of getting people together and processing information; it became possible with the coming of mass transportation; it is a true expression of a new social order.

629. Griffin, Ernst and Larry Ford. "Tijuana: Landscape of a Culture Hybrid." *Geographical Review* 66 (1975): 435–47.

A description of convergent regional patterns at a time of great change. For several reasons (e.g., wages, establishment of free zone): Tijuana has had a population boom. Housing ranges from huts made of cardboard and trash to a Los Angeles-style display of wealth. The authors are particularly interested in the pervasiveness in all social classes of the need for fences, which they tie in with the Latin courtyard style. In " A Model of Latin American City Structure," *Geographical Review* 70 (1981), pp. 397–422, the authors contrast the evolution of Latin American city form to that in North America.

630. Harris, Richard Colebrook. "The Historical Geography of North American Regions." *American Behavioral Scientist* 22 (1978): 115–30.

One of several recent efforts to characterize the evolution of cultural regions in the United States. Harris draws from Conzen, Vance, and Pred in arguing that information flow and economic development are basic to the establishment of regions. Colonial hearth areas along the east coast lose influence as the population moves west. Tocqueville's emphasis on individualism sounds the proper central note, says the author. See also Harris, "The Simplification of Europe Overseas," *Annals of the Association of American Geographers* 67 (December 1977), pp. 469–83.

631. ———. *The Seigneurial System in Early Canada: A Geographic Study*. Madison: Univ. of Wisconsin Press, 1966.

Examines how a medieval pattern of land grants affected actual settlement and use. Harris studies the effect of title on settlement, land alienation, crops grown and town settlement, concluding that the medieval patterns had little practical effect.

632. Hart, John Fraser. *The Look of the Land*. Englewood Cliffs, N.J.: Prentice-Hall, 1975.

A readable and succinct description of rural landscape patterns throughout the country by the leading expert on the subject. It includes an interesting discussion of landscape as amenity (e.g., as the setting for the blue-grass gentleman farmer). See also *The Southeastern United States* (Princeton, N.J.: Van Nostrand, 1967) for a discussion of agricultural subregions in the old cotton belt.

633. ———, ed. *Regions of the United States*. New York: Harper and Row, 1972.

Many articles cited in this bibliography are collected in this reprint of *Annals of the Association of American Geographers* 62 (1972), pp. 155–373: Meinig on the American West (cited in item 492 under Geography: Region as Concept); Vance on California (item 704): Pierce Lewis on a small Pennsylvania city (item 662): Prunty and Aiken on the Piedmont Cotton region (item 686); and Borchert on urban regions (item 736). There are also essays on the Colorado Plateau, the Great Plains, the Middle West and northern New England, as well as a brief essay by John B. Jackson.

634. Hart, John Fraser and Ennis Chestang. "Rural Revolution in East Carolina." *Geographical Review* 68 (1978): 435–58.

Describes regional change in the Piedmont tobacco country with the coming of mechanization (1954–1976). Most farmers gave up tobacco farming and went to work in nearby factories while continuing to live on the land. The size of tobacco farms has increased dramatically. The old and new technologies, as well as the landscape, are carefully described.

635. Hecht, Melvin E. "The Decline of the Grass Lawn Tradition in Tucson." *Landscape* 19 (May 1975): 3–10.

Studies regional integration. Latinos originally did not have grass lawns. American immigrants brought them to the Tucson area. Gradually, pebbles and desert flora yards became fashionable among the better-off "Anglos," even as Latinos made the grass lawn their own. Schools and other public institutions, as of the time of the article, still preferred grass.

636. Hewes, Leslie. *The Suitcase Farming Frontier: A Study in the Historical Geography of the Central Great Plains.* Lincoln: Univ. of Nebraska Press, 1973.

Hewes describes the "suitcase farmer" as a harbinger of change in Colorado and Kansas, from cattle raising to the raising of grain, during the 1920–1950 period. Sixty pages of maps and charts.

637. Hilliard, Sam B. "Headright Grants and Surveying in Northeastern Georgia." *Geographical Review* 72 (1982): 416–429.

A model study of land granting and land alienation, in an area measured by the metes and bounds system and granted by head right (one hundred acres to the head of family, fifty acres for each dependent and slave). The main land rush was during the 1785–1800 period.

Much more land was granted than existed. Illustrations of relevant documents support the text.

638. Hugill, Peter J. "Houses in Cazenovia: The Effects of Time and Class." *Landscape* 24:2 (1980): 10–15.

A study of changes in vernacular housing in a New York City over a century and a half. Early houses were imitative of New England and built in the spirit of the Greek Revival. In the 1890s, there was a housing boom, involving the building of huge Victorian-style residences. Over entire period, interesting patterns of imitation of fashion and individually eccentric patterns of remodeling. The city is now becoming a suburb of Syracuse.

639. Hudson, John C. "Cultural Geography in the Upper Great Lake Region." *Journal of Cultural Geography* 5 (1984): 19–32.

Mines county histories in upper great lakes region to determine birthplaces of residents. Hudson argues that the St. Lawrence Valley constitutes a distinct region because of patterns of generally due-west migration along the international boundary, with low-density occupations (e.g., lumbering). People in the area emphasize local values, and are relatively indifferent to national boundaries and concerns.

640. ———. *Plains Country Towns*. Minneapolis: Univ. of Minnesota Press, 1987.

A case-study of fourteen counties in north-central North Dakota. The central actors in the drama are the railroad companies, which decide where towns are to be placed and which towns are to survive, on which terms. The railroad towns typically provide crucial central-place functions without the usual supporting residential population. For a briefer version, see Hudson, "The Plains Country Town," *The Great Plains: Environment and Culture* (Lincoln: Univ. of Nebraska Press, 1979, edited by B.W. Blouet and F.C. Luebke, pp. 99–118.

641. Jackson, J.B. *American Space: The Centennial Years, 1865-1876*. New York: Norton, 1972.

Jackson, the dean of American landscape historians, here surveys the status of the national landscape at a time when its regional mosaic was undergoing a profound transformation. The railroad, especially, made Americans conscious of the changes underway, which Jackson reviews region by region. By the time of the Centennial Exposition in 1876, he argues, Americans were learning how to manage flow and change, and this was represented in the layout of the Exposition.

642. ———. *Discovering the Vernacular Landscape*. New Haven: Yale Univ. Press, 1984.

A summing-up of Jackson's thought, this collection of essays addresses the question of how to define landscape, pp. 1–8; the contrast between political and vernacular landscapes, pp. 9–55; and his typology of historical landscapes, pp. 147–59; moving from Landscape I (the medieval), to Landscape II (the modern), to Landscape III (the emergent, post-modern pattern).

643. ———. *The Necessity for Ruins*. Amherst: Univ. of Massachusetts Press, 1980.

Brilliant exercises in areal differentiation. This book exhibits Jackson at his best, in short, reflective essays on an amazing variety of topics. He describes the change in landscape affected by the U.S. military in Europe during World War II; traces the idea of the garden; contrasts the medieval to the modern town; describes the relation between theater and landscape; and talks of the "grove" as the locus for revivals in antebellum America, the shift in the meaning of monuments (in the title essay), and the evolution of the garage as an ingredient in the suburban landscape. A similarly varied range of topics is addressed in Jackson, *Landscapes: Selected Writings of J.B. Jackson* (Amherst: Univ. of Massachusetts Press, 1970), edited by Ervin H. Zube.

644. Jackson, Richard H. "Religion and Landscape in the Mormon Cultural Region." In *Dimensions of Human Geography: Essays on Some Familiar and Neglected Themes*, edited by Karl W. Butzer, 100–27. Chicago: Univ. of Chicago, Dept. of Geography, Research Paper 186.

An investigation of the interplay between Mormonism and the distinctiveness of the Mormon landscape, arguing that Smith's plan for the City of Zion was, largely, an adaptation of midwestern practice at that time; and, further, that focus upon a relict landscape has obscured the fact that since 1900 the Mormons have built in the approved suburban way, indistinguishable from building elsewhere.

645. Jakle, John. "Time, Space and the Geographic Past: A Prospectus for Historical Geography." *American Historical Review* 76 (1971): 1084–1103.

Argues for more attention to scientific, predictive, nomothetic study as the basis for interchange between geography and history. Jakle contrasts his agenda to that of Donald Meinig (item 670). In making his case, he reviews the evolution of historical geography over time, climaxing in the mathematical modeling of such geographers as Hagerstrand (item 753).

646. Johnson, Hildegard Binder. *Order Upon the Land: The U.S. Rectangular Land Survey and the Upper Mississippi Country.* New York: Oxford Univ. Press, 1976.

A model study of land-survey practices in the subject area, at once meticulously detailed and wide-ranging in its concerns. See also Johnson, "Rational and Ecological Aspects of the Quarter-Section: An Example from Minnesota," *Geographical Review* 47 (1957), pp. 330–48, which shows how early claimants manipulated the grid system so as to incorporate tree and bottom land within a single farm.

647. Jordan, Terry G. *German Seed to Texas Soil: Immigrant Farmers in Nineteenth Century Texas.* Austin: Univ. of Texas Press, 1966.

Traces farming practices from home areas in Germany to German immigrant settlements in Texas. Jordan studies farms, crops, settlement types, level of productivity, and persistency of ownership. He finds that the immigrants tended to discard traditional practices upon arrival in the interest of survival, but returned to some traditional practices once they were securely established.

648. ———. "The Imprint of the Upper and Lower South on Mid-Nineteenth Century Texas." *Annals of the Association of American Geographers* 57 (1967): 667–90.

Examines the state of origin of Texas settlers, crops raised, animals kept, and vote on secession and works out an index of "upper Southernness," and division between Lower South and Upper South as applied to Texas as of 1860–70 (as revealed in planting of wheat, number of slaves, states of origin, vote on secession, etc.).

649. ———. *Texas Graveyards: A Cultural Legacy.* Austin: Univ. of Texas Press, 1982.

An exercise in necrogeography. Jordan traces graveyard types by ethnic groups in Texas, notably southern (black and white), Hispanic and German. Jordan sees the book as a kind of material culture study and includes many pictures and careful descriptions of how cemetery traditions are kept up by the living.

650. ———. *Trails to Texas: Southern Roots of Western Cattle Ranching.* Lincoln: Univ. of Nebraska Press, 1981.

Argues that Texas cattle ranching derived from patterns developed in South Carolina that fused with patterns of the Spanish to form a Texas style.

651. Jordan, Terry G. and Lester Rowntree. *Human Mosaic: A Thematic Introduction to Cultural Geography.* New York: Harper and Row, 1982.

A first-rate text in cultural geography, reviewing ideas about region and discussing central ideas such as cultural diffusion, cultural ecology, cultural integration, cultural landscape, political patterns, settlement patterns, the geographies of religion, folk culture, popular culture, and urban geography. Concern is worldwide.

652. Kniffen, Fred. "The American Agricultural Fair: Time and Place." *Annals of the Association of American Geographers* 41 (1951): 42–57.

A study of regional influence. Kniffen maps diffusion of fairs over time from New England west, spreading to border South, and isochrones as to when in the year fairs are held. See also "The American Agricultural Fair: The Pattern," *Annals of the Association of American Geographers* 39 (1949), pp. 264–82, which describes the historical evolution of the fair, from an impromptu educational affair to its later form as an event at fixed locations with an emphasis upon amusements.

653. ———. "Folk Housing: Key to Diffusion." *Annals of the Association of American Geographers* 55 (1965): 549–557.

Annotated under Folk Studies, item 422.

654. ———. "Material Culture in the Geographic Interpretation of the Landscape." In *The Human Mirror: Material and Spatial Images of Man,* edited by Miles Richardson, 252–68. Baton Rouge: Louisiana State Univ., 1974.

Kniffen here argues that geography is getting more interested in the "mental" side of culture. As a demonstration of that approach, he talks about the Louisiana landscape as it was used by the French, the Spanish, Southerners and Midwesterners, as revealed in building and cadastral patterns. See also Kniffen, "Louisiana House Types," *Annals of the Association of American Geographers* 26 (1936), pp. 179–93.

655. Kniffen, Fred and Henry Glassie. "Building in Wood in the Eastern United States: A Time-Place Perspective." *Geographical Review* 56 (1966): 40–66.

Maps the distribution of folk housing built of wood in the eastern U.S. The authors argue that folk housing reflects the "fundamental needs and urges" of its builders, and that the need to document wood buildings is compelling, since they are disappearing from the scene without being documented. (See entries on vernacular architecture and by Glassie, especially, under Folk Studies.)

656. Kollmorgen, Walter M. "A Reconnaissance of Some Cultural-Agricultural Islands in the South." Parts 1,2. *Economic Geography* 17,19 (1941, 1943): 409–30, 109–17.

A stroll through the old cotton belt, to examine ethnic colonies there that have brought new techniques to southern farming. The general object is to promote experimentation. The colonies and their success or failure are described one by one. The second essay attempts to generalize, largely depending upon a federal type-of-farming atlas, to document the importance of these ethnic groups.

657. Lemon, James T. *The Best Poor Man's Country: A Geographical Study of Early Southeastern Pennsylvania*. Baltimore: Johns Hopkins Univ. Press, 1972.

Concerned with early settlement patterns of dispersed farms in the subject area. Lemon sees the pattern of middling people exploiting individual opportunities in a multi-ethnic culture as characteristic of the area and of what is to be the pattern for the new nation. The book charts settlement and land-use patterns for the settlers and their immediate descendants.

658. Lewis, Pierce F. "Common Houses, Cultural Spoor." *Landscape* 19 (January 1975): 1–22.

This general discussion of the diffusion of vernacular and folk house forms follows Glassie and Kniffen in relation to folk forms and emphasizes the diffusion of vernacular forms, especially after the Civil War. The general argument is that form triumphs over function and time as an indicator of cultural values. Lewis delights in describing the illogic of Italianate roofs in a snow belt and free-standing row houses with no side windows.

659. ———. "The Galactic Metropolis." In *Beyond the Urban Fringe: Land Use Issues of Nonmetropolitan America*, edited by Rutherford H. Platt and George Macinko, 23–49. Minneapolis: Univ. of Minnesota Press, 1983.

Argues that a new morphology and culture is now universal within the United States. With the coming of the car, the old Central Business District (CBD) became obsolete. Now a multinucleated urban complex, linked together by highways and interstates, makes everywhere available. The interchange, parking lots, and low-slung buildings have become universal; and old distinctions between urban and rural are now obsolete. Commentaries follow by Kirk H. Stone, pp. 51–56, and John Borchert, pp. 57–59.

660. ———. "Learning from Looking: Geographic and Other Writing About the American Cultural Landscape." *American Quarterly* 35 (1983): 242–61.

An excellent and wide-ranging review of the literature.

661. ———. *New Orleans: The Making of an Urban Landscape.* Cambridge, Mass.: Ballinger Publishing Co., 1976.

A model and concise study of urban landscape emphasizing morphology and changes over time, generously illustrated and mapped, probably the best known of the Ballinger series of urban biographies in the AAG Comparative Metropolitan Project (items 721, 724).

662. ———. "Small Town in Pennsylvania." *Annals of the Association of American Geographers* 62 (1972): 323–51.

Often cited. Lewis first surveys the literature about small towns in the United States, saying they have been central to American identity. He then analyzes Bellefonte, Pennsylvania, an early commercial center which enjoyed marked prosperity in the late nineteenth century because of its iron works, became stagnant with much outmigration thereafter, until the influence of a nearby state university introduced new growth patterns.

663. ———. "The Unprecedented City." In *The American Land*, edited by Alexis Doster, et al., 184–92. New York: Smithsonian Exposition Books, 1979.

Argues that American cities are dual in structure: an old spiderweb plan around a CBD, created by railroad and water transportation systems; and the "galactic city" created by the car which has no downtown (e.g., Los Angeles). Since the coming of the car, all growth in all towns and cities is galactic. Some CBDs keep some vitality; some are gutted. Regional concentrations make for high-rises in a Minneapolis or a Denver but not a revival of the old downtown. Lewis praises the virtues of the galactic city and wonders at the biases against it.

664. Ley, David and Roman Cybriwsky. "The Social Ecology of Stripped Cars." *Environment and Behavior* 6 (1974): 53–67.

Describes the patterns of deviant behavior as evidenced by the placement of stripped cars (in front of blind walls, abandoned buildings, vacant lots, etc.) Such a pattern only becomes evident with close study of small areas. See also Ley and Cybriwsky, "Urban Graffiti as Territorial Markers," *Annals of the Association of American Geographers* 64 (1974), pp. 491–505.

665. Malmberg, Torsten. *Human Territoriality*. The Hague: Mouton Publishers, 1980.

Overview of subject, describing basic concepts, animal territories, territories in man (primitive territories, rural territories, urban territories): special territories (cemeteries, playgrounds, etc.): an analysis of behavioral territoriality, and a general evaluation (relation to genes, evolution, overpopulation and freedom).

666. Marsh, George Perkins. *Man and Nature*. Edited by David Lowenthal. Cambridge: Harvard Univ. Press, 1965.

Originally published in 1864. An encyclopedic analysis of environmental change promoting a novel idea for the time: the notion that human beings were largely free to mold the earth and that much of the earth, for better or worse, was a man-made product. See Marsh's introduction, pp. 7–52, for a sweeping portrait of man as the dominant, often destructive, force in changing the physical world. For a relatively recent reprise on that general topic, see item 700.

667. Mayer, Harold and Richard C. Wade. *Chicago: Growth of a Metropolis*. Chicago: Univ. of Chicago Press, 1969.

A geographer and a historian pair up to create an invaluable visual record of change within an urban region. The book is dependent upon a rich collection of photographs and maps. The book is especially good on the evolution of the suburbs and the transportation system required to make the entire system work.

668. McManis, Douglas R. *Colonial New England: A Historical Geography*. New York: Oxford Univ. Press, 1975.

A matter-of-fact survey of area, early exploration, the development of English settlement and of commerce and early industries. McManis uses geographical concepts as the means of understanding the location and development of principal settlements.

669. McQuillan, D. Aiden. "Territory and Ethnic Identity: Some New Measures of an Old Theme in the Cultural Geography of the United States." In *European Settlement and Development in North America* (item 627), 136–60. Toronto: Univ. of Toronto Press, 1978.

A study comparing ethnic persistence (1885–1925) among three ethnic groups in selected Kansas townships. McQuillan finds Mennonites most persistent, French Canadians least, Swedes somewhere in between. The essay contrasts social assimilation (e.g., to market economy) with cultural assimilation (e.g., religion).

670. Meinig, Donald W. *The Great Columbia Plain: A Historical Geography*. Seattle: Univ. of Washington Press, 1968.

A detailed study of settlement and adaptation in relation to an area inland from the rain forest in the Washington-Oregon area. Meinig's concern is patterns, not process. The pattern in 1805 is contrasted with that in 1910 as the means of organizing the book. He describes the sequence of settlement, from entry through competition for use to conquest and empire. Many maps included.

671. ———. *Imperial Texas: An Interpretive Essay*. Austin, Texas: Univ. of Texas Press, 1969.

This small book applies Meinig's interest in core, domain and periphery (see item 492) to the development of the Texas culture area. The author sketches the historical interplay among cultural groups (Germans, lower South migrants, upper South migrants, Latinos) in relation to transportation, religion, and language. The study is synthetic, rather than detailed. See also Meinig, *Southwest: Three Peoples in Geographical Change, 1600–1970* (New York: Oxford Univ. Press, 1971), which applies the same strategy to another region (the three peoples are the Indians, the Hispanics and the Anglo-Saxons).

672. ———. *The Shaping of America: A Geographical Perspective on 500 Years of History*. Vol. I, *Atlantic America, 1492–1800*. New Haven: Yale Univ. Press, 1986.

This first of three volumes of a major historical-geographical synthesis chronicles the translation and implantation of European colonies in the new world, and the evolution of new-world regions, culminating in the establishment of the new nation. The emphasis is cultural and social, rather than topographical. Meinig describes, step by step, how international rivalry generated particular patterns of itinerant use, then fugitive settlement, then full-bodied culture areas. The account draws upon a very substantial bibliography, and is accompanied by original maps and diagrams. He outlines the case for a system of cultural hearths as the logic of historical geography in "The Continuous Shaping of America: A Prospectus for Geographers and Historians," *American Historical Review* 83 (1978), pp. 1185–1217 (see Jakle's rejoinder, item 645).

673. ———, ed. *The Interpretation of Ordinary Landscape: Geographical Essays.* New York: Oxford Univ. Press, 1979.

This good if uneven collection of essays is a useful introduction to the general subject of ordinary (or "vernacular") landscape. Meinig, Lewis, Tuan, Jackson and Sopher contribute. Meinig's appreciation of W. G. Hoskins and J.B. Jackson, pp. 195–244, is especially useful as an analysis of the work of two principal pioneers in landscape history.

674. Merrens, H. Roy. "Historical Geography and Early American History." *William and Mary Quarterly,* Series 3, 22 (1965): 529–48.

Workmanlike survey of historical geography addressed to historians, emphasizing colonial history. Merrens says there are three grand traditions involved: spatial distribution, man-land relationships, and chorographic or area analysis. He comments that geographers have only recently become seriously interested in historical data. He himself had just completed *Colonial North Carolina in the Eighteenth Century: A Study in Historical Geography* (Chapel Hill: Univ. of North Carolina Press, 1964).

675. Mitchell, Robert D. "American Origins and Regional Institutions: The Seventeenth-Century Chesapeake." *Annals of the Association of American Geographers* 73 (1983): 404–20.

Analyzes the early Chesapeake Bay area to test notions of cultural region. Mitchell generally argues against Zelinsky's three hearths (item 718), Henretta's notion of precommercial *mentalite* (item 868) and Lemon's exclusive attention to class difference (item 657). Mitchell describes the Chesapeake as devoted to individual gain, with land the currency. The church is weak, the market orientation strong. The pattern takes hold with the native-born after 1650.

676. ———. *Commercialism and the Frontier: Perspectives on the Early Settlement of the Shenandoah Valley.* Charlottesville: Univ. of Virginia Press, 1977.

A historical study on a county and regional level, focusing upon patterns of economic development during the eighteenth century. It describes the early distribution of land, the development of more specialized agriculture, and, finally, the evolution of a more stratified society by the end of the period. The Valley as a region fused patterns from Virginia with those from Pennsylvania. Commercial opportunity characterized the movement, more than anything else; religion was important; ethnicity became increasingly less important. These changes become important as the society moves further west.

677. ———. "The Formation of Early American Cultural Regions: An Interpretation." In *European Settlement and Development in North America* (item 627), 66–90.

Argues for a pattern of culture diffusion that corresponds neither to Turner nor Meinig. Mitchell argues that Americans shared materialistic, libertarian values generally; that hearth areas (Boston, Philadelphia, Chesapeake Bay, maybe Charleston) became basis for secondary areas, but that as culture moved west and especially over Appalachians variants occurred (deviation, fusion, replication). Most of the early cis-Appalachian migrants had earlier migrated inland from the coast.

678. ———. "The North American Past: Retrospect and Prospect." In *North America: The Historical Geography of a Changing Continent* (item 679), 3–21.

A useful summary of the history of historical geography, tracing the influence of Sauer, Wright, Brown, and Clark. The great themes of that history, Mitchell says, are the acquisition of geographical knowledge, cultural transfer from the old world, frontier expansion, spatial organization, resource exploitation, and landscape change.

679. Mitchell, Robert D. and Paul A. Groves, eds. *North America: The Historical Geography of a Changing Continent.* Totowa, N.J.: Rowman and Littlefield, 1987.

This text incorporates essays by leading historical geographers to tell the story from settlement to date. Each geographer treats a given region and/or period. Contributors include Nostrand, R.C. Harris, Hilliard, Earle, McIlwraith, Wishart, Ward, Lewis and Vance, as well as the editors.

680. Mook, Maurice A. and John A. Hostetler. "The Amish and Their Land." *Landscape* 6 (Spring 1957): 21–28.

Because the Amish valued the next world rather than this, they took a strictly utilitarian attitude toward architecture and farmscape, with the whole characterized by a severe geometry.

681. Morse, Jedidiah. *The American Geography, or a View of the Present Situation of the United States of America.* 1789. Reprint. New York: Arno Press, 1970.

The first comprehensive American geography. Morse argues that a text on geography is called for now that the United States has achieved nationhood. He says that he is making no attempt at originality, but rather is interested in compiling information otherwise inaccessible. The book is organized in terms of a general survey and then of more detailed information state by state, describing terrain, population, economy, institutions and history.

682. Newton, Milton, Jr. "Cultural Preadaptation and the Upland South." In *Man and Cultural Heritage: Papers in Honor of Fred B. Kniffen*, edited by M.J. Walker and W.J. Haag, 143–154. Baton Rouge: School of Geosciences, Louisiana State Univ., 1974.

Uses biological term (preadaptation) to argue that culture (form) invents functional patterns. Newton argues that the Upper South was formed in 1725–1775, then exploded over the upper and lower South from 1775 to 1825. Dominated by Scots-Irish and Germans, it carried with it dispersed settlement, the kin-structured hamlet, dispersed central place functions, generalized stockman-farmer-hunter economy, log construction, etc. The forms suited the new land. A fascinatingly detailed study of Louisiana rural settlement is Newton, "Settlement Patterns as Artifacts of Social Structure," in *The Human Mirror: Material and Spatial Images of Man* (Baton Rouge: Louisiana State Univ. Press, 1974), edited by Miles Richardson, pp. 339–61.

683. Noble, Allen G. *Wood, Brick and Stone: The North American Settlement Landscape.* Amherst: Univ. of Massachusetts Press, 1984.

Intended as survey of subject. Volume One, on houses, is organized according to cultural hearths, diffusion from those hearths, and resultant domains, with an emphasis on early patterns, although final sections of the book deal with the West and the nineteenth century. Volume Two discusses barns and outbuildings, concluding with a review of literature on material culture and discussion of distinctive ethnic landscapes.

684. Paullin, Charles O. and John K. Wright. *Atlas of the Historical Geography of the United States.* Washington D.C. and New York: Carnegie Institution and the American Geographical Society, 1932.

This basic resource contains maps of the natural environment, patterns of land cession and settlement, political changes, demography, military history, industries and transportation and much else (including reproductions of very early maps of America).

685. Price, Edward T. "The Central Courthouse Square in the American County Seat." *Geographical Review* 58 (1968): 29–60.

This classic essay describes regional variations in types of courthouse squares in the eastern United States. Price describes four types of squares, always placed in the center of town at the intersection of principal roadways. Patterns in the South differ from those in the old Northwest and the midwest.

686. Prunty, Merle C. and C.S. Aiken. "The Demise of the Piedmont Cotton Region." *Annals of the Association of American Geographers* 62 (1972): 283–306.

Reviews the movement away from cotton culture in the South (1940–60) and then concentrates on the Piedmont area, where acreage allotments discouraged traditional technologies. Only a few farmers switched to new technologies, and thus account for the few cotton "islands" that survive.

687. Raitz, Karl B. "Ethnic Maps of North America." *Geographical Review* 68 (1978): 335–50.

Bibliographical essay on the mapping of ethnic groups, emphasizing work done since 1950. Raitz suggests that large-scale maps are much more useful for tracing significant patterns of migration than are smaller-scale representations. See also Raitz, "Themes in the Cultural Geography of European Ethnic Groups in the United States," *Geographical Review* 69 (1979), pp. 77–94, suggesting general topics for geographical study.

688. Raitz, Karl B. and Richard Ulack. *Appalachia, A Regional Geography: Land, People and Development.* Boulder, Colo.: Westview Press, 1984.

A thorough traditional regional geography, surveying ideas as to the nature of the region, topographical diversity, settlement and cultural history, and demographic patterns, with a final section on prospects for development, emphasizing the last thirty years. The authors claim that geographers have given slight attention to the area.

689. Raup, H.F. "Transformation of Southern California to a Cultivated Land." *Annals of the Association of American Geographers* 49 (September 1959 supplement): 58–78.

Describes the development of techniques employed to bring water to Southern California. Irrigation techniques had to be perfected; irrigation districts had to make water common property. A long period of experimentation was required to decide what to plant, how to preserve products, and how to work the land.

690. Relph, Edward. *The Modern Urban Landscape: 1880 to the Present.* Baltimore: Johns Hopkins Univ. Press, 1987.

Examines modern and post-modern urban landscapes as total environments: billboards and parking meters as well as streets and buildings. The book traces developments in architecture, technology, planning and society since 1880.

691. Rice, John G. "The Role of Culture and Community in Frontier Prairie Farming." *Journal of Historical Geography* 3 (April 1977): 155–75.

Traces migration from the old world to a Minnesota county, showing how Scandinavian immigrants cluster according to regional origins in old world, around rural churches. English-speaking and Danish migrants follow different patterns. See also *Patterns of Ethnicity in a Minnesota County, 1880–1915* (Department of Geography, Univ. of Umea [Sweden], 1973), a more extended treatment of the same general subject.

692. Rooney, John F., Jr., et al., eds. *This Remarkable Continent: An Atlas of the United States and Canadian Society and Cultures.* College Station: Texas A&M Univ. Press, 1982.

A basic resource, with sections on cultural and popular regions (Zelinsky): settlement (Raitz): division of land (Jordan): structures (Bastian): social organization and behavior, language and place names, ethnicity, religion (Shortridge): politics, music and dance, sports and place perception.

693. Rubin, Barbara. "A Chronology of Architecture in Los Angeles." *Annals of the Association of American Geographers* 67 (1977): 521–37.

Studies changes in vernacular architecture within the Los Angeles region. Rubin examines housing in the area as the product of economic and social conditions, reigning construction techniques, changes in technical and design options, and shifts in popular taste. She traces the development of boomtown architecture (1880s), ranch bungalows (1880–1900), and "Mediterranean" styles (1900–20), leading to the development of types accommodating denser populations (e.g., bungalow courts).

694. Salter, Christopher L., ed. *The Cultural Landscape.* Belmont, Calif.: Duxbury Press, 1971.

This anthology of miscellaneous and short pieces is broadly interdisciplinary in approach. It has four sections: migration, husbandry, organization of space, and contemporary cultural landscape. Worldwide in scope.

695. Sauer, Carl O. "The Settlement of the Humid East." U.S. Department of Agriculture. *Climate and Man: The Yearbook of Agriculture*, 157–66. Washington, D.C.: Government Printing Office, 1941.

A masterful summary of the characteristics of the natural environment east of the Mississippi, and its effect on adaptations made by the first settlers. American flora was amazingly similar to that in Europe. Theories as to the tropicality of the South were slow to give way to the reality of a continental American climate much more extreme than that in Europe.

696. ———. *Land and Life: A Selection of the Writings of Carl Ortwin Sauer.* Edited by John Leighly. Berkeley: Univ. of California Press, 1963.

These essays sample the work of a man who may well be America's greatest geographer. It includes essays on the Midland frontier, the Southwest and Mexico, the origins of plant and animal domestication, and prehistory and geographical theory. Especially important are two essays in the final section, pp. 315–60: "The Morphology of Landscape" and "Foreword to Historical Geography" (see items 508–509 under Geography: Region as Concept).

697. Semple, Ellen Churchill. *Influences of Geographic Environment.* New York: Henry Holt, 1911.

Semple, a disciple of the German geographer Ratzel, makes out the case for geography determining history. An American "school" of geography was for some time distinguished by its subscription to that kind of determinism. See also Semple, *Influences of Geographic Environment: On the Basis of Ratzel's System of Antropo-Geography* (New York: Henry Holt & Co., 1911).

698. Shortridge, James R. "Patterns of Religion in the United States." *Geographical Review* 66 (1976): 429–34.

Maps by county and region describing areal divisions between liberal and conservative denominations, degree of denominational diversity, and number of church members in relation to total population yielding regionally distinct combinations of those patterns (e.g., South relatively undiversified, conservative, with high proportion of church members).

699. Sopher, David. *Geography of Religions.* Englewood Cliffs, N.J.: Prentice-Hall, 1967.

This short book offers an overview of the subject from a historical-diffusionist point of view. Sopher develops types of religions on a worldwide basis (universalizing, tribal, other): describes their areal patterns and ends up with maps describing present distribution in the world and the U.S.

700. Thomas, William L., ed. *Man's Role in Changing the Face of the Earth.* Chicago: Univ. of Chicago Press, 1956.

This massive collection of essays amounts to a compendium of intelligent opinion of the time, with many essays still readable. The book was occasioned by the idea that the mid-century marked a new stage in human affairs, in which the question in man-land relationships had become that of how man would manage his habitat. Includes essays by Sauer, Evans, Lewis Mumford, Teilhard de Chardin, Malin, and Glacken.

701. Thrower, Norman J.W. *Original Survey and Land Subdivision: A Comparative Study of the Form and Effect of Contrasting Cadastral Systems.* Chicago: Rand McNally, 1966.

Studies the effects of contrasting cadastral systems by closely examining two counties in Northwest Ohio, one part of the Virginia Military District, the other subject to the new national system. It traces the consequences of the original survey methods as relates to property and field lines, roads, communications systems, and educational and political districting. Many maps.

702. Trewartha, Glenn T. "Some Regional Characteristics of American Farmsteads." *Annals of the Association of American Geographers* 38 (1948): 169–225.

An essay by a pioneer in mapping American settlement patterns. Here Trewartha develops a method in studying patterns in Southeastern Wisconsin, and then suggests national applications. See also "The Unincorporated Hamlet," *Annals of the Association of American Geographers* 33 (1943), pp. 32–81, and "Types of Settlement in Colonial America," *Geographical Review* 36 (1946), pp. 568–96.

703. Tyman, John Langton. *By Section, Township and Range: Studies in Prairie Settlement.* Brandon, Manitoba: Assiniboine Historical Society, 1972.

Concentrates on western Manitoba in the 1870–1890 period. Tyman is interested in human ecology historically considered, taking into account land quality, topography, government policy, and the culture of the settlers.

704. Vance, James E., Jr. "California and the Search for the Ideal." *Annals of the Association of American Geographers* 62 (1972): 182–210.

Distinguishes between "Concordian" (exurban) and Arcadian notions of ideal landscape. Vance makes out a continuity between a very early fondness for rural mineral springs and the later idea of California as a habitat for utopian notions, as well as (later) a vast exurbia.

705. ———. *This Scene of Man: The Role and Structure of the City in the Geography of Western Civilization.* New York: Harper's College Press, 1977.

This text surveys the history of urban role and structure from the time of the Greeks to date. It is complemented by Vance, *Capturing the Horizon: The Historical Geography of Transportation Since the Transportation Revolution of the Sixteenth Century* (New York: Harper and Row, 1986).

706. Vidal de la Blache, Paul. *Principles of Human Geography.* Translated by Millicent T. Bingham. New York: Henry Holt & Co., 1926.

Vidal is a principal influence on all study of landscape since his time, as well as on the development of the *Annaliste* school of historians (referred to throughout the History section). On Vidal, see *International Encyclopedia of the Social Sciences* 16 (1968), pp. 316–318.

707. Wacker, Peter O. *Land and People: A Cultural Geography of Preindustrial New Jersey.* New Brunswick: Rutgers Univ. Press, 1975.

First of two projected volumes. This volume is concerned with the pre-European environment, on how that environment was perceived by Europeans and Africans, with landscape the organizing principle in discussing these two groups. Wacker says he is following Sauer rather than Clark in his emphasis on landscape study. New Jersey was caught between culture hearths, and was made up of mingled peoples. This volume ends at 1800–1820. See also *The Musconetcong Valley of New Jersey: An Historical Geography* (New Brunswick: Rutgers Univ. Press, 1968).

708. Wagner, Philip L. "The Themes of Cultural Geography Rethought." *Association of Pacific Geographers Yearbook* 37 (1975): 7–14.

Here Wagner rejects what he had said in the introduction to his earlier collection of readings on cultural geography (see item 710). He says he was there too concerned with the "ghostly" influence of past diffusion. He sees cultural ecology as stalemated, and cultural history as the great hope. Such history should be tied to specific acts within an institutional structure, and not to statements about whole peoples or mere individuals.

709. ———. *Environments and People.* Englewood Cliffs, N.J.: Prentice-Hall, Inc., 1972.

This admirable little book, worldwide in its concerns, expounds upon Wagner's central emphasis upon culture as communication (see item 708). It is especially interesting in its treatment of language spread through cultural encounters and on the varying attitudes historical religions have taken toward terrain, as well as in his discussion of the relation between settlement patterns and communications.

710. Wagner, Philip L. and Marvin W. Mikesell, eds. *Readings in Cultural Geography.* Chicago: Univ. of Chicago Press, 1962.

An exemplary collection of classic statements on general themes, assembled, the authors say, because of the low current repute of cultural geography among professional geographers. Carl Sauer's historical, genetic approach, concerned with areal differentiation, central to the selections. The general introduction, pp. 1–29, sets out the major themes: culture, culture area, cultural landscape, cultural history and cultural ecology.

711. Wallach, Bret. "Logging in Maine's Empty Quarter." *Annals of the Association of American Geographers* 70 (1980): 542–52.

Masterful landscape description of an uncared-for region exploited by corporate owners and worked by pieceworkers at low wages. Spruce budworm has induced clearcutting of the timber, which in turn produces perfect conditions for future budworm outbreak. See also "The Potato Landscape: Aroostook County, Maine," *Landscape* 23 (1979), pp. 15–22, describing the lonely, stark life around Presque Isle, Maine, with its declining potato culture.

712. ———. "The West Side Oil Fields of California." *Geographical Review* 70 (1980): 50–59.

A lively portrait of oil fields west of Bakersfield, California, where single-minded exploitation of oil resources has left a landscape littered with obsolete machinery and largely abandoned by humans to the last and most automated technology. Taft, a nearby town, is largely abandoned. See also "Sheep Ranching in the Dry Corner of Wyoming," *Geographical Review* 71 (1981), pp. 51–63, describing another desolate landscape caught between a declining sheep industry and a new boom industry in coal.

713. Ward, David, ed. *Geographical Perspectives on America's Past: Readings on the Historical Geography of the United States.* New York: Oxford Univ. Press, 1979.

A first-rate collection of essays, for college use, by historical geographers. Abridgements of several essays cited in this bibliography are included. The essays are grouped under The Land and Its People, with subheading on landscape and on migration; The Regional Mosaic; and Urbanization. Ward comments that historical geography has just lately become something of a crowded field.

714. Watson, James Wreford. *North America: Its Countries and Regions.* London: Longman, Green and Co., 1968.

Originally published in 1963. This richly detailed text surveys the continent, giving geomorphology central stage but (Watson says) giving more attention to "human factors" than is usually the case. History and economic geography are discussed in tandem. See also *The United States: Habitation of Hope* (London: Longman, Green and Co.,

1982), an update and revision of the subject book, focusing upon contemporary issues and arguing that the American West is characterized by its emphasis upon amenities rather than economic need.

715. Whittlesey, Derwent. "The Impress of Effective Central Authority upon the Landscape." *Annals of the Association of American Geographers* 25 (1935): 85–87.

Even after a half century this brief essay reads well. Whittlesey reviews the ways in which political causes enter into the nature of landscape (walled versus open cities, grid versus enclosed street plans, the emphasis on the political capital, the nature of the political borderland, the effect of laws, the emphasis on transportation as a dimension of national interest, etc.) Perhaps a more influential essay, although now dated, is "Sequent Occupance," *Annals of the Association of American Geographers* 19 (1929), pp. 162–165. See also "The United States: The Origin of a Federal State," in *The Changing World* (Yonkers-on-Hudson N.Y.: World Book Co., 1956), edited by W. Gordon East and E.A. Moodie, pp. 239–60, for a discussion of the interplay between colonists and land in relation to an emergent drive for independence.

716. Wood, Joseph S. "Village and Community in Early Colonial New England." *Journal of Historical Geography* 8 (1982): 333–46.

This essay involves careful quotation from contemporary sources to establish the fact that the notion of the New England village came into use in the late eighteenth century and originally did not refer to nucleated or any other particular kind of settlement. Many villages were scattered in their settlement pattern.

717. Zelinsky, Wilbur. "An Approach to the Religious Geography of the United States: Patterns of Church Membership in 1952." *Annals of the Association of American Geographers* 51 (1961): 139–93.

Describes religious regions as a step toward establishing the cultural regions of Anglo-America. Zelinsky outlines seven major religious regions: New England, Midland, Upper Midwest, Southern, Mormon, Southwest and West. The article includes maps of distributions for twenty-one denominations as well as a map summing up regional patterns.

718. ———. *The Cultural Geography of the United States*. Englewood Cliffs, N.J.: Prentice-Hall, 1973.

Part Two, pp. 65–140, is almost universally cited. In it, Zelinsky maps out historical boundaries for American cultural regions. He also invents the idea of a "voluntary" region, into which people move by choice, in search of particular amenities.

719. ———. "The Pennsylvania Town: An Overdue Geographical Account." *Geographical Review* 67 (1977): 127–147.

Studies towns built before 1860 sharing a set of traits: brick construction, a type of alley, scattered service institutions, a diamond at the town center, and many trees and little front lawn. Zelinsky maps the incidence of the town type and finds that it coincides with an earlier mapping of Pennsylvania barns. He thus sees the two kinds of evidence as confirming the existence of a Pennsylvania Culture Area (PCA), strangely uninfluenced by Philadelphia. He says urban and rural patterns have been emphasized in past studies, to the neglect of the town. See also "Where the South Begins: The Northern Limit of the Cis-Appalachian South in Terms of Settlement Landscape," *Social Forces* 30 (1951), pp. 172–78.

Geography: Distributional Studies

Entries under this heading are generally concerned with analyses of abstract patterns of spatial distribution rather than the study of landscape. In the 1960s, most geographers became absorbed in a drive for quantitative and theoretical rigor, for the development of a locational and regional science. Work by Berry, Hagerstrand, and Pred was especially influential. Such an emphasis went along with a new interest in urban patterns and a long-standing traditional interest in economic and political geography. Migration studies were often statistical and aggregate in nature, although they have recently given more attention to the particularities of places left behind and places newly settled (see, e.g., Hudson and Ostergren). Quantitative methods now no longer have the field so much to themselves. Radical geographers (e.g., Harvey and Taylor) note the lack of concern for social justice in the location science paradigm; landscape study enjoys a new vogue (see introduction for the previous subsection); and phenomenological geographers (see introduction for Geography: Perception Studies) make a point of calling themselves humanistic in pointed contrast to what they consider a "scientistic" bias.

Except where the emphasis of the study is clearly upon landscape and settlement, treatments of urban, economic, and political geography are included under this heading. Migration studies are included here, as long as the emphasis is upon the migration experience rather than settlement patterns (see, e.g., how Hudson's entries are divided between this and the preceding subheading). World-scale study and "secondarily relevant" entries (see general Introduction) are included here as in other subsections under Geography and History, to suggest the academic context for the concerns of this subheading.

C.M.

720. Abler, Ronald. "Monoculture or Miniculture? The Impact of Communication Media on Culture in Space." In *An Invitation to*

Geography, edited by David A. Lanegran and Risa Palm, 186–95. New York: McGraw-Hill, 1973. Reprinted in *Human Geography in a Changing World*, 122–131. North Scituate, Mass.: Duxbury Press, 1975.

Speculates on the implications of new technologies for territorially defined communities. "Formal" mass communications are one-way and give the impression of cultural uniformity but "informal" mass communications (cable television, the underground press) cater to specialized interests without regard to territory. Face-to-face communications are crucial to territorially defined community but "formal" interpersonal communications (e.g., the telephone) make territory less central.

721. Abler, Ronald and John S. Adams, eds. *A Comparative Atlas of America's Great Cities: Twenty Metropolitan Regions*. Minneapolis: Univ. of Minnesota Press, 1976.

Final volume of the Association of American Geographers Comparative Cities Project, mapping demography, ethnic groups, age, growth, etc., for each of twenty cities. Part Two of this volume addresses urban problems, health, segregation, etc., with data divided by city under such general topics. See also items 723, 724.

722. Adams, John. "Directional Bias in Intraurban Migration." *Economic Geography* 45 (1969): 302–23.

Studies migration patterns within Minneapolis over the 1890–1950 period, discovering that migrants move short distances, in a sectoral pattern running out from the Central Business District. The housing stock and the shape of the city affect patterns followed. The length of the move increases over time.

723. ———. "The Geography of Riots and Civil Disorders in the 1960s." *Economic Geography* 67 (1972): 24–42.

A sophisticated analysis of which cities were involved in the race riots of the 1960s, and which neighborhoods. Adams sees relative deprivation in relation to whites, and blocked opportunity, as basic. New migrants from the South are especially frustrated. The expansion of the ghettos themselves reduces interracial contact and affects the resultant patterns of violence.

724. ———, ed. *Contemporary Metropolitan America: Twenty Geographical Vignettes*. vol. 1. Cambridge, Mass.: Ballinger Publishing Co., 1976.

This is Volume One (a four-book series) of the Association of American Geographers 20–cities project. It is made up of urban biographies for those twenty cities. Biographies are grouped according to the historic metropolitan core (Book One), nineteenth-century ports (Book Two), nineteenth-century inland centers (Book Three), and twentieth-century cities (Book Four). These urban biographies were also published as books under separate covers, by the same publisher (see, e.g., item 659). A second volume of the 20–cities project emphasizes problems of urban life and policy: *Urban Policymaking and Metropolitan Dynamics: A Comparative Geographical Analysis*, edited by John Adams (Cambridge, Mass.: Ballinger Publishing Co., 1976).

725. Allen, James P. "Migration Fields of French Canadian Immigrants to Southern Maine." *Geographical Review* 62 (1972): 366–83.

Studies the migration of French Canadians into Maine, before and after the railroad, and with the availability of more printed information. With the new information and technology, the migration fields spread out, but early patterns persist despite new mobility.

726. Archer, J. Clark and Peter J. Taylor. *Section and Party: A Political Geography of American Presidential Elections, from Andrew Jackson to Ronald Reagan*. Chichester, England: Research Studies Press, 1981.

Study using factor analysis of election results to describe sectional patterns over course of American history, self-consciously in the tradition of V.O. Key and Frederick Jackson Turner. The book divides U.S. history into periods of sectional competition (to 1860), sectional dominance (to 1944), and sectional volatility (since 1944). The 1896 election was an attempt by periphery groups to wrest control from the core. The authors assume that material interests dictate politics.

727. Omitted.

728. Berry, Brian J.L. *Growth Centers in the American Urban System*. 2 vols. Cambridge, Mass.: Ballinger Publishing Co., 1973.

Volume One attempts to develop a research strategy for describing growth patterns. Volume Two is a compendium of data on urban centers and regions, emphasizing the new importance of amenities.

729. ———, ed. *Perspectives in Geography 3: The Nature of Change in Geographical Ideas*. DeKalb: Northern Illinois Univ. Press, 1978.

This anthology is based on the assumption that geography has moved beyond "theory-less" attention to areal differentiation (as in traditional regional geography) to a new emphasis upon quantitative methods, theory-building, theory testing, and theory refining. The heart of the new approach, Berry says, is location theory.

730. Berry, Brian J.L. and Donald C. Dahmann. "Population Redistribution in the United States in the 1970s." In *Population Redistribution and Public Policy*, edited by Berry and Lester P. Silverman, 8–49. Washington, D.C.: National Academy of Sciences, 1980.

A statistical analysis of the topic, going from national to interregional to intrametropolitan patterns of population movement. The authors describe a dispersal from the central city and a movement to the sunbelt on the part of particular cohorts of the population.

731. Berry, Brian J.L. and Quintin Gillard. *The Changing Shape of Metropolitan America: Commuting Patterns, Urban Fields and Decentralization Processes, 1960–1970.* Cambridge, Mass.: Ballinger Publishing Co., 1970.

Presents data on the title subject as to commuting and reverse commuting patterns, by individual metropolitan areas.

732. Berry, Brian J.L. and Thomas D. Hankins, eds. *A Bibliographic Guide to the Economic Regions of the United States.* Chicago: Univ. of Chicago Press, 1963.

Annotated under Economics (item 318).

733. Berry, Brian J.L. and Frank E. Horton. *Geographic Perspectives on Urban Systems.* Englewood Cliffs, N.J.: Prentice-Hall, 1970.

Combined textbook and reader focused on locational analysis of city size and growth, urban systems, urban hierarchies, problems of defining the metropolis, patterns of density, concepts of social space, individual mobility and waves of succession, and internal structure. Readings supply case studies.

734. Beyers, William B. "Contemporary Trends in the Regional Economic Development of the United States." *Professional Geographer* 31 (February 1979): 34–44.

A dense analysis of interregional economic changes during the 1965–75 period. Beyer calculates shifts in employment, total earnings, and location quotients for individuals not depending upon earnings, in relation to 173 daily urban systems. The significant new factor for the decade is the last group (retirees, individuals living off investments, etc.). During the decade the Northeast declines relatively and the West grows.

735. Bohland, James R. and Lexa Treps. "County Patterns of Elderly Migration in the United States." In *Geographical Perspectives on the Elderly* (item 787), 139–58.

A study of census-derived patterns of migration of the elderly in 1950–60 and 1960–70. In the first of the two decades, migration went to Florida, California-Arizona, and east-coast suburbs. In the second decade, new retirement regions develop in the Ozarks, the Piedmont, and the upper Northwest. Net migration changes are mapped on page 151.

736. Borchert, John R. "The Changing Metropolitan Regions." In *Regions of the United States* (item 633), pp. 352–73.

Excellent synoptic article on the topic as of the time it was written. It suggests the range of evidence used to determine the size of metropolitan regions, and describes the patterns of growth of polycentric urban complexes in the recent past.

737. ———. "American Metropolitan Evolution." *Geographical Review* 57 (1967): 301–32.

An important analysis of how American cities have changed over time. Working back from 1960 and dividing cities according to "class" (higher classes dominant, lower classes subordinate), Borchert divides urban history into epochs defined by important technological changes: steamboat and railroad (1830–1870); steel rails and coal-fired electric power (1870–1920); and auto-air-amenities (1920+). He then maps the growth and decline of metropolitan areas by epoch. Over the course of history, American emphasis has been on immediate exploitation of natural resources.

738. Bowen, William A. "American Ethnic Regions, 1880." *Proceedings of the Association of American Geographers* 8 (1976): 44–46.

The principal feature of this brief note is a map describing migration patterns from out of country and out of state (p. 45): as disclosed by state and country-of-birth information in the 1880 census. (The map and data have to do with migrants generally, and not just ethnic groups.)

739. Browning, Clyde E. and Wil Gesler. "The Sun Belt-Snow Belt: A Case of Sloppy Regionalizing." *Professional Geographer* 31 (1979): 66–74.

A factor analysis of items usually identified with the sunbelt (sunshine, rate of migration, economic well-being, etc.) The authors conclude that what is called the snow belt really refers to the western end of the old industrial core (Ohio and points west, through Illinois): and that the traits attributed to the sunbelt are those to be found in the West rather than in the old South.

740. Brunn, Stanley D. *Geography and Politics in America.* New York: Harper and Row, 1974.

A pioneer text on American political geography emphasizing the behavioral sciences. It is divided into sections on political institutions and on political behavior. See especially chapters on "Political Cultures," pp.237–70, and "Political Geography of the Future," pp.409–30.

741. ———. "Geography and Politics of the United States in the Year 2000." *Journal of Geography* 72 (1973): 42–49.

Recommends futurology as a dimension of political geography. Brunn predicts that boundaries will increasingly have less meaning, cities will become more important than states, new political cultures will emerge with new voting patterns, centralized authority at the national level will continue to be important, and political considerations will play a key role in environmental planning and protection.

742. Campbell, Robert D. "Personality as an Element of Regional Geography." *Annals of the Association of American Geographers* 58 (December 1968): 748–58.

Advocates the study of personality as an element in regional geography. Campbell argues that the social sciences generally have demonstrated a new interest in personality and national character and suggests how the whole subject might be approached by geographers.

743. Clark, Gordon L. "Capitalism and Regional Inequality." *Annals of the Association of American Geographers* 70 (June 1980): 226–37.

Critique of radical theorists who argue the necessity of regional inequalities and underemployed populations, as a consequence of the capitalist system. Clark focuses on issue of reproduction of firms and systems, as defined by neo-marxians.

744. Cohen, Saul B. *Geography and Politics in a World Divided.* 2d ed. New York: Oxford Univ. Press, 1973.

Discusses geopolitics on the world scale, in the Mackinder tradition. Cohen sees the world as divided necessarily into spheres of influence even as interconnections among those spheres become more articulate. Certain areas in the world (especially Southeast Asia and the Near East) are "shatterbelts," where the world order is most severely tested.

745. Conzen, Michael P. "The American Urban System in the Nineteenth Century." In *Geography and the Urban Environment: Progress in Research and Applications* (item 758), vol. 4, 295–347.

A detailed review of literature having to do with the historical development of urban system analysis in U.S. Conzen agrees with Vance that central place theory is unsuited to much of the American story, working best in the low-level analysis of rural areas. He sees Pred as good on his analysis of initial advantage but weak on the development of urban-industrial regions. The article includes maps of urban expansion, differentiation, and integration over time.

746. ———. "The Maturing Urban System in the United States, 1840–1910." *Annals of the Association of American Geographers* 67 (1977): 88–108.

Studies bank correspondence data to describe multi-level interdependencies in which old first-order cities retain relative advantages even as other cities jockey for advantage and specialization as between manufacturing and commerce becomes more pronounced, yielding a pattern of overlapping hinterlands. See also Conzen, "A Transport Interpretation of the Growth of Urban Regions: An American Example," *Journal of Historical Geography* 1 (1975), pp. 361–82, a study of passenger traffic in the Midwest during the 1850–1908 period, in which an early east-west bias in growth gives way in time to circular hinterland patterns, even as the metropolis increasingly dominates the small city.

747. ———. *Frontier Farming in an Urban Shadow: The Influence of Madison's Proximity on the Agricultural Development of Blooming Grove, Wisconsin.* Madison, Wis.: State Historical Society, 1971.

Examines the development of this area over time from its beginnings to stages of non-specialized agriculture, specialized agriculture, and urban land use, looking to demographics, figures on farm size and value, statistics on mechanization and marketing patterns, and social patterns thereto related.

748. Dilger, Robert J. *The Sunbelt-Snowbelt Controversy: The War Over Federal Funds*. New York: New York Univ. Press, 1982.

This book studies the emergence of "snowbelt" concern in the career of the Northeast-Midwest Congressional Coalition, formed to counteract what was perceived to be a tilt in federal policy toward sunbelt interests. It follows the career of that caucus during its first two years (1976–78), assessing the success of the effort.

749. East, W. Gordon and J.R.V. Prescott. *Our Fragmented World: An Introduction to Political Geography*. London: Macmillan, 1975.

This book offers a brisk overview of political geography on a worldwide basis. It sums up what is known about states, from a historical-areal differentiation perspective. Headings have to do with types of states, varieties of inhabitants, the nature of territories, frontiers and boundaries, economic structures, administrative structures, the political geography of oceans, groupings of states, and world geopolitics.

750. Goheen, Peter G. *Victorian Toronto, 1850 to 1900: Pattern and Process of Growth*. Chicago: University of Chicago, Department of Geography, Paper no. 127, 1970.

Surveys census data and reconstructs residential patterns and journeys to work during the 1850–1900 period. Goheen subjects his data to factor and regression analysis, concluding that Toronto of 1870 was premodern in landscape but modern in segregation according to money, occupation, and status. With the coming of mass transportation after 1870, segregation increases and separation of home from work becomes pronounced. He is interested throughout in how people of the time perceived geographical pattern and change.

751. Gottman, Jean. *Megalopolis: The Urbanized Northeastern Seaboard of the United States*. New York: Twentieth Century Fund, 1961.

A central document in American urban geography. Gottman is convinced that the complex of cities running from Boston to Richmond represents the type of the future. He therefore subjects the area to an

encyclopedic analysis of its history, topography, economy, social order
(the new prominence of white-collar occupations) and land use patterns,
to determine patterns within the urban complex and between that
complex and the rest of the nation.

752. ———. *The Significance of Territory*. Charlottesville: Univ.
Press of Virginia, 1973.

Lucid, learned, historically-oriented overview of changes in the
nature of territory, from city-state, to Roman imperium, to nations
(with an attendant dramatic shift in the sophistication of cartography):
to present need for supranational order. Territory is defined by what is
accessible to a people. It is understood to offer security and opportunity.
The present attempts to define air space and outer space is like that
earlier in relation to territorial waters and deep seas.

753. Hagerstrand, Torsten. "Migration and Area." In *Land Studies in
Geography*, edited by David Hammerberg, et al., 27–158. Series B,
Human Geography, no. 13, 1957.

This landmark study of a small Swedish area emphasizes the
networks of information available to migrants as crucial to their
movements. Hagerstrand distinguishes between passive migrants,
following movement of kin, and active migrants, who move for
particular reasons. The object of the study is to develop a statistical
model that predicts migrant behavior. The author discovers that early
patterns of migration have an inordinate influence on later patterns.

754. ———. *Innovation Diffusion as a Spatial Process*. Translated by
Allan R. Pred. Chicago: Univ. of Chicago Press, 1967.

Originally published in 1953. Hagerstrand amasses data on patterns
of innovation (e.g., control of tuberculosis, introduction of mechanized
farming, patterns of telephone calls, etc.) as the basis for describing
patterns of diffusion dependent on networks of interpersonal
communications. His interest is in developing a probabilistic model
describing such patterns. Pred's afterword assesses Hagerstrand's
contributions to geography and to the social sciences generally.

755. Hart, John Fraser. "The Changing Distribution of the American
Negro." *Annals of the Association of American Geographers* 50 (1960):
242–66.

Thorough statistical analysis of the subject. Interregional
movement was pronounced in 1810–60 (to the Old Southwest): static
from 1860 to 1910, and then pronounced again, to the cities of the

North and West, from 1910 on. Hart maps contrasts between 1910 and 1950 in regional trends and dates of maximum Negro population, and patterns of migration during 1940–50.

756. Hart, John Fraser, Neil E. Salisbury and Everett G. Smith, Jr. "The Dying Village and Some Notions About Urban Growth." *Economic Geography* 44 (1968): 343–49.

A survey of thirty villages throughout the midwest discloses that villages are not dying away but rather seem to have achieved a new equilibrium. They offer inexpensive housing, which seems to be one appeal, but, more basically, are properly seen as parts of a regionally "dispersed city," spread over space, many of them housing some "outsized function" (e.g., a lumberyard) serving a translocal function.

757. Harvey, David W. *Social Justice and the City*. Baltimore: Johns Hopkins Univ. Press, 1973.

These essays allow the reader to trace the development of Harvey's thought, as he moves from a liberal (Part One) to a neomarxian socialist (Part Two) perspective. He is concerned with integrating analysis of process along with structure and with incorporating a concern for social justice (thus his emphasis upon reciprocity and redistribution in discussion of economic integration and space economy).

758. Herbert, David T. and R. J. Johnston, eds. 6 vols. *Geography and the Urban Environment: Progress in Research and Applications*. London: John Wiley and Sons, 1976–1984.

Collections of essays in urban geography, representing positivistic as well as humanistic approaches.

759. Herbert, David T., R.J. Johnston, and Colin J. Thomas. *Urban Geography: A First Approach*. Chichester, England: John Wiley and Sons, 1982.

This text is at once brisk, dense, and informed. It takes into account new interest in "subjective" and structural and radical approaches to the general subject. Phenomenological geography is described but represented as reactive rather than a fully articulated theory (see chapter two). The authors generally argue for an opening out to the social sciences on the part of urban geographers. The book includes a very extensive bibliography.

760. Hudson, John C. "Migration to an American Frontier." *Annals of the Association of American Geographers* 66 (1976): 242–65.

Traces migration by ethnic group and occupation into North Dakota at the turn of the century. To do so, Hudson draws upon a state archive of individual migration accounts. The author shows how each group follows its own geographical pattern. Overall, the author concludes, the idea of culture area does not seem to apply to North Dakota at that time. See also "Two Dakota Homestead Frontiers," *Annals of the Association of American Geographers* 63 (1973), pp. 442–62, which compares migration patterns to selected counties in the Dakotas (much related to land policy and land use).

761. Hugill, Peter J. "Good Roads and the Automobile in the United States, 1880–1929." *Geographical Review* 72 (1982): 327–49.

History of the evolution of automobile and road technologies, up to mid-1920s. Interest in the automobile limited to the well-off and the city in early days. A kind of motorized buggy became popular in rural areas. The government comes into the act in 1916 with the Good Roads Act. By 1926 the first atlas was published.

762. Johnson, Hildegard Binder. "Factors Influencing the Distribution of the German Pioneer Population in Minnesota." *Agricultural History* 19 (1945): 39–57.

Traces German migration to Minnesota by use of the censuses of 1860 and 1870, and relates patterns of movement to old-country backgrounds as to soil, transportation, religion and urban and rural backgrounds. The great influx came in 1856–62, followed rivers and was largely rural. Letters from kinsmen and the activity of the church helped guide movement. Old-world patterns persist in clustered settlements, patterns of marriage, and clear preference for wooded land.

763. Knight, David B. "Identity and Territory: Geographical Perspectives on Nationalism and Regionalism." *Annals of the Association of American Geographers* 72 (1982): 513–31.

A wide-ranging discussion of the shifting relationships between regional and national identities in Europe, North America, and the Third World, with the suggestion that geographers devote more attention to subnational territorial identity and movements for ethnic separatism. Extensive bibliography.

764. Lee, D. and R. Schultz. "Regional Patterns of Female Status in the United States." *The Professional Geographer* 33 (1982): 32–41.

Calculation of relative status of women by area. Status of women higher where income and education highest, but women are relatively better off, compared to men, in the Southeast and in the Great Plains, and not so well off in New England and the old Northeast core.

765. Lewis, G.J. *Human Migration: A Geographical Perspective*.New York: St. Martin's Press, 1982.

Attempt to clarify migration theory. Since the 1950s, Lewis argues, there has been a massive growth in interest in migration study. Early study focused too much on aggregate patterns, and on constraints as among income groups. Review of literature, with case studies.

766. Lowenthal, David and Lambros Comitas. "Emigration and Depopulation: Some Neglected Aspects of Population Geography." *Geographical Review* 52 (1962): 195–210.

A study of outmigration as a steady state. Especially interesting is the description of a Greek island, where remittances from outside are depended upon but where outmigration is considered dishonorable. Outmigration occurs, but is not recognized; everyone says he or she intends to return, even if such return is unlikely.

767. Mikesell, Marvin W. "The Myth of the Nation State." *Journal of Geography* 82 (November/December 1983): 257–60.

Mikesell points out that very few nation states are culturally uniform and that geographers must examine the reality of "cultural discord" in terms of national, regional,and ethnic identities throughout the world.

768. Morrill, Richard L. *The Spatial Organization of Society*. Belmont, Calif.: Wadsworth Publishing Co., 1970.

An economic geography survey and text. Most of the book has to do with applications of central place theory to industry, settlement, trade, movement of people and ideas, and patterns of urbanization. Its principal focus is the U.S. Long bibliography and many maps included.

769. Muller, Edward K. "Selective Urban Growth in the Middle Ohio Valley,1800–1860." *Geographical Review* 66 (1976): 178–99.

Describes urban development in the Cincinnati area in terms of movement toward a system of interdependent cities. Muller emphasizes the fact that a manufacturing system had not yet developed by the end of his period and that the economy then largely depended on specialized agriculture and the processing of primary products. During the period studied, the cities first settled have an initial advantage; however, each major change in transportation shifts the interurban balance.

770. Muller, Peter O. *Contemporary Suburban America*. Englewood Cliffs, N.J.: Prentice-Hall, 1981.

This book is a thorough and lucid overview of the subject which includes a good-sized section on the historical evolution of the suburbs, as well as sections on social and regional organization. Muller is convinced that a new kind of urban structure has now emerged, with the suburban area itself multicentered, and with great diversity among suburbs. He says that he has had to depend largely upon sociologists and historians, since geographers have done so little with the subject.

771. ———. "Everyday Life in Suburbia." *American Quarterly* (1982): 262–77.

A reliable review of literature on the subject, emphasizing recent developments: segregation by class and race is more extreme and fragmented than ever; residential microcommunities provide a base for family life; residents fan out to individually defined macrocommunities for work, leisure, and shopping; increasingly the minicities in the suburbs become the center for cultural life as well as for shopping.

772. Ostergren, Robert. "A Community Transplanted: The Formative Experience of a Swedish Immigrant Community in the Upper Middle West." *Journal of Historical Geography* 5 (1979): 189–212.

A model description of movement from a particular Swedish parish to Isanti County, Minnesota. An emphasis on the small scale allows comparisons of data on individuals from manuscript censuses, tax rolls, and church registers. The author studies sources in Sweden as well as in the U.S. See also "Prairie Bound: Migration Patterns to a Swedish Settlement on the Dakota Frontier," in *Ethnicity on the Great Plains* (item 1004), pp. 73–91, on movement into an area in South Dakota; and "The Immigrant Church as a Symbol of Community and Place in the Upper Midwest," *Great Plains Quarterly* 1 (April 1979), pp. 189–212, emphasizing a town in Minnesota.

773. Pred, Allan R. "Manufacturing in in the American Mercantile City, 1800–1840," *Annals of the Association of American Geographers* 56 (1966): 307–38.

Surveys the national urban scene in terms of how the development of manufacturing was served by transportation, labor and capital systems in place. Pred concludes that the cities of the time are commerce-dominated, Atlantic-facing, with new money being invested in land rather than manufactures. New York City is described as this type of pre-1840 city, with people highly concentrated and with pedestrian patterns of journey to work.

774. ———. *The Spatial Dynamics of U.S. Urban-Industrial Growth, 1800–1914: Interpretive and Theoretical Essays.* Cambridge: Harvard Univ. Press, 1966.

Pred distinguishes his approach from that of merely descriptive geography, in that he is attempting to develop a scientific model of the changes being studied. He contrasts his effort, also, to that of economist, saying his subject matter is "irrational" to the economist (involving terrain, psychology, etc.) The three essays in this book concern innovation and industrialization in relation to urban growth, locational interrelationships, and the formation of what he calls the mercantile city.

775. ———. *Urban Growth and City-Systems in the United States, 1840–1860.* Cambridge: Harvard Univ. Press, 1980.

Investigates the development of key cities of the antebellum period in regard to interrelations among cities, relations between cities and their hinterlands, and between cities and small cities outside their hinterlands. Crucial to the growth of cities was the control of information, made possible by new technologies, especially the telegraph. The developing city-system became the means for accumulation of capital and the development of a network of industries. The city-system is biased against the South and is dominated by New York. See also *Urban Growth and the Circulation of Information: The United States System of Cities, 1790–1840* (Cambridge: Harvard Univ. Press, 1973).

776. Rooney, John F., Jr. *A Geography of American Sport: From Cabin Creek to Anaheim.* Reading, Mass.: Addison-Wesley, 1974.

An overview of major sports on all levels (high school, college, professional). Rooney traces patterns of movement of players and coaches, as well as franchises and leagues. He speaks of "fan regions." He is also interested in how sports structures fit into the landscape. See also "Up from the Mines and out from the Prairies: Some Geographical Implications of Football in the United States," in *An Invitation to Geography* (New York: McGraw-Hill, 1973), edited by David A. Lanegran and Risa Palms, pp. 97–111.

777. Shortridge, Barbara Gunla. *Atlas of American Women*. New York: Macmillan, 1987.

A valuable reference with sections on demographics, labor force, earnings and income, occupations, education, sports, relationships, pregnancy, health, crime, and politics.

778. Smith, David M. *The Geography of Social Well-Being in the United States: An Introduction to Territorial Social Indicators*. New York: McGraw-Hill, 1973.

Develops statistical techniques in order to develop social indicators as to well-being within and among cities and states. Smith's hope is that such social indicators can become part of a process of monitoring the effectiveness of government programs and discovering new areas of need.

779. Svart, Larry M. "Environmental Preference Migration: A Review." *Geographical Review* 66 (1976): 314–30.

This sweeping review of the literature, from a statistical-behavioral perspective, is especially good on relations between tourism and retirement, footloose industries moving South, tourism as support for other industries and as preceding settlement. Patterns in the U.S. are similar to those in England and France. The whole phenomenon, Svart says, is understudied, having more to do with weather and landscape than with money.

780. Swauger, John. "Regionalism in the 1976 Presidential Election." *Geographical Review* 70 (1980): 157–66.

This county-by-county study of pluralities for Ford and Carter in the 1976 election in the continental U.S. focuses upon interregional variations. Swauger finds patterns of diffusion of political culture from east to west, like those described by Elazar (items 1420–1424 under Political Science). Political cultures, urban-suburban differences, and traditional habits seem to have determined the outcome.

781. Taylor, Peter J. "Political Geography." *Progress in Human Geography* 1,2 (1977, 1978): 130–35, 153–62.

Taylor provides a brief overview of research in political geography, defending it against an undue emphasis on value-neutral statistics (as with Berry) and an exclusive interest in nation states (as with Prescott), at a time when the central issue is that of giving coherence to a new urban order.

782. ———. *Political Geography: World-Economy, Nation-State and Locality*. London: Longman, Green and Co., 1985.

Taylor applies Wallerstein's world-systems approach to the general topic. He takes a radical approach, on the side of everyday life (as against elite versions of reality, and the value-neutrality of social science orthodoxy). Taylor sees liberalism as a way of blurring issues as to political equity. He assumes that general principles work themselves out historically.

783. Ullman, Edward L. "The Nature of Cities, Reconsidered." In Regional Science Association, *Papers and Proceedings* 9 (1962): 7–23.

A historically sensitive account of the movement away from the city and toward the amenities with the coming of the car. All growth since the car became dominant is in the direction of the multicentered urban complex. The CBD is fated to be one among many urban nodes.

784. ———. "Regional Development and the Geography of Concentration." In Regional Science Association, *Papers and Proceedings* 4 (1958): 179–98.

Argues that initial advantages in location make for economies of scale and thus for concentration in a single core area (the New York-Chicago belt): with concentration itself introducing certain economies making for yet more concentration. Prospects for fringe areas (the rest of the country) relatively dim, for reasons outlined. Canada's core (around Toronto) is also described.

785. Vance, James E. Jr. *The Merchant's World: The Geography of Wholesaling*. Englewood Cliffs, N.J.: Prentice-Hall, 1970.

A historical treatment of wholesaling, especially in the United States during the nineteenth century. Vance finds central place theory inadequate to describe the patterns he discovers, and a mercantile model better suited. The book is both an overview of the subject and a theoretically influential discussion.

786. Ward, David. *Cities and Immigrants: A Geography of Change in Nineteenth-Century America*. New York: Oxford Univ. Press, 1971.

Ward here combines investigation of the regional economic growth and migration that resulted in the formation of the nation's urban core (the first two chapters) and the internal differentiation of urban settlements. He aspires to develop quantitative models for spatial patterns.

787. Warnes, Anthony, ed. *Geographical Pespectives on the Elderly.* Chichester, England: John Wiley and Sons, 1982.

This exciting collection of essays, emphasizing England but including France and the United States in its concerns, discusses demography and migration, daily activity patterns, spatial aspects of service provision, analysis of "senior" housing, retirement regions (item 735) and reviews of research. Warner's introductory essay surveys the field.

788. Watson, James Wreford. *Social Geography of the United States.* London: Longman, Green and Co., 1979.

This somewhat eccentric book offers a lively overview of relations between social and landscape order. It surveys the history and current state of affairs as to Indians, blacks, immigrants, social classes, poverty and crime, urban change, and communitarian experiment. Watson says he assumes environment to be central to the human condition and is attempting to interrelate ecology, technology, and the cultural framework.

789. Woods, Robert. *Population Analysis in Geography.* London: Longman, Green and Co., 1979.

A concise, readable text on demography in all its geographical aspects: family, migration, fertility, mortality, population structure and change, from a quantitative perspective. The book is oriented toward England. Extensive bibliography included.

790. Zelinsky, Wilbur. "Changes in the Geographical Patterns of Rural Population in the United States, 1790–1960." *Geographical Review* 52 (1962): 492–524.

A remarkably thorough description of the data, county by county and census by census, outlining regional patterns of growth and decline and repetitions thereof. Causes for changes ascribed to urbanization, mines discovered and abandoned, development of the urban fringe, and placement of second homes. (See especially map, p. 519.)

791. ———. "Selfward Bound? Personal Preference Patterns and the Changing Map of American Society." *Economic Geography* 50 (1974): 145–79.

Uses multi-dimensional factoral analysis to test the idea that personal preferences have a new significance in relation to traditional regional patterns. Data on areal patterns for subscription to interest magazines and membership in special interest associations reflect old regional patterns to some degree, but also a new emphasis on innovation and recreation, particularly typical of states in the West and Southwest.

History

Historians are second only to geographers in the range and depth of their contribution to regional studies. Geographical and historical perspectives are interconnected and complementary, supplying a sense of space and time to our comprehension of experience in general and regionalism in particular. "History and geography," D.W. Meinig has noted," are bound together by the very nature of things: history takes place and places are created by history."[1] Geographers are primarily interested in explaining differences over space, while historians are primarily concerned with tracing changes over time. Each perspective is vital, as Meinig stressed, and each is enhanced by the other: the geographer must know that places change over time, while the historian must understand that places influence the course of events.

Such interdisciplinary sensibility is especially vital for regional studies. Put all too simply, geography provides an invaluable spatial understanding of the nature and function of regions, while history traces the significance of regions through time, providing a vision of regionalism as a *process* subject to forces of change. This geohistorical perspective—a vivid sense of the fact that "history takes place and places are created by history"—forms a basic foundation and starting point for all students of region and regionalism.

At a more concrete level, regionalism is an inevitable concern for anyone interested in the history of a nation as vast and various as the United States. The nation's continental scale and cultural diversity often confound even the most cautious generalizations. One can argue that the United States is most vivid and comprehensible when seen as a composite of regions; without them it slides out of focus, becomes a blank abstraction. "In a nation as vast and diverse as ours," historian David Potter shrewdly argued, "there is really no level higher than the regional level at which one can come to grips with the concrete realities of the land."[2]

Pushing Potter's observation one step further, it can be argued that regions capture the historian's interest not simply because they are more palpable than the nation, but because they *are* the nation and constitute a driving force behind American history. William Hesseltine has asserted, for example, that "The nation was born in the region and the region has remained the dominant force in the nation. . . . The dynamic force in American history has been the struggle of rival groups for the control of regions." With equal conviction, Frederick Jackson Turner believed that even the frontier paled before the significance of the region in American experience. "There is no more enduring, no more influential force in our history," he bluntly declared, "than the formation and interplay of the different regions of the United States."[3]

The study of regions and regionalism in American history has generated an immense amount of scholarship as well as intense controversy. Mere mention of the word "region" among a group of historians is likely to provoke a flurry of such emotionally weighted words as "sectionalism," "balkanization," "antimodernism," "provincialism," "antiquarianism," "federalism," "decentralization," and "environmental determinism." Many historians, from Woodrow Wilson to Daniel Boorstin, have denounced regionalism as a divisive force and a detriment to national unity. Many others, from Frederick Jackson Turner to William Appleman Williams, have acclaimed the flowering of regional diversity as the key to national fulfillment.

Whatever one's attitude toward regionalism, it remains a potent, inescapable issue in American history. The spatial diversity of our culture—the dramatic differences, for example, between New England, the South, and the Far West—is an essential feature of the American experience, and regional analysis provides a further framework for understanding the development of such a multifarious society.

A host of American historians have been regional specialists. Ulrich B. Phillips, David Potter, C. Vann Woodward, and Eugene Genovese are a few who have written about the South; Frederick Jackson Turner, John D. Hicks, Theodore Blegen, Merle Curti, and many others have studied the Midwest; and Francis Parkman, Walter Prescott Webb, Ray Billington, and Robert Hine are some who have examined the West. The list of names and places could be expanded indefinitely, especially when one considers that all of history "takes place," that all people and events are influenced by where they exist, and that historians should be alert to the many spatial contexts of life.[4]

Because of the immense amount of historical scholarship related to region and regionalism, the following bibliography is highly selective and divided into sections. Reflecting the dual perspective of our book and paralleling our treatment of geography, these sections approach region and regionalism in history from two basic points of view. The first section examines the *region as concept* and includes sources that develop regional theories and discuss the larger significance of regionalism in American history. Shifting attention from regionalism as a general historiographical issue, the other sections consider the *region as object of study* and concentrate upon specific approaches to regional analysis: perceptual-intellectual studies of regional symbols and myths, analysis of frontiers and rural landscapes, family and community histories, and an assortment of approaches related to urban history. In all of these sections, there is considerable cross fertilization with regional scholarship in American Studies, architecture and planning, art, geography, and literature.

M.S

---

[1] D.W. Meinig, "The Continuous Shaping of America: A Prospectus for Geographers and Historians," *American Historical Review* 83 (December 1978): 1205.

[2] David M. Potter, *The South and the Sectional Conflict* (Baton Rouge: Louisiana State Univ. Press, 1968), 4.

[3] William B. Hesseltine, "Regions, Classes, and Sections in American History" in *Sections and Politics: Selected Essays by William H. Hesseltine*, ed. Richard N. Current. (Madison: State Historical Society of Wisconsin, 1968), 97 and Frederick Jackson Turner, typescript, "The Significance of the Section in the U.S.," May 1922, File Drawer 14 A #24, Frederick Jackson Turner Papers, Henry E. Huntington Library, San Marino, California.

[4] For further discussion of this view, see John A. Jakle, "Time, Space, and the Geographic Past: A Prospectus for Historical Geography," *American Historical Review* 76 (October 1971): 1084–1103, as well as the introduction to the Geography chapter, above.

History: Region as Concept

Anyone interested in the history of American regionalism is challenged by a series of haunting questions. How important has regional culture been in American life? What has been the relationship between region and nation throughout our history? Which has exerted the most compelling and lasting force? Has regionalism been a largely harmful or healthful impulse in our culture? Does it seem to be fading or flourishing over time? To begin to answer such vital questions requires a theoretical orientation, a familiarity with basic regional concepts, and acquaintance with the work of other historians who have wrestled with these very issues.

As the following list demonstrates, many American historians have grappled with these large questions, and at least three of them have made profound and lasting contributions to regional theory in general. Frederick Jackson Turner, Walter Prescott Webb, and James C. Malin are the pre-eminent regional theorists in American history. Their work, along with the pioneering scholarship of George Perkins Marsh in historical geography, Howard W. Odum in regional sociology, and Lewis Mumford in cultural history and planning, comes close to matching the finely tuned geohistorical sensibilities of English historians Jacquetta Hawkes and W.G. Hoskins and French historians Lucien Febvre, Marc Bloch, and Fernand Braudel.

Many American historians in addition to Turner, Webb, and Malin have made significant contributions to regional theory. The work of David Potter, William Hesseltine, Ray Billington, C. Vann Woodward, Carl Degler, George Tindall, William Appleman Williams, and others is important for any student of American regionalism as is the work of an emerging group of historians including Carl Abbott, David Goldfield, and Timothy Mahoney who analyze American cities within larger regional contexts.

This section contains at least three types of sources that enhance our conceptual understanding of region and regionalism. A highly selective group of sources, including work by Webb, Malin, Degler,

Braudel, and Michel Foucault, examines causes of regionalism by tracing the interaction of nature and culture over time. A second and much larger collection of sources, including work by Turner, Potter, Woodward, Tindall, Henry Shapiro, Robert Wiebe, and others, discusses the general significance of region and regionalism in American history by exploring such issues as the changing relationship between region and nation, or the connections between regionalism, modernization, and cultural pluralism. A final group, including Fulmer Mood, Vernon Carstensen, Warren Susman, Richard Maxwell Brown, David Noble, Richard Pells, R. Alan Lawson, Dewey Grantham, Michael O'Brien, and others, analyzes regionalism as an aspect of intellectual history, tracing the development of regional thought, ideologies, and movements in our culture.

M.S.

792. Abbott, Carl. "The American Sunbelt: Idea and Region." *Journal of the American West* 17 (July 1979): 5–18.

In this useful history of the "Sunbelt" as an idea and fact, Abbott suggests that the decentralization of war industries during the early 1940s triggered the rise of the southern rim and that metropolitan areas constitute the core of this region. "Houston," he writes, "is the symbol of the new America."

793. ———. "Frontiers and Sections: Cities and Regions in American Growth." *American Quarterly* 37 (Bibliography issue 1985): 395–410.

This perceptive analysis of the relationship between American cities and regions carefully surveys a variety of influential urban-regional theories in geography, economics, political science, sociology, and history to throw light upon the current tension between Sunbelt and Frostbelt, core and periphery. Turner's sense of the frontier and section; Norman Gras's theory of metropolitan regions; D.W. Meinig's model of regional core, domain, and sphere; and Jean Gottmann's portrait of the Megalopolis are a few of the issues developed. Other sources by Abbott are listed under History: Other (items 1032–1034).

794. Billington, Ray Allen. *Frederick Jackson Turner: Historian, Scholar, Teacher.* New York: Oxford Univ. Press, 1973.

This masterful biography contains thorough discussions not only of Turner's sectional theory but also of the varieties of regional thought in the United States and Europe during Turner's lifetime. "The Genesis of the Sectional Thesis, 1893–1910," pp. 209–32; "The Persistence of a Theory: The Frontier and Sectional Hypothesis," pp. 444–71; and "The Significance of Frederick Jackson Turner," pp. 472–97 offer exceptionally insightful background to Turner's influential vision of regionalism. Another source by Billington is listed under History: Perception Studies (item 858).

795. Blegen, Theodore. *Grass Roots History.* Minneapolis: Univ. of Minnesota Press, 1947.

The opening chapters of this book vigorously promote the use of a regional focus and folk materials in the writing of history. Echoing the folk-regional exuberance of Whitman, Sandburg, Odum, and Botkin, Blegen argues that the essence of regionalism is "a creative concern with the development of the region to its maximum for the culture of the nation. Adding up non-entities, someone has said, is like adding up a column of zeroes; the result remains zero. Add up regions that lack cultural richness and strength, and you cannot achieve an impressive total in terms of national culture.... The pivot of history is not the uncommon, but the usual, and the true makers of history are 'the people, yes.'" See "Inverted Provincialism," pp. 3–13, and "Literature of the Unlettered," pp. 14–27.

796. Block, Robert H. "Frederick Jackson Turner and American Geography." *Annals of the Association of American Geographers* 70 (March 1980): 31–42.

A detailed discussion of Turner's extensive professional and intellectual ties to the discipline of geography.

797. Bogue, Allan G. "The Heirs of James C. Malin: A Grasslands Historiography." *Great Plains Quarterly* 1 (1981): 105–31.

After evaluating Malin's contributions to regionalism, especially as expressed in his major work, *The Grasslands of North America* (1947), Bogue traces how subsequent historians, geographers, sociologists, and economists have picked up the challenges of Malin's scholarship. Stressing the contribution of geographers such as Walter Kollmorgen, Leslie Hewes, Martyn Bowden, and Terry Jordan, Bogue argues that "in matters of environmental perception it is they who are truly Malin's heirs."

798. Braudel, Fernand. *Afterthoughts on Material Civilization and Capitalism.* Translated by Patricia M. Ranum. Baltimore: Johns Hopkins Univ. Press, 1977.

Braudel's magisterial studies such as *The Mediterranean and the Mediterranean World in the Age of Philip II* and *Capitalism and Material Life* are deeply sensitive to the power of place and geography in human history. In this brief book, especially in "Capitalism and Dividing Up the World," pp. 79–117, Braudel discusses some of the regional theories and models implicit in his larger, more empirical works. His discussions of the spatial divisions of the world-economy from antiquity to the present parallels the work of Immanuel Wallerstein and Eric Wolf, annotated under Sociology and Anthropology, respectively. For a detailed discussion of Braudel, see Kinser below (item 822).

799. Brown, Richard Maxwell. "The New Regionalism in America, 1970–1981." In *Regionalism in the Pacific Northwest*, edited by William G. Robbins, Robert J. Frank, and Richard E. Ross, 37–96. Corvallis: Oregon State Univ. Press, 1983.

This important, richly documented essay carefully compares two periods of heightened regional consciousness—the 1920s and 1930s and the 1970s. After analyzing the many manifestations of regionalism in both eras and giving special attention to the recent flowering of regional literature in the West and Northwest, Brown points to the tenacity of regional attachments and myths and concludes that "It is just barely possible that ... culture, regionalism will not only rival but surpass nationalism in America as a source for good in human life."

800. Carstensen, Vernon. "The Development and Application of Regional-Sectional Concepts, 1900–1950." In *Regionalism in America* (item 820), 99–118.

This essay succinctly outlines some of the contributions of geographers, historians, sociologists, and others to regional thinking in the first half of the twentieth century. Fulmer Mood's companion essay (item 827) traces these concepts through the eighteenth and nineteenth centuries.

801. Curti, Merle. *The Roots of American Loyalty*. New York: Columbia Univ. Press, 1946.

"The Loyalty of Time and Place," pp. 30–64, contains an insightful discussion of the impact of an immense landscape upon American identities and the interplay between regional and national loyalties during the antebellum years.

802. ———. "The Section and the Frontier in American History: The Methodological Concepts of Frederick Jackson Turner." In *Methods in Social Sciences*, edited by Stuart Rice, 353–67. Chicago: Univ. of Chicago Press, 1931.

Along with Billington's biographical analysis, Curti's essay remains one of the most insightful discussions of the relationship between the frontier and the section in Turner's thought.

803. Degler, Carl. "Does Land Make a People?" In *Out of Our Past: The Forces That Shaped Modern America*. rev. ed., 121–134. Evanston, Ill.: Harper and Row, 1970.

In clear, logical fashion, this portion of Degler's text investigates the question of whether particular landscapes dictate particular cultural patterns. After observing that similar regions often support very different cultures and that the same region often sustains a variety of cultures, Degler concludes that "Geography may set the limits within which men must live, but it does not determine which of the several alternatives available to man actually will be pursued."

804. ———. *Place Over Time: The Continuity of Southern Distinctiveness*. Baton Rouge: Louisiana State Univ. Press, 1977.

Degler eloquently argues that reports of the death of southern distinctiveness have been greatly exaggerated. His concluding catalog of southern particularisms is a beautifully wrought prose poem to an "enduring sense of personal and regional identity born from a history no other American shares."

805. Etulain, Richard W. "Frontier, Region and Myth: Changing Interpretations of Western American Culture." *Journal of American Culture* 3 (Summer 1980): 268–84.

Etulain argues that Turner's general lack of interest in twentieth century cultural history has set a pattern for subsequent generations of American historians and urges greater attention to scholars, such as Josiah Royce, Walter Prescott Webb, Henry Nash Smith, and Kevin Starr, who have deviated from this pattern.

806. Fite, Gilbert C. "Regionalism: The Historical Perspective-Northern Plains." *South Dakota Review* 18 (Winter 1981): 17–38.

After discussing the emergence of sectional-regional concepts by the late nineteenth century, Fite carefully analyzes the work of three eminent twentieth century regional theorists and historians: Walter Prescott Webb, James C. Malin, and Elwyn B. Robinson.

807. Foucault, Michel. "Questions on Geography." In *Power/Knowledge*, edited by Colin Gordon, 63–76. New York: Pantheon, 1980, 63–76.

In this lively interview, Foucault examines the root meanings of the words "region" and "regionalism" and encourages historians to be more sensitive to geography and the power of place.

808. Goldfield, David R. "The New Regionalism." *Journal of Urban History* 10 (February 1984): 171–86.

In this well-informed review essay of seven books in urban-regional history published since 1978—including Allan Pred's *Urban Growth and City Systems in the U.S., 1840–1860*, Robert Balstad Miller's *City and Hinterland,* and Thomas Cochran's *Frontiers of Change*—Goldfield applauds the authors' vision of cities developing within larger regional and national frameworks. He also carefully compares this "new regionalism" with the influential regional approaches of Howard Odum and Fernand Braudel.

809. ———. "The Urban South: A Regional Framework." *American Historical Review* 86 (December 1981): 1009–34.

Building upon the insights of Howard Odum, Wilbur Cash, Brian J.L. Berry, and others, Goldfield stresses the need to study cities in the context of their surrounding regions rather than analyze them as unique environments set apart from the countryside as Louis Wirth had argued. Goldfield then proposes a "regional framework for the study of the urban South" emphasizing economic, religious, and social factors that distinguish southern cities from their counterparts elsewhere.

810. Goldman, Eric F. "Middle States Regionalism and American Historiography." In *Historiography and Urbanization*, edited by Eric F. Goldman, 211–20. Baltimore: Johns Hopkins Univ. Press, 1941.

Stressing the "deregionalizing influence" of the Mid-Atlantic states, Goldman believes that their sense of "inbetweeness" will eventually characterize the rest of the nation. Now that "historians are looking at the country more along horizontal lines of social groupings than along vertical lines of regionalism," the characteristics of New York, New Jersey, and Pennsylvania are closer to the future shape of the nation.

811. Grantham, Dewey. *The Regional Imagination: the South and Recent American History.* Nashville: Vanderbilt Univ. Press, 1979.

Two essays in this book are particularly valuable to a general understanding of American regionalism. "The South and the Politics of Sectionalism," pp. 1–22, essentially updates V.O. Key's classic analysis by outlining the factors that have produced a southern brand of politics and by discussing the nationalizing forces that "will eventually complete the erosion of southern sectionalism." "The Regional Imagination: Social Scientists and the American South," pp. 153–84, explains how Howard Odum, Rupert Vance, T.J. Woofter, Charles S. Johnson, V.O. Key, and others influenced southern regionalism in the twentieth century by adding "a new dimension to the regional imagination, a creative dimension that presents southern reality more fully than the mythology or even the perception growing out of experience itself." Their theoretical work, furthermore, has "provided an extraordinary demonstration of the ways in which society can be studied within a spatial framework."

812. Green, Fletcher. "Resurgent Southern Sectionalism, 1933–1955." *North Carolina Historical Review* 33 (April 1956): 222–40.

In contrast to many consensus historians, Green believes that the Great Depression and the New Deal aroused a dormant southern sectionalism which continued to swell into the 1950s. Green analyzes the emotional, aesthetic, economic, and political strands of this regional revival and concludes that, with proper guidance, it could enrich both the region and the nation.

813. Gressley, Gene M. "Regionalism and the Twentieth Century West." In *The American West: New Perspectives, New Questions,* edited by Jerome Steffen, 197–234. Norman: Univ. of Oklahoma Press, 1979.

In this densely footnoted, wide-ranging essay, Gressley traces manifestation of western regional consciousness from the 1890s to the 1970s. A potentially powerful regional identity has gradually emerged since the 1930s—an identity that has coalesced around environmental issues and western efforts to end eastern economic exploitation. Gressley has refined the theme of western identity in the face of continued colonialization in "The West: Past, Present, and Future," *Western Historical Quarterly* 17 (January 1986), pp. 5–23.

814. Hacker, Louis. "Sections—or Classes?" *Nation* (July 26 1933): 108–10.

Hacker forcefully criticizes Turner's sectional thesis and much of regional theory in general as a subterfuge hiding the more pressing problems of class conflict.

815. Handlin, Oscar. "Yankees." In *The Harvard Encyclopedia of American Ethnic Groups*, Cambridge: Harvard Univ. Press, 1980.

Echoing historian George B. Tindall and sociologists Andrew Greeley and John Shelton Reed, Handlin argues that American regional groups—in this case New England Yankees—can be categorized as ethnic groups.

816. Hesseltine, William B. "Regions, Classes, and Sections in American History." In *Sections and Politics: Selected Essays by William B. Hesseltine*, edited by Richard N. Current, 97–113. Madison: State Historical Society of Wisconsin, 1968.

In a few pages of this essay originally published in 1944, Hesseltine effectively refurbishes Turner's sectional vision in light of the work of regional social science in the 1930s and 1940s. "The nation was born in the region," he asserts, "and the region has remained the dominant force in the nation. The dynamic force in American history has been the struggle of rival groups for the control of regions." The essay ends with an appeal for a meeting of minds between historians and regional planners.

817. ———. "Sectionalism and Regionalism in American History." *Journal of Southern History* 26 (February 1960): 25–34.

In addition to reemphasizing Hesseltine's and Turner's beliefs that the competitive scramble for regional resources has been the driving force in American history, this essay urges historians to do comparative regional studies.

818. Holtgrieve, Donald G. "Frederick Jackson Turner as a Regionalist." *Professional Geographer* 26 (May 1974): 159–65.

In this brief survey of Turner's regional thought, Holtgrieve discusses Turner's changing perception of the culture/nature relationship and his fairly inconsistent use of the terms "section," "region," "province," and "area." Despite some theoretical and definitional vagueness, Turner's regional thought was more advanced than most of his "geographic brethren."

819. Jacobs, Wilbur R., ed. *Frederick Jackson Turner's Legacy: Unpublished Writings in American History.* San Marino, Calif.: Huntington Library, 1965.

This valuable collection contains a number of previously unpublished lectures and essays that demonstrate the centrality of sectionalism to Turner's historical vision and the sophistication of his regional theory. Especially useful are Jacobs's headnotes and Turner's "Introduction to a Lecture on Sectionalism," pp. 47–48; "Draft on Sectionalism," pp. 48–51; "Lecture on Sectionalism," pp. 52–69; and "Class and Sectional Struggles," pp. 77–78. The sectional speculation Turner published during his lifetime is listed under Turner (items 847–848).

820. Jensen, Merrill, ed. *Regionalism in America.* Madison: Univ. of Wisconsin Press, 1951.

An indispensable summation of American regional theory, this collection is comparable in importance to Turner's, Odum's, and Mumford's regional masterpieces of the 1930s. Classic essays published here include Fulmer Mood's "The Origin, Evolution, and Application of the Regional Concept, 1750–1900" (item 827); Vernon Carstensen's "The Development and Application of Regional-Sectional Concepts, 1900–1950" (item 800); Benjamin T. Spencer's "Regionalism in American Literature" (item 1291); E.P. Richardson's "Regionalism in American Painting" (item 298); Rexford Newcomb's "Regionalism in American Architecture" (item 203); Rupert Vance's "The Regional Concept as a Tool for Social Research" (item 1640); Louis Wirth's "The Limitations of Regionalism" (item 1648); and Howard W. Odum's "The Promise of Regionalism," pp. 395–425 (item 1608). (All annotated elsewhere.)

821. Jensen, Richard. "On Modernizing Frederick Jackson Turner: The Historiography of Regionalism." *Western Historical Quarterly* 11 (July 1980): 307–22.

After stressing many of the weaknesses of the Turnerian approach to American history—including a lack of comparative studies of frontiers and regions in other cultures, a general avoidance of issues of class structure and economic inequality, and an underdeveloped sense of the historical role of women and children—Jensen argues that some value can be salvaged from Turner's vision of the frontier and section if it is tied to the theme of modernization.

822. Kinser, Samuel. "'Annaliste' Paradigm? The Geohistorical Structuralism of Fernand Braudel." *American Historical Review* 86 (December 1981): 63–105.

Kinser traces the evolution of Braudel's geohistorical vision, from the 1920s until the publication of the second edition of *The Mediterranean and the Mediterranean World in the Age of Philip II* in 1966. The influence of Paul Vidal de la Blache, Lucien Febvre, Marc Bloch, Gaston Roupnel, and others is carefully analyzed as are Braudel's discussions of geographical personality and the relationships between time and space and culture and nature. Kinser writes, "The rhetoric of space with its intoxicating vastness, of exchange with its ceaseless activity, and of life with its alluring warmth have inspired many others to construct equally new and compelling visions of the past."

823. Lawson, R. Alan. *The Failure of Independent Liberalism, 1930–1941*. New York: Capricorn Books, 1971.

Lawson analyzes several of the regionalisms of the 1930s as parts of the larger effort of independent liberal reform "directed at replacing the old capitalist order with a more cooperatively organized society." With this unifying theme in mind, Lawson compares the regional ideas of such figures as Herbert Agar, Ralph Borsodi, W.Y. Elliott, Howard Odum, and Lewis Mumford.

824. Luebke, Frederick C. "Regionalism and the Great Plains: Problems of Concept and Method." *Western Historical Quarterly* 15 (January 1984): 19–38.

Luebke's highly perceptive essay accomplishes two general tasks. First, it provides a vivid overview of the course of American regional thought and practice in the fine arts, humanities, and social sciences from the 1920s to the 1970s. Second, this spectrum of regional thought is applied to the study of the Great Plains, and in the process, Luebke formulates a systematic method for regional analysis. Regional study, he wisely suggests, must focus upon the interaction of culture and environment over time and must involve careful comparisons between selected social groups in selected environments in order to more accurately gauge the impact of geographical factors upon cultural identity.

825. Mahoney, Timothy R. "Urban History in a Regional Context: River Towns on the Upper Mississippi, 1840–1860." *Journal of American History* 72 (September 1985): 318–39.

Because of the extremely varied and interrelated nature of American cities, Mahoney urges urban historians to abandon isolated case studies in favor of larger studies of towns and cities within regional systems. He proposes a three tiered model of urban-regional analysis, applies it to antebellum urban development on the Upper Mississippi, and concludes that "Examining the continual interaction of regional and local change is the basis of an urban history able to view reality in all its complexity."

826. Malin, James C. *History and Ecology: Studies in Grassland.* Edited by Robert P. Swierenga. Lincoln: Univ. of Nebraska Press, 1984.

This anthology gathers together the most crucial elements of Malin's widely scattered work in regional theory. Four essays published between 1944 and 1960 are especially important to students of the regional concept in American history. "Space and History: Reflections on the Closed-Space Doctrines of Turner and Mackinder," pp. 68–84, criticizes the American historian and English geographer for imputing an unnecessary sense of crisis to the end of the American and global frontiers and for ignoring air transportation as a continuation of frontier expansiveness. "Webb and Regionalism," pp. 85–104, takes Webb and others to task for their general ignorance of ecological theory and for their inability to demonstrate culture's dynamic, often positive, role in shaping regional environments. "Ecology and History," pp. 195–111, outlines the uses of ecological principles in historical analysis and underscores Malin's belief that technological innovation can counter environmental depletion. "On the Nature of the History of Geographical Area," pp. 129–43, urges regional historians to define the object of their study as accurately as possible, taking into account the work of natural science and geography; to perceive a region from "the ground up," building upon the insights of geologists, paleontologists, and anthropologists; and to understand "technology" in its largest sense as a reflection of human versatility in responding to nature. Swierenga's introduction and selected bibliography are extremely useful. This and other items by Malin are listed under History: Frontier and Landscape (items 918–921).

827. Mood, Fulmer. "The Sectional Concept, 1750–1900." In *Regionalism in America* (item 820), 5–98.

This richly detailed essay contains useful information regarding the origins and meanings of the words "section" and "region" as well as a catalog of regional schemes from Jedediah Morse to John Wesley

Powell. Vernon Carstensen's essay (item 800) continues the narrative to the mid-twentieth century.

828. Noble, David W. *The End of American History: Democracy, Capitalism, and the Metaphor of Two Worlds in Anglo-American Historical Writing, 1880–1980.* Minneapolis: Univ. of Minnesota Press, 1985.

This important critique of the myth of American exceptionalism culminates with an analysis of William Appleman Williams's development from internationalist to regionalist. Turner, Beard, Niebuhr, and Hofstadter receive careful attention, and "William Appleman Williams: Universal Capitalism, Universal Marxism, or American Democracies, 1955–1980," pp. 115–40, contains a perceptive, largely favorable, analysis of Williams's radical regionalism.

829. ———. "William Appleman Williams and the Crisis of Public History." In *Redefining the Past: Essays in Diplomatic History in Honor of William Appleman Williams,* edited by Lloyd C. Gardner, 45–62. Corvallis: Oregon State Univ. Press, 1986.

A highly perceptive analysis of the evolution of William's regional vision of American history. After comparing Beard's and Williams's lifelong commitments to the writing of public history, Noble carefully traces the reasons behind Williams's shift from a nationalistic Progressive position in the 1940s to a radical decentralist stance in the 1980s. Other sources by Noble are listed under American Studies (item 30) and History: Perception Studies (item 875).

830. O'Brien, Michael. *The Idea of the American South, 1920–1942.* Baltimore: Johns Hopkins Univ. Press, 1979.

This lucid study of the intensification of southern identity during the interwar decades makes important contributions to our understanding of the forces behind American regionalism in general. O'Brien's opening chapter, "On the Idea of the South," pp. 3–27, perceptively places the rise of southern regional consciousness in the eighteenth century within the context of European intellectual history, stressing the influence of European cultural nationalism and romantic folk-regional enthusiasms upon southern culture. A vivid account of Howard W. Odum's regional thought and practice is at the heart of O'Brien's book, and "Odum: The Failure of Regionalism," pp. 70–93, is highly perceptive. Other chapters are devoted to such major American regionalists as John Donald Wade, John Crowe Ransom, Frank Owsley, Donald Davidson, and Wilbur J. Cash.

831. Pells, Richard. *Radical Visions and American Dreams: Culture and Social Thought in the Depression Years.* New York: Harper and Row, 1973.

In "The Search for Community," pp. 96–150, Pells perceptively explores reasons for the widespread interest in folk life and regionalism in the United States during the 1930s.

832. Potter, David M. *The South and the Sectional Conflict.* Baton Rouge: Louisiana State Univ. Press, 1968.

This important book contains three vital contributions to understanding the region as a concept: "The Enigma of the South," pp. 3–16; "The Historian's Use of Nationalism and Vice Versa," pp. 34–83; and "Depletion and Renewal in Southern History," pp. 177–98. In the first essay Potter underscores the importance of regional analysis in a nation as vast and various as the United States and describes the tenacious "folk culture" that has sustained a strong sense of place in the South. The second essay discusses various meanings and uses of regionalism and nationalism in which Potter stresses that the two impulses are closely connected and can flourish together. The final piece abounds with pertinent suggestions for continued study of the South and American regionalism.

833. Robbins, William G. "The 'Plundered Province' Thesis and the Recent Historiography of the American West." *Pacific Historical Review* 55 (November 1986): 577–97.

After examining a persistent regional theme—the image of the West as victim of economic imperialism—Robbins suggests that this theme has renewed relevance in light of recent uneven economic development within the West itself and the possibility of the West becoming a resource colony for expanding Asian economies.

834. Rodgers, Daniel T. "Regionalism and the Burdens of Progress." In *Region, Race, and Reconstruction: Essays in Honor of C. Vann Woodward,* edited by J. Morgan Kousser and James M. McPherson, 3–26. New York: Oxford Univ. Press, 1982.

In the process of explaining why Howard Odum's progressive brand of regionalism vanished so quickly in the 1940s, Rodgers analyzes an impressive spectrum of American regional thought and highlights a pervasive tension between folk-regional sentiments and the drive for technological progress—a tension that eased somewhat during the Great Depression.

835. Ross, Robert. "Regional Illusion, Capitalist Reality." *Democracy* 1 (October 1981): 93–99.

Responding to William Appleman Williams's historical analysis of regionalism as a constructive alternative to the American empire, Ross argues that such "Jeffersonian dreams" are "dangerously sentimental" and play into the hands of the capitalist global hegemony. Williams's "Procedure Becomes Substance," *Democracy* 2 (April 1982), pp. 100–102, is a brisk rebuttal of Ross's article.

836. Russo, David J. *Families and Communities: A New View of American History*. Nashville: American Society for State and Local History, 1974.

Russo urges historians to view American culture from the inside out—to begin at the local level with families and communities and then build outward toward a sense of the nation. "The Intermediary Communities: Cities, States, and Regions," pp. 32–104, develops a useful scheme of a hierarchy of communities in which Americans live, argues for greater attention to regional analysis, and asks historians to avoid the habitual "regionalism-is-just-sectionalism" approach that has so often hindered effective regional study.

837. Shannon, Fred A. *An Appraisal of Walter Prescott Webb's "The Great Plains: A Study in Institutions and Environment."* New York: Social Science Research Council, 1940.

This remains a highly useful resource for anyone venturing into the field of regional historiography. Shannon's meticulous critique of Webb's regional masterpiece and the flurry of scholarly opinions surrounding the Webb-Shannon debate demonstrate the provocative nature of regional theory and the pleasures and perils of writing regional history. In addition to containing Shannon's often overly zealous criticisms of Webb's regional generalizations and environmental determinism and Webb's formal response to these charges, pp. 3–112 and 112–35, respectively, this volume also contains the transcript of a daylong scholarly conference devoted to the controversy in 1937. The exchanges between conference members Arthur Schlesinger, John Hicks, Louis Wirth, Clark Wissler, Charles Colby, Shannon, Webb, and others offer invaluable insights to regional-environmental theory.

838. Shapiro, Henry D. "The New Pluralism and the New Local History." *Appalachian Journal* 12 (Winter 1985): 142–46.

In reviewing a collection of essays on Kentucky history, Shapiro distinguishes between three periods of pluralistic scholarship in America: the old pluralism of the 1920s and 1930s, the new pluralism of the 1960s and 1970s, and less polemical studies of place and cultural diversity in the 1980s.

839. ———. "The Place of Culture and the Problem of Identity." In *Appalachia and America: Autonomy and Regional Dependence*, edited by Allen Batteau, 111–41. Louisville: Univ. of Kentucky Press, 1983.

Shapiro argues that in the late nineteenth century social scientists began to give fresh importance to regional place. Daniel G. Brinton, an ethnologist, argued that territoriality was crucial to understanding the United States, and Frederick Jackson Turner, during his middle period, made the "section" his key concept. Shapiro believes that the regional logic inherited from Brinton and Turner has encouraged an oversimplified notion of Appalachia. Another source by Shapiro is listed under History: Perception Studies (item 881).

840. Singal, Daniel. *The War Within: From Victorian to Modernist Thought in the South, 1919–1945*. Chapel Hill: Univ. of North Carolina Press, 1982.

In the process of examining southern regional consciousness between the world wars as a response to modernist thought, Singal perceptively analyzes the self-conscious regional theories of Howard Odum, Rupert Vance, Guy B. Johnson, and others at the University of North Carolina and John Crowe Ransom, Donald Davidson, Allen Tate, and others at Vanderbilt. Other southern writers and intellectuals studied include Ulrich B. Phillips, Broadus Mitchel, Ellen Glasgow, William Faulkner, William Terry Couch, Arthur Raper, and Robert Penn Warren.

841. Susman, Warren I. "Introduction." *Culture and Commitment, 1929–1945*, 1–24. New York: George Braziller, 1973, 1–24. Reprinted as "Culture and Commitment" in *Culture as History*, 184–210. New York: Pantheon, 1984.

Susman brilliantly analyzes regionalism as part of the search for cultural security and commitment that accompanied the depression and war years.

842. Thomas, John L. *Alternative America: Henry George, Edward Bellamy, Henry Demarest Lloyd and the Adversary Tradition.* Cambridge: Harvard Univ. Press, 1983.

Thomas's final chapter, "The Legacy," pp. 354–66, perceptively links the ideas and values of a late nineteenth century utopian adversary tradition to the regional movements of the 1920s and 1930s. Thomas argues, in part, that the widespread regional programs and theories of the interwar decades "derived from the adversary culture of Bellamy, Lloyd, and George with its emphasis on balance and symmetry, measure and pace, the indigenous and the participatory."

843. ———. "Lewis Mumford: Regionalist Historian." *Reviews in American History* 16 (March 1988): 158–72.

Thomas traces the growth of Mumford's regional vision during the 1920s and 1930s, compares Mumford's theory with other regionalisms of the period, and evaluates its historical significance.

844. Tindall, George B. *The Ethnic Southerners.* Baton Rouge: Louisiana State Univ. Press, 1977.

By forcefully arguing that Southerners comprise a distinct American subculture analogous to an ethnic subculture, Tindall explores the larger theme of cultural pluralism in American life. "Since the mid-1960s," he writes," the existence, certainly the appearance, of consensus in American life has been visibly shaken. The suspicion grows that the legend of a homogenized American culture had all along the shimmering quality of mirage, like those situation comedies where people live in boxes made of ticky-tacky and all look the same. It is not the South that has vanished but the mainstream, like one of those desert rivers that run out into the sand, consumed by heat." This important book also contains valuable discussions of the regional theories of the Southern Agrarians, Odum, Webb, and Woodward.

845. ———. ed. "The Status and Future of Regionalism—A Symposium." *Journal of Southern History* 26 (February 1960): 22–24.

This interdisciplinary symposium contains four valuable essays: Tindall's "Introduction," pp. 22–24, which outlines the rise and fall of the Chapel Hill and Vanderbilt versions of regionalism; William B. Hesseltine's "Sectionalism and Regionalism in American History" (item 817); Cleanth Brook's "Regionalism in American Literature (item 1176); and Rupert Vance's "The Sociological Implications of Southern Regionalism" (item 1641).

846. Tobin, G.M. "Landscape, Region, and the Writing of History: Walter Prescott Webb in the 1920s." *American Studies International* 16 (Summer 1978): 285–304.

Tobin carefully traces the evolution of Webb's regional consciousness, from his childhood at the turn of the century until the publication of *The Great Plains* in 1931. Webb resolved the tension between the eastern imagery contained in books and the seemingly empty open land around him by gaining a scientific understanding of the physical environment. "Once he had done that," Tobin writes, "he could begin to discover for the first time the harsh beauty of his region, to see meaning in its gaunt shapes and formidable terrain."

847. Turner, Frederick Jackson. *The Frontier in American History*. New York: Henry Holt and Co., 1920.

Turner's career-long interest in sections and sectionalism is at the heart of this book concerning the frontier. Many of the essays collected here reflect Turner's belief that with the death of the frontier the section would emerge as a dominant force in American life. A careful reading of such essays as "The Old West," pp. 67–125; "The Middle West," pp. 126–55; "The Significance of the Mississippi Valley in American History," pp. 177–204; "The Problem of the West," pp. 205–21; "The West and American Ideals," pp. 290–310; "Social Forces in American History," pp. 311–34; among others, reveals Turner's growing conviction that "There is no more enduring, no more influential force in our history than the formation and interplay of the different regions of the United States."

848. ———. *The Significance of Sections in American History*. New York: Henry Holt and Co., 1932.

Published the year of his death, this Pulitzer Prize winning book collection contains Turner's most important contributions to regional theory. Written between 1904 and 1925, essays such as "Problems in American History," "Geographical Influences in American Political History," "Is Sectionalism Dying Away?" and especially "Sections and Nation" and "The Significance of the Section in American History" are quintessential contributions to American regional theory. The latter two essays, the most effective summaries of the sectional thesis, are reprinted in Ray Allen Billington, ed., *Frontier and Section: Selected Essays of Frederick Jackson Turner* (Englewood Cliffs, N.J.: Prentice-Hall, 1961), pp. 115–35 and 136–53. For a thorough bibliography of Turner's work, including miscellaneous essays on sectionalism, see Vernon E. Mattson and William E. Marion, *Frederick Jackson Turner:*

A Reference Guide. (Boston: 1985). Other sources by Turner are listed under History: Frontier and Settlement (items 940–942).

849. Webb, Walter Prescott. "The American West—Perpetual Mirage." *Harper's Magazine* 214 (May 1957): 25–31.

This article, which sparked a firestorm of denial from many of Webb's fellow Westerners, asserts that the desert is the dominant force, and aridity the fundamental fact of life, in the western half of the United States. The desert makes the West a land of deficiencies supporting tenuous oasis cities, and a pervasive sense of scarcity conditions the culture and personality of Westerners. Webb refines this theory and describes the furor surrounding the article in "The West and the Desert," *An Honest Preface and other Essays* (Boston: Houghton-Mifflin, 1959), pp. 175–93.

850. ———. *Divided We Stand: The Crisis of a Frontierless Democracy.* rev. ed. Austin, Tex.: Acorn Press, 1944.

Originally published in 1937, this book opens with a sweeping image of fundamental "fault lines" that separate the United States into "three fairly distinct cultures": the North, the South, and the West. Webb describes the distinctive geography, history, and culture of each region and argues that the primary force that keeps them from being separate nations is the North's economic stranglehold upon the South and the West. While the fierce indignation of this book makes it seem the western counterpart of Donald Davidson's *The Attack on Leviathan* (1938), Webb ultimately echoes Howard Odum's conciliatory hopes for the growth of an equitable, balanced nationalism to replace the economic suzerainty of the North.

851. ———. "Geographical-Historical Concepts in American History." *Annals of the Association of American Geographers* 50 (June 1960): 85–93.

In this crisply argued essay, Webb describes the personal and intellectual sources of his most famous regional works: *The Great Plains* (1931), *The Great Frontier* (1952), and "The American West— Perpetual Mirage" (1957). In addition to stressing the purpose of each work, Webb discusses his method of regional analysis—sequent occupance—and reiterates his conviction that the physical environment is a key to understanding culture. Urging historians to start their work "solidly on the ground," Webb argues that for every culture "The whole action occurred on some piece of land, and is related in numerous ways to the land and the climate. . . . .The land is the matrix out of which culture grows." Webb's essay is followed by D.W. Meinig's appreciative and highly insightful commentary, pp. 95–96. Webb's article is reprinted in his *History as High Adventure* (Austin, Tex.: Pemberton Press, 1969), pp. 55–69. Other items by Webb are listed under History: Frontier and Landscape (items 945–946).

852. Wiebe, Robert. *The Segmented Society: An Introduction to the Meaning of America.* New York: Oxford Univ. Press, 1975.

In analyzing the abiding diversity of American culture, Wiebe pays particular attention to the centrifugal, segmenting influence of American space. "Open land," he writes, "was a vacuum as well as a magnet. From the earliest days of settlement it invited people who had differences to solve their problems by separation instead of accommodation. Rather than adjust, they parted.... Differences were spread across space rather than managed within it."

853. Williams, William Appleman. "Radicals and Regionalism." *Democracy* 1 (July 1981): 87–98.

This important essay is Williams's most effective discussion of the significance of regionalism in American culture. It outlines the historical and intellectual sources of his vision of regionalism as a necessary response to the overweening forces of empire. This sense of regional renewal informs much of Williams's work—e.g., his "Postlude: From Empire to Community," in *The Roots of the Modern American Empire* (New York: Random House, 1969), pp. 447–53, and his call for "replacing the American empire with a federation of regional communities" in the final chapter of *America Confronts a Revolutionary World, 1776–1976* (New York: William Morrow, 1976)—and this stance has generated historiographical debate. For a bibliography of Williams's work, see Lloyd C. Gardner, ed., *Redefining the Past: Essays in Diplomatic History in Honor of William Appleman Williams* (Corvallis: Oregon State Univ. Press, 1986), pp. 221–26. See Ross and Noble in this subsection for positive and negative evaluations of Williams's radical regionalism (items 835, 828).

854. ———. "Regional Resistance: Backyard Autonomy." *Nation* 233 (September 5, 1981): 161, 178–80.

Williams praises a spectrum of regional environmental protest groups, ranging from Mormons rejecting MX missiles to New Englanders stopping oil refineries, as signs of healthy resistance to centralized authority.

855. Woodward, C. Vann. *The Burden of Southern History*. rev. ed.
Baton Rouge: Louisiana State Univ. Press, 1968.

This influential book contains at least three vital contributions to
American regional theory, particularly to our understanding of the
changing relationships between regional and national identities. "The
Search for Southern Identity," pp. 3–25, analyzes the South's gradual
pull toward the national mainstream and urges Southerners to preserve
constructive aspects of their collective experience as antidotes against
the "disintegrating effect of nationalism and the pressure of
conformity." "The Irony of Southern History," pp. 187–211, discusses
the role of history or collective memory in the development of regional
identity and sense of place. Woodward argues that unlike the rest of the
nation the South has experienced "large components of frustration,
failure, and defeat" and that this fall from innocence has evoked a
profound sense of place. "A Second Look at the Theme of Irony," pp.
213–33, views the war in Vietnam and nationwide racial hatred and
somberly concludes that "If there was ever a time when America might
profit from the un-American heritage of the South, it would seem to be
the present." For an insightful analysis of Woodward's sense of
regionalism, see David M. Potter's "C. Vann Woodward and the Uses
of History," in *History and American Society: Essays of David M.
Potter* (New York: Oxford Univ. Press, 1973), edited by Don E.
Fehrenbacher, pp. 135–79. Other sources by Woodward are listed under
History: Perception Studies (items 887–889).

History: Perception Studies

Most of the entries under this subheading derive from scholars interested in intellectual history and in the history of ideas, who look to statements by the most articulate (usually verbal, sometimes visual) as more or less representative of the larger population. The Higham collection, generally, derives from that tradition. What we have here is a very partial listing of important work by historians in that tradition so far as it relates to ideas of nature and region. The Bender article (item 857) is at once intellectual history and a depiction of *mentalité*, in the manner of the French *Annales* tradition, here represented by Breen and Henretta.

For related entries, see the Perception Studies subheading under Geography; and the many relevant entries under American Studies, Literature, Art, and Architecture and Planning.

C.M.

856. Bender, Thomas. *Toward an Urban Vision: Ideas and Institutions in Nineteenth-Century America*. Baltimore: Johns Hopkins Univ. Press, 1975.

Bender treats ideas and imagery related to the development over the course of the nineteenth century of a genuinely urban vision. Lowell, Massachusetts, first pictured as nestled in the countryside, is later represented as divided from the countryside with its own urban identity. Thus the pastoral ideal becomes urbanized. The ideas of Bushnell, Brace, and Olmsted are seen as efforts in that same general direction.

857. ———. "The Cultures of Intellectual Life: The City and the Professions." In *New Directions in American Intellectual History* (item 869), 181–95.

Argues that there was a shift in the social and epistemic communities of American intellectuals during the nineteenth century. In the early part of that century, professionalism was locally oriented; by the latter part of that century, professionalism was organized according to a trans-local discipline (e.g., medicine).

858. Billington, Ray Allen. *Land of Savagery/Land of Promise: The European Image of the American Frontier in the Nineteenth Century.* New York: W.W. Norton, 1980.

Describes European images of the American West, from early times to the present. The book draws upon travel accounts, guidebooks, and novels. Billington concludes that until the restriction of immigration in the 1920s, those images were of a divided nature, seeing the new world as both savage and promising. Since the 1920s, the savage image, where rule is by force, has dominated.

859. Boorstin, Daniel J. *The Image, or What Happened to the American Dream.* New York: Atheneum, 1962.

Evaluates the importance of pseudo-events that foster a sense of unreality, as news-making replaces news-gathering, the celebrity the hero, the tourist the traveler, the image the ideal, and the illusion the dream. The general approach is historical and thematic. Boorstin is arguing that we need to be conscious of the degree to which we live in an Age of Contrivance.

860. Breen, T.H. *Tobacco Culture: The Mentality of the Great Tidewater Planters on the Eve of Revolution.* Princeton: Princeton Univ. Press, 1985.

A history of *mentalité* (in the manner of the French *Annales* school). Breen tries to recast how we think about the relation between ideas and experience. He is not concerned with abstract ideas but rather with how a group (the wealthy tobacco planters) gave meaning to daily experience, how they perceived agricultural and economic changes (and particularly the incurrence of debt) in such a way as to bring them individually and then collectively to contemplate revolution.

861. Brownell, Blaine A. *The Urban Ethos in the South: 1920–1930.* Baton Rouge: Louisiana State Univ. Press, 1975.

Examines urban images as they are articulated in southern urban publications during the subject decade as the embodiment of a business-commercial ideology in a region that was still agrarian in nature.

862. Cash, Wilbur J. *The Mind of the South.* New York: Vintage Books, 1941.

A classic statement as to the historical career of a southern "mind," taking form in the Greater South (the old Southwest) and persisting down to the time of writing, making for a nation within a nation, or the next thing to it. Cash passionately admires certain traits of the "mind" he describes (e.g., its attention to manners) and passionately detests others (e.g., an inability to face reality, particularly the reality of the modern condition).

863. Drinnon, Richard. *Facing West: The Metaphysics of Indian-Hating and Empire-Building.* Minneapolis: Univ. of Minnesota Press, 1980.

A radically critical psychohistorical analysis of what the West has meant to Americans, centering upon repression, racism and the spread of "civilization." Drinnon sees the basic problem as that of Europeans dealing with the "other," particularly the Indians. The book follows the changes in attitudes toward the West from the Maypole in Massachusetts Bay to Vietnam.

864. Ekirch, Arthur. *Man and Nature in America.* New York: Columbia Univ. Press, 1963.

A general history of ideas about conservation which deplores the displacement of harmonious man-land relationships by a worship of technology. The book relates conservation to the agrarian dream, the romantic impulse, the idea of progress, the contributions of George Perkins Marsh, debates about population and nuclear energy, and, finally, to the current ecological movement.

865. Elliott, John Huxtable. *The Old World and the New,* 1492–1650. Cambridge: Cambridge Univ. Press, 1970.

This brief, synoptic book surveys the intellectual as well as the economic and political consequences of new world discoveries throughout Europe down to 1650. The general story is that of the evolution of an Atlantic world. The emphasis is upon Spanish and Portuguese discovery and conquest.

866. Fleming, Donald. "Roots of the New Conservation Movement." *Perspectives in American History* 6 (1972): 7–91.

Briskly surveys the intellectual history of the conservation movement, involving an Emersonian strain running down through Muir and Rachel Carson; a strain growing out of natural history and forestry, that begins with Marsh and climaxes in Leopold; and a strain that relates such concerns to economics and planning, climaxing in Mumford.

867. Funnell, Charles. *By the Beautiful Sea: The Rise and High Times of That Great American Resort, Atlantic City.* New York: Knopf, 1975. New edition published in 1983.

Concentrating upon the 1890–1908 period, this book tries to define the meaning of a major resort to the popular culture of the time by means of a study of newspapers and literature (including promotional literature). In the tradition of Henry Nash Smith and Leo Marx (see American Studies), Funnell discerns a move toward more hedonistic values in continuing debates about the city as against nature and pleasure as against morality.

868. Henretta, James A. "Families and Farms: *Mentalité* in Pre-Industrial America." *William and Mary Quarterly* 35 (1978): 3–32.

Tries to derive *mentalité* from an analysis of methods of production and distribution. The preindustrial frame of mind combined the idea of freeholding with that of property by lineal descent, with the market system only becoming basic as the period ended. In making that case, the author is taking issue with the idea that late eighteenth-century Americans were already modern in their perspectives.

869. Higham, John and Paul K. Conkin, eds. *New Directions in American Intellectual History.* Baltimore: Johns Hopkins Univ. Press, 1977.

This important collection of essays assesses the current status of intellectual history in the U.S. It includes essays on intellectual history in relation to the new social history, the relation between print culture and *mentalité*, the present interpretation of the New England sense of mission, the relation between ideas and iconography, and between ideas and personality (includes item 857).

870. Hobsbawm, Eric and Terence Ranger, eds. *The Invention of Tradition.* Cambridge: Cambridge Univ. Press, 1983.

A provocative collection of essays, emphasizing Great Britain and the nineteenth century, arguing that traditions were invented (e.g., Scottish plaids by a London businessman) as a means of coming to terms with social puzzlement and disruption. The argument of the book (particularly Hobsbawm's concluding essay) can easily be extended to the way in which late-nineteenth-century Americans used flags, monuments, and museums to help contrive an identity.

871. Kramer, Frank R. *Voices in the Valley: Mythmaking and Folk Belief in the Shaping of the Middle West.* Madison: Univ. of Wisconsin Press, 1964.

Tells how wave after wave of interacting folk cultures shaped the larger regional culture of the Ohio Valley, from the wilderness of the Indians and French to the agrarian landscapes of Yankees, Pennsylvania Germans, and Southern Scotch-Irish, to the industrial landscapes of the European immigrants.

872. Lawson, R. Alan. *The Failure of Independent Liberalism, 1930–1941.* New York: Capricorn Books, 1971.

By independent liberals, Lawson means individuals who were at once non-Marxist and to the political left of the New Deal. The issue of region, especially as put forward by Lewis Mumford, is part of the story. Such liberal-radical thought, the author concludes, loses credence with the coming of World War II.

873. Marshall, Peter James and Glyndwr Williams. *The Great Map of Mankind: British Perceptions of the World in the Age of the Enlightenment.* Cambridge: Harvard Univ. Press, 1982.

This book describes the images and conceptions influential in England in the seventeenth and eighteenth centuries as a result of explorations in Asia, Africa, North America and Oceania.

874. Nash, Roderick. *Wilderness and the American Mind.* rev. and enl. New Haven and London: Yale Univ. Press, 1973. Revised and enlarged edition.

Originally published in 1967. This influential book recounts the history of the wilderness idea in the U.S. A Christian condescension to nature gives way to a romantic sympathy with the wilds, which in turn gives rise to the wilderness preservation movement, climaxing in the wilderness bill of 1964. Nash devotes special attention to Thoreau, Muir, and Leopold. The 1973 edition includes new chapters on the Grand Canyon dam controversy and discussion about the management of the National Wilderness Preservation system. The book includes a good "Note on the Sources."

875. Noble, David. *Historians against History: The Frontier Thesis and the National Covenant in American Historical Writing Since 1830.* Minneapolis: Univ. of Minnesota Press, 1965.

Noble argues that the central tradition of American historians is one in which the United States is represented as exempted from the historical processes that obtain in the rest of the world, and has the chance to live in timeless harmony with nature. (He cites Turner, Parrington and Beard as instances in point.) See also *The Eternal Adam and the New World Garden: The Central Myth in the American Novel Since 1830* (New York: George Braziller, 1968) which applies a similar argument to the work of American novelists. (See also items 828–829 by Noble, under History: Region as Concept).

876. O'Gorman, Edmundo. *The Invention of America: An Inquiry into the Historical Nature of the New World and the Meaning of its History.* 1961. Reprint. Westport, Conn.: Greenwood, 1972.

An examination of the progress of Columbus's thought as he amends his initial notion that he is exploring the eastern extremity of a single land mass to a theory that he had discovered something of continental size of unsettled location. The recognition of the New World meant the end of the idea of Europe as the God-ordained human home.

877. Pocock, John G.A. *The Machiavellian Moment: Florentine Political Thought and the Atlantic Republican Tradition.* Princeton: Princeton Univ. Press, 1975.

This very influential book argues that Americans of the Revolutionary period conceived of the republic and of citizen participation in it in a manner first devised by Florentine intellectuals. This is to conceive of intellectual influences in terms of an Atlantic world, in which America is on the periphery of the European world of ideas.

878. Potter, David M. "The Historian's Use of Nationalism and Vice Versa." In *History and American Society: Essays of David M. Potter*, edited by Don E. Fehrenbacher, 60–108. New York: Oxford Univ. Press, 1973.

In this well known essay by a very influential southern historian, the author argues that there is no simple contrast between nationalism and local and group loyalties. Loyalty to the nation may in fact be a by-product of loyalty to group and region. Potter discusses the coming of the Civil War to make his point: for the North, sectional and national interests coincided, for the South they did not; it was not cultural differences (which were declining) that occasioned the war, but differences in interests. See also, in the same volume, "C. Vann Woodward and the Uses of History," pp. 135–79.

879. Runte, Alfred. *National Parks: The American Experience*. Lincoln: Univ. of Nebraska Press, 1979.

Runte argues that the parks movement had more to do with national identity than with the environment. Parks were seen as isolated natural wonders and as monuments; they were placed so as not to impede economic development.

880. Schuyler, David. *The New Urban Landscape: The Redefinition of City Form in Nineteenth-Century America*. Baltimore: Johns Hopkins Univ. Press, 1986.

The vast expansion of the cities in the nineteenth century offered opportunities for urban reformers of the time to give large scope to their vision of nature as an antidote to urban excess. Suburbs, Central Park, cemeteries, parkways, landscape architecture, and the interplay between decentralization and all of the above are the major issues as relates to landscape.

881. Shapiro, Henry D. *Appalachia on our Mind: The Southern Mountains and Mountaineers in the American Consciousness, 1870–1920*. Charlotte: Univ. of North Carolina Press, 1978.

Traces the attractiveness of the idea of Appalachia in postbellum times, as the subject of local color fiction, as an arena for Protestant home missionaries, as the home of unsullied Anglo-Saxon tradition, and as an escape from the complexities of change. See also items 838–839 by Shapiro, under History: Region as Concept.

882. Sheehan, Bernard W. *Savages and Civility: Indians and Englishmen in Colonial Virginia*. London: Cambridge Univ. Press, 1980.

Studies English misperceptions of Virginia Indians down to the second decade of the eighteenth century, concluding that the experience of the new world did not compel any changes in the conventional categories of civilization and savagery that the British used to distinguish between themselves and the natives. The unfamiliar is made to conform to expectations.

883. Strout, Cushing. *The American Image of the Old World*. New York: Harper and Row, 1963.

Supplies a generalized treatment of how articulate Americans conceived of Europe, and how such conceptions changed over the course of time (Europe as origin of the American dream, Europe as home of Saxonism, etc.).

884. Tindall, George B. *The Ethnic Southerners.* Baton Rouge: Louisiana State Univ. Press, 1977.

These essays on somewhat miscellaneous themes stress the shared ethnic identity of Southerners, a sense of history in the bones. They concentrate upon the postbellum and progressive South. A more general historical treatment is Tindall, *The Emergence of the New South* (Baton Rouge: Louisiana State Univ. Press, 1967)—see especially Chapter Seventeen, "Southerners Discover the South."

885. Whisnant, David E. *All That Is Native and Fine: The Politics of Culture in an American Region.* Chapel Hill: Univ. of North Carolina Press, 1983.

Whisnant's general subject is the politics of culture. His particular topic is the effort of educated female reformers to intervene in mountain culture, generally as an effort to preserve what they suppose to be traditional culture. In contrast to a Jane Addams, these reformers were politically timid and sometimes reactionary.

886. White, G. Edward. *Eastern Establishment and Western Experience: The West of Frederick Remington, Theodore Roosevelt and Owen Wister.* New Haven: Yale Univ. Press, 1968.

The subjects of this book all reach prominence in the first decade of the twentieth century and all formulate meanings of East and West that respond to the massive changes in status they are then experiencing. Along with concern for the idea of the West goes an emphasis on the badges of status among an upper class formed in a preindustrial time.

887. Woodward, C. Vann. *American Counterpoint: Slavery and Racism in North-South Dialogue.* Boston: Little, Brown and Co., 1971.

This collection of essays on intra- and inter-regional debate about North, South and the Negro, in which such terms are used in counterpoint, emphasizes nineteenth-century issues (the southern ethic, the southern war against capitalism, the northern war against slavery, etc.).

888. ———. *The Burden of Southern History*. New York: Random House, 1969.

These essays argue that the South experienced history in a different way than did the rest of the country. The key essays are "The Search for Southern Identity," pp. 3–25, saying that the South persists as an exception to national norms, out of which has come the southern literary renaissance of the 1920s and since; and "The Irony of Southern History," pp. 167–91, which argues that the Southerners, like Europeans and unlike Northerners, never supposed themselves exempt from history. See also item 855 by Woodward under History: Region as Concept.

889. ———. *Tom Watson: Agrarian Rebel*. New York: MacMillan, 1938.

This classic study of an important southern populist and radical centers on mind-set and ideology. It represents Watson's life as a tragedy of a class and a section. For a brief while, Watson put economic interests above racial differences. From 1904 on, his politics become futile and reactionary. Woodward attempts to explain both the southern basis for the radical politics and the southern adoption of a futile and racist ideology.

History: Frontier and Landscape

Under this subheading are combined two distinct subjects. The largest number of entries are devoted to the study of the frontier, which often involves, along with it, the study of agriculture. Turner remains the dominant frontier historian but the approach of James C. Malin, with its emphasis upon the study of ecology, is clearly in the ascendant. Swieringa, arguing for a "new rural history," has Malin in mind, but also the example of the *Annales* school. Treatments of land and park policy are also included here, as are works in ethnohistory (e.g., Axtell). The other distinct subject is landscape study in the tradition of W.G. Hoskins, the English historian, and a related interest, in England, in a kind of local history. Hoskins's landscape study, thus far, seems to have had more influence upon American geographers and folklorists than upon historians.

See American Studies, Cronon (items 5–6), Steiner (items 51–52) and Worster (items 64–66), for related studies, as well as History: Region as Concept and Geography: Landscape and Settlement.

C.M.

890. Aston, Michael. *Interpreting the Landscape: Landscape Archaeology in Local Studies*. London: B.T. Batsford, 1985.

This text on landscape archaeology states its indebtedness to Hoskins, Beresford, and Darby. It brings such sources up to date in discussions of estates and boundaries, deserted villages, surviving villages, farms and hamlets, sites and patterns, land uses, field systems, and forms of communications with the outside world. Aston wants students to be concerned with analysis, not simple description. The book includes an extensive bibliography.

891. Atherton, Lewis. *Main Street on the Middle Border*. Chicago: Quadrangle Books, 1966.

A cultural and economic history of midwestern farm towns (1865–1950) in a region including the Old Northwest as well as Minnesota, Iowa, and Missouri. Atherton draws upon novels, autobiographies, reminiscences, and newspapers in an attempt to recreate attitudes and the rhythms of everyday life.

892. Axtell, James. *The Invasion Within: The Contest of Cultures in Colonial North America*. New York: Oxford Univ. Press, 1985.

The first of three projected volumes on the Cultural Origins of North America. Axtell, an ethnohistorian, is concerned with fully representing the role of Indian cultures, in their rivalry with the French and English. He tells how the French were able to convert many Indians to Christianity, whereas the English insisted that the Indians adopt their culture, with disastrous results. For an earlier collection of essays on the same subject, see Axtell, *The European and the Indian: Essays in the Ethnohistory of Colonial North America* (New York: Oxford Univ. Press, 1981). For a review of the literature on ethnohistory for the time period, see Axtell, "The Ethnohistory of Early America: A Review Essay," *William and Mary Quarterly*, 3d ser., 35 (1978): 110–44.

893. Barron, Hal S. *Those Who Stayed Behind: Rural Society in Nineteenth Century New England*. Cambridge: Cambridge Univ. Press, 1984.

In the manner of the *Annalistes*, Barron studies Chelsea, Vermont, 1784–1900, a settled area of slow growth with high rates of outmigration, examining changes in occupation, population and *mentalité*. The usual rural-urban continuum does not seem to apply. The effects of migration are a principal concern of the study.

894. Beresford, Maurice. *The Lost Villages of England*. London: Lutterworth Press, 1954.

The author is an economic historian, inspired by Hoskins. He traces out lost village sites in England with some excellent aerial photographs and abundant statistics, along with references to accounts by contemporaries and from government officials. Separate chapters discuss occasions of destruction, motives, and locale. See also Beresford and J.K.S. St. Joseph, *Medieval England: An Aerial Survey* (Cambridge: Cambridge Univ. Press, 1979, originally published in 1958), a pioneer attempt to combine aerial photographs with other kinds of evidence as to the nature of medieval landscapes.

895. Berkhofer, Robert F., Jr. "Space, Time, Culture and the New Frontier." *Agricultural History* 38 (1964): 21–30.

In this influential essay, Berkhofer applies culture theory (e.g., Kroeber) to frontier history. He distinguishes between culture, which changes very slowly, and behavior, which changes much more rapidly. Turner, a product of his time, represented topography as basic and culture as secondary. Berkhofer argues that culture was primary, so that settlers in the seventeenth century valued social hierarchy and land, while settlers in the nineteenth century valued free enterprise. Technology created a secondary environment that reinforced received cultural values.

896. Billington, Ray Allen, and Martin Ridge. *Westward Expansion: A History of the American Frontier.* New York: Macmillan, 1982.

Originally published in 1949. This text, revised and updated over the years, applies Turner's frontier thesis to the entire span of American history down to the end of the nineteenth century, telling the story of the colonial, and then the trans-Appalachian, and then the trans-Mississippi frontiers. A first chapter describes the thesis; a final chapter describes the frontier heritage. The book celebrates the lusty expansion of American culture and generally accepts the idea that the American experience is an exception to experience elsewhere. An extensive bibliography reviews scholarly work on the subject.

897. Bogue, Allan G. *From Prairie to Corn Belt: Farming on the Illinois and Iowa Prairies in the Nineteenth Century.* Chicago: Univ. of Chicago Press, 1963.

Farmers, in adapting to the prairie, faced a whole range of problems. Bogue describes the gradual process of agricultural adaptation to the prairie terrain. Those farmers succeeded who worked out a mix of large-scale enterprise with a particular rotation of crops. The approach is derived from Malin and from Gates. See also, *Money at Interest: The Farm Mortgage on the Middle Border* (Ithaca, N.Y.: Cornell Univ. Press, 1955).

898. ———. "The Heirs of James C. Malin: A Grassland Historiography." *Great Plains Quarterly* 1 (Spring 1981): 105–31.

A review of scholarship since World War II on the settlement of the grasslands. Malin is represented as the great exemplar, moving from Turner's emphasis upon the frontier to study of persistence and adaptation on the local level, as a means of understanding what was happening in the region. Bogue concludes that geographers have contributed more to following up on Malin than have historians.

899. ———. "Social Theory and the Pioneer." *Agricultural History* 34 (1960): 21–34.

This critique of Turner applies social science and behavioral studies to frontier behavior. It focuses upon patterns of settlement in the prairie frontier, 1840–1900. Bogue argues that the effect of migration was to shatter primary groups, to put money in short supply, and to create a vacuum in leadership. Out of such conditions came social maladjustments (crime, evangelical religion, ceaseless moving on).

900. Buley, R. Carlyle. *The Old Northwest: Pioneer Period, 1815–1840.* 2 vols. Bloomington: Indiana Univ. Press, 1950.

This encyclopedic treatment of its subject still reads well. Buley argues that for the period studied, the region had a unity that was crucial to the delicate political and cultural balance within the union. A shared dependence on the Great Lakes and the Mississippi was basic to the sense of regional identity. Chapters are devoted to the cultural and social backgrounds of the settlers, land use, material culture, medical practice and lore, trade and transportation, banking, politics, education and literature. The study attempts to recreate the feel of regional life as well as describe institutional development.

901. Carstensen, Vernon, ed. *The Public Lands: Studies in the History of the Public Domain.* Madison: Univ. of Wisconsin Press, 1968.

A collection of the best essays on the subject published in the preceding half-century, on the origins of the public land system, land distribution, and protection and management of the public domain. The book includes a brief, lucid introduction by the editor.

902. Clawson, Marion. *Man and Land in the United States.* Lincoln: Univ. of Nebraska Press, 1964.

This brief survey traces patterns of land use over the course of American history: old world patterns, use and tenure in the colonies, origins of public domain, land survey titles and records, public land disposal, and the permanent reservation of public lands. Five final chapters review the current situation.

903. Conzen, Kathleen N. "Historical Approaches to the Study of Rural Ethnic Communities." In *Ethnicity on the Great Plains* (item 1004), 1–18.

An authoritative survey of the literature on rural ethnic communities, looking at patterns of clustering as a clue to ethnic persistence. Types of settlement patterns are related to types of cultural clustering. Chain migration from the old world, shared information and community ties, especially to family and locale, were more important than self-conscious ethnicity. Urban ethnicity, Conzen remarks, has received much more study than its rural counterpart.

904. Cowdry, Albert E. *This Land, This South: An Environmental History.* Lexington: Univ. of Kentucky Press, 1983.

This study begins with and returns to the geological and climatic patterns of the South as it recites the story of Indian uses of the land, early white survival techniques, land exploitation with row crops, a developing interest in conservation, and the arrival of the new culture of the sun belt. Cowdry is particularly interested in disease as an interconnection between man and land. He finally asserts that there is a mystical union between Southerners and their environment.

905. Curti, Merle. *The Making of an American Community: A Case Study of Democracy in a Frontier County.* Stanford: Stanford Univ. Press, 1959.

An exhaustive study of Trempeleau County, Wisconsin, 1860–80, based upon all available data and information (including census data), intended as a test of the Turner thesis. The thesis is confirmed on the basis of data on political participation, the development of initiative and self-reliance, and the equality of economic and cultural opportunities.

906. De Voto, Bernard. *The Course of Empire.* Boston: Houghton-Mifflin, 1960.

Originally published in 1952. This volume is the first of a three-volume narrative history of the discovery and exploration of the West beginning with the earliest explorations and concluding with the Lewis and Clark expedition. The other volumes, treating later years, are *Across the Wide Missouri* (Boston: Houghton Mifflin Co., 1947) and *The Year of Decision, 1846* (Boston: Little Brown and Co., 1943). Wallace Stegner argues that De Voto's work rivals that of Parkman.

907. Dykstra, Robert R. *The Cattle Towns: A Social History of the Kansas Cattle Trading Centers Abilene, Ellsworth, Wichita, Dodge City and Caldwell, 1867 to 1895.* New York: Atheneum, 1976.

Originally published in 1968. Sees cattle towns as shot through with rivalries among cattle entrepreneurs, uplifters, and farmers, and with rivalries within each group. In each town, the ambition was to become a city, and agriculture was turned to only after city building failed.

908. Elkins, Stanley and Eric McKitrick. "A Meaning for Turner's Frontier." *Political Science Quarterly* 69 (1954): 321–53, 565–602.

Still cited, this article argues that Turner was not systematic in testing his theory. The authors attempt to develop a model to explain frontier behavior. They find Turnerian conditions (homogeneity, need for cooperation) in the Old Northwest but not in colonial Massachusetts or in the Old Southwest.

909. Everitt, Alan. *Landscape and Community in England*. London: Hambledon Press, 1985.

Collection of essays on English landscape, emphasizing regional patterns and historical origins of regions. See also *Perspectives of English Urban History* (New York: Barnes and Noble, 1973), edited by Everitt.

910. Finberg, H.P.R. *The Agrarian History of England and Wales*. 4 vols. to date. Cambridge: Cambridge Univ. Press, 1967–.

Eight projected volumes, with four published to date: Volume One, Part One, Prehistory (edited by Stuart Piggott); Volume Two, A.D. 43–1042; Volume Four, 1500–1640; and Volume Eight, 1914–1939 (edited by Edith H. Whetham). Finberg was editor until his death in 1974; he was succeeded by Joan Thirsk. These volumes make available a remarkably rich array of documentation on their subject. See also Finberg, *West-Country Historical Studies* (New York: Augustus M. Kelley, 1969).

911. Gates, Paul W. *Fifty Million Acres: Conflicts over Kansas Land Policy, 1854–1890*. Ithaca, N.Y.: Cornell Univ. Press, 1954.

Argues that Kansas was representative of patterns of disposal of public lands in the Great Plains and of the corruption and demoralization that went along with it, involving disposal of Indian lands, grants to railroads and tax policies toward them, and other patterns of sales and settlement.

912. Hawkes, Jacquetta. *A Land*. New York: Random House, 1951.

This classic effort to evoke a feeling for England as a land "in which past and present, nature, man and art appear all in one piece" emphasizes geology and archaeology, with a final section devoted to describing how the several succeeding cultures responded to that land. Illustrations, including drawings by Henry Moore, are crucial to the argument.

913. Hibbard, Benjamin H. *A History of Public Land Policies.* Madison: Univ. of Wisconsin Press, 1965.

Originally published in 1924. A pioneer treatment of the subject, much of it written by 1910. Hibbard was a Turner disciple, emphasizing the effects of the Homestead Act and taking the side of conservation.

914. Hoskins, W.G. *The Making of the English Landscape.* Harmondsworth, England: Penguin Books, 1970.

Originally published in 1955. Hoskins is the great pioneer in landscape history. In this book he surveys landscape history on the basis of present and visible evidence, showing how one can read in that evidence traces of prehistoric, Roman, Viking, medieval, and Georgian cultures. The account is richly documented and illustrated. See also *Provincial England: Essays in Social and Economic History* (London: Macmillan, 1964), a collection of essays. For an appreciation of Hoskins, see Meinig, item 673.

915. Hurt, R. Douglas. *The Dust Bowl: An Agricultural and Social History.* Chicago: Nelson Hall, 1981.

Narrative of the agricultural and social history of the dust bowl beginning with early problems in the nineteenth century and continuing to date. The dust bowl is said to be the consequence of new technologies as well as indifference to soil conservation in an area given to drought and wind storms.

916. Ise, John. *Our National Park Policy: A Critical History.* Baltimore: Johns Hopkins Univ. Press, 1961.

An encyclopedic history of particular parks and of the U.S. Park Service, limited to scenic and archaeological parks and monuments, as told by a parks advocate. See also *The United States Forest Policy* (New Haven: Yale Univ. Press, 1920).

917. Lamar, Howard and Leonard Thompson, eds. *The Frontier in History: North America and Southern Africa.* New Haven: Yale Univ. Press, 1981.

This book is representative of a mounting interest in comparative study of frontier histories. An introduction redefines frontier as an area in which two previously unrelated cultures come in contact. Comparative study of slave history supplies a precedent. The essays in the book systematically contrast America to southern Africa in relation to particular topics (settlement, politics, social and economic processes, the role of religion).

918. Malin, James C. *The Grassland of North America: Prolegomena to its History.* Lawrence, Kansas: Author, 1947.

Malin's thought is now understood to constitute a major alternative to the Turner thesis in the understanding of frontier history. It was his conviction that the environmental historian needed an understanding of earth sciences and ecological equilibrium if he was to avoid resorting to impressions and stereotypes (in chapter fifteen he criticizes Webb on that count). Malin was trained in biology as well as history. This is his major work, which includes chapters on plant ecology, geography and geology, climatology, etc., as well as a chapter on grasslands regionalism (chapter thirteen).

919. ———. *History & Ecology: Studies of the Grassland.* Lincoln: Univ. of Nebraska Press, 1984.

Brings Malin's major essays together under one cover. The essays are divided by major topics: ecological theories and critiques of Turner and Webb, case studies of how Kansans adapted to the grasslands, and examples of innovative quantitative methods.

920. ———. "Space and History: Reflections on the Closed Space Doctrines of Turner and MacKinder and the Challenge of Those Ideas by the Air Age." *Agricultural History* 18 (April 1944): 65–74.

Surveys the American idea of closed space and its implications for public policy. Turner, Malin says, had no vision of the future, tying the American Dream to free land, as if agriculture was all there was.

921. ———. *Winter Wheat in the Golden Belt of Kansas: A Study in Adaptation to Subhumid Geographical Environment.* New York: Octagon Books, 1973.

Originally published in 1941. This is one of three book-length studies by Malin of environmental adaptation. It examines transition counties, which are marginal to both wheat and pasture use. Over time, early experiment gives way to a soft winter wheat boom until the area is finally given over to winter wheat. New technologies are crucial to these several changes.

922. Malone, Michael P., ed. *Historians and the American West.* Lincoln: Univ. of Nebraska Press, 1983.

Essays appraising western history in relation to such topics as mining, transportation, women, Indians, and minorities. In the introduction, Malone surveys the main trends in regional history (Bolton, Turner, Webb); he sees new emphases on urban, social, and cultural history, and on comparative frontiers.

923. Merk, Frederick. *History of the Westward Movement.* New York: Knopf, 1978.

Merk co-lectured with Turner in a Harvard course on "The History of the Westward Movement." This book surveys that topic, emphasizing topography, agriculture, land use and land policy, and reclamation in the Far West in the twentieth century. Merk represents the story as that of a vast unplanned migration by means of which a raw wilderness was converted into a world power. The book is richly detailed and includes an impressive array of maps.

924. Petulla, Joseph M. *American Environmental History: The Exploitation and Conservation of Natural Resources.* San Francisco, Calif.: Boyd and Fraser Publishing Co., 1977.

Intended for the general reader and informed by the sense of the current ecological crisis. The book emphasizes an American zest for exploitation and indifference to waste. There are suggestions for further reading throughout.

925. Pomeroy, Earl. "Toward a Reorientation of Western History." *Mississippi Valley Historical Review* 41 (March 1955): 579–600.

Pomeroy argues that western history has been captive to the Turner tradition and has undervalued the importance of eastern precedent and involvement in the region. A narrow emphasis on environment and radical change has kept historians of the West separate from historians generally, and from progress in the discipline.

926. Power, Richard Lyle. *Planting Corn Belt Culture: The Impress of Upland Southerner and Yankee in the Old Northwest.* Indianapolis: Indiana Historical Society, 1953.

Power tries to get close to everyday life in evaluating the diffusion of Yankee and Upland Southern cultures in Southern Indiana and Illinois over the 1830–60 period. During that time, the area became the granary of the nation and the seedbed for states further west.

927. Robbins, Roy. *Our Landed Heritage: The Public Domain, 1776–1936*. Princeton: Princeton Univ. Press, 1962.

Robbins claims that this is the first attempt to put land use policy in social and cultural context. The executive withdrawal of all public lands from private entry in 1935 marks the conclusion of a major phase of our history. This narrative emphasizes the rise of sections, the growth of democracy and the conflict between settler and speculator.

928. Rohrbaugh, Malcolm J. *The Land-Office Business: The Settlement and Administration of American Public Lands, 1789–1837*. New York: Oxford Univ. Press, 1968.

A regional study of land-offices rather than an archival review of literature related to them. The accessibility of land was central to the stupendous migration west following the War of 1812. Land values rose rapidly and land ownership became an increasingly valuable prize.

929. ———. *The Trans-Appalachian Frontier: People, Societies and Institutions, 1775–1850*. New York: Oxford Univ. Press, 1978.

Takes issue with both the Turner and the myth-symbol approaches (see American Studies). The book examines small-scale as well as large-scale settlement patterns: county formation, the role of the militia, the local functioning of the economy. It concentrates on two waves of migrants following up on first settlement, in 1815–30 and in 1830–50. The settlers bring with them English traditions and prior experience with frontier settlement. The development of cities is important to the whole story.

930. Salisbury, Neal. *Manitou and Providence: Indians, Europeans and the Making of New England, 1500–1643*. New York: Oxford Univ. Press, 1982.

Salisbury draws upon ethnohistory to better understand Indian values and areal dispositions. Whereas Indians survived elsewhere, in New England the combination of disease (which claimed ninety percent of the Indians) and incompatible English land-use practices (centered on profit and high intensity) destroyed them.

931. Savage, Henry, Jr. *Discovering America, 1700–1875.* New York: Harper, 1979.

This workmanlike survey studies "those who first effectively made known the physical face of America" during the period studied.

932. Schafer, Joseph. *Four Wisconsin Counties: Prairie and Forest.* Wisconsin Domesday Book: General Studies, vol. 2. Madison: State Historical Society of Wisconsin, 1927.

An exhaustive study of thirty-one towns in four counties examining the whole range of life among early settlers, concentrating upon the fit between social background and topography. A prairie area was quickly settled by Yankees; a forest area in what became Milwaukee was left for German immigrants. The book includes 120 pages of tables and maps. A first volume studies twenty-three towns scattered throughout Southern Wisconsin.

933. Shannon, Fred A. *The Farmer's Last Frontier: Agriculture, 1865–1900.* New York: Holt, Rinehart & Winston, 1961.

Originally published in 1945. A highly readable narrative about what happened to farming as commercial replaced frontier values. Shannon tries to convey the feel of everyday life (at school, home, church, etc.) The story concludes with the agrarian uprising of the late nineteenth century. Richly detailed and illustrated.

934. Shover, John L. *First Majority—Last Minority: The Transforming of Rural Life in America.* DeKalb: Northern Illinois Univ. Press, 1976.

This book underscores the great disjunctures in rural life since 1945. A first part of the book concentrates on rural life prior to that date, with close description of particular rural communities. The second section describes the disappearance of such communities and the subsequent technological degradation of the environment.

935. Steffen, Jerome O. *Comparative Frontiers: A Proposal for Studying the American West.* Norman: Oklahoma Univ. Press, 1980.

Brief synoptic treatment of varieties of American frontiers, rating them according to their insularity from the outside world. The mining, ranching, and Great Plains frontiers, he argues, were linked to the larger culture and so had slight influence of their own. Western historians, Steffen says, remain isolated from the rest of the historical fraternity because of their assumptions about the uniqueness of the American frontiers.

936. ———, ed. *The American West.* Norman: Univ. of Oklahoma Press, 1979.

Essays by scholars in a number of disciplines (geography, literature, psychology), most of whom are historians. Range of concerns include western literature, frontier psychology, the nature of the ecology, comparative frontier studies, western urban development, and native American history. Gene M. Gressley, "Regionalism and the Twentieth-Century West," pp. 197–234, argues that the present-day West, in view of new movement to the South and revenue-sharing, must map out a strategy for political self-protection.

937. Stilgoe, John R. *Common Landscape of America, 1580 to 1845.* New Haven: Yale Univ. Press, 1982.

A wide-ranging discussion of vernacular landscapes of all kinds (mines, cemeteries, mills, and roads, as well as farms and farmsteads), arguing that by 1845 the traditional colonial landscapes had attained an "equilibrium" with more rationalized uses of the land (e.g., the grid survey system), which was soon to give way to the coming of cities and industries. The book draws upon a very impressive bibliography.

938. ———. *Metropolitan Corridor: Railroads and the American Scene.* New Haven: Yale Univ. Press, 1983.

Examines how the railroad, as agent and symbol, reshaped the American environment between 1880 and 1930 and how people responded to this altered cultural landscape. Stilgoe beautifully evokes the railroad landscape, the imposing terminals, its streamliners and Pullmans, the sooty industrial zones, and the bucolic retreats.

939. Swieringa, Robert P. "The New Rural History: Defining the Parameters." *Great Plains Quarterly* 1 (1981): 211–23.

Argues for a reassertion of rural concerns, in a new scholarly context supplied by the French *Annales* school and by Malin. Rural culture must be seen in terms of the entire social order. A good review of recent literature.

940. Turner, Frederick Jackson. *The Frontier in American History.* New York: Henry Holt & Co., 1921.

This collection of essays includes Turner's famous 1893 pronouncement of the frontier thesis, as well as discussions of the successive frontiers as settlers moved west. Other writings by and about Turner can be found under History: Region as Concept.

941. ———. *The United States, 1830–1850: The Nation and Its Sections*. Gloucester, Mass.: Peter Smith, 1958.

Originally published in 1935. Here Turner argues that sections are central to the politics of the time. Each section, equal in size to a nation, had to work out its relation to other sections and to the whole. This edition includes a spirited defense of Turner by Avery Craven.

942. ———. *The Rise of the New West, 1819–1829*. New York: Harper and Brothers, 1906.

This book tells the story of the movement from the era of good feelings to an adjustment of interests among sections with the West the prize.

943. Unruh, John D. *The Plains Across: The Overland Emigrants and the Trans-Mississippi West*. Urbana: Univ. of Illinois Press, 1979.

This exhaustive treatment of the topic up to 1860 tells the story of the relation between the overlanders and the army, Indians, Mormons and traders, as well as the relation between the overlanders and the flora and fauna of the West. It is abundantly documented and illustrated.

944. Washburn, Wilcomb E. *Red Man's Land—White Man's Land: A Study of the Past and Present Status of the American Indian*. New York: Scribner's, 1971.

An examination of the present-day legal status of the Indians and its historical precedents. From the time of Spanish conquest on, there was a ready-made set of assumptions about Indians that moved them to dependency.

945. Webb, Walter Prescott. *Divided We Stand: The Crisis of a Frontierless Democracy*. rev. ed. Austin, Tex.: Acorn Press, 1944.

In this book Webb argues from the fact that the frontier is gone and that the South and West must form an alliance against the dominating East to protect their interests.

946. ———. *The Great Plains*. Boston: Ginn and Co., 1931.

Webb tells the story of the region in the Turner way, beginning with the distinctiveness of the environment and moving on to early attempts at adaptation by successive cultures, and concluding with the spiritual consequences of the historical experience. In *The Great Frontier* (Boston: Houghton-Mifflin, 1952), Webb applied the argument on a worldwide basis, arguing that European exploration of the world was analogous to the American experience.

947. White, Richard. *Land Use, Environment and Social Change: The Shaping of Island County, Washington.* Seattle: Univ. of Washington Press, 1980.

This sensitive study, in the tradition of Marsh (item 666 under Geography: Landscape) and Malin, traces the relation between man and landscape over time in two islands located at the mouth of Puget Sound. White finds them interesting because unremarkably typical. Basing his study upon scientific surveys, surveyors' notes and technical reports, he describes the several transformations, from frontier farming, to market agriculture, to forest economy, to logged-off lands, to the world of promoters and tourists today.

948. Willis, F. Roy. "The Contribution of the Annales School to Agrarian History: A Review Essay." *Agricultural History*, 52 (1978): 538–48.

This essay reviews the history of the *Annales* school of history and its central concepts, in relation to its abiding concern for geography and agriculture.

949. Young, Mary E. "Congress Looks West: Liberal Ideology and Public Land Policy in the Nineteenth Century." In *The Frontier in American Development*, edited by David M. Ellis, 74–112. Ithaca, N.Y.: Cornell Univ. Press, 1969.

Argues that federal land policy in the nineteenth century, generally and overall, was centrally concerned with turning public land over to private interests as rapidly as possible.

History: Family and Community Studies

Entries were placed under this heading if they put a central emphasis upon family and the local community, even if in relation to a larger geographical area. Entries placing a primary emphasis upon large-scale study appear under the next subheading.

The general theme for this subheading is that described by Kathleen Neils Conzen in "Community Studies, Urban History and American Local History" (item 972), the emergence of "truly local studies" by American historians, i.e., studies that examine the distinctly local on its own (everyday, familiar) terms. As she says, the example of the *Annales* school has been important to that development as well as work in historical demography by the Cambridge group (see items 1027–1028). Earlier community studies tended to give only passing attention to the effects on and of particular environments. Zunz in *The Changing Face of Inequality* (item 1031) and Hershberg in *Philadelphia: Work, Space, Family and Group Experience* (item 990) put spatial concerns front and center. Earlier studies tended to examine the small-scale on its own terms, or in relatively abstract relation to large-scale changes. Zunz (item 1031A), calls for a more sophisticated understanding of how study of the distinctly local can become a means for understanding large-scale concerns. Bailyn (item 950) argues that the many small-scale studies of recent years, complemented by work in historical geography, now makes feasible a study of core and periphery areas in relation to American history (of Atlantic, Middle European, and African arenas) that was formerly impracticable. Because of the present theoretical ferment in matters of local studies, entries here include an unusual number of "secondarily relevant" works addressing questions of scholarly context.

A subtheme in the entries is migration study of a particular kind. Migration, studied in terms of its effects upon family and small-scale community, brings geographical concerns to the fore. Old home and new home must be understood in relation to one another, as is especially evident in studies of immigrant communities; and migrant groups tend to geographically "cluster," moving and living with people of their own kind.

See Anthropology, Psychology, and Sociology for various kinds of community studies. For migration studies see also Geography: Landscape and Settlement and Geography: Distributional Studies.

C.M.

950. Bailyn, Bernard. "The Challenge of Modern Historiography." *American Historical Review* 87 (1982): 1–24.

This important review of the state of the discipline makes explicit connections between history of the everyday and small-scale and awareness of culture areas. Bailyn makes brief mention of his extensive "peopling of America" project (see item 951) as an introduction to this American Historical Association Presidential Address. He argues that there is a need for a synthesis between new and old approaches to history. New approaches (from France and England, especially) have made us newly aware of the "latent" dimensions of history. A new interest in history on the large scale redefines centers and peripheries of culture areas (Bailyn here acknowledges a debt to cultural geographers, especially Gottman), making the English colonies part of an Atlantic world.

951. ———. *Voyagers to the West: A Passage in the Peopling of America on the Eve of the Revolution.* New York: Knopf, 1986.

This richly detailed analysis of British migration to the Atlantic coast is made possible because of the documents listing every emigrant officially known to have come to America during the 1773–1776 period. Using that material as a basis, Bailyn sought out supplementary information on the migrants in other sources. Two types of migration are described: young males traveling as indentured servants from London to the middle colonies; and farm families moving to improve their fortunes, from Northern England and Scotland to northern and southern backcountry. The movement of migrants is part of an Atlantic world, of the kind argued for in the preceding entry. The book includes some very useful maps charting patterns of settlement.

952. Baines, Dudley. *Migration in a Mature Economy: Emigration and Internal Migration in England and Wales, 1861-1900.* Cambridge: Cambridge Univ. Press, 1985.

This book is part of the Cambridge Series on Population, Economy and Society in Past Time, based upon a new sophistication in demographic history (referred to in introduction, above). This book exhaustively analyzes characteristics of migrants, counties of birth, incidence of return migration, patterns of step migration, and migration from Wales in relation to the Atlantic economy.

953. Ballard, Allen B. *One More Day's Journey: The Story of a Family and a People*. New York: McGraw-Hill, 1984.

Traces the cultural connections between Greenwood, South Carolina, and Philadelphia caused by the Great Migration of blacks from South to North. Ballard describes the two areas prior to migration, the migration experience, and then the ways in which natives and migrants drew upon common traditions in defining their common culture.

954. Barton, Josef J. "Land, Labor and Community in Nueces: Czech Farmers and Mexican Laborers in South Texas, 1880–1930." In *Ethnicity on the Great Plains* (item 1004), 190–209.

Contrasts patterns of migration into Texas by two very different ethnic groups. The Czechs emphasize the bond between family and land; the Mexicans form very different kinds of mutual aid arrangements. Culture during migration, Barton remarks, is a matter of "immediately experienced personal relationships" tied to specific social contexts, rather than a matter of general orientations.

955. Beeman, Richard. *The Evolution of the Southern Backcountry: A Case Study of Lunenburg County, Virginia, 1746–1832*. Philadelphia: Univ. of Pennsylvania Press, 1985.

Lunenberg County was selected because of the richness of its data on the history of everyday life. In the frontier stage, the county was governed by Virginia but found outlet through North Carolina; it was ethnically very diverse, with high through-migration. Eventually, tobacco took over and the area took on a southern identity.

956. Bender, Thomas. *Community and Social Change in America*. New Brunswick: Rutgers Univ. Press, 1978.

This brief book argues that historians have adopted from social scientists and from the larger culture the notion that a community must be territorially based. Bender argues that the old territorial community was replaced, some time back, by geographicaly indefinite social networks, and that historians should take it upon themselves to describe that change and to give historical dimensions to the typically ahistorical community studies in the social sciences.

957. Berlin, Ira. "Time, Space and the Evolution of Afro-American Society in British Mainland North America." *American Historical Review* 85 (1980): 44–78.

A spirited argument for placing discussion of slavery within its historical and geographical contexts. Berlin makes out three slave culture areas by the end of the colonial period (after an unsettled frontier period), in the deep South, the Chesapeake Bay area, and the northern cities. After 1750, there is a huge jump in the number of blacks coming directly from Africa.

958. Bethel, Elizabeth Rauh. *Promiseland: A Century of Life in a Negro Community.* Philadelphia: Univ. of Pennsylvania Press, 1981.

Studies a black town on the edge of the Black Belt in South Carolina showing how patterns of land ownership and kinship and institutions of church and school kept the community intact down to the present day. When great numbers moved to northern cities during the Great Migration, they retained their connections to the town.

959. Blegen, Theodore. *Grass Roots History.* Port Washington, N.Y.: Kennikat Press, 1969.

Originally published in 1947. These gracefully written essays constitute an early plea for serious attention by historians to local subjects and everyday life, citing the work of Merle Curti and Carl Becker, and urging attention to such subjects as tourism, advertisements, migration as experienced, and reading habits.

960. Bloch, Marc. *Feudal Society.* Translated by L. A. Manyon. London: Routledge and Kegan Paul, 1961.

Originally published in two volumes in 1939–40. This work is by a key figure in the *Annales* school. Bloch sees history as a science of the total society. He is concerned with the round of everyday life, mental as well as behavioral, in this attempt to describe feudalism as a type of society.

961. Bodnar, John et al. *Lives of Their Own: Blacks, Italians and Poles in Pittsburgh, 1900–1960.* Urbana: Univ. of Illinois Press, 1982.

A comparative study of migration and settlement experiences on the part of three ethnic groups (Italians, Poles, blacks). The book combines statistical analysis with oral-historical materials in emphasizing the tie between the place of departure and the new home, emphasizing attitudes toward religion, home ownership, work and ethnic community. The migrants are traced as they move from initial urban settlements to subsequent ethnic clusters in the suburbs. See also Bodnar, "Immigrants, Kinship, and the Rise of Working-Class Realism in Industrial America," *Journal of Social History* 14 (Fall 1980), pp. 45–65, anticipating the above book and arguing that kinship is crucial to migration patterns, and that ethnicity emerges after settlement.

962. Borchert, James. *Alley Life in Washington: Family, Community, Religion and Folklife in the City, 1850–1970*. Urbana: Univ. of Illinois Press, 1980.

A close examination of the culture that attended alley dwelling on the part of black migrants to Washington. Borchert makes the case that traditional values were crucial to adapting to the city; and that the alley community served to enclose black culture in relation to the white culture that faced the streets. He relies on photographs as well as census data to make his case.

963. Breen, T.H. *Puritans and Adventurers: Change and Persistence in Early America*. New York: Oxford Univ. Press, 1980.

Examines the connections among local, provincial and imperial levels of history. Breen argues that the precise circumstances of local life are crucial to understanding the adjustment of migrants to the New World situation in Massachusetts and Virginia. He finds persistence more significant than innovation.

964. Breen, T.H. and Stephen Innes. *'Myne Owne Ground': Race and Freedom in Virginia's Eastern Shore*. New York: Oxford Univ. Press, 1980.

This close study of black life in Northampton County, Virginia, down to the slave codes of 1685, describes a time when blacks held property and enjoyed near-equality with whites. Once black rights to property were gone, white assumptions as to their inferiority led to the institution of slavery, then common in the Atlantic world.

965. Burke, Peter, ed. *Economy and Society in Early Modern Europe: Essays from Annales*. New York: Harper and Row, 1972.

These essays are intended to introduce the English readers to the *Annales* historians. Authors include Febvre, Bloch, Braudel, and Le

Roy Ladurie. An introductory essay sketches the debt of English and American historians to that group.

966. Burton, Orville. *In My Father's House Are Many Mansions: Family and Community in Edgefield Country, South Carolina.* Chapel Hill: Univ. of North Carolina Press, 1982.

Burton here makes an exhaustive analysis of a good-sized Carolina Piedmont town, involving statistical analysis of census data on every household, family and farm, and thorough study of letters and family history, newspapers, former slave narratives and local government and church records, in attempting to describe how the actual experiences of black and white families embodied a set of southern values.

967. Burton, Orville and Robert C. McMath, Jr., eds. *Toward a New South? Studies in Post-Civil War Southern Communities.* Westport, Conn.: Greenwood, 1982.

See also Burton and McMath, eds., *Class, Conflict and Consensus: Antebellum Southern Community Studies* (Westport, Conn.: Greenwood, 1982). These two collections of essays approach southern history on a local, small-scale basis, to see how behavior at that level embodied and intersected with the larger world, with particular attention to the everyday aspects of political culture. Both books include extensive bibliographies.

968. Bushman, Richard L. *Joseph Smith and the Beginnings of Mormonism.* Urbana: Univ. of Illinois Press, 1984.

Interested in the immediate influences in family and village on the young prophet, and in how early Mormons reported their experiences. Bushman argues that Mormonism drew from its upstate New York influences but outgrew them.

969. Caroli, Betty Boyd. *Italian Repatriation from the United States, 1900–1914.* New York: Center for Migration Studies, 1973.

Consults Italian sources and conducts interviews in this brief but highly suggestive study of the phenomenon of remigration (migration back home) as a basic dimension of movement between Southern Italy and the United States. Such remigration was actively encouraged by the Italian government.

970. Chudacoff, Howard P. *Mobile Americans: Residential and Social Mobility in Omaha, 1880–1920.* New York: Oxford Univ. Press, 1972.

A close study of two city wards as to migration rates, migration from the city, degree of clustering by ethnic group, and movement to the suburbs. Chudacoff does not find the floating proletariat as hypothesized by Thernstrom in *Poverty and Progress* (item 1021), but he does find very high migration rates and generally low rates of clustering.

971. Cinel, Dino. *From Italy to San Francisco: The Immigrant Experience*. Stanford: Stanford Univ. Press, 1982.

A reconstruction of the families of two thousand Italian migrants to San Francisco. Cinel describes reasons for migrating (80 percent intended to return to Italy), why the migrants came from particular parts of Italy, and the development of regional (northern or southern Italian) loyalties among the new settlers. Such regional loyalties were ultimately displaced by a sense of common ethnicity.

972. Conzen, Kathleen Neils. "Community Studies, Urban History and American Local History." In *The Past Before Us*, edited by Michael G. Kammen, 270–91. Ithaca, N.Y.: Cornell Univ. Press, 1980.

This authoritative summary of scholarship in local history argues that the convergence of several strands of scholarship now opens the prospect for the first time of a "true" local history in which the distinctly local has its distinct signficance. Conzen reviews work in family and community studies, especially of the colonial period; new social history from the bottom up; and a new attention to the local dimension of urban history, as well as to related interest in landscape and material culture.

973. ———. *Immigrant Milwaukee: Accommodation and Community in a Frontier City*. Cambridge: Harvard Univ. Press, 1976.

Studies German migration to a frontier commercial city, emphasizing the ways in which an opportunity structure developed within the German-American community that at once depended upon German-American culture and represented a resourceful accommodation to American conditions. Integral to the experience were patterns of geographical clustering. On immigrant neighborhoods generally, see Conzen, "Immigrants, Immigrant Neighborhoods and Ethnic Identity: Historical Issues," *Journal of American History* 66 (1979), pp. 603–15.

974. Darroch, Gordon A. "Migrants in the Nineteenth Century: Fugitives or Families in Motion?" *Journal of Family History* 6 (1981): 257–77.

This wide-ranging review of the literature on migration makes it clear that the emphasis of a Thernstrom on "man in motion" undervalues the conservatism of migrants; and that the several kinds of migration described by Tilly (item 1023), chain, career, and circular, all centrally involve family and kin.

975. Demos, John. *A Little Commonwealth: Family Life in Plymouth Colony.* London: Oxford Univ. Press, 1970.

In this landmark study, Demos applied theory from the anthropology and social psychology to an understanding of family life in the Old Colony. He bases the study upon wills, inventories, official records (including a census) and artifacts, as a means of getting at the texture of everyday life for the colonists, and getting beyond merely impressionistic or literary sources.

976. Doyle, Don Harrison. *The Social Order of a Frontier Community: Jacksonville, Ill., 1825–1870.* Urbana: Univ. of Illinois Press, 1978.

This study of a small frontier city emphasizes the ways in which institutions accommodated to ceaseless through-migration, combining conservative with innovative features (e.g., churches thrive but alter the way in which members are received and involved).

977. Edwards, Owen Dudley. "Effects of Migration." In *Other Voices, Other Views*, edited by Robin W. Winks, pp. 99–112. Westport, Conn.: Greenwood, 1978.

Sprightly general review of issues relating to migration, with special reference to Irish migration to England and the U.S. Migration is the proper topic, Edwards says, rather than immigration or emigration. A very gray area separates involuntary from voluntary migration; implications of migration for the sending country vary by period and region; elite migrants color picture of new country as well as of old; much new-world behavior derived from old-world traditions (e.g., Molly Maguires).

978. Erickson, Charlotte. *Invisible Immigrants: Scottish and English Immigrants to Nineteenth-Century America.* Coral Gables, Fla.: Univ. of Miami Press, 1972.

Interested in coming as close as possible to the actual experience of migration. Erickson selects from immigrant letters organized according to trade (farming, industry, white collar), since that seemed to be crucial to the nature of the migration. The letters show the intimate interplay between old world and new. See also Erickson, *British Immigrants in Industrial America* (Cambridge: Harvard Univ. Press, 1953).

979. Gjerde, Jon. *From Peasants to Farmers: The Migration from Balestrand, Norway, to the Upper Middle West.* New York: Cambridge Univ. Press, 1985.

Detailed small-scale study of social conditions in Norway and in the Illinois, Wisconsin, and Minnesota prairies to which the Norwegians moved. Gjerde argues that changes in Norway from medieval to modern ways of life were echoed in adjustments required in the United States. The one prepared for the other.

980. Golab, Caroline. *Immigrant Destinations.* Philadelphia: Temple Univ. Press, 1977.

Attempts to place the story of Polish migration to Philadelphia in the context of changes in Poland and in the Atlantic community. Golab's treatment of the geography of ethnic neighborhoods is especially interesting.

981. Greven, Philip. *Four Generations: Population, Land and Family in Colonial Andover, Mass.* Ithaca, N.Y.: Cornell Univ. Press, 1970.

Studies land transactions, wills, and vital statistics as a means of following the history of the first twenty-seven settlers in Andover and their descendants. Over time, a patriarchal community with abundant land is transformed into a declining and crowded agricultural community with problems of social order. Greven states his debt to Wrigley in developing his methodology.

982. Gross, Robert. *The Minutemen and Their World.* New York: Hill and Wang, 1976.

A model study of the transformation of sense of community in a key Massachusetts town, from corporatist to proto-modern in structure. Gross makes an exhaustive search of town records as to property and vital statistics and gracefully and succinctly describes the interplay between such fundamental change and the coming of the Revolution.

983. Hahn, Steven. *The Roots of Southern Populism: Yeoman Farmers and the Transformation of the Georgia Upcountry, 1850–1890.* New York: Oxford Univ. Press, 1983.

This close study of a small area examines all locally relevant materials (U.S. manuscript census, probate records, newspapers, journals), focusing upon social change and popular consciousness thereof in this study of political culture. Hahn describes this study as subregional in scope.

984. Handlin, Oscar. *The Uprooted: The Epic Story of the Great Migrations that Made the American People.* New York: Grosset and Dunlap, 1951.

This influential book, following up on a pioneer study of Irish migration to Boston in the antebellum period, represents the experience of migration as a movement from a settled peasant life to the disorganization of American conditions. Yans-McLaughlin (item 1029) and others cited here argue that Handlin overemphasized discontinuities.

985. Hansen, Marcus Lee. *The Atlantic Migration, 1607–1860: A History of the Continuing Settlement of the United States.* Cambridge: Harvard Univ. Press, 1961.

Hansen revolutionized migration study by thoroughly studying European source materials in many languages, insisting on careful documentation, and studying colonization and immigration as continuous with one another. See also Hanson, *The Immigrant in American History* (Cambridge: Harvard Univ. Press, 1948), and Hansen and John Barlet Brebner, *The Mingling of the Canadian and American Peoples* (New Haven: Yale Univ. Press, 1940).

986. Hareven, Tamara. *Family Time and Industrial Time: The Relation Between Family and Work in a New England Industrial Community.* Cambridge: Cambridge Univ. Press, 1982.

Companion to the succeeding entry. The records of the Amoskeag Mills allows reconstruction of the family lives of people who worked there. Hareven attempts to describe the connections among individual time, family time, and industrial time, and between internal and external clocks. Clearly the family and work environments were intimately interrelated.

987. Hareven, Tamara and Randolph Langenbach. *Amoskeag: Life and Work in an American Factory-City.* New York: Pantheon Books, 1978.

This book, based upon oral histories from workers in a factory town, emphasizes the tie-ins between family life and work life for a first generation of French-Canadians along with the attitudes and practices of those working for the corporation, and continues the story down to the time of a worker strike in the 1930s, which was the beginning of the end.

988. Henri, Florette. *Black Migration: Movement North, 1900–1920.* Garden City, N.Y.: Anchor Press, 1976.

Charts the paths of changes—demographic, geographic, economic, political, social, psychological, even semantic—between the (southern) invisibility of blacks in 1900 and their increased (northern) self-assertion after World War I.

989. Hershberg, Theodore. "The New Urban History: Toward an Interdisciplinary History of the City." *Journal of Urban History* 5 (1978): 3–40.

The materials here were later published as the introduction to the succeeding entry. Hershberg calls for truly urban history, which sorts out what is distinctly urban as against whatever happens to occur in a city. Microstudies needed to determine what social experiences went with which social settings, and how both change as the city changes (e.g., from commercial to industrial in basis). Hershberg takes issue with Thernstrom because he treated urbanization without reference to spatial and environmental variables.

990. ———, ed. *Philadelphia: Work, Space, Family and Group Experience in the Nineteenth Century: Toward an Interdisciplinary Study of the City.* New York: Oxford Univ. Press, 1981.

Hershberg and his Philadelphia Social History Project have accumulated machine-readable data of residence, job, migration, ethnicity and neighborhood, from a wide range of sources. This collection of essays by scholars involved in the Project is specifically interested in how space functions in giving pattern to home, work, and their interrelationships.

991. Hoerder, Dirk, ed. *Labor Migration in the Atlantic Economies: The European and North American Working Classes During the Period of Industrialization.* Westport, Conn.: Greenwood, 1985.

Hoerder organizes this collection of essays to demonstrate that migration to America must be seen in the much larger context of migration within Europe. Return migration to cultures of origin has not received the attention it deserves. An introductory essay makes that general argument; an extensive bibliographical essay concludes the book. See also Hoerder, ed., *American Labor and Immigration History, 1870–1920s: Recent European Research* (Urbana: Univ. of Illinois Press, 1983).

992. ———, ed. *"Struggle a Hard Battle": Essays on Working-Class Immigrants.* DeKalb: Northern Illinois Univ. Press, 1986.

These essays, like those in the previous entry, see migration to America as part of a larger intra-European migration, that mixed cultures and languages and ways of life. Hoerder is concerned to work out the interconnections between work and home for the immigrants. His emphasis here is upon Chicago.

993. Horton, James O. and Lois E. Horton. *Black Bostonians: Family Life and Community Struggle in the Antebellum North.* New York: Holmes and Meier, 1979.

Close analysis of census data, 1850–60, supplemented by directories, newspapers, tax records, and vital statistics, are used to reconstruct families and households and community institutions in antebellum Boston. Appendices address occupational classifications, black household patterns, marriage patterns, and school attendance figures.

994. Hvidt, Kristian. *Flight to America: The Social Background of 300,000 Danish Emigrants.* New York: Academic Press, 1975.

Based upon the examination of fifty-eight volumes of official handwritten registers concerning Danes who emigrated from the home country to the United States after 1868. The book examines public opinion about emigration, the emigrants before departure, the range of occupations represented, return migration and trans-Atlantic contacts. The book is translated from the Danish.

995. Isaac, Rhys. *The Transformation of Virginia, 1740–1790.* Chapel Hill: Univ. of North Carolina Press, 1982.

Examines dramaturgy, particular scenes of action and complexes of performances in order to describe the changes occurring in Virginia during the subject period. Social and political authority, Isaac argues, was rooted in such scenes. His particular concern is change in religion as related to the larger social transformation. Evidence from material culture is central to his argument. A long essay on method is included.

996. Joyner, Charles Winston. "The South as a Folk Culture: David Potter and the Southern Enigma." In *The Southern Enigma*, edited by Walter J. Fraser, Jr., and Winfred B. Moore, Jr., pp. 157–67. Westport, Conn.: Greenwood, 1983.

Argues that study of southern folk culture must include city culture, must take historical change into account and must study white folk along with black folk. A sweeping review of relevant literature supports that contention. See also item 421 by Joyner under Folk Studies.

997. Katz, Michael B. *The People of Hamilton, Canada West: Family and Class in a Mid-Nineteenth Century City.* Cambridge: Harvard Univ. Press, 1975.

A model statistical analysis of family and class mobility in relation to urban change. Over the 1851–61 period, there was much through-migration, distinct differences in male and female roles at home and in the work place, an entrepreneurial class that was unstable but dominant, and families that were becoming smaller, with fewer boarders and relatives. See also Katz, "Migration and Social Order in Erie County, New York, 1855," *Journal of Interdisciplinary History* 8 (Spring 1978), pp. 669–701, an analysis of much the same kind.

998. Kulikoff, Allan. *Tobacco and Slaves: The Development of Southern Culture in the Chesapeake, 1680–1800.* Chapel Hill: Univ. of North Carolina Press, 1986.

A regional study tracing how geographically contiguous places go through similar stages of development. Kulikoff assumes that demography and economics are basic to the formation of social classes. After a pioneer phase, tobacco culture triumphed, and a three-tier class system resulted (planters, yeomen, slaves), which was maintained after tobacco became less profitable. Shifts and interrelations among family and community are related to that general pattern.

999. Laslett, Peter. *The World We Have Lost Further Explored.* London: Methuen and Co., 1983.

An entirely rewritten version of *The World We Have Lost*, originally published in 1965–68. It thus represents a new summing-up of research by the Cambridge Group for the History of Population and Social Structure (see also item 1028 by Wrigley and Schofield, *The Population History of England*), describing nuclear and extended family patterns in medieval and early-modern England, as well as the demographic effects of disease, patterns of bastardy and sexual non-conformity, etc. See also Laslett, *Family Life and Illicit Love in Earlier Generations* (Cambridge: Cambridge Univ. Press, 1977) and *Household and Family in Past Times* (Cambridge: Cambridge Univ. Press, 1972), edited by Laslett with Richard Walls, which includes essays by Demos and Greven.

1000. Le Roy Ladurie, Emmanuel. *Montaillou: The Promised Land of Error*. Translated by Barbara Bray. New York: George Braziller, 1978.

Originally published in 1975. An important current product of the *Annales* school. The book examines a village of 250 which, because it was the center of the Albigensian heresy, was carefully investigated and described in an inquisition register of the 1318–1325 period. The author tries to allow the peasants to speak for themselves, and tries to examine the full round of everyday life. See also Le Roy Ladurie, *Love, Death and Money in the Pays D'Oc* (New York: George Braziller, 1982), translated by Alan Sheridan, which examines the interplay among legend, folk culture and popular culture in an eighteenth-century French village.

1001. Lees, Lynn H. and John Modell. "The Irish Countryman Urbanized: A Comparative Perspective on the Famine Migration." *Journal of Urban History* 3 (August 1977): 391–407.

Compares Irish migrants to England with Irish migrants to the United States. The authors find that the two migrant groups share more with each other than they do with Irishmen back home. The groups move directly from farm to metropolis, without step migration en route. They reverse the classic terms used to describe movement off the farm as defined in Brinley Thomas, *Migration and Economic Growth: A Study of Great Britain and the Atlantic Economy* (Cambridge: Cambridge Univ. Press, 1954).

1002. Levine, Lawrence W. *Black Culture and Black Consciousness: Afro-American Folk Thought from Slavery to Freedom*. New York: Oxford Univ. Press, 1977.

An analysis of change in black folk tales, humor, music, and religion, as Afro-American culture moves from Africa to the South and then north. The book is particularly good in its analysis of the interplay between popular and northern influences and earlier tradition.

1003. Lockridge, Kenneth A. *A New England Town, The First Hundred Years: Dedham, Massachusetts, 1636–1736*. New York: Norton, 1970.

In the manner of Peter Laslett, Lockridge turns to statistical and demographic evidence to describe "the world we have lost" (the corporatist community as originally established) and its evolution toward a more libertarian and individualistic society as the Revolution approaches. The author attempts to sort out what was "American" about the patterns described. See also Lockridge, *Settlement and Unsettlement in Early America: The Crisis of Political Legitimacy Before the Revolution* (Cambridge: Cambridge Univ. Press, 1981), in which the author, on the strength of recent work by Breen, Isaac, and others, attempts to recreate the *mentalité* of pre-Revolutionary years, which he describes as caught between localism and piety, on the one hand, and hierarchy on the other.

1004. Luebke, Frederick C., ed. *Ethnicity on the Great Plains.* Lincoln: Univ. of Nebraska Press, 1980.

This collection of essays breaks with the Turner and Webb tradition in emphasizing ethnic diversity and continuity on the frontier. Especially valuable are the essays on rural ethnicity by Kathleen Neils Conzen, an essay on Volga German settlements in Argentina and in the Great Plains, Ostergren on the clustering of Swedish settlement in South Dakota, and Barton on Mexicans and Czechs in Texas (item 954).

1005. McDaniel, George W. *Hearth and Home: Preserving a People's Culture.* Philadelphia: Temple Univ. Press, 1981.

Studies slave and ex-slave life in an area southeast of the District of Columbia, based upon artifacts, records and oral history. House types are described, as well as the round of everyday life. (See also entries on vernacular housing under Folk Studies.)

1006. McMath, Robert C., Jr. "Community, Region and Hegemony in the Nineteenth-Century South." In *Toward a New South? Studies in Post-Civil War Southern Communities* (item 967), pp. 281–300.

This review of literature argues a particular approach to the study of the small-scale community. McMath invokes the tradition of Howard Odum (see Sociology) in arguing for a two-dimensional approach to the subject: one internal (family and the familiar); the other external (the larger society). The right focus is local; the right emphasis is upon the economic and political.

1007. Miller, Kerby A. *Emigrants and Exiles: Ireland and the Irish Exodus to North America.* New York: Oxford Univ. Press, 1985.

An overview of Irish migration to the United States, understood as trans-Atlantic history, relying on emigrant letters and memoirs, in addition to poems, songs and folklore. Miller argues that the Irish disliked the idea of migration and carried with them to the U.S. a feeling of exile, which was itself part and parcel of Irish nationalism.

1008. Mills, Gary B. *The Forgotten People: Cane River's Creoles of Color*. Baton Rouge: Louisiana State Univ. Press, 1977.

A close study of a small but remarkable *gens de couleur libre* community, living within a compact area in the heart of rural Louisiana, that flourished before the Civil War, and remained intact until 1877, when the historically separate status for such a group was extinguished.

1009. Monkkonen, Eric H., ed. *Walking to Work: Tramps in America, 1790–1935*. Lincoln: Univ. of Nebraska Press, 1984.

These essays address the topic of industrial "tramping" after the period of the preindustrial wandering poor and before the coming of the New Deal. The introductory essay argues that the tramps were simply a fluid work force of young men riding the rails from city to city, taking advantage of a social and informational network to find jobs where available. Topics include tramping in eighteenth-century Massachusetts; tramping by carpenters, cigar makers and women; and regional differences in tramping patterns. Good bibliographies throughout.

1010. Morgan, Edmund S. *The Puritan Family: Religion and Domestic Relations in Seventeenth-Century New England*. New York: Harper and Row, 1966.

Originally published in 1944. This book is an important early effort to describe everyday Puritan life (family, work, education), drawing upon literary sources.

1011. Nelli, Humbert. *The Italians of Chicago: A Study in Ethnic Mobility*. New York: Oxford Univ. Press, 1970.

An examination of the 1880–1930 period in Chicago as a means of describing the ways in which Southern Italians formed core-area colonies, in the process transcending Old World parochialisms in the formation of churches, societies and clubs. After World War I, Nelli claims, there was a pattern of group dispersion.

1012. Patterson, Orlando. "Migration in Caribbean Societies: Socioeconomic and Symbolic Resource." In *Human Migration: Patterns and Policies*, edited by William H. McNeill and Ruth S. Adams, 106–45. Bloomington: Indiana Univ. Press, 1978.

A remarkably sensitive and wide-ranging examination of the experience of exile and migration. The topic is movement among blacks in the Caribbean. The great growth in slavery came with sugar culture. After emancipation, blacks were pushed into the interior of the islands or forced to migrate elsewhere (e.g., Panama), and outmigration became basic to island economies. The resultant folklore involved a return to Africa after death and an emphasis upon tricksterism on the part of the gods. The best Caribbean writers, Patterson says, citing V.S. Naipaul among others, make exile central to the lives they describe.

1013. Russo, David J. *Families and Communities: A New View of American History.* Nashville, Tenn.: American Association of State and Local History, 1974.

Russo cites Boorstin (item 1042, under History: Other) and Page Smith (item 1017) in arguing for more attention to local history. He supposes that part of the story is the decline of the importance of locale in the recent past. Conzen (item 972) says the book is a first try in a new direction.

1014. Rutman, Darrett B. and Anita H. Rutman. *A Place in Time: Middlesex County, Virginia, 1650–1750.* New York: W.W. Norton, 1984.

An exhaustive study of a single county as to its everyday routines, family patterns, distribution of wealth and status, etc., describing the way in which social networks change over time. A companion volume, *A Place in Time: Explicatus,* supplies the computerized data used as evidence (12,200 biographies).

1015. Slayton, Robert A. *Back of the Yards: The Making of a Local Democracy.* Chicago: Univ. of Chicago Press, 1986.

Studies an urban Slavic community, emphasizing that local control of neighborhood life (in contrast to a total lack of control at work) allowed the development of a rich network of informal and formal neighborhood institutions, that eventually led to the formation of an effective neighborhood political organization.

1016. Smith, Daniel Scott. "Parental Power and Marriage Patterns: An Analysis of Historical Trends in Hingham, Mass." *Journal of Marriage and the Family* 35 (1973): 419–29.

A sample of the work of an important contemporary working in the Cambridge way. Smith here argues that the paternal power to determine marriage patterns declined in the eighteenth century, before the drop in fertility (in which New England led the nation) occurred. The Revolution, he argues, coincided with a period of crisis.

1017. Smith, Page. *As a City Upon a Hill: The Town in American History.* Cambridge: MIT Press, 1973.

An eccentric if provocative study arguing that the town was the basic form of social organization in the United States down to 1920, and that it has yet to receive its historian. Although other places and types are mentioned, the focus is upon the secularization of the New England style of covenant community as it moves west.

1018. Stone, Lawrence. "The Revival of Narrative: Reflexions on a New Old History." *Past and Present* 85 (November 1979): 3–24.

An often-cited article arguing that scientific history has run its course, and is now being replaced by a kind of bottom-up narrative history alive to analytic issues. Stone argues that Marxist historians (to the 1940s), *Annalistes* and Cambridge School historians (1945–75), and the new social history of American cliometricians have each had their effect on the nature of the new kind of narrative history. The article makes a sweeping review of literature.

1019. Tate, Thaddeus W. and David L. Ammerman, eds. *The Chesapeake in the Seventeenth Century: Essays on Anglo American Society.* Chapel Hill: Univ. of North Carolina Press, 1979.

A valuable collection of important recent work on the history of the Chesapeake Bay region, examining migration patterns, marriage and the family, vital statistics, settlement patterns, and class formation.

1020. Taylor, Philip. *The Distant Magnet: European Emigration to the U.S.A.* New York: Harper and Row, 1971.

A workmanlike and wide-ranging survey of the subject for the 1830–1930 period from the European perspective. It attempts to balance presentation between agricultural and urban and early and late, and among the religious groups involved. An Atlantic world supplies the arena for the story.

1021. Thernstrom, Stephan. *Poverty and Progress: Social Mobility in a Nineteenth-Century City.* New York: Atheneum, 1975.

Originally published in 1964. A landmark statistical study of mobility among manual laborers and their families in Newburyport,

Massachusetts, during the 1850–1880 period, showing the usefulness of data from the manuscript census for such study. It was argued that Thernstrom's work represented a new social history (but see, e.g., item 989). See also Thernstrom and Peter R. Knights, "Men in Motion: Some Data and Speculations about Urban Population Mobility in Nineteenth-Century America," *Journal of Interdisciplinary History* 1 (1970), pp. 7–35, an influential study of mobility and persistence in Boston, and Thernstrom, *The Other Bostonians: Poverty and Progress in the American Metropolis, 1880–1970* (Cambridge: Harvard Univ. Press, 1973).

1022. Thernstrom, Stephan and Richard Sennett, eds. *Nineteenth-Century* Cities: Essays in the New Urban History. New Haven: Yale Univ. Press, 1969.

An important early collection of essays on urban class and mobility patterns, urban residential patterns, urban elites and political control and urban families.

1023. Tilly, Charles. "Migration in Modern European History." In *Human Migration: Patterns and Policies*, edited by William H. McNeill and Ruth S. Adams, 48–72. Bloomington: Indiana Univ. Press, 1978.

Tilly's typology of migration is the one usually cited by contemporary scholars. He distinguishes among the following types: circular (involving remigration); chain (supported at point of arrival by fellow countrymen); career (required by job, of increasing importance in the more recent past); and local (the shifting of the individual or the household within a contiguous market area).

1024. Vinovskis, Maris, ed. *Studies in American Historical Demography*. New York: Academic Press, 1979.

An anthology of the best articles on the subject as of that time, interdisciplinary and often technical in nature. It includes work by Demos, Smith, Greven, Wells, Rutman, Modell, Hareven, and others. A useful general resource.

1025. Walkowitz, Daniel J. *Worker City, Company Town: Iron and Cotton-Worker Protest in Troy and Cohoes, New York, 1855–84.* Urbana: Univ. of Illinois Press, 1981.

Originally published in 1978. An examination of work life in two very different situations: the iron workers of Troy and the cotton workers in Cohoes. In both cases management is able to have its way. In Troy a lively labor protest, with a solid Irish neighborhood base, involves Old World forms of disruption, even as the iron industry itself is being transformed from a local to a corporate enterprise. The neighborhood base also allows the Irish certain forms of political leverage.

1026. Warner, Sam Bass. *Province of Reason.* Cambridge: Harvard Univ. Press, 1984.

An interesting attempt to describe the interplay between the everyday life of fourteen Bostonians (born after 1850) and changes in the larger world. Warner wants to ground public events in the patterns of everyday experience. He includes lives of the prominent (e.g., Rachel Carson) in his discussion. For other Warner entries, see next subheading.

1027. Wrigley, E.A. *Industrial Growth and Population Change: A Regional Study of the Coalfield Areas of Northwest Europe in the Later Nineteenth Century.* Cambridge: Cambridge Univ. Press, 1962.

A pioneer historical-demographic study of family and work across national borders. See also Wrigley, *Population and History* (New York: McGraw-Hill, 1969), a general overview of its topic, as well as the following entry. See also item 999 by Peter Laslett.

1028. Wrigley, E.A. and Roger S. Schofield. *The Population History of England, 1541–1871. A Reconstruction.* Cambridge: Harvard Univ. Press, 1981.

This monumental work by the Cambridge group affords a relatively complete record of population change into modern times for a complete nation. Robert I. Rotberg and Theodore K. Rabb, eds., *Population and Economy* (Cambridge: Cambridge Univ. Press, 1986), is a collection of essays exploring the implications of data made available in the title book.

1029. Yans-McLaughlin, Virginia. *Family and Community: Italian Immigrants in Buffalo, 1880–1930.* Ithaca, N.Y.: Cornell Univ. Press, 1977.

Argues that earlier discussions of migration, that supposed social disorganization or radical transformation the manifest result, do not apply to Italians moving to Buffalo. The migrants did not experience high divorce rates; the unemployed husbands did not desert the family. Italian traditions were crucial in cushioning the shock of the move by peasants to an industrial city.

1030. Zuckerman, Michael, ed. *Friends and Neighbors: Group Life in America's First Plural Society*. Philadelphia: Temple Univ. Press, 1982.

These essays discuss changes in family patterns, visiting patterns among women, diversity within the eighteenth-century town, etc. Zuckerman's introductory essay argues that community history has centered on New England and the South because they needed explanation. The mid-Atlantic region, up until now, has seemed self-explanatory. See also Zuckerman, *Peaceable Kingdoms: New England Towns in the Eighteenth Century* (New York: Knopf, 1970).

1031. Zunz, Olivier. *The Changing Face of Inequality: Industrial Development and Immigrants in Detroit, 1880–1920*. Chicago: Univ. of Chicago Press, 1982.

Zunz concentrates upon sociospatial patterns during the process of industrialization in a major American city. Study of small-scale patterns becomes the means for describing general changes. Ethnic neighborhoods (1880) give way to a mixture between ethnic and class bases for settlement patterns (1900), which in turn leads to an assimilation of old immigrant ethnic groups and segregation of blacks. Zunz argues that spatial arrangements were basic in a way that was not understood by studies in the Thernstrom tradition.

1031A. ———. "The Synthesis of Social Change: Reflections on American Social History." In *Reliving the Past: The Worlds of Social History*, edited by Olivier Zunz, 53–114. Chapel Hill: Univ. of North Carolina Press, 1985.

This important essay picks up the theme of the book within which it appears: that treatment of the local and everyday must be seen as basic to understanding of changes in the larger society, and must be placed in a comparative perspective (other essays discuss other times and other parts of the world). Zunz argues that the new social history has redefined migration, the industrial and urban experience and the family. Now the need is for reintegration. The Marxist and modernization models, he says, are simplistic. Application of models from the social sciences to the past has been historically naive. Emphasis on the everyday life of the underclasses must be complemented by emphasis on the means by which ethnic leaders emerged and a middle class was formed.

History: Other

A number of strands within the discipline of history not addressed under the preceding subheadings have important implications for the study of region. Many urban historians address issues systemically rather than as subjects for small-scale and community study. As was remarked in the introduction to the last subheading, Thernstrom and his early followers tended to slight the importance of particular environments. In the very recent past, urban historians have begun again to speak of region: Abbott (item 1034) attempts to describe Sun Belt cities in regional terms, with a central emphasis upon social geography; and Goldfield (item 1057) sees southern cities, because they are southern, as different in kind from cities outside the South. When studies included here use community study as the means of commenting upon larger urban and suburban patterns, that fact is parenthetically noted in the annotations below. In a few cases, it seemed necessary to list the entry under this heading as well as under the preceding, since the entry seemed important to both subheadings. Political and economic studies not fitting under earlier subheadings appear here. A traditional kind of history concentrating upon social and political affairs and emphasizing large-scale study is represented below (e.g., Boorstin, item 1042; Woodward, item 1093). Brown (item 1043), Jensen (item 1068) and Wyatt-Brown (item 1094) combine such traditional concerns with new emphases (modernization, *mentalité*). Entries having to do with certain urban-related subthemes within history—planning, suburbanization and popular culture—are represented here.

See Geography: Distributional Studies and Sociology for related entries.

C.M.

1032. Abbott, Carl. *Boosters and Businessmen: Popular Economic Thought and Urban Growth in the Antebellum Middle West.* Westport, Conn.: Greenwood, 1981.

Examines the relationship between the structure of regional development opportunities in the Old Northwest during the 1840–50 period and commercial strategies articulated by the business leadership of Cincinnati, Indianapolis, Chicago, and Galena. Abbott argues that booster literature was often realistic and gave expression to a vision of the future.

1033. ———. "Frontiers and Sections: Cities and Regions in American Growth." In *American Urbanism: A Historiographical Review* (item 1055), 271–90.

The best single bibliography on recent developments in the study of city-regions.

1034. ———. *The New Urban America: Growth and Politics in Sunbelt Cities.* Chapel Hill: Univ. of North Carolina Press, 1981.

This book has two major objectives: to describe the Sun Belt in terms of its economic and demographic characteristics; and to study shifting intrametropolitan political patterns within Sun Belt cities (from downtown control, to partnership with downtown, to new neighborhood activism). The author's general approach is social-geographical. The book includes a twenty-page bibliography on Sun Belt cities, which is especially good on periodical literature.

1035. Arnold, Joseph. *The New Deal in the Suburbs: A History of the Greenbelt Programs, 1935–1939.* Columbus: Ohio Univ. Press, 1971.

Analyzes interaction among the New Deal, city planners, and a welter of private groups. Greenbelt towns were intended to counter suburban segregation-by-income through overall planning for balance among social classes, with public services under the control of residents. The actual history of physical planning anticipates what private industry did after World War II. Socioeconomic planning never had a chance given suburban opposition to planning and to integration among classes and the general suburban devotion to the profit motive.

1036. Barth, Gunther. *City People: The Rise of Modern City Culture in Nineteenth Century America.* New York: Oxford Univ. Press, 1980.

Attempts to describe the distinctive institutions of the late nineteenth-century pre-automobile American city: parks, stadium sports, vaudeville, department stores, a new journalism, commuting, etc. Traditional formal cultural categories did not apply to the emergent flow, variety and movement. See also *Instant Cities: Urbanization and the Rise of Nineteenth-Century Denver and San Francisco* (New York: Oxford Univ. Press, 1975), which tells of how frontier cities had to "invent" cultures to suit radically transient populations.

1037. Berger, Michael L. *The Devil Wagon in God's Country: The Automobile and Social Change in Rural America, 1893–1939.* Hamden, Conn.: Archon Books, 1979.

Explores relationship between automobile and social change in rural America, drawing upon contemporary commentary as to the effect of the car on family, community, leisure activities, etc.

1038. Bernard, Richard M. and Bradley R. Rice, eds. *Sunbelt Cities: Politics and Growth Since World War II.* Austin: Univ. of Texas Press, 1983.

In the introduction, the editors argue that the Sun Belt has become a vernacular region (appearing in telephone and business directories) as a result of its big growth in population in the area as a result of World War II. The essays are largely biographies of particular cities in the region.

1039. Berthoff, Rowland. *An Unsettled People: Social Order and Disorder in American History.* New York: Free Press, 1971.

Intended as a history of social structures, moving from the relatively well ordered colonial societies to a society of individuals (1775–1875) to attempts to reconstitute social order on new basis (1875–), subsuming economic motivations to larger concerns. See also Berthoff, "The American Social Order: A Conservative Hypothesis," *American Historical Review* 45 (1960), 495–514, which argues that excessive migration, especially in the nineteenth century, made for a disorganized society.

1040. Binford, Henry C. *The First Suburbs: Residential Communities on the Boston Periphery, 1816–1860.* Chicago: Univ. of Chicago Press, 1985.

Studies Cambridge and Somerville, Massachusetts, on Boston's northwest periphery. Binford argues that antebellum suburbs were not the simple product of mass transit and commuting, but instead represented a complex of factors: communities in place, the advantages of being on the city's margin, and commuting. (A community study.)

1041. Blumin, Stuart. *The Urban Threshold: Growth and Change in a Nineteenth-Century American Community.* Chicago: Univ. of Chicago Press, 1976.

Kingston, New York, during the 1820–60 period is transformed from a rural town to a small city integrated with an expanding regional industrial-commercial network. (A community study.)

1042. Boorstin, Daniel J. *The Americans: The Colonial Experience.* New York: Random House, 1958.

This first volume of a three-volume survey of American social history features a regional analysis of the colonies. *The Americans: The National Experience* (New York: Vintage, 1965) has sections on New England, the South and "The Vagueness of the Land." *The Americans: The Democratic Experience* (New York: Random House, 1973) argues that an urbanized popular culture has made for an "everywhere community." The general pattern in the three volumes is movement from a culture in which geographical distinctions were crucial to one in which they count for very little.

1043. Brown, Richard D. *Modernization: The Transformation of American Life, 1600–1865.* New York: Hill & Wang, 1976.

Brown sees modernization and tradition as polar opposites. He represents modernization as a concept that allows historians to incorporate current work on family and community history and to avoid arbitrary periodization schemes. Society moves in the direction of rational, complex, integrated structures, with bureaucracy as a principal product. Along with this shift in structure goes the emergence of a modern personality type, that is rational, open to risk, etc. See also "Modernization and the Modern Personality in Early America, 1600–1865," *Journal of Interdisciplinary History* 2 (1971), pp. 201–28.

1044. Brownell, Blaine and David Goldfield, eds. *The City in Southern History: The Growth of Urban Civilization in the South.* Port Washington, N.Y.: Kennikat Press, 1977.

These essays attempt to describe an urban process rather than simply to recite urban biographies. They describe the colonial city, cities in the Old South, cities of the postbellum era and urbanization down to 1940 and since. The essays are intended as a status report on work in urban history as applied to the South.

1045. Callow, Alexander B., Jr., ed. *American Urban History: An Interpretive Reader with Commentaries.* New York: Oxford Univ. Press, 1982.

This urban history reader steers a middle way between an emphasis on the interplay between city and nation and one on the distinctly urban aspects of history. The essays represent a wide range of interests and a variety of academic disciplines.

1046. Cross, Whitney. *The Burned-Over District: The Social and Intellectual History of Enthusiastic Religion in Western New York, 1800–1850.* Ithaca, N.Y.: Cornell Univ. Press, 1950.

This classic historical-geographical study describes the movement of New England culture attending the establishment of the Erie Canal. Cross argues that there was a coincidence betweeen that particular geographical area and a remarkable burst of spiritual enthusiasms of all kind. Wilbur Zelinsky, in *The Cultural Geography of the United States* (item 718), describes the area as a "secondary hearth" of American culture.

1047. Curry, Leonard P. *The Free Black in Urban American, 1800–1850: The Shadow of the Dream.* Chicago: Univ. of Chicago Press, 1981.

A comparative study of free blacks in fifteen cities during the 1800–50 period. Chapter four, "Lofts, Garretts and Cellars, in Blind Alleys and Narrow Courts: Urban Black Housing and Residential Patterns," includes maps of the population distribution of free blacks in selected cities.

1048. Cutler, William, III, and Howard Gillette, Jr, eds. *The Divided Metropolis: Social and Spatial Dimensions of Philadelphia, 1800–1975.* Westport, Conn.: Greenwood, 1980.

These essays have to do with the processes of spatial dispersion and segregation, even as governmental functions expand to cope with city-wide and area-wide problems. See especially Meredith Savery, "Instability and Uniformity: Residential Patterns in Two Philadelphia Neighborhoods," pp. 193–226, which describes how neighborhoods keep identity even as people move through, because of stable housing values.

1049. Edel, Matthew, Elliott D. Sclar, and Daniel Luria. *Shaky Palaces: Homeownership and Social Mobility in Boston's Suburbanization.* New York: Columbia Univ. Press, 1984.

This "radical" critique of the suburbanization process for the working class for the 1890–1970 period argues that the people involved lived on a precarious margin, with the home the principal investment and its value uncertain or declining. Land developers, with government agencies in their pockets, were the principal beneficiaries of suburban development.

1050. Ernst, Joseph A. and H. Roy Merrens. "'Camden's Turrets Pierce the Skies': The Urban Process in the Southern Colonies During the Eighteenth Century." *William and Mary Quarterly* 30 (1973): 548–74.

A critique of the notion that the eighteenth-century South lacked cities. Literature on the general topic is reviewed, and then Camden, South Carolina, is used as an instance of a small town that carried out urban functions (jail, court house, tobacco warehouse, stores) and linked the area to larger world.

1051. Fein, Albert. *Frederick Law Olmsted and the American Environmental Tradition.* New York: George Braziller, 1972.

Fein argues that Olmsted is one of the great national heroes, on a par with Franklin and Jefferson, and uses this book to describe Olmsted's democratic vision and to assemble some eighty pages of illustrations of Olmsted projects for cities, parks, campuses, etc.

1052. Fogelson, Robert M. *The Fragmented Metropolis: Los Angeles, 1850–1930.* Cambridge: Harvard Univ. Press, 1967.

A geographically sensitive portrait of the evolution of one kind of urban sprawl, as an early search by Midwesterners for the amenities becomes more generalized, all made possible by new technologies in transportation (electric railroad, automobile).

1053. Folsom, Burton W., Jr. *Urban Capitalists: Entrepreneurs and City Growth in Pennsylvania, Lackawanna and Lehigh Regions, 1800–1920.* Baltimore: Johns Hopkins Univ. Press, 1981.

Examines two regions in Pennsylvania at three points in time: 1850, the outset of coal and iron exporting; 1900, after the first stage of economic development matures; and 1920, when the local economies become integrated into national and corporate structures. The study concentrates upon economic elites and urban development.

1054. Genovese, Eugene. *Roll, Jordan, Roll: The World the Slaves Made.* New York: Vintage Books, 1976.

Originally published in 1972. The author sees antebellum slave society in Marxian terms. The slaves had to learn to survive in a society in which they were kept in a subject condition. The book traces the round of everyday life for them (work, play, religion) in rich detail and discovers therein the cultural means for independence from and resistance to the official order.

1055. Gillette, Howard, Jr., and Zane L. Miller, eds. *American Urbanism: A Historiographical Review.* New York: Greenwood, 1987.

Essays reviewing historiography in all aspects of U.S. urban history. Particularly related to regional concerns are Edward K. Muller, on stages in the geographical development of the American city; Michael H. Ebner, on deconcentration; Carol A. O'Connor, on varieties of suburbs; Patricia Money Melvin, on urban neighborhood studies; and, especially, Carl Abbott, bibliography on city-regions (see item 1033).

1056. Goen, C.C. "Broken Churches, Broken Nation: Regional Religion and North-South Alienation in Ante-Bellum America." *Church History* 52 (March 1983): 21–35.

Argues that divisions within the major protestant denominations after 1840 broke primary bonds of national unity, furnished examples of sectional independence, encouraged the myth of peaceable secession, reinforced alienation between the sections and heightened the moral outrage each section felt toward the other, clearly preparing the way for the Civil War.

1057. Goldfield, David. *Cottonfields and Skyscrapers: Southern City and Region, 1608–1980.* Baton Rouge: Louisiana State Univ. Press, 1982.

This controversial book argues that southern cities are different in kind from cities elsewhere in the country. Goldfield says that they are distinguished from cities outside the region by their racial composition and by their tie to the countryside. They were not flooded with immigrants, and are characterized by traditional seasonal movements into and out of the city, as well as by building styles reminiscent of plantation architecture.

1058. Goldfield, David and Blaine A. Brownell. *Urban America: From Downtown to No Town.* Boston: Houghton-Mifflin Co., 1979.

This text emphasizes the evolution of urban space. It has four sections, organized by spatial types: a colonial kind of clustering; a focus upon the market place; an organization in a radial way around an urban center; and, most recently, growth on the part of a vital fringe. The authors argue that urban forms reveal the interplay among economic activity, political organization and spatial arrangements. They are concerned with small cities as well as large, and with continuity over time.

1059. Guest, Avery. "Ecological Succession in Puget Sound." *Journal of Urban History* 3 (1977): 181–210.

A study of the effects of transportation on regional integration. With steamship and railroad innovations there was a distinct jump in the number of communities in the region; with the automobile the established pattern (of metropolitan dominance) is the basis for a fuller, regionally coordinated social system.

1060. Gutman, Herbert. *Work, Culture and Society in Industrializing America: Essays in American Working-Class and Social History.* New York: Knopf, 1976.

Gutman argues for a new kind of labor history that goes beyond labor organization to labor culture, in the manner of the English historian E.P. Thompson. In the American case, he says, one wave of immigrants replaced another, so that modernization of the work force was a continuing process. Thus premodern work-ways and family arrangements persist into the twentieth century. This influential argument (see especially the title essay) leads naturally to an emphasis upon "traditional" spatial arrangements on the part of the immigrant working class.

1061. Haites, Erik, James Mak and Gary Walton. *Western River Transportation: The Era of Early Internal Development.* Baltimore: Johns Hopkins Univ. Press, 1975.

This study of the regional development of the early river transportation system in the West attempts to be systematic and rigorous in its quantitative analysis of the workings of the markets and the mix between private and public interests characteristic of that time and place.

1062. Handlin, Oscar and John Burchard, eds. *The Historian and the City.* Cambridge: MIT Press, 1963.

This collection of essays, the result of a 1961 conference, was important to the development of urban history as a field of study. It attempts to stake out broad areas of concern (technological innovation and economic development; comparative urban study; the city in the history of ideas; the city as artifact; planners and interpreters) demanding further study.

1063. Hays, Samuel P. *American Political History as Social Analysis.* Knoxville: Univ. of Tennessee Press, 1980.

In a long introduction to this collection of essays, on pp. 1–45, this influential political historian describes the evolution of his thought, toward an emphasis upon migration, family and locale, in relation to the analytically distinct concerns of middle-range and national politics. See also Hays, "Society and Politics: Politics and Society," *Journal of Interdisciplinary History* 15 (1985), pp. 459–99.

1064. Hershberg, Theodore, ed. *Philadelphia: Work, Space, Family and Group Experience in the Nineteenth Century.* New York: Oxford Univ. Press, 1981.

For annotation see item 990 under previous subheading.

1065. Hirsch, Arnold. *The Making of the Second Ghetto.* Cambridge: Cambridge Univ. Press, 1983.

This study of racial politics and geography in Chicago of the post-World War II period is excellent in describing how a sharply defined black ghetto suited white policy makers and white ethnic communities. It offers a careful analysis of the interplay among the dual (black and white) social system, urban renewal and ethnic rioting. For earlier times in the same city see Thomas Lee Philpott, *The Slum and the Ghetto: Neighborhood Deterioration and Middle-Class Reform in Chicago, 1880–1930* (New York: Oxford Univ. Press, 1978).

1066. Jackson, Kenneth T. *Crabgrass Frontier: The Suburbanization of America.* New York: Oxford Univrsity Press, 1985.

This ambitious work attempts to integrate intellectual, architectural, urban, and transportation history with public policy analysis, and to place American experience in its world context. Jackson argues that American suburbs are distinct in their middle-class composition, their distance from work, and their emphasis upon ownership of detached houses in large yards. He emphasizes the shifts in ideology and technological change in describing the rapid decentralization that made for the present shape of the metropolis. See also Jackson, "Urban Deconcentration in the Nineteenth Century: A Statistical Inquiry," *The New Urban History: Quantitative Explorations by American Historians* (Princeton: Princeton Univ. Press, 1975), edited by Leo F. Schnore, pp. 110–42.

1067. Jaynes, Gerald David. *Branches without Roots: Genesis of the Black Working Class in the American South, 1862–1882.* New York: Oxford Univ. Press, 1986.

Attempts to show how Southerners went about transforming their black population from slaves to free laborers. Jaynes looks to contemporary documents to recreate how planters and freedmen viewed the issue. By the end of the period, a color line had been established, along with a non-slave black working force.

1068. Jensen, Richard J. *Grass Roots Politics: Parties, Issues and Voters, 1854–1983.* Westport, Conn.: Greenwood, 1983.

Jensen maintains that modernization is a governing principle in American political history: the Democrats have appealed to traditional and local loyalties, the Republicans to business and commercial interests. Maps plot the geography of financial support, reforms, conservative caucuses, etc., in support of that argument. See also Jensen, *The Winning of the Midwest: Social and Political Conflict, 1888–1896* (Chicago: Univ. of Chicago Press, 1971), which makes that kind of analysis of a region's politics in relation to religious piety, temperance, ethnic groups and the business creed.

1069. Kasson, John F. *Amusing the Million: Coney Island at the Turn of the Century.* New York: Hill & Wang, 1978.

A new edition was published in 1983. Kasson argues that Coney Island represented new institutions of mass culture, in revolt against genteel proscriptions. Unlike baseball and boxing, which were new and popular, but passive, the amusement park demanded active participation in mass amusements, which displayed the latest technology and catered to popular fantasies. By the 1920s, the genteel culture had been displaced. See also item 867 by Charles Funnell under History: Perception Studies.

1070. Kusmer, Kenneth L. *A Ghetto Takes Shape: Black Cleveland, 1870–1930.* Urbana: Univ. of Illinois Press, 1976.

Studies blacks in Cleveland taking into account changing white attitudes, contrasts with immigrant groups, class differences within the black community, and comparisons and contrasts with other cities. The book emphasizes the shift from origins in the Upper South to origins in the Deep South at the time of the Great Migration. Prior to that time, an earlier abolitionist tradition had had its effect.

1071. Lubove, Roy. *Community Planning in the 1920s: The Contribution of the Regional Planning Association of America.* Pittsburgh: Univ. of Pittsburgh Press, 1963.

This brief book summarizes the achievement of the RPAA, with Lewis Mumford (see Architecture and Planning) a principal spokesman in insisting on incorporating environmental with urban planning, attempting to give integrity to urban communities, and placing human above commercial values.

1072. Mandelbaum, Seymour J. *Boss Tweed's New York.* New York: John Wiley and Sons, 1965.

An analysis of why it took until the 1870s for New York to begin to develop the means of communication (mail, transport, organization) that would make possible a regional integration of politics and economy. Mandelbaum is unusually sensitive to the importance of geography in influencing social and political patterns. He is interested in how people of the time perceived the issues he describes.

1073. Nash, Gerald D. *The American West Transformed: The Impact of the Second World War.* Bloomington: Indiana Univ. Press, 1985.

Nash surveys the many changes in the region during the 1941-45 period, economic, technological and cultural, particularly in the cities. He gives special attention to minority groups (blacks, Latinos, Indians).

1074. O'Connor, Carol A. *A Sort of Utopia: Scarsdale, 1891–1981.* Albany: State Univ. of New York Press, 1983.

Narrative history of Scarsdale emphasizing demography and political issues (planning, education, etc.) as statements of community policy. Scarsdale represents one version of the American dream, O'Connor argues; the history of Scarsdale tells much about what control by upper-middle-class progressives was able to achieve. (A community study.)

1075. Osofsky, Gilbert. *Harlem: The Making of a Ghetto: Negro New York, 1890–1930.* New York: Harper and Row, 1963.

An early and workmanlike attempt to describe the society and geography of the formative period of an urban ghetto. The account is sensitive to dwelling and neighborhood conditions from beginning to end.

1076. Reps, John W. *Cities of the American West: A History of Frontier Urban Planning.* Princeton: Princeton Univ. Press, 1979.

This richly illustrated encyclopedic treatment of its subject moves from the Ohio and Mississippi valleys, to the Spanish Southwest, to the Pacific, to the story of mining towns and railroad cities. See also Reps, *Town Planning in Frontier America* (Columbia: Univ. of Missouri Press, 1980).

1077. ———. *The Making of Urban America: A History of City Planning in the United States.* Princeton: Princeton Univ. Press, 1965.

This comprehensive and documentary history of American city planning tries to make out national traditions (the gridiron shape was not universal) and the fate of original plans over time. It ends at about World War I. It contains chapters on various types of cities (including discussion of suburbs, utopian communities, company towns, boulevards, parks, etc.) Some three hundred maps, plans and views included. See also Reps, *Views and Viewmakers of Urban America: Lithographs of Towns and Cities in the United States and Canada, Notes on the Artists and Publishers, and a Union Catalog of Their Work, 1825–1925* (Columbia: Univ. of Missouri Press, 1984).

1078. Schaffer, Daniel. *Garden Cities for America: The Radburn Experience.* Philadelphia: Temple Univ. Press, 1982.

Sees Radburn as the crystallization of the idea of the garden city and as a model for controlled land use, of how to preserve regional stability in a rapidly changing situation. The RPAA (see item 1071 by Roy Lubove) wanted to preserve undeveloped land, stabilize the idea of region and oppose blind real estate development.

1079. Schlereth, Thomas J. "Regional Studies in America: The Chicago Model." In *American Studies: Topics and Sources,* edited by Robert H. Walker, 224–37. Westport, Conn.: Greenwood, 1976.

Updated in *Sources for American Studies* (Westport, Conn.: Greenwood, 1983), edited by Jefferson B. Kellogg and Walker, pp. 518–32. Recommends Chicago as a subject for regional study, surveying the literature on the topic, especially during the 1870–1920 period.

1080. ———. *U.S. 40: A Roadscape of the American Experience.* Indianapolis: Indiana Historical Society, 1985.

Describes the historical development and physical environment of U.S. 40 within Indiana, drawing upon many old and new photographs and many maps. It concludes with a bibliography on the subject of "roadscape."

1081. Schnore, Leo F., ed. *The New Urban History: Quantitative Explorations by American Historians.* Princeton: Princeton Univ. Press, 1975.

These excellent essays survey the field, addressing such general topics as the growth and function of cities, social accommodations to the urban environment, and patterns of urban economic development.

1082. Scott, Mel. *American City Planning Since 1890.* Berkeley: Univ. of California Press, 1969.

Written in commemoration of the fiftieth anniversary of the American Institute of Planners. The book presents an overview of planning history of the past seventy years, going from the City Beautiful, to the City Functional, etc., up to the present date. Scott concludes that professional planners had a relatively slight influence on the shape of cities.

1083. Singleton, Gregory H. *Religion in the City of the Angels: American Protestant Culture and Urbanization.* N.P.: UMI Research Press, 1979.

Singleton describes the transformation of an eccelesiastical into a secular social order. Early Protestant migrants brought with them the neighborhood church and the covenantal idea. A growth in interinstitutional voluntarism (e.g., the Woman's Christian Temperance Union, Bible societies) led to the development of the large downtown church and its large professional staff. By the 1930s, the author argues, the society is post-Protestant and pluralistic.

1084. Tarr, Joel C. "From City to Suburb: The 'Moral' Influence of Transportation and Technology." In *American Urban History*, edited by A.B. Callow, 202–13. New York: Oxford Univ. Press, 1973.

In this brief article, Tarr argues that the streetcar enjoyed the popularity it did because it combined free enterprise, technological development, and access to a pastoral landscape.

1085. Thernstrom, Stephan. *Poverty and Progress: Social Mobility in a Nineteenth-Century City.* New York: Atheneum, 1975.

Originally published in 1964. Annotated in item 1021 in the previous subsection.

1086. Thernstrom, Stephan and Richard Sennett, eds. *Nineteenth-Century Cities: Essays in the New Urban History*. New Haven, Conn.: Yale Univ. Press, 1969.

Annotated in item 1022 in the previous subsection.

1087. Thompson, E.P. "Time, Work-Discipline and Industrial Capitalism." *Past and Present* 38 (1967): 56–97.

A very influential historian of class consciousness among the workers here describes in rich detail the emergence of clock time as a social and economic force during the early stages of industrialization in England. As many have remarked, how time is conceived is strictly related to ideas of place and region.

1088. Warner, Sam Bass. *The Private City: Philadelphia in Three Periods of Its Growth*. Philadelphia: Univ. of Pennsylvania Press, 1968.

Argues that American tradition leaves the fate of the city to "the unplanned outcomes of the private market." Up to 1850, private money found sufficient return in investment in the "big" city. Thereafter the private search for profit went beyond the city and the city suffered. The "three cities" refer to Philadelphia in 1770–80, 1830–60, and 1920–30. Warner gives most of his attention to the middle period, as the time when the limits of private enterprise first become obvious. He is interested in spatial patterns throughout. See also Warner, "If All the World Were Philadelphia: A Scaffolding for Urban History, 1774–1930," *American Historical Review* 74 (October 1968), pp. 26–43.

1089. ———. *Streetcar Suburbs: The Process of Growth in Boston, 1870–1900*. New York: Atheneum, 1973.

Originally published in 1962. This important early study of suburban growth emphasizes the interplay between the built environment and the new street railway technology. It is based upon study of the building trades, income distribution and demography.

1090. ———. *The Urban Wilderness: A History of the American City*. New York: Harper and Row, 1972.

In this survey of the subject, Warner describes three major phases in American urban development: a pedestrian city, of highly variegated neighborhoods, down to 1870; a trolley and railroad city, 1870–1920, of ring-and-center form; and the multi-centered automobile city taking shape since.

1091. Warner, Sam Bass and Colin P. Burke. "Cultural Change and the Ghetto." *Journal of Contemporary History* 4 (1969): 173–87.

The authors argue that the cultural "ghetto" is the product of very particular circumstances: the introduction of new transportation technologies, removing work from home, especially for the better-off; and immigrant groups wanting cheap housing and a central place for common services. Thus ghettoes are the creature of late-nineteenth-century conditions in big urban centers. See also "Community Studies, Urban History and American Local History" by Kathleen Conzen in the previous subsection (item 972).

1092. Wiebe, Robert. *The Search for Order*. New York: Hill & Wang, 1967.

This influential work traces the evolution of American society during the progressive period from a nation of "island communities" to a new interdependence articulated in developing bureaucracies and in a new emphasis upon professionalism with nationwide standards and loyalties. See also Wiebe, *The Segmented Society: An Introduction to the Meaning of America* (New York: Oxford Univ. Press, 1975) which says an earlier territorial notion of community has been displaced by a "segmentation" of interrelations between small-scale social units and the larger society. (Several entries under previous subheading address the same issue. See especially Thomas Bender's *Community and Social Change in America* (item 956).

1093. Woodward, C. Vann. *Origins of the New South, 1877–1913*. Baton Rouge: Louisiana State Univ. Press, 1971.

Originally published in 1951. Woodward issued in a whole new school of southern history. This book, part of the same series as George B. Tindall, *The Emergence of the New South* (referred to in item 884 under History: Perception Studies), examines a time when, Woodward says, the South was perhaps more distinct from the rest of the nation than previously, politically unified in a new way, and poor while the rest of the nation prospered. This new edition contains an extensive bibliography for the 1951–1971 period. The text itself is unchanged from the original version. See also *Reunion and Reaction: The Compromise of 1877 and the End of Reconstruction* (Boston:

Little, Brown and Co., 1951). See also Woodward entries under History: Perception Studies, items 887–89.

1094. Wyatt-Brown, Bertram. *Southern Honor: Ethics and Behavior in the Old South.* New York: Oxford Univ. Press, 1982.

The effort in this book is to discover why honor played the role it did in the Old South. It was integral to regional rhetoric, it reinforced power, it legitimated violence. It gave pattern to a whole range of regionally specific behavior: the emphasis on manners, the love of gambling, the patterns for policing slaves, gender roles within the family, and notions of sexual honor. An abridged version of this book, without footnotes, is *Honor and Violence in the Old South* (New York: Oxford Univ. Press., 1986).

Language

The study of language and the study of region are always intimately interrelated. Both have to do with primordial loyalties that antecede conscious thought, with one's "second nature." Techniques used to study language will come into increasing use as the understanding of cultural region becomes less a matter of concurrent uniformities (of the sort emphasized by the idea of culture areas) and more a matter of group loyalties and cultural codes related thereto (see introduction to Folk Studies). Because of the current ferment in language theory, and its importance to study of region, a considerable number of "secondarily relevant" entries have been included.

Linguistics as an academic discipline was for decades deeply split within itself. One very important school, led by Kurath and McDavid in the United States, was historically and dialectally oriented. Its pioneer project, the model for those that have come since, is the *Linguistic Atlas of New England* (LANE). The Kurath school is still active in generating a series of linguistic atlases and a dictionary of regional speech. Its members have corporately depicted linguistic versions of traditional regions. They characteristically map out early settlement patterns and go to elderly and native informants in order to discover the most traditional elements of language use. A wonderful monument to this general approach is the *Dictionary of American Regional English* (DARE), now in process of publication. Classically, dialectology has to do with geography. In the American case, from the beginning and more so with time, it has had to do with matters of social class and education as much as with place.

A second school, following Bloomfield and, more recently, Chomsky, concerns itself with formal analysis of the structure of a language, with language "competence" as against language "performance." Henry Glassie and his many disciples in Folk Studies are indebted to Chomsky. Generally, the interest in formal analysis and theory ran counter to the empiricism of the Kurath school. One can understand why Kurath in *Studies in Area Linguistics* (item 1121) would welcome a rebirth of interest in field-study, related to a third development in American linguistics.

Haugen and Weinreich (and Labov, Hymes and Fishman and many other younger scholars) insist that language be studied in real-life situations. Many of them speak of a "structural dialectology," a competence that straddles the heterogeneities of actual language use. Consistent with this last approach is the spectacular growth of interest in areas of overlap between language study and sociology, anthropology and psychology. Trudgill, for example, is determined to bring to this new approach the traditional concern with geography and region. Haugen, in speaking of "the ecology of language," makes multidimensional place primary, and language a dimension of that.

A generally separate concern is that for place names and family and given names, the product of which is likely to be a dictionary or a word list. Zelinsky, the geographer, illustrates how one can use place names as evidence of historical cultural regions.

For related entries see Folk Studies.

C.M.

1095. Allen, Harold B. *The Linguistic Atlas of the Upper Midwest.* 3 vols. Minneapolis: Univ. of Minnesota Press, 1973–1976.

Covers Minnesota, Iowa, Nebraska and the Dakotas. Volume One is introductory and lexical; Volume Two, syntactic; Volume Three, phonetic. These volumes follow the approach of the Kurath atlas, but do not insist on English origins in informants. They trace settlement patterns (1, 125, map 10); and map general regional patterns boundaries (1, 127, map 11). The boundary between the northern and midland speech areas runs across the top third of Iowa, then up the Missouri River. The boundary in the Upper Midwest is much less distinct than that in the North Central States. Allen stresses schooling as a major reason for the blurred boundaries.

1096. Atwood, E. Bagby. "Grease and Greasy: A Study of Geographical Variations." *Univ. of Texas Studies in English* 29 (1950): 249–60.

Using worksheets from fieldworkers on the Kurath project for the Atlantic coast area, Atwood establishes northern limits for "greazy," which runs from Philadelphia northwest to about Buffalo, which corresponds to the boundary between the northern and midland speech areas.

1097. ———. *The Regional Vocabulary of Texas.* Austin: Univ. of Texas Press, 1962.

Essentially a word geography. Atwood had intended to follow this study with studies of phonetics and syntax.

1098. ———. *A Survey of Verb Forms in the Eastern United States.* Ann Arbor: Univ. of Michigan Press, 1953.

Based on worksheets from East Coast research by Kurath group. Atwood worked out thirty-one maps of verb form distributions with commentary. He distinguishes between usage informants of Type 1 (old, uneducated) and Type 3 (middle-aged, educated), and charts usage by blacks. He discovers that "might could" is standard use in the South by Type 3 informants.

1099. Bernstein, Basil. *Class, Codes and Control: Theoretical Studies Toward a Sociology of Language.* 2d. rev. ed. New York: Schocken Books, 1974.

Collection of Bernstein's best-known essays. The introduction by Bernstein describes the development of sociolinguistic theory, from Durkheim through Sapir and Whorf. The author worked out a vocabulary for a kind of sociolinguistics that has wide currency. He is interested in codes of communication according to social class and among people within a class. Elaborated code (relatively independent of context) is contrasted to restricted code (context-dependent).

1100. Bloomfield, Leonard. *Language.* New York: Henry Holt & Co., 1933.

Bloomfield was devoted to the establishment of a science of linguistics, stressing formal definitions and suspicious of subjective evaluations. See also "A Set of Postulates for the Science of Language," *Language* 2 (1926), pp. 153–64. Bloomfield anticipates the emphasis upon formal analysis found in Chomsky.

1101. Bruner, Jerome S. "From Communication to Language: A Psychological Perspective." *Cognition* 3 (1974–1975): 255–87.

A meticulously argued case from a psycholinguistic perspective. (On Bruner, see item 1488 under Psychology.) The author emphasizes the "pragmatic" dimension of language (see item 1139 by Charles W. Morris) in making his argument, as a comment on Chomsky's nearly exclusive interest in syntax. He argues a developmental logic in linguistic competence, e.g., predication is implicit in taking any given object and testing it by hitting, sucking, etc. The effect of the argument is to base language situationally, relating its study to the social sciences generally.

1102. Burkett, Eva M. *American English Dialects in Literature.* Metuchen, N.J.: Scarecrow Press, 1978.

This extensive bibliography contains a detailed list of general studies in regional American dialects, pp. 9–19, as well as extensive listings of scholarship on regional dialects.

1103. Carver, Craig M. *American Regional Dialects: A Word Geography.* Ann Arbor: Univ. of Michigan Press, 1986.

A massively detailed overview of American dialect regions. Carver studies the country as a whole, drawing particularly from data for the *Dictionary of American Regional English.* He comments that the data for the linguistic atlases is difficult to come by and only covers sections of the country. DARE, in contrast, is national in scope and its research is current. Carver studies dialects as their histories and meanings throw light upon the cultural underpinnings of a region. A summary map as to dialect regions appears on p. 248. Some one hundred maps define dialect boundaries and individual isoglosses.

1104. Cassidy, Frederic G., ed. *Dictionary of American Regional English.* Cambridge: Harvard Univ. Press, 1985.

First of several projected volumes, which includes a general introduction and entries from A to C. It is a dictionary of general, non-standard English. Informants tend to be elderly (66 percent over sixty years of age) because the focus is upon the traditional and folk patterns of speech. The interest is in oral, not printed, tradition. This magisterial work combines materials from linguistic atlases and from miscellaneous word lists with results of interviews and questionnaires designed by DARE.

1105. Chomsky, Noam. *Aspects of the Theory of Syntax.* Cambridge: MIT Press, 1964.

One of the many books and articles by Chomsky that revolutionized contemporary linguistics. Chomsky is interested in competence rather than performance, and performance, generally, is the subject of region-related language study. (But for application of Chomsky's thought to a regional analysis, see Glassie's *Folk Housing in Middle Virginia,* item 407 under Folk Studies.) Chomsky looks to "deep structure" rather than to surface variation. Deep structure performs according to invariant rules, which underlie all language behavior. A limited number of "deep" rules generate an indefinite number of sentences.

1106. Craigie, Sir William and James R. Hulbert. *A Dictionary of American English on Historical Principles*. 4 vols. Chicago: Univ. of Chicago Press, 1938–1944.

Exhibits features of English in the colonies and states that distinguish it from English elsewhere. The dictionary includes words of American origin, words more common in the U.S. than elsewhere, and words clearly tied to the development of the country and the history of the people. Words included must come into use before 1900. Slang and dialect words are restricted to those of early use or special prominence. These volumes emphasize the connections between English and American usage. This source now needs to be supplemented by consulting *A Dictionary of Americanisms on Historical Principles* (item 1131).

1107. Davis, Lawrence M., ed. *Studies in Linguistics in Honor of Raven I. McDavid, Jr.* University: Univ. of Alabama Press, 1972.

The introduction summarizes McDavid's career. Section One contains essays on dialectology: an update on the North Central atlas, pp. 9–24; on Pennsylvania-Ohio phonology, pp.49–61; an update on LANE in relation to speech on Martha's Vineyard, pp.81–121 (item 1125); a mapping of speech patterns in California and Nevada, pp.135–43; and an article on black and white speech in Northern Georgia, pp. 123–34.

1108. Duckert, Audrey R. "The Second Time Around: Methods in Dialect Revisiting." *American Speech* 46 (1971): 66–72.

Discusses how to go about revisiting sites consulted in LANE. See also "The Linguistic Atlas of New England Revisited," *Publications of the American Dialect Society*, no. 39 (Birmingham: Univ. of Alabama Press, 1963).

1109. Fishman, Joshua A. *Language Loyalty in the United States: The Maintenance and Perpetuation of Non-English Mother Tongues by American Ethnic and Religious Groups*. The Hague: Mouton Press, 1966.

A statistically and conceptually sophisticated study of most aspects of the subject. It contains chapters on the historical and social contexts of language maintenance, the mother tongues and nativities of the

American population, the non-English press, foreign language broadcasting, ethnic education, ethnic parishes, organizations in language maintenance, and neighborhood dynamics in relation to maintenance and language planning.

1110. ———. "The Sociology of Language: An Interdisciplinary Social Science Approach to Language in Society." In *Advances in the Sociology of Language*, 2 vols, edited by Joshua A. Fishman. vol. 1, 217–404. The Hague: Mouton Press, 1976.

A summary of the status of the sociology of language as an area of study. Fishman is concerned with standardizing terminology. He defines speech community, speech domains, social situations as terms of special importance, extensively citing his sources.

1111. ———, ed. *Readings in the Sociology of Language*. The Hague: Mouton Press, 1968.

An exhaustive and reliable anthology on the subject (808 pages). Includes items 1113, 1117.

1112. Gilbert, Glen G. *Linguistic Atlas of Texas German*. Austin: Univ. of Texas Press, 1972.

Part of a long-term project to record and study the use of the German language in Texas. The *Deutscher Sprachtatlas* was point of reference and model. Dialectal differences in the use of German in Texas are mapped by pronunciation and idiom on 148 large-scale maps.

1113. Gumperz, John J. "Types of Linguistic Communities." In *Readings in the Sociology of Language* (item 1111), pp. 460–72.

Gumperz says he is trying to follow up on Dell Hymes' essay on the ethnography of speaking (included in this same volume). He argues (in contrast to Chomsky) that linguists, in their emphasis upon homogeneity of code, do not give attention to the fact that all speech communities are heterogeneous and bicodal, with dialects, styles, and levels of speech.

1114. Harder, Kelsie B. *Illustrated Dictionary of Place Names, United States and Canada*. New York: Van Nostrand Reinhold Co., 1976.

Intended for the generalist looking for location and origin. States, counties, capitals, and county seats are canvassed. Geographical features are included according to their historical importance and linguistic interest.

1115. Haugen, Einar. *The Ecology of Language.* Edited by Anwar S. Dil. Stanford: Stanford Univ. Press, 1972.

A collection of Haugen's essays from 1938 to date, sampling his thought over the years. His very early work on Norwegian-American bilingualism prepares the way for later work on language planning and on analysis of interlingual communication of all types, culminating in title essay which asks that we place language in its total context, psychological, social, etc., as in actual use. He suggests the need for "variable" as against the "pure" competence hypothesized by Chomsky. Haugen's great study of bilingualism, wonderfully suggestive for students of region, is *The Norwegian Language in America* (Philadelphia: Univ. of Pennsylvania Press, 1953), 2 vols.

1116. ———. "The Semantics of Icelandic Orientation." In *Cognitive Anthropology*, edited by Stephen A. Tyler, 330–42. New York: Holt, Rinehart & Winston, 1969.

A detailed discussion of space orientation as embedded in language in Iceland as a means of making a more general point. Icelanders spoke of directions "incorrectly," in terms of compass and meridian. They knew what was "correct," but in practice, because of lay of land and mode of travel, needed only to distinguish between two directional choices. They therefore spoke of directions in a precise but not a precisely "correct" way. As always, usage depended upon the kind of discourse involved.

1117. Hymes, Dell. "The Ethnography of Speaking." In *Readings in the Sociology of Language* (item 1111), 99–138.

Hymes, looking for an area of joint concern among anthropologists and linguists, argues that the speech act like language is patterned and subject to formal analysis. In attending to language and competence, we have neglected the actual speech situation.

1118. ———. *Language in Culture and Society: A Reader in Linguistics and Anthropology.* New York: Harper and Row, 1964.

A general reader, reviewing all aspects of the interrelation of culture and language, including an extensive bibliography.

1119. Krapp, George Philip. *The English Language in America.* 2 vols. New York: Century Co., 1925.

The first systematic study of the American language. Krapp uses a comparative perspective, contrasting and comparing American to

English usage. Volume One discusses mother tongue, vocabulary, proper names, literary dialects, spelling, and dictionaries. Volume Two addresses pronunciation (254 pages), inflection and syntax (18 pages), and includes a bibliography and an index of subjects and names and an index of words, pp. 299–355.

1120. Kurath, Hans. "Dialect Areas, Settlement Areas and Cultural Areas in the United States." In *The Cultural Approach to History*, edited by Caroline F. Ware, 331–45. New York: Columbia Univ. Press, 1940.

Argues that national culture has its foundation in regional cultures. Kurath's work with linguistic atlases shows how small pockets of speech (vocabulary and pronunciation) formed in early days, how breaks developed between coastal and western and mountain speech, how the coming of cities led to dominance of one kind of speech over another, how trans-Appalachian speech areas are much larger than coastal areas, and how education affects what urbanites say.

1121. ———. *Studies in Area Linguistics*. Bloomington: Indiana Univ. Press, 1972.

Surveys issues of method and vocabulary, as well as principal findings. Kurath outlines connections between English and American dialects, as well as area dialects as determined in Europe. He hails the recent revival of interest in dialectology (citing Gumperz and Hymes, among others) after several decades of exclusive attention to synchronic studies, and looks forward to a new fusion of the two approaches. An extensive bibliography is included.

1122. ———. *A Word Geography of the Eastern United States*. Ann Arbor: Univ. of Michigan Press, 1949.

Argues, by use of isoglosses, for three principal divisions of speech in the eastern U.S.: Northern (mid-New Jersey to Buffalo); Midland (Ocean City, Maryland to Wheeling, West Virginia, including the Shenandoah Valley); and Southern (the rest). This corrects old speech area typology of northern, southern, and "general." For a digest of conclusions reached see Kurath, " Linguistic Regionalism," in *Regionalism in America* (Madison: Univ. of Wisconsin Press, 1951), edited by Merrill Jensen, pp. 331–51.

1123. ——— et al., eds. *The Linguistic Atlas of New England*. Providence: Brown Univ. Press, 1939–1943.

As is remarked in the introduction to this heading, LANE is the pioneer American linguistic atlas after which all since have been modeled. Kurath arrived at a division between eastern and western New England speech areas. He interviewed in all original coast settlements, and sampled those further west. He divided informants by age and education. He wanted common, not just folk, speech. This very ambitious project was intended to be ongoing, with the wealth of data generated available as a basis for later study. See also *The Linguistic Atlas of the Middle and South Atlantic States*, Fascicles 1 and 2 (Chicago: Univ. of Chicago Press, 1980), edited by Raven I. McDavid and Raymond K. O'Cain.

1124. Kurath, Hans and Raven I. McDavid, Jr. *Pronunciation of English in the Atlantic States*. Ann Arbor: Univ. of Michigan Press, 1961.

Analyzes worksheets from field study in eastern part of the country. The emphasis here is upon phonology, especially vowels. The book argues for dialect boundaries on that basis, and for differences in standard English from one area to the next (on the basis of the most educated informants).

1125. Labov, William. "The Recent History of Dialectic Markers on the Island of Martha's Vineyard, Massachusetts." In *Studies in Linguistics in Honor of Raven I. McDavid, Jr.* (item 1107), 81–121.

An exemplary revisit study of earlier atlas work, concluding that language habits crucial to LANE do not apply today. Differences according to the section of the island were found to be significant, as well as social differences (as among Indians, native islanders, and the educated).

1126. ———. *The Social Stratification of English in New York City*. Washington, D.C.: Center for Applied Linguistics, 1966.

An important study on several counts. Labov was careful to choose a statistically representative sample as to education and income (as against the partially arbitrary sample for the atlases); and, in contrast to atlas work, he took into account the varieties of social situations (formal, informal, etc.) in which the interviews occurred. The upper middle class is more standard in speech behavior than other groups, and the formal interview situation made for more formal speech generally.

1127. ———. *Sociolinguistic Patterns*. Philadelphia: Univ. of Pennsylvania Press, 1972.

Collection of essays, including materials from the preceding entry. The introduction is a kind of proclamation on behalf of the study of real-life usage rather than the formalistic analysis inspired by Saussure, Bloomfield, and Chomsky. Labov identifies Weinreich as the principal inspiration for this approach. People speak in heterogeneous situations, without pure structures, so what scholars must understand is structured heterogeneity.

1128. Leighly, John B. "Town Names of Colonial New England in the West." *Annals of the Association of American Geographers* 68 (1978): 233–48.

Workmanlike mapping of New England names throughout eastern U.S. Leighly finds the highest incidence of New England place names in areas identified as northern by students of folk life. He traces the connection between settlement patterns and town names and the "contamination" because of place names common to other colonies as well as New England. The resulting map is on p. 234.

1129. Marckwardt, Albert H. *American English*. New York: Oxford Univ. Press, 1958.

Contains chapters on regional and social dialects, pp. 131–50, and place names, pp. 151–69. A readable and brief general introduction to the subject.

1130. ———. "Principal and Subsidiary Dialect Areas in the North-Central States." *Publications of the American Dialect Society* 27 (April 1957): 3–15.

Analyzes data from work for atlases for north-central and upper midwest states. Marckwardt concludes that divisions obtaining between major speech areas in the East hold in the north-central area, although they become more complex. The midland boundary remains pretty well defined through Ohio, Indiana, and Illinois, but becomes vague in the Upper Midwest.

1131. Mathews, Mitford M., ed. *A Dictionary of Americanisms on Historical Principles*. 2 vols. Chicago: Univ. of Chicago Press, 1951.

Updates and complements item 1106.

1132. McDavid, Raven I., Jr. "New Directions in American Dialectology." In *Varieties of American English* (item 1134), 257–95.

Thorough review of the history and progress of American dialectology, describing the several atlases, DARE, and interest in sociolinguistics (especially as in Labov), and climaxing with a final plea for field-based study. An extensive bibliography is included. McDavid distinguishes between sociolinguistics and dialect study in making the second a branch of historical linguistics, looking to the usages of the most stable element of population as the clue to historical linkages among language patterns.

1133. ———. "Postvocalic /r/ in South Carolina: A Social Analysis." *American Speech* 23 (1948): 194–203.

The geographic pattern of postvocalic /r/ use seemed haphazard until McDavid thought of the effects of social distinctions. He finds its use (as in 'barn,' which around Charleston loses the /r/ sound) to be a product of education in England, which diffused from the city to the hinterland. The use of the constricted /r/, common to much of the rest of country, remained common to the uneducated in the Charleston area.

1134. ———. *Varieties of American English.* Edited by Anwar S. Dil. Stanford: Stanford Univ. Press, 1980.

Collection of McDavid's essays, over the course of his career, on regional and social dialects.

1135. ———. "The Dialects of American English." In *The Structure of American English*, edited by W. Nelson Francis, 480–543. New York: Ronald Press, 1958.

Part of an introductory text in linguistics. McDavid surveys techniques, research to date, settlement patterns, and markers for each regional dialect. He reviews the influence of foreign languages and social change (urbanization, education, and industrialization). He says that there is least linguistic variation in American areas most recently settled but that no one standard language is dominant. He ends by commenting on the literary use of dialects as found in Twain, Lardner, and others.

1136. McMillan, James B. "The Naming of American Dialects." In *Papers in Language Variations: SAMLA-ADS Collection*, edited by David L. Shores and Carole P. Hines, 119–24. University: Univ. of Alabama Press, 1977.

Concise statement about the status of terms for regions used by dictionaries, and their current status.

1137. Mencken, Henry Louis. *The American Language: An Inquiry into the Development of English in the United States.* 4th rev. ed. New York: Knopf, 1936.

Originally published in 1919. See also Supplement I (1945) and Supplement 2 (1948), as well as the abridged and revised edition, with annotations and new material, edited by Ravid I. McDavid (New York: Knopf, 1963). A groundbreaking work, addressed to a general audience, written in a lively style and wonderfully rich in detail. Supplement One follows up on chapters 1–6 of the 1936 edition; Supplement Two on the next five chapters; and the Appendix discusses non-English languages in the United States. McDavid (1963), in "Editor's Introduction," pp. v-xi, summarizes Mencken's contribution to popular understanding and to scholarship, as well as the history of this work. Elsewhere McDavid especially recommends chapter 9 (1936) on everyday speech, and its follow-up, Supplement 2, chapter nine.

1138. Montgomery, Michael B. and Guy Bailey. *Language Variety in the South: Perspectives in Black and White.* University: Univ. of Alabama Press, 1986.

Papers presented at a 1981 conference on the subject. In a brief foreword, pp. ix-x, James B. McMillan remarks that known data do not justify a comprehensive descriptive grammar or a coherent account of its evolution. The atlases for the Gulf States (item 1141) and DARE (item 1104) help, but they give scant attention to syntax. He says there is a need to be more systematic in the study of the many southern dialects, and to show the connections among them.

1139. Morris, Charles W. "Foundations of the Theory of Signs." In *International Encyclopedia of Unified Sciences.* vol. 1, no. 2, 71–137. Chicago: Univ. of Chicago Press, 1938.

This influential early essay outlines the theory of semiotics, the science of sign-usage (semiosis). Semiosis is broader than language. It has three dimensions: syntactic, pragmatic, and semantic. Morris cites Carnap, Cassirer, Husserl, Mead, Pierce, and Wittgenstein in developing his argument. He looks at signs from a behavioral perspective.

1140. Pederson, Lee. "Chicago Words: The Regional Vocabulary." *American Speech* 46 (1971): 163–92.

Adapted format of the north-central states atlas (see item 1130) to work with Chicago informants. The article includes a description of which items had to be added to the standard questionnaire to represent varieties of Chicago English. Pederson concludes that adapting the traditional format of the regional linguistic atlas is more useful than trying to set up a format unique to Chicago.

1141. ———, ed. *Linguistic Atlas of the Gulf States*. Vol 1. *Handbook for the Linguistic Atlas of the Gulf States*. Athens: Univ. of Georgia Press, 1986.

Complemented by *LAGS: The Basic Materials* (Ann Arbor: University Microfilms International, 1981), edited by Pederson et al. Study area includes eastern Texas, Mississippi, Alabama, Tennessee, Arkansas, and the part of Georgia not covered in McDavid and O'Cain (cited in item 1122). The book includes a thorough review of settlement history, topography, and the influence of urban areas on diffusion patterns of usage. Chapter Two, "The Geography of the Gulf States," sketches regional culture areas, showing how cities have acted as staging grounds for the diffusion of usage patterns. An exhaustive bibliography, pp. 315–363, is included.

1142. Pickford, Glenna R. "American Linguistic Geography: A Sociological Analysis." *Word* 12 (1956): 211–33.

Criticizes the procedures of the Kurath group. Pickford argues that their sampling of informants, use of worksheets, and conclusions all were methodologically primitive. She says that geography is not the key ingredient in a society such as ours. The Kurath group emphasized culturally subordinate communities, not the cities, and imputed too much importance to education.

1143. Pyles, Thomas. *Thomas Pyles: Selected Studies of English Usage*. Edited by John Algeo. Gainesville: Univ. Presses of Florida, 1979.

Essays over a thirty-four-year period including discussion of popular culture and usage patterns, folk linguistics, and namegiving in the Bible Belt. See also John Algeo and Adele Algeo, "Bible Belt Onamastics Revisited," *Names* 3 (1983), pp. 103–116.

1144. Reed, Carroll E. and David W. Reed. "Problems of English Speech Mixture in California and Nevada." In *Studies in Linguistics in Honor of Raven I. McDavid* (item 1107), 135–43.

Summarizes settlement history of the area. The authors discuss markers among geographical and social groups, as to types of eastern speech prevailing. San Francisco and Los Angeles are different in words used. In Los Angeles some Spanish words (e.g., *arroyo*) are in common use. The Upper Northwest is distinct in usage as compared to California and Nevada. The essay is based upon linguistic atlas work at Berkeley.

1145. Sapir, Edward. *Selected Writings*. Edited by D.G. Mandelbaum. Berkeley: Univ. of California Press, 1949.

Collection of Sapir essays, including the classic essay on "Language" from the *Encyclopedia of the Social Sciences* (1933), on pp. 1–44. That wide-ranging essay explores nearly all aspects of its large subject: the formal units of speech, the way in which language gives structure to reality, the ways in which language differs from culture and culture depends upon language, and the sociology and psychology of language use.

1146. Schach, Paul, ed. *Languages in Conflict: Linguistic Acculturation on the Great Plains*. Lincoln: Univ. of Nebraska Press, 1980.

Essays on ethnic language use on the Great Plains, in the Haugen tradition. The book focuses upon bilingualism, usually of a recessive kind. Among Amish, though, bilingualism seems stable, because of the isolation of language users.

1147. Sealock, Richard B. and Pauline A. Seely. *Bibliography of Place Names in the United States and Canada*. 3d ed. Chicago: American Library Association, 1982.

Records by state and province available published material and some basic manuscript compilations which can be consulted at historical societies or libraries. Its detailed index allows a search for types of names, language origins, and relation to particular geographical features. Gazeteers are included.

1148. Stewart, George R. *American Place-Names: A Concise and Selective Dictionary for the Continental United States*. New York: Oxford Univ. Press, 1970.

Intended as a general reference, the book omits personal names, obvious names, and merely local names and focuses upon
famous or curious names, trying to determine the motivation of the namer (in contrast to the practice of English name dictionaries)

1149. ———. *Names on the Globe*. New York: Oxford Univ. Press, 1975.

Very general treatment of topic. Part One discusses what a name is and how it relates to the grammar of a language, as well as relations among languages; Part Two sorts out names as products of various kinds of motives; Part Three is historical, following the story of name-giving from prehistoric to present times; Part Four argues that names are useful to history, archaeology, and poetry.

1150. ———. *Names on the Land: An Historical Account of Place-Naming in the United States.* Boston: Houghton-Mifflin, 1967.

Originally published in 1945. A path-breaking work, supported by abundant notes and references but addressed to the general reader. The general structure is historical. The book is wonderfully readable and rich in detail.

1151. Trudgill, Peter. "Linguistic Geography and Geographical Linguistics." *Progress in Geography* 7 (1975): 227–52.

Excellent survey of literature. Trudgill first discusses linguistic geography, surveying European as well as American work; then areal patterns holding among unlike languages (e.g., French 'r' found in Denmark). He recommends "geographical linguistics," bringing recent progress in geography to bear on linguistics (e.g., cartography reflecting variations in use by social class, and concern about why isoglosses come where they do).

1152. Underwood, Gary N. "American English Dialectology: Alternatives for the Southwest." *International Journal of the Sociology of Language* 2 (1976): 19–40.

Formerly the director for the linguistic atlas for the Southeast, Underwood says that the Kurath approach is outdated. Questionnaires of the Kurath kind are biased in a rural direction, few blacks or "ethnics" are chosen, and other interested academic disciplines are not involved.

1153. Voegelin, C.F., F.M. Voegelin and Noel W. Schutz, Jr. "The Language Situation in Arizona as Part of the Southwest Culture Area." In *Studies in Southwestern Ethnolinguistics*, edited by Dell H. Hymes and William E. Bittle, 402–51. The Hague: Mouton Press, 1967.

Argues that students of the language situation should begin with the area, the general setting, rather than with the language itself. The many languages in the subject-area intermix because they share the area.

1154. Weinreich, Uriel. "Is a Structural Dialectology Possible?" *Word* 10 (1954): 388–400.

Says structural linguistics and dialectology have been separate worlds, and that there is an urgent need to fuse them by means of a structural dialectology. Dialects need to be studied rigorously, employing systematic comparison, opposition, and contrast among them. If one employs a structural approach, one can discover distinctions otherwise missed.

1155. Weinreich, Uriel, William Labov and Marvin I. Herzog. "Empirical Foundations for a Theory of Language Change." In *Directions for Historical Linguistics*, edited by Winfred P. Lehmann and Yakov Malkiel, 97–188. Austin: Univ. of Texas Press, 1968.

Argues that the tradition of Saussure, Bloomfield, and Chomsky ignored patterns of linguistic change. This essay sketches rules for patterns of change, in transmission from parents to children, among social classes and age groups, as well as between areas. The authors insist on the heterogeneity of language competence, with variability in any language; a need to switch among codes; the coexistence of different language systems; etc. Dependence on isoglosses on the part of linguistic geographers is criticized for achieving pattern by selection of evidence.

1156. Whorf, Benjamin Lee. *Language, Thought and Reality*. Edited by John B. Carroll. Cambridge: MIT Press, 1956.

Language, Whorf argues, structures experience: " ... all observers are not led by the same physical evidence to the same picture of the universe, unless their linguistic backgrounds are similar or can in some way be calibrated" (p. 214). Language shapes perception of the world in terms of basic categories, of space and time. Whorf emphasizes American Indian languages (especially Hopi) in contrast to English to make his point. Scholars often speak of a Sapir-Whorf approach to language.

1157. Wood, Gordon R. *Vocabulary Change: A Study of Variation in Regional Words in Eight of the Southern States*. Carbondale: Southern Illinois Univ. Press, 1971.

In the Kurath tradition, based upon mailed questionnaire, distinguishing among words that are Northern, Midland, Coastal Southern, and General Southern (borrowing from Atwood, *The Regional Vocabulary of Texas*, item 1097). Wood sees Gulf Southern as basically different from Coastal Southern, and talks of mid-Southern rather than South Midland. The bulk of book consists of graphs, maps, and word lists. The master map appears on pp. 358–59. The area includes Georgia, Florida, Mississippi, Alabama, Tennessee, Arkansas, Louisiana, and Oklahoma.

1158. Zelinsky, Wilbur. "Cultural Variations in Personal Name Patterns in the Eastern United States." *Annals of the Association of American Geographers* 60 (1970): 743–69.

Tries to establish scientific criteria for "markers" of a culture. The author conducts a factor analysis of British-derived names in 1790 and in 1968, deriving regional patterns. Overall, he finds regional differences in personal name patterns diminishing.

1159. ———. "Classical Town Names in the United States: The Historical Geography of an American Idea." *Geographical Review*, 57 (1967): 463–97.

Traces diffusion patterns of classical place names. The author makes out an explosive diffusion in the use of such names from New York (1790+) to Ohio, the Ohio River valley, Michigan (1830–40), Wisconsin/Illinois (1840–50), and Minnesota/Iowa (1850–60). Thereafter there is a "hollow frontier" where the edge of the naming patterns keeps moving out but changes stop at the core. The pattern is not important to industrial areas and suburbs; its area of greatest influence is that of New England extended. The influence of classical town names seems unique to the U.S. (it is not found in Canada or Brazil).

1160. ———. "Nationalism in the American Place-Name Cover." *Names* 31 (March 1983): 1–28.

Follows procedure similar to that in the previous entry, examining the diffusion of place-names derived from the names of national heroes and events. Zelinsky finds that New England extended is the area of greatest occurrence, and that the South is strangely resistant to the pattern.

Literature

Creative literature that evokes the texture and sense of a place is an indispensable source of regional knowledge. Much of our greatest literature is inextricably rooted in particular portions of the land. A sense of New England lies at the heart of the works of Hawthorne, Robinson, and Frost. The South haunts the imaginations of Twain, Faulkner, Tennessee Williams, and Eudora Welty, just as the Midwest informs the work of Garland, Dreiser, Anderson, Sinclair Lewis, and Garrison Keillor. Cather and Rolvaag would lose much of their meaning apart from the Great Plains and prairie as would Wallace Stegner and Joan Didion apart from the Far West.

The list could continue, but the point is clear: sense of place often imbues the highest forms of literature, and the vast space and sprawling diversity of the American scene encourage regional rather than national creative focus. Paradoxically, it has often been argued that only by descending into the rich detail of our culture can the artist discover what Americans share in common. It is through the particular and the commonplace that creative literature is most likely to discover the universal. As William Stafford has observed, "the more local the self that art has, the more all people can share it, for that vivid encounter with the stuff of the world is our common ground." Hawthorne's declaration that "New England is quite as large a lump of this earth as my heart can readily take in" combined with John Dewey's belief that "the locality is the only universal" could serve as guiding principles for regional aesthetics and for much of American literature.[1]

Like all art forms, regional literature does have besetting weaknesses and possible excesses. At one extreme, regional expression can lapse into folksy nostalgia or strident provincialism: into quaint laments for the misty past or barbaric yawps against mass culture. Yet in the other extreme, regional sensibility can sustain the most profound works of art and affirm William Carlos Williams's belief that "The classic is the local fully realized, words marked by place." Arguing that all arts celebrate the mystery of place, Eudora Welty has stressed that "fiction depends for its life on place. Location is the crossroads of circumstance, the proving ground of 'What happened? Who's here? Who's coming?'—and that is the heart's field."[2]

Regionalism has always been a driving force in American literature, but discussions of regional aesthetics have peaked during three periods of American history. The widespread local color movement of the 1880s and 1890s sparked the first significant discussion of literary regionalism in the United States, a debate that captured the interest of critics as varied as William Dean Howells, Hamlin Garland, and Josiah Royce. The flowering of regional art during the 1920s, 1930s, and early 1940s—the outpouring of regional novels, poems, and painting, of regional magazines and theater—attracted widespread critical attention. The ensuing debate over the strengths and weaknesses of regional art generated a large body of literature, much of it relevant for contemporary regional studies while some of it is weighted with vague, predictable allusions to the need for roots and a feel for the land and the folk. As in other fields and disciplines, there has been a revival of interest in literary regionalism in the 1970s and 1980s. Motivated by the desire to uncover a more pluralistic vision of American literature as well as a renewed respect for place in light of the environmental crisis, writers as varied as Wendell Berry, Edward Abbey, Gary Snyder, and Eudora Welty have revived questions of sense of place and region in American literature.

The following list includes important sources from each of these periods; it also contains sources that contribute to our understanding of American regional literature in four general areas. A large group of sources, first of all, is directly concerned with the strengths and weaknesses of regionalism in creative literature. Included here are important regional manifestos and critiques by Hamlin Garland, Mary Austin, Donald Davidson, John Crowe Ransom, Allen Tate, Benjamin Botkin, Bernard DeVoto, J. Frank Dobie, Marjorie Kinnan Rawlings, T.S. Eliot, Flannery O'Connor, Paul Horgan, Gary Snyder, Jim Wayne Miller, and others. Also included are perceptive studies of regional literature by Alfred Kazin, Alexander Karanikas, Benjamin Spencer, Jules Chametzky, Lawrence Buell, and David Wyatt to name a few.

A second group of sources examines the general significance of place in literature. American writers as varied as Gertrude Stein, T.K. Whipple, Charles Olson, Edward Dahlberg, Eudora Welty, Richard Wilbur, Wendell Berry, Floyd Watkins, and Leonard Lutwack contribute to our understanding of the relationship between creativity and sense of place as do English writers Wyndham Lewis, Lawrence Durrell, Alan Sillitoe, Raymond Williams, and Ronald Blythe. A number of literary scholars, including Annette Kolodny, Vera Norwood and Janice Monk,

Lewis Simpson, and Cecilia Tichi, extend a theme of American Studies scholarship by exploring symbols and myths associated with American regions and landscapes.

A third, highly selective, group is composed of anthologies of and guides to the literature of particular regions. Various collections of essays on the literature of at least seven regions—New England, the South, the Midwest, the Great Plains, the Southwest, the Far West, and California—are included throughout this list. Finally, an unusually large number of bibliographies of regional literature are available, and bibliographical guides by Otis Coan and Richard Lilliard, Richard Etulain, Clarence Ghodes, Martha Khede, and Lewis Leary constitute a fourth group of materials.

In addition to the above areas of interest, this chapter also contains sources devoted to a number of literary subthemes including: regional theater analyzed by Herbert Blau, Kenneth MacGowan, Paul Nolan, Felix Sper, and Joseph Ziegler; regional literary magazines examined by Frederick Hoffman, Charles Allen, and Carolyn Ulrich and Milton Reigelman; teaching regional literature commented on by Lenore Hoffmann and Deborah Rosenfelt, Paul Lauter, and Emily Toth; and regional children's literature studied by Fred Erisman. The large number of special magazine issues included here reflects the depth and persistence of regional concerns in American literature.

There is considerable cross-fertilization and overlap between regional studies in literature and in other disciplines. The creative dimension of regionalism has been an important concern of scholars in American Studies, art history, folk studies, geography, language, philosophy, and religious studies. For the sake of convenience, literary discussions by a small group of "outsiders"—by sociologist Howard Odum and geographers D.W. Meinig, Christopher Salter, and Yi-Fu Tuan—have been included here. Many other connections can be made and further areas of research uncovered by consulting our chapters devoted to these closely related disciplines, particularly American Studies.

M.S.

---

[1]William Stafford, "Regionalism, Localism, and Art," cited in *South Dakota Review* 12 (Autumn 1975): 47. Nathaniel Hawthorne to Horatio Bridge, January 15, 1857, cited by Randall Stewart, *Regionalism and Beyond: The Essays of Randall Stewart*, George Core, ed., (Nashville: Vanderbilt Univ. Press, 1973), 157. John Dewey, "Americanism and Localism," *Dial* 68 (1920): 686.

[2]William Carlos Williams, "Kenneth Burke," cited by David Wyatt, *The Fall into Eden: Landscape and Imagination in California* (New York: Cambridge Univ. Press, 1986), xvii. Eudora Welty, "Place in Fiction," *The Eye of the Story: Selected Essays and Reviews* (New York: Random House, 1978), 118.

*   *   *

1161. Allen, Gay Wilson. "The Influence of Space on the American Imagination." In *Essays in Honor of Jay B. Hubbell*, edited by Clarence Gohdes, 329–42. Durham: Duke Univ. Press, 1967.

Using Whitman's poetry as a case study of the impact of geographical expansiveness upon the imagination, Allen examines the spatial sensibilities of such writers as Crevecoeur, Emerson, Thoreau, Dickinson, Hart Crane, Archibald MacLeish, Robinson Jeffers, William Carlos Williams, and Wallace Stevens. See Jules Zanger, "Whitman and the Influence of Space on American Literature," *Newberry Library Bulletin* 5 (December 1961), pp. 299–314, for a summary of the critical response to Allen's essay.

1162. Austin, Mary. "Regionalism in American Fiction." *English Journal* 21 (January 1932): 97–107.

From her vantage point in New Mexico, Austin criticizes fiction with a "bird's-eye view of the American scene, what you might call an automobile-eye view, something slithering and blurred," and she upholds local art "which has come up through the land, shaped by the author's adjustment to it." An insightful comment on Austin's regional fiction and speculation is Henry Nash Smith's "The Feel of the Purposeful Earth: Mary Austin's Prophecy," *New Mexico Quarterly* 1 (February 1931), pp. 17–33.

1163. Baker, Joseph E. "Four Arguments for Regionalism." *Saturday Review of Literature* 15 (November 28, 1936), 3–4 and 14.

Taking the affirmative side of an insightful debate with Paul Beath on "Regionalism: Pro and Con," Baker argues for the value of regionalism from historical, aesthetic, political, and antimetropolitan perspectives.

1164. Beath, Paul Robert. "Four Fallacies of Regionalism." *Saturday Review of Literature*, 15 (November 28, 1936): 3–4 and 14–16.

The thrust of Beath's argument is that regional movements usually wall themselves off from vital contact with the larger world.

1165. Berry, Wendell. "Poetry and Place." In *Standing By Words*, 92–199. San Francisco: North Point Press, 1983.

This wide-ranging essay analyzes the meaning of place in the poetry of Dante, Spenser, Shakespeare, Milton, Dryden, Pope, Shelley, Wordsworth, and others, eventually connecting their ideas and imagery to contemporary principles of ecology and bioregionalism.

1166. ———. "The Regional Motive." In *A Continuous Harmony: Essays Cultural and Agricultural*, 63–70. New York: Harcourt, Brace, Jovanovich, 1970.

After listing many of the besetting weaknesses of regionalism—aesthetic and otherwise—Berry develops an understanding of regionalism as "local life aware of itself" that he believes to be necessary to counter the destructive "urban nomadism" of contemporary life.

1167. ———. "Writer and Region." *Hudson Review* 40 (Spring 1987): 15–30.

Berry discusses the many strengths and weaknesses of *Huckleberry Finn* as echoes of the strengths and weaknesses of American regional literature. On the positive side, Twain "taught American writers to be writers by teaching them to be regional writers. The great gift of *Huckleberry Finn* ... is its ability to be regional without being provincial." On the negative side, the desire to "light out for the Territories" reinforces an American impulse to reject community and commitment to place. Other sources by Berry are listed under Philosophy and Religion (items 1330–1331).

1168. Bingham, Edwin R. and Glen A. Love, eds. *Northwest Perspectives: Essays on the Culture of of the Pacific Northwest*. Eugene: Univ. of Oregon Press, 1979.

The results of a symposium in honor of Harold G. Merriam, founder and editor of *The Frontier* and an "early leader in helping the Northwest find its distinctive voice," this book contains a number of essays on regional creative expression. Especially useful are essays on Oregon Indian literature, Northwest regional folklore, the regional perspectives of Vardis Fisher, H.L. Davis, and Theodore Roethke, and an annotated bibliography, pp. 219–35. An earlier, still useful anthology, is V.L.O. Chittick, ed., *Northwest Harvest: A Regional*

Stock-Taking (New York: MacMillian, 1948). (See Robbins et al. for a closely related source (item 1269).

1169. Blackmur, R.P. *Psyche in the South.* Tyron, N.C.: Tyron Pamphlets, n.d.

Obviously written during the 1930s, this is a thorough critique of the political, economic, and aesthetic "sectionalism" championed by the Southern Agrarians, especially by Donald Davidson and Allen Tate. Centralization and urbanism, Blackmur argues, are incontrovertible, potentially positive, forces requiring intelligent planning rather than blind rejection. Genuine regional art ought to emerge from urban as well as rural experience, and such art is most compelling when least ideological.

1170. Blau, Herbert. *The Impossible Theater: A Manifesto.* New York: MacMillian, 1964.

A central theme of Blau's critique of Broadway-dominated American drama is the need for decentralized, regional theater. "New Frontiers," pp. 54–84, examines the historical roots of the tension between center and periphery—between New York and outlying regions—and promotes a vigorous decentralized theater that will be more than a "new provincialism." For an earlier form of this argument, see Blau's "Decentralization: New Frontiers and Old Dead Ends," *Tulane Drama Review* 7 (Summer 1963), pp. 55–85.

1171. Blythe, Ronald. *Characters and Their Landscapes.* New York: Harcourt, Brace, Jovanovich, 1982.

Especially important is "An Inherited Perspective," pp. 1–13, which discusses the significance of local landscape consciousness in English literature, with emphasis upon the regional expressions of John Clare, Norman Nicholson, and Richard Jeffries. Other essays touch upon the significance of place in the work of Hazlitt, Hardy, Tolstoy, and others. Two other books by Blythe which are less literary in orientation but which effectively evoke the significance of place through oral history are *Akenfield: Portrait of an English Village* (New York: Random House, 1969) and *The View in Winter: Reflections on Old Age* (New York: Penguin Books, 1980).

1172. Botkin, Benjamin. "The Folk in Literature: An Introduction to the New Regionalism." *Folk-Say: A Regional Miscellany* 1 (1929): 9–20.

An influential regional manifesto and an insightful description of the rise of folk-regional aesthetics during the 1920s. For an inside account of the Oklahoma based regional revival nurtured by little magazines, see Botkin's *"Folk-Say* and *Space*: Their Genesis and Exodus," *Southwest Review* 20 (July 1935), pp. 321–35. A vivid survey of regional activities throughout the nation is found in Botkin's "We Talk About Regionalism—North, East, South, and West," *The Frontier* 13 (May 1933), pp. 286–96.

1173. ———. "Regionalism and Culture." *Writers in a Changing World*, edited by Henry Hart, 140–57. New York: Equinox Cooperative Press, 1937.

After outlining the limitations of two largely reactionary regional literary groups—the Southwest regionalists and the Southern Agrarians—Botkin draws attention to more progressive manifestations of regionalism. The novels of Grace Lumpkin and Fielding Burke are offered as examples of a "proletarian regionalism" that "can help make the masses articulate by letting them tell their own story, in their own words. . . . it can create new forms, styles, and modes of literature by drawing upon place, work, and folk for motifs, images, symbols, slogans, and idioms. . . . Such a literature is truly regional in the etymological sense of giving a direction and a straight line to walk in." Other regional items by Botkin and reference to a complete bibliography of his work are listed in the Folk Studies (item 392). For further discussions of proletarian regionalism, see Conroy and LeSueur (items 1186, 1239) and Rourke under American Studies (items 33–35).

1174. ———. "Regionalism: Cult or Culture?" *English Journal* 25 (March 1936): 181–85.

In this critical analysis of the plethora of regional ideologies that competed for attention during the 1930s, Botkin concludes that "regionalism, properly controlled, becomes a valuable social adjunct to literature, along with ethnology, folklore, and Marxist economics."

1175. Bracher, Frederick. "California's Literary Regionalism." *American Quarterly* 7 (Fall 1955): 275–84.

In addition to analyzing California's regional literature, Bracher adeptly criticizes the cliche-ridden state of many discussions of regional aesthetics. This theme is elaborated by Houston and Wyatt (items 1221, 1325) and Veysey under American Studies (items 57–58).

1176. Brooks, Cleanth. "Regionalism in American Literature." *Journal of Southern History* 26 (February 1960): 35–43.

After comparing southern regional writing with the "powerful emergence" of provincial art throughout the western world, Brooks wisely observes that the strongest regional literature is the least self-conscious and chauvinistic. Great regional writers such as Hardy, Yeats, and Frost, he concludes, often serve as gadflies in urban-industrial society. Brooks has expanded several of these ideas in "Southern Literature: The Past, History, and the Timeless," *Southern Literature in Transition: Heritage and Promise* (Memphis: Memphis State Univ. Press, 1983), edited by Philip Castille and William Promise, pp. 3–16.

1177. Broyard, Anatole. "Country Fiction." *New York Times Book Review* (December 19, 1982): 31.

Like critics Ellen Douglas, Ann Hulbert and Robert Tower (items 1197, 1224, 1307), Broyard reviews the work of Bobbie Ann Mason, Cormac McCarthy, and others who seem to be part of "a new generation of regional writers."

1178. Buell, Lawrence. *New England Literary Culture: From Revolution Through Renaissance.* New York: Cambridge Univ. Press, 1986.

Building upon the earlier work of Lewis Mumford, Van Wyck Brooks, F.O. Matthiessen, and others, Buell carefully examines the regional dimensions of the efflorescence of American creative expression during the 1830s, 1840s, and 1850s. Departing from earlier studies, Buell's analysis is supported by dense biographical data regarding some 276 professional writers active in New England between 1770 and 1865. Especially germane to considerations of literary regionalism are "Part Three, Reinventing Puritanism: The New England Historical Imagination," pp. 193–280; and Part Four, "New England as a Country of the Imagination: The Spirit of Place," pp. 283–370.

1179. Burke, John Gordon, ed. *Regional Perspectives: An Examination of America's Literary Heritage.* Chicago: American Library Association, 1973.

This somewhat uneven anthology contains wide-ranging, discursive essays on the regional imaginations of the Midwest, New England, South, Southwest, and Far West. Especially useful are John Knoepfle's "Crossing the Midwest," Hayden Karruth's "The New England Tradition," Larry Goodwyn's "The Frontier Myth and Southwestern

Literature," and William Everson's "Archetype West." A fairly detailed bibliography is included.

1180. Calverton, V.L. *American Literature at the Crossroads.* Chapbook no. 48. Seattle: Univ. of Washington, 1931.

In Calverton's straightforward morality play, the regressive, anti-modern forces of regional writing are arrayed against the progressive, constructive qualities of proletarian literature.

1181. Caughey, John and LaRee Caughey, eds. *California Heritage: An Anthology of History and Literature.* Los Angeles: Ward Ritchie Press, 1964.

This thorough and wide-ranging collection of images of California from Native American creation myths to the poetry of Ginsberg and Ferlinghetti, contains a useful bibliography of California literature, pp. 527–32. John and LaRee Caughey's *Los Angeles: Biography of a City* (Los Angeles: Ward Ritchie Press, 1976) follows a similar pattern. Closely related sources include Lawrence Clark Powell, ed., *California Classics: The Creative Literature of the Golden State* (Los Angeles: Ward Ritchie Press, 1971); Jonathan Eisen and David Fine, eds., *Unknown California* (New York: MacMillian, 1985); and David Fine, ed., *Los Angeles in Fiction* (Albuquerque: Univ. of New Mexico Press, 1984).

1182. Chametzky, Jules. *Our Decentralized Literature: Cultural Meditations in Selected Jewish and Southern Writers.* Amherst: Univ. of Massachusetts Press, 1986.

A central theme of this collection of ten previously published essays is the need for a more profound sense of regional literature as a source of empowerment for marginalized, often oppressed groups of Americans. For Chametzky, "decentralization" has geographical as well as psychological and political connotations; borrowing from Foucault, he argues that "'decentering' and deconstructing presumably fixed and coherent structures of meaning are a necessary prelude to less imperial approaches to knowledge and understanding." Valuable discussions of literary regionalism are found in his "Introduction," pp. 3–18; "Our Decentralized Literature: The Significance of Regional, Ethnic, Racial, and Sexual Factors," pp. 22–45; "Realism, Cultural Politics, and Language as Meditation in Mark Twain," pp. 109–24; "Thomas Wolfe and the Cult of Experience," pp. 123–36; and "Styron's *Sophie's Choice*: Jews and Other Marginals," pp. 135–46.

1183. ———. "Regional Literature and Ethnic Realities." *Antioch Review* 31 (Fall 1971): 385–96.

In this modification of the argument of "Our Decentralized Literature," Chametzsky focuses on the relationship between ethnicity and regionalism in the work of Abraham Cahan and Charles Chestnutt.

1184. Clough, Wilson O. *The Necessary Earth: Nature and Solitude in American Literature.* Austin: Univ. of Texas Press, 1964.

Like T.K. Whipple, Howard Mumford Jones, Wright Morris, and others, Clough explores how the "frontiers of nature and solitude" have influenced American writers from Cotton Mather to Wallace Stevens. The opening section, "The Shock of Geography," contains essays examining how "enthusiasm over open landscape and wildness" helped lay the foundations for a national literature. "Not From Landscape, Not From Flight," pp. 153–68, perceptively discusses the regional literatures of the West, Midwest, New England, and the South, and explores possible requirements for stronger regional writing in the West and the emergence of the "greater western novel."

1185. Coan, Otis W. and Richard G. Lilliard, eds. *America in Fiction: An Annotated List of Novels that Interpret Aspects of American Life in the United States, Canada, and Mexico.* 5th ed. Palo Alto, Calif.: Pacific Press, 1967.

A carefully annotated bibliography of prose fiction, stressing works which convey a "picture" of particular aspects of American life. Major headings are pioneer life in forests, plains, deserts, and mountains; farm and village life by regions, including the Northeast, Midwest, Plains and Northwest, South, Southern Highlands, and Southwest and California; business, industry, and city; life during given historical periods; religious life; and the culture of ethnic groups.

1186. Conroy, Jack and Curt Johnson, eds. *Writers in Revolt: The Anvil Anthology, 1933–1940.* New York: Lawrence Hill, 1973.

A vivid collection of the radical midwestern regionalism fostered by three little magazines during the 1930s: *The Rebel Poet, The Anvil,* and *The New Anvil.* Early works by Nelson Algren, Erskine Caldwell, Jack Conroy, James T. Farrell, Langston Hughes, Meridel Le Sueur, Karl Shapiro, and others are reprinted. Conroy's introduction is the most thorough history of this vital marriage of regional and proletarian literature in print.

1187. Cunliffe, Marcus. "The Conditions of an American Literature." *American Literature to 1900*, 1–22. New York: Peter Bedrick Books, 1987.

Cunliffe discusses the "quest for nationality" and its relationship with regional literary expression during the eighteenth and nineteenth centuries. The particular qualities of southern and western literature and their contributions to the general development of an American literature before 1900 are perceptively analyzed. Cunliffe's "New England: The Universal Yankee Nation," pp. 253–72 of the same volume, effectively traces the rise and fall of New England's cultural dominance between 1815 and 1900.

1188. Dahlberg, Edward. "Word-Sick and Place-Crazy." In *Alms for Oblivion*, 20–27. Minneapolis: Univ. of Minnesota Press, 1964.

Dahlberg uses William Carlos Williams's *Paterson* as a source for discussing the tension between sense of place and rootlessness in American literature. America's oceanic vastness hampers the growth of earth bound culture. Thoreau, Melville, Parkman, Prescott, Williams, and others are "wild, watery men.... river and sea and plateau geniuses, ranging a continent for a house, and all of the outdoors."

1189. Davidson, Donald. "A Mirror for Artists." In *I'll Take My Stand: The South and the Agrarian Tradition* (item 1309), 28–60.

Davidson argues against the notion that urban-industrial culture stimulates the arts—the art gallery or art museum theory of art. Industrial leisure, he contends, is corrupted by the work that attends it. Great art is produced in stable, religious, agrarian cultures; it is centrally concerned with values and with the depiction of nature. Achievements in the arts of the contemporary South are brought forth as evidence.

1190. ———. *The Attack on Leviathan: Regionalism and Nationalism in the United States*. Chapel Hill: Univ. of North Carolina Press, 1938.

A seminal, multidisciplinary study of American regionalism comparable to Turner's, Odum's, and Mumford's classics. Written from the perspective of an ardent Southern Agrarian, this book contains important essays on regionalism in American history, the social sciences, arts, politics, and economics. "Still Rebels, Still Yankees," pp. 131–54, and "Howard Odum and the Sociological Proteus," pp. 285–311, are essential documents of the regional fervor of the 1930s. Davidson's remarks concerning regional aesthetics abound with useful information and remain especially insightful. See "Regionalism and the

Arts," pp. 65–101; "Regionalism and Nationalism in American Literature," pp. 228–39; and "the Southern Poet and His Tradition," pp 339–46. For a complete bibliography of Davidson's work, much of which bears upon literary regionalism, see Thomas Daniel Young and M. Thomas Inge, *Donald Davidson: An Essay and a Bibliography.* (Nashville: Vanderbilt University Press, 1965).

1191. ———. "Sectionalism in America." *Hound and Horn* 6 (July–September 1933): 561–89.

Building upon Turner's notion of sectionalism, Davidson makes a distinction between divisive political sectionalism and harmonious "organic sectionalism," which is a necessary function of national life. This article is the seed for many of the ideas developed in *The Attack on Leviathan* (item 1190). Other sources by Davidson are listed under Political Science (items 1417–1418).

1192. DeVoto, Bernard. *The Literary Fallacy.* Bloomington: Indiana Univ. Press, 1944.

A powerful, at times vitriolic, condemnation of American writers who spurned their native grounds during the 1920s and 1930s. "All roots," DeVoto writes, "will be winter killed and all the sweet green shoots will die except as they are warmed and fertilized by the common experience of America."

1193. ———. "Regionalism, or the Coterie Manifesto." *Saturday Review of Literature* 15 (November 28, 1936): 8.

A wry critique of the plethora of self-conscious regional cliques of the 1930s. For examples of DeVoto's ability to both praise and scorn regional art, see his "New England, There She Stands," *Harper's Magazine* 164 (March 1932), pp. 413–15 and "Horizon Land," *Saturday Review of Literature* 15 (April 24, 1937), p. 8.

1194. Didion, Joan. *Slouching Towards Bethlehem.* New York: Farrar, Straus and Giroux, 1968.

A collection of essays, mostly concerned with California, and all conveying a sense of place. If one wants to understand the mental map of an educated Californian, one can hardly do better than read Part One, "Life Styles in the Golden Land," pp. 3–128, and Part Three, "Seven Places of the Mind," pp. 171–238, which includes evocative essays on the Sacramento Valley, Hawaii, Mexico, Newport, Rhode Island, Los Angeles, and New York City. Several of these themes are continued in

Didion's *The White Album* (New York: Simon & Schuster, 1979), especially the section, "California Republic," pp. 51–105.

1195. Dobie, J. Frank. *Guide to Life and Literature of the Southwest.* rev. ed. Dallas: Southern Methodist Univ. Press, 1952.

A lively tour through southwestern writing by one of the region's most ardent champions, this book contains an extensive bibliography of regional literature.

1196. ———. "The Writer and His Region." *Southwest Review* 35 (Spring 1950): 81–87.

The highest form of regional art, Dobie argues, must be anchored to the particular at the same time that it aspires to the universal. "Nothing is too trivial for art, but good art treats nothing in a trivial way. Nothing is too provincial for the regional writer, but he cannot be provincial-minded toward it."

1197. Douglas, Ellen. "Provincialism in Literature." *New Republic* 173 (July 5/12, 1975): 23–25.

Aware of many of the weaknesses and excesses of provincialism and parochialism, Douglas argues that some provincialism is inevitable and desirable. "The ground of all art is the particular.... all human experience is provincial in the sense that it is the experience of a particular time and place."

1198. Durrell, Lawrence. *Spirit of Place: Letters and Essays on Travel.* Edited by Alan G. Thomas. New York: E.P. Dutton, 1969.

Especially useful is "Landscape and Character," pp. 156–63. Echoing Ronald Blythe, D.H. Lawrence, Alan Sillitoe, and other English writers, Durrell believes that the spirit of place is the primary determinant of any culture, and that just as people are molded by the particular qualities of their physical environment, so also the greatest works of art are "well and truly anchored in nature.... tuned in to the sense of place."

1199. Eliot, T.S. *Notes Toward a Definition of Culture.* London: Faber and Faber, 1948.

In "Unity and Diversity: The Region," pp. 49–60, Eliot shrewdly observes that "We have not given enough attention to the ecologies of cultures" and that national cultures can only flourish if they are composed of "a constellation of cultures."

1200. Erisman, Fred. "Regionalism in American Children's Literature." In *Society and Children's Literature*, edited by James H. Fraser, 53–75. Boston: David R. Goudine, 1978.

Erisman traces how juvenile literature mirrored stages in adult regional fiction, from sentimental local color writing in the 1870s and 1880s to the "broader integration of the total regional experience" by the 1930s and 1940s. Children's regional literature in both rural and urban settings is discussed along with such authors as Laura Ingalls Wilder, Marjorie Kinnan Rawlings, Elizabeth Enright, and Lois Lensky. "By demonstrating the ways in which diverse persons have effectively come to terms with their place and their time," Erisman writes, "the literature suggests to the young reader that he, too, can create a zone of stability.... that makes him a balanced person."

1201. ———. "Western Regional Writers and the Uses of Place," *Journal of the West* 19 (January 1980): 36–44.

An effective discussion of the differences between local color and regionalism in western writing as well as the distinctive qualities of five western regional writers: Willa Cather, A.B. Guthrie, Jr., John Steinbeck, Paul Horgan, and John Graves. For a closely related argument see Erisman's "Literature and Place: Varieties of Regional Experience," *Journal of Regional Cultures* 1 (Fall-Winter 1981), pp. 144–53.

1202. Etulain, Richard W. "Local Color and Regionalism." In *A Bibliographical Guide to the Study of Western American Literature*, 48–53. Lincoln: Univ. of Nebraska Press, 1982.

An extensive bibliography that extends beyond western writers.

1203. Faulkner, Virginia and Frederick C. Luebke, eds. *Vision and Refuge: Essays on the Literature of the Great Plains*. Lincoln: Univ. of Nebraska Press, 1980.

This anthology includes effective essays on Ole Rolvaag, Scandinavian-American literature, Willa Cather, and Black Elk, as well as discussions of major literary themes of the Great Plains region. The editors comment that Great Plains writers have always had difficulty gaining recognition from the eastern literary establishment.

1204. Fiedler, Leslie A. "Boxing the Compass." In *The Return of the Vanishing American*, 16–28. New York: Stein and Day, 1968.

Fiedler argues that "much of our most distinguished literature arises out of a geographical mythology" and then discusses this vital, regionally-rooted literature as it is expressed in four kinds of books: "Northerners," "Southerners," "Easterners," and "Westerns."

1205. Fisher, Vardis. "The Western Writer and the Eastern Establishment." *Western American Literature* 1 (Winter 1967): 244–59.

An irascible attack from the hinterlands against the New York literary establishment and a call for an independent, truly indigenous western art.

1206. Fishman, Solomon. *The Disinherited of Art: Writer and Background.* Berkeley: Univ. of California Press, 1953.

"The National Center," pp. 40–60, and "Traditional Society and the New Criticism," pp. 61–92, contain sophisticated, richly detailed analyses of the relationship between literary nationalism and regionalism and between so-called "primitive" and regional aesthetic impulses in our culture.

1207. Flanagan, John T., ed. *America Is West: An Anthology of Middlewestern Life and Literature.* Minneapolis: Univ. of Minnesota Press, 1945.

This important collection of midwestern writing focuses upon various ethnic groups and symbolic landscapes throughout the region—including the farm, the river, the small town and city—and contains selections from the work of such writers as Garland, Rolvaag, Lewis, Sandburg, and Anderson. For a more updated collection, see Walter Havighurst, ed., *Land of Long Horizons* (New York: Coward-McCann, 1960), which contains useful interpretive essays by Glenway Wescott, Frank Lloyd Wright, Theodore Dreiser, Robert and Helen Lynd, and others.

1208. Fletcher, John Gould. "Regionalism and Folk Art." *Southwest Review* 14 (July 1934): 429–34.

Fletcher, an imagist poet and staunch Southern Agrarian, describes folk culture as the seed bed of genuine art and the bulwark against the spread of industrialized mass culture.

1209. Garland, Hamlin. *Crumbling Idols: Twelve Essays on Art and Literature.* Chicago: Stone and Kimball, 1894.

This fiery manifesto announcing the birth of an indigenous midwestern literature echoes another manifesto also delivered at the Columbian Exposition in Chicago—Turner's famous essay on the significance of the frontier. Particularly important to an understanding of the history of American literary regionalism is Garland's discussion of his notion of "veritism" and its relationship to literary naturalism and realism. The chapters concerning "Provincialism," "New Fields," "Local Color in Art," "The Local Novel," and "Literary Centers," pp. 3–18, 21–29, 57–66, 69–79, and 145–62, respectively, are especially useful. For a useful discussion of Garland's pioneering effort in critical regionalism, see Warren Motley, "Hamlin Garland's *Under the Wheel*: Regionalism Unmasking America," *Modern Drama* 26 (December 1983), pp. 477–85.

1210. Gibson, Arrell Morgan. *The Santa Fe and Taos Colonies.* Norman: Univ. of Oklahoma Press, 1983.

A thorough account of the surge of regional aesthetics in New Mexico between 1920 and 1942, a renaissance that included painters John Sloan, Marsden Hartley, and Georgia O'Keefe, and writers Mary Austin, Mabel Dodge Luhan, and D.H. Lawrence.

1211. Gohdes, Clarence. "Exploration of the Provinces," in *The Literature of the American People*, edited by Arthur H. Quinn, 639–60. New York: Appleton-Century-Crofts, 1951, 639–60.

A fairly detailed discussion of the local color movement from 1870 until 1900.

1212. Gohdes, Clarence and Sanford E. Marovitz. "Literary Regionalism and Selected Studies of of American Regional Literature." In *Bibliographical Guide to the Study of the Literature of the U.S.A.* 5th ed., 156–65. Durham: Duke University Press, 1981.

This, along with Gohdes's earlier bibliographical work, *Literature and Theater in the States and Regions of the U.S.A.: An Historical Bibliography* (Durham: Duke Univ. Press, 1967), especially pp. 270–74, provides a useful introduction to literary regionalism.

1213. Hardwick, Elizabeth. "Southern Literature: The Cultural Assumptions of Regionalism." In *Southern Literature: Heritage and Promise*, edited by Philip Castille and William Osborne, 17–28. Memphis: Memphis State Univ. Press, 1983.

Hardwick questions the standard assumption that southern literature emerges from reverence for a distinctive past and place. "The conditions for all literature," she concludes, "are unknown, accidental, and unpredictable. The South is as much a part of the television, highway world as any other part of the country. It depends upon all that we are as a nation and is in some ways more quick to accept the expediencies of the moment than are other regions—no matter the conflict with the 'idea' of the South."

1214. Haslam, Gerald W. and James D. Houston, eds. *California's Heartland: Writings from the Great Central Valley.* Santa Barbara: Capra Press, 1978.

An imaginative collection of Central Valley literature ranging from Native American perspectives to such writers as Steinbeck, McWilliams, and Didion.

1215. Hazard, Lucy Lockwood. *The Frontier in American Literature.* 1927. Reprint. New York: Frederick Ungar, 1961.

Applying Turner's frontier thesis to the development of American fiction, Hazard examines the imaginative development of four frontier regions: New England, the South, the Midwest, and the Far West.

1216. Heiney, Donald W. "Between the Wars: Regionalism and Rural Naturalism." In *Recent American Literature*, 179–261. Woodbury, N.Y.: Barron, 1958.

After making a distinction between literary regionalism, with its pastoral settings and psychological concerns, and rural naturalism, with its more economic and social interests, Heiney carefully analyzes the writings of Ellen Glasgow, Willa Cather, Ole Rolvaag, Pearl Buck, William Faulkner, John Steinbeck, Erskine Caldwell, Robert Penn Warren, William Saroyan, and Eudora Welty in terms of this distinction.

1217. Hoffman, Frederick, Charles Allen, and Carolyn F. Ulrich. *The Little Magazine: A History and a Bibliography.* Princeton: Princeton Univ. Press, 1946.

"Regionalism and the Little Magazine," pp. 128–147, is a richly detailed and insightful discussion of an important manifestation of American regionalism. The detailed bibliography of magazines, pp. 233–411, is a useful resource.

1218. Hoffmann, Leonore and Deborah Rosenfelt, eds. *Teaching Women's Literature from a Regional Perspective*. New York: Modern Language Association of America, 1982.

The materials gathered here are the results of an MLA-sponsored project to develop literature courses "in which students conducted original research in noncanonical texts—out-of-print books, autobiographies, letters, diaries, memoirs, oral testimonies—of the women in their region." Leonore Hoffmann's "Introduction," pp. 1–14, describes the advantages of this grass roots regional approach. Useful theoretical essays include Elizabeth Meese's "The Whole Truth: Frameworks for the Study of Women's Noncanonical Literature," pp. 15–22; Julian Bader's "The 'Rooted' Landscape and the Woman Writer," pp. 23–30; and Douglas Jones's "Civilization and Geologic Consent: Region from a Geologist's Perspective," pp. 208–13. There are several perceptive essays on the interpretation of women's letters, diaries, and oral histories, as well as a general bibliography and a guide to regional resources in the South.

1219. Horgan, Paul. "The Pleasures and Perils of Regionalism." *Western American Literature* 8 (Winter 1974): 167–71.

Like many other accomplished regional writers, Horgan urges artists to avoid the pitfalls of corrupting self-conscious, exploitive regionalism. "Where once the term (regionalism) stood for uncommon local ways," he warns, " it now stands for almost any comic cartoon-like view of the varied life-styles to be found in the physical variations of the land."

1220. ———. "Preface to an Unwritten Book." *Yale Review* 65 (Spring 1976): 321–35. Reprinted in *Of America East and West: Selections From the Writings of Paul Horgan*, edited by Paul Horgan, 153–65. New York: Farrar, Straus, Giroux, 1984.

The author of the monumental regional study *Great River: The Rio Grande in North American History* (1954), describes his western background and its relationship to his work and sense of regionalism. Although the Great Depression, with its surge of self-conscious regionalism, was a crucial force in the development of western writing, it also paved the way for exploitive forms of literature. "The minute regionalism 'sees' itself," Horgan writes, "it disappears, and a counterfeit takes its place, with every likelihood of a long and profitable run." Another source by Horgan is listed under Art (item 271).

1221. Houston, James D. *One Can Think About Life After The Fish Is In The Canoe*. Santa Barbara: Capra Press, 1985.

A collection of five essays and short stories examining the relationship between place and creativity in parts of California. Especially insightful are "The Light Takes Its Color From the Sea," "The Psychology Of Heavy Weather, Parts I & II," and the title essay, pp. 7–20, 21–30, and 59–65, respectively. The title essay contains a discussion of a "new and upgraded regional feeling" among writers and intellectuals that is less sentimental than the "old provincialism."

1222. Howells, William Dean. "American Literary Centers." In *Literature and Life*, 173–86. New York: Harper and Brothers, 1902.

Like Hamlin Garland, Howells describes the vigorous growth of literary centers in California, the Midwest, the South, and New England independent of New York City and praises "our decentralized literature" for "its honesty, its fidelity to our decentralized life." In two utopian novels, *A Traveller from Altruria* (1894) and *Through the Eye of a Needle* (1907), Howells's ideal society is a decentralized commonwealth of regions.

1223. Hubbell, Jay. *The South in American Literature*. Durham: Duke Univ. Press, 1954.

This massive 987–page study testifies to the incredible amount of regionally-related literature that can be uncovered in only one area of the nation.

1224. Hulbert, Ann. "Rural Chic." *New Republic* 685 (September 2, 1985): 25–30.

A thoughtful analysis of the recent "bumper crop of regional fiction and earthy movies" that includes Bobbie Ann Mason's *In Country*, Larry McMurtry's *Lonesome Dove*, Garrison Keillor's *Lake Wobegon Days*, and such films as "Places in the Heart," "Country," and "Witness."

1225. James, Stuart B. "Western American Space and the Human Imagination." *Western Humanities Review* 24 (Spring 1970): 147–55.

A perceptive discussion of the impact of the geographical immensity and open space of the West upon such artists as A.B. Guthrie, Ole Rolvaag, Willa Cather, Vardis Fisher, Georgia O'Keefe, and D.H. Lawrence. James argues that a stark clarity of vision—an unadorned confrontation with the meaning of existence itself—is a central feature of the greatest western regional literature.

1226. Junkins, Donald. "New England As Region and Idea: Looking Over the Tafferel of our Craft." *Massachusetts Review* 26 (summer Autumn 1985): 198–207.

In discussing the impact of his native region upon his poetry, Junkins explores the general relationship between place and creativity. "The aim," he writes, "is to begin in New England and to explore life to the ends of the earth.... Shakespeare's Anthony and Cleopatra sail up the Nile of our own hearts. The only difference for a New England writer is that he takes his Walden Pond with him, and though he may never speak of it again, it resides somewhere near his pen, and the memory of it clarifies in some indefinable way, everything that he will ever write."

1227. Karanikas, Alexander. *Tillers of a Myth: Southern Agrarians as Social and Literary Critics*. Madison: Univ. of Wisconsin Press, 1966.

Of the many studies of the Nashville-based Southern Agrarians, this book contains the most thorough account of their regional ideology as well as an intelligent analysis of American regional theory in general. Valuable sections include "Agrarian Economic Thought," pp. 33–58, and "The Aesthetic of Regionalism," pp. 100–22.

1228. Kazin, Alfred. *On Native Grounds: An Interpretation of Modern American Prose Literature*. New York: Reynal and Hitchcock, 1942.

At the heart of this classic study of American literature is a sensitive account of the creative tension between cultural nationalism and regionalism. Especially important is "America! America!" pp. 485–518, an exuberant narrative of the discovery of meaning in the "indigenous" during the 1930s. This chapter stands as one of the most penetrating explanations of the regional impulse of the interwar decades.

1229. Kehde, Martha. "Regionalism in American Literature: A Bibliography." In *Regional Perspectives: An Examination of America's Literary Heritage*, edited by John Gordon Burke, 307–10. Chicago: American Library Association, 1973.

This fairly useful bibliography focuses upon classic regional literature rather than discussion of literary regionalism.

1230. Kemp, John C. *Robert Frost and New England: The Poet as Regionalist*. Princeton: Princeton Univ. Press, 1979.

A literary-biographical exploration of the evolution of Frost's regionalism. After a long period of exploration and expatriation, Frost became a poet "of New England," adopting a New England identity and subject matter. After 1915, he became a poet "in New England," living in New Hampshire and Vermont. Frost's best New England poems transcend local color writing in their complexity and universality. An appendix, pp. 237–81, supplies "A Chronological Listing of Commentary on Frost's Regionalism."

1231. King, Richard. *A Southern Renaissance: The Cultural Awakening of the American South, 1930–1955*. New York: Oxford Univ. Press, 1980.

King examines why the South experienced an efflorescence of creativity from the 1930s until the 1950s. He combines intellectual history, literature, and sociology in discussing such topics as the southern family romance, social thought in the 1930s, Faulkner in relationship to Allen Tate, Wilbur J. Cash, Lillian Smith, Walker Percy, and other recent writers and historians.

1232. Kolodny, Annette. *The Land Before Her: Fantasy and Experience of the American Frontiers, 1630–1860*. Chapel Hill: Univ. of North Carolina Press, 1984.

A vivid analysis of the private responses of pioneer women to forests and prairies and frontier environments in New England and the South, Texas and the Ohio Valley, California and Oregon, from the seventeenth to the nineteenth century. Describing the differences between male and female perceptions of the land, Kolodny concludes, in part, that "Massive exploitation and alteration of the continent do not seem to have been part of women's fantasies. They dreamed, more modestly, of locating a home and a familial community within a cultivated garden."

1233. ———. *The Lay of the Land: Metaphor as Experience and History in American Life and Letters*. Chapel Hill: Univ. of North Carolina Press, 1975.

An influential study of a central and consuming male response to the New World environment from Thomas Morton to Norman Mailer: the image of the land-as-woman and symbol of sexual fantasy. The largely negative implications of this environmental ethos are explored and the stage set for the analysis of female environmental responses in *The Land Before Her* (item 1232).

1234. Kramer, Dale. *Chicago Renaissance: Literary Life in the Midwest, 1900–1930.* New York: Appleton-Century-Crofts, 1966.

This aesthetic counterpart to Ray Ginger's *Altgeld's America* (1958) examines the flowering of midwestern literature in the work of eight Chicago-based writers: Floyd Dell, Theodore Dreiser, Sherwood Anderson, Carl Sandburg, Edgar Lee Masters, Vachel Lindsay, Harriet Monroe, and Margaret Anderson. For related studies, see Bernard Duffy, *The Chicago Renaissance in American Letters: A Critical History* (1954. Reprint. Westport, Conn.: Greenwood, 1972) and Carl S. Smith, *Chicago and the American Literary Imagination, 1880–1920* (Chicago: Univ. of Chicago Press, 1984) which, among other things, examines the image and meaning of the railroad, skyscraper, and stockyard in Chicago literature.

1235. Krauth, Leland. "Mark Twain: A Man For All Regions." *Studies in American Fiction* 13 (Autumn 1985): 239–46.

Assessing the strengths and weaknesses of regional interpretations of Twain's work, Krauth points out that four regions—the South, the West, the East, and the Midwest—have claimed Twain as their literary spokesman.

1236. Lauter, Paul, ed. *Reconstructing American Literature: Courses, Syllabi, Issues.* Old Westbury, N.Y.: Feminist Press, 1983.

An entire section of this anthology of course outlines is devoted to "Place and Region in American Literature," pp. 197–208. Also useful are two courses concerned with women and regional literature, pp. 194–96.

1237. Lawrence, D.H. *Studies in Classic American Literature.* 1923. Reprint. New York: Viking Press, 1961.

This often-cited, brilliantly idiosyncratic analysis of the American imagination contains an influential vision of the "white" man's sense of place in America. Every continent, every region, Lawrence argues, sustains a vital "spirit of place." In North America, the true spirit of place belongs to the Indians, not to the European interlopers. "The American landscape," he writes, "has never been at one with the white man. Never. And white men have probably never felt so bitter anywhere, as here in America, where the very landscape, in its very beauty, seems a bit devilish and grinning, opposed to us." Especially useful are "The Spirit of Place," pp. 1–8, and "Fenimore Cooper's Leatherstocking Novels," pp. 47–63. Further comments concerning the relationship between landscape and creativity are included in Edward G.

McDonald, ed., *Phoenix: The Posthumous Papers of D.H. Lawrence* (London: William Heinemann, 1936), section two, "Peoples, Countries, Races," pp. 71–147.

1238. Leary, Lewis. "Regionalism." In *Articles on American Literature*, 691–707. Durham: Duke Univ. Press, 1979.

An unusually thorough bibliography.

1239. Le Sueur, Meridel. "Proletarian Literature in the Middle West." In *American Writers' Congress*, edited by Henry Hart, 135–38. New York: International Publishers, 1935.

Echoing Benjamin Botkin, Jack Conroy, and Constance Rourke, Le Sueur argues that regional literature can go hand in hand with proletarian literature and that regionalism need not be the sole property of reactionaries. Le Sueur's classic portrait of the Upper Midwest, *North Star Country* (New York: Book Find Club, 1945), realizes this theme. A perceptive analysis of Le Sueur's on-going radical regionalism is Neala J. Schleuning's "Meridel Le Sueur: Toward a New Regionalism," *Books at Iowa* (Iowa City, 1980), pp. 37–41.

1240. Lewis, Wyndham. *America and Cosmic Man*. New York: Doubleday, 1949.

In "American Regionalism," "The Case Against Roots," and "Cosmic Society and Cosmic Man," pp. 178–81, 182–94, and 195–203, respectively, Lewis argues that a crowning glory of American culture is its vigorous, all-embracing sense of mobility and cosmopolitanism and its weak sense of region and place. "It is American to be open to all winds of heaven," he writes, "to be eclectic, promiscuous—universal.. Nobody will ever get anywhere in America by shutting himself up in a region, and trying to find *roots* there. . . ."

1241. Lindsay, Vachel. *Adventures While Preaching the Gospel of Beauty Together With Rhymes to be Traded For Bread, The Village Improvement Parade, and Selections from the Village Magazine*. Edited by Robert F. Sayre. New York: Eakins Press, 1968..

This anthology is a useful source for understanding Lindsay's notion of a "new localism." Ann Massa's *Vachel Lindsay: Field Worker for the American Dream* (Bloomington: Univ. of Indiana Press, 1970) contains an extended analysis of Lindsay's flamboyant regional schemes and theories.

1242. ———. *The Golden Book of Springfield*. New York: Macmillan, 1920.

Moving beyond literary regionalism, Lindsay combines his "new localism" with regional planning, utopian speculation, and Frank Lloyd Wright's architectural theories.

1243. Lutwack, Leonard. *The Role of Place in Literature*. Syracuse: Syracuse Univ. Press, 1984.

This richly detailed, wide-ranging study connects a fresh spatial-environmental sensitivity in literature with the "widespread recognition that earth as place ... is being radically changed and perhaps rendered uninhabitable by more and more pervasive and powerful technologies." Contains lucid, interdisciplinary essays on how essential properties of space—including sense of centrality, place and things, place and motion—are depicted in modern English and American literature as well as an extended discussion of the meaning of the metaphor of place and body. "Place and National Literature: The American and His Land," pp. 138–81, and "Placelessness: The Concern of Twentieth Century Literature," pp. 182–245, are particularly relevant to the current revival of regional themes in literature.

1244. MacGowan, Kenneth. *Footlights Across America: Toward a National Theater*. New York: Harcourt, Brace & Co., 1929.

MacGowan documents the fervor of the Little Theater movement of the 1920s, describing the need for a regional, decentralized theater as the foundation for a truly national vision. The historical roots of this movement are analyzed as well as the role of such dramatists as Frederick Koch, Percy MacKaye, and Paul Green. Especially valuable is "Toward a New Native Drama," pp. 200–18.

1245. MacLeod, Norman, ed. "Regionalism: A Symposium." *Sewanee Review* 39 (October-December 1931): 456–83.

This brief symposium contains three valuable articles: McLeod's introductory "Notes on Regionalism," which focuses upon developments in the Southwest; Helen Hill's "A Local Habitation," which provides a wide-ranging, cross-cultural summary of contemporary regional ideas and art forms; and Caroline B. Sherman's "Farm Life Fiction Reaches Maturity," which concentrates on the midwestern fiction of Hamlin Garland, Herbert Quick, Glenway Wescott, Willa Cather, and Ruth Suckow.

1246. McDowell, Tremaine. "Regionalism in American Literature." *Minnesota History* 20 (June 1939): 105–18.

Next to Benjamin Spencer's densely detailed essay (item 1291), McDowell's analysis remains the best introduction to the history and variety of American literary regionalism before World War II.

1247. McWilliams, Carey. *The New Regionalism in American Literature.* Chapbook No. 46. Seattle: Univ. of Washington, 1930.

Primarily a critique of Benjamin Botkin's efforts to cultivate a "new regionalism" in the Southwest, McWilliams's pamphlet also contains a valuable list of regional writers and centers of regionalism in the 1920s. McWilliams updated his critique in "Localism in American Criticism," *Southwest Review* 14 (July 1934), pp. 410–28.

1248. ———. *Southern California: An Island on the Land.* 1946. Reprint. Santa Barbara, Calif.: Peregrine Smith, 1979.

McWilliams's portrait of Southern California is a regional masterpiece comparable in scope and sensitivity to F.O. Matthiessen's, W.J. Cash's, and Walter Prescott Webb's classic studies of New England, the South, and the Great Plains. Although literary regionalism is not the primary focus of McWilliams's book, his narrative is sustained by a keen literary-aesthetic sensibility as well as a sharp social-political vision. The connections between artistic expression and regional myths are carefully explored in such chapters as "The Growth of a Legend," pp. 70–83 (regarding Helen Hunt Jackson and the Mission Myth), "The Island of Hollywood," pp. 330–49, and "A Slight Case of Cultural Confusion," pp. 350–70.

1249. Major, Mabel and T.M. Pearce. *Southwest Heritage: A Literary History with Bibliographies.* 3d rev. ed. Albuquerque: Univ. of New Mexico Press, 1972.

In addition to updating Dobie's *Guide* (item 1195), this book contains an extensive bibliography of Southwest literature, pp. 315–64. A glance at other studies, including Lawrence Clark Powell's *Southwest Classics* (1974), William T. Pilkington's *My Blood's Country: Studies in Southwestern Literature* (1973), and C.L. Sonnichsen's *The Southwest in Life and Literature* (1962), demonstrates the abundance of literary material related to this region.

1250. Mallory, William E. and Paul Simpson-Housley, eds. *Geography and Literature: A Meeting of Disciplines.* Syracuse: Syracuse Univ. Press, 1987.

The essays in this collection analyze the significance of place and region in American, Latin American, and European literature. Particularly relevant essays include Jim Wayne Miller's "Anytime the Ground Is Uneven: The Outlook for Regional Studies" (item 1253); Kenneth Mitchell's "Landscape and Literature," pp. 23–30; and essays on sense of place in the novels of Willa Cather and Harriet Arnow by Susan J. Rosowski and Joan Griffin, pp. 81–94 and 95–114, respectively.

1251. Meinig, D.W. "Geography as Art. " *Transactions, Institute of British Geographers*, New Series 8 (1983): 314–28.

A vigorous plea not only for the use of creative literature as a source of geographical knowledge but also for the creation of geographical analysis that is in itself a work of art. In the tradition of geographers John K. Wright, John Leighly, Christopher Salter, John Fraser Hart, and Yi-Fu Tuan, Meinig advocates the uses of the imagination and subjectivity in geography.

1252. Meyer, Roy W. *The Middlewestern Farm Novel in the Twentieth Century*. Lincoln: Univ. of Nebraska Press, 1954.

In some ways a companion volume to Hoffman, Allen, and Ulrich's *The Little Magazine*, Meyer's book documents the extensive revival of literary regionalism in the Midwest, especially during the 1920s and 1930s. Hundreds of regional novels are analyzed, and an extensive bibliography is included.

1253. Miller, Jim Wayne. "Anytime the Ground Is Uneven: The Outlook for Regional Studies and What to Look Out For." In *Geography and Literature: A Meeting of Disciplines* (item 1250), 1–20.

This essay, along with Richard Maxwell Brown's survey, annotated under History: Region as Concept (item 799), is a central manifesto of the "new regionalism" of the 1970s and 1980s. Miller traces the history of regional thought and sentiment in twentieth century America and argues that the time is ripe for the growth of a "cosmopolitan regionalism—a regional perspective which does not exclude a knowledge of the wider world, but is concerned with and appreciative of the little traditions within the great traditions of human history, and of ways in which small and great traditions are connected."

1254. Milton, John R. *The Novel of the American West*. Lincoln: Univ. of Nebraska Press, 1980.

Milton's discussion of the development of a distinctively western American literature in the twentieth century focuses upon the novels of Vardis Fisher, A.B. Guthrie, Frederick Manfred, Walter Van Tilburg Clark, Harvey Fergusson, and Frank Waters. "The Writer's West," pp. 41–64, contains a perceptive analysis of the relationship between sense of place and creativity in the West as well as a useful discussion of the differences between eastern and western fiction.

1255. ———— , ed. "The Realities of Regionalism: A Symposium." *South Dakota Review* 18 (Winter 1981).

This issue contains useful essays on regional writing, especially in the Great Plains and the West. Included are Lois Phillips Hudson's "'A Sweet Little Nest Somewhere in the West'," pp. 7–16; Gilbert Fite's "Regionalism: The Historical Perspective," pp. 17–38 (see History: Region as Concept, item 806); William Stafford's "The Realities of Regionalism," pp. 54–63; Frederick Manfred's "Usable Wests," pp. 64–80; and a panel discussion among the four contributors.

1256. ————. ed. "The Writer's Sense of Place." *South Dakota Review* 13 (August 1975).

The comments and short essays of more than fifty writers and painters regarding the meaning of place and region to their art are gathered here. Gary Snyder, William Stafford, Wallace Stegner, Frederick Manfred, Frank Waters, Grace Paley, Erskine Caldwell, James T. Farrell, Andrew Nelson Lytle, and others provide vivid remarks concerning the uses and abuses of sense of place and regionalism.

1257. Morris, Wright. *The Territory Ahead.* New York: Harcourt, Brace, 1959.

A probing analysis of how two pervasive themes—the beckoning raw material of a new landscape and the retreat to a mythic natural past—have enhanced as well as thwarted American writers from Thoreau, Whitman, Melville, and Twain to Hemingway, Wolfe, Fitzgerald, and Faulkner. Important discussions of the "ravages of raw material," the lure of nostalgia, and the eclipse of genuine regionalism are found in the opening chapters "Technique and Raw Material," pp. 3–17, and "The Mythic Past," pp. 19–36. Many of these themes are further developed in Morris's *Earthly Delights, Unearthly Adornments: American Writers as Image Makers* (New York: Harper and Row, 1978).

1258. Nolan, Paul T., ed. *Provincial Drama in America, 1870–1916: A Casebook of Primary Materials*. Metuchen, N.J.: Scarecrow Press, 1967.

A survey of more than forty thousand largely unperformed American plays copyrighted between 1870 and 1916. Nolan contends that this massive body of "lost plays of provincial America" represents a neglected source for understanding late Victorian American culture. Plays from nearly every state of the union are listed as well as detailed suggestions for further study. For a closely related study, see Carl F.W. Larson, *American Regional Theatre History to 1900: A Bibliography* (Metuchen, N.J.: Scarecrow Press, 1972).

1259. Norwood, Vera and Janice Monk, eds. *The Desert Is No Lady: Southwestern Landscapes in Women's Writing and Art*. New Haven: Yale Univ. Press, 1987.

This wide-ranging anthology contains essays concerning the regional sensibilities of novelist Willa Cather, photographers Nancy Newhall and Laura Gilpin, and artists Georgia O'Keefe, Nancy Holt, and Michelle Stuart. Other subjects include the sense of landscape found in frontier women's narratives, Chicano and Hispanic literature, and the creative expression of southwestern Indian women. Norwood and Monk's "Introduction: Perspectives on Gender and Landscape," pp. 1–9, is an impressive, interdisciplinary overview of the literature on gender, place, and regional landscape. For a closley related source, see Janice Monk, "Approaches to the Study of Women and Landscape," *Environmental Review* 8 (Spring 1984), pp. 23–33.

1260. O'Connor, Flannery. "The Regional Writer." In *Mystery and Manners: Occasional Prose*, edited by Sally and Robert Fitzgerald, 51–59. New York: Farrar, Straus, and Giroux, 1961.

Paralleling C. Vann Woodward's argument in "The Irony of Southern History," O'Connor suggests that the South has more than its share of good writers because as Southerners "we have all had our Fall. We have gone into the modern world with an inburnt knowledge of human limitations and with a sense of mystery which could not have been developed in our first state of innocence—as it has not sufficiently developed in the rest of the country." See John F. Desmond's "Flannery O'Connor's Sense of Place," *Southern Humanities Review* 10 (Summer 1976), pp. 251–58, for critical commentary.

1261. Odum, Howard W. "American Blend: Regional Diversity and National Unity." *Saturday Review of Literature* 32 (August 6, 1949):

92, 96, 169–72. Reprinted in *Folk, Region, and Society: Selected Papers of Howard W. Odum*, edited by Katharine Jocher et al., 192–201. Chapel Hill: Univ. of North Carolina Press, 1964.

A vivid roll call of regional fiction is at the heart of Odum's effort to describe regionalism as an essential component of healthy nationalism and global harmony. Other works by Odum are listed under Sociology, items 1607–1611.

1262. ———. "On Southern Literature and Southern Culture." In *The Literature of the Modern South.* edited by Lois D. Rubin and Robert W. Jacobs. Baltimore: Johns Hopkins Univ. Press, 1953. Reprinted in *Folk, Region, and Society: Selected Papers of Howard W. Odum*, edited by Katharine Jocher, et al., 202–18. Chapel Hill: Univ. of North Carolina Press.

Rising to Donald Davidson's challenge to develop a socio-economic explanation of southern literary renaissance, Odum discusses qualities of southern folk-regional culture that have sparked and haunted the imagination.

1263. Odum, Howard W. and Harry E. Moore. "Culture Regions: Literary and Aesthetic Regionalism." In *American Regionalism: A Cultural-Historical Approach to National Integration*, 168–87. New York: Henry Holt, 1938.

In addition to guiding the reader through the debates over literary regionalism in the 1930s, Odum and Moore list regional fiction from each of their six basic American regions. Sifting through the book titles listed in *Publishers Weekly* between 1927 and 1936, they uncovered more than two thousand volumes with regional titles. New England had by far the most titles, followed by the Northwest with its "westerns," the South, the Midwest, the Southwest, and the Far West.

1264. Olson, Charles. *Call Me Ishmael: A Study of Melville*. San Francisco: City Lights Books, 1947.

Within this idiosyncratic, powerful insightful study of *Moby-Dick* is an important analysis of the impact of American space and place upon the American psyche and creative imagination. "I take SPACE to be the central fact to man born in America, from Folsom cave to now," Olson argues. "I spell it large because it comes large here. Large, and without mercy." This is one among many of Olson's works profoundly shaped by sensitivity to place.

1265. Ransom, John Crowe. "The Aesthetic of Regionalism." *American Review* 2 (December 1933): 290–310. Reprinted in *Selected Essays of John Crowe Ransom*, edited by Thomas Daniel Young and John Hindle, 45–58. Baton Rouge: Louisiana State Univ. Press, 1984.

Ransom eloquently describes the connections between the aesthetic and economic principles of the Southern Agrarians and the New Mexico regionalists.

1266. ———. "Happy Farmers." *American Review* 1 (October 1933): 513–35.

Obviously a poet's venture into economic theory, this rhapsodic and utopian essay captures much of the spirit of Southern Agrarianism and provides a link with the economic and aesthetics of the New Mexico regionalists. For closely related sources see: Twelve Southerners, Karanikas, John Stewart, Tate, and Warren (items 1309, 1227, 1300, 1303–1304, 1314) in this chapter; Agar and Tate, Cauley, Crichton et al., and Hoepfner under Economics (items 313, 327, 330, 350); Rock and Smith under American Studies (items 32, 45–48).

1267. Rawlings, Marjorie Kinnan. "Regional Literature in the South." *College English* 1 (February 1940): 381–89.

Like her fellow southern writers, such as Robert Penn Warren, James Agee, and Wendell Berry, Rawlings vigorously condemns the faddish, exploitative quality of most of what passes for "regional literature." "Regionalism written on purpose," she asserts, "is perhaps as spurious a form of literary expression as ever reaches print. It is not even a decent bastard, for back of illegitimacy is usually a simple, if ill-timed, honesty." Only a few writers—including Ellen Glasgow, Julia Peterkin, and Zora Neale Hurston—have avoided these pitfalls to produce an honest "native regionalism" in the South.

1268. Reigelman, Milton R. *The Midland: A Venture in Literary Regionalism.* Iowa City: Univ. of Iowa Press, 1975.

An ably written study of an important force in literary regionalism in the early twentieth century: John T. Frederick and his Iowa-based little magazine, *The Midland* (1915–1933). Especially useful is "Editorial Policy—Regionalism," pp. 41–74, which compares *The Midland's* version of regionalism—especially the encouragement it gave to black and Native American literature—to the many regional movements and magazines of the period.

1269. Robbins, William G., Robert J. Frank, and William E. Ross, eds. *Regionalism in the Pacific Northwest*. Corvallis: Oregon State Univ. Press, 1983.

Two essays in this useful anthology perceptively discuss literary regionalism in general and the literature of the Northwest in particular. Richard Maxwell Brown's "The New Regionalism in America, 1970–1981," pp. 37–97, discusses, among other things, the regional work of Gary Snyder, Tom Robbins, Ivan Doig, and others. Edwin R. Bingham's "Pacific Northwest Writing: Reaching for Regional Identity," pp. 151–74, focuses upon the literature of William L. Adams, Charles Erskine Scott Woods, H.L. Davis, and Richard Hugo.

1270. Rothfork, John. "The Failure of Southwest Regionalism." *South Dakota Review* 19 (Winter 1982): 85–99.

Rothfork argues that despite the achievements of writers like Oliver La Farge, Frank Waters, or William Eastlake, southwestern writing remains largely a literature of local color rather than regionalism. This "new kind of local color" is characterized by "a broad romanticism and rose-hued appreciation of Native American and Hispanic life. But it is local color nonetheless."

1271. Rovit, Earl. "Region Versus Nation: Critical Battle in the Thirties." *Mississippi Quarterly* 8 (Spring 1960): 89–98.

Rovit examines regionalism as a literary cause that began in the 1920s and crested in a storm of controversy in the 1930s.

1272. Rubin, Louis D., ed. *The American South: Portrait of a Culture*. Baton Rouge: Louisiana State Univ. Press, 1980.

A skillfully edited collection of essays, broad-ranging but emphasizing literature. In the lead essay for Part One, Rubin surveys the historical roots of southern distinctiveness and stresses that separate southern identity remains in the present. Part Two treats contemporary southern society in terms of demographics, politics, religion, outdoor recreation, stock car racing, country music, and a resurgence of southern identity. Part Three examines regional literature, with essays on Twain, Caldwell, Faulkner, the Agrarians, as well as particular literary themes.

1273. ———, ed. *A Bibliographic Guide to the Study of Southern Literature*. Baton Rouge: Louisiana State Univ. Press, 1969.

Rubin's richly detailed guide is divided into two parts. Part One contains some twenty-three bibliographical essays on general topics such as the negro in southern literature, the South in northern eyes, agrarian themes, local color, southern folklore, and popular literature. Part Two contains bibliographies for more than 130 southern writers from John Smith to Walker Percy.

1274. ———, ed. *The History of Southern Literature.* Baton Rouge: Louisiana State Univ. Press, 1985.

The sixty-eight essays included here add a narrative and analytical dimension to Rubin's earlier *Bibliographic Guide* (annotated above.) Insightful essays include Fred Hobson on "The Rise of the Critical Temper," Herschel Gower on "Regions and Rebels," and Thomas Daniel Young on "The Agrarians," as well as analyses of Mark Twain, Kate Chopin, William Faulkner, Thomas Wolfe, Richard Wright, James Agee, Eudora Welty, William Styron, Ralph Ellison, Truman Capote, and other southern writers. Rubin's "Scholarship in Southern Literature: Its History and Recent Developments," *American Studies International* 21 (April 1983), pp. 3–34, is a useful summary of this vast subject.

1275. Salter, Christopher. "Signatures and Settings: One Approach to Landscape in Literature." In *Dimensions of Human Geography: Essays on Some Familiar and Neglected Themes.* Research Paper no. 186, edited by Karl W. Butzer, 69–83. Chicago: Univ. of Chicago, Department of Geography.

A plea for the use of creative literature in geographical teaching and research. Spatially sensitive fiction, Salter argues, enhances environmental sensitivity and understanding of various cultural "signatures" upon the land.

1276. Salter, Christopher and William J. Lloyd. *Landscape in Literature.* Resource Paper for College Geography no. 76–3. Washington, D.C.: Association of American Geographers, 1977.

Although written primarily to add an imaginative dimension to the teaching of cultural geography, this monograph, like Coan and Lilliard's bibliography (item 1185), provides an abundance of literary images for particular environments including landscapes of settlement, agriculture, livelihood, sacred space, transportation, home and garden, and entertainment. Examples are largely drawn from twentieth century American literature.

1277. Sillitoe, Alan. "A Sense of Place." *Geographical Magazine* 47 (August 1975): 685–89..

Sillitoe recalls the relationship between sense of place and his development as a creative writer. He also argues that a sense of place is a prerequisite for a sense of community. "I have always felt," he writes, "that real love begins with one's feeling for the earth, and that if you do not have this love, then you cannot begin to love people."

1278. Simpson, Lewis P. *The Dispossessed Garden: Pastoral and History in Southern Literature.* Athens: Univ. of Georgia Press, 1975.

Paralleling Leo Marx and Raymond Williams, Simpson examines southern versions of the pastoral myth of America as a new Garden of Eden. Attempts "to reconcile slavery with pastoral pieties" by Thomas Jefferson, John P. Kennedy, William Gilmore Simms, and other antebellum writers are discussed as well as the meaning of the pastoral for such twentieth century writers as William Faulkner, Allen Tate, Robert Penn Warren, and William Styron.

1279. ———. *The Man of Letters in New England and the South: Essays on the History of the Literary Vocation in America.* Baton Rouge: Louisiana State Univ. Press, 1973.

Like Randall Stewart, Simpson skillfully relates the creative imaginations of New England and the South. The most useful essays regarding literary regionalism in general are "The Southern Novelist and Southern Nationalism," pp. 201–28, which brilliantly compares the myth of New England as a "redemptive community" that culminated in the mid-nineteenth century with the southern literary consciousness that flowered after the First World War; and "The Southern Writer and the Great Literary Secession," pp. 229–55, which analyzes the Southern Agrarians and their use of that "species of American nationalism known as regionalism." Simpson continues many of these themes in *The Brazen Face of History: Studies in Literary Consciousness* (Baton Rouge: Louisiana State Univ. Press, 1980) by discussing, among other things, the functions of the pastoral mode and sense of history in southern writing.

1280. Snyder, Gary. *Earth House Hold.* New York: New Directions, 1969.

Especially relevant to literary regionalism is "Poetry and the Primitive: Notes on Poetry as an Ecological Survival Technique," pp. 117–30, an impressionistic discussion of poetry as a medium for renewing a holistic sense of nature.

1281. ————. *The Old Ways*. San Francisco: City Lights Books, 1977.

Three of the essays in this anthology are vital discussions of the relationship between creative literature, sense of place, and the bioregional movement. "The Politics of Ethnopoetics," pp. 15–43, examines the ecological insights of "primitive" poetry and lore. "Re-Inhabitation," pp. 57–66, argues the need for renewed sense of region and place in the modern world. "The Incredible Survival of Coyote," pp. 67–93, points to the enduring relevance of native American environmental perception as a possible source for American regionalism and regional expression in the future. The West, he predicts, will be the source of a fresh regional vision grounded in ecological knowledge and American Indian lore—a regional literature depicting far more than the European conquest and exploitation of an alien land. For a closely related source, see Peter Berg, ed., *Reinhabiting a Separate Country: A Bioregional Anthology for Northern California* (San Francisco: Planet Drum Foundation, 1978).

1282. ————. *The Real Work: Interviews and Talks, 1964–1979*. Edited by William Scott McLean. New York: New Directions, 1980.

At least three interviews abound with regional insights. "On Earth Geography," pp. 23–30, reveal Snyder's deep understanding of the regional theories of Alfred Kroeber, Raymond Dasmann, Carl Sauer, and others. "The Bioregional Ethic," pp. 138–58, is an important summary of the sources of the bioregional movement. "Poetry, Community & Climax," pp. 159–74, eloquently promotes poetry that evokes sense of place, community and bioregional consciousness—a return to a "healthy side of the original American vision." Locally rooted, environmentally attuned poetry, Snyder argues, can encourage "new definitions of territory and region, and fresh ways to see local government—watershed politics, bioregion consciousness. Sense of community begins to include woodpeckers and cottontails. Decentralization includes the decentralization of 'culture,' poetry." For other bioregional sources, see Bookchin, Capra and Spretnak, Sale, and Special Issues under Political Science (items 1410–1411, 1412, 1460–1462, 1470–1471) as well as Devall and Sessions under Philosophy and Religion (item 1342).

1283. Special Issue. *Southwest Review* 14 (Summer 1929).

The entire issue is devoted to discussions of Southwestern literary regionalism, containing valuable comments by Mary Austin, Stanley Vestal, J. Frank Dobie, Howard Mumford Jones, B.A. Botkin, and others. Later issues of the *Southwest Review*, especially volume 19 (July 1934), contain important essays by Henry Nash Smith (items 45–48), Carey McWilliams, and John Gould Fletcher (item 1208).

1284. Special Issue. *New Mexico Quarterly* 4 (May 1934).

This issue contains essays on the New England poetry of Frost and Robinson, on southern literature by John Crowe Ransom, on northwestern literature by H.G. Merriam, and on southwestern art by T.M. Pearce.

1285. Special Issue. *New Mexico Quarterly* 5 (February 1935).

This issue focuses upon southwestern folk arts and regionalism with valuable essays by Dudley Wynn, "The Southwestern Regional Straddle," pp. 7–14, and Phillip Stevenson, "The Outlook for Folk Art," pp. 40–47. The next issue of *New Mexico Quarterly* focused upon economic-political aspects of southwestern regionalism. See Crichton et al. under Economics (item 330).

1286. Special Issue. *Virginia Quarterly Review* 11 (April 1935).

This issue includes six important essays on southern literary regionalism: Allen Tate's "The Profession of Letters in the South," pp. 161–76; John Crowe Ransom's "Modern With the Southern Accent," pp. 184–200; John Donald Wade's "Old Wine in a New Bottle," pp. 239–52; Stark Young's "Encaustics For Southerners," pp. 264–80; and Cleanth Brooks's "The Modern Southern Poet and Tradition," pp. 305–20.

1287. Special Issue. "Regionalism: Pro and Con." *Saturday Review of Literature* 15 (November 28, 1936).

Largely devoted to debating the strengths and weaknesses of regionalism—see Baker, Beath, and DeVoto, above—this remains the most useful of the several special regional issues of this magazine during the 1930s and 1940s.

1288. Special Issue. "Sense of Place: Mississippi." *The Southern Quarterly* 17 (Spring/Summer 1979).

This issue contains twenty-four essays examining a wide range of regional and place related issues, including Mississippi's contributions to literature and music and the role of preservation and planning in perpetuating sense of place. Vital essays on regionalism and sense of place, paralleling those gathered by John R. Milton (item 1255), are

Willie Morris's "A Sense of Place and the Americanization of Mississippi," Will D. Campbell's "Staying Home or Leaving," and Pierce Lewis's magnificent "Defining a Sense of Place," pp. 3–13, 14–23, and 24–46, respectively.

1289. Special Issue. "A Stubborn Sense of Place: Writers and Writings on the South." *Harper's* 273 (August 1986): 35–45.

Nine contemporary southern fiction writers discuss the impact of the Sun Belt South upon their art. Also see "Naming the Land: Poetic Variations on an American Theme," *Harper's* 269 (August 1984), pp. 37–49, for a collection of contemporary poetry concerning place and region.

1290. Spencer, Benjamin F. "Nationality Through Region and Locale, 1815–1892." In *The Quest for Nationality: An American Literary Campaign*, 252–89. Syracuse: Syracuse Univ. Press, 1957.

An insightful account of the largely creative relationship between regional and national sentiments in American literature, from the New England renaissance to the end of the century local colorists. Spencer pushed this analysis into the early twentieth century in "Nationality During the Interregnum," *American Literature* 32 (January 1961), pp. 434–45.

1291. ———. "Regionalism in American Literature." In *Regionalism in America* (item 820), 219–61.

The best single discussion of American literary regionalism in print, Spencer's essay has broad historical sweep as well as impressive critical depth. It is an indispensable source.

1292. Sper, Felix. *From Native Roots: A Panorama of Our Regional Drama*. Caldwell, Idaho: Caxton Printers, 1948.

Heavily influenced by the work of Benjamin Botkin, Percy MacKaye, Lynn Riggs, and Paul Green, this lively book evokes much of the regional enthusiasm of the interwar decades. In addition to describing thirteen folk-drama regions, Sper's book contains an impressive bibliography of regional literature, drama, and folklore.

1293. Spiller, Robert E. et al. *Literary History of the United States*. 3 vols. 3d rev. ed. New York: MacMillian, 1963.

Especially useful is the section on the rise of literary regionalism, pp. 843–77 of Volume One. Bibliographical guides to regional literature are located on pp. 304–25 of Volume Two and pp. 62–64 of Volume Three.

1294. Stafford, William. "Regionalism, Localism, and Art," "The Fiction of Not Being Local," and "Starting With Little Things" (poem). *South Dakota Review* 13 (Autumn 1975): 47–48.

Part of a symposium on "The Writer's Sense of Place" (item 1255), these three items succinctly express Stafford's belief in the universality of local and regional experience. Further reflections on regionalism by Stafford are found in Lars Nordstrom, "Willingly Local: A Conversation With William Stafford About Regionalism and Northwest Poetry," *Studia Neophilogica: A Journal of Germanic and Romance Languages and Literature* 59 (1987), pp. 41–63. An extensive bibliography of work by and about Stafford is included with the interview.

1295. Stegner, Wallace. "Myth, History, and Western Literature" In *The Sound of Mountain Water*, 186–201. Garden City, New York: Doubleday, 1969.

This influential essay compares western, midwestern, and southern regional expressions and then focuses upon factors that have inhibited the full development of regional literature in the West. In addition to analyzing the impact of mobility and pluralism upon regional writing, Stegner, like Wright Morris, criticizes the tendency of western authors to separate the past from the present to despise contemporary life and glorify the pioneer past. Other important essays in this book include "Coda: Wilderness Letter," pp. 145–53 and Stegner's discussion of three western writers: Bret Harte, Willa Cather, and Bernard De Voto, pp. 223–75.

1296. Stegner, Wallace and Richard W. Etulain. *Conversations With Wallace Stegner on Western History and Literature*. Salt Lake City: Univ. of Utah Press, 1983.

Looking back over fifty years of regional writing, Stegner comments upon such subjects as environmentalism, sense of place, and the significance of regional expression in the West. For further discussions of Stegner's contributions to regional aesthetics, see the tribute to the author in the *South Dakota Review* 23 (Winter 1985). Of the nine essays in this special issue, James D. Houston's "Wallace Stegner: Universal Truths Rooted in a Region," pp. 6–10, and Wendell Berry's "Wallace Stegner and the Great Community," pp.10–19, contain the most perceptive discussions of literary regionalism.

1297. Stein, Gertrude. *The Geographical History of America: or The Relation of Human Nature to the Human Mind*. New York: Random House, 1936.

A meditation upon literature with intermittent attention to America and geography. Among other things, Stein asserts that the experience of living in a vast and flat land invites abstraction and wandering and has the effect of "loosing" the individual from the usual preoccupation with the vagaries of human nature. Memorable epigrams include "In the United States there is more space where nobody is than where anybody is" and "Think not the way the land looks but the way it lies that is now connected with the human mind." Many of Stein's observations on American places and regions are gathered in Robert Bartlett Haas, ed., *How Writing is Written: The Previously Uncollected Writings of Gertrude Stein*. vol. 2 (Los Angeles: Black Sparrow Press, 1974), especially in the section, "America," pp. 67–105.

1298. Stewart, George R. "The Regional Approach to Literature." *College English* 9 (April 1948): 370–75.

A vigorous appeal for the necessity of regional literature and "an intelligent provincialism" in the modern world.

1299. ———. *U.S. 40: Cross Section*. Boston: Houghton-Mifflin, 1953.

This is a pioneer treatment of highway landscape, tracing what can be seen from U.S. 40 at intervals across the country, using written descriptions and photographs. An effective follow-up study, tracing Stewart's path and comparing scenes then and now is Thomas R. Vale and Geraldine R. Vale, *U.S. 40 Today* (Madison: Univ. of Wisconsin Press, 1983). Another spin-off from Stewart's book is Thomas J. Schlereth, *U.S. 40: A Roadscape of the American Experience* (Indianapolis: Indiana Historical Society, 1985), which, although focused upon Indiana, goes beyond Stewart's book in its historical reach and its bibliography on "The Road in American Life."

1300. Stewart, John L. *The Burden of Time: The Fugitive and Agrarians*. Princeton, N.J.: Princeton Univ. Press, 1965.

Along with Alexander Karanikas's *Tillers of a Myth* (item 1227), this is a most thorough study of the regional ideology of such Southern Agrarians as John Crowe Ransom, Allen Tate, Donald Davidson, Robert Penn Warren, and others. Especially useful are "Toward Agrarianism," pp. 91–171, and "Agrarianism and After," pp. 172–205.

1301. Stewart, Randall. *Regionalism and Beyond: Essays of Randall Stewart.* Edited by George Core. Nashville: Vanderbilt Univ. Press, 1968.

The most valuable portions of this book for a general understanding of American regionalism are Stewart's discussions of regional consciousness in New England and the South, particularly his vivid comparison of Hawthorne's and Faulkner's senses of place. See "Hawthorne and Faulkner," pp. 126–35, "Regional Characteristics in the Literature of New England," pp. 143–61, "The Relationship Between Fugitives and Agrarians," pp. 234–40, "Donald Davidson," pp. 241–54, and "The Outlook for Southern Writing," pp. 255–66. A complete bibliography of Stewart's work is included.

1302. Suckow, Ruth. "The Folk Idea in American Life." *Scribner's Magazine* 88 (September 1930): 245–55.

This eloquent discussion of the rise of interest in the American land and folk during the 1920s contains vital observations concerning the relationship between folk-regional and nationwide mass culture.

1303. Tate, Allen. "The New Provincialism." *Virginia Quarterly Review* 21 (April 1945): 262–72. Reprinted in *Collected Essays*, 282–93. Denver: Swallow Press, 1959.

Tate prophesizes that one of the most important consequences of the Second World War will be the decline of creative regional consciousness and the domination of a parochial internationalism lacking any unifying sense of civility. The advent of this arrogant internationalism—a worldwide "new provincialism"—is irreversible and must be understood by contemporary writers. Such somber realism contrasts sharply with Tate's earlier declaration that "Only a return to the provinces, to the small self-contained centers of life, will put the all-destroying abstraction America, safely to rest," in his "American Poetry Since 1920," *Bookman* 58 (1929), p. 508.

1304. ———. "Regionalism and Sectionalism." *New Republic* 69 (December 23, 1931): 158–61.

Applying the distinction between regionalism and sectionalism to art, Tate contends that "Sectionalism is a doctrine, philosophical at its rare best, at its worst propaganda. . . . Regionalism is, or should be, self-contained and unaware of whatever value it may have." A year earlier, in *I'll Take My Stand* (1930), he had committed himself to a self-conscious sectional doctrine—a political and economic stance he refined along with Herbert Agar in *Who Owns America? A New Declaration of Independence* (1936), annotated under Economics (item 313).

1305. Tichi, Cecelia. *New World, New Earth: Environmental Reform in American Literature From the Puritans Through Whitman*. New Haven: Yale Univ. Press, 1979.

Tichi traces the zeal with which Americans have literally "reformed" their continent to the Puritan belief that such activities were necessary to transform the New World into the utopian New Earth envisioned in Revelation. Contrary to many scholars, Tichi locates a positive strain in this tradition of stewardship and wise intervention as it was initiated by the New England Puritans and last expressed by Olmsted, Marsh, and Whitman. Tichi has continued her study of the American urge for environmental mastery in *Shifting Gears: Technology, Literature, and Culture in Modern America* (Chapel Hill: Univ. of North Carolina Press, 1987).

1306. Toth, Emily, ed. *Regionalism and the Female Imagination: A Collection of Essays*. New York: Human Services Press, 1985.

The eleven essays in this collection—essays formerly published in the *Kate Chopin Newsletter*—examine the work of women regional writers in New England, the Midwest, the Appalachians, the South, Mormon Country, and Canada. Writers discussed include Sarah Orne Jewett, Mary E. Wilkins Freeman, Lisel Mueller, Harriet Arnow, and Alice Dunbar-Nelson. A useful bibliography is included.

1307. Tower, Robert. "Good Pix From Stix." *New York Review of Books* 31 (May 31, 1984): 35–36.

A generally positive review of the resurgence of rural or "country" novels in the early 1980s.

1308. Tuan, Yi-Fu. "Literature and Geography: Implications for Geographical Research." In *Humanistic Geography: Prospects and Problems*, edited by David Ley and Marwyn S. Samuels, 194–206. Chicago: Maaroufa Press, 1978.

Tuan convincingly argues three basic points: "geographical writing should have greater literary quality, literature is a source material for geographers, and literature provides a perspective for how people experience their world." For a closely related discussion, see Tuan's "Literature, Experience, and Environmental Knowing," in *Environmental Knowing: Theories, Research and Methods*

(Stroudsburg, Penn.: Dowden, Hutchinson, and Ross, 1976) pp. 260–72.

1309. Twelve Southerners. *I'll Take My Stand: The South and the Agrarian Tradition*. New York: Harper and Brothers, 1930.

This famous work begins with a manifesto on behalf of the Southern Agrarian order at the onset of the Great Depression. Vigorously written, often cited essays discuss politics, economics, literature and the arts, religion and race as evidence of a Southern Agrarian alternative to the national industrial "dispensation." The contributors—who included John Crowe Ransom, Allen Tate, Andrew Lytle, Robert Penn Warren, Donald Davidson, Stark Young, and others—went on to distinguished literary careers and have made important contributions to American regional theory. *Fifteen Southerners, Why the South Will Survive* (Athens: Univ. of Georgia Press, 1981), commemorating the fiftieth anniversary of *I'll Take My Stand*, imitates the original and proclaims its present relevance.

1310. Von Frank, Albert J. *The Sacred Game: Provincialism and Frontier Consciousness in American Literature, 1630–1860*. New York: Cambridge Univ. Press, 1985.

Von Frank analyzes how the transit of culture from Europe to America and the frontier experience shaped American creative expression from the seventeenth to the nineteenth century. The tension between two perspectives—an enduring provincial mentality and a more rigorous frontier consciousness—is traced in the words of Anne Bradstreet, Royall Tyler, Timothy Dwight, Hawthorne, Fuller, Emerson, and others.

1311. Walcutt, Charles C. "The Regional Novel and Its Future." *Arizona Quarterly* 1 (Summer 1945): 17–27.

After describing the dialectic between literary nationalism and regionalism in the nineteenth and twentieth centuries, Walcutt defines three types of contemporary regionalism: the "polemical regionalism" of many southern and western writers, the "unconscious regionalism" of writers like Robert Penn Warren and Ole Rolvaag, and the "decentralism" of regional planners and sociologists. Truly distinguished regional novels, such as Rolvaag's *Giants in the Earth* or Warren's *At Heaven's Gate*, can be achieved only by the avoidance of self-conscious polemics or politics.

1312. ———. " Regionalism—Practical or Aesthetic?" *Sewanee Review* 49 (1941): 165–72.

Using the literature of New England's "Golden Day" as an example, Walcutt argues that the finest aesthetic regionalism is the unself-conscious and is directed outward toward the rest of the world. While "one can be aesthetically regional only by not trying to be so," practical regionalism—e.g., planning and sociology—must be deliberate and focused.

1313. Warren, Austin. "Regional Retrospective." *American Review* 8 (December 1936): 245–51.

In the same manner that Southerner Donald Davidson or Westerner Bernard Voto were drawn to New England's firm sense of itself, New Englander Austin Warren explains how "We in New England have looked with some envy upon the alert movement in progress among our brethren of Nashville and its circumjacent South."

1314. Warren, Robert Penn. "Some Don'ts for Literary Regionalists." *American Review* 8 (October 1936): 142–50.

Although appreciating what Allen Tate called "the immediate organic sense of life in which a fine artist lives," Warren describes how regional writing can easily lapse into the repetition of simple-minded formulas.

1315. Watkins, Floyd C. *In Time and Place: Some Origins of American Fiction*. Athens: Univ. of Georgia Press, 1977.

Watkins discusses the cultural, historical, and geographical backgrounds of eight important American novels: the Oklahoma and California settings of *The Grapes of Wrath*; the southern plantation in *Gone With the Wind* and *The Confessions of Nat Turner*; Nebraska in *My Antonia* and New Mexico in *Death Comes for the Archbishop*; the Jemez Pueblo in *House Made of Dawn*; Mississippi in *As I Lay Dying*; and rural Minnesota in *Main Street*. The erosion of a sense of place and community in twentieth century America is a common theme of this body of literature.

1316. Welty, Eudora. "Place in Fiction." In *The Eye of the Story: Selected Essays and Reviews*, 116–33. New York: Random House, 1978.

Avoiding the treacherous and worn meanings of the word "regional," Welty prefers to examine the meaning of place for herself as a writer as well as for authors such as Flaubert and Faulkner. In words that underscore much of the purpose and significance of regional studies, she writes: "it is by knowing where you stand that you are able to judge where you are. Place absorbs our earliest notice and attention, it bestows on us our original awareness; and our critical powers spring up from the study of it and the growth of experience inside it. It perseveres in bringing us back to earth when we fly too high. It never really stops informing us, for it is forever astir, alive, changing, reflecting, like the mind of man itself. One place comprehended can make us understand other places better. Sense of place gives equilibrium; extended, it is sense of direction too.... It is the sense of place going with us still that is the ball of golden thread to carry us there and back and in every sense of the word to bring us home."

1317. Western Literature Association. *A Literary History of the American West*. Fort Worth: Texas Christian Univ. Press, 1987.

This massive compendium of more than eighty original essays is an essential resource for studying western creative expression. Part One, "Encountering the West," surveys basic expressive forms and genres of the West with essays concerning native oral traditions, folklore, adventure narratives, nature essays, and the western novel and film. Part Two, "Settled In: Many Wests," contains essays on the literature of four subregions: the Far West, the Southwest, the Midwest, and the Rocky Mountains. Some forty writers are separately analyzed, including Mary Austin, Theodore Roethke, William Stafford, and Gary Snyder from the Far West; Paul Horgan, Edward Abbey, and Larry McMurtry from the Southwest; Ole Rolvaag, Willa Cather, Wright Morris, and Robert Bly from the Midwest; and Bernard De Voto, Frank Waters, and Wallace Stegner from the Rocky Mountains. Part Three, "Rediscovering the West," examines contemporary developments in western creativity, particularly an emphasis upon popular culture and cultural pluralism. Useful bibliographies accompany every essay.

1318. Whipple, Thomas King. *Spokesmen*. 1928. Reprint. Berkeley: Univ. of California Press, 1963.

Paralleling efforts of Van Wyck Brooks, Lewis Mumford, and Constance Rourke (see items 4, 14, 33–35), Whipple's essays document an emerging interest in the land and folk and regional culture during the 1920s. Whipple's discussions of such literary "spokesmen" as E.A. Robinson, Robert Frost, Theodore Dreiser, Sherwood Anderson, Carl Sandburg, Vachel Lindsay, Sinclair Lewis, and Willa

Cather abound with a keen sense of the creative influence of New England, the Midwest, and the Great Plains.

1319. ———. *Study Out the Land*. 1943. Reprint, New York: Books for Libraries Press, 1971.

More effectively than perhaps any other literary critic, Whipple uses creative literature to elucidate the often tenuous relationship between Americans and their land. Especially insightful are "The American Predicament," "The American Land," and "The Myth of the Old West," pp. 31–41, 43–57, and 59–68, respectively. "The story of the American people," he writes, "is the story of the process of interaction between the American country and the foreign heritage of the American people.... Our desires must be accommodated to geography and climate; we must accept the spirit of the materials in which we work, for the shape, and the lines, of the nation to be are already implicit in the soil. We, the people, need remaking worse than the land does."

1320. Wilbur, Richard. Introduction to *A Sense of Place: The Artist and the American Land*, by Alan Gussow. San Francisco: Friends of the Earth, 1971.

Wilbur discusses how a "feeling for the lay and character of the land" has informed much American poetry and painting in the past and how such art may have renewed relevance in light of the environmental crisis.

1321. ———. "Poetry and the Landscape." In *The New Landscape in Art and Science* (item 278), 86–96.

After describing his personal responses to the natural and increasingly artificial landscapes of the contemporary world, Wilbur laments that "any confident lyric relationship between man and the landscape has been invalidated.... The modern poet commonly writes through nature but not about it." Poetry might help us understand this separation and ultimately help "our culture to repair its relations with the natural world,—to see our mills, railroads and airways as a part of that world,—to feel our surroundings as an ensemble and to take them personally."

1322. Williams, Raymond. *The Country and the City*. New York: Oxford Univ. Press, 1973.

This influential, wide-ranging study of rural and urban imagery in English literature contributes to our general understanding of the origins of self-conscious regional literature in England and America during the Romantic Era. Paralleling Leo Marx's *The Machine in the Garden* (1964), Williams's perceptive analysis of the relationship between nostalgic pastoralism and industrialization provides a wider, cross-cultural understanding one aspect of regional literature.

1323. ———. "Region and Class in the Novel." In *The Uses of Fiction: Essays on the Modern Novel in Honour of Arnold Kettle,* edited by Douglas Jefferson and Graham Martin, 59–68. Milton Keynes: Open Univ. Press, 1982.

After tracing the origins of the word "region" and analyzing forms of English regional novels in the nineteenth and twentieth centuries, Williams discusses the links between regional and working class novels. Both genres depict distinct, often neglected groups of people, and both forms often suffer from an inability to draw connections between these special groups of people and larger economic and social forces.

1324. Winther, Sophus K. "The Limits of Regionalism." *Arizona Quarterly* 8 (Spring 1952): 30–36.

Echoing Marjorie Kinnan Rawlings, Winther vigorously condemns the majority of regional literature. Although regionalism is an indispensable tool for "every aspect of the practical life of man," it is "a misfortune that it was ever applied to the realm of the arts." "Perhaps the greatest flaw in the whole regional concept," Winther writes, "is that it gravitated toward an insular point of view which expressed itself in an outward bravado to conceal a deep inferiority complex."

1325. Wyatt, David. *The Fall Into Eden: Landscape and Imagination in California.* New York: Cambridge Univ. Press, 1986.

Paralleling classic studies of regional creativity in New England and the South, Wyatt analyzes the relationship between sense of place and the literary imagination in California. Chapters are devoted to the regional sensibilities of Richard Henry Dana, John Muir, Clarence King, Mary Austin, Frank Norris, John Steinbeck, Raymond Chandler, Robinson Jeffers, and Gary Snyder. Wyatt's "Prologue: The Mythology of the Region," pp. xv-xviii, and "Epilogue: Fictions of Space," pp. 206–10, provide important insights to the relationship between place, region, and the creative process.

1326. Zeigler, Joseph Wesley. *Regional Theatre: The Revolutionary Stage.* Minneapolis: Univ. of Minnesota Press, 1973.

This thorough account of the rise of regional theater in the 1960s contains perceptive discussions of the "centrifugal" impulse in American drama from the founding of the Cleveland Play House in 1916 to the beginning of the Guthrie Theater in Minneapolis in 1963. The on-going tension between New York, outlying regional theaters, and the desire for a truly national theater is intelligently analyzed in "The Regional Dilemma," pp. 199–209, and "A More Suitable Dream," pp. 234–52. A useful bibliography is included.

Philosophy and Religion

George Santayana once warned that "It would . . . be a gross and false geography of morals that should paint upon the map bands and tracts of different pure colours, to represent the territory of different religions, arts or moralities. If these things really flourished in blocks, like corn in one field and grasses in the next, there would not be that terrible insecurity and those painful moral and religious conflicts which prevail within states and within families, and even within individual minds . . . . "[1] As if aware of Santayana's shrewd criticism, few American philosophers or theologians have attempted a geography of morals or have directly confronted the issue of regionalism. Yet despite the relative dearth of explicit regional theory among American philosophers and theologians, more abstract discussions of space and place, pluralism and spatial diversity, abound in American and European thought.

For simplicity's sake and because of considerable thematic overlap, philosophical and religious studies have been merged into one category in this chapter. A few philosophers—among them Josiah Royce, John Dewey, and Martin Heidegger—have developed specific theories of regionalism. Recently, the bioregional and deep ecology movements have emerged from a philosophical position described by Bill Devall and George Sessions. Other philosophers contribute to regional theory in a less direct fashion. Many who are phenomenologically inclined, such as Edmund Husserl, Maurice Merleau-Ponty, Gaston Bachelard, William Gass, Walker Percy, and John J. McDermott, have investigated the nature of environmental perception and spatial experience. Other philosophers and philosophically-oriented scholars such as Horace Kallen, Rene Dubos, Paul Ricoeur, Morris Berman, and others have explored the spatial dimension of cultural pluralism.

Theologians are equally sensitive to spatial-regional issues, especially to questions of sacred and profane space, local and universal faith, and the impact of religious belief upon environmental attitude and behavior. The following section contains a fairly wide selection of

Protestant, Catholic, and Jewish thought as well as Native American and some Eastern religious speculation regarding place and region. Theological scholars as varied as Harvey Cox, Mircea Eliade, Richard Rubenstein, Paul Tournier, Alan Watts, and Simone Weil are represented here.

Once again, geographers, historians, and sociologists offer invaluable cross-disciplinary insights, and because of the fairly limited nature of this list much of their work is included here rather than under their separate disciplines. The philosophical and religion-related work of Catherine Albanese, Edwin Gaustad, William Halvorson and Peter Newman, Samuel Hill, Wendell Berry, Anne Buttimer, Nicholas Entrikin, Yi-Fu Tuan, Erich Isaacs, David Sopher, Peter Shortridge, Roger Stump, Wilbur Zelinsky, and others helps us begin to construct a sophisticated geography of morals and religion.

M.S.

---

[1]George Santayana, "Geography and Morals," in *Physical Order and Moral Liberty: Previously Unpublished Essays of George Santayana*, edited by John Lachs and Shirley Lachs (Nashville: Vanderbilt Univ. Press, 1969), 207.

*   *   *

1327. Albanese, Catherine L. "Exploring Regional Religion: A Case Study of the Eastern Cherokee." *History of Religions* 23 (May 1984): 344–71.

Among the Cherokee who remained in North Carolina after the removal of 1838, Albanese observes the development of a distinct regional religion as a "response to crisis of a conquered people." The evolution of this specific, place-oriented religion "made the Eastern Cherokee a people" and exemplifies "the ways in which, in such a strongly marked region, the common experiences of the land merges with the history and interactions of peoples to yield a distinctive religious expression."

1328. Bachelard, Gaston. *The Poetics of Space.* Translated by Maria Jolas. Boston: Beacon Press, 1969.

In this often-cited classic, Bachelard uses creative literature, philosophical and psychological concepts to interpret the meaning of "felicitous space" in human experience. His phenomenological analysis of "the space we love," of "eulogized space," ranges from the intimate interiors of our houses to the immensity of external nature.

1329. Berman, Morris. *The Reenchantment of the World*. New York: Bantam Books, 1984.

After depicting the progressive alienation from nature—a contemporary "disenchantment of the world"—fostered by modern scientific consciousness, Berman locates sources of renewal and reenchantment in the holistic thought of Carl Jung, Wilhelm Reich, and Gregory Bateson and in the promise of economic decentralization, "green" politics, and bioregional consciousness. The final chapter, "The Politics of Consciousness," pp. 267–304, is an especially useful survey of recent regional thought and practice.

1330. Berry, Wendell. "The Body and the Earth." In *The Unsettling of America: Culture and Agriculture*, 97–140. New York: Avon Books, 1977.

A wide-ranging, discursive analysis of the essential connections between the human spirit, body, and the earth. "While we live," Berry writes, "our bodies are moving particles of earth, joined inextricably both to the soil and to the bodies of other living creatures. It is hardly surprising, then, that there should be some profound resemblances between our treatment of our bodies and our treatment of the earth."

1331. ———. "The Gift of Good Land." In *The Gift of Good Land: Further Essays Cultural and Agricultural*, 267–81. San Francisco: North Point Press, 1981.

Using Lynn White's "The Historical Roots of Our Ecologic Crisis" as a starting point, Berry develops a Biblical argument for environmental stewardship and explores the practical implications of this argument. (Other works by Berry are included under Literature.)

1332. Brauer, Jerald C. "Regionalism and Religion in America." *Church History* 54 (September 1985): 366–78.

After pointing out that historians of American religion from Robert Baird to Sydney Ahlstrom have depicted New England Puritanism as the dominant force in American religion, Brauer urges greater attention to other regional varieties of Protestantism. People in the Mid Atlantic and southern regions developed distinct and influential religious cultures, and Brauer suggests that the orthodox vision of New England hegemony might be applied to the South, "that from the time of the Great Awakening the South exhibited an escalating hegemony of pietistic revivalism" that was felt nationally.

1333. Brown, Stuart Gerry. "From Provincialism to the Great Community." In *The Social Philosophy of Josiah Royce*, edited by Stuart Gerry Brown, 1–29. Syracuse: Syracuse Univ. Press, 1950.

An insightful overview of the evolution of Royce's regional and communitarian philosophy. Other discussions of Royce's theory of provincialism include Sollers (item 49), and Entrikin, Pomeroy, White and White (items 1353, 1375, 1400).

1334. Buttimer, Anne. "Grasping the Dynamism of Lifeworld." *Annals of the Association of American Geographers* 66 (June 1976): 277–92.

Buttimer effectively describes possible connections between phenomenology and human geography, especially how the "lifeworld" concept and other ideas of Heidegger, Bachelard, and Eliade can help clarify three basic research areas: sense of place, social space, and time-space rhythms.

1335. Capps, Walter, ed. *On Seeing With a Native Eye*. New York: Harper and Row, 1976.

Of central importance for understanding the relationship between religion and sense of place are W. Richard Comstock's "On Seeing With the Eye of the Native European," pp. 58–78, and N. Scott Momaday's "Native American Attitudes to the Environment," pp. 79–85.

1336. Clark, Michael D. *Coherent Variety: The Idea of Diversity in British and American Conservative Thought*. Westport, Conn.: Greenwood, 1983.

A lucid discussion of a central tenet of classical conservatism: the vision of a society composed of a diversity of groups rather than one based upon individual atomism or centralized authority. Clark's analysis of American regional theory—especially that of Madison and Calhoun in the early republic and that of the Southern Agrarians and their heirs today—is contained in, "Federalism and Diversity in the United States," pp. 104–24, and "Southern Demons," pp. 125–37.

1337. Clarke, Clifford J. "Religion and Regional Culture: The Changing Pattern of Religious Affiliation in the Cajun Region of Southwest Louisiana." *Journal for the Scientific Study of Religion* 24 (December 1985): 384–95.

Focusing upon changes in denominational membership within the Cajun subregion between 1950 and 1980, Clarke finds that the denominational mix has moved closer to the national norm. This finding lends some support to the argument that regional differences in American religion are becoming less distinct or "converging" due to mobility and general forces of modernization. See Newman and Halvorson, Shortridge, and Stump (items 1372, 1384–1385, 1389–1390) for critiques of the "religious convergence" thesis.

1338. Cox, Harvey. "The Restoration of a Sense of Place: A Theological Reflection on the Visual Environment." *Ekistics* 25 (June 1968): 422–24.

The author of *The Secular City* depicts the depletion and disappearance of a sense of place as "one of the deplorable characteristics of our times." Rather than urge a return to a now archaic "sacral" sense of place, Cox advocates the fostering of "human space" in which "places are understood as giving pace, variety, and orientation to man." The notion of a progression from "magical" to "sacral" to "secular" and finally to "human" space is imaginatively linked to specific urban-regional planning issues.

1339. Cross, Whitney. *The Burned-Over District: The Social and Intellectual History of Enthusiastic Religion in Western New York, 1800–1850.* Ithaca: Cornell Univ. Press, 1950.

In this classic study of the relationship between religion and region, Cross describes the cultural and geographical factors that helped give birth to a variety of religious movements in western New York. Vivid portraits of such religious leaders as Joseph Smith, Charles Finney, John Humphrey Noyes, and William Miller are interspersed with sensitive accounts of regional conditions and folkways.

1340. Davis, W.D. *The Gospel and the Land: Early Christianity and Jewish Territorial Doctrine.* Berkeley: Univ. of California Press, 1974.

A detailed analysis of the meaning of "land"—as particular place and as a general sensibility—in early Judeo-Christian thought. Davis's detailed biblical exegesis reveals a movement from devotion to specific place in the Old Testament to the "spiritualization of 'holy space'" and general detachment from the land in the New Testament and subsequent Christian doctrine. "If it was the Hellenists and Paul who broke asunder the territorial chrysallis of Christianity," Davis concludes, "they did so in the name of Christ, to whom all space, like all time, was subordinated, and who has become in the Christian tradition—to adopt and adapt a metaphor from Rainer Maria Rilke—'for every ship a haven; for every land a ship.'"

1341. Deloria, Vine. *God Is Red*. New York: Grossett and Dunlap, 1973.

A central feature of Deloria's analysis is the contrast between sense of time and place in Native American and Judeo-Christian religions. The implications of worshipping a "God of Place" as opposed to a "God of Time" are effectively explored in "Thinking in Time and Space," pp. 75–109; "The Concept of History," pp. 111–28; and "The Spatial Problem of History," pp. 129–50. See Highwater and Rubenstein (items 1360, 1380–1382) for closely related arguments.

1342. Devall, Bill and George Sessions. *Deep Ecology*. Salt Lake City, Utah: Peregrine Smith, 1985.

"Deep ecology" is a term coined by Norwegian philosopher Arne Naess in 1973 to "describe the deeper, more spiritual approach to Nature exemplified in the writings of Aldo Leopold and Rachel Carson." In many ways this treatise serves as a philosophical/ethical handbook for bioregionalists. Especially germane is "Ecotopia: The Vision Defined," pp. 161–91, which examines the thought of Loren Eisley, Baker Brownell, Aldous Huxley, Gary Snyder, and Paul Shepard. An extensive bibliography is included. Other sources closely connected with the bioregional movement include Berry and Dubos (items 1330–1331, 1346), Snyder under Literature, Shepard under Art, and Bookchin, Capra, Louv, Parsons, Sale, and Spretnak under Political Science.

1343. Dewey, John. "Americanism and Localism." *Dial* 68 (June 1920): 684–88.

Dewey vigorously contends that the local, immediate community provides a more satisfying sense of identity than the national frame of reference and that ultimately "the locality is the only universal." "The wider the formal, the legal entity," he shrewdly observes, "the more intense becomes the local life."

1344. ———. *The Public and Its Problems*. New York: Henry Holt & Co., 1927.

In "The Search for the Great Community," pp. 143–84, Dewey, like Royce before him, argues for the need of local and regional community as an intimate source of identity in mass society.

1345. Doughty, Robin W. "Environmental Theology: Trends and Prospects in Christian Thought." *Progress in Human Geography* 5 (June 1981): 234–48.

In addition to providing a useful bibliography of the extensive debate regarding the environmental implications of Christian theology, Doughty reviews the contributions of Lynn White, Aldo Leopold, Teilhard de Chardin, Martin Buber, and others to this issue.

1346. Dubos, René. *A God Within.* New York: Scribners, 1972.

A central theme of this book is Dubos's belief that by cultivating regionalism Americans could develop a much needed social identity and spirit of place to counteract the homelessness of mass society. "Modern societies," he argues, "will have to find some way to reverse the trend toward larger and larger agglomerations and to create units compatible with the limits of man's comprehension.... By cultivating regionalism, the United States could derive from its rich geographical diversity cultural values and also forms of economic wealth far more valuable.... than those measured by the artificial criteria of a money economy."

1347. ———. "A Theology of Earth." In *Western Man and Environmental Ethics,* edited by Ian G. Barbour, 43–54. Menlo Park, Calif.: Addison-Wesley, 1973.

In this powerful rejoinder to Lynn White's "Historical Roots of the Ecologic Crisis," Dubos finds a viable tradition of environmental responsibility in Christianity and offers St. Benedict, with his practice of "creative intervention," as a patron saint for the environmental movement.

1348. ———. "The Despairing Optimist." *American Scholar* 46 (Spring 1977): 152–58.

The rise of global awareness, Dubos argues, logically coincides with a worldwide resurgence of regional identity. Similarly, greater physical and social mobility in the United States will "increasingly enhance regionalism as more and more people can choose the place where they settle."

1349. ———. "The Despairing Optimist." *American Scholar* 47 (Spring 1978): 152–56.

Just as diversity has been a crucial factor in biological evolution, Dubos believes that cultural regionalism rather than centralization is the surest path toward a global health and harmony "in which natural regions will recapture their identity by cultivating their *genius loci*, yet interplay symbiotically in a creative way ... "

1350. ———. "Think Globally, But Act Locally." In *Celebrations of Life*, 83–127. New York: McGraw-Hill, 1981.

An eloquent summation of Dubos's thought concerning the need for regional variety and consciousness within an increasingly unified planet. Dubos provides vivid examples of working human scale communities that nurture the genius of a particular place as well as global consciousness.

1351. Eliade, Mircea. *The Sacred and the Profane: The Nature of Religion*. Translated by Willard R. Trask. New York: Harcourt, Brace & Co., 1959.

Of Eliade's many works, this is his most influential analysis of the significance of space and place in religious experience. "Sacred Space and Making the World Sacred," pp. 20–65, employs examples from a spectrum of religions to discuss, among other things, the differences between sacred and secular conceptions of space; the meaning of a sacred center for home, village, city or region; and the cosmic symbolism inherent in built environments.

1352. Entrikin, J. Nicholas. "Contemporary Humanism in Geography." *Annals of the Association of American Geographers* 66 (December 1976): 615–30.

An excellent survey of the relationship between various strands of twentieth century philosophy and humanistic geography, with emphasis upon the work of Husserl, Heidegger, Merleau-Ponty, Buttimer, Tuan, Relph, and others.

1353. ———. "Royce's 'Provincialism': A Metaphysician's Social Geography." In *Geography, Ideology and Social Concern*, edited by D.R. Stoddart, 208–26. Towota, N.J.: Barnes and Noble Books, 1981.

A detailed study of the personal and intellectual sources of Royce's theory of "provincialism" and its relevance to contemporary social thought. (Another source by Entrikin is listed under Geography: Region as Concept.)

1354. Gass, William H. "The Face of the City: Observations of a Post-Modern Boulevardier." *Harper's* 272 (March 1986): 37–46.

Like his fellow philosopher and creative writer, Walker Percy (item 1373), Gass examines the meaning of sense of place and environmental perception. After noting that "We soon cease to see what we are accustomed to.... The sightless, who bump along on Braille, don't care to count what their fingers read. That would be twice blind...." he nevertheless suggests ways to sharpen our sense of the distinctive "surfaces" of cities and places.

1355. Gaustad, Edwin Scott. *Historical Atlas of Religion in America.* New York: Harper and Row, 1962.

This richly illustrated atlas contains essays and maps depicting the spatial distribution of American religious groups from 1650 to 1960. Eight colonial religious groups are treated along with sixteen major religious bodies in the twentieth century. The changing spatial distribution of Baptists, Congregationalists, Disciples of Christ, Episcopalians, Jews, Lutherans, Methodists, Mormons, Presbyterians, Quakers, Roman Catholics, and others are vividly illustrated on separate and cumulative maps.

1356. Goen, C.C. "Broken Churches, Broken Nation: Regional Religion and North-South Alienation in Ante-Bellum America." *Church History* 52 (March 1983): 21–35.

A straightforward account of denominational dispute and schism— an "inner civil war" in which Christianity was twisted "to the purposes of regional identity and defense"—that served as a prelude to the larger conflict.

1357. Graber, Linda. *Wilderness as Sacred Space.* Washington, D.C.: Association of American Geographers, 1976.

A useful discussion of how the general sense of wilderness as sacred space has been refined and intensified in American culture where a wilderness ethic functions as a religious belief system and wilderness purists form a community of true believers.

1358. Heidegger, Martin. *Being and Time.* Translated by John Macquarrie and Edward Robinson. New York: Harper and Row, 1962.

Sections 22, 23, and 24, pp. 135–48, of Heidegger's book, originally published in 1927, contain the heart of his notion of region as the "concernful" realm within which familiar objects and places function together. Such intimate horizons of interrelationships and belonging are taken for granted and assume a "character of inconspicuous familiarity"; only when this ecology is disrupted, do we become aware of our region. "Often the region of a place does not become accessible explicitly," he argues, "until one fails to find something in its place." For commentary on Heidegger's influential concepts of space and notions of "being-in-the-world," "thing," "ready-to-hand," "dwelling," and "region," see Vincent Vycinas's *Earth and Gods: An Introduction to the Philosophy of Martin Heidegger* (The Hague: Martinus-Nijhoff, 1969).

1359. ———. *Poetry, Language, Thought*. Translated by Albert Hofstadter. New York: Harper and Row, 1971.

Three essays are central to the phenomenological understanding of space, place, and region: "Building Dwelling Thinking," pp.143–61; "The Thing," pp. 165–82; and "Poetically Man Dwells," pp. 213–29. Like Bachelard, Heidegger poetically evokes the subjective meanings and associations of buildings and dwellings, things, space, and language to grasp man's proper place on earth. In a world where "Everything gets lumped together into increasing distancelessness," he argues, people must learn to appreciate the immediacy of things in themselves—both man-made and natural—in order to "dwell humanly on this earth." Another source by Heidegger is listed under Art (item 268).

1360. Highwater, Jamake. *The Primal Mind: Vision and Reality in Indian America*. New York: Harper and Row, 1981.

Highwater's discussion of "Place," pp. 119–32, is a useful analogue to Deloria's discussion of place and region in Native American religion. See J. Donald Hughes, *American Indian Ecology* (El Paso: Texas Western Press, 1983), for a related source.

1361. Hill, Samuel S. "Religion and Region in America." *Annals of the Academy of Political and Social Science* 480 (July 1985): 132–41.

This essay effectively reviews recent studies of American religious regionalism—especially the work of Zelinsky, Shortridge, and Stump—and concludes that religion continues to demonstrate strong regional variations in the United States.

1362. ———. *The South and the North in American Religion*. Athens: Univ. of Georgia Press, 1980.

Complementing John Shelton Reed's study of contemporary religious distinctiveness in *The Enduring South*, Hill examines the changing relationships between southern and northern varieties of Protestantism during three "epochs" of American history: 1795–1810, 1835–1850, and 1885–1900.

1363. Houston, James M. "The Concepts of 'Place' and 'Land' in the Judaeo-Christian Tradition." In *Humanistic Geography: Prospects and Problems,* edited by David Ley and Marwyn S. Samuels, 224–37. Chicago: Maaroufa Press, 1978.

This densely-documented, insightful survey of the implications of "place" and "land" in western religion vividly outlines how contemporary theologians seek to understand and remedy the sense of placelessness and homelessness pervading modern life.

1364. Isaac, Erich. "The Act and the Covenant: The Impact of Religion on the Landscape." *Landscape* 11 (Winter 1961–62): 12–17.

After arguing that "the key to the study of religion as a landscape transforming factor lies in *rite,*" Isaac describes a variety of religions in Africa, Europe, and the Near East whose landscape transformations range from profound to insignificant.

1365. ———. "God's Acre." *Landscape* 14 (Winter 1945–65): 28–32.

A thoughtful exploration of the meaning of sacred place in early Greek, Jewish, and Christian thought and how the notions of personal property and boundary may be rooted in this general religious sensibility.

1366. ———. "Religion, Landscape and Space." *Landscape* 9 (Winter 1959–60): 14–18.

Isaac describes how the "urge to 'put heaven on earth'" may be the source of the radical landscape transformations often "wielded by magical-cosmic religion." The dwindling of such powerful land-molding religion in modern times parallels a fundamental shift in spatial perception from an earlier sense of "symbolic" space redolent with cosmic and mythical meaning to a contemporary sense of "abstract" space that is homogeneous and value-free.

1367. Kallen, Horace M. *Culture and Democracy in the United States.* New York: Boni and Liveright, 1924.

Influenced by William James's notion of a "pluralistic universe," philosopher Kallen first developed the concept of "cultural pluralism" in the opening chapter of this book. In "Culture and the Ku Klux Klan," pp. 9–43, as well as "Democracy Versus the Melting Pot," pp. 67–125, Kallen stressed regional diversity as an essential component of cultural pluralism. Kallen continued to perceive regionalism as an ingredient of pluralism in his later work, especially *Cultural Pluralism and the*

American Idea: An Essay in Social Philosophy (Philadelphia: Univ. of Pennsylvania Press, 1956).

1368. McDermott, John J. *The Culture of Experience: Philosophical Essays in the American Grain.* New York: NYU Press, 1976.

In these clearly argued, highly literate essays, many of them concerned with the "press of environment" upon the American temperament, McDermott examines how Americans respond to space and place, to nature and to the "artifactual" backgrounds of their lives. Especially useful for a philosophical and cultural understanding of American regionalism and sense of place are "Deprivation and Celebration: Suggestions for an Aesthetic Ecology," pp. 82–98, which treats the issues of landscape perception and urban planning; "Nature Nostalgia and the City," pp. 179–204, which, among other things, soundly criticizes the self-destructive American tradition of unreserved nature loving and city hating; and "Space, Time, and Touch: Philosophical Dimensions of Urban Consciousness," pp. 205–31, which points the way toward a much needed love of place, or topophilia, in the city.

1369. ———. *Streams of Experience: Reflections on the History and Philosophy of American Culture.* Amherst: Univ. of Massachusetts Press, 1986.

Many of the essays in this collection support McDermott's general belief that America's bequest to global survival involves the cultivation of "our wisest positions, that is, meliorism, pluralism, positive provincialism, the avoidance of closure, and a commitment to the affairs of time as sacred." "Transcience and Amelioration: An American Bequest for the New Millennium," pp. 63–75, carefully spells out the regionally-related American legacies of pluralism, positive provincialism, and interrelatedness; "America: The Loneliness of the Quest," pp. 76–91, describes, in part, the global relevance of Royce's and Dewey's concepts of pluralism and community; "Classical American Philosophy: A Reflective Bequest to the Twenty-First Century," pp. 92–106, contains insightful discussions of James's pluralism and Royce's wise provincialism; and "Glass Without Feet: Dimensions of Urban Aesthetics," pp. 196–209, expands McDermott's contention that Americans must develop a more positive urban sense of place.

1370. Matore, Georges. "Existential Space." *Landscape* 15 (Spring 1966): 5–6.

A succinct discussion of the the heightened need for place aroused among people subjected to the "rootlessness and discontinuity" of contemporary life. "All gains of activity in space," Matore argues, "should be compensated for by a gain of stability in one particular spot in space."

1371. Mead, Sidney. "The American People: Their Space, Time, and Religion." In *The Lively Experiment: The Shaping of Christianity in America*, 1–15. New York: Harper and Row, 1963.

A crisply written, sweeping account of the impact of mobility and sense of place upon Euro-American religious faith.

1372. Newman, William M. and Peter L. Halvorson. "Religion and Regional Culture: Patterns of Concentration and Change Among Religious Denominations, 1925–1980." *Journal for the Scientific Study of Religion* 23 (September 1984): 304–15.

Although the authors challenge Shortridge and Stump's assumption that denominational affiliation is a firm measure of regional culture, they agree that there is little evidence to suggest a decrease of religious regionalism throughout the United States over the past thirty years.

1373. Percy, Walker. "The Loss of the Creature." In *The Message in the Bottle*, 46–63. New York: Farrar, Straus & Giroux, 1975.

In this stimulating discussion of how environmental perception is deeply colored by factors external to the experience itself—especially by cultural expectations and the advice of experts and educators—Percy urges individuals to recover the "direct" experience of places and objects in an untutored fashion.

1374. Pickles, John. *Phenomenology, Science and Geography: Spatiality and Human Sciences*. Cambridge: Cambridge Univ. Press, 1985.

Especially useful is "Toward an Understanding of Human Spatiality," pp. 154–70, which attempts "to retrieve two basic concepts of geographic concern—place and space—for a viable and vital regional ontology of the geographical." Using several of Heidegger's concepts, Pickles argues that the region is the arena within which things and places "appear in their necessary connection," and he contrasts this intimate "region of dwelling" with the abstract, undifferentiated "technological space" that threatens to dominate contemporary life. "Dwelling-places, with their horizons or regions of concernful involvement with world, things, and others," he writes "are gradually forgotten when technological conceptions of space are projected for worldless and not-yet human beings."

1375. Pomeroy, Earl. "Josiah Royce: Historian in Quest of Community." *Pacific Historical Review* 40 (February 1971): 1–20.

Although Royce's unsparing criticism of the rootless frontier and his advocacy of provincial community ran against the grain of popular and professional thought during his lifetime, Pomeroy argues that this quest for community is increasingly valued in the late twentieth century.

1376. Ricoeur, Paul. "Universal Civilization and National Cultures." In *History and Truth.* Evanston: Northwestern Univ. Press, 1961.

Ricoeur discusses the tension between the universal and the particular in terms of human social organization and argues, in part, that a healthy "world culture" requires a balance between rooted culture, on the one hand, and universal civilization, on the other. Cultures must partake of the universal as well as the particular, must face the paradox of "how to become modern and return to sources; how to revive an old dormant civilization and take part in universal civilization ... "

1377. Royce, Josiah. "The Hope of the Great Community." In *The Hope of the Great Community*, 25–70. New York: Macmillan. Reprinted in *The Basic Writings of Josiah Royce*. vol. 2, edited by John J. McDermott, 1145–63. Chicago: Univ. of Chicago Press, 1969.

Responding to the war in Europe, Royce connects his earlier vision of the a harmonious balance between province and nation to a larger vision of a spiritually sustained and peaceful world order.

1378. ———. "Provincialism: Based Upon a Study of Early Conditions in California." *Putnam's Magazine* 7 (November 1909): 232–40.

Drawing upon personal memories as well as his vivid history of his native state, *California ... A Study of American Character* (1886), Royce depicts the transition from the anarchy of the frontier to the order of provincial life and argues that a "wise provincialism" is now needed "to serve as a check upon mob psychology on a national scale, and to furnish that variety which is essential to vital growth and originality."

1379. ———. *Race Questions, Provincialism, and Other American Problems*. 1908, Reprint. New York: Books for Libraries, 1967.

This book contains two important essays: "Provincialism," pp. 55–109, which is an expanded version of the essay published in *Putnam's Magazine*, and "The Pacific Coast, A Psychological Study of the Relations of Climate and Civilization," pp. 169–255, which examines the impact of the physical environment upon regional culture. Royce's theory of provincialism has influenced American regional theorists, from Frederick Jackson Turner and John Dewey to Robert Nisbet and Peter Berger. Royce's central treatment of the subject "Provincialism" is reprinted in John J. McDermott, ed., *The Basic Writings of Josiah Royce*. vol. 2. (Chicago: Univ. of Chicago Press, 1969), pp. 1067–88.

1380. Rubenstein, Richard L. "The Cave, the Rock, and the Tent: The Meaning of Place in Contemporary America." In *Morality and Eros*, 164–82. New York: McGraw-Hill, 1970.

Rubenstein compares the restless nature of American life to the long enforced nomadic quality of the Jewish experience. The return to the homeland of Israel represents a renewal of place and a reorientation of Jewish theology that contrasts vividly with persistent American placelessness and lack of sacred place and presents American Jews with a choice between rootedness and continued mobility. "Whoever participates in American life," Rubenstein concludes, " must be prepared to accept both the blessings and the shortcomings of our nomadic estrangement from the earth," and for the perpetually wandering American, the only fixed point of reference is internal.

1381. ———. "Homeland and Holocaust: Issues in the Jewish Religious Situation." In *The Religious Situation: 1968*, edited by Donald Cutler, 39–64. Boston: Beacon Press, 1968.

This essay elaborates Rubenstein's call for a "new paganism" in response to the holocaust and the return to Israel: for a reorientation of faith from belief in an omnipotent sky-god of time to a more finite earth-god of place. This essay is followed by commentaries by Milton Himmelfarb, Zalman M. Schachter, and Irving Greenberg and a reply by Rubenstein.

1382. ———. "The Rebirth of Israel in Contemporary Jewish Theology." In *After Auschwitz: Radical Theology and Contemporary Judaism*, 130–42. Indianapolis: Bobbs-Merrill, 1966.

Rubenstein argues that the return to the Jewish homeland will allow the renewal of an "archaic earth religion" and joyous paganism missing from Judaism during nineteen hundred years of exile and wandering. His discussion of the differences between time- and place-oriented religions, and between gods of history and nature, is a valuable contribution to the understanding of religion and region.

1383. Santayana, George. "Geography and Morals." In *Physical Order and Moral Liberty: Previously Unpublished Essays of George Santayana*, edited by John Lachs and Shirley Lachs, 207–9. Nashville: Vanderbilt Univ. Press, 1969.

While not discounting the influence of geography upon values and beliefs, Santayana warns against simplistic environmental determinism. "It would ... be a gross and false geography of morals," he argues, "that should paint upon the map bands and tracts of different pure colours, to represent the territory of different religions, arts or moralities. If these things really flourished in blocks, like corn in one field and grass in the next, there would not be that terrible insecurity and those painful moral and religious conflicts which prevail within states and within families, and even within individual minds ... "

1384. Shortridge, James R. "A New Regionalization of American Religion." *Journal for the Scientific Study of Religion* 16 (June 1977): 143–53.

Pushing beyond Zelinsky's influential anatomy of American religion, Shortridge describes five basic religious types and maps their spatial distribution. The types are (1) intense, conservative Protestant, concentrated in the South, Utah, and parts of the northern plains, (2) diverse, liberal Protestant, concentrated in the Middle West and West Coast, (3) Catholic, found in the Northeast and upper Middle West, (4) super Catholic, located in French Louisiana and the Spanish Southwest and (5) a transition type, found in the upper South, Southwest, and West Coast. In addition to arguing that "a religious regionalization is as close to an objective general cultural regionalization as we are to get," Shortridge asserts that religious regionalism is increasing due to the rise of "voluntary regions"—the conscious clustering of like-minded people.

1385. ———. "Patterns of Religion in the United States." *Geographical Review* 66 (October 1976): 420–34.

Shortridge maps the spatial variations of three aspects of American religion: (1) the distribution of liberal and conservative Protestants, (2) areas of marked religious diversity or pluralism, and (3) levels of religious commitment indicated by the percentage of church membership.

1386. Smith, Jonathan Z. "Earth and Gods." *Journal of Religion* 49 (January 1969): 103–25. Reprinted in Smith, Jonathan Z. *Map Is Not Territory: Studies in the History of Religions*, 104–28. Leiden, Netherlands: Brill, 1978.

A densely documented, effective overview of studies of sacred space—especially the work of Eliade and Rubenstein—with a focus upon Israel as a holy land, a sacred enclave, and exiles' goal.

1387. Sopher, David E. "Geography and Religion." *Progress in Human Geography* 5 (December 1981): 510–24.

This fine review essay of recent scholarship in the geography of religions also contains a detailed bibliography.

1388. ———. *Geography of Religions*. Englewood Cliffs, N.J.: Prentice-Hall, 1967.

Sopher's global survey contains several valuable general discussions remindful of earlier work by Isaacs and Eliade: "Ecology and Religious Institutions," pp. 17–23; "Religion and the Land," pp. 24–46; and "Sacred Space and Sacred Territory," pp. 47–55.

1389. Stump, Roger. "Regional Divergence in Religious Affiliation in the United States." *Sociological Analysis* 45 (Winter 1984): 283–99.

Contrary to the popular regional convergence thesis, Stump demonstrates that regional differences in religious affiliations among Catholics and white Protestants have increased during the twentieth century.

1390. ———. "Regional Migration and Religious Commitment in the United States." *Journal for the Scientific Study of Religion* 23 (September 1984): 292–303.

Stump's study indicates that Americans who migrate from one region to another are likely to adopt the religious values of the host region. He concludes that "migration need not lead to the decay of regional differences; indeed, if migrants readily conform to regional norms, migration should reinforce those differences."

1391. Tournier, Paul. *A Place for You: Psychology and Religion*. New York: Harper and Row, 1968.

Using insights from theology and psychotherapy and paralleling the arguments of fellow French-speaking theorists like Bachelard, Halbwachs, and Weil, Tournier argues that sense of place is a primal human need. From an impressive array of evidence, Tournier examines the impact of place upon psychological development and the life-cycle, the consequences of uprootedness and spatial deprivation, and the significance of sacred places, patriotism, family, and home. "The relationship of people with places," he argues, "may be more stable than their relationships with other people.... All our experiences, emotions, and feelings are indissolubly linked in our memories with places....Nothing happens in pure abstraction." "Biblical Perspectives," pp. 39–52, examines the tension between localizing and universalizing forces in the Judaeo-Christian tradition, a theme also analyzed by Davis, Deloria, Dubos, Rubenstein, Smith, White, and others (see items 1340, 1346–1350, 1380–1382, 1386).

1392. Tuan, Yi-Fu. "Geography, Phenomenology, and the Study of Human Nature." *Canadian Geographer* 15 (1971): 181–92.

Tuan argues that phenomenology can provide a model for humanistically oriented geographers interested in exploring the immediate, subjective experiences of space and place.

1393. ———. "Sacred Space: Explorations of an Idea." In *Dimensions of Human Geography: Essays on Some Familiar and Neglected Themes*, edited by Karl W. Butzer, 84–99. Chicago: Univ. of Chicago, Department of Geography, 1978.

After exploring the root meanings of such words as "sacred," "profane," "holy," "power," and "purity," Tuan compares the significance of sacred space in premodern and modern societies. Although the "sense of holiness and of otherworldly splendor has dimmed in modern times," Tuan discusses how the nation-state, the suburb, and the neighborhood may function as contemporary sacred spaces.

1394. ———. "Structuralism, Existentialism, and Environmental Perception." *Environment and Behavior* 4 (September 1972): 319–31.

Tuan succinctly describes how structuralism, as developed by Levi-Strauss, and existentialism, as expressed by Sartre, "contribute to our knowledge of how people perceive and organize their worlds and behave in them."

1395. Vecsey, Christopher. "American Indian Environmental Religions." In *American Indian Environments*, edited by Christopher Vecsey and Robert W. Venables, 1–37. Syracuse: Syracuse Univ. Press, 1980.

In this sweeping survey, Vecsey discusses how Native American religions evoked environmental reverence as well as environmental despoliation.

1396. Watts, Alan. *Nature, Man, and Woman*. New York: Pantheon, 1958.

An influential rumination on the environmental sensibilities of western and eastern religions. Christianity encourages a sense of isolation from the natural world and estrangement from our essential selves, while elements of Taoist, Zen Buddhist, and Neo-Confucian thought can be used to elicit an "understanding of nature in which man is something more than a frustrated outsider." Especially useful for understanding possible relationships between religion and region are Watts's "Introduction," pp. 1–22, and "Urbanism and Paganism," pp. 25–50.

1397. ———. "The World Is Your Body." In *The Book: On the Taboo Against Knowing Who You Are*. New York: Pantheon, 1966.

As the title suggests, Watts argues that the Newtonian conception of a universe composed of separate objects should be replaced with an ecological vision of the continuity of man and nature, organism and environment.

1398. Weil, Simone. *The Need for Roots*. Translated by Arthur Wills. New York: G.P. Putnam's Sons, 1952.

Written during the Nazi occupation of her native France, Weil examines the forces of alienation and uprootedness that contributed to the collapse of Western Europe and proposes a core of human rights and obligations necessary to sustain free societies after the war. A profound sense of the human need for place, community, and region is at the heart of her passionate plea for the recovery of spiritual roots. "To be rooted," Weil writes, "is perhaps the most important and least recognized need of the human soul ... Every being needs to have multiple roots. It is necessary for him to draw well-nigh the whole of his moral, intellectual, and spiritual life by way of the environment of which he forms a natural part." Part Two of her book, "Uprootedness," pp. 43–184, especially the section, "Patriotism and Nationalism," pp.

99–184, examines the consequences of the erosion of intimate local-regional sources of identity and the rise of the impersonal nation-state.

1399. White, Lynn. "The Historical Roots of Our Ecologic Crisis." In *Western Man and Environmental Ethics*, edited by Ian Barbour, 18–30. Menlo Park, Calif.: Addison-Wesley, 1973.

Originally published in *Science* 155 (March 10, 1967), pp. 1203–07, this often-cited article meticulously traces environmental attitudes and behaviour encouraged by Christianity. White concludes that the mainstream Christianity of the Latin West "bears a huge burden of guilt" for the late twentieth century environmental crisis—a crisis that can only be countered by rethinking our fundamental religious axioms and perhaps resurrecting Francis of Asissi as the "patron saint for ecologists." Rene Dubos's response to White (item 1349) is included in this anthology, as is White's retort, "Continuing the Conversation," pp. 55–64.

1400. White, Morton and Lucia White. "Provincialism and Alienation: An Aside on Josiah Royce and George Santayana." In *The Intellectual Versus the City: From Thomas Jefferson to Frank Lloyd Wright*, 181–9. Cambridge: Harvard Univ. Press, 1962.

An insightful analysis of the anti-urban bias in Royce's theory of provincialism and Santayana's estrangement from modernism.

1401. Zelinsky, Wilbur. "An Approach to the Religious Geography of the United States: Patterns of Church Membership in 1952." *Annals of the Association of American Geographers* 51 (June 1961): 139–93.

This is an influential effort to locate the nation's religious regions and to "contribute some material toward our still quite shadowy delineation of the general cultural regions of Anglo-America " After carefully summarizing previous scholarship in the field, Zelinsky isolates seven admittedly impressionistic major religious regions: *New England*, with its Congregationalist base and emerging Catholicism; the *Midland*, dominated by Methodism; the *Upper Middle West*, dominated by Lutheranism; the *South*, with a Baptist-Methodist-Fundamentalist flavor; the *Mormon* region; the Spanish Catholic *Southwest*; and a highly heterogeneous *Western* region. This article includes maps of the spatial distributions of twenty-one denominations as well as a cumulative map of the major religious regions.

Political Science

Theories regarding the territorial extent of loyalty and sovereignty have been a staple of political thought since Plato's and Aristotle's visions of the ideal polis. Hobbes, Locke, Montesquieu, Rousseau, Hegel, Marx, Kropotkin, and many others have examined the nature of loyalty to various social units ranging from the immediate family and neighborhood to the far flung nation-state and empire. Such issues have been especially pertinent in the United States, for the sheer size and complexity of the nation raise persistent questions regarding the territorial dynamics of patriotism and power.

Region and regionalism have been central concerns of American political thought. For two centuries Americans have witnessed a perpetual debate regarding the relationship between political parts and the whole—between local and central, state and federal, regional and national sources of authority. Such issues have concerned politicians from Jefferson and Hamilton to Lincoln and Douglas to Roosevelt and Hoover. Political regionalism has imbued debates regarding states' rights, civil rights, and environmental protection, and it informs recent controversies concerning the new federalism, decentralization, reindustrialization, revenue sharing, the rise of the Southern Rim, and the Sagebrush Rebellion.

American politicians and political theorists of all persuasions have discussed patterns of governmental power within the nation. Conservatives from John C. Calhoun to James J. Kilpatrick, liberals from Thomas Jefferson to Franklin Roosevelt, radicals from Thomas Paine to Murray Bookchin—all have been interested in the spatial distribution of political power and ideology at the subnational level.

An essential feature of federalism, perhaps our most important contribution to political thought, is its understanding of the significance of territorial parts within a large scale nation and its deliberate combination of the democratic and representative possibilities of local and national governments. Madison's belief that "in a democracy, the people meet and exercise the government in person; in a republic they assemble and administer it by their representatives and agents. A democracy consequently will be confined to a small spot. A republic may be extended over a large nation," has profoundly shaped the areal division of powers within the United States.[1]

Foreign observers have often confirmed the strength of this spatial system by praising American local government and provincial patriotism as mainstays of democracy and nationalism. In the 1830s Alexis de Tocqueville admired the vigor of subnational politics and observed that the "The public zeal of the Union is nothing more than an abstract of the patriotic zeal of the provinces," and sixty years later James Bryce noted that "It is from their local government that the political ideals of the American people have been formed: and they have applied to their State assemblies and their national assembly the customs which grew up in a smaller area."[2]

An immense amount of scholarship has been devoted to understanding the regional dimensions of American government and politics, the geographical patterns of public opinion and political belief, and the relationship between various levels of loyalties within the nation. The materials in this chapter are highly selective and represent at least three general approaches to regional political theory. Political theorists in one group are largely interested in a global overview and theoretical understanding of the relationship between regionalism and nationalism. Scholars such as Walker Connor, Robert Dahl, Leopold Kohr, Harold Isaacs, John Schaar, John Armstrong, Louis J. Snyder, and others provide valuable understanding of the relationships between local, regional, and national patriotisms and the significance of the rise of cultural pluralism, ethno-nationalism, and decentralization throughout the world.

A second, more empirically-oriented group of political scientists is primarily concerned with mapping and analyzing the regional distribution of party loyalty, political beliefs, and governmental power within the United States. Heavily influenced by the pioneering work of Frederick Jackson Turner and V. O. Key, scholars such as Daniel Elazar, Ira Sharkansky, James Fesler, Julius Turner, and Richard Bensel have developed detailed regional anatomies of American political culture. Taking a slightly different tack than the regional model builders, a number of commentators, including James Q. Wilson, Kevin Phillips, Horace Sutton, Kirkpatrick Sale, Joel Garreau, Richard Lamm and Michael McCarthy, Neal Peirce and Jerry Hagstrom, have analyzed the political realignments caused by the post-World War II rise of the Southern Rim.

As in other disciplines, some political scientists explain the way things are, while others visualize the way things ought to be. A third and final approach is represented by normative political thinkers such as Murray Bookchin, Kirkpatrick Sale, David Morris, Karl Hess, Donald Davidson, W.Y. Elliott, William Munro, and others who have advocated a spectrum of regional solutions to political problems. They promote permutations of anarchism, decentralism, bioregionalism, ecofeminism, green politics, agrarianism, and federalism; their regional solutions range from adjusting the federal system to dismantling the nation into autonomous regional commonwealths. (The interdisciplinary bioregional movement, in particular, is well represented here with several special magazine issues and contributions by Bookchin, Sale, Fritjof Capra, James Parsons, Charlene Spretnak, and Richard Louv.) Such disparate visions of the way society ought to be add a vital moral dimension to understanding the spatial dynamics of power.

The political dimension of regionalism is such an immense subject that it has been necessary to slight several areas of related interest. The innumerable case studies of the politics of localities, single states, and single regions, for example, are generally excluded unless they explicitly contribute to a larger understanding of political regionalism. The vast body of scholarship devoted to theories of nationalism—e.g., the work of Carlton Hayes, Hans Kohn, Karl Deutsch, Boyd Shafer, John Herz, and others—while often useful for understanding the region as a source of loyalty predating the nation, is largely excluded except for those sources in which region and regionalism receive central attention. Out of the myriad of studies of federalism, only those that focus upon regionalism and the spatial division of powers have been included here.

Finally, there is a tremendous amount of cross-disciplinary work in political regionalism. See entries under Architecture and Planning, Economics, and Geography: Distributional Studies for related studies.

M.S.

---

[1]James Madison, "The Federalist No. 14," in *The Federalist*, ed. Jacob E. Cooke. (New York: World Publishing Co., 1961), 84.

[2]Alexis de Tocqueville, *Democracy in America*. Translated by Henry Reeve (London : Oxford Univ. Press, 1946), 107. James Bryce, *The American Commonwealth*. vol. 1, 3d ed. (New York: Macmillan, 1899), 192.

*　　　　　*　　　　　*

1402. Adrian, Charles. "Regional Analysis in Political Science." *Social Science Quarterly* 49 (June 1968): 27–32.

Adrian describes a revival of interest in the region as a unit of political analysis—a revival stemming largely from the work of V.O. Key—and urges political scientists to refine their sense of the region by looking to the regional theory of historians, planners, and sociologists and by carefully considering the strengths and weaknesses of the traditional groups of states approach. This essay is part of a published symposium, "On Regionalism and State Public Policy," containing useful articles by political scientists Adrian, Clarence Ayres, and Ira Sharkansky (items 1407, 1466), rural sociologist Alvin Bertrand (item 1537), and historian Joe Frantz.

1403. Anton, Thomas J. "Power, Pluralism, and Local Politics." *Administrative Science Quarterly* 7 (March 1963): 425–57.

After describing the contrast between sociologists such as C. Wright Mills and Floyd Hunter, who perceive local political power concentrated in the hands of an elite, and political scientists such as Edward Banfield and Robert Dahl, who argue that such power is scattered among a plurality of interests groups, Anton urges social scientists in general to measure how much power local communities exercise in relationship to larger social units.

1404. Armstrong, John A. *Nations Before Nationalism.* Chapel Hill: Univ. of North Carolina Press, 1982.

This impressively researched, wide-ranging study carefully examines the emergence of territorial identity among groups of people thousands of years before the rise of far-flung nationalism as a self-conscious ideology. Especially germane to understanding the evolution of various forms and levels of patriotism and the historical relationship between regionalism and nationalism are "An Approach to the Emergence of Nations," pp. 3–13; "Sedentary versus Nomad: The Emergence of Territorial Identity," pp. 14–53; "Polis and Patria," pp. 93–128; and "Imperial Polities: The Centralization Imperative," pp. 168–200. For closely related sources in this chapter, see Connor, Isaacs, Schaar, and Snyder (items 1413–1415, 1434, 1463, 1469).

1405. Ashford, Douglas E. *Democracy, Decentralization, and Decisions in Subnational Politics.* Beverly Hills, Calif.: Sage Publications, 1976.

After pointing out the paradox that "economic progress does not necessarily enhance democratic government, and may indeed handicap participation and active party politics" at the local level, Ashford describes how political scientists might study the effectiveness of efforts to bolster local political activity. Such central/subunit governmental studies, he argues, should be cross cultural, and these studies are likely to indicate that "drastic institutional change" is needed to insure the survival of meaningful local democracy in advanced industrial nations. See also Fesler and Sharpe (items 1426–1427, 1468).

1406, ———. "Territorial Politics and Equality: Decentralization in the Modern State." *Political Studies* 27 (March 1979): 71–83.

After pointing out the inevitability of territorial differences within modern states and the rise of decentralist politics over the last twenty years, Ashford argues that the most vital understanding of centralization and decentralization in the modern state can be obtained from studying fiscal policies and the spatial distribution of revenue.

1407. Ayres, Clarence E. "Some Reflections on Regionalism." *Social Science Quarterly* 49 (June 1968): 33–35.

Ayres stresses, among other things, that state boundaries are often either too small or too large for the purposes of discerning political patterns and that social scientists and policy makers interested in the problem of uneven regional development must be sensitive to historical-cultural factors perpetuating so-called "underdevelopment." "Has any area a right to be other than it is?" he asks. "If it is poor and mean and ugly, has it a right to be affluent and beautiful? Is it our duty to make it so?"

1408. Bartley, Numan V. "The South and Sectionalism in American Politics." *Journal of Politics* 38 (August 1976): 239–57.

Reviewing the history of the five party systems that have functioned in the United States since the 1790s, Bartley locates a persistent southern brand of politics that is rooted in ethnocultural values. The enduring mark of southern politics, he argues, is a continuing sense on the part of Southerners, both black and white, of being part of a culturally homogeneous island surrounded by a swirling, heterogeneous nation.

1409. Bensel, Richard Franklin. *Sectionalism and American Political Development, 1880–1980.* Madison: Univ. of Wisconsin Press, 1984.

This important, sweeping study of historical patterns of American political sectionalism is the sort of book Frederick Jackson Turner anticipated. "The central thesis of this book," Bensel writes, "is that sectional competition—grounded in a geographical division of labor between economically advanced northern core and the underdeveloped southern and western periphery has been and remains the dominant influence in the American political system." This geographical split—reflecting global core/periphery tensions—has been more important, he argues, than class or ideological differences and will endure despite the much-touted power shift from Frostbelt to Sun Belt. For an insightful review of Bensel's book, see Allan J. Lichtman, "Geography as Destiny," *Reviews in American History* 13 (September 1985), pp. 438–43.

1410. Bookchin, Murray. *The Ecology of Freedom: The Emergence and Dissolution of Hierarchy.* Palo Alto, Calif.: Cheshire Books, 1982.

This is a grand summation of Bookchin's anarchist, decentralist vision of a balanced ecological society.

1411. ———. *Post-Scarcity Anarchism.* Berkeley, Calif.: Ramparts Press, 1971.

In this series of essays written between 1965 and 1968, Bookchin describes how social and economic conditions are ripe for the creation of the "non-repressive utopia envisioned by anarchism," namely a "stateless, classless, decentralized society." Especially useful for understanding the anarcho-communalist vision of decentralization are: "Post-Scarcity Anarchism," pp. 31–54; "Ecology and and Revolutionary Thought," pp. 55–82; and "Towards a Liberatory Technology," pp. 85–139. These arguments are pushed toward a "bioregional" vision in Bookchin's more recent collection, *Toward an Ecological Society* (Montreal: Black Rose Books, 1980). See also Capra and Spretnak, Hess, Kohr, Kropotkin, Louv, and Morris and Hess (items 1412, 1431–1432, 1443, 1446, 1448, 1451) under this heading and Borsodi, Goodman and Goodman, Henderson, and Schumacher under Economics (items 321, 339, 349, 381–382).

1412. Capra, Fritjof and Charlene Spretnak. *Green Politics.* New York: E.P. Dutton, 1984.

Although this book is largely devoted to analyzing the West German Green political movement, "The Green Alternative: It Can Happen Here," pp. 193–222, describes the surge of decentralist, bioregional movements in the United States. A useful appendix of "100 Green Oriented Organizations in the United States" is included. See Bookchin, Louv, Sale, Spretnak, and Special Issues for related sources (items 1410–1411, 1448, 1460–1462, 1473, 1470–1472), as well as numerous entries under Economics.

1413. Connor, Walker. "Nation-Building or Nation-Destroying?" *World Politics* 24 (April 1972): 319–55.

After pointing out that the vast majority or 91 percent of contemporary nation-states are ethnically diverse, Connor argues that most theories of "nation-building" are flawed because of their ignorance or misunderstanding of the significance of ethnic identity. The persistence of cultural diversity within nation-states as well as the resurgence of ethnoregional movements weaken the assumptions of Karl Deutsch and other "nation-building" theorists that modernization inevitably replaces ethnic loyalty with state loyalty. Their theories are also weakened by a misunderstanding of the basic distinction between "nation," whose root meaning connotes primordial ethnic-regional loyalties, and "state," which is a fairly recent legal and administrative construct used to encompass a variety of ethnic or nationality groups. Connor effectively discusses the tension between notions of geopolitical unity and the reality of cultural diversity in "Myths of Hemispheric, Continental, Regional, and State Unity," *Political Science Quarterly* 85 (December 1969): 555–82.

1414. ———. "A nation is a nation, is a state, is an ethnic group is a. . . ." *Ethnic and Racial Studies*, 1 (October 1978): 377–400.

After carefully explaining the fundamental differences between "nation" and "state," "ethnic group" and "citizenry," Connor clarifies our understanding of ethnonational movements by defining such elusive terms as "ethnicity," "primordialism," "pluralism," "tribalism," "regionalism," "communalism," "parochialism," and "subnationalism."

1415. ———. "The Politics of Ethnonationalism." *Journal of International Affairs* 27 (1973): 1–21.

Connor traces the concept of "self-determination" as it was articulated by such disparate figures as Locke and Rousseau, Karl Marx, and Woodrow Wilson. The twentieth century has witnessed a mounting conflict between the centrifugal force of ethnic self-determination and the centripetal pull of the centralized state, and Connor soberly concludes that it is unlikely that "ethnonationalism can be accommodated within existing political structures." (For closely related sources, see Armstrong, Isaacs, and Snyder in this chapter (items 1404, 1434, 1469), Whisnant under American Studies (item 59), and Hechter under Sociology (item 1576).

1416. Dahl, Robert and Edward R. Tufte. *Size and Democracy.* Stanford: Stanford Univ. Press, 1973.

This ambitious book probes questions central to politics and regionalism: "How large should a political system be in order to facilitate rational control by its members? What are the comparative advantages and disadvantages enjoyed by political systems of different sizes?" After surveying opinions of political theorists from Plato to Madison and examining a range of political systems from San Marino to India, Dahl and Tufte conclude that there is no optimal size for a political entity, that neither the small-scale city-state nor the large-scale nation-state are necessary models, and that "Different problems require political units of different sizes." In particular, they urge democratic theorists to focus their attention upon the myriad of interacting political units that exist between the nation-state and the city; they also argue that the larger the nation-state, the more important small-scale units become in the minds of ordinary citizens. See also Fesler and Maass (items 1426–1427, 1449).

1417. Davidson, Donald. "The Political Economy of Regionalism." *American Review* 6 (February 1936): 410–36. Reprinted as "Federation or Disunion: The Political Economy of Regionalism." In *The Attack on Leviathan*, 102–28. Chapel Hill: Univ. of North Carolina Press, 1938.

This Southern Agrarian foray into political science raises many pertinent issues. In addition to arguing that "the diversity of regions rather enriches the national life than impoverishes it," Davidson vigorously indicts the Northeast's political-economic domination of the United States. "The greatest threat to the Federal Union," he feels, "comes not from any rising sectional movement, but from the growth of the Leviathan State which, like the young cowbird, hatching where it did not build, shoulders the native brood from the nest."

1418. ———. "Political Regionalism and Administrative Regionalism." *Annals of the American Academy of Political and Social Sciences* 207 (January 1940): 138–43.

Davidson describes a "gross" form of political regionalism—the common tendency of dominant regions to impose their peculiar ways upon the rest of the nation—and proposes a new form of administrative regionalism to counter such imperialistic political regionalism. The Tennessee Valley Authority, he argues, is an example of the Northeast continuing its exploitation of the South under the guise of regional planning, and careful administrative regionalism is required to ward off such foreign ventures. Other sources by Davidson are listed under Literature (items 1189–1191).

1419. Derthick, Martha. *Between State and Nation: Regional Organizations of the United States.* Washington, D.C.: The Brookings Institute, 1974.

A practical guide to the maze-like limbo of regional organizations between federal and state bureaucracies, this book compares the functions of a variety of regional bodies, ranging from the Tennessee Valley Authority and the Appalachian Regional Council to scores of Federal Regional Councils.

1420. Elazar, Daniel J. *American Federalism: A View From the States.* 3d ed. New York: Harper and Row, 1984.

Heavily influenced by Frederick Jackson Turner, this important book offers a sweeping regional image of American politics. Elazar's description of three "political cultures"—Moralistic, Individualistic, and Traditionalistic—and their geographical distribution has had a major conceptual impact. Especially useful is "The States and the Political Setting," pp. 109–49, which contains a "geology" of American politics. Asserting that political beliefs are the glue that holds sections or regions together, Elazar locates three basic "spheres"—the greater Northeast, the greater South, and the greater West—and eight smaller "sections" within the nation. For useful critiques of Elazar's thesis, see Ira Sharkansky, "The Utility of Elazar's Political Culture: A Research Note," *Polity* 2 (Fall 1969) and Charles A. Johnson, "Political Culture in the American States: Elazar's Formulation Examined," *American Journal of Political Science* 20 (August 1976), pp. 491–509.

1421. ———. *Cities of the Prairie: The Metropolitan Frontier and American Politics.* New York: Basic Books, 1970.

Essentially a case study of the theory of sectional politics developed in the first edition of *American Federalism* (1966): this book carefully examines the political cultures of ten medium sized cities in Illinois, Wisconsin, Minnesota, and Colorado. The case studies are interspersed with useful general discussions of the nature of political cultures, the relationship between the frontier and sectionalism, and an elaboration of the three spheres, eight section scheme. Elazar's "Political Culture on the Plains," *Western Historical Quarterly*, 11 (July 1980), pp. 261–83. is a state by state study of the distribution of Moralistic, Individualistic, and Traditionalistic political cultures from North Dakota to Texas. Elazar's book and its focus upon local political or civic cultures has been amplified and updated in Daniel J. Elazar et al., *Cities of the Prairie Revisited: The Closing of the Metropolitan Frontier* (Lincoln: Univ. of Nebraska Press, 1986).

1422. ———. "Megalopolis and the New Sectionalism." *Public Interest* 11 (Spring 1968): 67–85.

Elazar analyzes the political consequences of the rise of the Sunbelt economies since World War II. Speculating whether the new political sectionalism "will manifest itself in radical or progressive or reactionary ways," he concludes that "the nation as a whole may be in for a rather sensational epoch of ill-will."

1423. ———. "The New Federalism: Can the States be Trusted?" *Public Interest* 53 (Spring 1974): 89–102.

In the process of refuting five common criticisms of moves toward stronger local control, Elazar argues that state and local politics have carried the "brunt of domestic governmental progress in the United States" and represent an essential well-spring of democracy and safeguard against totalitarianism. "Increasingly," he writes, "we are rediscovering the special virtues of local self-government which the Founding Fathers understood so well."

1424. Elazar, Daniel J. and Joseph Zikmund, eds. *The Ecology of American Politics*. New York: Thomas Y. Crowell, 1975.

Elazar's theory of regional political cultures and subcultures constitutes the core of this anthology devoted to the spatial variations of American politics. Useful materials include introductory essays on the concept of political culture in America by Daniel Elazar and Samuel Patterson; a series of historical essays by Page Smith, Sam Bass Warner, Charles Syndor, Wilbur Zelinsky, and others on the ethnic-regional origins and diffusion of moralistic, individualistic, and traditionalistic political subcultures; and essays on state political styles in Wisconsin, Massachusetts, Illinois, and California.

1425. Elliott, W.Y. *The Need for Constitutional Reform*. New York: Whittlesey House, 1935.

Elliott, who was associated with the Vanderbilt regionalists in the 1920s and later taught political science at Harvard, proposes that the United States be reorganized into eleven regional commonwealths. This "United Regions of America," he believes, "would revive drooping federalism and stay the present march of centralization in Washington." This is perhaps the most influential of the many schemes proposed during the interwar decades to formally regionalize American government. For closely related arguments, see Frankfurter and Landis and Munro (items 1428, 1453).

1426. Fesler, James W. "Approaches to the Understanding of Decentralization." *Journal of Politics* 27 (August 1965): 536–66.

Fesler seeks to clarify our understanding of decentralization by distinguishing various forms that it can take and by exploring common misconceptions and contradictions applied to it. These troublesome issues include the linguistic tendency to treat "decentralization" and "centralization" as antithetical when in fact they often function together; the impulse to romanticize decentralization as being rooted in a golden age of village democracy when in reality democracy usually emerged from cities, and democratic reforms were often imposed upon autocratic villages from above; and the paradox inherent in having national governments assume responsibility for decentralization. See Ashford, Sharpe, and Tarrow (items 1405–1406,1465,1475) for directly related studies.

1427. ———. *Area and Administration*. Tuscaloosa: Univ. of Alabama Press, 1949.

This classic study of the spatial distribution of governmental authority reflects a detailed understanding of the regional concept in geography, planning, and sociology. Stressing that "The legal areas of particular governments seldom coincide with or wholly embrace the natural areas defined by the problems with which society must deal," Fesler also describes the difficulties of determining the boundaries of such "composite areas based upon a multiplicity of factors." Arguing that American society is too intricate "to be neatly cut into rectangles by a governmental Paul Bunyan armed with a giant cookie cutter," Fessler outlines the dimensions and functions of different types of governmental areas, distinguishes between vertical and horizontal distributions of authority within these areas, and examines the relationship between governmental centralization and decentralization. See Dahl and Tufte and Maass (items 1416, 1449) for closely related studies.

1428. Frankfurter, Felix and James M. Landis. "The Compact Clause of the Constitution: A Study in Interstate Adjustments." *Yale Law Journal* 34 (1925): 685–758.

Frankfurter and Landis describe the interstate compact as a crucial tool for the formulation of regional government to direct regionally-related problems. Problems such as flood control and the generation and distribution of electrical power, they argue, are usually regional issues and "political thinking must respond to these realizations. Instead of leading to parochialism, it (regional government) will bring fresh ferment of political thought whereby national aims may be achieved through various forms of political adjustment."

1429. Garreau, Joel. *The Nine Nations of North America*. Boston: Houghton Mifflin, 1981.

This widely-read, sprightly written account of the "real" nations that lie beneath the standard political map of North America reflects much of the sentiment behind the "new regionalism" of the 1970s and 1980s. Nine of Garreau's eleven chapters are journalistic portraits of each of the nine nations: New England, the Foundry, Dixie, the Islands, Mexamerica, Ecotopia, the Empty Quarter, the Breadbasket, and Quebec. A lively opening chapter discusses such issues as the sources of subnational identity and the differences between regional diversity and balkanization. A useful, highly eclectic, bibliography is included.

1430. Gibbins, Roger. *Regionalism: Territorial Politics in Canada and the United States*. Toronto: Butterworth and Co., 1982.

Regionalism is an extremely volatile issue in Canadian politics, and this book contrasts the relative decline of political regionalism in the United States to its resurgence in Canada. (For closely related sources, see Schwartz (item 1464) and Jacobs (items 356–358, under Economics).

1431. Hess, Karl. *Community Technology*. New York: Harper and Row, 1979.

Hess describes ways to achieve neighborhood power and local self-sufficiency based upon his experiences in the Adams-Morgan neighborhood in Washington, D.C. and later in rural West Virginia.

1432. ———. *Dear America*. New York: William Morris and Co., 1975.

An appeal for political and economic decentralization is at the heart of Hess's account of his political odyssey from writing speeches for Barry Goldwater in the early 1960s to promoting industrial democracy and community power in the early 1970s. Deeply critical of large-scale systems, either in the form of corporate capitalism or state socialism, Hess promotes the growth of small-scale, worker controlled economic and social units and uncovers the roots of such a pluralist-decentralist vision in American culture. "Thinking Small," pp. 235–50, and "Coming Home," pp. 251–79, are especially effective. For closely related sources see Morris and Hess, Bookchin, Kropotkin, and Kohr (items 1451, 1410–1411,1446, 1443) and Borsodi, Goodman, Goodman and Goodman, Schumacher (items 321, 339, 340, 381–382, under Economics).

1433. Hintze, Hedwig. "Regionalism." *Encyclopaedia of the Social Sciences,* vol 13, 208–18. New York: Macmillan, 1934.

This highly perceptive historical survey of regionalism as cultural and political force in Europe and North America is a classic, indispensable introduction to regional theory. (For a similar sweeping definitional essay, see Vance under Sociology (items 1638–1641).

1434. Isaacs, Harold R. *Idols of the Tribe: Group Identity and Political Change.* New York: Harper and Row, 1975.

This powerful book addresses a central paradox in modern society: the coexistence of forces of global unity and cultural pluralism, of globalization and fragmentation. Never have the possibilities of human unity been greater, yet never have people been more eager to worship the idols of their separate tribes. Isaacs analyzes the fundamental sources of the need for group identity, and he vividly describes the historical, cultural, and psychological dynamics of the "compulsive ingathering" of people into ever smaller tribal units since World War II. He carefully analyzes the ethnic, racial, religious, national, and regional forms of this "great clustering into separatenesses" in Africa, the Middle East, Europe, and the United States, and he evaluates the strengths and weaknesses of this pervasive pluralism. This book is a vital source for understanding the relationship between regionalism and other forms of cultural pluralism in a global context. For closely related sources, see Connor, Kohr, and Snyder (items 1413–1415, 1443, 1469).

1435. Key, V.O. Jr. *American State Politics: An Introduction.* New York: Knopf, 1956.

A firm sense of the regional political patterns pervades this important book. In "Federalism, Sectionalism, One-Partyism," pp. 21–28, Key argues that although traditional forms of political sectionalism are declining, fresh versions will continue to shape state politics.

1436. ———. "The Erosion of Sectionalism." *Virginia Quarterly Review* 31 (Spring 1955): 161–79.

Although focused upon the South, Key's argument has national implications. He asserts that in the near future "internal cleavages within the South will deepen, that both the sentiment and the reality of sectionalism will decline, and that kindred interests in South and North will become more interwoven." In many ways this essay is a theoretical summary of Key's masterpiece, *Southern Politics in State and Nation* (New York: Vintage Books, 1949).

1437. ———. "Sectionalism, Urbanism, and Party." In *Politics, Parties, and Pressure Groups*, 5th ed., 223–53. New York: Thomas Y. Crowell, 1964, 228–53.

This is a masterful summary of the significance of sectionalism in American politics from the formation of the Constitution to the beginning of the Civil Rights movement. The impact of "dual sectionalism" and the influence of urbanization and suburbanization upon traditional sectional alignments are also analyzed.

1438. Kilpatrick, James Jackson. "The Case for 'States' Rights'." In *A Nation of States: Essays on the American Federal System*. Edited by Robert Goldwin, 88–105. Chicago: Rand McNally, 1963, 88–105.

Like a latter day Donald Davidson, Kilpatrick skillfully musters the words of Jefferson, Madison, Marshall, and Tocqueville to argue that vigorous, independent local government is the ultimate bulwark against centralized despotism. Describing "today's zealous centralizers," Kilpatrick warns that "Their god is the the brutal bulldozer, squat as a pagan idol, whose function is to bring down the mountains and to fill the valleys up."

1439. Kincaid, John. "Dimensions and Effects of American Political Cultures." *Journal of American Culture* 5 (Fall 1982): 84–92.

After discussing the notion of political and civic cultures, Kincaid describes and maps the geographical distribution of individualistic, moralistic, and traditionalistic political cultures as defined by Daniel Elazar.

1440. ———. "Toward the Third Century of American Federalism: New Dynamics and New Perspectives." *American Studies International* 22 (April 1984): 86–122.

In addition to surveying traditional scholarship on American federalism, Kincaid discusses studies of such recent developments as the New Federalism and the renewal of state and local government since the 1960s. An extensive bibliography is included.

1441. ———, ed. "The Study of American Political Subcultures." *Publius* 10 (Spring 1980).

This special issue includes such particularly useful essays for understanding political regionalism as Kincaid's "Political Cultures of the American Compound Republic," pp. 1–15, and Daniel Elazar's "Afterword: Steps in the Study of American Political Culture," pp. 127–39.

1442. Kirk, Russell. "The Prospect for Territorial Democracy in America." In *A Nation of States: Essays on the American Federal System,* edited by Robert Goldwin, 42–64. Chicago: Rand McNally, 1963.

Kirk asserts that centralization has had few champions in America and that most Americans have agreed with the Founding Fathers that "American democracy is essentially territorial or local in character."

1443. Kohr, Leopold. *The Breakdown of Nations.* New York: Routledge and Kegan Paul, 1986.

First published in 1957, this increasingly influential book develops a "new and unified political philosophy centering in the theory of size." Contradicting much orthodox political thought and nationalistic ideology, Kohr bluntly asserts that "there seems only one cause behind all forms of social misery: bigness. . . . Whenever something is wrong, something is too big." With impressive interdisciplinary breadth and historical sensitivity, Kohr catalogues the miseries arising from large scale socio-political systems and argues that individual well-being and global harmony would be enhanced by the breakdown of massive nation-states into small-scale commonwealths. Insightful sections include: "Disunion Now," pp. 55–69; "The Glory of the Small: The Cultural Argument," pp. 115–31; "The Efficiency of the Small: The Economic Argument," pp. 132–69; and "The American Empire," pp. 198–216. A series of maps of possible divisions of the United States and Europe are included. For closely related sources, see Bookchin, Kropotkin, Morris, and Morris and Hess (items 1410–1411, 1446, 1451) and Jacobs and Schumacher (items 356–358, 381–382, under Economics).

1444. Kollmorgen, Walter. "Political Regionalism in the United States—Fact or Myth." *Social Forces,* 15 (October 1936): 102–22.

Kollmorgen applies a geographer's expertise to the political regionalisms of the 1920s and 1930s—particularly the enthusiasms of Turner, Davidson, Munro, Elliott, and various New Deal administrators—and concludes that their hopes for the regional reorganization of American government are highly utopian and fly in the face of inevitable national centralization.

1445. Krich, Aron and Vincent Garofollo. "Regionalism and Politics." *New Mexico Quarterly* 8 (November 1937): 261–69.

Focusing upon the New Mexico regionalists and the Southern Agrarians, Krich and Garofollo warn against the reactionary, possibly fascist, tendencies of regionalist thought.

1446. Kropotkin, Peter. *Fields, Factories, and Workshops Tomorrow.* Edited by Colin Ward. London: Allen and Unwin, 1974.

Originally published in 1898, Kropotkin's vision of a decentralized, stateless society composed of small-scale industrial-agrarian communities has deeply influenced generations of anarcho-communalists. For closely related sources, see Bookchin and Morris and Hess (items 1410–1411, 1451) and Borsodi, Goodman and Goodman, Henderson, and Schumacher (items 321, 339, 349, 381–382, under Economics).

1447. Lamm, Richard D. and Michael McCarthy. *The Angry West: A Vulnerable Land and Its Future.* Boston: Houghton Mifflin, 1982.

Echoing the fierce indignation of Henry Caudill's account of the environmental exploitation of Appalachia in *My Land Is Dying* (1971): Lamm and McCarthy protest the narrowing of the West by outside forces. Surveying the ruthless exploitation of their region by energy hungry corporate forces to the East, the authors lament the "desecration of the land and air and water...the shattering of a way of life" and warn against trading such qualities for the "bubble wealth" of a mining economy. The West, they argue, "is the Matchbelt, not the Sunbelt, where economies blaze brilliantly, then die." This book contains valuable discussions of such regional political issues as the allocation of energy resources, the Sagebrush Rebellion, and the deployment of MX missiles.

1448. Louv, Richard. *America II.* Los Angeles: Jeremy P. Tarcher, 1983.

This journalistic survey of the upsurge of regional-preservationist-environmentalist sentiments since the 1960s urges Americans to adopt some bioregional principles to "build communities, cities, and towns that approach some semblance of self-reliance, but in a way that assures a greater degree of equity; instead of a new countrified population that destroys the land it seeks to enjoy, a people who accept their stewardship of the land."

1449. Maass, Arthur, ed., *Area and Power: A Theory of Local Government.* Glencoe, Ill.: Free Press, 1959.

Taking a slightly different approach to spatial dynamics than Dahl and Tufte (item 1416), the contributors to this volume explore the proper areal division of powers within democracies. Five essays are especially relevant to a conceptual grasp of political regionalism. Maass's "Division of Powers: An Areal Analysis," pp. 9–26, distinguishes various ways to divide power to analyze such divisions. Paul Ylvisaker's "Some Criteria for a 'Proper' Areal Division of Governmental Powers," pp. 27–49, develops basic maxims for the construction of an ideal model. Stanley Hoffmann's "The Areal Division of Powers in the Writings of French Political Thinkers," pp. 113–49, surveys French spatial-political thought from Bodin and Montesquieu to Taine, Tocqueville, and Proudhon. Samuel Huntington's "The Founding Fathers and the Division of Powers," pp. 130–205, is perhaps the most thorough discussion available of the spatial implications of Adams's, Jefferson's, and Madison's thought. The appendix, H.G. Wells's "A Paper on Administrative Areas" (1903), vigorously advocates realigning subnational political boundaries to reflect current social-economic realities.

1450. Mezerik, A.G. *The Revolt of the South and the West.* New York: Duell, Sloan, and Pearce, 1945.

Building upon Walter Prescott Webb's *Divided We Stand* (1937) and anticipating Lamm and McCarthy's *The Angry West* (1982) (item 1447), political scientist Mezerik urges greater regional balance and an end to the economic and political domination of the eastern "corporate aristocracy."

1451. Morris, David and Karl Hess. *Neighborhood Power: The New Localism.* Boston: Beacon Press, 1975.

In many ways a mixture of Paul and Percival Goodman's utopian *Communitas* (1947) and Saul Alinsky's pragmatic *Rules for Radicals* (1971), this book is both a theoretical manifesto and a practical guide for building local self-reliance. Based upon their experience in the Adams Morgan community in Washington, D.C., Morris and Hess argue, in part, that "People are not galactic atoms floating in space... people live in particular places and work in particular places," and that politics should thrive where people live. Large-scale economic and political units, on the other hand, "are actually social dinosaurs, lumbering toward a time when the urgent demands of practical nature will make them extinct and obsolete." For closely related sources, see, Bookchin and Kropotkin (items 1410–1411, 1446); Alperovitz and Faux, Borsodi, Goodman and Goodman, Henderson, and Schumacher under Economics (items 315, 321, 339, 349, 381–382).

1452. Moynihan, Daniel P. "The Politics and Economics of Regional Growth." *Public Interest* 51 (Spring 1978): 3–21.

Moynihan deftly traces patterns of national response to regional decline, from New Deal programs to aid the "benighted South" in the 1930s to the War on Poverty with its spotlight upon Appalachia in the 1960s. With the history of such efforts in mind, Moynihan reminds the prospering Sunbelt that it is time to return the favor and help the declining Northeast.

1453. Munro, William B. *The Invisible Government.* New York: Macmillan, 1928.

Echoing Frederick Jackson Turner and Josiah Royce, Munro argues in his final chapter, "Our Strengthening Sectionalism," pp. 136–64, that political sectionalism is "inevitable and desirable" in a nation as vast and varied as ours and that a "stabilizing provincialism" is necessary for a sense of identity amid mass society. Munro points out that "North Dakota and Louisiana, although under the same flag, are less alike than Denmark and Sicily," and he believes that the region ought to be our primary subnational entity. Munro refined this regional proposal in "Regional Governments for Regional Problems," *Annals of the American Academy of Political and Social Science* 183 (May 1936), pp. 123–32. For closely related arguments, see Elliott, and Frankfurter and Landis (items 1425, 1428).

1454. Parsons, James J. "On 'Bioregionalism' and 'Watershed Consciousness'." *Professional Geographer* 37 (February 1985): 1–6.

A succinct, carefully researched discussion of the origins and implications of two intertwined regional political movements.

1455. Patterson, Samuel. "The Political Cultures of the American States." *Journal of Politics* 30 (February 1968): 187–209.

After surveying the concept of political culture as developed by Gabriel Almond, Lucien Pye, Daniel Elazar, and others, Patterson describes American political culture at two levels: the political attitudes, values, and beliefs shared by all Americans and those shared by state and regional groups within the United States.

1456. Peirce, Neal R. and Jerry Hagstrom. *The Book of America: Inside Fifty States Today.* New York: W.W. Norton, 1983.

A massive synthesis of Peirce's many books on the politics, economics, and culture of particular American regions, this book discerns general regional patterns in the early 1980s, including the spread of political and economic decentralization, the rise of Frost Belt/Sun Belt tensions, gentrification of inner city neighborhoods and revival of remote rural areas. It also contains detailed state-by-state analyses of the economic-political conditions of eight American regions: the Mid-Atlantic, New England, the Great Lakes, the Border South, the Deep South, the Great Plains, the Mountains, and the Pacific Coast.

1457. Phillips, Kevin P. "The Balkanization of America." *Harper's* 256 (May 1978), 37–47.

Phillips, who coined the word "sun-belt" in the late 1960s, roundly criticizes the resurgence of economic, political, and cultural regionalism in the late 1970s as symptoms of the possible "decomposition of the American polity." See Phillips's *The Emerging Republican Majority* (New Rochelle, N.Y.: Arlington House, 1969) for the initial use of the term "sun-belt" and an influential analysis of the politics of that emerging region. For closely related sources, see Bensel, Price, Sale, and Sutton (items 1409, 1458, 1460–1462, 1474).

1458. Price, Kent A., ed. *Regional Conflict and National Policy.* Washington, D.C.: Resources for the Future, 1982.

This book contains seven papers from a 1981 public forum regarding regional conflict over oil, gas, coal, water, and agricultural resources in the 1970s. The Arab oil embargo of 1973–74 intensified the tension between energy producing and energy consuming regions, and these papers explore the political and economic ramifications of this contrast. Particularly useful essays include Senator Paul Tsongas's "Foreword," pp. xi-xiv; Nathan Rosenberg's "History and Perspective," pp. 18–33; Hans H. Landsberg's "Energy 'Haves' and 'Have-Nots'," pp. 34–58; and Gilbert F. White's "Epilogue," pp. 126–31.

1459. Rafuse, Robert W. *The New Regional Debate: A National Overview.* Washington, D.C.: National Governors' Conference, Center for Policy Research and Analysis, 1977.

This 25–page monograph describes the resurgence of regional political organizations in the 1970s and analyzes a flurry of newspaper and periodical articles on regional tensions that appeared in 1976. Critical of the alarmist nature of these articles, Rafuse calls for a more deliberate analysis of the many issues lumped under the term "regionalism."

1460. Sale, Kirkpatrick. *Dwellers on the Land: The Bioregional Vision.* San Francisco: Sierra Club Books, 1985.

Dedicated to the emerging, bioregional movement, this book is an attempt to "lay some of its groundwork, suggest some of its basic outlines, and gather in one place some of its wisdom." Sale examines, among other things, the primeval Gaea myth and its contemporary relevance; the principles of the present bioregional paradigm and the myriad of grass roots organizations within it; the economic, political, and social implications of bioregionalism; and the theoretical contributions of Frederick Jackson Turner, Lewis Mumford, Howard Odum, E.F. Schumacher, Gary Snyder, Peter Berg, and others. An effective bibliography of regional and bioregional thought is included.

1461. ———. *Human Scale.* New York: Coward, McCann & Geoghegan, 1980.

Building upon the insights of Leopold Kohr, E.F. Schumacher, Lewis Mumford, and others, this encyclopedic study graphically depicts the "burden of bigness" in human affairs. With impressive historical depth and disciplinary breadth, Sale outlines the economic, political, and environmental problems spawned by the large scale, centralized nation-state and suggests regional alternatives rooted in decentralist and anarcho-syndicalist visions of small-scale work democracies.

1462. ———. *Power Shift: The Rise of the Southern Rim and Its Challenge to the Eastern Establishment.* New York: Random House, 1975.

In vivid terms, Sale argues that since World War II the political and economic power and even the central cultural values of the nation have shifted "from the older and colder sections of the Northeast to the younger and sunnier sections of the South and Southwest." Although the entire book is concerned with the political consequences of this shift, Sale's discussions of "The Cowboy Conquest," pp. 207–72, and "The Yankee Counterattack," pp. 273–310, are especially insightful. This was one of the first, and remains one of the most perceptive, analyses of this fundamental regional realignment.

1463. Schaar, John. "The Case for Patriotism." In *Legitimacy and the Modern State,* edited by John Schaar, 285–311. New Brunswick, N.J.: Transaction Books, 1981.

Schaar's contrast between the diffuse, aggressive nature of nationalism and the more focused, intimate nature of genuine patriotism has profound implications for the understanding of regionalism. "Nationalism," he argues, is "patriotism's bloody brother." His belief in the need for a "natural" or "primary patriotism of place" rooted in a familiar environment is echoed throughout regional literature.

1464. Schwartz, Mildred A. *Politics and Territory: The Sociology of Regional Persistence in Canada.* Montreal: McGill Univ. Press, 1974.

An immense literature is devoted to Canadian political regionalism, and this book is a perceptive analysis of Canadian political culture as a case study of the relationship between cultural pluralism and modernization. Such studies heighten our understanding of regional and ethnic politics in the United States. For directly related sources, see Gibbens (item 1430) and Bennett and Vallee (items 75–75, 136, under Anthropology).

1465. Sharkansky, Ira. "Economic Development, Regionalism and State Political Systems." *Midwest Journal of Political Science* 12 (February 1968): 41–61.

Along with Daniel Elazar and Richard Bensel, Sharkansky is one of the foremost contemporary proponents of regional political analysis. In this article he urges political scientists to pay greater attention to the impact of "regional historical experiences" upon political behavior. Sharkansky offers several examples of how regional identity has been more salient than economics as a factor in voter turnout and concludes that the region is an important independent variable in the "systematic study of the American states."

1466. ———. "Regionalism, Economic Status and the Public Policies of American States." *Social Science Quarterly* 49 (June 1968): 10–26.

Sharkansky argues that local and state public policies are largely determined by a mixture of economic and regional factors. While immediate economic circumstances influence policies, it is also necessary "to weigh heavily the likelihood that historical experiences shared by neighboring states have had a lasting impact on public policies." Economic and historical-regional factors are often intertwined and neither offer sufficient explanations of local public policy by themselves.

1467. ———. *Regionalism in American Politics*. Indianapolis: Bobbs-Merrill, 1970.

This important book attempts to correct shortcomings in regional political theory by employing multiple definitions of American regions, searching for historically ingrained regional patterns beneath current economic circumstances, and going beyond single region studies to cross-regional comparisons. The most useful portions of this book for the regional generalist are Sharkansky's introduction, pp. 3–16; dissection of the United States into seventeen political regions and subregions in "The Empirical Analysis of Regions," pp. 17–48; and masterful overview of regionalism in political theory in "The Literature of Regionalism and Comparative State Politics," Appendix A, pp. 163–83. Sharkansky has refined and updated his regional analysis in *The Maligned States* (New York: McGraw-Hill, 1978), especially "Justification for Strong State Governments: Diversity in Culture, Economics, and Politics," pp. 19–51.

1468. Sharpe, L.J., ed. *Decentralist Trends in Western Democracies*. Beverly Hills, Calif.: Sage Publications, 1979.

This wide-ranging anthology explores the resurgence of decentralist, pluralistic movements within western nations since World War II. The various analyses of theories of spatial decentralization and discussions of neighborhood councils and regional ethnic nationalisms in Europe and America are especially useful. See, for example, Nelson Polsby's preface, pp. 1–7; L.J. Sharpe's "Decentralist Trends in Western Democracies: A First Appraisal," pp. 9–79; Warren Magnusson's "The New Neighborhood Democracy: Anglo-American Experience in Historical Perspective," pp. 119–56; and Anthony Mughan's "Modernization and Regional Relative Deprivation: Towards a Theory of Ethnic Conflict," pp. 279–312. For directly related sources, see Ashford, Fesler, Isaacs, Kohr, Morris and Hess, Snyder, and Zwerin (items 1405–1406, 1426–1427, 1434, 1443, 1451, 1469,1479).

1469. Snyder, Louis L. *Global Mini-Nationalism: Autonomy or Independence*. Westport, Conn.: Greenwood, 1982.

Paralleling the work of Connor, Isaacs, Kohr and others, Snyder analyzes the dramatic rise of separatist movements since the 1940s and the possibility of the fragmentation of the present system of nation-states. Snyder's book develops vivid continent by continent analyses of scores of ethnic-religious groups—e.g., Quebecois, Basques, Kurds, Sikhs, Tamils—seeking regional freedom. It also contains a firm vision of the sources of nationalism and its continuing relationship to regionalism. Particularly useful for understanding American political and cultural regionalism are "Nationalism and Its Peripheries," pp. 1–10; "Characteristics of Mini-Nationalisms," pp. 11–24; and especially "The American Mosaic," pp. 199–222, with its analyses of Native American, black, and Puerto Rican separatism.

1470. Special Issue. "Bioregions." *CoEvolution Quarterly* 32 (Winter 1981).

Twenty-four essays on bioregional theory and practice in North America, Africa, Europe, and the Far East are included. Especially useful essays include Jim Dodge's "Living by Life: Some Bioregional Theory and Practice," pp. 6–12; Murray Bookchin's "The Concept of Social Ecology," pp. 14–23; Peter Berg's "Devolving Beyond Global Monoculture," pp. 24–30; and a survey of "American Bioregional Experience," pp. 86–90.

1471. Special Issue. "Bioregionalism and the Politics of Place." *Utne Reader* 14 (February/March 1986).

A central section of this issue contains five essays debating the strengths and weaknesses of bioregional politics. Included are excerpts from Kirkpatrick Sale's *Dwellers in the Land* (item 1460); Walter Truett Anderson's "The Pitfalls of Bioregionalism," pp. 35–38; Ted Relph's "Seeing With the Soul of the Eye," pp. 40–43; and a useful guide to bioregional groups across the United States.

1472. Special Issue. "Green Politics." *Utne Reader* 23 (September/October 1987).

Six essays assess the significance of the Green Movement in the United States, including Jay Walljasper's "Prospects for Green Politics in the U.S.," pp. 37–39; Norman Atkin's "The New Activists: Politics Among the Post-Boom Generation," pp. 40–43; and essays on sacred space and geomancy.

1473. Spretnak, Charlene. *The Spiritual Dimension of Green Politics.* Santa Fe, N.M.: Bear & Company, 1986.

In addition to stressing the need for a spiritual foundation to sustain the groundswell of environmental politics of the 1980s—including bioregionalists, ecofeminists, greens, and others—Spretnak outlines a spiritual platform for these various groups. See "Four Goals for the

Green-at-Heart," pp. 70–74, and "Appendix: Ten Key Values of the American Green Movement," pp. 75–82.

1474. Sutton, Horace. "Sunbelt vs. Frostbelt: A Second Civil War?" *Saturday Review* (April 15 1978): 28–37.

Characteristic of a flurry of sectional forebodings in the late 1970s, Sutton argues that the rising political-economic power of the the South and Southwest has provoked a dangerously defensive posture on the part of members of Congress from the Northeast and Midwest. Comparing such activities to regional-separatist movements around the world, Sutton warns that "From the sharp edge of partisan regionalism it is not too long a step to separatism.... once in the the bloodstream, regionalism is as hard to expunge as dengue fever."

1475. Tarrow, Sidney G., Peter J. Katzenstein, and Luigi Graziano, eds. *Territorial Politics in Industrial Nations.* New York: Praeger, 1978.

Tarrow's "Introduction," pp. 1–27, is a perceptive survey of recent literature examining the changing relationships between central governments and their territorial subunits in western, industrialized nations. Theories of decentralization, ethnonationalism, and center-periphery relationships are analyzed. Essays focus on decentralization and grassroots movements in Italy, Israel, France, Austria, Poland, and the northeast United States.

1476. Turner, Julius. *Party and Constituency: Pressures on Congress.* rev. ed. by Edward V. Schneier, Jr. Baltimore: Johns Hopkins Press, 1970.

In this important book, Turner and Schneier demonstrate how regional interests along with rural-urban, ethnic, racial, and religious differences have influenced voting patterns in the House of Representatives since the 1930s. "Sectionalism: The Democratic Party," pp. 165–89, and "Sectionalism: The Republican Party," pp. 191–209, are highly perceptive overviews. For closely related sources, see Bensel, Elazar, Key, and Sharkansky (items 1409, 1420–1424, 1435, 1465–1467).

1477. Wilson, James Q. "A Guide to Reagan Country: The Political Culture of Southern California." *Commentary* 43 (May 1967): 37–45. Reprinted in *The Ecology of American Political Culture*, edited by Daniel J. Elazar and Joseph Zikmund, 228–44. New York: Thomas Y. Crowell, 1975.

This witty, insightful discussion of the political world view of newly arrived, rootless suburbanites in Southern California and their impact upon national politics anticipates Phillips's and Sale's analyses of Sun Belt individualistic conservatism.

1478. Wolfinger, Raymond E. and Fred I. Greenstein. "Comparing Political Regions: The Case of California." *American Political Science Review* 63 (1969): 74–85.

Using the ideological contrasts between Northern and Southern California as a case study of "the regional differences that abound within political systems," Wolfinger and Greenstein carefully analyze the possible sources of Bay Area liberalism and Southern California conservatism.

1479. Zwerin, Michael. *A Case for the Balkanization of Practically Everyone.* London: Wildwood House, 1976.

Zwerin's book is a journalistic, personal account of the rise of regional separatism in Europe and North America, particularly among the Basques, Welsh, Gypsies, Bretons, American Iroquois, Catalans, and Lapps. Swiss federalism is examined as a possible model for resolving tensions between center and peripheral.

Psychology

The literature cited in this section has little to say about region as concept. It has a great deal to say about region as object of study. A very few of the sources cited do speculate about "regional states of mind," but such concerns are more likely to surface among social psychologists listed under the next heading than among the psychologists listed here. Studies here cited are focused upon the spatial experience of the individual and the small group.

Over the past decade and a half there has been an explosion of interest in "man-environment" studies and in "environmental design." This is reflected in the range and quality of materials to be found in important anthologies of essays on those subjects (for example, the Proshansky volumes and the collection edited by Moore and Golledge) and in series of volumes on subtopics as summaries of research and as a means to make that research accessible to the undergraduate student and the general reader (notably the series put out by Plenum Press and the series being published by Brooks/Cole and Cambridge).

One can distinguish two general approaches to man-environment studies, psychologically considered. Originally poles apart, they now converge and overlap. One approach is experimental, growing out of the work of such scholars as Lewin and Bruner. As relates to our topic, experimentation has moved out of the laboratory and into the field. Coincidentally there has been an increasing research interest in real-life (as against "controlled") behavior. Such study has also moved away from notions of man as passively responding to stimulus from the outside toward notions of "stimulus information," representing man as actively ordering, and reordering, information at hand. The essay by Ittleson (item 1504) describes that change. The other general approach, with increasing numbers of converts, is phenomenological, growing out of the work of Heidegger, Husserl and Sartre. An earlier emphasis upon philosophical issues has supplied the groundwork for a present emphasis upon application to design of homes and neighborhoods. The essay by Korosec-Serfaty (item 1506) reviews the progress of phenomenological psychology.

The importance of these developments to region as object of study can hardly be overstated. Experimentalists and phenomenologists are both interested in cognitive maps, which of course is an important emergent interest among geographers. Both are interested in design and planning, and are insisting upon a shift from top-down planning to a bottom-up approach, responding to real-life use. Yet more comprehensively, both increasingly represent man's relation to the environment as active, or, more exactly, interactive. In such terms, region becomes centrally important, as one dimension of "home;" as well as radically problematic, the uncertain product of innumerable interactions.

For related entries see also Architecture and Planning, Geography: Perception Studies, Philosophy, and Sociology.

C.M.

1480. Altman, Irwin. *Culture and Environment*. Monterey, Calif.: Brooks/Cole Publishing Co., 1980.

Like other books in this Brooks/Cole series (and the parallel Cambridge Univ. Press series), this is addressed to interested undergraduates and laymen. The book surveys the literature, employing a systems approach including physical environment as a principal factor. It incorporates cross-cultural perspectives on the subject and approaches values in terms of dialectics between public and private, stability and change. There is a good discussion of the meanings of privacy and the American home, and a good, brief bibliography. See also *The Environment and Social Behavior: Privacy, Personal Space, Territory, and Crowding* (Monterey, Calif.: Brooks/Cole Publishing Co., 1975).

1481. ———— et al., eds. *Human Behavior and Environment: Advances in Theory and Research*. New York: Plenum Press, 1976. Vols. 1 and 2.

The lead volumes in a series devoted to the general topic. Subsequent volumes address more particular topics: Volume Three, Children and Environment; Volume Four, Environment and Culture; Volume Five, Transportation and Environment; Volume Six, Behavior and the Natural Environment; Volume Seven, Elderly People and the

Environment; Volume Eight, Home Environments; Volume Nine, Neighborhood and Community Environments.

1482. Altman, Irwin and Carol M. Werner, eds. *Home Environments.* New York: Plenum Press, 1985.

Essays on temporal aspects of home, home and homelessness, experience and the use of dwelling, ritual establishment of home, house as symbol, home and near-home territories, thinking about home, the role of housing in the experience of dwelling, and comparative treatments of policy and homes in U.S. and elsewhere. Includes Dovey (item 1498) and Korosec-Perfaty (item 1506).

1483. Altman, Irwin and Joachim F. Wohlwill, eds. *Children and the Environment.* New York: Plenum Press, 1978.

Essays on children's home environment, children outdoors, school environments, childhood and privacy, cognitive maps and children as planners. Includes Moore and Young (item 1519) and Siegal (item 1525). All articles in the book have good bibliographies.

1484. Barker, Roger G. *Ecological Psychology: Concepts and Methods for Studying the Environment of Human Behavior.* Stanford: Stanford Univ. Press, 1968.

Field-study on site at the Midwest Psychological Field Station at Oskaloosa, Kansas, 1947–1968. Barker studies "behavior settings" as causes of behavior (classroom, playground, baseball field, etc.) Such settings, Barker argues, have structure and are replicable. He develops his own vocabulary, and argues that he is in pursuit of a new science. See also Barker and Herbert F. Wright, *One Boy's Day* (New York: Harper and Row, 1951); and, by the same authors, *Midwest and Its Children* (New York: Harper and Row, 1955).

1485. ———. *Habitats, Environments and Human Behavior.* San Francisco, Calif.: Jossey-Bass, 1978.

Essays summarizing the work of Barker and his colleagues at their Kansas field station. They trace a general shift in thinking from ecological psychology to eco-behavioral science during the twenty-five year history of their fieldwork. Several essays compare environment and behavior in an English town with that in the Midwest. A comprehensive bibliography of Field Station publications is included. As one summary of Barker-style psychology, see Wicker (item 1529).

1486. ———. "The Influence of Frontier Environments on Behavior." In *The American West: New Perspectives, New Dimensions*, edited by Jerome E. Steffen, 61–93. Norman: Univ. of Oklahoma Press, 1959.

Applies behavior-setting theory to frontier experience ideally considered. Barker argues that because the frontier was undermanned and unfinished, it gave certain qualities to frontier experience like those identified by Frederick Jackson Turner.

1487. Bollnow, Otto F. "Lived Space." In *Readings in Existential Phenomenology*, edited by Nathaniel Lawrence and Daniel O'Connor, 178–86. Englewood Cliffs, N.J.: Prentice-Hall, 1967.

Seminal essay in the phenomenological mode. Lived-space is described as always involving leaving and return, centering on dwelling, and radiating out from the individual. Doors and windows keep a house from becoming a prison. The world beyond the protective boundaries of the home has its own exciting and fearful qualities. Roads and roaming area also invested with particular qualities.

1488. Bruner, Jerome S. and C.C. Goodman. "Value and Need as Organizing Factors in Perception." *Psychology* 42 (1947): 33–44.

Article sets forth opposition to stimulus-response theory, arguing for behavioral as well as autochthonous (elecrochemical) behavior. It shows how children distort perception (e.g., poor children perceive coins as being larger than do those who are better off). For a sampling of Bruner's later work see *Beyond the Information Given* (1973), and its introductory essay by Jeremy M. Anglin, reviewing Bruner's work.

1489. Campbell, Robert D. "Personality as an Element of Regional Geography." *Annals of the Association of American Geographers* 58 (December 1968): 748–58.

Reviews literature on personality: individual (motive, self-view, world-view), collective or group (uniformity as against diversity, modal personality), national character (arguments for and against). The psychological dimension of man-land relationships, Campbell says, needs to be taken into account by geographers.

1490. Canter, David. *The Psychology of Place*. New York: St. Martin's Press, 1977.

Uses distance estimates, cognitive maps, and verbal descriptions of areas, and takes into account differences in class and gender. Canter tries to call upon all related disciplines. Place, large or small, is the basic unit of the environment. Canter's general objective is to improve planning, so that place is seen as locus of action, and not as an object. See also Canter and Terrence Lee., eds., *Psychology and the Built Environment* (New York: John Wiley and Sons, 1974).

1491. Canter, David and Peter Stringer, eds. *Environmental Interaction: Psychological Approaches to our Physical Surroundings.* New York: International Universities Press, 1975.

Chapters on thermal, acoustic, luminous and spatial environments; on life in the city; and on public decision-making. In the introductory chapter, Canter argues against environmental psychology as a term, and for a term that denotes human interaction with the environment, in physics and geography as well as psychology.

1492. Cobb, Edith. *The Ecology of Imagination in Childhood.* With an Introduction by Margaret Mead. New York: Columbia Univ. Press, 1977.

A remarkable synthesis of materials from all quarters, the physical sciences and the creative arts included, emphasizing the formal techniques of psychological study and field observation. Cobb argues that creativity and individuation in childhood is necessary to human evolution. Unlike the young of other animals, the human child must create a cosmos in order to be biologically fulfilled. The book includes a bibliography of Cobb's collection of biographies and autobiographies of childhood from around the world, pp. 119–36.

1493. Coles, Robert. *Migrants, Sharecroppers, Mountaineers.* Vol. 2, *Children of Crisis.* Boston: Little, Brown and Co., 1971.

Oral histories of the three populations, all living in a South in which the traditional rural economy can no longer sustain itself. The emphasis is upon the children involved. Coles is wonderfully sensitive to the geographical dimensions of the dislocation being described.

1494. ———. *The Old Ones of New Mexico.* Photographs by Alex Harris. Albuquerque: Univ. of New Mexico Press, 1973.

Interviews with Mexican-American elders in a village outside Albuquerque. Coles attempts to capture the tradition and faith of his subjects, emphasizing habit, daily rhythms and the wisdom of experience. The final passage, describing tourists stalled by a herd of sheep crossing a highway, underscores the incommensurateness between old ways and new. Coles's text is attended by a photographic essay.

1495. ———. *The South Goes North*. Vol. 3, *Children of Crisis*. Boston: Little, Brown and Co., 1971.

Companion volume to *Migrants, Sharecroppers, Mountaineers* (item 1493). An oral-historical treatment of the experience of moving from the agricultural South to northern cities. It conveys a detailed sense of the trauma involved. As always with Coles, there is a wonderful sensitivity to the geographical dimensions of the experiences being described.

1496. Cone, John and Steven Hayes. *Environmental Problems/Behavior Solutions*. Monterey, Calif.: Brooks/Cole Publishing Co, 1980.

A primer on behavior modification (behavioral "technology"), as a dimension of technological modifications addressing environmental problems. The emphasis is on a straightforward stimulus-response kind of psychology.

1497. Cooper, Clare. "The House as Symbol of the Self." In *Designing for Human Behavior: Architecture and the Behavioral Sciences*, edited by Jan T. Lang et al., 130–45. Stroudsburg, Penn.: Dowden, Hutchinson and Ross, 1974.

Argues that the house is an archetype of the self, in Jungian fashion. Cooper cites a variety of evidence to suggest how this works (e.g., a woman when pregnant puts peculiar intensity into cleaning house). She says that "normal" Americans lack identity with the extra-human environment, in a way that people called abnormal do not.

1498. Dovey, Kimberly. "Home and Homelessness." In *Home Environments* (item 1482), 33–64.

A lucid, compact summary of the phenomenology of home. The home is basic to spatial and temporal identity. It is best seen in terms of binary opposites, e.g., home/journey, inside/outside, certainty/doubt. There are social dialectics involved: self/other, private/public, etc., as well as dialectics of appropriation (e.g., ours/theirs). Dovey talks of the homelessness which occurs when the external world is seen as threatening and boundaries harden. As an architect, Dovey is particulary interested in the implications for design. See also Dovey, "Home: An Ordering Principle in Space," *Landscape* 22 (Spring 1978), pp. 27–30.

1499. Edney, J.J. "Human Territories: Comment on Functional Properties." *Environment and Behavior* 8 (1976): 31–48.

Review of literature from a behavioral point of view, taking off from E.T. Hall (see item 1502). Edney argues that humans are different from animals in that control of relationships, not dominance over others, is the principal motive in ordering communities, small groups, and individual life. He suggests that there is a need for studies of deterritorialization.

1500. Estvan, F.J. and E.W. Estvan. *The Child's World: His Social Perception.* New York: G.P. Putnam's Sons, 1959.

A study of first- and sixth-grade pupils in two midwestern communities. Both groups were shown pictures of various types of landscapes. The first-graders reacted to ingredients in the landscapes, especially people, rather than to the landscape as a whole. The sixth-graders recognized the landscapes as units and could discuss their social and economic contexts.

1501. Freedman, Johnathan L. *Crowding and Behavior.* San Francisco, Calif.: W.H. Freeman and Co., 1975.

Argues that crowding is not bad, that humans do not have a territorial instinct like in kind with that of animals, and that crowding, generally, does not make for more crime or reduce sex urges. Density, Freedman argues, intensifies whatever emotions a person has.

1502. Hall, Edward T. *The Hidden Dimension.* Garden City, N.Y.: Doubleday, 1966.

A landmark discussion of proxemics (non-verbal communication through manipulation of interpersonal space). Hall posits spatial zones (intimate, personal, social, public). Distances between individuals are regulated according to the zone involved, and vary by culture. Hall is the author of many other books on the same general topic. (See items 99–100, under Anthropology).

1503. Hayward, D. Geoffrey. "Home as an Environmental and Psychological Concept." *Landscape* 29 (October 1975): 2–9.

Home a label for several things: physical structures, area, neighborhood or territory, locus in space (in terms of which other places are located), as the base of self and self-identity (citing Cooper, item 1497), and as a social and cultural unit (in distinction from those who are homeless, for example).

1504. Ittleson, W. H. "Environmental Perception and Perceptual Theory." In *Environment and Cognition*, edited by Ittleson, 1–19. New York: Seminar Press, 1973.

Summarizes research on the subject: an old emphasis on stimulus-response has been replaced by an emphasis on stimulus information subject to continuous reordering by the mind. Short-term memory is photographic; long-term memory is symbolic. The environment is not an object; it is that which surrounds, always ambiguous, incomplete, and contradictory. The book itself is a collection of essays by scholars in psychology and in related disciplines (geography, architecture, health care, etc.).

1505. Klein, Donald C., ed. *Psychology of the Planned Community: The New Town Experience*. New York: Human Sciences Press, 1978.

A series of brief articles, mostly by psychologists and behavioral scientists, on new towns, and especially on Columbia, Maryland. The editor concludes by remarking that psychologists have not dealt with behavior of entire communities, have not sufficiently understood the need for sense of place, and have undervalued the importance of freedom of choice to residents of a new community.

1506. Korosec-Serfaty, Perla. "Experience and Use of Dwelling." In *Home Environments* (item 1482), 65–86.

The first half of this article is a wide-ranging analysis of terms important to phenomenology in relation to dwelling, citing Husserl, Heidegger and Sartre, especially. The author criticizes Bachelard (item 1328, under Philosophy) for ignoring the economic dimension of his subject. The article concludes with an analysis of interviews with elderly individuals whose houses had been burglarized. Those individuals felt personally violated by the burglar's act.

1507. Kron, Joan. *Home-Psych: The Social Psychology of Home and Decoration*. New York: Clarkson N. Potter, 1983.

A wide-ranging popularized study of the social and psychological significance of dwelling and decoration in contemporary American culture. Chapters are devoted to the meanings of various rooms of the house as well as to considerations of how gender, age, class, and lifestyle differences are reflected in domestic environments. Richly documented.

1508. Krupat, Edward. *People in Cities: The Urban Environment and Its Effects*. Cambridge: Cambridge Univ. Press, 1985.

Summarizes research on the topic for the general reader or the college undergraduate. Krupat distinguishes among levels of description: objective (as from above), sociocultural (as in a subway map); and subjective (of the sort described by Kenneth Lynch, items 183–185, under Architecture and Planning). The city is an arena for contrasting views, but people must retain a sense of control.

1509. Ladd, Florence C. "Black Youths View Their Environment: Neighborhood Maps." *Environment and Behavior* 2 (1970): 74–99.

Children of low-income black families are asked to draw maps of their neighborhoods, in which the author looks for landmarks, complexities, and types of maps drawn.

1510. ———. "Black Youths View Their Environments: Some Views of Housing." *American Institute of Planners Journal* 38 (1972): 108–16.

Follow-up on prior entry, reporting on the same group of youngsters. Ladd analyzes verbal descriptions the youngsters give of their homes. Such descriptions emphasize the interior of the home, especially the kitchen and bedrooms. Exteriors are relatively unimportant. The youngsters talk of particular rooms, though shared, as theirs. They share the dream of living in a suburban home when adults.

1511. Lee, Terrence. "The Urban Neighborhood as a Socio-spatial Schema." *Human Relations* 21 (1968): 241–68.

An elegant and compact argument relating social to spatial patterns. Each individual develops a "schema" of his immediate area, on the basis of which he is able to sketch a rough map of his neighborhood. Individual maps overlap and reinforce one another. Lee argues that planners should plan from the bottom up, taking such individual schemas into account. His conclusions are based upon interviews in Cambridge, England.

1512. Lewin, Kurt. *Principles of Topological Psychology*. New York: McGraw-Hill, 1936.

Applies topology as used in mathematics to psychology, in the interest of making psychology more scientific. Behavior is a function of person and environment. Environment introduces opportunities and constraints, e.g., food costs, time of preparation, enter into choice of food. Lewin is more interested in perception than in the environment itself. This influential work is still often cited (particularly by Barker, items 1484–86).

1513. Lindeman, Edward. "Notes on Psychological Aspects of Regionalism." *Social Forces* 19 (March 1941): 301–06.

Examines "motivational elements" that generate regional thought and practice, including fear of bigness, fear of standardization, fear of modernization and fear of mobility. While sometimes making for reactionary excess, more generally regionalism serves to make the democratic process compatible with the continental expanse of the nation.

1514. Loyd, Bonnie. "Woman's Place, Man's Place." *Landscape* 20 (October 1975): 10–13.

An application of research by Erik Erikson to an analysis of gender and place. Boys in play orient themselves to adventure outside the house walls, girls to domestic activity. Loyd suggests that Erikson may have underemphasized the role of acculturation in causing such differences.

1515. Mehrabian, Albert. *Public Places and Private Spaces: The Psychology of Work, Play and Living Environments*. New York: Basic Books, 1976.

In the manner of Barker (items 1484–1486), talks of behavior and environment in terms of behavior settings. Mehrabian moves from intimate environments (skin, sheets), to the residence, to the work setting, to therapeutic environments, to communal settings. He does so in terms of avoidance/approach, dominance/passivity continua. He talks in terms of exploration, affiliation, and performance.

1516. Michelson, William, Saul V. Levine and Ellen Michelson, eds. 2 vols. *The Child in the City*. Toronto: Univ. of Toronto Press, 1979.

Volume One, subtitled "Today and Tomorrow," contains a series of lectures by well-known scholars in a range of disciplines (e.g., Robert Bremner in history, Jerome Kagan in psychology, Kevin Lynch in planning). Volume Two, subtitled "Changes and Challenges," is made up of papers by a research group in Toronto studying interaction with real-life environments, with the focus on social change, scale, services, and child development.

1517. Milgram, Stanley. "The Experience of Living in Cities." *Science* 167 (1970): 1461–68.

Discusses defense mechanisms used to combat stimulus overload in big cities. People block out and repress stimulation, turn to others for services, distance others through rituals of interaction, give less time to each input, etc. The general result is a complex of devices establishing social distance of one person from another.

1518. Moore, Gary T. and Reginald G. Golledge, eds. *Environmental Knowing: Theories, Research and Methods.* Stroudsburg, Penn.: Dowden, Hutchinson and Ross, 1976.

Encyclopedic collection of articles having to do with environmental cognition. Of particular value is the review of literature by the editors, pp. 3–24; David Stea, "Program Notes on a Spatial Fugue," pp. 106–120; the section on social perspectives and on literature, pp. 196–293, which includes excellent articles by Amos Rapoport and Yi-Fu Tuan, and superb commentary by Anne Buttimer and David Lowenthal; and an extensive bibliography, pp. 393–423.

1519. Moore, Robin and Donald Young. "Childhood Outdoors: Toward a Social Ecology of the Landscape." In *Children and the Environment* (item 1483), 83–130.

An attempt to analyze the "phenomenal" landscape of the child. That landscape has physiographic, social and inner dimensions. Behavior-mapping, tracking, diary use, and child-guided trips are recommended as means to discover that landscape. A set of terms is proposed: the child's landscape is composed of place, pathway, and territorial range; range extension is a venturing out, and range development makes use of those discoveries. Children hide aspects of their landscape from adults, putting them to their own use. Social factors and gender affect those patterns.

1520. Piaget, Jean. *The Child's Conception of the World.* New York: Littlefield, Adams and Co., 1969.

Originally published in 1929. One of many works by Piaget, outlining his influential theory of cognitive development in children, as the child moves from infancy to adolescence, from pre-representational to representational, from egocentric to coordinated systems of reference, from route-type to survey-type representations. Piaget is one of the great theorists on how cognitive maps take shape.

1521. Proshansky, Harold M. et al., eds. *Environmental Psychology: Man and His Physical Setting.* New York: Holt, Rinehart and Winston, 1970.

Bulky collection of previously published articles, intended as means of establishing the field of environmental psychology, having to do with theory and applications. Authors come from many disciplines, psychology among them.

1522. ——— et al., eds. *Environmental Psychology: People and Their Physical Settings*. 2d ed. New York: Holt, Rinehart and Winston, 1976.

A follow-up on the 1970 volume. The essays, mostly reprinted from other sources, only slightly overlap with those in the earlier volume. Like that volume, this one is intended to bring together from many disciplines the materials defining the state of the art in environmental psychology.

1523. Rubenstein, Carin. "Regional States of Mind." *Psychology Today* 16 (February 1982): 22–30.

Popular article drawing upon data from the Institute for Social Research (1976, 1978) and the National Opinion Research Center (1980), along with census data on income, education, etc. Regions are ranked according to outlook on life, stress, negative/positive feelings, personal competence, and overall satisfaction with geographical area.

1524. Searles, Harold F. *The Nonhuman Environment: In Normal Development and in Schizophrenia*. New York: International Universities Press, 1960.

A study of the impact of the nonhuman physical environment upon psychological growth and development throughout the life-cycle. Searles makes a plea for greater awareness among psychologists of the interplay between the physical world and mental growth.

1525. Siegal, Alexander et al. "Stalking the Elusive Cognitive Map: The Development of Children's Representations of Geographic Space." In *Children and the Environment* (item 1483), 223–58.

Develops a scheme of levels of cognition: enactive, allowing movement; perceptual, sorting out landmarks; and symbolic, allowing for a Euclidean perspective. The child goes from one to another level as it develops, so that the negotiation of the environment for the more developed child is a combination of all three. Good bibliography included.

1526. Sommer, Robert. *Personal Space: The Behavioral Basis of Design*. Englewood Cliffs, N.J.: Prentice-Hall, 1969.

An early and influential study of human behavior in public places. Sommer studies real-life situations, attempting to understand the orientation of users, with the object of improving design.

1527. Tolman, E. C. "Cognitive Maps in Rats and Men." *Psychological Review* 55 (1948): 189–208.

A pioneer article on the subject of cognitive maps. Most of the article discusses maze behavior in rats, but at its conclusion Tolman speculates about human cognitive maps, arguing against any simple stimulus-response model. Faulty cognitive maps (in rats and men) may be due to fear of threat, an undue fixation of response and/or a reaction to outgroups.

1528. Whiting, Beatrice B. and John W.M. Whiting. *Children of Six Cultures: A Psycho-Cultural Analysis.* Cambridge: Harvard Univ. Press, 1975.

Review of real-life activity in behavior settings in six cultures. The authors look to home and village environments as clues to the nature of socialization. They develop a paradigm (p. 172). In subsistence cultures children are more nurturant-responsible. In more competitive societies, there is more dominance by symbolic means, with more ego-centered behavior. Children are acculturated by the time they are six.

1529. Wicker, Allan. *An Introduction to Ecological Psychology.* Monterey, Calif.: Brooks/Cole Publishing Co., 1979.

An introduction to Barker's approach, involving all his terms: behavior setting, manning (under, over), maintenance of behavior setting, etc. Analysis is focused upon interaction between the goal-oriented individual and the behavior setting.

1530. Wohlwill, Joachim F. and Gerald D. Weisman. *The Physical Environment and Behavior: An Annotated Guide to the Literature.* New York: Plenum Press, 1981.

A book-length bibliography.

1531. Wolfenstein, Martha. *Disaster: A Psychological Essay.* Glencoe, Ill.: Free Press, 1957.

A study of how people are affected by disasters. There are three sections to the book: threat, impact, aftermath. Data is derived from materials supplied largely by government agencies. Disaster studies are recommended as one way of studying "deterritorialization" (see Edney, item 1499).

Sociology

The sociological study of American regions has followed a pattern familiar in other disciplines. As in anthropology, folk studies, geography, history, and the creative arts, regional sociology had its roots in the 1880s and 1890s, flowered in the 1920s and 1930s, faded in the wake of World War II, and has revived in the 1970s and 1980s.

Franklin Giddings initiated the study of regional social groups at the end of the nineteenth century just as Franz Boas, John Wesley Powell, William Morris Davis, Frederick Jackson Turner, Josiah Royce, and Hamlin Garland were beginning regional work in their respective fields. By the mid-1920s, regional sociology was a thriving subdiscipline, and two full-fledged schools of regional sociology began exerting national and international influence.[1] At the University of North Carolina, Howard Odum, Rupert Vance, Guy Johnson, Katharine Jocher, Arthur Raper, and others analyzed regions largely from the perspective of the rural folk and promoted nationwide regional planning. At the University of Chicago, Robert Park, Ernest Burgess, Roderick McKenzie, Harvey Zorbaugh, Louis Wirth, and their associates visualized regions as areas dependent upon metropolitan cores and were concerned with the human ecology or interrelations of people and communities within these urban regional environments.

Both the Chapel Hill regionalists under Odum and the Chicago human ecologists under Park have made lasting contributions to our understanding of the spatial structure of society. Although enthusiasm for regional sociology waned after the 1940s, there has been a renewal of interest since the 1960s. More diffuse than the earlier movement, the contemporary revival is, nevertheless, indebted to the past. Odum's and Vance's vision of large-scale regions and their folk cultures has been carried on by Don Martindale, John Shelton Reed, Lewis Killian, Raymond Gastil, Andrew Greeley, Stephen Olsen, and others. Park's and Burgess's sense of the human ecology of the metropolis their focus upon neighborhood networks and small scale regions within the city has continued in the work of Amos Hawley, Walter Firey, Herbert

Gans, Gerald Suttles, Albert Hunter, Claude Fischer, and others. As our list indicates, the study of urban regionalism, in particular, has passed through several productive phases, from the delineation of "zones" and "natural areas" of the city in the 1920s and 1930s to "social area analysis" in the 1940s and 50s to the present day use of "factorial ecology" to map the urban mosaic. See Burgess (items 1543–1545), Park item 1614), Zorbaugh (item 1652), Abu-Lughud (item 1533), Bell (item 1534), Hatt (item 1571), Hamm (item 1570), Herbert and Johnston (item 1577) and Shevky and Bell (item 1624) for sources related to these developments.

During the past twenty years sociological theorists in the United States and Europe have devoted increasing attention to the spatial organization of society. At the level of macro-theory, Robert Nisbet, Peter Berger, Edward Shils, Michael Hechter, Henri Lefebvre, and Immanuel Wallerstein have developed influential concepts of spatial order involving mediating structures, intermediate associations, and center-periphery relationships within national and global contexts. At the level of micro-theory, Erving Goffman, Anthony Giddens, Joshua Meyrowitz, Mihaly Csikzentmihaly, and Eugene Rochberg-Halton have developed equally valuable models for understanding the intimate spatial contexts and social regions of everyday life.

Paralleling these vital spatial perspectives is an implicit debate between sociologists like Maurice Halbwachs, Marc Fried, and Kai Erikson who stress the centrality of sense of place and region in people's lives and sociologists like Melvin Webber, Sanford Labovitz, and Joshua Meyrowitz who describe the decreasing significance of place and region in modern society. At a more empirical level, sociologists have a long tradition of measuring regional variations in American society, from the hundreds of statistical "indices" included in Odum's massive studies of the 1930s to Donald Bogue's continuing analyses of regional demographics. Added to this are innumerable sociological studies of regional differences in specific variables, including agriculture (Nelson, Taylor); social stress, crime, and illness (Linsky and Straus); quality of life (Liu, Wilson); violence (Dixon and Lizotte, Gastil, Hackney, Lofton and Hill, Messner, and Reed); racial and ethnic prejudice (Middleton, Tuch); political intolerance (Abrahamson and Carter, Stouffer); television viewing (Morgan); and music (Peterson and Di Maggio.)

The following list elaborates each of these regional perspectives in sociology, from Franklin Gidding's pioneering work at the turn of the century to the contributions of the Chapel Hill and Chicago schools during the interwar decades to the many strands of regionally related sociology in the present. This chapter traces the development of rural-flavored theories of regional consciousness and of folk, agricultural, and ethnic regionalism often stemming from Chapel Hill as well as the evolution of urban-flavored theories of human ecology, metropolitan regionalism, natural and social areas, and factorial ecology often emerging from Chicago. Attention has been given to a spectrum of large, middle, and small-scale regional perspectives, ranging from Wallerstein's vast "world system" to Goffman's intimate "behavioral regions." An overwhelming number of sociological studies of individual American communities have been written during this period, and in the interest of precision, only those keenly sensitive to the spatial structure of society have been included.[2]

The current revival of spatial-regional theory is international in scope, and the influential studies of Anthony Giddens and John Urry in England and Maurice Halbwachs and Henri Lefebvre in France are included. Finally, there are valuable connections between regional studies in sociology and regional scholarship in anthropology, regional planning, economics, geography, and political science—documented in chapters three, four, six, eight, and thirteen, respectively. Social geographers such as David M. Smith, Keith D. Harries, Richard L. Morrill, and Ernest H. Wohlenberg have mapped out the regional contours of social well-being, inequality, crime, justice, and poverty, and much of their their work is listed under Geography: Distributional Studies.

M.S.

---

[1]The first book devoted entirely to regional sociology was published by Indian sociologist, Radhakamal Mukerjee in 1926. Mukerjee's title was suggested by the poet, Rabindranath Tagore. See Mukerjee (item 1603).

[2]For a glimpse at the hundreds of community studies generated by the Chapel Hill and Chicago Schools alone, see Katharine Jocher's bibliography, "Toward Regional Documentation," in *In Search of the Regional Balance of America*, ed. Howard W. Odum and Katharine Jocher (Chapel Hill: Univ. of North Carolina Press, 1945), 60–86, and Lester R. Kurtz's detailed bibliography in his *Evaluating Chicago Sociology: A Guide to the Literature* (Chicago: Univ. of Chicago Press, 1984), 113–266. Maurice Stein's *The Eclipse of Community* (New York: Harper and Row, 1960) discusses and lists scores of classic community studies from Robert and Helen Lynd's Middletown studies in the 1920s and 1930s to W. Lloyd Warner's Yankee City series in the 1940s to William H. Whyte's suburban studies in the 1950s.

*　　　　　*　　　　　*

1532. Abrahamson, Mark and Valerie J. Carter. "Tolerance, Urbanism, and Region." *American Sociological Review* 51 (February 1986): 287–94.

Insights from urban and regional sociology are used to understand spatial variations of tolerance within the United States. Louis Wirth's and Samuel Stouffer's theories that urbanization generally encourages higher levels of tolerance and the regional convergence hypothesis that visualizes the inevitable dwindling of spatial variations in culture over time are discussed. Analysis of data from national opinion surveys taken between 1947 and 1982 reveals that general levels of tolerance—measured in terms of attitudes toward civil rights, euthanasia, epileptic workers, and prohibition—have risen over time. Yet tolerance is not necessarily greater in larger cities as expected and regional divergence in levels of tolerance has remained fairly constant, with the East and West registering higher levels than the Midwest and South.

1533. Abu-Lughod, Janet L. "Testing the Theory of Social Area Analysis: The Ecology of Cairo Egypt." *American Sociological Review* 34 (April 1969): 198–212.

· Most of this insightful article assesses the social area hypothesis developed by Eshref Shevky, Wendell Bell, and others during the 1940s and 1950s. Abu-Lughod perceptively describes the strengths and weaknesses of various sociological "regionalizations" of the city, from the composite patterns of "natural areas" delineated by early human ecologists to the separate dimensions of socio-economic rank, family structure, and ethnicity measured by social area analysts. Suggestions for the cross-cultural study of urban spatial patterns are included as well as an extensive list of social area and factorial ecology studies.

1534. Bell, Wendell. "Social Areas: Typology of Urban Neighborhoods." In *Community Structure and Analysis*, edited by Marvin B. Sussman, 61–92. New York: Thomas Y. Crowell, 1959.

This effective overview of the theory and method of social area analysis describes in detail how to use census tract statistics to measure the distribution of three important variables: socio-economic status, family structure, and ethnic identity.

1535. Berger, Peter L. *Facing Up to Modernity: Excursions in Society, Politics, and Religion.* New York: Basic Books, 1977.

Two essays in this collection are germane to understanding the social significance of region and regionalism. Both "Reflections on Patriotism," pp. 118–29, and "In Praise of Particularity: The Concept of Mediating Structures," pp. 130–41, praise local, communal patriotism as the primordial building block for wider, more abstract, and often dangerous forms of loyalty. Much of this critique of modernity—although with a less explicit spatial orientation—was developed in Peter Berger, Bridgitte Berger, and Hansfried Kellner's *The Homeless Mind: Modernization and Consciousness* (New York: Random House, 1973).

1536. Berger, Peter L. and Richard John Neuhaus. *To Empower People: The Role of Mediating Structures in Public Policy.* Washington, D.C.: American Enterprise Institute for Public Policy Research, 1977.

Paralleling Nisbet's analysis of the need for "intermediate institutions," Berger and Neuhaus discuss how identity within neighborhoods, churches, families, voluntary associations, and other "particularities" can mediate between the individual and the vast "megastructures" of mass society.

1537. Bertrand, Alvin L. "Comments by a Regional Sociologist." *Social Science Quarterly* 49 (June 1968): 36–38.

Commenting upon Ira Sharkansky's appeal for greater attention to regional analysis in political science, Bertrand urges social scientists in general to pay greater attention to folk-cultural factors in defining regions and to be more careful in distinguishing regionalism from sectionalism.

1538. ———. "Regional Sociology as a Special Discipline." *Social Forces* 31 (December 1952): 132–36.

Bertrand carefully carves out a place for regional sociology within the larger discipline. He describes the subdiscipline's content as "the study of all forms of human association within a regional environment," its relationship to regionalism, and its importance as a tool for research.

1539. Birenbaum, Arnold and Edward Sagarin, eds. *People in Places: The Sociology of the Familiar.* New York: Praeger, 1973.

Building upon Erving Goffman's pioneering studies of small-scale behavioral regions, the ethnographic essays in this collection examine such subjects as the sociology of sleep, the behavior of pedestrians, bar sociability, subway behavior, and the social structure of the restaurant.

1540. Bogue, Donald J. *The Population of the United States: Historical Trends and Future Projections.* New York: Free Press, 1985.

Much of this book is devoted to regional demographics, especially the section, "Internal Migration," pp. 327–46, which analyzes internal migration patterns and changing regional distributions of population, especially since 1980. The 1959 edition of this book pays equal attention to regional demographics. Also useful for historical studies is Donald J. Bogue and Margaret Jarman Hagood, *Subregional Migration in the United States, 1935–1940* (Oxford, Ohio: Miami Univ. Press, 1953). Another source by Bogue is listed under Economics (item 320).

1541. Boskoff, Alvin. *The Sociology of Urban Regions*. New York: Appleton-Century-Crofts, 1962.

Boskoff integrates many of the findings of the Chicago School of urban regionalism into this clearly argued and carefully organized text. Depicted as "modern man's increasingly typical habitat," the urban region is defined as a "constellation of communities about a politically delimited urban center." Boskoff's chapters discuss, among other things, the historical development of urban life from rural villages to complex urban regions, various types and stages of growth for urban regions, the ecology of urban regions, various approaches to regional planning. "The Urban Regional System: A Changing Equilibrium," pp. 278–93, contains an impressive summary of sociological regional theory as expressed by Spengler, Durkheim, Mumford, Park, McKenzie, Odum, and others.

1542. Brunn, John G. "Human Ecology: A Unifying Science." *Human Ecology* 2 (April 1974): 105–25.

Brunn carefully traces the use of ecological concepts in four social sciences—geography, anthropology, sociology, and psychology—and concludes that the highly specialized and compartmentalized development of human ecology in each discipline has inhibited the development of a unifying science of man-environment relations. The section devoted to sociology is especially thorough and well-documented, especially in terms of the contributions of Robert Park, Roderick McKenzie, Amos Hawley, and others.

1543. Burgess, Ernest W. "The Growth of the City: A Research Project." In *The City*, edited by Robert E. Park, Ernest W. Burgess, and Roderick D. McKenzie, 47–62. Chicago: University of Chicago Press, 1925. Reprinted in *Urban Patterns*, edited by George A. Theodorson, 35–41. University Park: Pennsylvania State Univ. Press, 1982.

This classic essay develops two influential theories based upon empirical studies of Chicago: the notion that cities expand outward in concentric zones from central business districts to outlying commuter suburbs and the belief that people are arranged in "natural economic and cultural groupings" throughout urban regions. Burgess's scheme of five concentric zones and delineation of natural community areas has generated extensive scholarship and debate.

1544. ———. "Urban Areas." In *Chicago: An Experiment in Social Science*, edited by T.V. Smith and Leonard D. White, 113–38. Chicago: Univ. of Chicago Press, 1929.

In this central expression of his belief in the existence of an urban mosaic of "natural" or "community areas," Burgess writes: "A human community, like a biological organism, grows up by a process of subdivision. As a city grows, its structure becomes more complex and its areas more specialized." After reiterating his five zone model of urban expansion, Burgess delineates seventy-five community areas for Chicago.

1545. ———, ed. *The Urban Community*. Chicago: Univ. of Chicago Press, 1926.

This collection contains several important contributions to the study of urban and metropolitan regionalism, including Robert Park's "The Urban Community as a Spatial Pattern and a Moral Order," pp. 3–18; R.D. McKenzie's "The Scope of Human Ecology," pp. 167–82; N.S.B. Gras's "The Rise of the Metropolitan Community" (item 344); and Harvey Zorbaugh's "The Natural Areas of the City" (item 1652), pp. 219–29.

1546. Cahnman, Werner. "The Concept of *Raum* and the Theory of Regionalism." *American Sociological Review* 9 (October 1944): 455–62.

Doing for sociologists what Richard Hartshorne did on a much larger scale for geographers, Cahnman outlines German contributions to regional theory. He discusses the work of Carl Ritter, Friedrich Ratzel, Kurt Lewin, and others and focuses upon such concepts as *raum*, *landschaft*, and *gestalt* and their regional implications.

1547. ———. "Outline of a Theory of Area Studies." *Annals of the Association of American Geographers* 37 (December 1948): 233–43.

Anticipating anthropologist Julian Steward's espousal, Cahnman forcefully argues that large-scale area studies should be an integral part of higher education—that such interdisciplinary courses provide a framework for studying total social change and a means to perceive the similarities and differences between cultures within America and throughout the world.

1548. Csikzentmihaly, Mihaly and Eugene Rochberg-Halton. *The Meaning of Things: Domestic Symbols and the Self.* New York: Cambridge Univ. Press, 1981.

In many ways a social scientific version of Gaston Bachelard's *The Poetics of Space* (item 1328), this provocative, somewhat extravagant, book raises important questions about the social and psychological significance of domestic objects and places. Based upon interviews with some three hundred middle-class Chicago-Evanston area residents, the authors examine the meaning of such cherished objects as furniture, visual art, photographs, books, stereos, and television sets; they also analyze the significance of various places and rooms within the home for different family members at different stages of life. Useful sections for understanding the ecology of domestic place are "The Most Cherished Objects in the Home," pp. 55–89; "The Home as Symbolic Environment," pp. 121–45; and "Characteristics of Happy Homes," pp. 146–71.

1549. Dixon, Jo and Alan J. Lizotte. "Gun Ownership and the 'Southern Subculture of Violence.'" *American Journal of Sociology* 93 (September 1987): 383–405.

After effectively surveying the extensive literature regarding regional variations in violence, especially the southern subculture of violence thesis, the authors carefully analyze patterns of gun ownership to test that thesis. Their study indicates, among other things, that gun ownership is unrelated to the values of subcultures of violence and that a *non*regional subculture of violence exists—one that is related to age, education, race, income, and city size rather than to distinctly southern factors.

1550. Erikson, Kai T. *Everything In Its Path: Destruction of Community in the Buffalo Creek Flood.* New York: Simon & Schuster, 1976.

This sensitive analysis of the social trauma caused by a natural disaster—the flood that destroyed Buffalo Creek, West Virginia on February 26, 1972—underscores the centrality of familiar landmarks and landscapes in maintaining personal and collective identities. Paralleling the work of psychologist Robert Coles, Erikson listens to the words of more than 140 survivors, and the disorientation caused by the sudden loss of familiar surroundings and the pain of placelessness is a central theme of their narratives. The sections, "The Furniture of the Self," pp. 174–85, "Disorientation," pp. 209–14, and "Loss of Connection," pp. 214–28, stress the relationship between sense of place and sense of self and community.

1551. Firey, Walter. "Sentiment and Symbolism as Ecological Variables." *American Sociological Review* 10 (April 1945): 140–48. Reprinted in *Urban Patterns*, edited by George A. Theorson, 129–136. rev. ed. University Park: Pennsylvania State Univ. Press, 1982.

In this succinct and accessible essay, Firey urges sociologists and planners to consider the impact of non-economic forces in human ecology. Examining three areas in Boston—the upper class Beacon Hill neighborhood, Boston Common and other colonial burial sites, and the Italian North End neighborhood—Firey stresses the symbolic power of each place. Aesthetic, historical, familial, and sacred landmarks, symbols, and memories shape and sustain environments as much as economic forces. Firey elaborates this and other concepts in *Land Use in Central Boston* (Cambridge: Harvard Univ. Press, 1947) and *Man, Mind and Land* (New York: Free Press, 1960).

1552. Fischer, Claude S. et al. *Networks and Places: Social Relations in an Urban Setting*. New York: Free Press, 1977.

These essays use data from the Detroit Area Study (1965–66) and a National Opinion Research Center survey (1967) to understand what constitutes a sense of community in urban society. Part One examines the role of social *networks* in the creation and maintenance of community; Part Two focuses upon the significance of *place* in sustaining community. Essays in Part Two directly relevant to regional studies include Claude S. Fischer and Robert Max Jackson, "Suburbanism and Localism," pp. 117–38; Kathleen Gerson, C. Ann Stueve, and Claude S. Fischer, "Attachment to Place," pp. 139–61; and Claude S. Fischer and Ann Stueve, "'Authentic Community': The Role of Place in Modern Life," pp. 163–86. These essays, as well as Fischer's introduction and conclusion, generally describe the diminishing role of place and locality as ingredients of community and challenge the "authentic community thesis that social relations turned inward to a locality are richer and deeper than specialized relations with people outside of it."

1553. Fried, Marc. "Grieving for a Lost Home." In *The Urban Condition: People and Policy in the Metropolis*, edited by Leonard J. Duhl, 151–71. New York: Basic Books, 1963.

This classic study of the psychological and physiological problems experienced by people relocated from Boston's West End underscores the significance of place and local region in society—that "a sense of spatial identity is fundamental to human functioning." This argument is expanded in Marc Fried and Peggy Gleicher's "Some Sources of Residential Satisfaction in an Urban Slum," *Journal of the American Institute of Planners* 27 (November 1961), pp. 305–15.

1554. Gans, Herbert J. *People and Plans: Essays on Urban Problems and Solutions.* New York: Basic Books, 1968.

Most of the essays in this important anthology examine the relationship between the built environment and the social order. Gans is particularly sensitive to the differences between urban and suburban ways of life and the problems of urban renewal and planned communities. Especially perceptive essays include "Urban Vitality and the Fallacy of Physical Determinism," pp. 25–33, a highly favorable review of Jane Jacobs's *The Death and Life of Great American Cities* (see Economics, item 357); "City Planning in America: A Sociological Analysis," pp. 57–77, an insightful survey of American urban and regional planning from the turn of the century City Beautiful Movement to the contemporary New Town Movement stressing the split between social and physical planning approaches; and "Diversity and Homogeneity in American Culture," pp. 141–51, in which the "old diversities" of region and ethnic group are depicted as being replaced by "new diversities" based upon class, education, and lifestyle.

1555. ———. *The Urban Villagers: Group and Class in the Life of Italian-Americans.* Updated and exp. ed. New York: Free Press, 1982.

Originally published in 1962, this classic study of the impact of relocation upon Boston's West End Italian-American community contributes to our understanding of the relationship between sense of place and sense of community. Like Marc Fried, Gans analyzes the trauma of dislocation yet unlike Fried, Gans argues that the loss of familiar people was felt much more keenly than the loss of familiar places. See "Redevelopment of the West End," pp. 323–46, and "An Evaluation of the Redevelopment Process," pp. 347–77, as well as the 1982 "Postscript" to these chapters, pp. 378–95, in which Gans discusses the debate with Fried regarding the priority of people or place.

1556. Gastil, Raymond D. *Cultural Regions of the United States.* Seattle: Univ. of Washington Press, 1975.

In this sweeping, sometimes idiosyncratic, portrait of American society, Gastil argues that regional identity is a central though often underestimated source of identity in mass society. Gastil's separate analyses of eleven regions are less useful than the opening and closing chapters, which examine regional theory and the general significance of regional variations, respectively. A fairly thorough bibliography is included.

1557. ———. "Homicide and a Regional Culture of Violence." *American Sociological Review* 36 (1971): 412–27.

Using qualitative historical evidence as well as statistical data, Gastil stresses that since the 1850s southern homicide rates have been consistently higher than in other American regions, and that "it is a predisposition to lethal violence in Southern regional culture that accounts for the greater part of the relative height of the American homicide rate" in comparison to other nations. For further discussion, see Gastil's "Comments," *Criminology*, 16 (1978), pp. 60–65. For closely related sources, see Dixon and Lizotte (item 1549), Hackney (item 1568), Linsky and Straus (item 1591), Lofton and Hill (item 1592), Messner (item 1598), and Reed (items 1617–1621).

1558. ———. "The Pacific Northwest as a Cultural Region." *Pacific Northwest Quarterly* 64 (October 1973): 147–56.

Gastil skillfully applies general regional theory to the analysis of the Pacific Northwest as a distinct cultural region taking into account migration statistics and religious, educational, and political values. This article is followed by commentaries by Norman Clark, Richard Etulain, and Otis Pease, as well as a response by Gastil.

1559. Giddens, Anthony. *The Constitution of Society: Outline of a Theory of Structuration.* Berkeley: Univ. of California Press, 1984.

Sensitivity to the spatial contexts of the day-to-day flow of life lies at the heart of Giddens's social theory. His "Introduction," pp. xiii-xxxvii, and "Time, Space and Regionalization," pp. 110–61, urge sociologists to greater awareness of the limits of time and space that condition every action of our lives. The "locales" of human interaction, Giddens writes, range in size from the "shop floor of a factory ... to the territorially demarcated areas occupied by nation-states," and the "regions" within these locales constitute the immediate contexts of human behavior. Giddens uses Torsten Hagerstard's concept of "time-geography" to analyze the locales, regions, and pathways of everyday life; he also uses Goffman's notion of "front" and "back" regions as well as "center/periphery" distinctions to examine the arrangements of people and things in space. The concluding comment, "Critical Notes: Foucault on Timing and Space," pp. 145–61, is insightful.

1560. Giddings, Franklin. *The Elements of Sociology*. New York: Macmillan, 1898.

Giddings pioneered the sociological study of American regionalism. His influential concept of "consciousness of kind," like Edward Shil's notion of "primordial ties," has been used to understand regional consciousness and identity, and Giddings's spatial analyses of society have influenced many sociologists, including his student, Howard Odum. In "Where Aggregations of People Are Formed," Giddings divides North America into four primal regions determined by their ability to sustain human life: the Grainless North, the Western Desert, the Region of Fertility, and the Pacific Coast.

1561. ———. *Inductive Sociology*. New York: Macmillan, 1901.

This text contains Giddings' regional social psychology for the "habitable areas" of the United States. Forceful personality types, Giddings argued, dominated both seacoasts, the Ohio Valley, and the Great Plains; convivial types would be formed in the Southwest; austere personalities in New England and the Upper Midwest; and rational, conscientious types in urban centers. For other discussions of regional social psychology, see Heberle (item 1574), Hertzler (items 1578–1580) and Zimmerman (items 1650–1651).

1562. Glenn, Norval D. "Massification Versus Differentiation: Some Trend Data from National Surveys." *Social Forces* 46 (December 1967): 172–80.

A careful analysis of public opinion polls taken since the 1940s, indicates a stronger trend toward differentiation than toward massification of attitudes and values among Americans. While value differences between men and women and between rural and urban dwellers have diminished somewhat, value differences between regions, manual and non-manual workers, whites and non-whites, and Protestants and Catholics have increased.

1563. Glenn, Norval D. and J.L. Simmons. "Are Regional Cultural Differences Diminishing?" *Public Opinion Quarterly* 31 (Summer 1967): 176–93.

After analyzing the "cultural" questions in a series of public opinion polls taken in the northeastern, southern, central, and western states, the authors conclude that, contrary to many sociological projections, regional differences in values are increasing somewhat. For sources closely related to both articles, see Greeley (item 1567), Labovitz (item 1589), McKinney and Bourque (item 1596), and Webber (item 1644); and Newman and Halvorson (item 1372), Shortridge (items 1384–1385), and Stump (items 1389–1390) under Philosophy and Religion.

1564. Goffman, Erving. *Frame Analysis: An Essay on the Organization of Experience.* Cambridge, Mass.: Harvard Univ. Press, 1974.

Framing is the means by which everyday life is given meaning on an interactive, phenomenological, micro-scale. We frame certain activities from the welter of ongoing experience, and Goffman develops terms to describe aspects of this process including style (relates framing to persons involved), flooding out (framing dissolved in anger, humor, etc.), and keying (to particular moods and modes). Such microregional activity provides a basis for understanding larger spatial patterns.

1565. ———. *The Presentation of the Self in Everyday Life.* New York: Doubleday, 1958.

This important contribution to microsociology analyzes human behavior as performance taking place within a variety of small-scale settings or regions. In the section, "Regions and Region Behavior," Goffman defines a "region" as "any place that is bounded to some degree by barriers to perception," and then describes behavioral regions that are common in Anglo-American society, a society in which performances are usually indoors and are tightly bounded. The function of three generalized types of regions are examined—the decorous "front region," the more private "back region," and the distant "outside region"—and the implicit rules of decorum for sacred places, work places, recreation places, and various rooms of domestic places are analyzed.

1566. ———. *Relations in Public: Microstudies of the Social Order.* New York: Basic Books, 1971.

Goffman expands his analysis of the intimate regions of everyday life in two chapters of this book. "The Territories of the Self," pp. 28–61, discusses the need for territorial and psychological "preserves of the self" which can be "fixed," "situational," or "egocentric" in their organization. He then analyzes the boundaries, functions, and ways of violating a variety of common, protected places, including one's personal space, the "sheath" of one's skin, the personal "stall" one can temporarily occupy within a public place, "possessional territory," "information preserves," and "conversational preserves." "Normal Appearances," pp. 238–333, carefully analyzes how people feel at ease and ill-at-ease, protected and vulnerable, within the places of their lives.

1567. Greeley, Andrew M. "Ethnicity Among 'WASPS.'" In *Ethnicity in the United States: A Preliminary Reconnaissance*, 53–70. New York: John Wiley and Sons, 1974.

Asserting that "American social science has paid scant attention to the possibility of regional diversity in the country's population," Greeley uses a variety of public opinion polls to measure possible regional value differences first among white Anglo-Saxon Protestants and then among American Catholics. Distinct regional variety is apparent within both groups, especially within Protestant ranks, and Greeley argues that regional identity may play a "quasi-ethnic role" for "WASPS." For equally vigorous, often stronger cases for the equation of ethnic and regional identity see, Killian (item 1585) and Reed (items 1617–1621); Whisnant under American Studies (items 59–61), and Handlin under History: Region as Concept (item 815).

1568. Hackney, Sheldon. "Southern Violence." *American Historical Review* 74 (1969): 906–25.

Examining historical statistics related to violence, Hackney stresses that Southern states have had persistently high rates of homicide and assault, moderate rates of property crimes, and low rates of suicide compared with northern states. The possible racial, economic, social-psychological causes of this pattern are explored, with particular attention given to the existence of a regional "siege mentality." "From the southern past," Hackney writes, "arise the symbiosis of profuse hospitality and intense hostility toward strangers and the paradox that the southern heritage is at the same time one of grace and violence."

1569. Halbwachs, Maurice. *The Collective Memory*. Translated by Francis J. Ditter and Vita Y. Ditter. New York: Harper and Row, 1980.

In "Space and the Collective Memory," pp. 128–57, Halbwachs argues that personal and collective memories exist *only* as they are anchored to places or objects. He believes that "space is a reality that endures: since our impressions rush by, one after another, and leave nothing in the mind, we can ... recapture the past only by understanding how it is, in effect, preserved by our physical surroundings.... it is the spatial image alone that, by reason of its stability, gives us the illusion of not having changed through time and of retrieving the past in the present.... Space alone is stable enough to endure without growing old or losing any of its parts."

1570. Hamm, Bernd. "Social Area Analysis and Factorial Ecology: A Review of Substantive Findings." In *Urban Patterns: Studies in Human Ecology*, 316–37. rev. ed., edited by George A. Theodorson, 316–37. University Park: Pennsylvania State Univ. Press, 1982.

Along with R.D. Johnston's work, Hamm's essay provides the most thorough and contemporaneous evaluation of theories and methods of urban regional analysis. After describing the evolution from the classical human ecology paradigm of concentric zones and natural urban areas to the increasingly complex mapping of variables in social area analysis and factorial ecology, Hamm argues that "all three approaches ... are necessary to gain more cumulative knowledge on the structure and processes of urban socio-spatial differentiation."

1571. Hatt, Paul. "The Concept of Natural Area." *American Sociological Review* 11 (August 1946): 423–27. Reprinted in *Urban Patterns: Studies in Human Ecology*, 78–81. rev. ed., edited by George A. Theodorson, 78–81. University Park: Pennsylvania State Univ. Press, 1982.

Based upon his study of a multi-ethnic residential section of Seattle, Hatt argues that the concept of natural areas developed by Burgess, Park, Zorbaugh, and others is useful primarily as a tool for mapping the distribution of selected variables rather than as a description of reality.

1572. Hawley, Amos. *Human Ecology: A Theory of Community Structure*. New York: Ronald Press, 1950.

In many ways a grand synthesis of the work of the Chicago School of human ecology, this book contains a masterful analysis of the meaning and significance of region in the social sciences. "Habitat and Population," pp. 80–103, perceptively analyzes a variety of regional paradigms, including the "natural area" concept of anthropogeographers Ratzel, Semple, and Herbertson, the "culture area" concept of anthropologists Wissler and Kroeber, and the rural and urban regions delineated by the Chapel Hill and Chicago Schools. Chapters thirteen and fourteen, both entitled "Spatial Aspects of Ecological Organization," pp. 234–63 and 264–87, discuss the actual spatial patterns of human activity and settlement, stressing concepts of community center, community area, and administrative area, region and metropolitan region, concentric and linear zones of urban expansion and multicentered patterns of urban growth.

1573. ———. *Human Ecology: A Theoretical Essay*. Chicago: Univ. of Chicago Press, 1987.

In the process of developing a "unified theory of human ecology," Hawley provides a succinct summary of the subdiscipline, from the early use of principles from plant ecology to later applications of general systems theory. "Cumulative Change: Expansion in Time and Space," pp. 88–108, carefully delineates the various territorial patterns and scales in which human ecosystems operate.

1574. Heberle, Rudolf. "Regionalism: Some Critical Observations." *Social Forces* 21 (March 1943): 280–86.

Among other things, Heberle urges greater precision in the application of the concept of "folk culture" to regional analysis; he also urges regional sociologists to move from empirical studies of economic differences to more penetrating social psychological analyses of regional identity and consciousness.

1575. Hechter, Michael. *Internal Colonialism: The Celtic Fringe in British National Development, 1536–1966*. Berkeley: Univ. of California Press, 1975.

Hechter's wide-ranging analysis of the imperialistic relationship between the English core and the Celtic periphery in Britain has had a large impact upon recent studies of ethnoregionalism in Europe and America. His sociological model of internal colonialism within a larger world system—drawn partially from the social theories of Antonio Gramsci, Fernand Braudel, Frantz Fanon, and Immanuel Wallerstein— has been used to understand uneven regional development and ethnoregional pluralism in the United States, especially among Appalachians, black nationalists, Hispanics, and Native Americans. The internal colonization and core/periphery models are developed in "Introduction" and "Toward a Theory of Ethnic Change," pp. 3–43. "Industrialization and Regional Economic Inequality,1851–1961," pp. 127–63, and "The Persistence of Sectionalism, 1885–1966," pp. 208–33 are also highly perceptive. For closely related sources see Shils and Wallerstein (items 1625–1626, 1642–1643), Peet and Wolf under Anthropology (items 117, 145), and Braudel under History:Region as Concept (item 798).

1576. Hechter, Michael and Margaret Levi. "The Comparative Analysis of Ethnoregional Movements." *Ethnic and Racial Studies* 2 (July 1979): 260–74.

After asserting that ethnoregional movements "represent the most important source of armed conflict in the world at this time," Hechter and Levi explore some of the causes of ethnoregionalism, explain why it is stronger in certain places among certain ethnic groups, and why it seems to rise and fall in historical cycles. A "full analysis" of ethnoregionalism, they conclude, must account for at least three "levels of aggregation"—"starting at microscopic settings for interaction, then moving to the level of the state, and finally to the international system as a whole."

1577. Herbert, D.T. and R.J. Johnston. *Social Areas in Cities.* vol 1. London: John Wiley and Sons, 1976.

This collection analyzes the increasingly complex residential mosaic of large cities in the United States and England. Although written by English and American social geographers, these essays contain some of the most perceptive summaries of urban regional sociology available. Especially perceptive essays include D.W.G. Timms's "Social Bases to Social Areas," pp. 19–39, which surveys much of the sociological literature on neighborhoods and social areas and stresses the significance of mental images in the maintenance of local identity; F.W. Boal's "Ethnic Residential Segregation," pp. 41–79, which analyzes the role of ethnic identity in neighborhood formation; and, especially, R.J. Johnston's "Residential Area Characteristics: Research Methods for Identifying Urban Sub-areas— Social Area Analysis and Factorial Ecology," pp. 193–235, which is the most thorough analysis of two sociological models of urban regionalization in print.

1578. Hertzler, J.O. "Some Sociological Aspects of American Regionalism." *Social Forces* 18 (October 1939): 17–29.

In this extensively documented retrospective analysis, Hertzler advances reasons for the rise of regional interest during the 1930s and concludes that sociologists must continue to probe "this new, meaningful areal unit of maturity, the region, which is a constellation of communities bound together by natural and cultural uniformities, on the one hand, and a natural, logical, convenient subdivision of the national society on the other."

1579. ———. "Some Notes on the Social Psychology of Regionalism." *Social Forces* 18 (March 1940): 331–37.

Hertzler suggests that the shared background of regional experience must give rise to common psychological responses and that sociologists should explore the psychological dimension of regionalism. With the frontier ended and the continent settled he believes that "regional consciousness" is increasing and that "a regional 'sense of community' is developing." "We are thinking of our relationships with others," Hertzler continues, "in terms of the regions we inhabit; here are elicited our basic interests; here is the ideal tangible areal unit to which we attach our loyalties."

1580. ———. "American Regionalism and the Regional Sociological Society." *American Sociological Review* 3 (October 1938): 738–48.

Hertzler describes the surge of sociological interest in regions stemming from Chapel Hill and Chicago and suggests how regional professional societies might encourage regional research, teaching, and planning.

1581. Hunter, Albert. "Persistence of Local Sentiments in Mass Society." In *Handbook of Contemporary Urban Life*, edited by David Street et al., 133–62. Washington, D.C.: Jossey-Bass, 1978.

After criticizing the nostalgic "community lost" tradition in sociology, Hunter develops an "emergent view" of community by arguing that local sentiments are becoming increasingly important in mass society. Local sentiments, he argues, are usually evoked by outside threats after which sense of community passes through several stages of increasing intensity and consciousness. "Within mass society," Hunter writes," the relatively autonomous, functionally and institutionally integrated local community may be lost, but the local sentiments of neighborhood persist and flourish.... Mass society will not disappear ... neither will the local sentiments of community."

1582. ———. *Symbolic Communities: The Persistence and Change of Chicago's Local Communities*. Chicago: Univ. of Chicago Press, 1974.

In this important book, Hunter compares Chicago's local communities in the 1970s with the "natural areas" delimited by Burgess in the 1920s. Using statistical methods of "social area analysis" or "factorial ecology" as well as extensive field interviews, Hunter locates some ninety local communities that correspond fairly closely to the seventy-five communities Burgess had mapped. Hunter's study attests to the remarkable persistence of local attachments over time and that such attachment "varies little by class, race, or characteristics of the area." Hunter's research also underscores the need for spatial symbols— especially a shared sense of place names, boundaries, landmarks, and memories of place—for the maintenance of community.

1583. Jocher, Katharine. "Toward Regional Documentation." In *In Search of the Regional Balance of America*, edited by Howard W. Odum and Katharine Jocher, 60–86. Chapel Hill: Univ. of North Carolina Press, 1945.

Honoring twenty years of regional study and interpretation promoted by the University of North Carolina's Institute for Research in Social Science and the journal *Social Forces*, Jocher's detailed bibliography lists all of the materials relating to the South and to regionalism published in the journal or sponsored by the Institute.

1584. Kantor, Harvey. "Howard W. Odum: The Implications of Folk Planning and Regionalism." *American Journal of Sociology* 29 (September 1973): 278–95.

In this insightful analysis of the evolution and application of Odum's folk-regional theory, Kantor focuses upon the utility of Odum's concepts of "folkways," "technicways," and "stateways," as well as his celebrated distinction between regionalism and sectionalism. For closely related sources, see Simpson (item 1627) and Vance (items 1638–1641) and O'Brien and Singal under History: Region as Concept (items 830, 840).

1585. Killian, Lewis W. *White Southerners*. New York: Random House, 1970.

This detailed study of white Southerners as an ethnic group helps clarify the possible relationships between regional and ethnic identity and has influenced later studies by historians George B. Tindall and Oscar Handlin and sociologists Andrew Greeley and John Shelton Reed.

1586. Kraenzel, Carl F. "Great Plains Regionalism Reconsidered." In *Perspectives on Regions and Regionalism*, edited by B.Y. Card, 77–90. Edmonton, Alberta: Western Association of Sociology and Anthropology, 1969.

After surveying much of the literature on Great Plains regionalism, especially the angry charges of northern exploitation by Webb and Mezerik, Kraenzel delivers an Odumesque plea for regional planning within a national context rather than divisive sectionalism.

1587. Kurtz, Lester R. *Evaluating Chicago Sociology: A Guide to the Literature, with an Annotated Bibliography.* Chicago: Univ. of Chicago Press, 1984.

In documenting the pervasive influence of the University of Chicago Sociology Department over the past hundred years, Kurtz discusses various theories and controversies in human ecology, pp. 21–29, and develops a lengthy bibliography, pp.113–266, that includes much of the Chicago School's contributions to regional sociology.

1588. Labovitz, Sanford. "Territorial Differentiation and Societal Change." *Pacific Sociological Review* 8 (Fall 1965): 70–75.

Labovitz develops a four-stage model of social change stressing the erosion of regional differences in economic activity as industrialization and technological change homogenize national societies. Based upon some historical statistics, Labovitz argues that regional convergence is the rule of urban-industrial society, and that "the United States is becoming more homogeneous—the different sectors of the country are converging and the whole system is increasingly moving together."

1589. Labovitz, Sanford and Ross Purdy. "Territorial Differentiation and Societal Change in the United States and Canada." *American Journal of Economics and Sociology* 29 (April 1970): 127–47.

After analyzing further economic data, the authors conclude that regional convergence is continuing in the United States and Canada despite some signs of divergence, especially in terms of primary industries. Economic and political specialists in uneven regional development would find much to debate regarding Labovitz and Purdy's insistence on convergence and their belief that "as regions become increasingly alike on most characteristics, they become unlike on primary industry.... it appears that territorial specialization in primary industries may be the only counter-acting force."

1590. Lefebvre, Henri. *The Survival of Capitalism: Reproduction of the Relations of Production.* Translated by Frank Bryant. New York: St. Martin's Press, 1976.

Like Wallerstein, Lefebvre sees spatial relationships and the manipulation of space as key factors in the perpetuation of capitalism. Beginning with Marx's belief that "*domination* over material nature was indissolubly linked with *appropriation* of it," Lefebvre argues that capitalism has survived primarily "*by occupying space, by producing a space.*" Defining the urban- industrial world as "produced space," he describes specific tactics for the capitalistic production and control of space and for the "spatial distribution of domination." These tactics include the expansion of core/periphery economic relationships on a global scale and "fragmentation" and "hierarchisation" of space in everyday life. Lefebvre's *Everyday Life in the Modern World* (New York: Harper and Row, 1971), translated by Sacha Rabinovitch, develops some of these themes. Unfortunately, few of Lefebvre's many books, including the important *La Production de l'Espace* (1974), are available in English translation.

1591. Linsky, Arnold S. and Murray A. Straus. *Social Stress in the United States: Links to Regional Patterns in Crime and Illness.* Dover, Mass.: Auburn House, 1986.

Pointing toward a dearth of "knowledge on regional and state differences in social well-being, including stressfulness of the environment," Linsky and Straus begin to fill that gap by gathering statistics on stress, crime, and illness and mapping their geographical distribution. Based upon previous research in "life event" theories of stress, the authors develop a "State Stress Index" of fifteen quantifiable variables (including business failures, bankruptcies, divorces, and infant deaths), and in mapping out the distribution of these events they develop a "geography of stress" with the Far West and Deep South ranking highest and New England and the Upper Midwest ranking lowest. The geographical distributions of violent crimes fit similar patterns, while regional patterns for illness are less discernible. This provocative, wide-ranging study will undoubtedly spark further research.

1592. Liu, Ben-Chieh. *Quality of Life Indicators in the United States Metropolitan Areas.* New York: Praeger, 1976.

Perhaps the most comprehensive of the many quality of life studies, this book carefully ranks metropolitan areas according to a variety of criteria. See Liu's *The Quality of Life in the United States: Index, Rating, and Statistics* (Kansas City: Midwest Research Institute, 1973) and John O. Wilson's *The Quality of Life in the United States: An Excursion Into a New Frontier of Socio-Economic Indicators* (Kansas City: Midwest Research Institute, 1969) for early state-by-state analyses. David M. Smith's work (item 728, under Geography: Distributional Studies) offers even more comprehensive view of the "geography of well-being."

1593. Lofton, Colin and Robert H. Hill. "Regional Subculture and Homicide: An Examination of the Gastil-Hackney Thesis." *American Sociological Review* 29 (October 1974): 714–24.

Lofton and Hill question the validity of the Southern culture of violence thesis. They argue that Gastil's and Hackney's conclusions are dubious because of failure to make clear distinctions between cultural factors peculiar to the South and situational factors without regional significance.

1594. McKenzie, Roderick D. *The Metropolitan Community*. New York: McGraw-Hill, 1933.

This book, coupled with Park, Burgess, and McKenzie's *The City* (1925) and Burgess's *The Urban Community* (1926), sums up the regional position of the Chicago School of human ecology. Like economist Norman Gras, McKenzie argues that metropolitan regions with dense urban centers and far-flung hinterlands of interdependent communities have emerged since 1900 as the basic spatial framework of American society. McKenzie provides a graphic bird's-eye view of "this new city regionalism" of "supercommunities throughout the nation"; Park and Burgess provide closer views of the structure and function of zones, neighborhoods, and natural areas within metropolitan regions. McKenzie summarized his findings in "The Rise of Metropolitan Communities," *Recent Social Trends: Report of the President's Research Committee on Social Trends* (New York: McGraw-Hill, 1933), vol 1, pp. 443–96.

1595. ———. *Roderick D. McKenzie on Human Ecology: Selected Writings*. Edited by Amos Hawley. Chicago: Univ. of Chicago Press, 1968.

This highly useful collection contains McKenzie's influential essays on the nature of human ecology, local community, and regionalism. "The Ecological Approach to the Study of the Human Community" (1924) and "The Scope of Human Ecology" (1926), pp. 3–18 and 19–32, respectively, stand as classic outlines of the purpose and orientation of the Chicago School. "Industrial Expansion and the Interrelations of Peoples" (1933), "Movement and the Ability to Live" (1926), and especially "The Concept of Dominance and World-Organization" (1927), pp. 121–33, 134–40, and 205–19, respectively, visualize the expansion of western metropolitan regionalism within a global context.

1596. McKinney, John C. and Linda Brookover Bourque. "The Changing South: National Incorporation of a Region." *American Sociological Review* 36 (June 1971): 399–411.

In this prime expression of the regional convergence hypothesis, a variety of socioeconomic and demographic data are used to demonstrate that over the past forty years the South has been losing its regional distinctiveness and is "becoming increasingly indistinguishable from the rest of American society." For closely related discussions see Glenn (item 1562), Glenn and Simons (item 1563), Labovitz (item 1588), and Reed (items 1617–1621); and Newman and Halvorson (item 1372), Shortridge (items 1384–1385), and Stump (items 1389–1390) under Philosophy and Religion.

1597. Martindale, Don. *American Social Community.* New York: Appleton-Century-Crofts, 1960.

Part Two, "The Regional Community," pp. 131–218, is a highly perceptive, deeply informed discussion of the significance of regionalism in American society. Martindale carefully analyzes the connections between local and regional communities and their relationship to the nation; he also vividly describes northern, southern, and western regional societies. Regions function, according to Martindale, as "slow countereddies within the general system of American society.... they add interest and variety beneath the superficial homogeneity of American society" and help sustain community life.

1598. Messner, Steven F. "Regional and Racial Effects on the Urban Homicide Rate: The Subculture of Violence Revisited." *American Journal of Sociology* 88 (March 1983): 997–1007.

After examining the homicide rates for 204 Standard Metropolitan Statistical Areas in order to evaluate the regional and racial aspects of the subculture of violence thesis, Messner concludes that "both southern region and the relative size of black population exhibit significant partial effects on the homicide rate even with controls for theoretically important socioeconomic and demographic variables."

1599. Meyrowitz, Joshua. *No Sense of Place: the Impact of Electronic Media on Social Behavior.* Berkeley: Univ. of California Press, 1985.

In this wide-ranging and provocative book, Meyrowitz argues that the increased use of such electronic media as radios, telephones, televisions, and personal computers has dramatically reduced the significance of "place" or "physical presence" in people's lives. Because of these ubiquitous media, "physically bounded spaces are less significant as information is able to flow through walls and rush across great distances. As a result, *where* one is has less and less to do with what one knows and experiences." After describing the demise of society rooted in direct experience and place-bound, face-to-face interaction, Meyrowitz analyzes the positive and negative aspects of media induced placelessness. Among other things, this book contains valuable discussions of McLuhan's media theory, Goffman's concept of "region behavior," changing notions of territoriality, and the impact of placelessness upon traditional distinctions between public and private spheres, men and women, adults and children.

1600. Middleton, Russell. "Regional Differences in Prejudice." *American Sociological Review* 41 (February 1974): 94–117.

Middleton carefully analyzes a 1964 nationwide survey that indicated few regional differences in anti-Semitic, anti-Catholic, and anti-immigrant prejudice but did reveal a much higher level of anti-black prejudice in the South than in other regions. The moderating impact of migration upon the anti-black prejudice of native white southerners is measured, and Middleton concludes that southern patterns of prejudice are shaped by uniquely regional, subcultural forces.

1601. Moore, Harry Estill. *What is Regionalism?* Chapel Hill: Univ. of North Carolina Press, 1937.

Heavily influenced by Howard Odum's thought, this pamphlet can be read as a handbook to the Chapel Hill School of regional thought and as a highly condensed version of Odum and Moore's massive *American Regionalism* (1938).

1602. Morgan, Michael. "Television and the Erosion of Regional Diversity." *Journal of Broadcasting & Electronic Media* 30 (Spring 1986): 123–39.

Morgan analyzes data from six National Opinion Research Center surveys to determine "the extent to which television may be associated with a reduction in the impact of geographic region on social and political attitudes and perspectives." While generally supporting the regional convergence thesis—i.e., "heavy" television viewers tend to show less deviation in values across regions than "light" viewers— Morgan's study also reveals regional persistence in the fact that the television programing and imagery has been increasingly dominated by rural southern rather than urban cosmopolitan values.

1603. Mukerjee, Radhakamal. *Regional Sociology*. New York: Century Co., 1926.

In this, the first general treatise on regional sociology, Mukerjee merges the sweeping environmental insights of Friedrich Ratzel and

Paul Vidal de la Blache with work in plant and animal ecology to visualize groups of people as parts of complex regional communities. Regional sociology is promoted as a unifying social science, and Mukerjee's text contains insightful discussions of "The Web of Life," pp. 3–21; "The Equilibrium of the Region," pp. 22–33; "Human Ecology," pp. 75–90; and "The Regional Basis of Social Types," pp. 91–114. Although largely concerned with agrarian societies, Mukerjee also analyzes regionalism in urbanindustrial settings.

1604. Nelson, Lowry. *Rural Sociology.* 2d ed. New York: American Book Co., 1955.

"Regional Patterns in the United States," pp. 29–46, contains a perceptive synopsis of regional theory and delineates a variety of rural regions. "Patterns of Land Settlement," pp. 47–70, analyzes the morphology of regional farmsteads, farm systems, and villages in New England, the South, the Midwest, and the Great Basin.

1605. Nisbet, Robert. *The Quest for Community: A Study in the Ethics of Order and Freedom.* New York: Oxford Univ. Press, 1953.

Nisbet's wide-ranging discussion of the rise of the centralized nation-state, the erosion of local communal loyalties, and the need to restore these small-scale, primordial affinities through economic and political decentralization—all have profound regional implications. There is a basic need, he argues, for "intermediate associations" such as the family, church, and local community to mediate between the isolated individual and the daunting nation-state, and the region could serve as the spatial framework within which these intimate forms of community would flourish.

1606. ———. *The Twilight of Authority.* New York: Oxford Univ. Press, 1979.

Region and regionalism are central themes of this Spenglerian vision of the twilight of western political society in the closing years of the twentieth century. After describing the decay of the values and institutions of the leviathan nation-state, Nisbet perceives signs of social renewal in the re-emergence of classical conservative and anarchist thought, the general rediscovery of ethnicity and pluralism, the rise of interest in family and kin, and the revival of localism and voluntary associations. "The Restoration of Authority," pp. 230–87, contains a sweeping discussion of the revival of localism and regionalism in late twentieth century western society.

1607. Odum, Howard W. *Folk, Region, and Society: Selected Papers of Howard W. Odum*. Arranged and edited by Katharine Jocher, Guy B. Johnson, George L. Simpson, and Rupert B. Vance. Chapel Hill: Univ. of North Carolina Press, 1964.

Odum has written more about region and regionalism than any American social scientist, and this posthumous tribute contains many of his most valuable contributions to regional theory. Part Two, "The Region and Regionalism," includes articles on specific southern topics—ranging from the Scopes Trial to Faulkner's literary regionalism—as well as sweeping discussions of regional theory. Part Three, "The Folk and Folk Society," pp. 219–354, contains Odum's most important contributions to folk-regional sociology. Part Four, "Sociology in the Service of Society," pp. 355–454, includes a thoughtful sample of Odum's contributions to regional planning theory. A complete bibliography of Odum's work, pp. 455–69, is included.

1608. ———. "The Promise of Regionalism." In *Regionalism in America*, edited by Merrill Jensen, 395–425. Madison: Univ. of Wisconsin Press, 1951.

In this stirring summation of nearly thirty years of regional speculation, Odum responds to an array of criticisms and envisions a "swelling tide of regionalism "throughout the world, regionalism that will be "a tool for democratic world reconstruction in the post-war world.... a tool for attaining balance and equilibrium between people and resources, men and machines, the state and the folk." For a closely related source, see Wirth's critique in this chapter.

1609. ———. *Southern Regions of the United States*. Chapel Hill: Univ. of North Carolina Press, 1936.

This massive study contains Odum's first fully developed folk-regional sociology and his influential division of the United States into six basic group-of-states regions. In addition to its theoretical contributions, the empirical depth of this book—its hundreds of cross-regional statistical indices underscoring regional social and economic deficiencies—had a deep impact upon New Deal domestic policy. Odum's more impressionistic, often lyrical and impassioned portraits of his native region include *An American Epoch: Southern Portraiture in the National Picture* (New York: Henry Holt & Co., 1930) and *The Way of the South* (New York: Macmillan, 1947).

1610. Odum, Howard W. and Katharine Jocher, eds. *In Search of the Regional Balance of America.* Chapel Hill: Univ. of North Carolina Press, 1945.

This brief book is the most effective summary of the development of Odum's regional theory. Particularly useful are Odum's personal narrative, "From Community Studies to Regionalism," pp. 3–16, and his capstone essay "The Regional Quality and Balance of America," pp. 27–43, a lyrical summation of his folk-regional theory. This book also contains Jocher's extensive bibliography of material related to the North Carolina approach to region and regionalism, pp. 60–86, and useful essays on regional planning and southern studies, including Rupert B. Vance's "The Place of Planning in Social Dynamics," pp. 9–91; William Ogburn's "Ideologies of the South in Transition," pp. 92–100; and Edgar T. Thompson's "Sociology and Sociological Research in the South," pp. 114–23.

1611. Odum, Howard W. and Harry Estill Moore. *American Regionalism: A Cultural-Historical Approach to National Integration.* New York: Henry Holt & Co., 1938.

In spite of its intimidating bulk and occasionally murky prose, Odum and Moore's book remains a monument of American regional thought and the most comprehensive survey of the subject. "The Implications and Meanings of Regionalism," pp. 3–34, stands as the most thorough, wide-ranging introduction to regional theory in print and "From Sectionalism to Regionalism," pp. 35–51, summarizes a crucial distinction between divisive and harmonious manifestations of subnational identity. Odum and Moore then devote nine chapters to specific types of regions, ranging from physiographic to literary and aesthetic divisions of the nation. Six chapters analyze the meaning of region and regionalism for geographers, anthropologists, ecologists, economists, political scientists, and sociologists. Finally, separate chapters examine each of the six basic group-of-states regions: the Middle States, the Northeast, the Southeast, the Far West, the Northwest, and the Southwest. An extensive bibliography, pp. 643–75, is included. Other sources by Odum are listed under Literature (items 1261–1263).

1612. Ogburn, William F. "Regions." *Social Forces* 15 (October 1936): 6–21.

In a few pages of succinct analysis, Ogburn begins to answer a fundamental question: How do cities influence cultural regions? After measuring the intensity of eighteen social factors in urban and rural parts of three regions, he concludes that "The rise of cities has not produced urban units that are more alike than rural units ... but they have produced differences within regions that overshadow regional differences themselves."

1613. Olsen, Stephen. "Regional Social Systems: Linking Quantitative Analysis and Field Work." In *Regional Analysis* (item 128), vol 2, 20–61.

In this thorough, richly documented guide to the interdisciplinary field of regional systems analysis, sociologist Olsen points out the limitations of the small-scale community study tradition and the need to analyze intermediate scale units within nation states. After outlining insights gained from rural sociology and regional sociology, cultural and political geography, central place theory, and human ecology, Olsen describes how multivariate statistical analysis and comparative community studies can help social scientists comprehend "middle- and large-scale systems in which they find particular communities embedded." For closely related sources, see Casagrande, Geertz, Miller, Redfield and Smith under Anthropology (items 79, 89–92, 114, 122–124, 126–128).

1614. Park, Robert Ezra. *Human Communities: The City and Human Ecology*. Edited by Everett C. Hughes et al. Glencoe, Ill.: Free Press, 1952.

The second volume of the collected papers of Robert Park, this book offers the fullest collection of Park's contributions of human ecology, community studies, and regional theory. Classic contributions to urban regionalism include "The City: Suggestions for the Investigation of Human Behavior in the Urban Environment" (1916), pp. 13–51, an early, wide-ranging discussion of the morphology of urban life; "The City as a Social Laboratory" (1929), pp. 73–87, which discusses the meaning of urban regions, "natural areas," and visualizes the city as "a constellation of natural areas"; "The Urban Community as a Spatial Pattern and Moral Order" (1926), pp. 160–77, which describes the ever-increasing regional differentiation of the expanding city; and "Newspaper Circulation and Metropolitan Regions" (1933), which develops a nationwide regional scheme based upon this important variable. Park effectively applies principles of plant ecology to the study of human society in such important papers as "Human Ecology" (1936), pp. 145–58; "Dominance: The Concept, Its Origin and Natural History" (1934), pp. 159–64; and "Succession, An Ecological Concept (1936), pp. 223–32. Many of these papers are reprinted along with a bibliography of Park's work in Ralph H. Turner, ed., *On Social Control and Collective Behavior: Selected papers of Robert E. Park* (Chicago: Univ. of Chicago Press, 1967).

1615. Park, Robert E., Ernest W. Burgess, and Roderick D. McKenzie. *The City.* 1967. Reprint. Chicago: Univ. of Chicago Press, 1925.

Important essays in this central statement of the Chicago School of human ecology include Park's "The City: Some Suggestions for the Investigation of Human Behavior in the Urban Environment," pp. 1–46 (included in annotation for item 1614); Burgess's "The Growth of the City," pp. 47–62 (annotated in item 1543); McKenzie's "The Ecological Approach to the Study of Human Community," pp. 63–79 (included in annotation for item 1595); Park's "Community Organization and the Romantic Temper," pp. 113–22, and "Magic, Mentality, and City Life," pp. 123–41; and Louis Wirth's "A Bibliography of the Urban Community," pp. 161–228.

1616. Peterson, Richard A. and Paul Di Maggio. "From Region to Class, The Changing Locus of Country Music: A Test of the Massification Hypothesis." *Social Forces* 53 (March 1975): 497–506.

Carefully tracing the diffusion of country music from local to regional to national audiences from the 1920s to the 1970s, the authors find that the regional distinctiveness of country music has diminished at the same time that the variety of musical styles available to distinct groups of consumers has increased. "The massification theorists," they conclude, "were right in observing that the old patterns of cultural diversity along ethnic, regional, and even class lines were destroyed or buried. They erred in their prediction of ever-increasing cultural homogeneity."

1617. Reed, John Shelton. *The Enduring South: Subcultural Persistence in Mass Society.* Chapel Hill: Univ. of North Carolina Press, 1974.

With an effective mixture of lucid, often witty, prose and substantive statistic analysis, Reed has brilliantly refined in this book and others much of the regional agenda started by Odum in the 1920s. Using a variety of public opinion polls and some historical studies, Reed examines attitudes toward religion, violence, and localism in various American regions and finds that "Southerners ... are more likely than non-Southerners to be conventionally religious, to accept the private use of force (or the potential for it), and to be anchored to their homeplace." And contrary to the commonly accepted notion of regional convergence, these differences in values seem to have increased in recent years.

1618. ———. *One South: An Ethnic Approach to Regional Culture.* Baton Rouge: Louisiana State Univ. Press, 1982.

The many lucid and insightful essays in this important collection demonstrate the social and cultural distinctiveness of the South and argue that Southerners constitute an "ethnic or quasi-ethnic group." Essays that make vital contributions to general regional theory include "The Sociology of Regional Groups," pp. 11–32, which explores the nature of group identity and the relationship between ethnicity and regionalism; "Whatever Became of Regional Sociology," pp. 33–44, which traces the rise and fall and current revival of regionalism as a sociological concern; and "The Same Old Stand?" pp. 162–85, which is a stirring summation of Reed's understanding of American regionalism and southern identity. Several essays, including "The Heart of Dixie: An Essay in Folk Sociology," pp. 61–77, and "Getting to Know You: Regional Stereotyping Among Southern Whites," pp. 88–100, use statistical analysis to determine content and boundaries of southern identity. Other essays examine the relationship between southern whites and southern blacks, southern Jews, and the new southern middle class. A final group of essays, including "Plastic Wrapped Crackers: Southern Culture and Social Change," pp. 129–38, and "Below the Smith and Wesson Line: Southern Violence," pp. 139–53, make important contributions to the on-going regional convergence/ divergence debate.

1619. ———. *Southern Folk, Plain & Fancy: Native White Social Types.* Athens: Univ. of Georgia Press, 1986.

Observing that "the psychic landscape of the South has always been peopled with strange and wonderful creatures," Reed classifies and analyzes the types of people who inhabit "this strange land, the South of the mind." "Social Types and How They Work," pp. 4–19, analyzes the general function of regional social types and their relationship to social reality. The remaining chapters draw upon a wide variety of popular culture and media imagery to analyze a spectrum of southern social types, ranging from southern gentlemen, good old boys, rednecks, and hillbillies, to Southern belles, good old girls, honkeytonk angels, and hillbilly gals.

1620. ———. *Southerners: The Social Psychology of Sectionalism.* Chapel Hill: Univ. of North Carolina Press, 1983.

In this important monograph, Reed enhances our understanding of the nature of regional identity by carefully analyzing a detailed survey of the attitudes and values of more than one thousand white and black North Carolinians. Separate chapters contain profound discussions of such issues as "Regional Consciousness," pp. 27–55; "Southern Grievances, Southern History, and Symbolic Sectionalism," pp. 70–94; and "Prejudice, Social Distance, and Boundary Maintenance," pp. 95–107. Reed concludes, among other things, that southern identity has dynamics similar to ethnic and racial identity, that urbanized, "cosmopolitan" southerners have stronger regional consciousness than more rural, isolated inhabitants, and that fresh forms of southern distinctiveness are emerging as old ones end.

1621. ———. "Southerners." In *The Harvard Encyclopedia of American Ethnic Groups*, edited by Stephan Thernstrom, Ann Orlov, and Oscar Handlin, 944–48. Cambridge: Harvard Univ. Press, 1980.

The inclusion of Southerners as a category in this important reference book lends authority to the regional ethnicity thesis. In addition to succinctly summarizing the ethnoregional argument, Reed describes distinctive southern patterns in politics, literature, music, and institutions and discusses the impact of migration to and from the South upon regional consciousness.

1622. Reimer, Svend. "Theoretical Aspects of Regionalism." *Social Forces* 21 (March 1943): 275–80.

In this positive survey of the North Carolina school of regional thought, Reimer praises Odum's sensitivity to the persistence of folkways and his insistence that theory lead to social action. Reimer also perceives such regionalism as a unifying science, arguing that "With the coordination of technology, biology, geography, economy, and sociology regionalism establishes itself as a new superscience."

1623. Schwarzweller, Harry K. et al. *Mountain Families in Transition: A Case Study of Appalachian Migration*. University Park: Pennsylvania State Univ. Press, 1971.

In this model study of a mass exodus from a particular rural Kentucky community to Ohio, Schwarzweller and associates describe how "stem family" arrangements preserve sense of family and community even as members move from and between the old place and the new.

1624. Shevky, Eshref and Wendell Bell. *Social Area Analysis: Theory, Illustrative Application and Computational Procedures.* Stanford: Stanford Univ. Press, 1955.

This monograph outlines an influential theory and method for understanding urban social-spatial patterns. Unlike the classical urban ecologists who mapped out a mosaic of all-purpose "natural areas" within the city, Shevky and Bell measure the intensity of three important variables—social rank, urbanization (later modified as family structure), and ethnicity—for every census tract within a city and then group together "the tract populations with similar configurations of scores on the three indexes ... into larger units called social areas." Basically an analytical tool for social scientists and planners, "the social area ... is not bounded by the geographical frame of reference as is the natural area, nor by the implications concerning degree of interaction between persons in the local community as is the subculture." Eshref Shevky and Marilyn Williams's *The Social Areas of Los Angeles: Analysis and Typology* (Berkeley: Univ. of California Press, 1949) is a frequently cited example of social area analysis.

1625. Shils, Edward. *Center and Periphery: Essays in Macrosociology.* Chicago: Univ. of Chicago Press, 1975.

Two essays in this collection make important contributions to regional theory: "Center and Periphery" (1961), pp. 3–16, and "Primordial, Personal, Sacred, and Civil Ties" (1957), pp. 111–26. The first essay develops a largely non-geographical model of relationship between the sacred central value system espoused by the ruling elites of a society and the profane margins inhabited by ordinary citizens that parallels core/periphery models developed by Hechter, Wallerstein, and others. The second essay eloquently argues that society is sustained by immediate ties or "primordial affinities" to family, friends, work group, and neighborhood rather than abstract allegiances to remote ideals and symbols of authority.

1626. ———. "Roots—The Sense of Place and Past: The Cultural Gains and Losses of Migration." In *Human Migration: Patterns and Policies,* edited by William H. McNeill and Ruth S. Adams, 404–26. Bloomington: Indiana Univ. Press, 1978.

Shils touches upon a spectrum of topics—the relationship between immigrant groups and host societies, tension between center and periphery and between assimilation and pluralism—but his central discussions of the meanings of "rootedness" and "sense of place" have direct relevance to regional theory.

1627. Simpson, George L. "Howard W. Odum and American Regionalism." *Social Forces* 34 (December 1955): 101–6.

This retrospective essay discusses Odum's sense of the dialectical tension between folk culture and state civilization, his crusade for regional planning on a national basis, and his fundamental vision of "strength and unity through diversity." For further analyses of Odum's regional theory, see Kantor (item 1584) and Brown, Singal, and O'Brien under History: Region as Concept (items 799, 840, 830).

1628. Stein, Maurice R. *The Eclipse of Community: An Interpretation of American Studies*. Expanded ed. Princeton: Princeton Univ. Press, 1972.

Originally published in 1960, Stein's book surveys and evaluates a myriad of American community studies. Several chapters have explicit regional orientations, including "Robert Park and the Urbanization of Chicago," pp. 13–46, which carefully analyzes the concept of "natural areas" within urban regions, and "Suburbia: Dream or Nightmare?" pp. 199–226, which evaluates the many studies of suburban human ecology. "The Lynds and Industrialization in Middletown," pp. 47–69; "Lloyd Warner and Bureaucratization in Yankee City," pp. 70–93; and "Deep South," pp. 153–74, examine classic midwestern, New England, and southern community studies.

1629. Stouffer, Samuel A. *Communism, Conformity, and Civil Liberties: A Cross-Section of the Nation Speaks Its Mind*. New York: Doubleday, 1955.

Regionalism is an important variable of this influential study of political intolerance. In "Does It Matter Where People Live?" pp. 109–30, Stouffer analyzes national public opinion polls to determine whether there are significant regional and rural-urban differences in levels of tolerance of nonconformity. Higher levels of tolerance are found in the West and East with lower levels in the Midwest and South. Furthermore, "Rural people in every region are less tolerant of nonconformists than city people, even when we compare urban and rural people with the same amount of schooling." "There is something about life in a small community," Stouffer concludes, "that makes it less hospitable to divergent opinions than is the case in urban centers. In the anonymity of city life it is much easier for deviant behavior to flourish than in the goldfish bowl of a small community."

1630. Strauss, Anselm. *Images of the American City*. Glencoe, Ill.: Free Press, 1961.

In "Era and Geography in Urban Symbolism," pp. 124–98, Strauss effectively analyzes a variety of American cities within their larger regional settings. Such settings include "The South: Urbane Agrarianism on the Defensive," "The East: Commerce, Manufacturing, and the Symbolism of Individual Success," "The Midwest: Ambiguities and Symbolization," and "The Country Town as a Symbolic Locale."

1631. Suttles, Gerald D. "The Cumulative Texture of Local Urban Culture." *American Journal of Sociology* 90 (September 1984): 283–304.

In discussing the importance of portraying the ambience of urban communities, Suttles describes how sociologists might begin to grasp the special character—the cultural and artifactual texture—of such vanguard "shock cities" as Chicago, Los Angeles, and Houston.

1632. ———. *The Social Construction of Communities*. Chicago: Univ. of Chicago Press, 1972.

Like Albert Hunter, Gerald Suttles has written several important revisions of Park's and Burgess's theories of urban regionalism and human ecology, and this book abounds with insights regarding the regional structure of urban life. "The Natural Community: Its Followers and Revisionists," pp. 3–20, evaluates the Chicago school's early notions of natural area and natural community and its use of concepts of primordial solidarity and territoriality. Chapters two, three, and four examine the social-spatial structure of a variety of community types, including the defended community, the community of limited liability, and the contrived community. Suttles's discussion of territoriality in "The Ideological Overburden in the Study of Territoriality," pp. 111–39, and "Territoriality and Distancing," pp. 156–88, are especially relevant to regional theory. While criticizing the extreme claims of Robert Ardrey, Konrad Lorenz, Desmond Morris, and others, Suttles describes the persistence of modified forms of territorial affiliation in modern society.

1633. ———. *The Social Order of the Slum: Ethnicity and Territory in the Inner City*. Chicago: Univ. of Chicago Press, 1968.

This detailed study of a multi-ethnic neighborhood in Chicago's Near West Side stresses the close relationship between sense of place and sense of community. Suttles's participant observation revealed that during times of threat Mexicans, Negroes, Italians, and Puerto Ricans living in the same neighborhood felt a stronger sense of community with each other than with members of their own ethnic groups in different neighborhoods. "The Ecological Basis of Ordered Segmentation," pp. 13–38, carefully analyzes the significance of territorial unity in the formation of community.

1634. Taylor, Carl C. et al. *Rural Life in the United States.* New York: Knopf, 1955.

Part Four, "Rural Regions," pp. 329–491, contains separate chapters on seven basic farming regions as well as several perceptive theoretical essays. Taylor and Arthur Raper's discussion of "Rural Culture," pp. 329–243, contains an effective survey of the regional concept from the perspective of rural sociology; Raper's "Comparisons and Contrasts of Major-Type Farming Areas," pp. 464–91, is a useful overview of agricultural regions.

1635. Theodorson, George A., ed. *Urban Patterns: Studies in Human Ecology.* rev. ed. University Park: Pennsylvania State Univ. Press, 1982.

This thorough anthology of fifty-six articles is an invaluable resource to the study of urban regionalism. Part One documents the rise and decline of "classical" human ecology through central essays by Park, Burgess, McKenzie, Zorbaugh, Hatt, Hawley, Firey, and others. Part Two surveys current uses of urban human ecology to understand ethnic and racial patterns, neighborhood structure, social area analysis, and factorial ecology. Part Three is devoted to cross-cultural human ecology studies.

1636. Tuch, Steven A. "Urbanism, Region, and Tolerance Revisited: The Case of Racial Prejudice." *American Sociological Review* 52 (August 1987): 504–10.

With Stouffer's findings of regional and urban-rural differences in political intolerance as a starting point, Tuch examines public opinion data to see whether racial intolerance follows similar spatial patterns. Tuch's analysis indicates that since 1977 regional differences in tolerance have been decreasing while rural-urban differences have increased. For a slightly different non-regional analysis, see Thomas C. Wilson's "Urbanism and Tolerance: A Test of Some Hypotheses Drawn From Wirth and Stouffer." *American Sociological Review* 50 (February 1985), pp. 117–23.

1637. Urry, John. "Localities, Regions and Social Class." *International Journal of Urban and Regional Research* 5 (December 1981): 455–74.

Urry urges mainstream sociologists to pay greater attention to regional differences in social class. Beginning with the general assertion that "social activity necessarily involves passing through time and space—in Pred's words, 'a weaving dance through time-space'," Urry then argues, along with other observers of uneven economic development, that "Important changes in contemporary capitalism are at present heightening the economic, social, and political significance of each locality." For a response to this argument, see Richard Harris, "Space and Class: A Critique of Urry," *International Journal of Urban and Regional Research* 7 (March 1983), pp. 115–20 and Urry's rejoinder in the same issue, pp. 122–26.

1638. Vance, Rupert B. *Human Geography of the South: A Study in Regional Resources and Human Adequacy.* Chapel Hill: Univ. of North Carolina Press, 1932.

This wide-ranging, well-written book is an exemplary regional study comparable to such masterpieces as Walter Prescott Webb's *The Great Plains* (1931) and Carey McWilliams's *Southern California* (1946). Vance displays a masterful grasp of regional theory, from the contributions of LePlay, Vidal, Brunhes, and Geddes in Europe to the theories of Marsh, Turner, Mumford, and Odum in the United States. Through the method of sequent occupance, he paints a vivid portrait of the South as a whole as well as its physiographic and cultural subregions. Vance's powerful book is in many ways a companion piece to Odum's more empirical and often ponderous *Southern Regions of the United States* (1936).

1639. ———. "Region." In *International Encyclopedia of the Social Sciences.* vol. 13, edited by David L. Sills, 377–82. New York: Macmillan, 1968. Reprinted in *Regionalism and the South: Selected Papers of Rupert Vance*, edited by John Shelton Reed and Daniel Joseph Singal, 308–16. Chapel Hill: Univ. of North Carolina Press, 1982.

This masterful exposition remains one of the most insightful introductions to the meaning of region and regional theory. In an earlier essay, "The Concept of the Region," *Social Forces* 8 (December 1929), pp. 208–18, Vance carefully traces the regional concept to its European roots.

1640. ———. "The Regional Concept as a Tool for Social Research." In *Regionalism in America* (item 820), 119–40. Reprinted in *Regionalism and the South: Selected Papers of Rupert Vance* (item 1641), 155–75.

Vance begins by stressing the integrative rather than the divisive function of regionalism and the complexity of the regional concept. He then discusses four levels of regional analysis for social scientists: (1) the delineation of single-factor regions, (2) the description of complex regions based upon many crucial variables (a method later described by urban ecologists as "factorial ecology"), (3) the monograph depicting "a region in process... the interplay and interaction of phenomena that create the regional *Gestalt*, and (4) the comparative analysis of several regions.

1641. ———. *Regionalism and the South: Selected Papers of Rupert Vance*. Edited by John Shelton Reed and Daniel Joseph Singal. Chapel Hill: Univ. of North Carolina Press, 1982.

This useful anthology contains many of Vance's most important contributions to regional reportage, planning, and sociology. In addition to the two seminal essays annotated above, this book includes such important papers as "Is Agrarianism for Farmers?" (1935), pp. 60–74; "Regional Family Patterns: The Southern Family" (1948), pp. 149–54; "Regionalism and Ecology" (with Charles M. Grigg, 1956), pp. 185–96; "The Sociological Implications of Southern Regionalism" (1960), pp. 208–219; and "Beyond the Fleshpots: The Coming Culture Crisis in the South" (1965), pp. 250–61. A complete bibliography of Vance's work, pp. 3336–41, is included.

1642. Wallerstein, Immanuel. *The Capitalist World-Economy*. New York: Cambridge Univ. Press, 1980.

Part One "The Inequalities of Core and Periphery," contains nine essays that explore socio-economic aspects of the world system model Wallerstein developed in the early 1970s and described below (item 1643). His sense of regionalization on a global scale—of various groups of states functioning within a world economy—is carefully developed in such essays as "The Rise and Demise of the Capitalist World System," pp. 1–36; "Three Paths of National Development in Sixteenth Century Europe," pp. 37–48; and "The Present State of the Debate on World Inequality," pp. 49–65. Many of the contemporary geo-political implications of this model are developed in Wallerstein's *The Politics of the World-Economy: The States, the Movements, and the Civilizations* (New York: Cambridge Univ. Press, 1984).

1643. ———. *The Modern World System: Capitalist Agriculture and the Origins of the European World-Economy in the Sixteenth Century*. New York: Academic Press, 1974.

The first volume of a projected four-part study, this book is the foundation for sociologist Wallerstein's sweeping concept of a capitalistic "world-system" composed of "core states" exploiting "peripheral areas." The "Introduction: On the Study of Social Change," pp. 2–11, argues that the history of social change—especially the process of modernization—must be viewed in the context of a single "world system" of interacting sovereign states driven by the forces of capitalism and scientific technology. The complex history of the transition from a medieval to modern world economy that follows is deeply influenced by Fernand Braudel and depicts the gradual rise and interaction of "core states" in northwest Europe exploiting "semiperipheral" and "peripheral areas" in eastern Europe, Africa, Asia, and America. The final chapter, "Theoretical Reprise," pp. 346–57, recapitulates the world system and core/periphery model and points toward further study published in *The Modern World System II: Mercantilism and the Consolidation of the European World-Economy, 1600–1750* (New York: Academic Press, 1980). Wallerstein is also general editor of a series on the "political economy of the world system" from which at least three volumes have been published since 1978. For closely related sources, see Hechter, Hechter and Levi, Lefebvre, and Shils (items 1575, 1576, 1590, 1625–1626); Peet and Wolf under Anthropology 117, 145); Johnston and Taylor under Geography: Region as Concept (item 475); and Braudel under History: Region as Concept (item 798).

1644. Webber, Melvin M. "Culture, Territoriality, and the Elastic Mile." *Regional Science Association Papers* 13 (1964): 283–304.

To demonstrate that the meaning of space varies dramatically between subgroups in American society, Webber contrasts the mobility of professional class "cosmopolites" with the rootedness of working class "locals." Cosmopolites engage in "spatially dispersed, *nonplace* communities," while locals develop "close-knit networks of association *based upon residence.*" Planners must be aware of these differences, and must know that "At the same time that social organization of cosmopolite groups is being largely freed from the restraints of territorial place, the 'urban villagers' live out their lives in territorially bounded and territorially perceived societies."

1645. ———. "The Urban Place and the Nonplace Urban Realm." In *Explorations into Urban Structure*, edited by Melvin M. Webber et al., 79–153. Philadelphia: Univ. of Pennsylvania Press, 1964.

In contrast with many community theories, Webber argues that place is rapidly disappearing as an important ingredient of group identity, and that for most people "the functional processes of urban communities are not placelike or regionlike at all." Observing the multiplicity of overlapping, nonplace communities of interest that every individual belongs to, Webber stresses that "We thus find no Euclidean territorial divisions—only continuous variation, spatial discontinuity, persisting disparity, complex pluralism, and dynamic ambiguity," and he suggests several models for analyzing the complex "nonplace urban realm" that dominates modern life. For an elaboration of this thesis, see Webber's "Order in Diversity: Community Without Propinquity," in *Environmental Psychology* (New York: Holt, Rinehart and Winston, 1970), edited by Harold M. Proshansky, et al., pp. 533–49.

1646. Wellman, Barry and Barry Leighton. "Networks, Neighborhoods, and Communities: An Approach to the Study of Community Question." *Urban Affairs Quarterly* 14 (March 1979): 363–90.

The authors effectively discuss the significance of space or propinquity in three general traditions of community theory. The "Community Lost" perspective mourns the passing of territorially rooted, face-to-face community and perceives no adequate replacement in mass society; the "Community Saved" position argues that geographically-oriented communities flourish in mass society; the "Community Liberated" orientation contends that placeless, "aspatial communities" dominate mass society and thrive through network systems and electronic media.

1647. Wirth, Louis. "Limitations of Regionalism." In *Regionalism in America*, edited by Merrill Jensen, 381–93. Madison: Univ. of Wisconsin Press, 1951.

While acknowledging the value of regional analysis, Wirth reminds social scientists that it is only one method among many. Over-reliance upon regional explanation, he argues, can mask the complexity of society, can lead toward simplistic environmental determinism, and can degenerate into a nostalgic sentimentality. Regionalism, Wirth concludes, "can lead to the falsification of facts. It can become a futile effort to squeeze life into a rigid mold, and it can become a vain gesture to retard the integration of life on a wider and more inclusive scale." Wirth's critique is followed by Odum's sweeping espousal, "The Promise of Regionalism" (item 1608).

1648. ———. "Localism, Regionalism, and Centralization." *American Journal of Sociology* 27 (January 1937): 493–509.

Wirth perceives regionalism—primarily in the form of the metropolitan community—as a means of mediating between the dangers of extreme centralization, on the one hand, and the fragmentation of "archaic localism," on the other.

1649. Young, Gerald L., ed. *Origins of Human Ecology*. Stroudsburg, Penn.: Hutchinson Ross Publishing, 1983.

In addition to the work of such sociological human ecologists as Park, McKenzie, Hawley and Milla Alihan, Young's anthology includes contribution from geography by Harlan Barrows and George Renner, anthropology by Julian Steward, Andrew Vayda and Roy Rappaport, psychology by Kurt Lewin and Roger Barker, economics by Kenneth Boulding, and interdisciplinary statements by F. Fraser Darling and Paul Shepard.

1650. Zimmerman, Carle C. *Outline of American Regional Sociology*. Harvard Square, Cambridge: Phillips Book Store, 1947.

The most original section of this book is an ambitious, highly impressionistic, analysis of regional personality types.

1651. Zimmerman, Carle C. and Richard E. DuWhors. *Graphic Regional Sociology*. Harvard Square, Cambridge: Phillips Book Store, 1952.

A reworking of Zimmerman's earlier discussion of "regional mentalities," this somewhat eccentric text is an extended plea for sociologists to focus more attention upon the large-scale regional configurations of society.

1652. Zorbaugh, Harvey W. "The Natural Areas of the City." *Publications of the American Sociological Society* 20 (1926): 188–97. Reprinted in *Urban Patterns: Studies in Human Ecology*. Rev. ed., edited by George A. Theodorson, 50–54. University Park: Pennsylvania State Univ. Press, 1982.

Zorbaugh, author of the classic urban study *The Gold Coast and the Slum* (1929), effectively summarizes many of the guiding theories of the Chicago School of urban regionalism. Reiterating Park, Burgess, and McKenzie, Zorbaugh visualizes the city as a mosaic of "natural areas" that are "unplanned, natural products of the city's growth." "The physical individuality of the natural areas of the city," he writes, "is re-emphasized by the cultural individuality of the populations segregated over them. Natural areas and natural cultural groups tend to coincide."

Author Index

Listed are names given as authors in entries. Numbers refer to entries and not to pages. When a title is cited in more than one chapter, the first entry to appear is listed followed by others for that title in parentheses.